Structured Assembler Language for IBM Computers

Structured Assembler Language for IBM Computers

Alton R. Kindred

Manatee Community College

HBJ

Harcourt Brace Jovanovich, Publishers
and its subsidiary, Academic Press

San Diego New York Chicago Austin Washington, D.C.
London Sydney Tokyo Toronto

ISBN: 0-15-584070-3
Library of Congress Catalog Card Number: 86-70503

Printed in the United States of America

Preface

As a student of computer science, you probably learned programming through a high-level language, such as Pascal, BASIC, FORTRAN, or COBOL. You also realize that much of the application programming in the business world is done in high-level languages. You might then wonder, "Why should I study assembler language?"

Benefits of Assembler Language

Assembler language provides a broad understanding of machine functions and processing techniques that cannot be matched through any other source. It offers alternative choices of instructions for data manipulation and calculations. It helps you to understand why certain file and data definitions cause more efficient operations than others do. You may find that subprograms written in assembler language can be called from high-level languages to perform specific tasks not otherwise possible.

Through assembler language you can gain a detailed understanding of address modification, register operations, table handling, and other functions common to many languages. Moreover, you can learn to analyze object code and diagnose storage dumps, both valuable tools in debugging.

Some people contend that assembler language should be avoided because programs must be rewritten every time the hardware is changed. But the IBM family of computers starting with the System/360 and progressing through the 370, 3030, 3080, and 4300 series—as well as a large group of IBM-compatible computers—has used the same assembler language for over 20 years. Although the language has been expanded, programs written in the 1960s can usually be run with few or no changes on hardware that has changed dramatically over the years. Few high-level languages have been so stable.

Shortcomings of Other Textbooks

Many assembler textbooks have certain shortcomings that I have tried to overcome here. They present too much detail early in the text, before the student has an opportunity to assimilate and apply it. They wait too long to provide enough information to produce a complete program. They show too few complete programs—and these usually appear late in the book. They depend on artificial tools, such as special housekeeping and input/output macros, and often ignore the use of disk files entirely.

But the most serious omission in many assembler books is lack of attention to the principles of structured programming. Students who have learned proper structure in their introductory courses are perplexed at the disregard of proper branching and modular design they often find in their assembler texts.

Features of This Book

This book employs many techniques to design and write correct programs. Structured programming is demonstrated and practiced throughout. Initially, each program is shown in flowchart form, pseudocode, and assembler language. Later the flowcharts are eliminated.

A new method is introduced by which each type of program structure—sequence, repetition, and selection—is clearly identified by the use of names such as IF, THEN, ELSE, ENDIF, DOWHILE, ENDDO, REPEAT, and UNTIL. Consistent use of these names helps to ensure proper structure.

Page heading subroutines are introduced with the first program and other subroutines are emphasized throughout as ways to improve and extend modular structure.

Programs begin with simple character operations and gradually move on to decimal arithmetic, editing, binary arithmetic, address modification, and table handling. Later chapters, which may be omitted without loss of continuity, deal with subprograms, advanced register operations, macro definitions, and floating-point numbers.

No special non-system macros are used. File definitions and processing macros for both DOS and OS are provided as a model that can be used for each of the programs.

Data types and machine instructions are introduced only as needed and are immediately utilized in examples and sample programs. Detailed summaries are presented in appendixes.

Early sample programs are based on the same data set to give continuity and relevance.

File creation and processing are covered with sequential, indexed sequential, and VSAM files. Sample programs illustrate each form of processing for each type of file.

Organization of the Text

The book contains 18 chapters and five appendixes. The intent is always to work from familiar concepts and material to new ones. The first seven chapters should be taken in sequence. Chapter 1 reviews basic hardware and software concepts, with special emphasis on structured program development. Chapter 2 covers types of assembler language statements, file and data definitions in both DOS and OS, and procedural instructions to permit development of a complete program utilizing a heading subroutine. Chapter 3 develops more complex program logic while continuing to work with data in character form.

Chapters 4 and 5 introduce packed decimal numbers, arithmetic operations, and editing. Standards modules are developed for reading records and printing lines.

Chapter 6 introduces more technical material on base-displacement addressing, machine instruction formats, the condition code and branching, and input/output channels.

Chapter 7 covers techniques to avoid errors in programs and detect those that do occur. Output from the assembler and linkage editor is examined, and detailed analysis of a core dump is explained.

Chapter 8 presents control break processing, with single-level and multiple-level totals. This chapter may by studied in sequence or deferred until later, when magnetic tape and disk files are covered.

Chapters 9 and 10 deal with operations on binary numbers, address modification, and table handling. Conversion between decimal and binary numbers, arithmetic operations, shifting within registers, and creating and searching tables are treated in detail.

Chapter 11 shows subroutines and subprograms as means of expanding modular structure of programs. Chapter 12 explains macro definitions and conditional assemblies as ways to simplify programming for definitions and routines that are frequently used.

Chapter 13 presents advanced logical operations for working on individual bits within a byte, translating data from one coding structure to another, or scanning strings of characters. This chapter can be studied immediately after Chapter 10 if desired.

Chapters 14 and 15 discuss sequential files on magnetic tape and disk. Topics include fixed-length and variable-length records, blocked records, volume and file labels, disk track capacity, and processing techniques.

Chapters 16 and 17 cover indexed sequential and VSAM files. Either or both may be omitted without affecting any of the book's other contents.

Chapter 18 concludes the text with a discussion of floating-point data, arithmetic operations, and conversion from fixed-point to floating-point data.

Each chapter contains a statement of objectives, numerous illustrations, and (except for Chapter 1) one or more complete illustrative programs. Each chapter concludes with a summary, a list of terms for review, questions for discussion, exercises, and programming problems.

The appendixes include a glossary, a summary of machine instructions, the IBM System/370 reference summary, data for programming problems, and answers to exercises.

Supplemental Materials

An instructor's manual is available with teaching suggestions and a large bank of test questions.

The following IBM publications will provide valuable additional information:

A22-6821 System/360 Principles of Operation
GA22-7000 System/370 Principles of Operation
GA22-7070 IBM 4300 Processors Principles of Operation
GC24-5099 OS/VS1 JCL Reference
GC24-5103 OS/VS1 Supervisor Services and Macro Instructions
GC33-4010 OS/VS-DOS-VS-VM-370 Assembler Language
GC33-4021 OS/VS-VM/370 Assembler Programmer's Guide
GC33-4024 Guide to the DOS/VSE Assembler
GC33-5372 DOS/VS Data Management Guide
GC33-5373 DOS/VS Supervisor and I/O Macros
G320-5774 VSAM Primer and Reference

Acknowledgments

Many people have contributed to the development and production of this book. My students at Manatee Community College have field-tested many of the structured concepts evolving over the past three years. My colleagues in the computer science department and the computer center have offered valuable support and assistance.

The manuscript was reviewed by Joseph S. McFarland, Dundalk Community College, who offered numerous helpful criticisms and suggestions. Dale Brown, of Academic Press, and Ralph Zickgraf, of EDP, Inc., lent their expertise in technical production.

Special thanks, as always, are reserved for my loving wife, Joy, who gave her unfailing inspiration and support throughout the long hours of creation and development of the book.

Alton R. Kindred

Contents

11. System Macros, Subroutines, and Subprograms 248

12. Macro Definitions and Conditional Assemblies 272

1
Basic Computer Concepts

OBJECTIVES

After studying this chapter, you should be able to:

- Name and describe the various parts of a computer system
- Explain the purpose and functions of the central processing unit
- Describe typical input/output devices
- Describe the parts and functions of the DOS/VSE and OS/VS operating systems
- Explain the steps in developing structured programs
- Describe the steps in assembling and relocating programs
- Name types of documentation used with programs
- Write EBCDIC code for letters, digits, and special characters
- Convert decimal numbers to hexadecimal and vice versa
- Perform elementary addition and subtraction on hexadecimal numbers

THE COMPUTER SYSTEM

People often speak of a "computer" as a means of processing data. More properly, we should speak of a "computer system" because many different parts and components must work together to accomplish the work we expect to do.

A system may be defined as a set of interrelated parts or components working together to accomplish some desired function or purpose.

A computer system consists of four major groups of components whose purpose is to process basic facts, called *data*, into meaningful *information* that is useful for record keeping and decision making. This function is usually called *data processing* or *information processing*. Processing includes such activities as recording, classifying, sorting, calculating, summarizing, storing, retrieving, and communicating.

The four major groups of components of the computer system are:

1. Hardware, or equipment.
2. Software, or programs with their supporting documents.
3. Personnel: programmers, systems analysts, operators, and others.

4. Procedures to direct personnel in handling transactions and papers outside the computer itself.

In this text, we shall concentrate on the hardware and software of the IBM family of computers that started more than 20 years ago with the System/360 and has evolved into the 370, 30xx, and 43xx series.

HARDWARE

The hardware of a computer system (Figure 1–1) consists of (1) main storage, (2) the central processing unit, and (3) various input/output (I/O) devices. Some of the I/O devices are employed as extensions of main storage and are thus called secondary or auxiliary storage. Main storage and the central processing unit are often housed in the same cabinet.

Main Storage

Main storage, often called *memory*, *primary storage*, or *internal storage*, consists of numbered *locations*, also called *addresses*. Each location is called a *byte*, and is capable of holding a code that represents one letter, digit, or special character. The code is made up of eight *bits*. A bit is a short name for

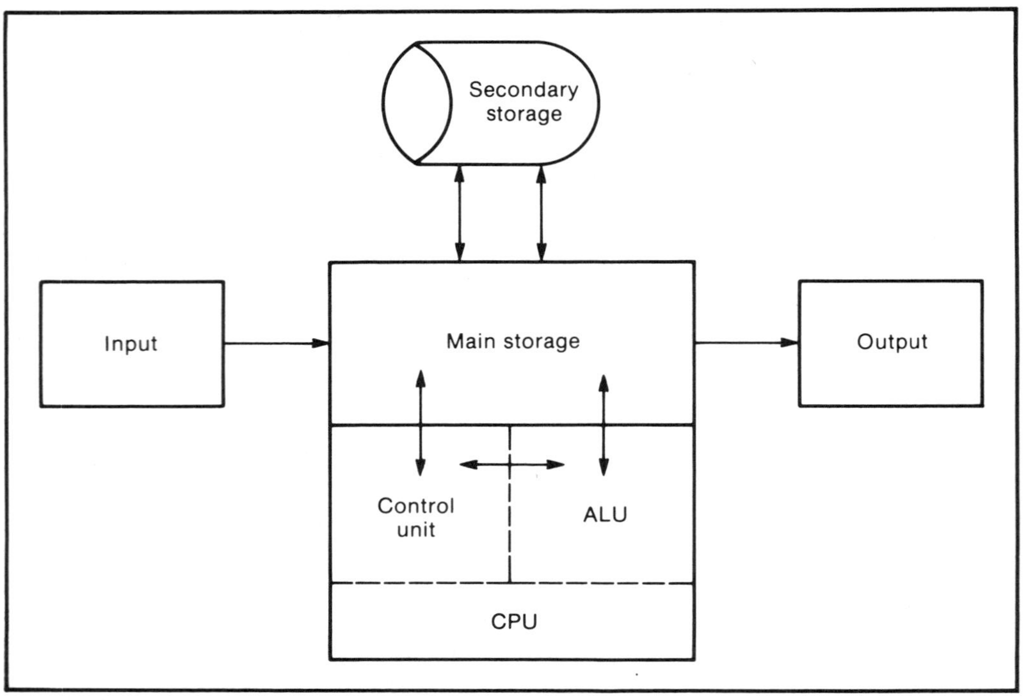

Figure 1–1 Hardware of a computer system

binary digit. The term "binary" refers to a number system consisting of only the digits 0 and 1.

The bits are in electronic form, so that a 1 might be represented as a pulse and a 0 as the lack of a pulse, or a 1 as a clockwise magnetic field and a 0 as a counterclockwise magnetic field. The bytes are numbered starting with location 0 and go consecutively to the maximum number available in any particular computer, often from 2 to 16 million bytes.

Bytes may be grouped together to form binary *words*. IBM uses a *halfword* of two bytes to represent a binary number of 64 bits. A *fullword* has four bytes, or 32 bits, while a doubleword has 64 bits. Other manufacturers may use words of 8, 24, 48, or 60 bits. Words may be either fixed-point (integer) form or floating-point (exponential) form.

Computer instructions are also represented in the form of bits in special codes called *machine language*. Each instruction occupies from two to six bytes. When programs are to be *run*, or *executed*, their instructions in machine language must be placed, or *loaded*, into main storage. Thus computers are said to have *stored programs*.

Central Processing Unit

The heart of any computer is the *central processing unit*, or CPU. The CPU generally controls operation of the entire system and performs arithmetic and logical operations. The CPU has two main parts:

1. The control unit.
2. The arithmetic-logic unit.

Control Unit The *control unit* directs the automatic execution of instructions. Normally instructions are executed in sequence, but jumps may be made backward or forward to change the order in which instructions are executed. Any transfer away from the next instruction in sequence is called a *branch*. If the branch is to be made only if some condition is true, it is called a *conditional branch*. If the transfer to another instruction is made without regard to any condition, it is an *unconditional branch*.

A special component in the control unit called the *instruction address register* gives the address of the next instruction to be executed, whether it is the next one in sequence or one in another part of the program.

Each instruction consists of one *operation code (op code)* and usually one or more *operands*. The op code corresponds to a verb saying what is to be done. The operands are either actual data or the addresses of the bytes holding the data that is to be processed by the instruction. Some operands may refer to general registers that perform binary arithmetic or to the length of data items in main storage.

There are two *cycles* involved with each instruction:

1. During the *instruction cycle* the control unit fetches the instruction from main storage, separates the op code and operands, and places different

parts of the instruction into special registers. Some of the registers used include:

a. The op code register.
b. The address, or location, register for each operand.
c. A register containing the length of each operand.
d. The instruction counter, giving the location of the next instruction.

2. During the *execution cycle* the control unit carries out the instruction. This may involve moving an operand from one location to another, performing arithmetic on two operands, branching to some other part of the program, starting an input or output operation, or performing other operations.

The control unit carries out data transfer between internal storage locations and between main storage and the arithmetic-logic unit. It also directs data transfer between main storage and external input/output devices.

The control unit also has a *storage protection* feature that prevents a program in one part of main storage from destroying data placed in another part of main storage.

The control unit also services *interrupts*, which allow the CPU to suspend operations on one program so that another program in main storage may run for a time.

Arithmetic-Logic Unit All arithmetic operations are carried out in the *arithmetic-logic unit* (ALU). Data items to be processed are moved by the control unit from main storage into ALU, and the results are returned by the control unit to main storage. The ALU is also able to compare two values, shift bits in registers to the right or left, and perform certain types of logical operations that change individual bits within a byte.

The ALU performs operations on numbers in three different forms.

1. *Binary arithmetic*, often called integer or fixed-point arithmetic, is performed in 16 general registers, each of which can hold one fullword of 32 bits. General registers are numbered from 0 through 15.
2. *Floating-point arithmetic* is performed in four floating-point registers, each of which contains a 64-bit doubleword. Both general registers and floating-point registers may be used alone or, for some types of operations, in pairs. Floating-point registers are number 0, 2, 4, or 6.
3. *Decimal arithmetic* is performed on two numbers having each decimal digit coded in a four-bit form. Both numbers are located in main storage.

Input/Output Devices

Entering data into main storage requires both *devices* and *media*. *Input devices* are the machines, such as keyboards, magnetic tape or disk units, or optical scanning equipment, that are able to record data in a form that can be converted into binary codes in main memory. The media are the materials, such as visual display screens, magnetic tapes or disks, paper, or punched cards, that actually hold the data.

After the data has been processed into meaningful information by the program in main storage, the information is sent from main storage to an *output device*, such as a printer, magnetic tape or disk drive, or visual display terminal. The device records, or *writes*, the information on media such as magnetic tape or disk, display screen, or paper.

The data is actually recorded on the media. The device is the equipment that reads or writes the data on the media.

Data travels between the I/O device and main storage along special-purpose devices called *channels* as directed by the control unit. A *byte-multiplexor channel* connects to slow-speed devices such as terminals, card readers, and printers. One or more *block-multiplexor channels* (called *selector* channels in older CPUs) connect main storage to high-speed devices such as magnetic tapes and disks. Channels may perform I/O operations at the same time the CPU is executing instructions located in main storage.

Data is sent to or from main storage in the form of *records*. A collection of records organized for a particular purpose is called a *file*, or *data set*. Each record is divided into *fields*, each of which contains one *data element*, such as name, address, age, or rate of pay.

Files on magnetic tape or disk devices are usually regarded as *auxiliary* or *secondary* storage, since they hold data needed for frequent reference, such as master files. To the program such files are *input files* if they send data to main storage and *output files* if they receive information from main storage.

SOFTWARE

A computer *program* is a set of instructions to the computer hardware along with the conditions under which they are to be carried out. The entire collection of programs, rules, procedures, and documentation is called *software*. Software is broadly classified as (1) systems software and (2) applications software.

Systems software is concerned with routines that are common to the needs of almost all users, such as loading programs, sorting records, maintaining libraries of files and programs, and carrying out input/output operations.

Applications software is designed to perform functions to meet the specific needs of the user, such as billing customers, paying employees, registering students, or making engineering calculations.

The Operating System

All medium- and large-scale modern computer systems and most small systems utilize an *operating system*. This term describes a collection of programs designed to assist in preparing, translating, storing, and executing our

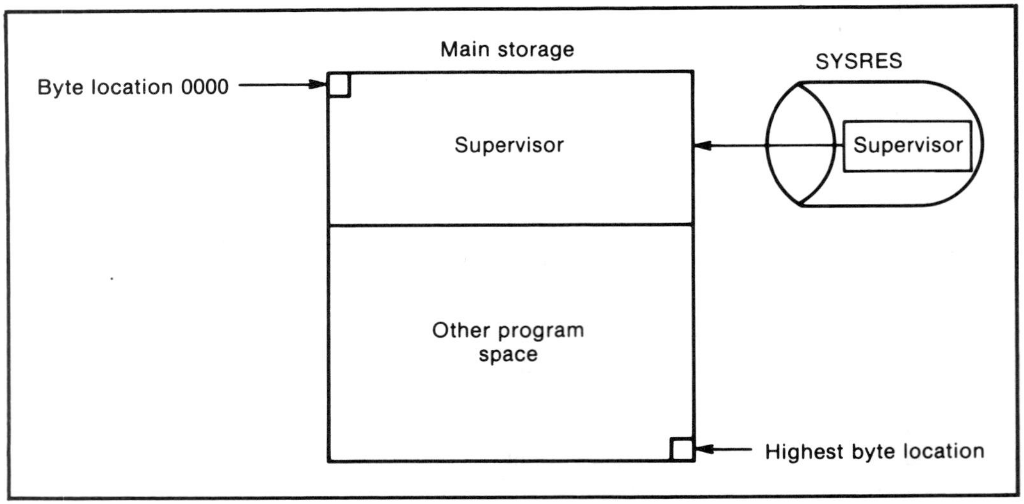

Figure 1–2 Initial program loading

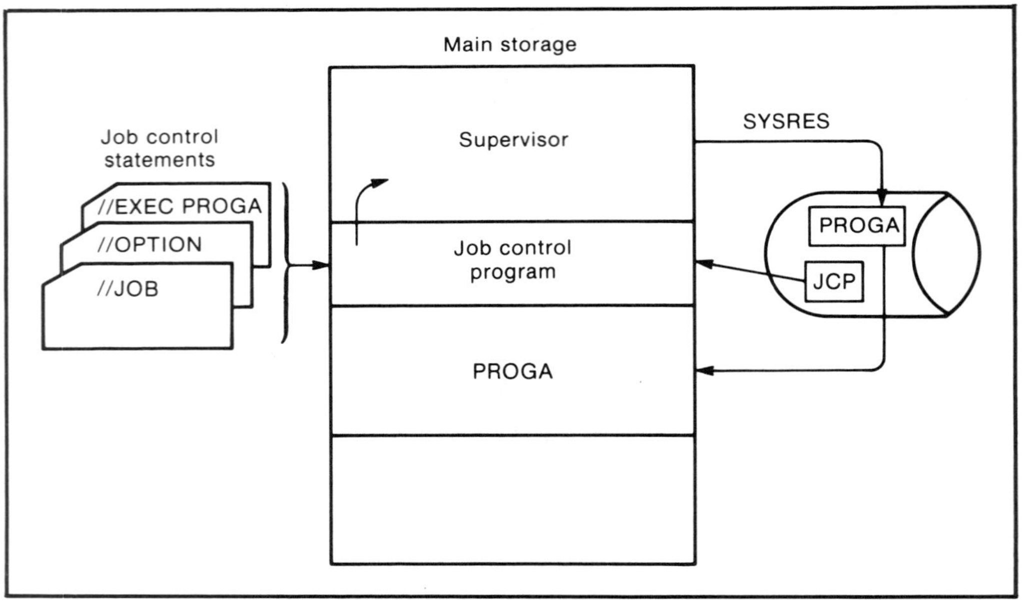

Figure 1–3 Job control statements and program loading

programs. The operating system is usually stored in *libraries* on magnetic disks and is therefore called a Disk Operating System, or DOS. The disk unit holding the operating system is the *system residence device*, or SYSRES. There are many different versions of operating systems, varying with the size and capacity of the computer system.

The most important single program of an operating system is the *supervisor*, sometimes called by such names as the executive, master control program, monitor, or controller. It normally is read, or *loaded*, from disk into the lowest numbered locations of main storage at the start of each day in an operation called *initial program loading* (IPL). The IPL operation is depicted in Figure 1–2. IPL may also be necessary following a power failure or other temporary interruption.

The supervisor is responsible for loading all other programs and for initiating all input/output operations. The supervisor works closely with a *job control program*, which deciphers statements in a *job control language* (JCL). Through JCL, the programmer or computer operator gives the supervisor necessary instructions to load and execute programs and handle input/output operations on files. (See Figure 1–3.) Job control statements may be supplied to the operating system in a continuous sequence. As soon as one job is finished, the job control program reads in the statements for the following job, and work continues. This continuous flow of work is called a *job stream*.

The supervisor also controls *multiprogramming*, whereby more than one program may reside in main storage and appear to be executing at the same time. Actually, only one machine instruction can be executed at a time, but internal operations of the computer are so fast that, while one program is waiting for an input/output operation to be completed, the supervisor transfers control to another program. That program runs until the first I/O operation is completed or another I/O operation is required. The third program can run for a while. As many as 12 to 15 different programs can each have a turn in this fashion. The supervisor can assign a different priority to each program, or take them purely in turn.

Other important programs supplied with the operating system include *language translators*. *Compilers* are programs that translate high-level languages such as COBOL, FORTRAN, PL/I, RPG, BASIC, Pascal, Modula 2, or C into machine language. The *assembler* is the program that translates statements written in assembler language into machine language.

The *linkage editor* is a program that combines (links) machine language program segments together and relocates certain addresses to indicate where in main storage the link-edited program will reside when it is executed. *File-to-file utility programs* permit copying of files from one medium to another, such as tape to printer, disk to tape, or card to disk. The *librarian* program catalogs, displays, retrieves, and deletes programs from several different libraries in the operating system.

DOS DOS is an acronym for Disk Operating System. It is usually pronounced "doss." DOS is used with many medium-to-large sized IBM computers. DOS is of direct concern to the assembler language programmer in two ways: (1) through job control statements outside your program and (2) through statements called *macros* within your program.

Through JCL, you may direct the assembler to translate statements you have written in assembler language, called a *source program*, into machine language instructions, called an *object program* or *object module*. You may later use JCL to direct that your object module be link edited with other modules that control various I/O devices. The link edited program is called a *load module*. You may then use JCL to direct the supervisor to load the load module into main storage and execute it. JCL may also be used to catalog all or part of the program into one of the libraries.

JOB CONTROL STATEMENTS	EXPLANATION
// JOB jobname	Start of job. Jobname must contain not more than 8 letters or digits and must start with a letter.
// EXEC ASSEMBLY	Directs supervisor to load assembler into main storage and execute it.
(Your source program appears here.)	
/*	End of data for your program.
/&	End of job.

Figure 1–4 DOS job control statements to assemble a program

JOB CONTROL STATEMENTS	EXPLANATION
// JOB jobname	Start of job.
// OPTION LINK	Indicates that linkage editor will be required later in the job.
// EXEC ASSEMBLY	Loads and executes assembler.
(Source program appears here.)	
/*	End of data for source program.
// EXEC LNKEDT	Loads and executes linkage editor, which links I/O modules to your object module to create a load module.
// EXEC	Loads and executes your load module.
(Test data for your program appears here.)	
/*	End of test data.
/&	End of job.

Figure 1–5 DOS JCL statements to assemble, link edit, and execute a program

JOB CONTROL STATEMENTS	EXPLANATION
//jobname JOB (password),name	Start of job. No space follows //. Jobname is 1 to 8 characters long, starting with a letter. Password and programmer name are determined by each installation.
// EXEC ASMFC	Load and execute assembler.
// ASM.SYSIN DD *	Indicates that source program follows.
(Source program appears here.)	
/*	End of source program.
//	End of job. Note difference from DOS.

Figure 1–6 OS JCL statements to assemble a program

JOB CONTROL STATEMENTS	EXPLANATION
//jobname JOB (password),name	Start of job.
// EXEC ASMFCLG	Initiate procedure for assembling, linking, and executing program.
// ASM.SYSIN DD *	Source program follows.
(Source program appears here.)	
/*	End of source program.
//GO.SYSPRINT DD SYSOUT=A	Direct all output to printer.
//GO.SYSIN DD *	Test data follows.
(Test data appears here.)	
/*	End of test data.
//	End of job.

Figure 1–7 OS JCL statements to assemble, link edit, and execute a program

Within the assembler language program, you must define each file by writing a DTF (Define the File) macro. A macro is a single statement you write that causes the assembler to generate many constants or instructions in assembler language. The macro gives characteristics of the hardware and tells how the records of the file are organized. DOS provides a special module to handle input or output for each type of file that you may define. Each module is attached to your object module by the linkage editor.

DOS job control statements begin with two slashes followed by a space followed by a keyword, such as JOB, OPTION, ASSGN, or EXEC. Each keyword is followed by a space and one or more operands. Operands are separated by commas. No space may normally appear between operands. The special code /* in the first two columns of a job control statement signifies end of data, and /& in the first two columns indicates end of job.

Some versions of DOS may have slightly different operands from those given below. You should verify exact statements before attempting to use them.

The JCL statements in Figure 1–4 cause the supervisor to load the assembler into main storage to translate your program into machine language. Keywords are in uppercase, and programmer-supplied names are in lowercase.

During the translation process, the assembler prints an error message following each statement that does not follow the rules for spelling, punctuation, or syntax. It also summarizes probable reasons for errors at the end of the program listing. You must locate and remove such errors and reassemble the program until the assembler indicates no errors are found. Then to test your program, use the JCL statements in Figure 1–5.

OS Operating System (OS) is a powerful operating system used with large-scale IBM computers. Its job control statements and organization differ from those of DOS. Like DOS, it has job control statements used to assemble, link edit, and execute programs. Also, within the assembler language program, it has statements used to describe the various files, which are called *data sets* in OS.

To assemble a program without executing it, use the JCL statements in Figure 1–6.

As with DOS, the assembler program listing will show any errors detected. You must remove errors and reassemble the program. When the assembler finds no errors in the source program, use the JCL statements in Figure 1–7 to link edit and execute your object program.

Application Programs

The programs that meet the specific information processing needs of the computer user are called *application programs*. They may be purchased commercially or written by in-house programmers. Most of the examples in this text are application programs. Typical applications include billing of customers, clients, or patients; registering students; reporting grades; receiving and disbursing funds; keeping accounting records; searching tables and files; and performing engineering or scientific calculations.

Systems programs perform functions common to almost all users. Applications programs differ widely depending on the nature of the business and the types of problems the computer is intended to solve.

STRUCTURED PROGRAM DEVELOPMENT

Structured programming is a formal approach to program design that starts with the broadest and highest level of program logic. It is often called *top-down* programming, because it first defines *what* is to be done before considering *how*. For example, you may know that certain accumulators must be cleared and certain initial values set at the start of a program before you decide just how you will do this.

Each major function or task to be performed is often written as a *module* that ideally can be printed on a single page, with only one entry point at the top and one exit at the bottom.

You may normally follow the same general steps toward program development, no matter what programming language you happen to use.

Defining the Problem

The first step in defining the problem is to determine what output is needed. A print chart such as Figure 1–8 is often used to show the placement of headings, detail lines, and totals. Xs are normally placed wherever variable information will print.

Much output nowadays appears on visual display screens. Such screens normally have a maximum of 80 characters per line and around 25 lines per screen. You may use a print chart to design the screen format, or a special screen layout chart.

Once the format of the output is determined, the data format of the input records must be determined. You may use a record layout form such as Figure 1–9 to show the relative locations and sizes of the fields of data. The format of tape or disk records may also be shown on a similar form. Or input records may be described by showing the starting and ending location of each

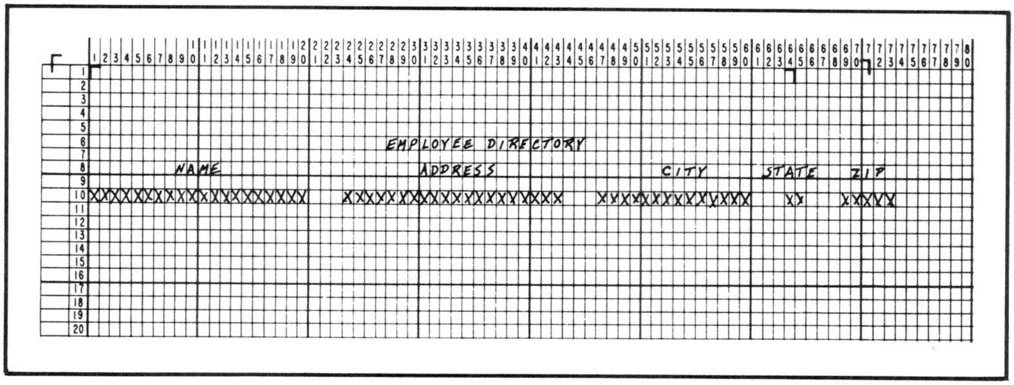

Figure 1–8 Print chart

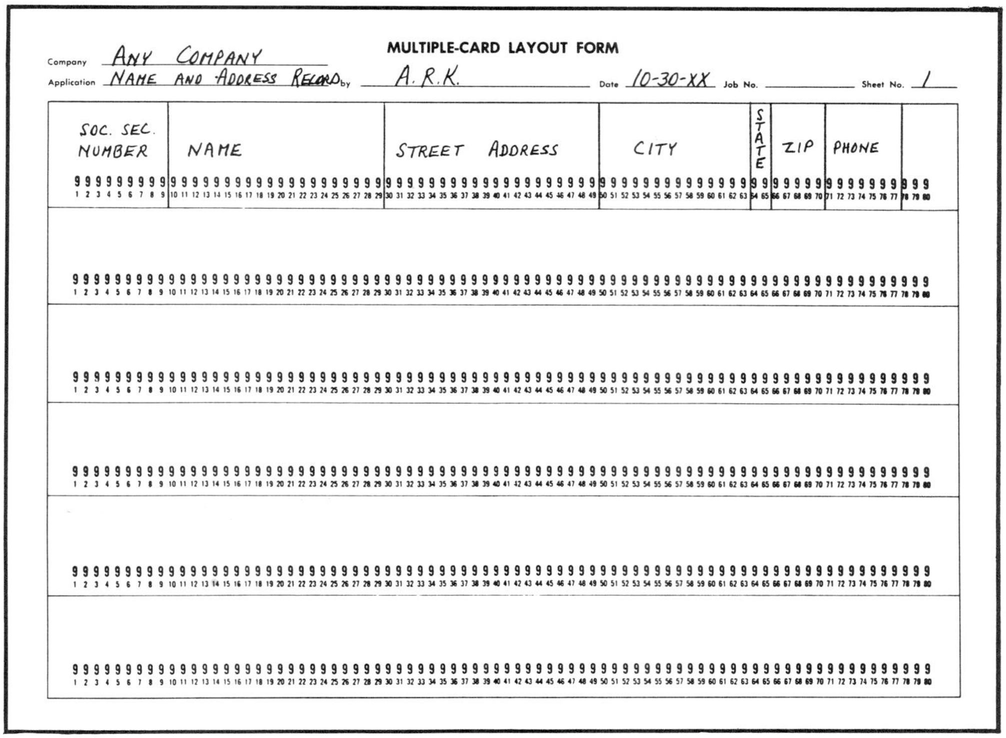

Figure 1–9 Record layout form

LOCATION	FIELD NAME
1–9	Social security number (999999999)
10–29	Customer name
30–49	Customer street address
50–63	City
64–66	State code
67–71	Zip code
72–81	Phone
82–87	Date of latest transaction (999999)
88–94	Balance (99999V99)

Figure 1–10 Record description

field within the record, the type of data, and the number of decimal places. In the example in Figure 1–10, each 9 represents one digit in the field, and the V represents the position where a decimal point is assumed to be, but is not actually present in the record.

Often you need additional information to define the problem accurately, such as maximum values fields may have, special codes used, or special processing requirements. All print charts, data layout forms, and other specifications become an important part of the documentation (working papers) that should be prepared and retained for each program.

Planning the Logical Solution

Program logic involves those steps necessary to transform input data into output information. The logic is normally expressed in the form of a structure chart, pseudocode, or a program flowchart. A *structure chart* shows the relationship of modules that make up the program. *Pseudocode* consists of a few capitalized keywords followed by ordinary English terms, indented in such a way as to show the relationships of the various statements. A *program flowchart* uses lines, arrows, and symbols to show the flow of the program logic. Figure 1–11 shows program flowcharting symbols and conventions.

Fundamentally, all program logic can be classified under one of three categories:

1. Sequence structure: a series of instructions executed in the order they appear.
2. Repetition structure (iteration or loop): a group of instructions that are repeated until some condition occurs that terminates the loop.
3. Selection structure: a choice of one logical path if a condition is true and a different path if the condition is false.

Every structure should have a *single entry point* and a *single exit*. In other words, we should never branch into or out of the middle of a structure.

Symbol	Name	Use
	Terminal	Placed at start and end of each program or subroutine.
	Processing block	Used to show data movement, arithmetic operations.
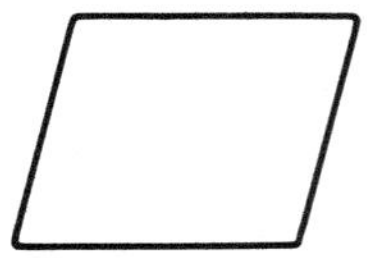	Input/output symbol	Used for any input or output operation.
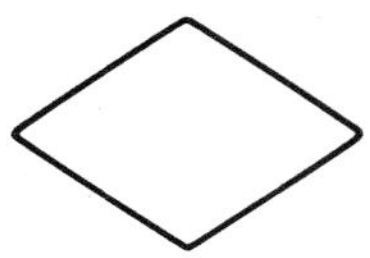	Decision block	Used to show any condition to be tested. If condition is true, line leaves one side of block. If false, line leaves the other side.
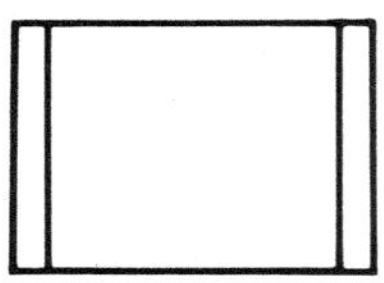	Predefined process symbol	Used to represent a subroutine or module that might occur at more than one place in a program. The detailed symbols showing logic of the subroutine or module must appear in some other part of the flowchart.
	Collector or connector	Used where two lines come together. Also to show exit at one part of chart and entry at another.
	Line and arrowhead	Used to connect blocks. Arrowhead shows direction of logical flow. If flow is downward or to the right, arrowhead may be omitted.

Figure 1–11 Program flowcharting symbols

Sequence Structure This is the simplest structure. Instructions are simply executed one after another. Only the most elementary program can be written using the sequence structure. Here is an example of pseudocode for a few instructions in sequence structure. Figure 1–12 shows a program flowchart for the same logic.

```
START PROGRAM
Open files
Move zeros to totals
Move spaces to print line
Read first record
```

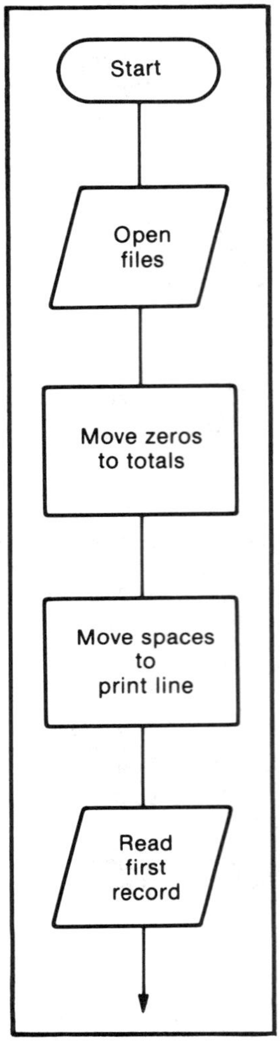

Figure 1–12 Flowchart showing sequence structure

Repetition Structure The repetition structure, or *loop*, has two main forms. In the first form, a condition is tested by asking a question before the other statements in the loop are performed. If the condition tested is true, that is, the answer to the question is YES, the loop is performed. If the condition is false (the answer is NO), the loop is not performed. This structure is usually called a *DOWHILE* (pronounced "do while") or *WHILEDO* structure, or a *pretest loop*. Note that if the condition is false the first time the test is made, the loop will not be performed at all. Each time the loop is repeated is called an *iteration*.

A loop is not terminated the instant the condition becomes false. Only when the condition is tested again before the loop is repeated can the loop be terminated. It is therefore important to know exactly where in the loop the condition to be tested is changed, or just how the condition is phrased.

In pseudocode, a loop to read and print all the records in a file might be:

```
Read first record
DOWHILE NOT end-of-file:
   Print record
   Read next record
ENDDO:
```

Figure 1–13 shows the same logic represented as a program flowchart.

In the second form, the loop is performed once before a condition is tested to see if the loop should be repeated. This form is usually called a *REPEAT-UNTIL* structure, or a *posttest loop*. Notice that under this structure the loop will always be performed at least once.

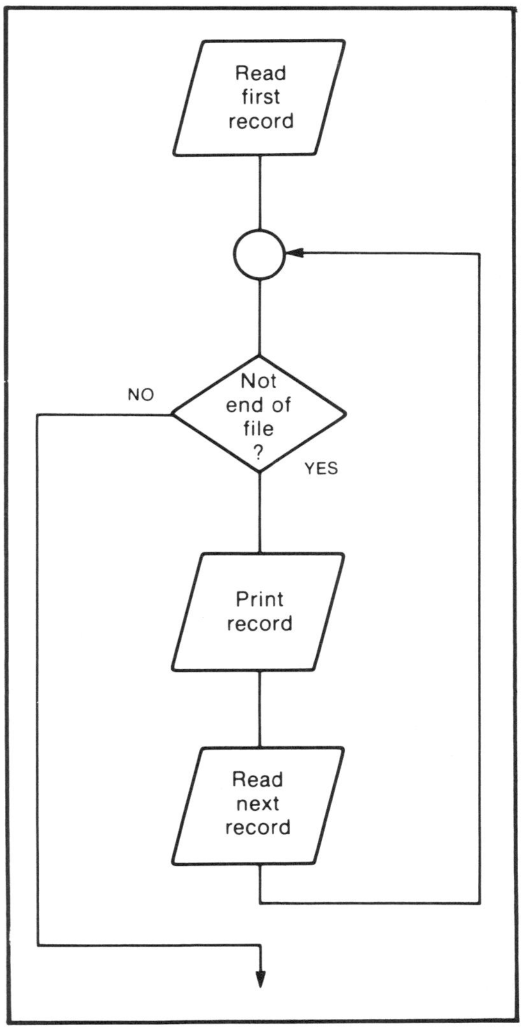

Figure 1–13 Flowchart showing pretest loop

```
Set counter to 50
Set table address at beginning
REPEAT:
   Read table record
   Put data into table
   Modify table address
   Subtract one from counter
UNTIL counter is not greater than zero
```

Figure 1–14 shows the program flowchart for this posttest loop.

Selection Structure The selection structure is often called the *IF-THEN-ELSE* structure. There are two variations. The first is a *one-way* test, of IF-THEN form. Here you take some action if the condition is true, but don't take it if the condition is false. In the pseudocode below, you skip to a new page and print the headings only if the line counter is equal to or greater than 50. If the line counter is less than 50, you omit these actions.

```
IF line-counter is equal to or greater than 50:
   THEN skip to a new page
   Print heading lines
   Set line-counter to 0
ENDIF:
```

A flowchart for one-way selection is shown in Figure 1–15.

The second variation on the selection structure provides a *two-way* test. If the condition is true, you execute the statements following THEN; if the condition is false, you execute the statements following ELSE. The THEN and ELSE statements will never both be executed for the same condition. Note the following pseudocode:

```
IF student-grade is equal to or greater than 70:
   THEN print "STUDENT PASSES"
ELSE
   Print "STUDENT FAILS"
ENDIF:
```

The flowchart logic for two-way selection is shown in Figure 1–16.

Coding and Assembling the Program

Once the program logic has been worked out, the next step is *coding* the program. Coding is writing the actual computer instructions in the language you have selected. For this book, of course, you will use assembler language. Depending upon the amount of detail in the pseudocode or program flowchart, you may write exactly one statement in assembler language for each flowchart symbol or line of pseudocode, or you may write more than one. You must exercise extreme care to be sure that all details of punctuation, spelling, sequence, and format are correct. The details of actual coding are covered more fully in Chapter 2.

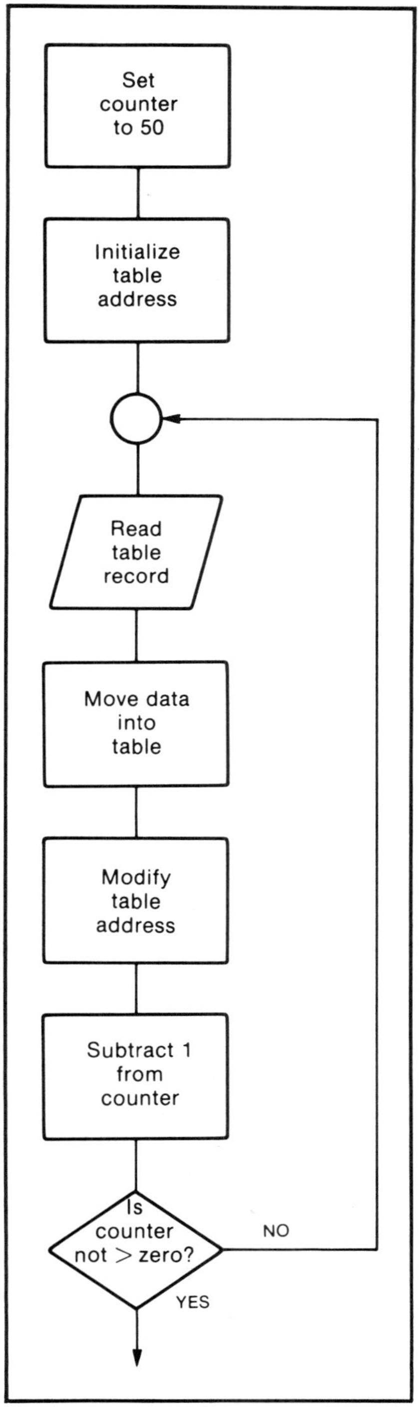

Figure 1–14 Flowchart showing posttest loop

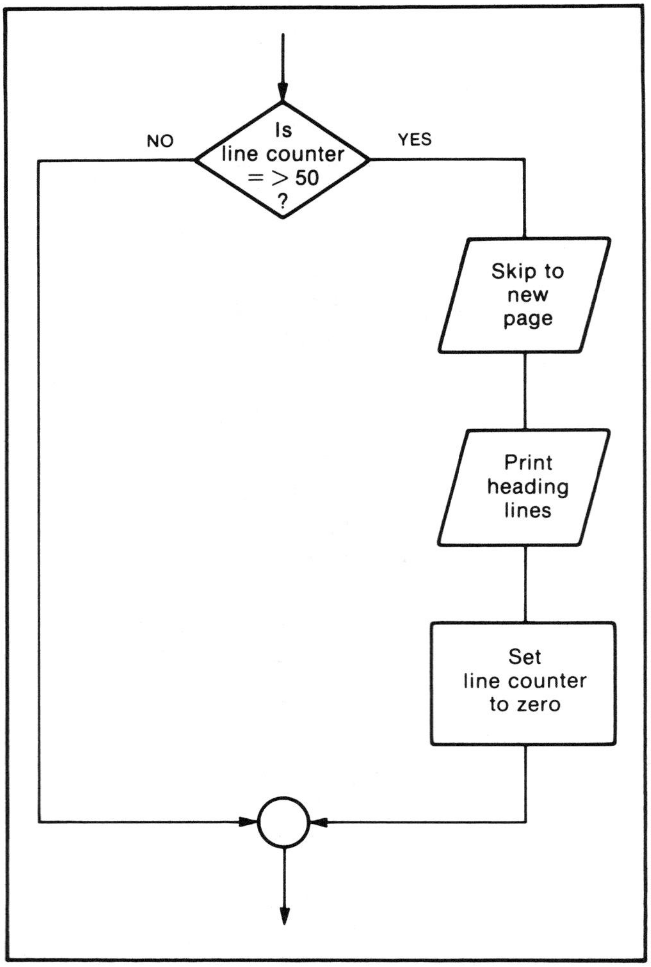

Figure 1–15 Flowchart showing one-way selection

The Assembly Process The statements you write during coding are called the *source statements*. You may write them on a standard coding form or on plain paper. When finished, you must enter them into a computer terminal or punch them into cards to form the *source program*. Verify carefully to be sure you have made no errors in keying in the source program.

The source program then becomes input to the assembler, which translates source statements into machine language to produce the *object program*, or *object module*. You normally ask the assembler to produce a listing, which shows the source and object programs side by side, along with a notation of any errors or diagnostic messages the assembler has detected.

If you have made errors, you must correct them and reassemble the revised source program. Continue this cycle until the listing indicates that the assembler has found no errors. Then you can make your program ready for testing. Figure 1–17 shows the steps for assembling and testing a program.

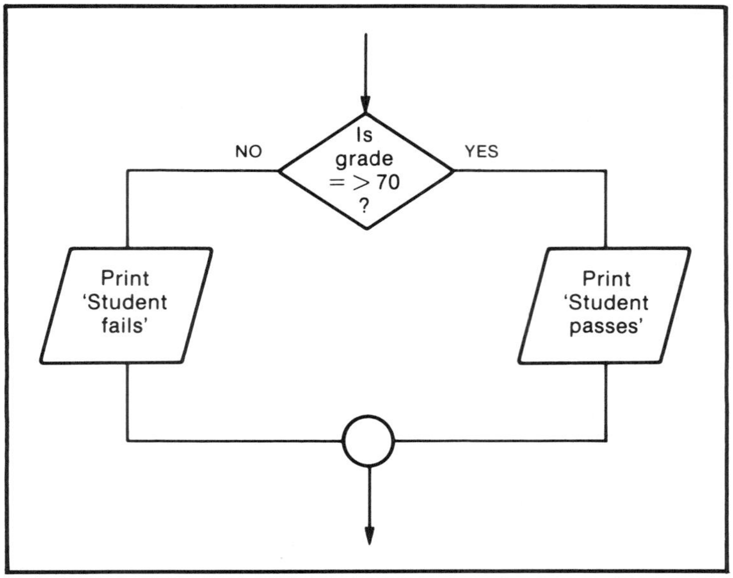

Figure 1–16 Flowchart showing two-way selection

Relocating the Program Programs are normally written as if they would be placed in main storage starting at location 0. However, the supervisor occupies the lowest-numbered locations of main storage. Our program must then be *relocated* so that it can be run in some other part of main storage. Relocation is done by changing addresses of data and instructions in the program. This is similar to what you would do in changing page numbers in a report if you had to insert additional material at some point.

Program relocation may be done by the *linkage editor* or by a *relocating loader*. The linkage editor, one of the programs supplied with the operating system, takes the object program from the assembler and relocates designated addresses. It also *links* standard I/O modules to your object program and creates a *load module*, ready for execution. The linkage editor produces a map giving the new addresses where the program will reside at execution time. In some operating systems, the functions of the linkage editor are carried out when the program is loaded for execution.

Testing the Program

You are now ready to test your load module. You should select or prepare test data of every type and condition so that every instruction in your program will be executed at least once. Do not be surprised if the program does not run correctly the first time. Even though the assembler may detect no errors, you still may have used incorrect logic or described some data incorrectly.

Examine all output to verify that all output information is in the correct form and position. Verify calculations and see that all exceptions or unusual situations have been correctly handled.

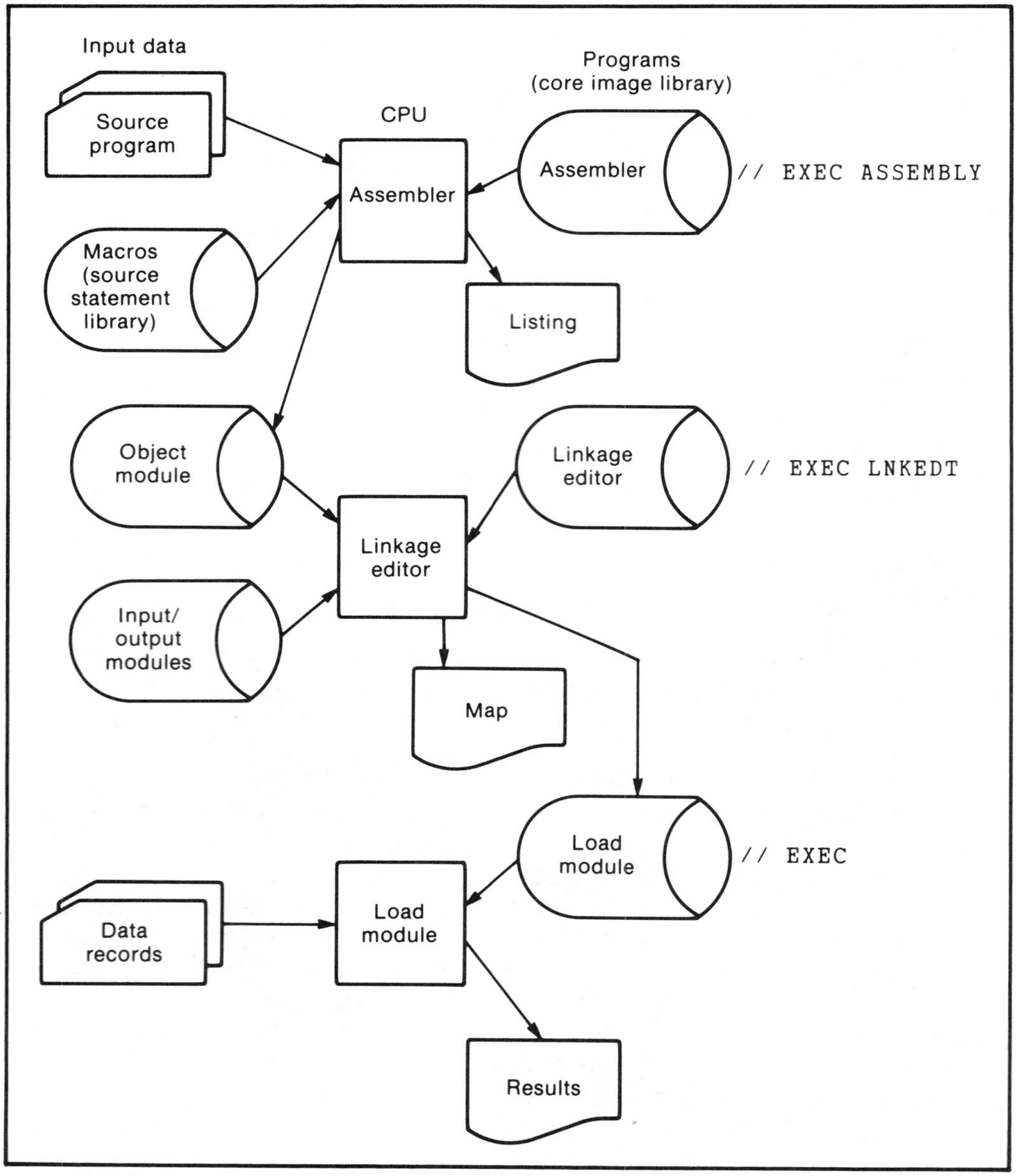

Figure 1–17 Assembling and testing a program

Completing the Documentation

When you are satisfied that your program runs correctly, you are ready to complete the program documentation. Items that should normally be included are:

1. Print chart or screen layout form.
2. Input record descriptions.

3. Additional program specifications.
4. Structure chart, pseudocode, or program flowchart.
5. Assembler listing.
6. Linkage editor map.
7. Program output.

DATA CODES

IBM computers use an eight-bit code to represent each letter, digit, and special character. Each eight-bit character fills one byte. Binary numbers are represented by 8, 16, 32, or 64 bits occupying more than one byte.

EBCDIC Code

The eight-bit code is called the Extended Binary-Coded Decimal Interchange Code, EBCDIC for short (pronounced "eb-si-dik"). There are 256 different ways in which eight bits can be arranged in one byte. The 256 combinations provide codes to represent upper- and lower-case letters, the 10 decimal digits, some 30 special characters, and a number of codes that are not printable characters.

Long strings of bits can be difficult to read and write. Hexadecimal (hex) digits are used as a short method of representing groups of bits. There are 16 digits in the hex number system, representing values of 0 through 15.

Any combination of four bits can be represented as one hexadecimal digit. The bits have values of 8, 4, 2, and 1 from left to right. For example, 1001 is equivalent to $(1*8) + (0*4) + (0*2) + (1*1) = 8 + 0 + 0 + 1 = 9$. The decimal, binary, and hex values from 0 through 15 are shown in Table 1–1. Notice that the hex digits A through F are used to represent decimal values of 10 through 15 respectively.

Table 1–1 Decimal, Binary, and Hexadecimal Equivalents

DECIMAL	BINARY	HEXADECIMAL
0	0000	0
1	0001	1
2	0010	2
3	0011	3
4	0100	4
5	0101	5
6	0110	6
7	0111	7
8	1000	8
9	1001	9
10	1010	A
11	1011	B

12	1100	C
13	1101	D
14	1110	E
15	1111	F

Two hex digits can represent any possible contents of one byte. Figure 1-18 shows the EBCDIC code in both binary and hex form for the characters most commonly found on a computer keyboard.

The leftmost, or high-order, four bits of a byte are called *zone* bits, while the rightmost, or low-order, four bits are the *numeric* bits. These terms originated with punched cards, where the upper three rows are called zone rows and the lower nine rows are called numeric rows. (Actually, the zero row on a card is considered either zone or numeric, depending upon its use.) Figure 1–19 shows punched card codes for numbers, letters, and special characters.

The order of the bits, when considered as binary numbers, is called the *collating sequence*. This sequence is important in sorting and comparing data. In EBCDIC, you will note that special characters generally have a lower collating sequence than letters, while letters are lower than the decimal digits. Other codes, such as ASCII (American Standard Code for Information Interchange), used on many microcomputers, have a different collating sequence.

Hexadecimal Numbers and Addresses

Hexadecimal numbers are used rather than decimal numbers for many purposes on IBM computers, because they can be more readily converted to and from binary numbers. As stated before, each hex digit can be converted directly to four bits.

Hex numbers are used to represent the contents of each storage byte. Thus they may show machine instructions, constants in assembler programs, addresses, and printouts of main storage.

Hex numbers can be converted to and from decimal numbers, but the process is more complex than conversion to and from binary. The simplest way to convert hex to decimal is to use a place value table (see Figure 1–20).

Place values of hex digits are in powers of 16, as contrasted with the place values of decimal digits in powers of 10. The place values of the hex digits, right to left, are 1, 16, 256, 4096, 65536, and so forth. Each place is 16 times the value of the digit to its right.

To distinguish hex numbers from decimal, we will precede hex numbers with the letter X and enclose them in single quotation marks, as in X'12A7'.

For practice, we might convert the hex number X'947' to decimal, using the place value table in Figure 1–20. The values of the X'900' in the third digit from the right is decimal (9 * 256), or 2304. The value of the X'40' in the second digit is decimal (4 * 16), or 64. The value of the X'7' in the rightmost

CHARACTER	HEX	BINARY	CHARACTER	HEX	BINARY
A	C1	1100 0001	Space	40	0100 0000
B	C2	1100 0010	.	4B	0100 1011
C	C3	1100 0011	<	4C	0100 1100
D	C4	1100 0100	(	4D	0100 1101
E	C5	1100 0101	+	4E	0100 1110
F	C6	1100 0110	&	50	0101 0000
G	C7	1100 0111	!	5A	0101 1010
H	C8	1100 1000	$	5B	0101 1011
I	C9	1100 1001	*	5C	0101 1100
J	D1	1101 0001	)	5D	0101 1101
K	D2	1101 0010	;	5E	0101 1110
L	D3	1101 0011	-	60	0110 0000
M	D4	1101 0100	/	61	0110 0001
N	D5	1101 0101	,	6B	0110 1011
O	D6	1101 0110	%	6C	0110 1100
P	D7	1101 0111	>	6E	0110 1110
Q	D8	1101 1000	?	6F	0110 1111
R	D9	1101 1001	:	7A	0111 1010
S	E2	1110 0010	#	7B	0111 1011
T	E3	1110 0011	@	7C	0111 1100
U	E4	1110 0100	‘	7D	0111 1101
V	E5	1110 0101	=	7E	0111 1110
W	E6	1110 0110	“	7F	0111 1111
X	E7	1110 0111			
Y	E8	1110 1000			
Z	E9	1110 1001			
0	F0	1111 0000			
1	F1	1111 0001			
2	F2	1111 0010			
3	F3	1111 0011			
4	F4	1111 0100			
5	F5	1111 0101			
6	F6	1111 0110			
7	F7	1111 0111			
8	F8	1111 1000			
9	F9	1111 1001			

Figure 1–18 EBCDIC code for common characters

digit is decimal (7 * 1), or 7. Adding the decimal values of the three digits, we get 2304 + 64 + 7 = 2375.

To get the decimal equivalent of X‘B97C’:

X‘B000’	=	11 *	4096	=	45056
X‘0900’	=	9 *	256	=	2304
X‘0070’	=	7 *	16	=	112
X‘000C’	=	12 *	1	=	12
X‘B97C’	=				47484

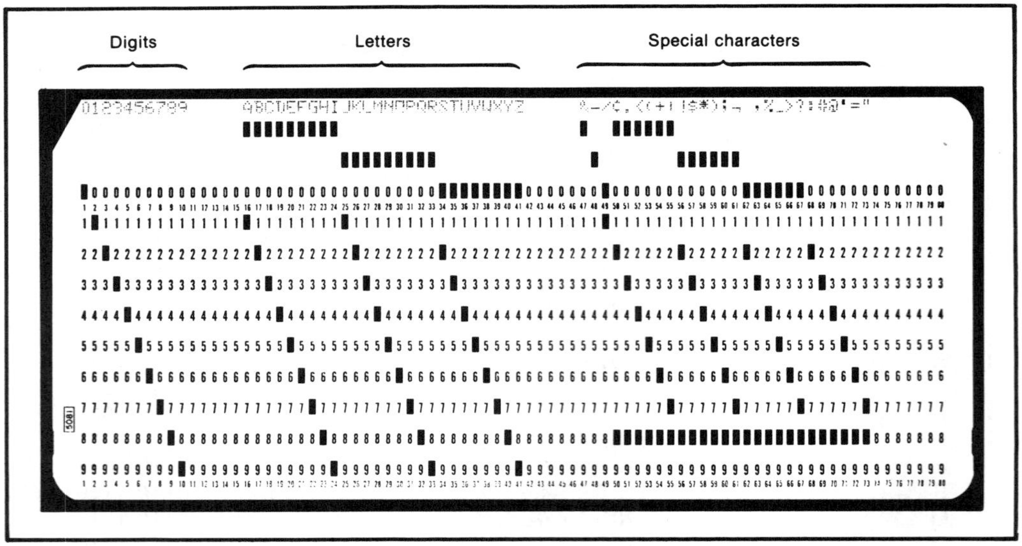

Figure 1–19 Punched card codes

To convert the decimal value 795 to hex, proceed as follows: Find the largest value in the table that does not exceed 795. This is 768 decimal, or X'300'. Subtract 768 from 795, leaving 27 still to be converted. The largest number on the table that does not exceed 27 is 16 decimal, or X'10'. Subtract 16 from 27, leaving 11 decimal, which is X'B'. Add the three hex values X'300' + X'10' + X'B' = X'31B', the hex number that is equivalent to decimal 795.

For another example, convert decimal value 4967 to hex.

Original value	4967	
Subtract largest value	4096	= Hex value X'1000'
Leaving	871	
Subtract largest value	768	= Hex value X'0300'
Leaving	103	
Subtract largest value	96	= Hex value X'0060'
Leaving	7	= Hex value X'0007'
Add hex values to give hex equivalent		= Hex value X'1367'

All addresses in assembler listings and linkage editor maps are given in hex. We often have to add or subtract hex numbers to determine the number of bytes between addresses. The simplest way to perform hex addition is to convert each digit mentally to decimal, add the two, and reconvert to hex. Instead of carrying when the sum reaches 10, as we do in decimal addition, we carry only when the sum reaches 16 (X'10') in hex addition. Note the following example:

X	16^6 X000000	16^5 X00000	16^4 X0000	16^3 X000	16^2 X00	16^1 X0	16^0 X
1	16777216	1048576	65536	4096	256	16	1
2	33554432	2097152	131072	8192	512	32	2
3	50331648	3145728	196608	12288	768	48	3
4	67108864	4194304	262144	16384	1024	64	4
5	83886080	5242880	327680	20480	1280	80	5
6	100663296	6291456	393216	24576	1536	96	6
7	117440512	7340032	458752	28672	1792	112	7
8	134217728	8388608	524288	32768	2048	128	8
9	150994944	9437184	589824	36864	2304	144	9
A	167772160	10485760	655360	40960	2560	160	10
B	184549376	11534336	720896	45056	2816	176	11
C	201326592	12582912	786432	49152	3072	192	12
D	218103808	13631488	851968	53248	3328	208	13
E	234881024	14680064	917504	57344	3584	224	14
F	251658240	15728640	983040	61440	3840	240	15

Figure 1–20 Hexadecimal place value table

09	X'09'
+12	X'0C'
=21	X'15'

The sum of the two decimal values is 21, which is 5 more than 16. In the hex number, we record the X'5' and carry the 16 (X'10') to the next position.

Here are some more examples:

Carries:		1	1	111
	X'456'	X'72D'	X'3AC'	X'0ABE'
	+X'789'	+X'657'	+X'83F'	+X'0FED'
	X'BDF'	X'D84'	X'BEB'	X'1AAB'

When we subtract hex numbers, we borrow not 10 as we do in decimal, but X'10', or 16 in decimal. (Remember that the place value of each digit is 16 times that of the digit to its right.) Also, whenever we borrow, the digit from which we borrow is reduced by 1 before the next subtraction is made. Here are some examples of hex subtraction:

Borrows:		1	1	1
	X'789'	X'72D'	X'83F'	X'FED'
	-X'456'	-X'657'	-X'3AC'	-X'ABE'
	X'333'	X'0D6'	X'493'	X'52F'

In the first example, no borrow is necessary. In the second example, for the rightmost digit we subtract 7 from 13 (X'D'), giving 6 (X'6'). For the second digit from the right, when we borrow we get X'10' to add to the X'2', giving X'12', or decimal 18. Subtracting 5 from 18 leaves 13, or X'D' as the second digit. The X'7' in the third position from the right was reduced to X'6' by the borrow. Subtracting X'6' for this leaves X'0' in the leftmost digit of the difference. The third and fourth examples use the same principle.

SUMMARY

A computer system is made up of four principal components:

1. hardware
2. software
3. personnel
4. procedures

Its main purpose is to convert data into meaningful information.

The principal hardware components are main storage, the central processing unit, and input/output devices. Main storage contains numbered locations, called bytes, that hold data to be processed as well as the instructions that direct the processing. The CPU contains the control unit and the arithmetic-logic unit. The control unit fetches and decodes each instruction. Then it carries it out by moving data back and forth between the various parts of the computer system. The arithmetic-logic unit performs calculations and comparisons.

Input devices sense data recorded on some medium such as magnetic tape or disk or punched cards, and send the data to main storage along special-purpose channels when directed by the control unit. The channels convey information processed in main storage to output devices that record it on a medium such as a display screen, printed page, or magnetic tape or disk.

Software consists of systems programs and application programs. Systems programs, usually called operating systems, perform duties that make the computer run efficiently. These include loading and executing programs, carrying out input/output operations, translating programs in different languages into machine language, maintaining libraries, sorting data, and maintaining files.

Application programs do the specific processing of the individual user. Applications vary according to the nature of the organization and the type of information desired.

Structured program development follows five steps:

1. defining the problem
2. planning the logical solution
3. coding and assembling the program

4. testing the program
5. completing documentation

The problem is defined by showing the format of the output desired and the arrangement of input data.

Program logic falls into three structures:

1. sequence
2. repetition
3. selection

Each structure has only one entry point and one exit. The programmer plans the logical solution by arranging the instructions into the proper structure. A structure chart shows the relationship between the modules that make up the program. Pseudocode represents the logic in ordinary English words. A program flowchart represents the logic with special symbols and connecting lines.

Instructions are written, or coded, following the program logic, producing the source program. The assembler converts the source program into a machine language object program. The linkage editor relocates certain addresses, attaches various I/O modules, and produces a load module which is ready for execution.

Test data should represent all types and conditions that the program is likely to encounter during normal operation. It should test every part of the program.

When the program operates as desired, documentation is completed. Usual documentation includes print charts or screen layout forms, input layouts, pseudocode or program flowcharts, assembler listings, output from test runs, and any other information necessary for full understanding of how the program operates.

Each byte contains eight bits, which can be represented as either 0 or 1. The eight-bit combinations form a code, called EBCDIC, that represents a letter, digit, or special character. There are 256 different possible combinations in each byte.

Hexadecimal numbers have 16 different digits, 0 through 9 and A through F. Each four bits can be converted directly to one hexadecimal digit. Instructions, addresses, and data in main storage are represented in hexadecimal form on the assembler listings.

TERMS FOR REVIEW

Arithmetic-logic unit (ALU)
Assembler
Binary numbers
Bit
Byte
Central processing unit (CPU)
Channel
Coding
Collating sequence
Conditional branch

Control unit
Device
Documentation
EBCDIC
Execution cycle
General register
Hardware
Hexadecimal numbers
Initial program load (IPL)
Instruction cycle
Job control language (JCL)
Job stream
Linkage editor
Load module
Main storage
Medium
Module
Multiplexor channel
Multiprogramming
Numeric bits
Object module
One-way test
Op code
Operand
Operating system
Posttest loop
Pretest loop
Program flowchart
Pseudocode
Repetition structure
Selection structure
Selector channel
Sequence structure
Software
Source statements
Structured programming
Supervisor
Two-way test
Unconditional branch
Zone bits

REVIEW QUESTIONS

1. What is the function of a computer system, and what are its four major components?
2. What are the parts of the central processing unit?
3. How is data represented in main storage? What is in main storage other than data while programs are running?
4. What are general registers, and why are they used?
5. What are the main functions of the control unit?
6. How are instructions decoded and executed? What part of the computer does these operations?
7. What is the difference between a medium and a device?
8. What types of channels are there, and what is their function?
9. What are the two major divisions of software?
10. What is meant by an operating system? What types of programs does it include?
11. Distinguish between DOS and OS. How are they used in assembling or running programs?
12. Briefly describe the five steps in structured program development.
13. What documents are used in defining the problem to be solved by a computer program?
14. What is pseudocode?
15. What symbols are used in program flowcharts?
16. What is the input to the assembler? What output does it produce?
17. What is the purpose of the linkage editor? What does it use for input and output?

18. What makes good test data for testing a program?
19. What items should be included in the final documentation for a program?

EXERCISES

1. Write pseudocode to show the difference between a pretest and a posttest loop.
2. Write the program flowchart symbols to illustrate an IF-THEN (one-way) and an IF-THEN-ELSE (two-way) test.
3. Write the hexadecimal form of the EBCDIC code for each of the following:
   a. CPU
   b. $37.48
   c. // JOB TEST
   d. Your first name
4. Show the decimal equivalent for each of these hexadecimal numbers:
   a. X'4375'
   b. X'2D7B'
   c. X'BEAD'
   d. X'FACE'
5. Convert each of these decimal numbers to hexadecimal:
   a. 4341
   b. 54321
   c. 5280
   d. 12345
6. Perform the following hexadecimal arithmetic operations:
   a. X'8792' + X'384A'
   b. X'FE79' + X'48C1'
   c. X'A73D' − X'3B09'
   d. X'FACE' − X'BEEF'
7. Convert each of these binary numbers to hex:
   a. 0101 1110
   b. 1111 0010
   c. 1001 0111
   d. 0001 0011
8. Convert each of these hex numbers to binary:
   a. X'37'
   b. X'59'
   c. X'EB'
   d. X'1F'

2

Getting Started in Assembler Language

OBJECTIVES

After studying this chapter, you should be able to:

- Name the various parts and columns of the coding form
- Describe the three types of statements in assembler language
- Define constants and storage areas
- Define files for card input and printer output in DOS and OS
- Show the relationship between program flowcharts and pseudocode
- Build a program shell to read and print records
- Write and describe a typical subroutine to print headings
- Describe the use of general registers for counting and linking to subroutines
- Use macros for reading cards and printing on the line printer
- Distinguish between conditional and unconditional branching

In the first chapter, we reviewed some basic computer concepts and saw the role of the operating system in assembling, link editing, and executing programs. We also went through the steps in developing a program in proper structured form. We examined the EBCDIC code and learned that hexadecimal numbers are used for addresses and other representations in assembler language. Now we are ready to write our first program.

THE CODING FORM

You may write assembler statements on any type of paper or even directly on the keyboard of your terminal or keypunch machine. However, a special form (Figure 2–1) is convenient to show statements in an attractive, readable format.

The heading portion of the form contains identifying information about the programmer, name of program, date written, and so forth. If anyone other than yourself will be keying in your program, you may specify in the graphics section exactly how you write certain numbers or letters that may be difficult

IBM IBM System/360 Assembler Coding Form — GX28-6509-6 U/M 050* Printed in U.S.A.

PROGRAM: EMPLOYEE NAME, OFFICE, AND PHONE LISTING — PROGRAMMER: A.R.K. — DATE: 10-29-XX — PAGE 1 OF 4

```
*              ALTON R. KINDRED, PROGRAM 1
* THIS PROGRAM LISTS NAME, OFFICE, AND PHONE NUMBER OF EACH EMPLOYEE.
*              REGISTERS USED:
*                R5  - LINE COUNTER
*                R9  - LINK TO MODULE
*                R12 - BASE REGISTER
*
         PRINT NOGEN
MAINLINE START Ø                       SET LOCATION COUNTER
         BALR  12,Ø                    LOAD BASE REGISTER
         USING *,12                    DESIGNATE BASE REGISTER
         OPEN  INFILE,PRINTER          OPEN FILES
         BAL   9,HEADING               PRINT HEADING
         GET   INFILE,INRECD           READ FIRST RECORD
DOWHILE  EQU   *                       DOWHILE NOT END OF FILE
         MVC   PRNAME,INNAME             SET UP PRINT LINE
         MVC   PROFFICE,INOFFICE         *
         MVC   PRPHONE,INPHONE           *
         PUT   PRINTER,PRLINE            PRINT LINE
         BCT   5,ENDIF                   SUBTRACT 1 FROM LINE COUNT
IF       EQU   *                         IF LINE COUNT = ZERO
THEN     BAL   9,HEADING                   THEN PRINT HEADING
ENDIF    EQU   *                         ENDIF
         GET   INFILE,INRECD             READ NEXT RECORD
```

* A standard card form, IBM electro 6509, is available for punching source statements from this form. Instructions for using this form are in any IBM System/360 assembler language reference manual. Address comments concerning this form to IBM Nordic Laboratory, Publications Development, Box 962, S-181 09 Lidingö 9, Sweden.

*No of forms per pad may vary slightly.

Figure 2–1 Assembler coding form

to distinguish, such as I and 1, 2 and Z, or the numeral 0 and the letter O. Use the entire heading area as you wish or as prescribed in programming standards for your installation.

The body of the coding form is divided into four areas:

1. Columns 1 to 8 are the *name* area. The name is sometimes called a *label* or *symbol*. Where a name is needed to identify a file, record, field, or instruction, it must begin in column 1 of this area. Names must begin with a letter, and may have no more than eight letters or numbers and no imbedded spaces. File names are an exception and are limited to seven letters or numbers. The special characters #, @, and $ are considered letters when used in names.
2. Columns 10 to 14 are for the *operation code*, often called *op code* for short. Op codes state what the instruction is to do or what is being defined.
3. Columns 16 to 71 are for *operands* and *comments*. Operands may be names of instructions, files, or data that have been defined elsewhere in the program. They may also be self-defining terms such as character strings or numbers. Most statements have two operands separated by commas. Operands specify what the op code will be operating on. Except as specified later in special cases, no spaces are allowed between operands.

   Comments may be written following the last operand on a line. At least one space must separate the comments from the operands. Comments often are started at or to the right of column 40 for easier reading.

4. Column 72 is the continuation column. If any statement cannot be contained on a single line, any nonblank character is placed in column 72 of that line to indicate that the statement is continued on the following line. Additional continuation lines may be used. Each line being continued from the preceding line must begin in column 16.
5. Columns 73 to 80 are for identification and sequence. Their use is entirely optional. Some programmers prefer to use columns 73 to 76 for a code to identify the program and 77 to 80 for line numbers to keep statements in sequence. Often an interval of 10 is left between line numbers to allow other statements to be inserted if necessary.

If we place an asterisk (*) in column 1 of the coding form, the entire line is a comment. Comments are not translated by the assembler, but do appear on the assembler listing as an important part of program documentation.

The assembler will accept source statements in free format if they meet the following rules:

1. The name, if used, must begin in column 1.
2. If no name is used, the op code must begin in or to the right of column 2.
3. There must be at least one space between name and op code, between op code and operands, and between operands and comments.

Statements in free format are difficult to read. Use of standard columns in the coding form is recommended.

TYPES OF STATEMENTS

Every statement written in assembler language is one of three types:

1. machine instructions
2. assembler instructions
3. macro instructions

Machine Instructions

Machine instructions are converted to machine language to direct the computer to carry out your program logic. Each op code must be the precise authorized *mnemonic* (aid to memory) code and every operand must be in exactly the correct form. Much of this text is devoted to learning the form and function of machine instructions.

Assembler Instructions

Assembler instructions may be divided generally into directives and declaratives. *Directives* are *not* converted into machine language to become a part of

NAME	OP	OPERANDS	REMARKS
Optional	TITLE	'Data to be printed'	Prints up to 100 characters at top of each page of assembler listing
Omit	EJECT	Omit	Skip assembler listing to new page
Omit	SPACE	An integer or omit	Skip the specified number of blank lines; omitted operand causes one line
Omit	PRINT	ON	Print assembler listing
	PRINT	OFF	Do not print listing
	PRINT	DATA	Print object code for constants in full
	PRINT	NODATA	Print only first 8 bytes of object code for constants
	PRINT	GEN	Print statements generated by macros in full from this point on; they will show a plus sign (+) to the right of the statement number
	PRINT	NOGEN	Do not print generated statements from this point on

Figure 2–2 Assembler listing control directives

the object program. They indicate something you wish the assembler to do while translating or printing your source statements. They may be used to indicate the name of the program, its starting location, printing options, and other details. *Declaratives* define constants and storage areas required in the program. Constants do become part of the object code.

Four directives, TITLE, EJECT, SPACE, and PRINT, are provided to control listing of source statements at assembly time. These statements have no effect whatever when the assembled program is executed at run time. Figure 2–2 summarizes the format and functions of these statements. Other directives will be discussed later.

The TITLE statement, when used, should be the first source statement written. The operand in single quotation marks usually indicates the name of the author and perhaps a program identifier, date, name of the course, or other information. The statement number of the TITLE statement is not printed.

Write EJECT in the op code field whenever you wish to advance the source listing to a new page. It is normally used to separate modules or major sections of a program. Neither the EJECT statement nor its statement number is printed.

The SPACE statement causes one or more blank lines to appear in the source listing as specified by the operand. SPACE without an operand shows one blank line. The blank lines may be used to separate file descriptions, data descriptions, or program structures. Neither the word SPACE nor the statement number is printed on the program listing. If the number of lines specified exceeds the lines remaining on the page, SPACE has the same effect as EJECT.

The PRINT statement allows options stated in the operand field to be exercised in printing the source statements. Certain options are made standard when the operating system is generated, but may be changed anywhere in the program by using PRINT statements. PRINT ON and PRINT NODATA are normally standard. PRINT options may be set and reset as often as desired in the source program.

Macro Instructions

Macro instructions are statements that cause the assembler to produce a predefined sequence of machine assembler instructions. Most input/output operations are carried out by macros provided in the operating system. Macros save programming time because a single statement can produce a large number of complex instructions. Later we will learn to write our own macro definitions.

PARTS OF A PROGRAM

Every program has three main parts:

1. file definitions
2. data definitions
3. procedural instructions

The file and data definitions describe the files and the records they contain; the instructions say what to do with them. We normally code the definitions first, even though the instructions appear first in the source program.

File Definitions

A *file* is made up of a group of logically related records. Each *record* contains fields holding data elements that describe the subject of the record. Every file resides on an input/output device. The *file definitions* give the assembler a description of each file we will use in our program.

Files are normally processed by special I/O routines supplied by the operating system. These routines are usually called the Input/Output Control System (IOCS). DOS and OS are the two versions of IOCS that we shall describe in this text. Information about each file is supplied to DOS by completing a DTF (Define the File) macro and to OS with a DCB (Define Control Block) macro. Files in OS are usually called *data sets*.

Every file must have an *input/output (I/O) area*, often called a *buffer*, reserved in main storage. The I/O area must be large enough to handle whatever data is actually transferred to or from the I/O device at one time. For card and printer files, IOCS usually transfers a single record at a time. For magnetic tape or disk files, IOCS usually builds a *block* of records, and the entire block is transferred at once. The I/O area is the size of one block, whether the block contains one or more than one record. The block is often called a *physical record*, since it represents what is actually transferred to or from the I/O device at one time. More than one I/O area may be defined for a file, but we shall limit our first programs to a single I/O area for each file.

It is often convenient to define a separate *work area* for each file in addition to the I/O area. The work area, when used, is the size of a single record, usually called a *logical record*, since it consists of logically related data about a single person, item, or transaction.

Data that must be supplied about each file include the name of the file, name of the I/O area, size of each record, size of the block if records are blocked, what kind of device is used for the file, whether it is used for input or output, whether a work area is to be used for records, and other data. The file description normally requires more than one line. It is common practice to use a separate line for each entry. The entry must be followed by a comma, and a nonblank character must be placed in column 72 to show that the statement is continued on the following line.

DOS The name of a file is given in the name field of the coding form. The name is limited to seven letters or numbers, must start with a letter, and cannot contain blanks. The op code field to define a card file contains the macro DTFCD. Each operand consists of a keyword, an equal sign (=), and a term completed by the programmer to give a characteristic of the file. Often only one operand is written on each line. On each line of the DTF except the last, the operand must be followed by a comma, and column 72 must contain a nonblank character to show that the statement is continued to the following line.

Figure 2–3 shows a typical input file definition. Some of the most commonly used operands in DOS for defining a card file using DTFCD are as follows:

DEVADDR Use SYSRDR, SYSIPT, or SYSnnn (where nnn can be 000 through 244). This is the device address, a symbolic name used in job control statements to assign the file to a specific input device. SYSRDR refers to the device that reads job control statements. SYSIPT is the device that reads input to the assembler or other language translators. SYSnnn refers to numbers assigned by the specific installation.

```
INFILE   DTFCD DEVADDR=SYSRDR,                                X
               DEVICE=2501,                                   X
               EOFADDR=ENDDO,                                 X
               IOAREA1=INAREA,                                X
               WORKA=YES
```

Figure 2–3 DOS input file definition

IOAREA1 Give name of I/O area, 80 bytes by default.

IOAREA2 Give name of optional second I/O area, if used.

WORKA Use YES as operand if record is processed in separate work area. The GET statement that reads records from file must name the work area.

DEVICE Give the model of the card reader. 1442, 2501, 2520, and 2540 are typical models. 2540 is the default.

EOFADDR Give the end-of-file address, the name of the instruction to which to branch when the end-of-file record is read. End of file is indicated by a /* in the first two bytes of a record. This entry is required for input files.

TYPEFLE Specify type of file, INPUT or OUTPUT. INPUT is the default.

BLKSIZE Specify the size of the I/O area, which must be 80 bytes or less. The default is 80.

We may omit any operands when their default values apply. We have omitted TYPEFLE and BLKSIZE operands in our DTFCD macro because their default values apply to almost all input files.

Many disk systems do not use punched card files. However, their input records are often logically considered to be card files even though the records have actually been stored in disk files. You will need to get precise file definition statements used by your computer installation.

We may define a printer file in DOS by using a DTFPR macro as illustrated in Figure 2–4. The more common DTFPR operands are:

DEVADDR Use the device address for the printer. SYSLST refers to the device that prints output from the operating system. SYSnnn refers to a code assigned by the installation, in which nnn may be 000 through 244.

IOAREA1 Give name of the I/O area for the printer. It is usually 132 or 133 bytes long.

IOAREA2 Give name of second optional I/O area, if used.

BLKSIZE Give length of I/O area, usually 132 or 133. Default is 121.

CONTROL Use YES as operand if the CNTRL macro will be used to control spacing and skipping. Do not use CTLCHR and CONTROL with the same file.

```
PRFILE    DTFPR BLKSIZE=132,                           X
                CONTROL=YES,                           X
                DEVADDR=SYSLST,                        X
                DEVICE=1403,                           X
                IOAREA1=PRINTIO,                       X
                WORKA=YES
```

Figure 2–4 DOS printer file definition

```
INFILE    DCB    DDNAME=INFILE,                          X
                 BLKSIZE=80,                             X
                 LRECL=80,                               X
                 MACRF=GM,                               X
                 DSORG=PS,                               X
                 EODAD=ENDDO
```

Figure 2–5 OS input data set definition

CTLCHR Use ASA or YES as operand if spacing and skipping are controlled by placing a special character in the first byte of the printer record. Omit CONTROL.

DEVICE Give the model of the printer. 1403, 1443, and 3211 are common models. Default is 1403.

WORKA Use YES as operand if output is created in a work area. The PUT macro gives the name of the work area.

The first two operands are required for all printer files. The others are optional for some kinds of files and required by others.

OS A card data set may be defined in OS with the statements shown in Figure 2–5. Here is an explanation of common entries for the DCB macro for a card data set:

DDNAME Give the data definition name, the name used in job control statements.

MACRF Give special codes indicating how records will be handled. G indicates that the GET macro will be used to read records. M specifies that each record will be moved from the input area to a work area.

BLKSIZE Give the size of the I/O area, normally 80.

LRECL Give the length of one logical record. With punched cards this is usually the same as BLKSIZE.

DSORG Use PS to indicate that the data set organization is in physical sequence order.

EODAD Write name of the instruction to which to branch when end of data is reached. Required for an input file.

A printer data set may be defined in OS with the statements shown in Figure 2–6. An explanation of these entries follows:

DDNAME Write the data definition name, the name used in job control statements.

MACRF Write code such as P, PM, or PMC. P means PUT macro will be used to write records. M indicates that the record will be moved to a work area. C indicates that the CNTRL macro will control spacing and skipping.

BLKSIZE Give size of the I/O area, normally 132 or 133 bytes.

```
PRINTER   DCB   DDNAME=PRINTER,                  X
                BLKSIZE-132,                     X
                LRECL=132,                       X
                MACRF=PMC,                       X
                DSORG=PS
```

Figure 2–6 OS printer data set definition

LRECL Write logical record length, same as BLKSIZE.

DSORG PS code indicates that data set organization is in physical sequence order.

Data Definitions

Data definitions describe the fields in each input record, each output record, and any working storage area. The Define Storage (DS) and Define Constant (DC) statements define the data.

An I/O area must be described for each file. Every record received from an input file is placed in the I/O area. Every record to be sent to an output file leaves from the I/O area. The I/O area may be regarded as a sort of loading dock in main storage for data routed to or from the file.

We will normally use a work area with each file. Thus the I/O area does not need to be subdivided into fields, but only needs to indicate the number of bytes in the record associated with that file. The work area will contain the detailed record description.

Defining Constants Constants are values that we wish to store in our program. They may be characters, addresses, or several types of numbers. Constants are used to set initial values in counters or totals, for comparing, for creating headings, and for many other purposes. Normally, they do not change when the program is running, but they may be changed by later processing.

An assembler declarative is used to define a constant. The op code is DC (for Define Constant). The form of the instruction is

```
DC dtLn'v'
```

where d = a duplication factor (1 is assumed if d is omitted)
t = the type of constant (C is used for character constants)
L = when followed by a decimal number n, the length in bytes (L50, for example)
'v' = the value of the constant enclosed in single quotes

The type and value are required for every constant. Duplication and length are optional. The specified constants are translated by the assembler into EBCDIC code and are printed in the assembler listing to the left of the DC statement.

If the length is omitted, the assembler determines the length from the value of the constant. If the stated length is longer than the value, the constant is padded to the right with blanks. If the stated length is shorter than the value, the rightmost characters will be truncated. The duplication factor permits more than one constant to be created from a single statement. If the duplication factor is zero, no constant is created. Figure 2–7 shows some examples.

Defining Storage Often we wish to reserve space in main storage for a record or field of data without placing a constant in it. This is done by an assembler instruction with an op code of DS (Define Storage). Operands may be the same as for defining constants. Normally no value is given, but if a value is given and no length is specified, then the assembler will reserve enough bytes to hold the value given. Figure 2–8 shows a few examples.

It is important to understand the relation between storage definitions and the *location counter* for the program. The location counter is normally set to zero by a START or CSECT statement at the start of the program. The assembler increases the location counter by the length of each machine instruction, macro, or DC or DS statement. The name of a field refers to the address in the location counter when that field was defined in the program. The location counter therefore gives the relative address of each field or instruction within the program. The location counter value is shown at the left of each statement in the assembler source program listing.

We often need to define a record having, say, 80 bytes that contains a number of different fields. To do so, we define the overall record with a DS statement showing a duplication factor of zero, followed by the definition of

EBCDIC CODE	DEFINITION	REMARKS
C1C2C3	DC C'ABC'	
F1F2F5	DC C'125'	
C1C2C34040	DC CL5'ABC'	Padded with blanks
C1C2C3C4	DC CL4'ABCDE'	Last byte truncated
4040404040	DC 5C' '	Duplication factor = 5

Figure 2–7 Character constant definitions

DEFINITION	REMARKS
DS CL5	Reserves 5 bytes
DS CL80	Reserves 80 bytes
DS 5CL4	Reserves 5 * 4, or 20 bytes
DS C'ABC'	Reserves 3 bytes, enough to hold ABC; does not create a constant

Figure 2–8 Storage definitions

the various fields. The DS gives the proper location and length of 80 to the name of the record, but the duplication factor of zero does not advance the location counter. The first field within the record therefore starts at the same location as the entire record, and the following fields are located within the 80 bytes instead of following them. The example in Figure 2–9 shows the description of an input record containing name, street address, city, state, and zip code. Assume the location counter is at location X'140' of the program at the time the DS statements are written. The location counter is shown in hex numbers.

After the last 18 bytes are defined, the next available location is X'190'. This is exactly 80 (X'50') bytes from the start of the definition of the card record. Note that the fields reserved within the record must exactly use up all 80 bytes. No name need be given to a field if it is not referred to within the program, but it must be allotted its required space.

Heading records for printer files are described by using a DS statement with zero duplication to give the name and length of the entire record. DC statements are used to define the constant words or blanks that appear in the headings. The total length of the constants must equal 132, the total length of the printer records. (We will see later that printer records may have 133 characters, with the first byte containing special code to control spacing and skipping.) Figure 2–10 shows a definition of a heading record.

Detail print lines require a combination of DS and DC statements. The entire line is named with a DS with duplication factor of 0. Each field into which variable data is to be moved is defined with a DS statement giving the

LOCATION		DEFINITION	COLUMNS	REMARKS
140	INRECD	DS 0CL80		Defines 80-byte area; does not increment location counter
140	INNAME	DS CL20	1–20	Reserves 20 bytes for name
154	INSTADDR	DS CL20	21–40	Reserves 20 more bytes
168	INCITY	DS CL15	41–55	Reserves 15 bytes for city
177	INSTATE	DS CL2	56–57	Reserves 2 bytes for state code
179	INZIP	DS CL5	58–62	Reserves 5 bytes for zip
17E		DS CL18	63–80	Last 18 bytes of record unnamed
190		(Next available location)		

Figure 2–9 Input record description

HEAD2	DS	0CL132	Name and length of entire record
	DC	CL10' '	First 10 bytes blank
	DC	CL20'ACCT. NO.'	Column heading followed by 11 blanks
	DC	CL19'NAME'	Column heading followed by 15 blanks
	DC	CL83'BALANCE'	Column heading followed by 76 blanks

Figure 2–10 Heading record description

```
PRLINE   DS   OCL132      Name and length of entire record
         DC   CL12' '     First 12 columns blank
PRACCT   DS   CL4         Name of 4-byte variable field
         DC   CL6' '      Six blanks between fields
PRNAME   DS   CL20        Name of 20-byte variable field
         DC   CL6' '      Six blanks between fields
PRBAL    DS   CL8         Name of 8-byte variable field
         DC   CL76' '     76 blanks to complete record
```

Figure 2–11 Detail line description

name of the field and its length. Spaces between fields are defined as constants containing blanks. Figure 2–11 illustrates the definition of a detail line.

Programming Tips

- Where possible, copy complete file descriptions, record descriptions, and processing modules from one program to another to save time and avoid keying errors.
- Define complete records using zero duplication factor. Then be sure that the total lengths of the individual fields add up to the length of the record.
- When defining headings, include trailing blank columns in the length of the character constants.
- When defining detail lines, make each field to which data is to be moved the exact length of the data itself. Define areas between fields separately.
- Leave a blank line between the last heading line and the first detail line.

Procedural Instructions

Procedural instructions generally have three main sections:

1. initialization
2. the mainline loop
3. the end-of-file routine

Initialization involves opening files, clearing totals, setting starting values, and reading the first input record. The mainline loop processes an input record, accumulates necessary totals, writes an output record, and reads the next input record. When the last input record has been read, the end-of-file routine prints final totals and closes files.

```
DOWHILE   EQU *
          These statements test if the loop should be performed. If not, a
          branch is made to ENDDO. Next are the statements executed by the
          loop. At least one of these statements must change some value that
          is tested to see if the loop is to be continued. The loop must end
          with a branch to DOWHILE.
          B    DOWHILE
ENDDO     EQU *
```

Figure 2–12 Format for pretest loop

```
REPEAT    EQU *
          These are statements to be executed by the loop. One or more
          statements must modify the condition tested to see if the loop is to
          continue. The last statements in the loop provide a test of the
          condition and a branch to REPEAT if the condition is met. If the
          condition is not met, the program falls through to the UNTIL.
UNTIL     EQU *
```

Figure 2–13 Format for posttest loop

Machine instructions and macros are used to process the files and data we have described. In Chapter 1, we saw the three basic structures into which all program logic may be divided. Assembler language does not readily adapt itself to structured programming. It is awkward to indent names, op codes, and operands as we do in other languages. Names must begin in column 1. We therefore build our repetition and selection structure by choosing certain key words as names for our machine instructions and macros. We can use comments to the right of our operands to show pseudocode to aid in describing the program logic.

We control the logical flow of our program by using branching instructions. Usually two items are compared, and the *condition code* is set to show that the first item is equal to, greater than, or less than the second. A *conditional branch* transfers control to some other part of the program if the condition code agrees with the condition that is tested. If it does not agree, the program proceeds to the next instruction in sequence. An *unconditional branch* goes to some other part of the program regardless of the condition code.

The EQU (Equate) assembler instruction, with an asterisk as an operand, is useful to allow us to give a name to a specific location without taking up any additional space in the program. The asterisk refers to the present value in the location counter. Wherever we might need to give more than one name to a location, we will use this instruction with names of DOWHILE and ENDDO or REPEAT and UNTIL to indicate the start and end of a loop. We

```
IF       EQU *
         Here the condition is tested. If not true, a branch is made to ENDIF.
THEN     EQU *
         Here are the statements to be executed if the condition is true.
ENDIF    EQU *
```

Figure 2–14 Format for one-way selection

```
IF       EQU *
         Here the condition is tested. If not true, branch to ELSE.
THEN     EQU *
         Here are the statements to be executed if the condition is true. They
         terminate with an unconditional branch:
         B    ENDIF
ELSE     EQU *
         Here are the statements to be executed if the condition is false. When
         they are finished, logic falls through to ENDIF.
ENDIF    EQU *
```

Figure 2–15 Format for two-way selection

will also use EQU as needed with names of IF, THEN, ELSE, or ENDIF in selection structures.

Remember from Chapter 1 that a pretest loop is one in which a test is made at the start of a loop to see if it should be performed. Under our programming standards, we will use DOWHILE as the name of the first statement in a pretest loop and ENDDO as the name of the first statement following the loop. The pretest loop follows the format shown in Figure 2–12.

For a posttest loop, the test is made at the end of the loop. Therefore, a posttest loop will always be executed at least once. The REPEAT-UNTIL format is used with a posttest loop as in Figure 2–13.

The selection structure requires names of IF, THEN, ELSE, and ENDIF. Usually a test is made at IF that causes a branch to the ELSE if the condition is *not* true. If the condition *is* true, the logic falls through to the THEN. One-way selection requires no ELSE, but if the condition is not true, a branch is made to the ENDIF. One-way selection uses the format shown in Figure 2–14.

With two-way selection, the main concern is to be sure that only the THEN or the ELSE is executed, and not both. This is done by having the last statement in the THEN group contain a branch to ENDIF regardless of any condition. Two-way selection uses the format shown in Figure 2–15.

Each name appearing in columns 1 to 8 of the coding form may be defined only once in the program. If we have more than one loop, the second may use DOWHILE2 and ENDDO2, or DOWHILEA and ENDDOA, to distinguish the loops. We may also add a number or letter to IF, THEN, ELSE, and ENDIF or to REPEAT and UNTIL where necessary.

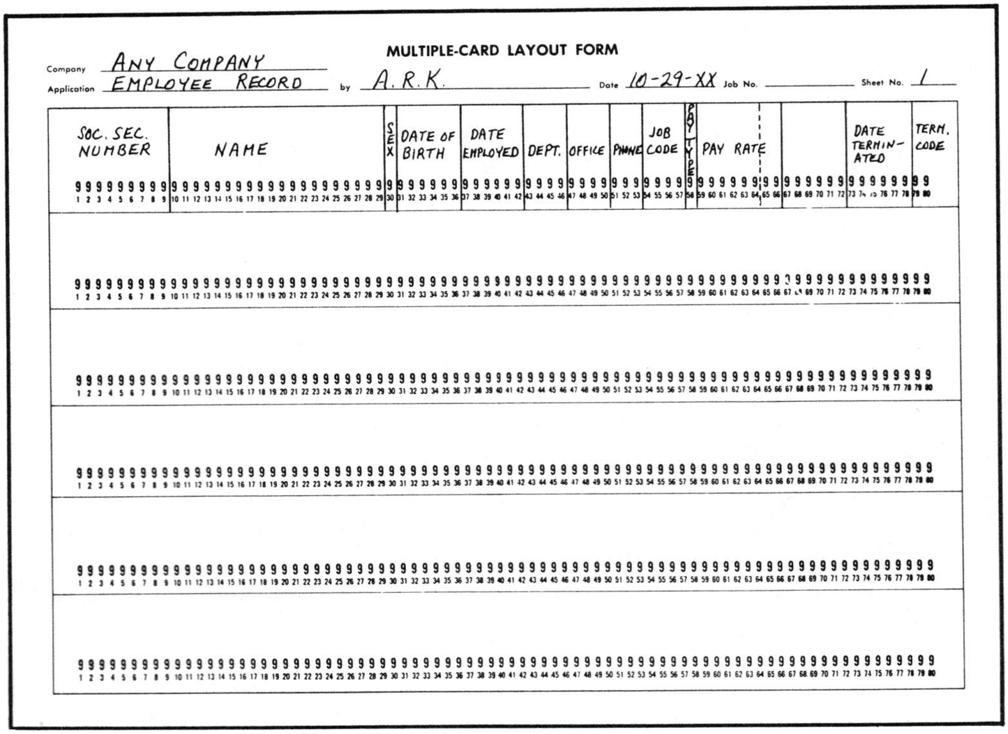

Figure 2–16 Employee record

PROGRAM 1: READING AND PRINTING RECORDS

Almost all business programs involve reading in data, processing it in some way, and printing it out. Our first few programs will use a typical employee record containing fields shown in Figure 2–16. Figure 2–17 shows the set of sample data to be used in these demonstration programs.

Our first program reads records from the employee file and selects employee name, office number, and phone number. It reverses the positions of the phone and office number in moving data to the output record. In addition, it prints headings over each column of output, counts 50 detail lines, prints headings on a new page after the 50 detail lines have been printed. A print chart on the output format is shown in Figure 2–18. The reading and printing of the data continues until the end-of-data signal is reached. End of data is indicated under DOS and OS with a record containing nothing but /* in the first two columns.

Pseudocode for our program is shown in Figure 2–19. Figure 2–20 shows a program flowchart. Figure 2–21 shows the assembler source program. The following discussion explains the various parts of the program.

```
0        1         2         3         4         5         6         7         8
12345678901234567890123456789012345678901234567890123456789012345678901234567890

123456789MARK DOWN           M0224340913561234020110100104A06200000
974635128CLYDE S DALE        M1207420403751234020310200204A05175000
443355777CARRIE AHN          F1015401210591234020210112004W00041500
821546379CLAIRE VOYANT       F0328500707721234020410212004W00039200
111773024DUNNAN BRADSTREET   M0707560321801234020510341304W00028300
202123242SALLY FORTH         F1125310216532143010110400504A04125000
789321654DELLA KATESSEN      F0108521028792143010210412004W00038000
625714903PETE MOSS           M0427621116832143010210567154W00027500
987654321BART ENDER          M1207410508593756012110600504A03800000
500311255JACK RABBETT        M0916500730813756012210612004W00035200
475612038BELLE TOWER         F0731531201793756012310756254H00001075
864208640BARRY MOORE         M0321570705823756012310856254H00000983
315426537LYON HART           M1026590916833756012410956254H00000945
611722833TOM KATZ            M0229600420843756012511056254H00000937
765123987SARAH MOANIE        F0308530814754028015111100504A03500000
021978645NORA GRETA          F0622541013794028015211112004W00029750
666333942PEARL STRAND        F0817551102834028015311212004W00029150
177283940HEDDA HARE          F0124580516844028015411312004W00028450
400155266STEVE EDORE         M1111370419595337100111400504A03612500
813243567SUZY KEW            F1209540326785337100211512004W00031750
087264519CONNIE SHURR        F0704580920785337100311532454H00000875
999234732NEIL DOWNE          M0612400110805337100211532454H00000858
221057326HAMMOND RYE         M0420490315805337100411632454H00000849
642753864CANDY KANE          F0515600104825337100411632454H00000842
375963842CLEMENT SEE         M0909611018825337100511732454H00000837
263241796ABBY WESTMINSTER    F0214330803586541120111800504A03178500
179664223LOTTA WAITE         F0117530915786541120211912504H00000815
664917322BETTA WAGER         F1031560409796541120211912504H00000810
923617469ROGER ANDOVER       M0401581115806541120312012504H00000805
009943726PERRY WINKLE        M0415481206816541120312012504H00000802
115226337ELLA MENTRY         F0728350314577409112112100604W00041200
640751862ANNE ARKIE          F0315520129757409112212277354H00000762
321798543BARBIE DAHL         F0108570907767409112312377354H00000738
780541619RICH PERSON         M0522401014648823200112400604W00039500
401215380SEYMOUR SEITZ       M0614261208568823200212586424H00000675
098176354OSCAR QUESTION      M0823330123588823200212586424H00000666
453671890BILL OLADING        M1104610425828823200312686424H00000651
803914725RICK SHAW           M0121630510838823200312686424H00000638
527419308BEN Z DREEN         M0718640328858823200412786424H00000625
419527830ARTHUR RYTUS        M0302660810858823200412786424H00000610
```

Figure 2–17 Sample data for employee record

Housekeeping and Initialization

Comments may occupy a full line if we place an asterisk (*) in column 1. Blocks of comments are useful to identify the program, author, date written, and purpose of the program. We will use comments rather than the TITLE statement for program identification. They may also identify and separate the various sections of the program.

The PRINT NOGEN statement is an assembler directive that tells the assembler not to print source statements that are generated by each macro instruction. These generated statements would make our program look longer and more confusing but tell us nothing useful at this point.

The START statement is an assembler directive that enables us to give a name (MAINLINE) to our program and also to set the location center to some starting value. In this text we will always set the location counter to 0 to start each program. The body of source statements that is assembled at one time is called *control section*. We could use a CSECT statement to show the name and first instruction in the control section. The CSECT statement sets the location counter to 0.

The BALR (Branch and Link Register) is a machine instruction that loads the address of the next instruction into the specified general register to be used as a base address for the program. The USING statement is an assembler directive that designates the base register and what address is to be in that register. BALR and USING are normally used together to establish and designate the base register. We will normally use general register 12 as a base register. We will explain more about base registers later.

OPEN is a macro to make the specified files available for use. Every file must be opened before it can be used. A single OPEN macro can open all files

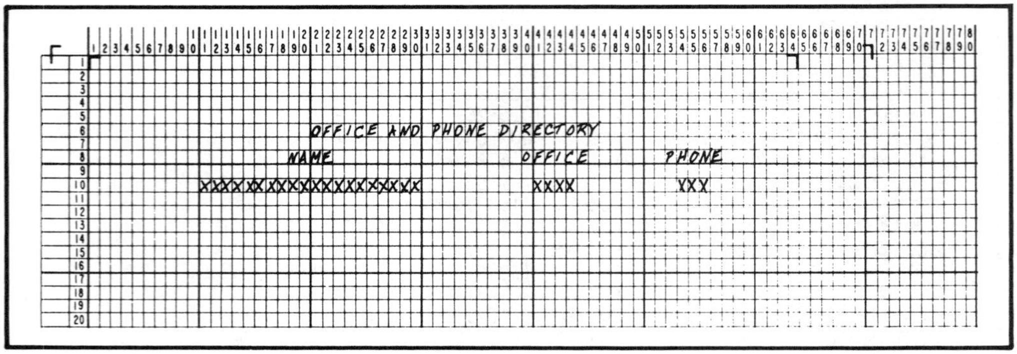

Figure 2–18 Print chart for Program 1

```
START PROGRAM
Open files
Print headings and set line counter
Read first record
DOWHILE NOT end of file
   Move input data to output record
   Print output record
   Subtract one from line counter
   IF line counter is not greater than zero
      THEN print headings and reset line counter
   ENDIF
   Read next record
ENDDO
Close files
END PROGRAM
```

Figure 2–19 Pseudocode for Program 1

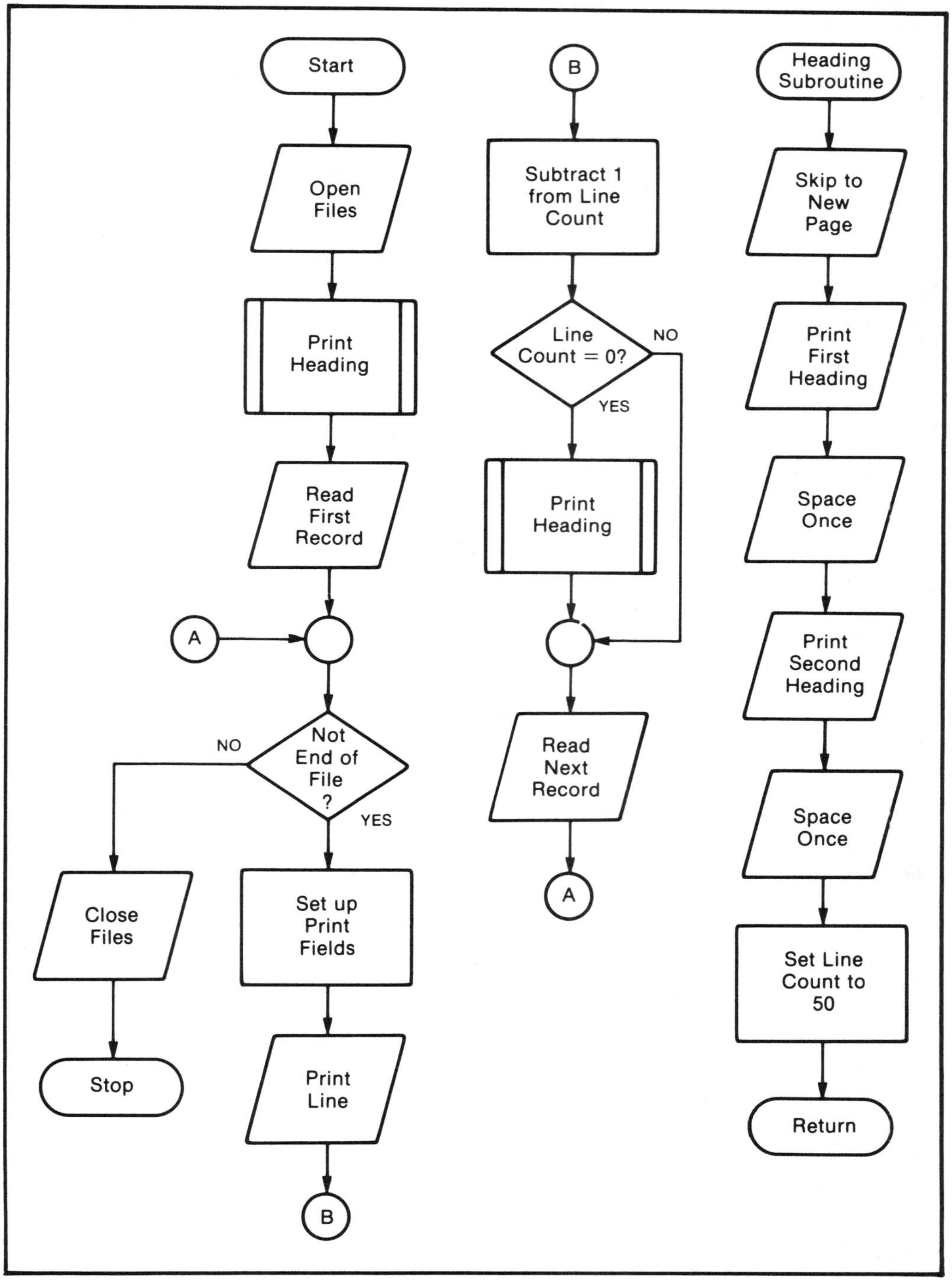

Figure 2–20 Program flowchart for Program 1

```
                                                                                                     PAGE    2
  LOC  OBJECT CODE     ADDR1 ADDR2  STMT   SOURCE STATEMENT                                DOS/VSE ASSEMBLER 14.49 86-03-27

                                       1 ********************************************************************** ******
                                       2 *                 ALTON R. KINDRED, PROGRAM 1
                                       3 * THIS PROGRAM LISTS NAME, OFFICE, AND PHONE NUMBER OF EACH EMPLOYEE.
                                       4 *           REGISTERS USED:
                                       5 *                 R5  - LINE COUNTER
                                       6 *                 R9  - LINK TO MODULE
                                       7 *                 R12 - BASE REGISTER
                                       8 **********************************************************************
                                       9           PRINT NOGEN
000000                                10 MAINLINE START 0     SET LOCATION COUNTER
000000 05C0                           11          BALR  12,0                    LOAD BASE REGISTER
                           00002      12          USING *,12                    DESIGNATE BASE REGISTER
                                      13          OPEN  INFILE,PRINTER          OPEN FILES
000016 4590 C07A           0007C      22          BAL   9,HEADING               PRINT HEADING
                                      23          GET   INFILE,INRECD           READ FIRST RECORD
                           0002A      29 DOWHILE  EQU   *                       DOWHILE NOT END OF FILE
00002A D213 C264 C213 00266 00215     30          MVC   PRNAME,INNAME             SET UP PRINT LINE
000030 D203 C282 C238 00284 0023A     31          MVC   PROFFICE,INOFFICE         *
000036 D202 C290 C23C 00292 0023E     32          MVC   PRPHONE,INPHONE           *
                                      33          PUT   PRINTER,PRLINE            PRINT LINE
00004C 4650 C052           00054      39          BCT   5,ENDIF                   SUBTRACT 1 FROM LINE COUNT
                           00050      40 IF       EQU   *                         IF LINE COUNT = ZERO
000050 4590 C07A           0007C      41 THEN     BAL   9,HEADING                   THEN PRINT HEADING
                           00054      42 ENDIF    EQU   *                         ENDIF
                                      43          GET   INFILE,INRECD             READ NEXT RECORD
000064 47F0 C028      0002A           49          B     DOWHILE                   *
                           00068      50 ENDDO    EQU   *                       ENDDO
                                      51          CLOSE INFILE,PRINTER          CLOSE FILES
                                      60          EOJ                           END JOB
                                      63 **********************************************************************
                                      64 *                 HEADING SUBROUTINE
                                      65 **********************************************************************
                                      66 HEADING  CNTRL PRINTER,SK,1            SKIP TO NEW PAGE
                                      72          PUT   PRINTER,HEAD1           PRINT FIRST HEADING
                                      78          CNTRL PRINTER,SP,1            SPACE ONCE
                                      84          PUT   PRINTER,HEAD2           PRINT SECOND HEADING
                                      90          CNTRL PRINTER,SP,1            SPACE ONCE
0000C6 4150 0032           00032      96          LA    5,50                    SET LINE COUNT TO 50
0000CA 07F9                           97          BR    9                       RETURN
                                      98 **********************************************************************
                                      99 *                 FILE DEFINITIONS AND I/O AREAS
                                     100 **********************************************************************
                                     101 INFILE   DTFCD BLKSIZE=80,IOAREA1=INAREA,DEVICE=2540,                 X
                                                        DEVADDR=SYS006,EOFADDR=ENDDO,WORKA=YES
                                     122 PRINTER  DTFPR BLKSIZE=132,IOAREA1=PRTAREA,DEVICE=1403,               X
                                                        CONTROL=YES,DEVADDR=SYS009,WORKA=YES
                                     143 *
000138                               144 INAREA   DS    CL80
000188                               145 PRTAREA  DS    CL132
                                     146 **********************************************************************
                                     147 *                 DATA DEFINITIONS
                                     148 **********************************************************************
00020C                               149 INRECD   DS    0CL80
00020C                               150          DS    CL9
000215                               151 INNAME   DS    CL20
000229                               152          DS    CL17
00023A                               153 INOFFICE DS    CL4
00023E                               154 INPHONE  DS    CL3
000241                               155          DS    CL27
                                     156 *
00025C                               157 PRLINE   DS    0CL132
00025C 4040404040404040              158          DC    CL10' '
000266                               159 PRNAME   DS    CL20
00027A 4040404040404040              160          DC    CL10' '
000284                               161 PROFFICE DS    CL4
000288 4040404040404040              162          DC    CL10' '
000292                               163 PRPHONE  DS    CL3
000295 4040404040404040              164          DC    CL75' '
                                     165 *
0002E0                               166 HEAD1    DS    0CL132
0002E0 4040404040404040              167          DC    CL20' '
0002F4 D6C6C6C9C3C540C1              168          DC    CL112'OFFICE AND PHONE DIRECTORY'
                                     169 *
000364                               170 HEAD2    DS    0CL132
000364 4040404040404040              171          DC    CL18' '
000376 D5C1D4C540404040              172          DC    CL21'NAME'
00038B D6C6C6C9C3C54040              173          DC    CL14'OFFICE'
000399 D7C8D6D5C5404040              174          DC    CL79'PHONE'
                                     175 *
                           00000     176          END   MAINLINE
0003E8 5B5BC2D6D7C5D540              177                =C'$$BOPEN '
0003F0 5B5BC2C3D3D6E2C5              178                =C'$$BCLOSE'
0003F8 000000D0                      179                =A(INFILE)
0003FC 0000020C                      180                =A(INRECD)
000400 00000108                      181                =A(PRINTER)
000404 0000025C                      182                =A(PRLINE)
000408 000002E0                      183                =A(HEAD1)
00040C 00000364                      184                =A(HEAD2)
```

Figure 2–21 Program 1 assembler listing of DOS version

that are named as operands and separated by commas. Usually all files are opened near the start of the program.

BAL is a machine instruction used to branch to the heading subroutine. Before branching, however, it places the address of the next instruction into the specified general register, called a *link register*. The subroutine refers to the same link register to branch back to the mainline of the program. General register 9 (R9) is our link register here.

The Heading Subroutine

We will leave the mainline of the program to discuss the heading subroutine, since logically it is performed at this point. The CNTRL (Control) macro is used to perform skipping to a new page and spacing on the printer. The first operand (PRINTER) gives the name of the printer file as defined in the DTFPR macro. The second operand is either SK (Skip) or SP (Space). After SK, the third operand gives the channel in the carriage control tape to which to skip before printing. Channel 1 in the carriage control tape is consistently used to refer to the first printing line on a page. With SP, the third operand gives the number of lines to space the paper downward before printing. If there is a fourth operand, it gives directions for skipping or spacing after printing the line.

The PUT macro is used to send a line of output to the printer. PUT, when used with WORKA=YES in the DTFPR macro, requires two operands. The first gives the name of the printer file. The second is the name of the work area that contains the desired heading line to be sent to the printer.

The LA (Load Address) is a machine instruction that allows us to load a number into a specified general register. In this case, general register 5 (R5) is loaded with the value 50 to be used as a line counter. Letter-sized paper is 11 inches long, with 6 lines per inch and 66 lines per page. Allowing for heading lines and about an inch for each of the top and bottom margins, we will print 50 detail lines per page.

The BR (Branch Register) machine instruction is an unconditional branch or transfer. It indicates that a branch is to be made to the address in general register 9 (R9). Recall that R9 is the link register in which the mainline return address was stored before branching to the heading subroutine. We have now completed our return to the main program.

The Priming Read

The GET macro is used to read in a record from the specified file (INFILE). When used with WORKA=YES in the DTFCD macro, GET requires two operands. The first is the file name. The second is the name of the work area (INRECD) into which the record is to be placed for processing. The GET macro also checks to see if the record is the end-of-file record that contains /* in the first two columns. If so, GET causes a branch to ENDDO, the address specified in the EOFADDR operand in the DTFCD macro to terminate the loop.

The Mainline Loop

The MVC (Move Characters) machine instruction causes data to be moved from a field in the input record to a field in the output record. Strictly speak-

```
***********************************************************************
*             ALTON R. KINDRED, PROGRAM 1, OS VERSION
* THIS PROGRAM LISTS NAME, OFFICE, AND PHONE NUMBER OF EACH EMPLOYEE.
*        REGISTERS USED:
*              R5  - LINE COUNTER
*              R9  - LINK TO MODULE
*              R12 - BASE REGISTER
***********************************************************************
         PRINT NOGEN
MAINLINE START 0                        NORMAL OS PROGRAM INITIALIZATION
         STM   14,12,12(13)             *
         BALR  12,0                     *
         USING *,12                     *
         ST    13,SAVE+4                *
         LA    13,SAVE                  *
         OPEN  (INFILE,(INPUT),PRINTER,(OUTPUT))  OPEN FILES
         BAL   9,HEADING                PRINT HEADING
         GET   INFILE,INRECD            READ FIRST RECORD
DOWHILE  EQU   *                        DOWHILE NOT END OF FILE
         MVC   PRNAME,INNAME              SET UP PRINT LINE
         MVC   PROFFICE,INOFFICE          *
         MVC   PRPHONE,INPHONE            *
         PUT   PRINTER,PRLINE             PRINT LINE
         BCT   5,ENDIF2                   SUBTRACT 1 FROM LINE COUNT
IF       EQU   *                          IF LINE COUNT = ZERO
THEN     BAL   9,HEADING                    THEN PRINT HEADING
ENDIF    EQU   *                          ENDIF
         GET   INFILE,INRECD              READ NEXT RECORD
         B     DOWHILE                    *
ENDDO    EQU   *                        ENDDO
         CLOSE (INFILE,,PRINTER)        CLOSE FILES
         L     13,SAVE+4                STANDARD OS TERMINATION
         LM    14,12,12(13)             *
         BR    14                       RETURN TO OS
***********************************************************************
*              HEADING SUBROUTINE
***********************************************************************
PRHEAD   CNTRL PRINTER,SK,1             SKIP TO NEW PAGE
         PUT   PRINTER,HEAD1            PRINT FIRST HEADING
         CNTRL PRINTER,SP,1             SPACE ONCE
         PUT   PRINTER,HEAD2            PRINT SECOND HEADING
         CNTRL PRINTER,SP,1             SPACE ONCE
         LA    5,50                     SET LINE COUNTER
         BR    9                        RETURN
***********************************************************************
*              DEVICE CONTROL BLOCKS AND SAVE AREA
***********************************************************************
INFILE   DCB   DDNAME=INFILE,BLKSIZE=80,LRECL=80,                      X
               MACRF=GM,DSORG=PS,EODAD=ENDDO
*
PRINTER  DCB   DDNAME=PRINTER,BLKSIZE=132,LRECL=132,                   X
               MACRF=PMC,DSORG=PS
*
SAVE     DS    18F
*
```

Figure 2–22 Program 1 assembler listing of OS version

```
**********************************************************************
*              DATA DEFINITIONS
**********************************************************************
INRECD   DS    0CL80
         DS    CL9
INNAME   DS    CL20
         DS    CL17
INOFFICE DS    CL4
INPHONE  DS    CL3
         DS    CL27
*
PRLINE   DS    0CL132
         DC    CL10' '
PRNAME   DS    CL20
         DC    CL10' '
PROFFICE DS    CL4
         DC    CL10
PRPHONE  DS    CL3
         DC    CL75' '
*
HEAD1    DS    0CL132
         DC    CL20' '
         DC    CL112'OFFICE AND PHONE DIRECTORY'
*
HEAD2    DS    0CL132
         DC    CL18' '
         DC    CL21'NAME'
         DC    CL14'OFFICE'
         DC    CL79'PHONE'
*
         END   MAINLINE
```

Figure 2–22 *(Concluded)*

ing, the data is not moved, but *copied*, since the original data is not destroyed. The data moves from the location named in the second operand to the location named in the first operand. Starting at the left of each field, one byte after another is moved to successive addresses until the first operand is filled. To avoid error, both operands should be the same length. The three MVC instructions move the name, office number, and phone number from the point record to the work area for the print line. The MVC instruction will be discussed in more detail later.

The PUT macro is used to print the detail line. The first operand is the file name, and the second is the name of the work area containing the fields to be printed.

The BCT (Branch on Count) machine instruction is often used to control loops. Here it is used for selection. First BCT subtracts 1 from the contents of general register R5. (Remember that R5 was loaded in the heading subroutine with the number 50 as a line counter.) Then BCT tests to see if R5 contains 0. If not, it branches to the instruction named as the second operand (ENDIF). If R5 contains 0 after 1 is subtracted, BCT does not branch but falls through to the BAL instruction to perform the heading subroutine again. BCT and BAL used in this way cause the heading routine to be performed after exactly 50 detail lines have been printed.

The GET macro is repeated at the end of the mainline loop to be consistent with structured programming in other languages. Most structured pro-all other records be read in the mainline loop after each record is processed and an output is written.

The B (Branch) machine instruction is an unconditional transfer or branch that returns to repeat the DOWHILE loop. The program flowchart in Figure 2–20 shows that, logically, the GET macro is divided into two parts: the input operation that reads, and the test for end of file. Logically, the card is read at the end of the loop, and the test for end of file is made at the start.

The End-of-File Routine

The CLOSE macro is used to deactivate files. Once a file is closed, it is no longer available for use. CLOSE will be explained more fully when we discuss different types of files. It is more efficient to close all files with a single CLOSE, although it is possible to use a separate CLOSE statement for each file.

The EOJ (End of Job) macro transfers control back to the supervisor at the logical end of the program. This is the last instruction actually executed. The remaining statements contain file and data definitions.

OS Version of Program 1

Figure 2–22 shows an assembler listing of the OS version of Program 1. You will note differences in addition to those between DTF and DCB statements previously mentioned.

OS considers every program to be a subroutine called by OS itself. OS places in register 13 the address of a 72-byte system save area to hold the contents of the general registers. The program itself must also define a save area if it in turn needs to save the contents of the registers. These instructions will be explained in detail in later chapters. For now, we will simply insert the following statements at the start of every OS program:

```
STM    14,12,12(13)    or SAVE (14,12) instead of STM
BALR   12,0
USING  *,12
ST     13,SAVE+4
LA     13,SAVE
```

Additional instructions must also appear at the end of the program to restore the registers to their original contents. These are used instead of the EOJ macro that appears at the end of the DOS version.

```
L      13,SAVE+4
LM     14,12,12(13)    or RETURN (14,12) instead of LM and BR
BR     14
```

Notice also several changes in the OS version of the OPEN macro from the DOS version. OS requires that the data set names be enclosed in parentheses and followed by the word INPUT or OUTPUT enclosed in another set of parentheses. The CLOSE macro also requires parentheses around the data set names.

Other sample programs will show only the DOS version. For OS systems, you change the DCBs, OPEN and CLOSE macros, and the initialization and termination statements. Many variations exist between versions of DOS and OS. You should get specific information about your own installation.

Figure 2–23 shows output produced by the program.

Programming Tips

- Use BAL instructions to utilize frequently used modules such as headings at more than one point in the program.
- For procedural statements, use IF, THEN, ELSE, DOWHILE, ENDDO, REPEAT, and UNTIL to match pseudocode in comments with each statement. Branch only to statements with these names to control program structure.

SUMMARY

Assembler language statements are written on a coding form, with one statement per line. The form is divided into four areas:

1. name or symbol
2. operation code
3. operands and comments
4. identification and sequence

Where a statement is continued to the next line, a nonblank character must be placed in column 72 of the line that is continued.

An asterisk in column 1 indicates that the full line is a comment. Comments may be placed on the same line as operands, following at least one space.

Three types of statements are used:

1. machine instructions
2. assembler instructions
3. macros

OFFICE AND PHONE DIRECTORY

NAME	OFFICE	PHONE
MARK DOWN	0201	101
CLYDE S DALE	0203	102
CARRIE AHN	0202	101
CLAIRE VOYANT	0204	102
DUNNAN BRADSTREET	0205	103
SALLY FORTH	0101	104
DELLA KATESSEN	0102	104
PETE MOSS	0102	105
BART ENDER	0121	106
JACK RABBETT	0122	106
BELLE TOWER	0123	107
BARRY MOORE	0123	108
LYON HART	0124	109
TOM KATZ	0125	110
SARAH MOANIE	0151	111
NORA GRETZ	0152	111
PEARL STRAND	0153	112
HEDDA HARE	0154	113
STEVE EDORE	1001	114
SUZY KEW	1002	115
CONNIE SHURR	1003	115
NEIL DOWNE	1002	115
HAMMOND RYE	1004	116
CANDY KANE	1004	116
CLEMENT SEE	1005	117
ABBY WESTMINSTER	1201	118
LOTTA WAITE	1202	119
BETTA WAGER	1202	119
ROGER ANDOVER	1203	120
PERRY WINKLE	1203	120
ELLA MENTRY	1121	121
ANNE ARKIE	1122	122
BARBIE DAHL	1123	123
RICH PERSON	2001	124
SEYMOUR SEITZ	2002	125
OSCAR QUESTION	2002	125
BILL OLADING	2003	126
RICK SHAW	2003	126
BEN Z DREEN	2004	127
ARTHUR RYTUS	2004	127

Figure 2–23 Output from Program 1

Machine instructions specify certain options performed at assembly time. Macros are used primarily for defining files and performing input/output operations.

The program is divided into three parts:

1. file definitions
2. data definitions
3. procedural instructions

Each input/output device is considered to be a file, which consists of logically related records. File definitions describe characteristics of each file. Data definitions describe records belonging to each file as well as working storage required by the program. Procedural instructions describe the logical processing steps.

DOS and OS are the two main operating systems used to interpret job control statements and carry out input/output operations. The two systems use somewhat different formats and statements.

The location center keeps track of the number of bytes required to hold the data and instructions of the program. Data definitions include DC statements to define constant data loaded with the program, and DS statements that reserve space into which data may be placed as the program progresses.

Instructions should be written to follow the principles of structured programming. The three principal structures are:

1. sequence
2. repetition
3. selection

The structure of the program should be indicated by use of names and by comments to the right of each instruction.

Program logic may be indicated by pseudocode or by a program flowchart. Instructions should follow the logic developed for solution of the programming problem.

Procedural instructions generally have three main sections:

1. initialization
2. the mainline loop
3. the end-of-file routine

Subroutines are modules to handle specific processing functions, such as printing headings. They are normally written outside the mainline of the program. The Branch and Link (BAL) instruction permits leaving the mainline, executing the subroutines, and returning to the next statement in the mainline.

TERMS FOR REVIEW

Assembler declarative	File definition	Mainline loop
Assembler directive	Link register	One-way selection
Carriage control tape	Location counter	Priming read
Data definition	Loop	Symbol
Data set	Machine instruction	Two-way selection
Duplication factor	Macro instruction	

REVIEW QUESTIONS

1. Name the four parts of the body of the assembler coding form. Describe the function of each.
2. In what two ways are comments indicated on the coding form?
3. What is the difference between assembler declaratives and assembler directives? Which is put into object code?
4. What types of operations are carried out principally by macro instructions? Name four or five of the most common macros.
5. What are file definitions? What type of statement is used in the definitions?
6. What two parts of a constant definition are required? What are optional?
7. What is meant by the duplication factor in a data definition? What effect does it have on the location counter? What happens if the duplication factor is zero?
8. What operands are typically used in a file definition? In what ways do DOS operands differ from OS operands?
9. Distinguish between a pretest loop and a posttest loop. What names identify the start and stop of a pretest loop? What names are used for a posttest loop?
10. What names are used with one-way selection to identify the parts of the structure? with two-way selection?
11. What types of operations are done during initialization of a program?
12. What is a subroutine? What statements are used to go to a subroutine and return to the proper place in the mainline routine?
13. What two instructions are used to load and designate a base register? Where in the program do they normally appear?
14. What is meant by opening and closing a file? Why is this done?
15. What two operands are used with GET and PUT statements? What do they refer to?
16. What determines the number of bytes to be moved in a Move Characters (MVC) instruction? What happens to the bytes in the destination field? In the source field?
17. What three separate operations are performed by the Branch on Count (BCT) instruction? What is the most common use?

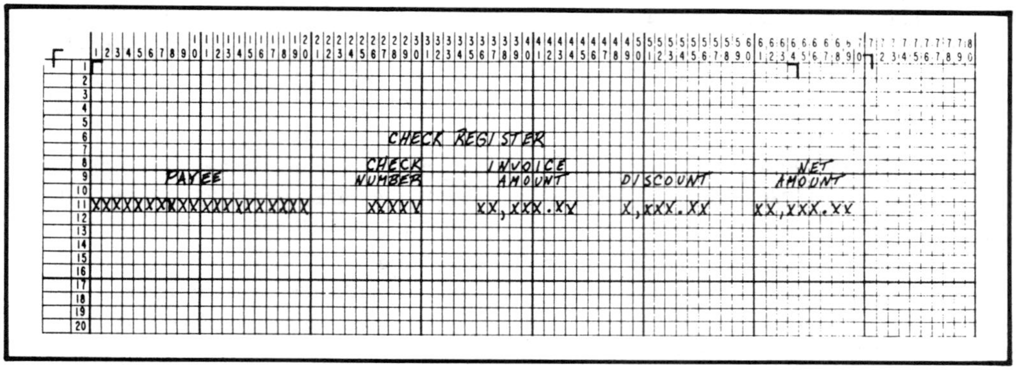

Figure 2–24 Heading lines to be defined

EXERCISES

1. Show the EBCDIC code produced by the assembler for each of the following constant definitions:
   DC C'XYZ'   DC C'347'   DC CL5'IBM'   DC 5C'*'
2. Write data definitions for an input record of 80 bytes that has an account number in columns 1 to 5, a description in columns 11 to 25, and a quantity on hand in columns 46 to 50.
3. Write DS and DC statements to describe the heading lines in Figure 2–24.
4. Write a heading subroutine to skip to a new page, print one heading line, double space, print a second heading line, and skip one more line between the heading and the first detail line. Set line counter to 40 before returning to the mainline program.
5. Write a statement to read a record from a file named INTRANS and place the record in a work area named INWORK.
6. Write instructions to load general register 8 with the address of the following instruction and designate R8 as the base register for the program.

PROGRAMMING PROBLEMS

1. Using Data Set 1 in Appendix D, write a program to print a report showing employee name, department, and date employed. The report would have the following format:

```
             EMPLOYEES WITH DATE OF EMPLOYMENT
     NAME                 DEPARTMENT     DATE EMPLOYED

     MARK DOWN            1234           091356
     CLYDE S DALE         1234           040375
```

The main heading starts in print position 16. Column headings start in print positions 11, 33, and 46, respectively. Columns in detail lines start in print position 6, 36, and 50, respectively. Use a line counter to print 50 detail lines per page. Use naming conventions for instructions and comments to show pseudocode as in Program 1.

2. Modify Problem 1 to leave only five blank print positions between columns, instead of the 10 as shown. Shift the headings to the left so that they will be properly centered over the detail lines. Print only 30 detail lines per page.
3. Using the same data set, print a directory showing name, social security number, sex, and date of birth. Print the columns in the detail line 10 spaces apart. Show headings of your own choice centered over the detail columns. Draw a program flowchart to show program logic.

3
More Operations with Characters

OBJECTIVES

After studying this chapter, you should be able to:

- Use relative addressing and explicit lengths with character operands
- Show the results of moving overlapping fields to the left or right
- Describe the literal pool and use literals as operands
- Explain and use immediate instructions
- Define hexadecimal constants
- Compare characters and perform conditional branching
- Use the selection structure in programs to print only certain records
- Create nested IF structures
- Employ compound conditions in selection and loops

EXPLICIT LENGTHS IN MOVING CHARACTERS

In our first program we found that the MVC (Move Characters) instruction would move (copy) the contents of one field, called the *source* field, into another location, called the *receiving* field. The defined length of the first operand, the receiving field, determines the number of bytes to be moved. The length given in a DS or DC statement is the *implicit* length of the field. However, we may override the implicit length by giving the operand an *explicit* length enclosed in parentheses. For example, if INRECD is defined as an 80-byte field and PRLINE as a 132-byte field and we write

```
MVC PRLINE,INRECD
```

the effect is to move 132 bytes (the implicit length) from the area starting at the first byte of INRECD into the 132 bytes starting at PRLINE. This would bring the 52 bytes following INRECD (whatever they might be) into the last 52 bytes of PRLINE. To move only the desired 80 bytes we write:

```
MVC PRLINE(80),INRECD
```

RELATIVE ADDRESSING

The address of any instruction, record, or field is the location of its first, or leftmost, byte. The length of the field is defined either implicitly in a DS or DC statement or explicitly within parentheses as a part of the operand.

We can refer to any location in storage in terms of its position relative to some other location. For example, if a location is defined as INRECD, then the byte next to it is INRECD + 1 and the fifth byte from it is INRECD + 5. We may also use a negative relative address. INRECD-1 is the byte just to the left of INRECD. There must be no space between any parts of the operands in relative addresses.

Whenever we use a relative address, we must normally be sure to use an explicit length; otherwise the assembler will assume the implicit length from the DS or DC statement. For example,

```
MVC PRLINE+50,INRECD
```

would cause 132 bytes to be moved from an area starting at INRECD to an area starting 50 bytes past PRLINE. To move, say, only the first 10 bytes of INRECD to PRLINE + 50, we should write

```
MVC PRLINE+50(10),INRECD
```

MOVING OVERLAPPING FIELDS

Two fields are said to *overlap* if some storage locations are common to both fields. For example, an eight-byte field starting at INRECD will overlap four bytes of an eight-byte field starting at INRECD + 4.

Whenever we move an overlapping field to one that starts to its left, we shift the data in that field left by the number of bytes between the two starting points. Suppose INRECD contains the alphabet starting in column 10, and we give the instruction

```
MVC INRECD+8(26),INRECD+9
```

The alphabet will now appear starting in column 9. As each letter is shifted left, it destroys the original letter that was there. In column 35, we will find the original letter Z next to the place where it was moved in column 34. Figure 3–1 illustrates the effect of this move.

If we give the instruction

```
MVC INRECD(26),INRECD+9
```

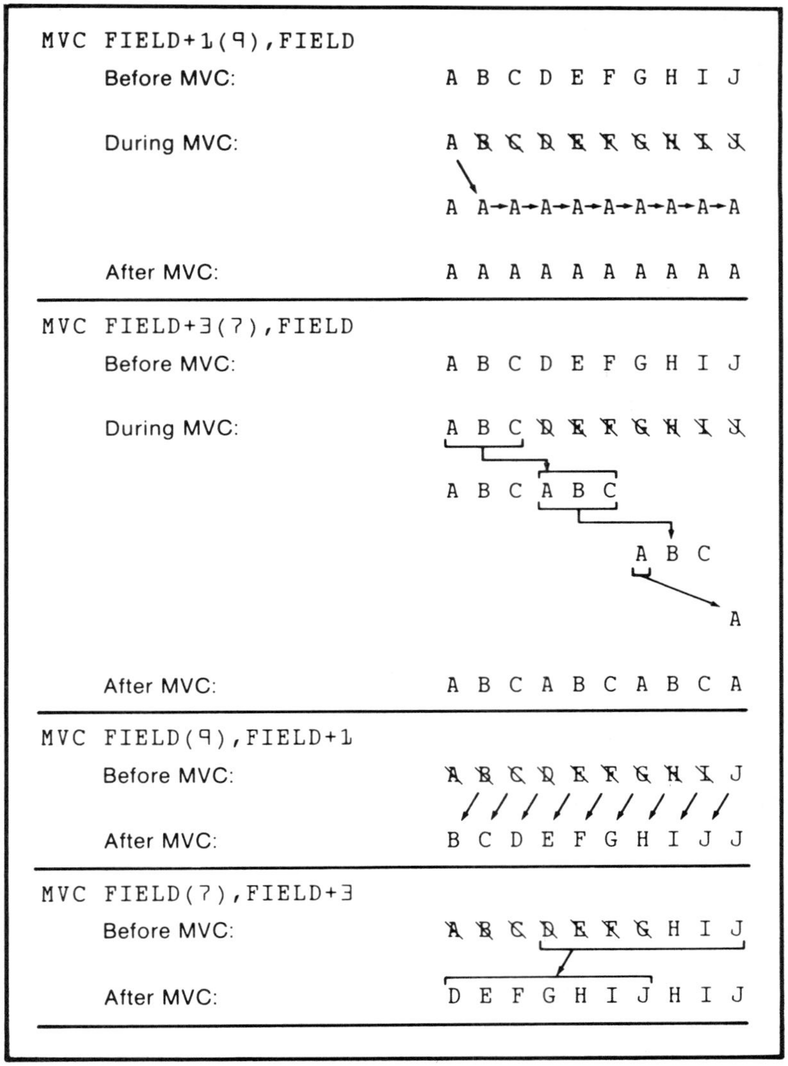

Figure 3–1 MVC instructions with overlapping fields

we will find that the alphabet has been shifted left nine columns and that the last nine letters of the alphabet appear once where they were moved and again in their original locations.

On the other hand, if we move a field to one which overlaps it starting to the right, we tend to repeat characters through the field. The instruction

```
MVC INRECD+10(26),INRECD+9
```

propagates the letter A through the next 26 bytes. Whenever the first byte of the receiving field is immediately right of the first byte of the sending field, the same character will be replicated through the entire receiving field. Each time the MVC instruction moves a byte, it picks up the same byte on the next machine cycle to move to the next byte.

If we give the instruction

```
MVC INRECD+14(26),INRECD+9
```

we find that the characters ABCD repeat themselves throughout the desination field.

We normally employ overlapping fields to fill a field with blanks, zeros, or any other character. The following two instructions clear a field, such as a print line, before moving in the data that is to be printed in the line:

```
MVI PRLINE,C' '
MVC PRLINE+1(131),PRLINE
```

There are actually two 131-byte overlapping fields. The source field starts at PRLINE and the destination field at PRLINE+1. The byte at PRLINE is propagated throughout the rest of the 132 bytes, clearing the field.

Programming Tips

- Always use an explicit length with a relative address in an SS type instruction where a length is required. Otherwise, the assembler will use the implicit length of the DS or DC statement defining the field.
- To propagate the same character through each position of a field or record, move it to the first byte of the field. Then, with a MVC instruction, move the byte to a destination field starting one byte to the right and continuing to the end of the field.

LITERALS

Suppose we wish to move the word 'TOTALS' to positions 20 through 25 of PRLINE. One way is move a field holding the constant 'TOTALS' to a field defined in PRLINE as in Figure 3–2.

With relative addressing and defining PRLINE DS CL132, we could eliminate defining three separate fields in PRLINE:

```
MVC PRLINE+19(6),WDTOTALS
```

but even this requires that we make a separate definition for WDTOTALS.

A *literal* allows us to define the constant right in the instruction in which we use it. The form of a literal is:

```
MVC PRLINE+19(6),=C'TOTALS'
```

The literal is made up of an equal sign (=) and a constant definition. The literal must include the type and value, just as any other constant does, and may include a duplication factor and a length. Each literal is placed at the end of the program in the *literal pool*. When the instruction is converted to machine language, the assembler replaces the literal with the address in the literal pool where the literal is stored. If the same literal is used more than once in a program, it is stored only once in the literal pool.

The literal pool need not always appear at the end of the program. The LTORG assembler declarative instructs the assembler to place the pool of all literals used in the program thus far so as to start wherever the LTORG is placed.

IMMEDIATE INSTRUCTIONS

Where we wish to move a single byte to a certain location, we might use

```
MVC PRLINE+131(1),=C'X'
```

A special class of instructions called *immediate instructions* handles operands consisting of a single byte. Immediate operands differ from other operands discussed so far in that the single byte is placed directly in the instruction itself. The second operand in an immediate instruction is not the address of a field in storage, but the byte itself. Immediate instructions require only four bytes in machine language form, whereas instructions like MVC that refer to two separate storage locations (called storage-to-storage instructions) require six bytes in machine language. (We will discuss types of machine instructions in Chapter 6.)

We write an immediate instruction in the form:

```
MVI LINE+131,C'X'
```

```
               MVC     PRTOTALS,WDTOTALS
                .
                .
                .
PRLINE         DS      0CL132
               DS      CL19
PRTOTALS       DS      CL6
               DS      CL107
WDTOTALS       DC      CL6'TOTALS'
```

Figure 3–2 Heading set up by MVC statements

We never need to use a length with immediate instructions, since the length of each operand is always one byte. The immediate operand does not require an equal sign as a literal does. It can be of any type of data and any value, so long as it is one byte only.

DEFINING HEXADECIMAL CHARACTERS

So far we have defined only type C (character) constants and literals. For type C, we use the actual numbers, letters, or special characters we use in everyday life, and the assembler translates them to the proper EBCDIC code. Or we can define characters as type X (hexadecimal) constants using the same hex digits that the assembler does in EBCDIC code. For example, EBCDIC code for the letters ABC is C1C2C3. We could define the letters ABC by writing:

```
DC X'C1C2C3'
```

In the following pairs, the type C entry in the left column produces the same constant as the corresponding type X entry in the right column. Notice that it requires two hex digits to produce one character.

```
DC C'125'                       DC X'F1F2F5'
DC C'   '   (three blanks)      DC X'404040'
DC 4C'*'                        DC X'5B5B5B5B'
```

There is one important difference between type C and type X constants. The assembler considers type C to be alphanumeric data, and pads excess length to the right of the constant with spaces. It regards type X data as numeric, and pads extra length to the left with zeros. Note the object code produced by the assembler from these constant definitions:

OBJECT CODE	CONSTANTS
C1C2C34040	DC CL5'ABC'
0000C1C2C3	DC XL5'C1C2C3'
0000000ABC	DC XL5'ABC'

Hex constants enable us to create bit patterns not used for the normal characters we find on the keyboard. For example, X'00' creates a byte containing eight 0 bits and X'FF' creates a byte of all 1 bits. These bit patterns cannot be expressed as type C constants.

COMPARING CHARACTERS

When any two fields are compared, there are three possible relationships: the first may be equal to, less than, or greater than the second field. A special hardware indicator called the *condition code* is set to indicate the result of the comparison. The condition code then may be tested by a *conditional branch* instruction to change the logical path of the program. (Technical details about the condition code are treated later in the text.)

EBCDIC characters are compared bit by bit, left to right, until one bit is found that is different from the corresponding bit in the other field. As an example, suppose we wish to compare the letter A with the letter C. The EBCDIC codes in hex and binary are shown below:

CHARACTER	HEX CODE	BINARY CODE
A	C1	11000001
C	C3	11000011

We can see that the first six bits of the binary codes are equal. In the seventh bit, A contains a 0 while C contains a 1. A is therefore less than C. The same sort of comparison continues throughout the entire field until a difference is found or both fields are determined to be equal.

To compare two fields we use CLC (Compare Logical Characters). The length of the first operand determines how many characters are compared. The maximum length of the fields being compared is 256 bytes. We may use relative addressing, length operands, and literals with the CLC instruction just as we did in moving data with the MVC instruction.

To compare one byte in storage with an immediate operand, we use CLI (Compare Logical Immediate). The first operand is always compared with the second operand, and the condition code indicates whether the first operand is equal to, less than, or greater than the second operand.

CONDITIONAL BRANCHING

A *conditional branch* instruction tests the condition code and branches if the tested condition is found to be true. The condition code has normally just been set by comparing two values, but it is also set by certain arithmetic operations.

To print every record that has an X in column 80, we might use the program segment described in Figure 3–3. We wish to print the records at THEN that have an X in column 80 in INRECD (INRECD + 79), but branch to ENDIF if the value in column 80 is not equal to X. This is an example of one-way selection, since there is no ELSE part to the selection structure.

The following op codes may be used for conditional branching following comparisons. These are not true op codes, but are called *extended mnemonics*. Chapter 6 will explain them more fully.

BE—branch if equal
BNE—branch if not equal
BL—branch if low (less than)
BNL—branch if not low
BH—branch if high (greater than)
BNH—branch if not high

The condition code is also set by some arithmetic operations to indicate if the result is equal to, less than, or greater than zero. The condition code is also set if the result of an arithmetic operation is *overflow*, that is, too large to fit into the space provided for it. We may use the following op codes to express these conditions:

BZ—branch if zero
BNZ—branch if not zero
BM—branch if minus (less than zero)
BNM—branch if not minus
BP—branch if positive (greater than zero)
BNP—branch if not positive
BO—branch if overflow
BNO—branch if not overflow

Note that the NOT condition really tests two conditions. For example, branch if not zero means branch if positive or branch if negative. If a value is not higher than another value, it may be equal or it may be lower.

Suppose we wish to move the word 'PASSES' to the print line if the student's grade is 70 or greater and the word 'FAILS' if the grade is less than 70. We could use the routine in Figure 3–4 to illustrate this two-way selection.

We must ensure that both operands in CLC instructions have the same length; otherwise, comparisons may be incorrect.

NESTED IF STATEMENTS

Once we have determined whether some condition is true or false, we often have to consider some other condition under either or both of the alternate paths. This requires that we use a *nested IF* structure, in which one IF structure is completely contained within either the THEN or the ELSE of another IF. Consider the pseudocode in Figure 3–5, which extends somewhat further the logic of the example of the student grade.

Note that the second IF structure is completely contained within the THEN portion of the first IF. That is, if the student grade is less than 70, the second IF is completely bypassed, and control passes to the ELSE that moves 'FAILS' to the print line. Each IF must be paired with an ENDIF (and often an ELSE) not already paired with another ENDIF. The indentation of the pseudocode helps to make this relationship clear.

COMPOUND CONDITIONS

Our program logic often requires that we consider two or more conditions before taking some action. Each separate condition is called a *simple* condition. For example, we may wish to print only the records that do not have an X in column 80 but do have a state code of 'FL'. This is called an AND *compound* condition, because *both* conditions must be true for the record to be printed. If *either* is false, the record is not printed.

The pseudocode and source statements for this AND condition are shown in Figure 3–6. Source statements for this logic phrase the conditions just the opposite and branch to ENDIF if either condition as stated is true. If column 80 does not have an X or the state code is not 'FL', we will bypass the record. Thus we will print the record only if both original conditions were true.

A second form of compound statement is called an OR condition. Here the action is taken if *either* of the simple conditions is true. For example, we may wish to print a record if the state code is either 'FL' or 'CA'. The pseudocode and source statements for this OR compound condition are shown in Figure 3–7.

In our source statements, we ask the first condition in a positive way and branch to THEN if it is true. We ask the second condition negatively; we branch to ENDIF if the negative condition is true, but fall through to THEN if the negative condition is false (positive condition is true).

Compound conditions may also be used to control loops. Suppose our records should be in alphabetic order by name and we wish to print out all names that start with the letters 'A' through 'H'. This requires an AND compound condition: to continue the loop, we must not be at end of file AND the

```
IF       CLI   INRECD+79,C'X'
         BNE   ENDIF
THEN     MVC   PRLINE(80),INRECD
         PUT   PRINTER,PRLINE
ENDIF    EQU   *
```

Figure 3–3 Program segment showing one-way selection

```
IF       CLC   GRADE(3),=C'070'
         BL    ELSE
THEN     MVC   PRLINE+80(6),=C'PASSES'
         B     ENDIF
ELSE     MVC   PRLINE+80(6),=C'FAILS '
ENDIF    EQU   *
```

Figure 3–4 Program segment showing two-way selection

```
If student grade is not less than 70
   THEN
   IF student grade is not less than 90
      THEN move 'HONORS' to print line
   ELSE move 'PASSES' to print line
   ENDIF
ELSE move 'FAILS' to print line
ENDIF
```

Figure 3–5 Pseudocode for nested IF statements

PSEUDOCODE	SOURCE STATEMENTS		
IF column-80 is not equal to X	IF	CLI	INRECD+79,C'X'
AND state code is equal to 'FL'		BE	ENDIF
THEN print record	AND	CLC	INSTATE,=C'FL'
ENDIF		BNE	ENDIF
	THEN	PUT	PRINTER,PRLINE
	ENDIF	EQU	*

Figure 3–6 Pseudocode and source statements for AND compound condition

PSEUDOCODE	SOURCE STATEMENTS		
IF state code is equal to 'FL'	IF	CLC	INSTATE,=C'FL'
OR state code is equal to 'CA'		BE	THEN
THEN print record	OR	CLC	INSTATE,=C'CA'
ENDIF		BNE	ENDIF
	THEN	PUT	PRINTER,PRLINE
	ENDIF	EQU	*

Figure 3–7 Pseudocode and source statements for OR compound condition

PSEUDOCODE	SOURCE STATEMENTS		
Read first record		GET	INFILE,INRECD
Save name		MVC	PREVNAME,INNAME
DOWHILE NOT end of file	DOWHILE	CLI	INNAME,C'H'
AND first letter of name not greater than 'H'		BH	ENDDO
AND name not less than previous name	AND	CLC	INNAME,PREVNAME
Move data to print line		BL	ENDDO
Print record		MVC	PRLINE(80),INRECD
Save name		PUT	PRINTER,PRLINE
Read next record		MVC	PREVNAME,INNAME
ENDDO		GET	INFILE,INRECD
		B	DOWHILE
	ENDDO	EQU	*

Figure 3–8 AND compound condition to control loop

first letter of last name must not be greater than ‘H’, AND the name must not be lower in sequence than the preceding name. We must stop if any of these conditions is found to be false. Pseudocode and source statements are shown in Figure 3–8.

In the source code shown, the test for end of file is automatically provided in the GET macro, while the other two conditions that terminate the loop are tested with Compare instructions. Note that the CLI instruction compares only the first byte of INNAME with ‘H’, while the CLC compares the entire field of INNAME with PREVNAME.

Programming Tips

- Use immediate instructions to move or compare a single byte. They require no explicit length operand and contain the second operand in the instruction itself.
- In a conditional branch for a DOWHILE or IF structure, test the opposite condition from that stated in the pseudocode. Branch to ENDDO, ELSE, or ENDIF if the test is true.

PROGRAM 2: PRINTING SELECTED RECORDS

This program uses the same data as the program in the last chapter but produces a different report. In this program we print name, date of birth, and date employed of all persons employed before 1960. To do so, we must compare the field giving year employed with 60 (1960) and branch to ENDIF if that year is not lower than 60. Thus we set up the print line and print the desired data only for those employed before 1960.

Data fields from the employee record needed for this program are:

10–29 Employee name
31–36 Date of birth
37–42 Date employed

The pseudocode for the program is shown in Figure 3–9. It shows an IF structure contained within the DOWHILE loop. The nested IF, which tests the line counter to determine if a heading should be printed, is necessary only if we do print the record. Data definitions and headings are somewhat different from Program 1 because this report contains different data elements.

Figure 3–10 shows the print chart, Figure 3–11 the program flowchart, Figure 3–12 the assembler output, and Figure 3–13 the expected output from this program.

```
START PROGRAM
Open files
Print headings and set line counter
Read first record
DOWHILE NOT end of file:
   IF year employed is lower than 1960
      THEN move input fields to output record
      Print output record
      Subtract 1 from line counter
      IF line counter = zero
         THEN Print headings and set line counter
      ENDIF
   ENDIF
   Read next record
ENDDO
Close files
END PROGRAM
```

Figure 3–9 Pseudocode for Program 2

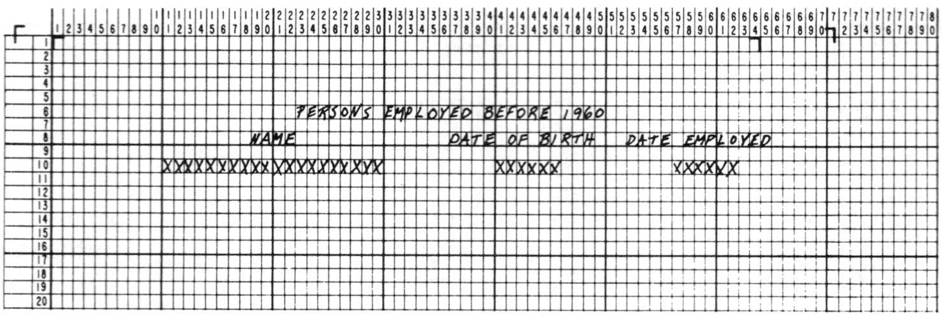

Figure 3–10 Program 2 print chart

Notice the zero duplication factor with the DS for the date employed field, so that the entire six digits can be moved as a unit for printing or the rightmost two digits can be used separately to compare date employed with 60 (1960).

PROGRAM 3: PRINTING SELECTED RECORDS

Our next sample program examines the employee record and prints the name, department, job code, and date of birth of all male employees born between 1955 and 1965. Selection of records with birth years between two val-

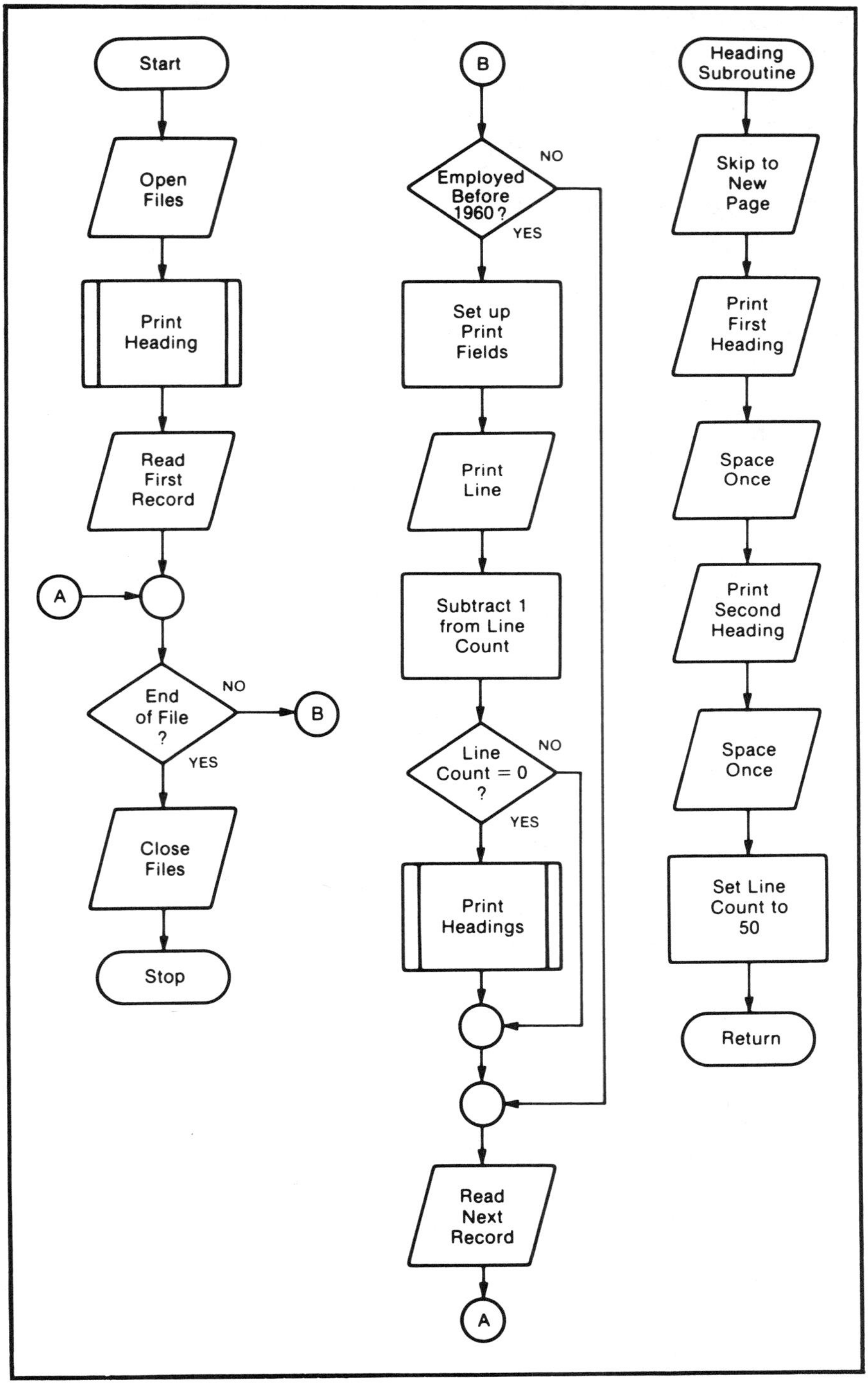

Figure 3–11 Program flowchart for Program 2

ues requires compound conditions. To eliminate the need for a print chart, we show in Figure 3–14 the fields needed from the employee record as input and the positions where they are to be printed.

For practice, we shall use relative addressing for all fields within the input record and the detail print line. We will need to show explicit lengths for MVC and CLC instructions. Length operands are not needed for CLI and MVI instructions, because the length of immediate operands is always 1.

Pseudocode is shown in Figure 3–15.

From this point on we shall omit the print chart and program flowchart for each program. Figure 3–16 shows the assembler output, and Figure 3–17 shows the expected program output.

SUMMARY

In this chapter, we have explored further uses of character instructions. An explicit length is written in parentheses following the name of a field. The explicit length overrides the implicit length in the DS or DC statement to move more or fewer than the defined number of bytes.

```
  LOC  OBJECT CODE    ADDR1 ADDR2  STMT   SOURCE STATEMENT                                         DOS/VSE ASSEMBLER 14.50 86-03-27

                                      1 ***********************************************************************
                                      2 *                    ALTON R. KINDRED, PROGRAM 2
                                      3 * THIS PROGRAM LISTS NAME, DATE OF BIRTH, AND DATE EMPLOYED OF ALL
                                      4 * PERSONS EMPLOYED BEFORE 1960.
                                      5 *          REGISTERS USED:
                                      6 *                    R5  - LINE COUNTER
                                      7 *                    R9  - LINK TO MODULES
                                      8 *                    R12 - BASE REGISTER
                                      9 ***********************************************************************
                                     10          PRINT NOGEN
000000                               11 MAINLINE START 0                             SET LOCATION COUNTER
                                     12 *        STM   14,12,12(13)                  SAVE REGISTERS FOR OS         OS
000000 05C0                          13          BALR  12,0                          LOAD BASE REGISTER
                           00002     14          USING *,12                          DESIGNATE BASE REGISTER
                                     15 *        ST    13,SAVE+4                     STORE REGISTER 13             OS
                                     16 *        LA    13,SAVE                       LOAD SAVE AREA ADDRESS        OS
                                     17 *        OPEN  (INFILE,(INPUT),PRINTER,(OUTPUT))                           OS
                                     18          OPEN  INFILE,PRINTER                OPEN FILES                    DOS
000016 4590 C086           00088     27          BAL   9,HEADING                     PRINT HEADING
                                     28          GET   INFILE,INRECD                 READ FIRST RECORD
                           0002A     34 DOWHILE  EQU   *                             DOWHILE NOT END OF FILE
00002A D501 C23A C416 0023C 00418    35 IF       CLC   INYREMPL,=C'60'                 IF HIRED BEFORE 1960
000030 47B0 C05C      0005E          36          BNL   ENDIF                             *
000034 D213 C26C C21B 0026E 0021D    37 THEN     MVC   PRNAME,INNAME                     THEN SET UP PRINT LINE
00003A D205 C28A C230 0028C 00232    38          MVC   PRDTBRTH,INDTBRTH                 *
000040 D205 C29A C236 0029C 00238    39          MVC   PRDTEMPL,INDTEMPL                 *
                                     40          PUT   PRINTER,PRLINE                    PRINT LINE
000056 4650 C05C           0005E     46          BCT   5,ENDIF2                          SUBTRACT 1 FROM LINE COUNT
                           0005A     47 IF2      EQU   *                                 IF LINE COUNT = ZERO
00005A 4590 C086           00088     48 THEN2    BAL   9,HEADING                           THEN PRINT HEADING
                           0005E     49 ENDIF2   EQU   *                                 ENDIF
                           0005E     50 ENDIF    EQU   *                               ENDIF
                                     51          GET   INFILE,INRECD                   READ NEXT RECORD
00006E 47F0 C028      0002A          57          B     DOWHILE                         *
                           00072     58 ENDDO    EQU   *                             ENDDO
                                     59          CLOSE INFILE,PRINTER                CLOSE FILES                   DOS
                                     68          EOJ                                 END PROGRAM                   DOS
                                     71 *        CLOSE (INFILE,,PRINTER)             CLOSE FILES                   OS
                                     72 *        L     13,SAVE+4                     LOAD SAVE AREA ADDRESS        OS
                                     73 *        LM    14,12,12(13)                  RESTORE REGISTERS             OS
                                     74 *        BR    14                            RETURN TO OS                  OS
                                     75 ***********************************************************************
                                     76 *                   HEADING SUBROUTINE
                                     77 ***********************************************************************
                                     78 HEADING  CNTRL PRINTER,SK,1                  SKIP TO NEW PAGE
                                     84          PUT   PRINTER,HEAD1                 PRINT FIRST HEADING
                                     90          CNTRL PRINTER,SP,1                  SPACE ONCE
                                     96          PUT   PRINTER,HEAD2                 PRINT SECOND HEADING
                                    102          CNTRL PRINTER,SP,1                  SPACE ONCE
0000D2 4150 0032           00032    108          LA    5,50                          SET LINE COUNTER
0000D6 07F9                         109          BR    9                             RETURN
```

Figure 3–12 Program 2 assembler listing

```
  LOC  OBJECT CODE     ADDR1 ADDR2  STMT   SOURCE STATEMENT                                          DOS/VSE ASSEMBLER 14.50 86-03-27

                                     111 ***********************************************************************DOS
                                     112 *                    FILE DEFINITIONS AND I/O AREAS                    DOS
                                     113 ***********************************************************************DOS
                                     114 INFILE    DTFCD BLKSIZE=80,IOAREA1=INAREA,DEVICE=2540,                 DOSX
                                                         DEVADDR=SYSIPT,EOFADDR=ENDDO,WORKA=YES                 DOS
                                     135 *                                                                      DOS
                                     136 PRINTER   DTFPR BLKSIZE=132,IOAREA1=PRTAREA,DEVICE=1403,               DOSX
                                                         CONTROL=YES,DEVADDR=SYS009,WORKA=YES                   DOS
                                     157 *                                                                      DOS
000140                               158 INAREA    DS    CL80                                                   DOS
000190                               159 PRTAREA   DS    CL132                                                  DOS
                                     160 ***********************************************************************OS
                                     161 *                    DEVICE CONTROL BLOCKS AND SAVE AREA               OS
                                     162 ***********************************************************************OS
                                     163 *INFILE   DCB   DDNAME=INFILE,BLKSIZE=80,LRECL=80,                     OSX
                                     164 *               MACRF=PM,DSORG=PS,EODAD=ENDDO                          OS
                                     165 *                                                                      OS
                                     166 *PRINTER DCB    DDNAME=PRINTER,BLKSIZE=132,LRECL=132,                  OSX
                                     167 *               MACRF=PMC,DSORG=PS                                     OS
                                     168 *                                                                      OS
                                     169 *SAVE     DS    18F                                                    OS
                                     170 ************************************************************************
                                     171 *               DATA DEFINITIONS
                                     172 ************************************************************************
000214                               173 INRECD    DS    0CL80
000214                               174           DS    CL9
00021D                               175 INNAME    DS    CL20
000231                               176           DS    CL1
000232                               177 INDTBRTH DS     CL6
000238                               178 INDTEMPL DS     0CL6
000238                               179           DS    CL4
00023C                               180 INYREMPL DS     CL2
00023F                               181           DS    CL38
                                     182 *
000264                               183 PRLINE    DS    0CL132
000264 40404040404040 40             184           DC    CL10' '
00026E                               185 PRNAME    DS    CL20
000282 4040404040404040              186           DC    CL10' '
00028C                               187 PRDTBRTH DS     CL6
000292 4040404040404040              188           DC    CL10' '
00029C                               189 PRDTEMPL DS     CL6
0002A2 4040404040404040              190           DC    CL70' '
                                     191 *
0002E8                               192 HEAD1     DS    0CL132
0002E8 4040404040404040              193           DC    CL22' '
0002FE D7C5D9E2D6D5E240              194           DC    CL110'PERSONS EMPLOYED BEFORE 1960'
                                     195 *
00036C                               196 HEAD2     DS    0CL132
00036C 4040404040404040              197           DC    CL18' '
00037E D5C1D4C540404040              198           DC    CL18'NAME'
000390 C4C1E3C540D6C640              199           DC    CL16'DATE OF BIRTH'
0003A0 C4C1E3C540C5D4D7              200           DC    CL80'DATE EMPLOYED'
                                     201 *
                          00000      202           END   MAINLINE
0003F0 5B5BC2D6D7C5D540              203                 =C'$$BOPEN '
0003F8 5B5BC2C3D3D6E2C5              204                 =C'$$BCLOSE'
000400 000000D8                      205                 =A(INFILE)
000404 00000214                      206                 =A(INRECD)
000408 00000110                      207                 =A(PRINTER)
00040C 00000264                      208                 =A(PRLINE)
000410 000002E8                      209                 =A(HEAD1)
000414 0000036C                      210                 =A(HEAD2)
000418 F6F0                          211                 =C'60'
```

Figure 3–12 *(Concluded)*

A relative address is written with a plus or minus and an offset following the name of a field to indicate how many bytes the relative position is away from the defined field. PRLINE + 24(10) refers to a ten-byte field located 24 bytes away from a location named PRLINE. We always need an explicit length when using relative addressing with the first operand of a Move Characters (MVC) instruction.

When two fields overlap, we may shift data to the left if the address of the destination field is lower than that of the source field. We may cause one or more bytes to be repeated within overlapping fields when the address of the destination field is higher than that of the source field.

A literal is a constant preceded by an equal sign used as an operand in a machine instruction. Literals are placed by the assembler in a pool at the end of the program. The address of the literal becomes the operand in the machine instruction when the program is assembled.

```
              PERSONS EMPLOYED BEFORE 1960

          NAME                    DATE OF BIRTH   DATE EMPLOYED

MARK DOWN                            022434          091356
CARRIE AHN                           101540          121059
SALLY FORTH                          112531          021653
BART ENDER                           120741          050859
STEVE EDORE                          111137          041959
ABBY WESTMINSTER                     021433          080358
ELLA MENTRY                          072835          031457
SEYMOUR SEITZ                        061426          120856
OSCAR QUESTION                       082333          012358
```

Figure 3–13 Output from Program 2

INPUT COLUMNS	FIELD NAME	PRINTING POSITIONS
10–29	Employee name	11–30
30	Sex	Not printed
31–36	Date of birth	60–65
43–46	Department	37–40
54–57	Job code	48–51

Figure 3–14 Input and output formats for Program 3

Immediate instructions contain the second operand, which is always a single byte, in the second byte of the machine instruction itself. No length code is necessary, and immediate instructions are shorter than instructions that refer to two separate fields in storage.

Hexadecimal constants may be used in place of characters. The hex digits making up the EBCDIC code are used to represent numbers, letters, or special characters. Two hexadecimal digits are required to represent each character.

When characters are compared or some arithmetic operations are done, the condition code is set. The condition code is tested in conditional branch instructions to control the sequence in which instructions are executed. If the tested condition is true, the branch is made. If not true, the program proceeds to the following instruction.

Compound conditions occur when more than one condition may have to be tested to see if some action is to be taken. The AND condition requires that all simple conditions be true before the action is taken. The OR condition requires that the action be taken if any one condition is true. Nested IF statements and nested loops may be used to test multiple conditions.

```
START PROGRAM
Open files
Print heading
Read first record
DOWHILE not end of file
   IF male
      THEN
      IF birth year => 1955
      AND birth year <= 1965
         THEN
         Set up print line
         Print line
         Subtract 1 from line count
         IF line count = zero
            THEN Print heading
         ENDIF
      ENDIF
   ENDIF
   Read next record
ENDDO
Close files
```

Figure 3–15 Pseudocode for Program 3

TERMS FOR REVIEW

Compound condition
Condition code
Conditional branch
Destination field
Explicit length
Immediate instruction
Implicit length
Literal
Multiple record format
Nested IF statements
Overlapping fields
Relative address
Source field

REVIEW QUESTIONS

1. Distinguish between implicit and explicit lengths. How is each defined?
2. You give the instruction MVC PRLINE+28,HEADING. HEADING has been defined as 20 bytes. PRLINE is defined as 132 bytes. How many bytes are moved? Why?
3. What is the effect of the following statements if WORKAREA has been defined to contain 20 bytes?
   a. `MVC WORKAREA,WORKAREA+1`
   b. `MVC WORKAREA+1(20),WORKAREA`
   c. `MVC WORKAREA+5(16),WORKAREA`
   d. `MVC WORKAREA(15),WORKAREA+5`

4. What advantages are there to using literals as opposed to defining constants, giving them names, and referring to the names in instructions?
5. Where does the assembler store literals, and how does it refer to them in instructions?
6. Give the brief differences between literals and immediate operands. In what instances would the immediate operand be more efficient?
7. What is the purpose of the condition code? What class of instructions are used primarily to set the condition code?
8. When two fields of characters are compared, what determines that one field is higher or lower than the other?
9. A field named A contains 783. Another field named B contains 543. If the instruction CLC A,B has been executed, which of the following instructions will cause a branch to ENDIF?
   a. `BL  ENDIF`
   b. `BNL ENDIF`
   c. `BE  ENDIF`
   d. `BNE ENDIF`

```
  LOC  OBJECT CODE    ADDR1 ADDR2  STMT   SOURCE STATEMENT                                  DOS/VSE ASSEMBLER 14.51 86-03-27

                                      1 *********************************************************************
                                      2 *                  ALTON R. KINDRÉD, PROGRAM 3
                                      3 * THIS PROGRAM PRINTS NAME, DEPARTMENT, JOB CODE, AND DATE OF BIRTH OF
                                      4 * ALL MALE EMPLOYEES BORN BETWEEN 1955 AND 1965.
                                      5 *          REGISTERS USED:
                                      6 *                  R5  - LINE COUNTER
                                      7 *                  R9  - LINK TO MODULE
                                      8 *                  R12 - BASE REGISTER
                                      9 *********************************************************************
                                     10          PRINT NOGEN
000000                               11 MAINLINE START 0                           SET LOCATION COUNTER
                                     12 *        STM   14,12,12(13)                SAVE REGISTERS FOR OS        OS
000000 05C0                          13          BALR  12,0                        LOAD BASE REGISTER
                          00002      14          USING *,12                        DESIGNATE BASE REGISTER
                                     15 *        ST    13,SAVE+4                   STORE REGISTER 13            OS
                                     16 *        LA    13,SAVE                     LOAD SAVE AREA ADDRESS       OS
                                     17 *        OPEN  (INFILE,(INPUT),PRINTER,(OUTPUT))                        OS
                                     18          OPEN  INFILE,PRINTER              OPEN FILES                   DOS
000016 4590 C0A6          000A8      27          BAL   9,HEADING                   PRINT HEADING
                                     28          GET   INFILE,INRECD               READ FIRST RECORD
                          0002A      34 DOWHILE  EQU   *                           DOWHILE NOT END OF FILE
00002A 9504 C24F    00251            35 IF       CLI   INRECD+29,C'M'                 IF MALE
00002E 4770 C07E    00080            36          BNE   ENDIF                            *
                          00032      37 THEN     EQU   *                                THEN
000032 D501 C254 C436 00256 00438    38 IF2      CLC   INRECD+34(2),=C'55'              IF YEAR OF BIRTH NOT < 55
000038 4740 C07E    00080            39          BL    ENDIF2                           *
00003C D501 C254 C438 00256 0043A    40 AND2     CLC   INRECD+34(2),=C'65'              AND NOT > 1965
000042 4720 C07E    00080            41          BH    ENDIF2                           *
000046 9240 C282    00284            42 THEN2    MVI   PRLINE,C' '                        THEN CLEAR PRINT LINE
00004A D282 C283 C282 00285 00284    43          MVC   PRLINE+1(131),PRLINE               *
000050 D213 C28C C23B 0028E 0023D    44          MVC   PRLINE+10(20),INRECD+9             SET UP PRINT LINE
000056 D203 C2A6 C25C 002A8 0025E    45          MVC   PRLINE+36(4),INRECD+42             *
00005C D203 C2B1 C267 002B3 00269    46          MVC   PRLINE+47(4),INRECD+53             *
000062 D205 C2BD C250 002BF 00252    47          MVC   PRLINE+59(6),INRECD+30             *
                                     48          PUT   PRINTER,PRLINE                     PRINT LINE
000078 4650 C07E          00080      54          BCT   5,ENDIF3                           SUBTRACT 1 FROM LINE COUNT
                          0007C      55 IF3      EQU   *                                  IF LINE COUNT = 0
00007C 4590 C0A6          000A8      56 THEN3    BAL   9,HEADING                            THEN PRINT HEADING
                          00080      57 ENDIF3   EQU   *                                  ENDIF
                          00080      58 ENDIF2   EQU   *                                ENDIF
                          00080      59 ENDIF    EQU   *                              ENDIF
                                     60          GET   INFILE,INRECD                  READ NEXT RECORD
000090 47F0 C028    0002A            66          B     DOWHILE                        *
                          00094      67 ENDDO    EQU   *                           ENDDO
                                     68          CLOSE INFILE,PRINTER              CLOSE FILES                  DOS
                                     77          EOJ                               END PROGRAM                  DOS
                                     80 *        CLOSE (INFILE,,PRINTER)           CLOSE FILES                  OS
                                     81 *        L     13,SAVE+4                   LOAD SAVE AREA ADDRESS       OS
                                     82 *        LM    14,12,12(13)                RESTORE REGISTERS            OS
                                     83 *        BR    14                          RETURN TO OS                 OS
                                     84 *********************************************************************
                                     85 *                  HEADING SUBROUTINE
                                     86 *********************************************************************
                                     87 HEADING  CNTRL PRINTEP,SK,1                 SKIP TO NEW PAGE
                                     93          PUT   PRINTER,HEAD1               PRINT FIRST HEADING LINE
```

Figure 3–16 Program 3 assembler listing

```
  LOC  OBJECT CODE    ADDR1 ADDR2  STMT   SOURCE STATEMENT                                  DOS/VSE ASSEMBLER 14.51 86-03-27

                                    99            CNTRL PRINTER,SP,1             SPACE ONCE
                                   105            PUT   PRINTER,HEAD2            PRINT SECOND HEADING LINE
                                   111            CNTRL PRINTER,SP,1             SPACE ONCE
0000F2 4150 0032           00032   117            LA    5,50                     SET LINE COUNT TO 50
0000F6 07F9                        118            BR    9                        RETURN
                                   119 *******************************************************************DOS
                                   120 *                FILE DEFINITIONS AND I/O AREAS                    DOS
                                   121 *******************************************************************DOS
                                   122 INFILE   DTFCD BLKSIZE=80,IOAREA1=INAREA,DEVICE=2540,              DOSX
                                                      DEVADDR=SYSIPT,EOFADDR=ENDDO,WORKA=YES              DOS
                                   143 *                                                                  DOS
                                   144 PRINTER  DTFPR BLKSIZE=132,IOAREA1=PRTAREA,DEVICE=1403,            DOSX
                                                      CONTROL=YES,DEVADDR=SYS009,WORKA=YES                DOS
                                   165 *                                                                  DOS
000160                             166 INAREA   DS    CL80                                                DOS
0001B0                             167 PRTAREA  DS    CL132                                               DOS
                                   168 *******************************************************************OS
                                   169 *                DEVICE CONTROL BLOCKS AND SAVE AREA               OS
                                   170 *******************************************************************OS
                                   171 *INFILE  DCB   DDNAME=INFILE,BLKSIZE=80,LRECL=80,                  OSX
                                   172 *              MACRF=PM,DSORG=PS,EODAD=ENDDO                       OS
                                   173 *                                                                  OS
                                   174 *PRINTER DCB   DDNAME=PRINTER,BLKSIZE=132,LRECL=132,               OSX
                                   175 *              MACRF=PMC,DSORG=PS                                  OS
                                   176 *                                                                  OS
                                   177 *SAVE    DS    18F                                                 OS
                                   178 *********************************************************************
                                   179 *                DATA DEFINITIONS
                                   180 *********************************************************************
000234                             181 INRECD   DS    CL80
                                   182 *
000284                             183 PRLINE   DS    CL132
                                   184 *
000308                             185 HEAD1    DS    0CL132
000308 4040404040404040            186          DC    CL18' '
00031A D4C1D3C540C5D4D7            187          DC    CL114'MALE EMPLOYEES BORN BETWEEN 1955 AND 1965'
                                   188 *
00038C                             189 HEAD2    DS    0CL132
00038C 4040404040404040            190          DC    CL18' '
00039E D5C1D4C540404040            191          DC    CL18'NAME'
0003B0 C4C5D7E34B404040            192          DC    CL9'DEPT.'
0003B9 D1D6C240C3D6C4C5            193          DC    CL11'JOB CODE'
0003C4 C4C1E3C540D6C640            194          DC    CL76'DATE OF BIRTH'
                                   195 *
                           00000   196          END   MAINLINE
000410 5B5BC2D6D7C5D540            197                =C'$$BOPEN '
000418 5B5BC2C3D3D6E2C5            198                =C'$$BCLOSE'
000420 000000F8                    199                =A(INFILE)
000424 00000234                    200                =A(INRECD)
000428 00000130                    201                =A(PRINTER)
00042C 00000284                    202                =A(PRLINE)
000430 00000308                    203                =A(HEAD1)
000434 0000038C                    204                =A(HEAD2)
000438 F5F5                        205                =C'55'
00043A F6F5                        206                =C'65'
```

Figure 3–16 *(Concluded)*

```
          MALE EMPLOYEES BORN BETWEEN 1955 AND 1965

          NAME                DEPT.    JOB CODE   DATE OF BIRTH

DUNNAN BRADSTREET             1234       4130         070756
PETE MOSS                     2143       6715         042762
BARRY MOORE                   3756       5625         032157
LYON HART                     3756       5625         102659
TOM KATZ                      3756       5625         022960
CLEMENT SEE                   5337       3245         090961
ROGER ANDOVER                 6541       1250         040158
BILL OLADING                  8823       8642         110461
RICK SHAW                     8823       8642         012163
BEN Z DREEN                   8823       8642         071864
```

Figure 3–17 Output from Program 3

EXERCISES

1. Write the instructions most commonly used to clear a print line of 132 characters to blanks.
2. Write instructions that would move asterisks to a 20-byte field called PRNAME using:
   a. MVI and MVC instructions
   b. MVC with a literal
3. Write instructions to move data as follows:
   a. From INAMOUNT to positions 31–38 of PRLINE.
   b. From positions 70–74 of INRECD to PRZIP.
   c. From position 30 of INRECD to a field called PRCODE.
   d. From the first three bytes of INRECD to positions 59–61 of PRLINE.
4. Write hexadecimal constants that would be equivalent to each of the following character constants:
   a. `DC C'987'`
   b. `DC CL3' '`
   c. `DC 2C'ABC'`
   d. `DC C'$98.75'`
5. Show the difference between the object code produced by the assembler for the following pairs of constant definitions:
   a. `DC C'ABD'`   `DC X'ABD'`
   b. `DC CL5'123'`   `DC XL5'123'`
6. Write instructions to branch to THEN if A is greater than 5 and B is less than 3; otherwise, branch to ELSE.
7. Write instructions to branch to THEN if A is greater than 5 or B is less than 3; otherwise, branch to ELSE.
8. Write instructions to branch to ELSE if bytes 21–25 of INRECD contain C'12345'; otherwise, drop through to THEN. Be sure that both THEN and ELSE are not executed for the same conditions.

PROGRAMMING PROBLEMS

1. Using the Data Set 1 in Appendix D, write a program to print a report showing the name, social security number, and date of employment of all women having pay type 'A' (annual salary). Use MVC and MVI instructions to print social security number in form 123-45-6789 and date employed in form mm/dd/yy. Design your own format with appropriate headings. Print 50 detail lines per page.
2. Modify Problem 1 to define the input record as INRECD DS CL80 and use relative addressing to refer to all input fields.
3. Write a program to list the name, date of birth (in form mm-dd-yy), department, and phone of all employees who were born during the current month. The president of your company wishes to send each a special birthday greeting. Show appropriate headings. Print 35 detail lines per page.
4. Modify Problem 3 to print an asterisk to the left of the name of any employee born this month who was employed more than 10 years ago.

4 Packed Decimal Addition, Subtraction, and Editing

OBJECTIVES

After studying this chapter, you should be able to:

- Differentiate between characters, packed decimal, and zoned decimal data
- Define packed decimal constants and work areas
- Define zoned decimal constants and work areas
- Write instructions to add and subtract packed decimal numbers
- Use the PACK and UNPACK instructions
- Explain the operation of the EDIT instruction
- Use the EDIT instruction in printing numeric amounts
- Use packed decimal arithmetic in counting and accumulating totals

To do meaningful processing, we must be able to perform arithmetic operations. So far, we have employed the Load Address (LA) instruction to initialize a register as a line counter and the Branch on Count (BCT) instruction to subtract from the register and branch if the contents of the register are not zero. These instructions permit us to control a loop that is repeated a definite number of times or a selection based on a count.

But we need to be able to do more arithmetic operations to count items, accumulate totals, figure percentages and averages, and generally do the calculations required in modern data processing. In this chapter, we shall see how to perform arithmetic operations on decimal numbers.

ZONED DECIMAL DATA

Numeric data with one digit per byte is called *zoned decimal* data. We define zoned decimal data as type Z in DC and DS statements. Like type C (character) data, type Z data requires one byte per digit, and contains zone bits of 1111, or X'F'. But character data is alphanumeric, while zoned decimal data is numeric. The two types of constants differ in two respects:

1. If the explicit length of a type Z constant is greater than the number of digits in its value, the field is padded to the left with zeros (X'F0'). Type C constants are padded to the right with blanks (X'40').
2. Zoned decimal numbers use the zone bits of the rightmost byte of the field to indicate the sign of the number. A sign in a type C constant is just another character.

This method of representing the sign dates from punched card usage. For many years, to save space in punched cards, the sign of a number was represented as an overpunch above the digit in the last column of a field. A punch in the top row of the card, called the 12 row, indicated a plus sign. A punch in the second row from the top, called the 11 row, indicated a minus sign. If there was no overpunch, the field was considered unsigned.

The overpunch above the digit of course makes two punches in the same column. This is the same as the punched card code used for letters of the alphabet. The digits 1 through 9 with no overpunch produce the EBCDIC code X'F1' through X'F9'. With an overpunch in the 12 row, the digits 1 through 9 produce EBCDIC codes X'C1' through X'C9', the same as the letters of the alphabet A through I. With an overpunch in the 11 row, the digits 1 through 9 make EBCDIC codes X'D1' through X'D9', the same as the letters J through R. Figure 4–1 illustrates these overpunches.

The zone bits of the last byte of the field indicate the sign of the number. X'F' indicate an unsigned field, X'C' a positive field, and X'D' a negative field.

The assembler follows the same conventions when we define a type Z zoned decimal field. The sign of a zoned decimal constant is always X'C' if positive or X'D' if negative. Unsigned zoned decimal data can only be read from an input source. The examples in Figure 4–2 show the difference between type C data and type Z data.

The designers of the System 360/370 family of computers did not provide instructions to do arithmetic on data in zoned decimal form. We must convert to one of three other forms, packed decimal, fixed point binary, or floating point binary, in order to perform arithmetic. In this chapter we shall explore packed decimal arithmetic. In later chapters we shall work with fixed point binary and floating point binary numbers.

PACKED DECIMAL DATA

A *packed decimal* number is formed by removing the zone bits from each zoned decimal digit and placing the code for two decimal digits into a single byte. The last byte of the field contains both a digit and the sign, but the positions occupied in a zoned decimal digit have now been reversed. Packed dec-

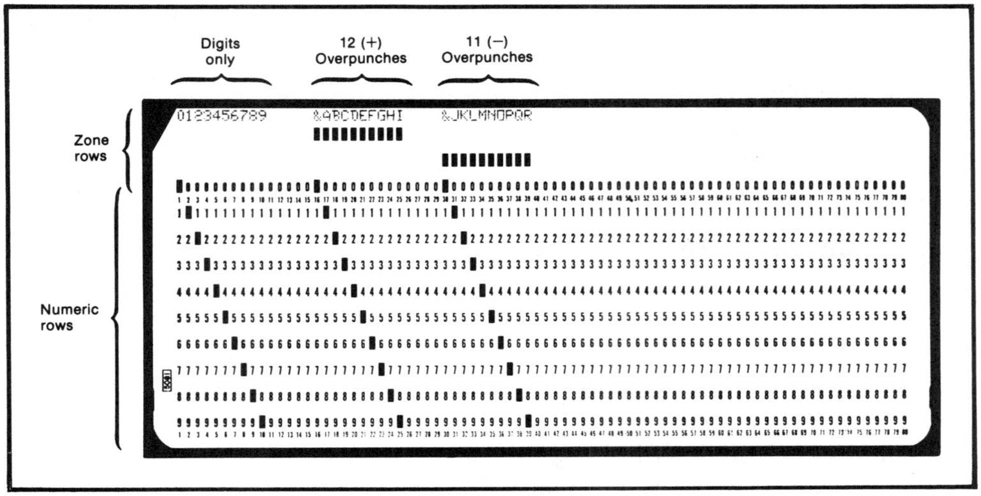

Figure 4–1 Codes for zone punches over numeric punches

OBJECT CODE	STATEMENT	COMMENTS
F1 F2 F5	DC C'125'	
F1 F2 C5	DC Z'125'	Plus sign assigned
F1 F2 F5 40 40	DC CL5'125'	Padded right with blanks
F0 F0 F1 F2 C5	DC ZL5'125'	Padded left with zeros
60 F1 F2 F5	DC C'-125'	Sign is just another character
F1 F2 D5	DC Z'-125'	Sign in rightmost byte
F1 F2	DC CL2'125'	Rightmost byte truncated
F2 C5	DC ZL2'125'	Leftmost byte truncated

Note: Spaces are shown between bytes in object code for clarity.

Figure 4–2 Difference between type C and type Z constants

imal data is valid only in the form

dd dd dd dd ds

where *d* is a four-bit code for a decimal digit, 0000 through 1001, and
s is the four-bit code for the sign.

Signs of X'C' for positive or X'D' for negative are produced by all decimal arithmetic instructions. Packed decimal constants are also assigned these signs by the assembler. However, X'A', X'E', and X'F' are also recognized as alternate positive signs by the hardware, and X'B' as an alternate negative sign.

Data cannot be printed in packed decimal form. We must convert to EBCDIC to print. EBCDIC may be thought of as the input/output form for data, while packed decimal is the calculation form. We therefore must go through these procedures:

1. Enter data from cards or keyboard in zoned decimal or character form.
2. Convert data to packed decimal to perform arithmetic.
3. Convert results back to EBCDIC for printing or display on a screen.

The PACK and UNPK Instructions

The PACK instruction converts zoned decimal or character data in the source field (first operand) to packed decimal form in the receiving field (second operand). It works right to left by reversing the position of the zone and numeric bits in the rightmost byte of the field. Then it strips off the zone bits in all other bytes of the field and packs two decimal digits in each byte.

The Unpack (UNPK) instruction converts packed decimal data back to zoned decimal. It reverses the zone and numeric bits in the rightmost byte of the packed decimal field. Then it selects each four-bit decimal digit, places it in the numeric bits of a byte, and fills the zone bits with ones (X'F') from the arithmetic-logic unit. Figure 4–3 shows the PACK and UNPK operations. The UNPK instruction will be discussed more fully in a later section.

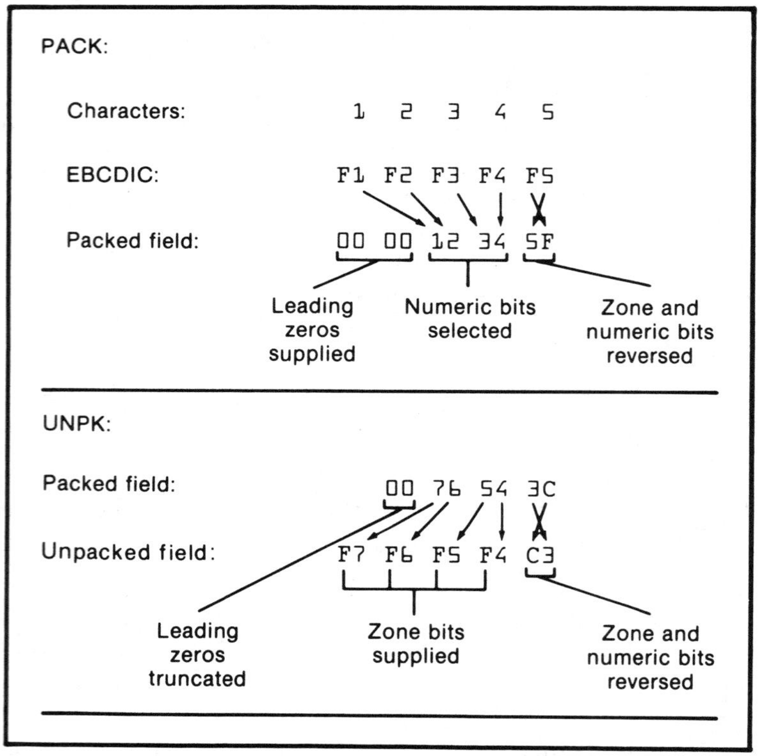

Figure 4–3 Operation of PACK and UNPK instructions

The source and destination fields in a PACK instruction may have different lengths but neither may be longer than 16 bytes. Each operand must have a length specified, either implicitly or explicitly. If the receiving field for the packed data is longer than required to hold the digits, leading zeros are supplied. If the receiving field is too short to hold the digits, the leftmost digits are truncated. In the examples in Figure 4–4, lengths are shown explicitly for each operand.

The five examples in Figure 4–5 illustrate problems that may occur with the PACK instruction. Any data at all may be packed; however, the resulting field may not be valid. In the first example, the letters A,B,C,D,E are packed. Their numeric bits are the same as the digits 1,2,3,4,5, and the zone bits of the last byte are a valid sign (X'C').

The second example illustrates why numeric fields should be filled with zeros rather than left blank, at least in the rightmost byte. The blank (X'40') in the rightmost byte of the field, when packed, produces a sign of X'4', which is invalid.

The third example shows a field of asterisks (X'5B'). When packed, the digits are not valid decimal digits (0–9), and the sign is also invalid (X'5').

The fourth example shows a field that is already packed being packed again. Only every other decimal digit appears in the resulting packed field, and the zone and numeric bits in the last byte are exchanged (X'5F' to X'F5'), giving an invalid decimal digit and invalid sign.

The last example has a length greater than 16 for the second operand. Neither operand may be longer than 16 bytes.

INSTRUCTION	DESTINATION FIELD	SOURCE FIELD	REMARKS
PACK DEST(3),SOURCE(5)	12 34 5F	F1 F2 F3 F4 F5	Unsigned field
PACK DEST(5),SOURCE(5)	00 00 12 34 5F	F1 F2 F3 F4 F5	Zeros padded
PACK DEST(2),SOURCE(5)	34 5F	F1 F2 F3 F4 F5	Truncated
PACK SOURCE(5),SOURCE(5)	00 00 12 34 5F	F1 F2 F3 F4 F5	Packed into itself

Figure 4–4 Examples of PACK instruction

INSTRUCTION	DESTINATION	SOURCE FIELD	REMARKS
PACK DEST(3),SOURCE(5)	12 34 5C	C1 C2 C3 C4 C5	Zone bits stripped
PACK DEST(3),SOURCE(5)	00 00 04	40 40 40 40 40	Invalid sign
PACK DEST(3),SOURCE(5)	BB BB B5	5B 5B 5B 5B 5B	Invalid digits and sign
PACK DEST(3),SOURCE(5)	00 24 F5	00 00 12 34 5F	Packed twice; invalid
PACK DEST(10),SOURCE(19)			Too long

Figure 4–5 Examples of PACK instructions on irregular data

Defining Packed Decimal Data

Packed decimal data are described with type P (packed). The assembler will place two decimal digits in each byte of the constant except the last, which must contain the sign. There will always be an odd number of decimal digits in every packed decimal field.

The assembler always supplies a positive or negative sign for constants. Unsigned data is created only by using the PACK instruction on input EBCDIC data. Leading zeros are added if the length is greater than the constant requires. Figure 4–6 shows some examples.

Commas, dollar signs, or other punctuation marks are not allowed in packed decimal constants. The plus sign may be written but is never required. The minus sign preceding the decimal digits is required to indicate a negative number. Note that decimal points in type P constants are ignored by the assembler. They may be used purely as information. Where a comma is used in a constant, the assembler creates separate packed decimal values. Observe:

VALUE	CONSTANT	REMARKS
1C 00 0C	DC P'1,000'	Two constants created: the first 1 and the other 000
3C 4C 5C	DC P'3,4,5'	Three constants created

We do not recommend this form and will not use it further in this text.

When DS statements define storage for packed decimal data, the assembler uses the explicit length if supplied by the programmer; otherwise, it creates an area large enough to hold the packed decimal value. No constant is actually created with a DS statement.

STATEMENT	REMARKS
DS PL3	The 3 bytes will hold 5 digits and sign
DS P'000'	2 bytes will be reserved for 3 digits
DS PL5	The 5 bytes will hold 9 digits and sign

VALUE	CONSTANT	REMARKS
0C	DC P'0'	One byte assigned; 0 is always positive
12 5C	DC P'125'	Two bytes required for three digits
04 56 7C	DC PL3'4567'	Leading zero padded
12 5D	DC P'-125'	Negative sign supplied
00 00 0C	DC PL3'0'	Leading zeros padded
18 75 0C	DC P'187.50'	Decimal point ignored in constant
18 75 0C	DC P'18750'	
75 0C	DC PL2'18750'	Leading digits truncated if too short

Figure 4–6 Packed decimal constants

Figure 4–7 indicates the number of digits that can fit into fields of various sizes. No packed decimal field can be longer than 16 bytes, which can hold 31 digits and a sign. The length of the field is the next integer greater than one-half the number of digits.

To summarize rules for valid packed decimal data:

1. Four-bit digit codes can only be bits 0000 through 1001 to represent decimal digits 0 through 9.
2. The four-bit sign code in the last byte of the field can only be the preferred bits 1100 or 1101 (X'C' or X'D') or the alternate sign bits 1010, 1011, 1110, or 1111 (X'A', X'B', X'E', or X'F').

DECIMAL ADDITION, SUBTRACTION, AND COMPARING

The Add Packed (AP) instruction performs decimal addition. The field named in the second operand is added to the field named in the first operand. The sum appears in the first operand location.

Fields may be of different length, so that two length operands are required. Lengths may be used implicitly from the DS or DC statement, or they may be shown explicitly in parentheses following the name of the operand. The maximum field length is 16 bytes, containing 31 digits plus a sign. The sign is considered as in any other addition: the sum of two negative numbers is negative, and the sum of one positive and one negative number may be either positive or negative, depending on which number is larger.

For example, assume that at the start of each of the instructions in Figure 4–8, two fields, NBR1 and NBR2, have packed decimal values of 125 and 37 respectively. The result of each instruction is shown in the figure.

DIGITS	LENGTH IN BYTES	LEADING ZERO SUPPLIED
1	1	No
2	2	Yes
3	2	No
4	3	Yes
5	3	No
6	4	Yes
7	4	No
8	5	Yes
9	5	No

Figure 4–7 Length of packed decimal fields

DEFINITIONS OF CONSTANTS AT START OF EACH OPERATION

```
00 12 5C     NBR1    DC    PL3'125'
03 7C        NBR2    DC    PL2'37'
```

INSTRUCTION	RESULT	COMMENTS
`AP NBR1,NBR2`	`00 16 2C`	Sum in NBR1
`AP NBR2,NBR1`	`16 2C`	Sum in NBR2
`AP NBR1,NBR1`	`00 25 0C`	Sum in NBR1
`AP NBR1,=P'-10'`	`00 11 5C`	Adding negative number subtracts
`AP NBR1,=P'1'`	`00 12 6C`	A literal may be added to a field
`AP NBR2,=P'999'`	`03 6C`	Overflow; sum too large for field
`AP NBR2,=P'-50'`	`01 3D`	Sum is negative

Figure 4–8 Results of packed decimal addition

OPERAND	DATA ASSUMED	COMMENTS
`NBR1(2)`	`00 12`	Wrong amount; invalid sign
`NBR1(4)`	`00 12 5C 03`	Invalid digit and sign
`NBR2(1)`	`03`	Invalid amount and sign
`NBR2(3)`	`03 7C ??`	Unknown content of third byte

Figure 4–9 Effect of explicit lengths

When a three-byte field is added to a two-byte field, as in the second example above, overflow often results. With the data given, the sum could be contained within two bytes, so that the result is valid.

Lengths must be carefully controlled in packed decimal addition. For example, note the effect of the explicit lengths shown in Figure 4–9.

If either operand in an AP instruction contains invalid data, the program is interrupted and control returns to the supervisor. Improper use of lengths is one major reason that this happens. Another reason is failing to initialize a field before adding to it. In this instance, an attempt is made to add to a field that does not contain a valid packed decimal value, and an interrupt results.

The Zero and Add Packed (ZAP) instruction is used to set a field to an initial value or to move a packed decimal field from one location to another. ZAP effectively sets the first operand to zero and then adds the second operand to it. Fields may be of different lengths up to a maximum of 16 bytes. Leading zeros are supplied if the first operand is longer than the second, and truncation of the leftmost digits occurs if the first operand is shorter. The second operand must contain valid packed decimal data, but the first operand can contain anything.

We often count records as a byproduct of other processing. The source statements in Figure 4–10 show how this may be done. RECCOUNT should be two bytes long to count up to 999 records or three bytes to count up to 99999 records.

Subtraction is done by the Subtract Packed (SP) instruction. The rules governing subtraction are like those for addition, except that the second operand is subtracted from the first. Use of signs, overflow, length operands, and interrupts are the same as with the AP instruction.

Now we may use either the Branch on Count (BCT) or the Subtract Packed (SP) instruction to control a posttest loop. Consider the examples in Figure 4–11.

In the first example, the value 50 is placed in general register 5 (R5) to initialize for the loop. The BCT instruction subtracts 1 from R5, tests to see if it contains zero, and if not branches to REPEAT. When R5 reaches zero, the loop is terminated. One disadvantage of BCT is that it stops branching only when the general register reaches exactly zero. If, by error, the register goes negative, the loop repeats almost indefinitely.

The use of the ZAP and SP instructions in the second example guards against a runaway loop. Since the SP instruction sets the condition code, we do not need a comparison before the conditional Branch if Positive (BP) instruction. Further, the branch is made only while COUNTER is positive, guarding against a possible runaway loop.

Programming Tips

- Take care in using explicit lengths with packed decimal fields. The rightmost byte of the field must contain a valid sign.
- You may pack an unpacked field into the same location it occupied before packing. You may never unpack a field into the same location.
- Use ZAP rather than MVC to move packed data from one field to another. ZAP preserves the sign and adjusts for different field lengths.
- Initialize accumulators and counters with ZAP instructions rather than defining the fields with DC statements.

Packed decimal numbers are compared by the Compare Packed (CP) instruction. Both operands must be valid packed decimal numbers. They may have different lengths. The shorter number is extended with leading zeros in the arithmetic-logic unit before the comparison is made. The sign of the numbers is taken into account, so that negative values compare lower than positive values.

```
         ZAP   RECCOUNT,=P'0'
         GET   INFILE,INRECD
DOWHILE  AP    RECCOUNT,=P'1'
         Write other processsing instructions here
         GET   INFILE,INRECD
         B     DOWHILE
ENDDO    EQU   *
```

Figure 4–10 Program segment to count records

```
         USE OF BRANCH ON COUNT

         LA    5,50
REPEAT   Write processing instructions
         here
         BCT   5,REPEAT
UNTIL    EQU   *


         USE OF ZAP, SP, AND BP INSTRUCTIONS

         ZAP   COUNTER,=P'50'
REPEAT   Write processing instructions here
         SP    COUNTER,=P'1'
         BP    REPEAT
UNTIL    EQU   *
```

Figure 4–11 Control of posttest loop

CP sets the condition code, which may be tested with conditional branch instructions to control selection or repetition structures. Relative addressing and explicit lengths may be used with either operand in the CP instruction.

EDITING DATA

As mentioned earlier, packed decimal data cannot be printed without being converted to EBCDIC. The Edit (ED) instruction not only converts packed data to printable form but also permits suppression of leading zeros, insertion of decimals and commas, and other operations that make output more readable and attractive.

The Edit Pattern

The first operand in an Edit instruction must be the address of a field holding an *edit pattern*. The pattern contains special codes indicating how the EBCDIC field is to appear. The second Edit operand is the packed decimal field. Normally the edit pattern is defined in working storage as a type X (hexadecimal) constant that is moved to the proper location in the output record where the edited data is to appear.

Four types of codes are used in edit patterns:

1. The first byte of the pattern is the *fill character*. It replaces leading zeros and message characters in front of the first significant (nonzero) digit.
2. *Digit select* characters show where the decimal digits are to be printed.
3. *Message characters* include decimal points, commas, or other characters inserted into the edited field.
4. *Field separators* permit more than one field to be edited with a single instruction. Field separators will be discussed later in the text.

The edit pattern is always longer than the packed decimal field being edited. Even though the fields are of different lengths, only the first operand (the edit pattern) uses a length code. The number of digits to be selected from the packed decimal field depends on the number of digit select characters in the edit pattern.

Zero Suppression

In its simplest form, the Edit instruction suppresses or eliminates leading zeros by converting them to blanks. If we have a three-byte packed decimal field named PKAMOUNT containing five digits, it can have any value from 00000C through 99999C, including the sign. If the value is, say, 00125, we would like to print it as bb125 (where b represents a blank, or space).

The first byte of the edit pattern, called the *fill character*, replaces all leading zeros in the value to be edited. A leading zero is any zero that is to the left of the first significant (nonzero) digit in the packed field. To replace leading zeros with blanks, our fill character is a blank (X‘40’). Sometimes the asterisk (*) or the dollar sign ($) is used as a fill character. A nonblank fill character is usually called a *check protection* symbol, since it is used to fill in blank spaces preceding the amount in computer-written checks.

The rest of our edit pattern consists of five *digit select* codes, each being X‘20’. As the edit operation proceeds from left to right, the digit select code selects one four-bit packed decimal digit, supplies four zone bits (X‘F’), and replaces the X‘20’ with the resulting zoned decimal digit. If the digit selected was a leading zero, the fill character replaces the zero. The pattern is defined by:

```
PATTERN DC X'402020202020'
```

An internal switch, called the *significance indicator*, is set OFF when the Edit instruction begins. So long as it is OFF, the fill character replaces any leading zeros. As soon as the first nonzero digit is selected from the packed field, the significance indicator is turned ON. While the indicator is ON, all digits are selected and printed, zero or not. We may print the edited five-byte field starting at PRLINE + 50 by using the following instructions. Remember that the fill character occupies a byte, so we will move the pattern to PRLINE + 49.

```
MVC  PRLINE+49(6),PATTERN
ED   PRLINE+49(6),PKAMOUNT
```

After editing, the six bytes at PRLINE + 49 contain 40 40 40 F1 F2 F5, which prints as bbb125.

If PKAMOUNT had contained nothing but zeros, the entire field at PRLINE + 49 would be blanked out, since the significance indicator was never turned ON. We can turn the indicator ON by using X'21' as a digit select code. This code, usually called a *significance starter*, selects a digit, turns on the significance indicator if the digit is nonzero as usual, but turns the indicator ON effective with the *following* character if the selected digit is zero. Thus, if we want to print one zero of a zero amount, we would use the pattern X'402020202120'. The first three examples in Figure 4–12 show how edited data would look if significance is forced.

Since there is always an odd number of decimal digits in any packed field (two digits per byte except for the last byte containing one digit with the sign), there should always be an *odd* number of digit select characters (X'20' or X'21') in any edit pattern.

Inserting Characters

In an edit pattern, any character after the first, except the digit selectors X'20' and X'21' and the field separator X'22', is called a *message character*. The message character is replaced by the fill character if the significance indicator is OFF, but remains where it is if the indicator is ON.

Now let us assume we have a three-byte field with five digits as before, but two of the digits are considered to be to the right of a decimal point. We will insert a period (X'4B') into our edit pattern before the last two digit select characters. We will also place a significance starter (X'21') just to the left of the decimal point, so that the decimal point will print with two digits to its right even if the entire field is zeros. The next four examples in Figure 4–12 show how data would be edited using the pattern X'402020214B2020'.

With longer fields, we may wish to insert commas. Suppose we now have a four-byte field with seven digits and no decimal point. The values can range from 0 to 9,999,999 and are printed accordingly. We insert two commas (X'6B') into the proper positions in the edit pattern. We place no significance

FORCING SIGNIFICANCE

PATTERN	PACKED FIELD	EDITED RESULT	PRINTS AS
X'402020202120'	00000C	4040404040F0	bbbbb0
X'402020212020'	00000C	40404040F0F0	bbbb00
X'402120202020'	00000C	4040F0F0F0F0	bb0000

FORCING DECIMAL POINT WITH PATTERN X '402020214B2020'

PACKED DATA	EDITED DATA	PRINTS AS
00125C	404040F14BF2F5	bbb1.25
00008C	404040404BF0F8	bbbb.08
99999C	40F9F9F94BF9F9	b999.99
00000C	404040404BF0F0	bbbb.00

SUPPRESSING LEADING COMMAS WITH PATTERN X'40206B2020206B202120'

PACKED DATA	EDITED DATA	PRINTS AS
1234567C	40F16BF2F3F46BF5F6F7	b1,234,567
0025000C	40404040F2F56BF0F0F0	bbbb25,000
0000075C	404040404040F7F5	bbbbbbbb75

Figure 4–12 Examples of editing

starter to the left of them, because we do not wish leading commas or leading zeros to print. The edit pattern is X'40206B2020206B202120', which is 10 bytes in length. Notice that we do put a significance starter before the last digit so that one zero will print if the entire field is zeros. Examples of output are shown in the last three lines of Figure 4–12.

The computer treats all packed decimal numbers as integers. The programmer is responsible for keeping track of the decimal point and putting it into the proper position in the edit pattern for printing. More examples of advanced editing will appear later in the text.

AN ALTERNATE EDITING APPROACH

Limited editing may be performed with the Unpack (UNPK) and the Move Zones (MVZ) instructions. Additional instructions are required to insert decimal points and commas and to suppress leading zeros.

The Unpack (UNPK) Instruction

The Unpack instruction may be used to convert packed decimal data to *zoned decimal*. UNPK is much less powerful than the Edit instruction and therefore less commonly used. It requires a length factor for each operand, since the operands are normally of different lengths. The first operand designates the destination (unpacked) field, normally twice the length of the second operand, the packed field, raised to the next higher integer.

UNPK works right to left. The zone and numeric bits of the rightmost byte are reversed as they are moved to the unpacked field. Then each decimal digit is selected from the packed field, zone bits of X'F' are supplied, and the resulting zoned decimal digit is placed in the destination field. If the length of the destination field is longer than necessary to hold the digits from the source field, the leftmost bytes are padded with zoned decimal zeros (X'F0'). If the destination field is too short, the leftmost digits are truncated.

Figure 4–13 shows a few examples of the UNPK instruction. Note that the first and third examples have a valid sign for zoned decimal numbers, but that the rightmost digit would print as a letter rather than a number. The X'C4' in the first example prints as a letter D rather than the digit 4. The X'C7' in the third example prints as the letter G rather than the digit 7.

The Move Zones Instruction

We may correct the zone bits in the last byte to print correctly by using the Move Zones (MVZ) instruction. This instruction works like Move Characters (MVC) except that only the leftmost (zone) bits of each byte are moved. The first operand must indicate the number of bytes to be moved. To correct the sign for printing we need move only one byte.

In the first example in Figure 4–13, PKAMT contained the packed decimal data X'23754C'. After unpacking into the five-byte field UPAMT, the data appeared as X'F2F3F7F5C4', which, if printed, would appear as 2375D, rather than 23754. We may move (copy) the zone bits from the next-to-last byte of UPAMT to the last byte of the field with

```
MVZ UPAMT+4(1),UPAMT+3
```

After this instruction is executed, UPAMT contains X'F2F3F7F5F4', which prints as 23754. To cause the result to print as 23,754 we would need a routine like that in Figure 4–14.

INSTRUCTION	UNPACKED FIELD	PACKED FIELD	REMARKS
`UNPK UPAMT,PKAMT`	F2 F3 F7 F5 C4	23 75 4C	
`UNPK UPAMT,PKAMT(2)`	F0 F0 F2 F3 57	23 75	Zeros padded; invalid sign
`UNPK UPAMT,PKAMT(4)`	F3 F4 F5 F6 C7	12 34 56 7C	Two digits truncated

Figure 4–13 Examples of UNPK instruction

INSTRUCTION	RECEIVING FIELD	SOURCE FIELD	REMARKS
`UNPK UPAMT,PKAMT`	F2F3F7F5C4	23754C	
`MVZ UPAMT+4(1),UPAMT+3`	F2F3F7F5F4	F2F3F7F5C4	Zone bits moved
`MVC PRAMT(2),UPAMT`	F2F3??????????	F2F3F7F5F4	First 2 bytes moved
`MVI PRAMT+2,C','`	F2F36B??????	6B	Comma inserted
`MVC PRAMT+3(3),UPAMT+2`	F2F36BF7F5F4	F2F3F7F5F4	Last 3 bytes moved

Figure 4–14 Editing without Edit instruction

Additional instructions would be necessary to change leading zeros to blanks. It seems clear that the Edit instruction, while complex, is far preferable to the Unpack and Move Zones combination.

Programming Tips

- Since the number of digits in a packed decimal field is always odd, be sure you have an odd number of digit select characters (X'20' or X'21') in every edit pattern.
- Define each edit pattern as a constant in working storage. Move it to the print area as needed before editing.
- Be sure each print field is the same size as the edit pattern that is to be moved into it.
- Put a significance starter (X'21') to the left of any decimal point appearing in an edit pattern.

PROGRAM 4: ACCUMULATING TOTALS

Our next program illustrates accumulation of totals, which are printed out after reaching end of file. Using the same employee personnel records that we used in our previous three programs, we will print out name, department, job code, and pay rate of all employees on weekly salary. As we go, we will accumulate the total of the weekly salary and the number of employees and print out these totals upon reaching end of file.

Data elements to be used from our input record are shown in Figure 4–15, along with their print positions. The pay rate is eight digits long, including two digits right of the assumed decimal point. We will therefore require a five-byte packed decimal field to hold the salary. Since five bytes can actually hold a nine-digit number, we will also use a five-byte field to hold our total salaries, since we do not expect our total weekly salaries to exceed $9,999,999.99.

COLUMNS	FIELD NAME AND FORMAT	PRINT POSITIONS
10–29	Employee name	11–30
43–46	Department	41–44
54–57	Job code	55–58
58	Pay type (A, W, H)	Not printed
59–66	Pay rate 999999V99	63–75 bZ,ZZZ,ZZZ.99
	Number of employees	16–19 bZZZ
	Total weekly salaries	63–75 bZ,ZZZ,ZZZ.99

Figure 4–15 Data elements for Program 4

```
START PROGRAM
Open files
Clear total pay and employee count
Print heading
Read first record
DOWHILE NOT end of file
   IF paytype = 'W'
      THEN add weekly pay to total pay
      Add 1 to employee count
      Setup print line
      Print line

      If line count = >50
         THEN print heading
      ENDIF
   Read next record
ENDDO
Print total pay and employee count
Close files
END PROGRAM
```

Figure 4–16 Pseudocode for Program 4

The formats bZZZ and bZZ,ZZZ,ZZZ.99 represent our edit pattern. The 'b' represents a blank position to be occupied by the fill character. Each 'Z' represents a digit position in which leading zeros will be suppressed, along with any leading commas. The decimal point and two digits to its right will always be printed.

We will need one edit pattern for the salary amount and total salaries, and another pattern for the number of employees.

As usual, we will print a maximum of 50 lines per page; however, in this program we shall use packed decimal arithmetic instead of the Load Address (LA) and Branch on Count (BCT) instructions for our line counter.

Pseudocode for the program is shown in Figure 4–16. Figure 4–17 is the assembler listing, and Figure 4–18 shows the program output.

SUMMARY

Zoned decimal numbers contain one digit per byte, just as characters do. However, zoned decimal numbers contain a sign in the zone bits of the rightmost byte. For constants, the assembler produces a sign of X'C' if positive and X'D' if negative. Zoned decimal constants are padded with zeros to left, whereas character constants are padded with blanks to the right. No arithmetic can be performed on zoned decimal numbers.

Before arithmetic operations can be carried out, numbers must be converted to packed decimal form and then (optionally) to binary or floating-point form. Each packed decimal digit is represented in a four-bit code, with two digits per byte, except in the rightmost byte, which contains one digit and the sign. Valid signs are X'A' through X'F' in the rightmost four bits of the last byte of the field. X'C' is the preferred sign for positive and X'D' for negative.

The Pack instruction converts data from zoned decimal or character form to packed decimal form. The first operand is the destination field, while the second operand is the source field. The two operands normally are of differ-

```
  LOC  OBJECT CODE     ADDR1 ADDR2  STMT   SOURCE STATEMENT                                 DOS/VSE ASSEMBLER 14.53 86-03-27

                                      1 *************************************************************************
                                      2 *                  ALTON R. KINDRED, PROGRAM 4
                                      3 * THIS PROGRAM PRINTS NAME, DEPARTMENT, JOB CODE, AND SALARY OF ALL
                                      4 * EMPLOYEES ON WEEKLY SALARY.  IT ALSO PRINTS OUT TOTAL WEEKLY
                                      5 * SALARIES.
                                      6 *          REGISTERS USED:
                                      7 *                  R9   - LINK TO MODULE
                                      8 *                  R12  - BASE REGISTER
                                      9 *************************************************************************
                                     10          PRINT NOGEN
000000                               11 MAINLINE START 0                          SET LOCATION COUNTER
                                     12 *        STM   14,12,12(13)               SAVE REGISTERS FOR OS          OS
000000 05C0                          13          BALR  12,0                       LOAD BASE REGISTER
                             00002   14          USING *,12                       DESIGNATE BASE REGISTER
                                     15 *        ST    13,SAVE+4                  STORE REGISTER 13              OS
                                     16 *        LA    13,SAVE                    LOAD SAVE AREA ADDRESS         OS
                                     17 *        OPEN  (INFILE,(INPUT),PRINTER,(OUTPUT))                         OS
                                     18          OPEN  INFILE,PRINTER             OPEN FILES                     DOS
000016 F840 C4E9 C534 004EB 00536    27          ZAP   PKTOTPAY,=P'0'             CLEAR TOTAL PAY
00001C F810 C4E7 C534 004E9 00536    28          ZAP   PKTOTEMP,=P'0'             CLEAR EMPLOYEE COUNT
000022 4590 C0EE             000F0   29          BAL   9,HEADING                  PRINT HEADING
                                     30          GET   INFILE,INRECD              READ FIRST RECORD
                             00036   36 DOWHILE  EQU   *                          DOWHILE NOT END OF FILE
000036 95E6 C2BB       002BD         37 IF       CLI   INPAYTYP,C'W'                IF WEEKLY RATE
00003A 4770 C090       00092         38          BNE   ENDIF                          *
00003E F247 C4E2 C2BC 004E4 002BE    39 THEN     PACK  PKRATE,INRATE                  THEN ADD SALARY TO TOTAL
000044 FA44 C4E9 C4E2 004EB 004E4    40          AP    PKTOTPAY,PKRATE                ADD RATE TO TOTAL PAY
00004A FA10 C4E7 C535 004E9 00537    41          AP    PKTOTEMP,=P'1'                 ADD 1 TO EMPLOYEE COUNT
000050 D213 C2DC C28B 002DE 0028D    42          MVC   PRNAME,INNAME                  SET UP PRINT LINE
000056 D203 C2FA C2AC 002FC 002AE    43          MVC   PRDEPT,INDEPT                  *
00005C D203 C308 C2B7 0030A 002B9    44          MVC   PRJOBCD,INJOBCD                *
000062 D20C C310 C4F4 00312 004F6    45          MVC   PRRATE,PATRN2                  *
000068 DE0C C310 C4E2 00312 004E4    46          ED    PRRATE,PKRATE                  *
                                     47          PUT   PRINTER,PRLINE                 PRINT LINE
00007E FA10 C4EE C535 004F0 00537    53          AP    LINECNT,=P'1'                  ADD 1 TO LINE COUNT
000084 F911 C4EE C532 004F0 00534    54 IF2      CP    LINECNT,=P'50'                 IF LINE COUNT => 50
00008A 4740 C090       00092         55          BL    ENDIF2                           *
00008E 4590 C0EE             000F0   56 THEN2    BAL   9,HEADING                        PRINT HEADING
                             00092   57 ENDIF2   EQU   *                              ENDIF
                             00092   58 ENDIF    EQU   *                            ENDIF
                                     59          GET   INFILE,INRECD                READ NEXT RECORD
0000A2 47F0 C034       00036         65          B     DOWHILE                      *
                             000A6   66 ENDDO    EQU   *                          ENDDO
0000A6 D203 C46D C4F0 0046F 004F2    67          MVC   PRTOTEMP,PATRN             MOVE EMPL. COUNT TO TOTAL LINE
0000AC DE03 C46D C4E7 0046F 004E9    68          ED    PRTOTEMP,PKTOTEMP          *
0000B2 D20C C49C C4F4 0049E 004F6    69          MVC   PRTOTPAY,PATRN2            MOVE TOTAL PAY TO TOTAL LINE
0000B8 DE0C C49C C4E9 0049E 004EB    70          ED    PRTOTPAY,PKTOTPAY          *
                                     71          CNTRL PRINTER,SP,1               SPACE ONCE
                                     77          PUT   PRINTER,TOTLINE            PRINT TOTAL LINE
                                     83          CLOSE INFILE,PRINTER             CLOSE FILES                    DOS
                                     92          EOJ                              END PROGRAM                    DOS
                                     95 *        CLOSE (INFILE,,PRINTER)          CLOSE FILES                    OS
                                     96 *        L     13,SAVE+4                  LOAD SAVE AREA ADDRESS         OS
                                     97 *        LM    14,12,12(13)               RESTORE REGISTERS              OS
                                     98 *        BR    14                         RETURN TO OS                   OS
```

Figure 4–17 Program 4 assembler output

```
  LOC  OBJECT CODE    ADDR1 ADDR2  STMT   SOURCE STATEMENT                                         DOS/VSE ASSEMBLER 14.53 86-03-27

                                    100 ***********************************************************************
                                    101 *                    HEADING SUBROUTINE
                                    102 ***********************************************************************
                                    103 HEADING  CNTRL PRINTER,SK,1                    SKIP TO NEW PAGE
                                    109          PUT   PRINTER,HEAD1                   PRINT FIRST HEADING LINE
                                    115          CNTRL PRINTEP,SP,1                    SPACE ONCE
                                    121          PUT   PRINTER,HEAD2                   PRINT SECOND HEADING LINE
                                    127          CNTRL PRINTER,SP,1                    SPACE ONCE
00013A F810 C4EE C534 004F0 00536   133          ZAP   LINECNT,=P'0'                   SET LINE COUNT TO ZERO
000140 07F9                         134          BR    9                               RETURN
                                    135 *******************************************************************DOS
                                    136 *                    FILE DEFINITIONS AND I/O AREAS                DOS
                                    137 *******************************************************************DOS
                                    138 INFILE   DTFCD BLKSIZE=80,IOAREA1=INAREA,DEVICE=2540,              DOSX
                                                       DEVADDR=SYSIPT,EOFADDR=ENDDO,WORKA=YES              DOS
                                    159 *                                                                  DOS
                                    160 PRINTER  DTFPR BLKSIZE=132,IOAREA1=PRTAREA,DEVICE=1403,            DOSX
                                                       CONTROL=YES,DEVADDR=SYS009,WORKA=YES                DOS
                                    181 *                                                                  DOS
000180                              182 INAREA   DS    CL80                                                DOS
000200                              183 PRTAREA  DS    CL132                                               DOS
                                    184 ********************************************************************OS
                                    185 *                    DEVICE CONTROL BLOCKS AND SAVE AREA            OS
                                    186 ********************************************************************OS
                                    187 *INFILE  DCB   DDNAME=INFILE,BLKSIZE=80,LRECL=80,                   OSX
                                    188 *              MACRF=PM,DSORG=PS,EODAD=ENDDO                        OS
                                    189 *                                                                   OS
                                    190 *PRINTER DCB   DDNAME=PRINTER,BLKSIZE=132,LRECL=132,                OSX
                                    191 *              MACRF=PMC,DSORG=PS                                   OS
                                    192 *                                                                   OS
                                    193 *SAVE    DS    18F                                                  OS
                                    194 ***********************************************************************
                                    195 *                    DATA DEFINITIONS
                                    196 ***********************************************************************
000284                              197 INRECD   DS    0CL80
000284                              198          DS    CL9
00028D                              199 INNAME   DS    CL20
0002A1                              200          DS    CL13
0002AE                              201 INDEPT   DS    CL4
0002B2                              202          DS    CL7
0002B9                              203 INJOBCD  DS    CL4
0002BD                              204 INPAYTYP DS    CL1
0002BE                              205 INRATE   DS    CL8
0002C6                              206          DS    CL14
                                    207 *
0002D4                              208 PRLINE   DS    0CL132
0002D4 4040404040404040             209          DC    CL10' '
0002DE                              210 PRNAME   DS    CL20
0002F2 4040404040404040             211          DC    CL10' '
0002FC                              212 PRDEPT   DS    CL4
000300 4040404040404040             213          DC    CL10' '
00030A                              214 PRJOBCD  DS    CL4
00030E 40404040                     215          DC    CL4' '
000312                              216 PRRATE   DS    CL13
00031F 4040404040404040             217          DC    CL57' '
                                    218 *
000358                              219 HEAD1    DS    0CL132
000358 4040404040404040             220          DC    CL30' '
000376 C5D4D7D3D6E8C5C5             221          DC    CL102'EMPLOYEES ON WEEKLY SALARY'
                                    222 *
0003DC                              223 HEAD2    DS    0CL132
0003DC 4040404040404040             224          DC    CL18' '
0003EE D5C1D4C540404040             225          DC    CL22'NAME'
000404 C4C5D7E34B404040             226          DC    CL12'DEPT.'
000410 D1D6C240C3D6C4C5             227          DC    CL17'JOB CODE'
000421 E2C1D3C1D9E84040             228          DC    CL63'SALARY'
                                    229 *
000460                              230 TOTLINE  DS    0CL132
000460 4040404040404040             231          DC    CL15' '
00046F                              232 PRTOTEMP DS    CL4
000473 40C5D4D7D3D6E8C5             233          DC    CL20' EMPLOYEES'
000487 E3D6E3C1D340E6C5             234          DC    CL23'TOTAL WEEKLY SALARIES'
00049E                              235 PRTOTPAY DS    CL13
0004AB 4040404040404040             236          DC    CL57' '
                                    237 *
0004E4                              238 PKRATE   DS    PL5
0004E9                              239 PKTOTEMP DS    PL2
0004EB                              240 PKTOTPAY DS    PL5
0004F0                              241 LINECNT  DS    PL2
0004F2 40202120                     242 PATRN    DC    XL4'40202120'
0004F6 40206B2020206B20             243 PATRN2   DC    XL13'40206B2020206B2020214B2020'
                                    244 *
                              00000 245          END   MAINLINE
000508 5B5BC2D6D7C5D540             246                =C'$$BOPEN '
000510 5B5BC2C3D3D6E2C5             247                =C'$$BCLOSE'
000518 00000148                     248                =A(INFILE)
00051C 00000284                     249                =A(INRECD)
000520 00000180                     250                =A(PRINTER)
000524 000002D4                     251                =A(PRLINE)
000528 00000460                     252                =A(TOTLINE)
00052C 00000358                     253                =A(HEAD1)
000530 000003DC                     254                =A(HEAD2)
000534 050C                         255                =P'50'
000536 0C                           256                =P'0'
000537 1C                           257                =P'1'
```

Figure 4–17 *(Concluded)*

EMPLOYEES ON WEEKLY SALARY

NAME	DEPT.	JOB CODE	SALARY
CARRIE AHN	1234	1200	415.00
CLAIRE VOYANT	1234	1200	392.00
DUNNAN BRADSTREET	1234	4130	283.00
DELLA KATESSEN	2143	1200	380.00
PETE MOSS	2143	6715	275.00
JACK RABBETT	3756	1200	352.00
NORA GRETZ	4028	1200	297.50
PEARL STRAND	4028	1200	291.50
HEDDA HARE	4028	1200	284.50
SUZY KEW	5337	1200	317.50
ELLA MENTRY	7409	0060	412.00
RICH PERSON	8823	0060	395.00
12 EMPLOYEES	TOTAL WEEKLY SALARIES		4,095.00

Figure 4–18 Output from Program 4

ent lengths, with the packed field being half the length of the unpacked field raised to the next higher integer.

Packed decimal constants may be defined as type P. If the specified length is longer than necessary to hold the constant, the field is padded to the left with zeros. If it is too short, leftmost digits of the constant will be truncated. A decimal point may be written in the constant as information, but it is ignored by the assembler.

Addition and subtraction may be performed on packed decimal fields that have valid decimal digits in each position except the rightmost four bits of the last byte, which must contain the sign. Fields may be of differing lengths. The second operand is added to or subtracted from the first, and the result replaces the first operand.

Packed decimal data must be edited to print correctly. The Edit instruction converts the packed data to character form and may eliminate leading zeros and insert commas and decimal points.

The edit pattern is defined as a hexadecimal constant that contains a fill character, digit selectors, message characters, and field separators. The edit pattern is moved to the position where the edited result is to be printed or displayed, and the packed decimal field is edited into the pattern.

The Unpack (UNPK) and Move Zones (MVZ) instructions may be used to convert packed decimal data to printable form. These instructions are less versatile than Edit and less commonly used.

TERMS FOR REVIEW

Check protection
Decimal digit
Digit selector
Edit
Edit pattern
Field separator
Fill character
Message character
Move Zones
Pack
Packed decimal
Padding

Sign
Significance indicator
Significance starter
Unpack
ZAP
Zero suppression
Zoned decimal

REVIEW QUESTIONS

1. In what ways does character data differ from zoned decimal data? What type codes are used to define constants of each kind?
2. What are the differences between zoned decimal and packed decimal numbers? On which kind can arithmetic be performed?
3. What are valid signs that may be used on zoned decimal and packed decimal numbers?
4. What besides the sign is necessary to make a packed decimal number valid?
5. What is meant by overflow in addition or subtraction? How can it be avoided?
6. What happens if you ZAP a source field into shorter destination field? What condition can cause an interrupt during a ZAP instruction?
7. Name the four types of codes that may be used in edit patterns and explain the purpose of each type.
8. Suppose you wish to suppress leading zeros to the left of a decimal point. Where in the edit pattern should the significance starter be placed?
9. What characters are sometimes used as a fill character in editing to cause check protection? Explain how this is done.

EXERCISES

1. Show the constant created by the assembler for each of the following definitions:
   a. `DC Z'237'`
   b. `DC ZL5'237'`
   c. `DC ZL5'-237'`
   d. `DC ZL2'237'`
   e. `DC C'237'`
   f. `DC CL5'237'`
   g. `DC PL5'-237'`
   h. `DC PL2'237'`
2. What characters would be printed for a field defined as Z'456'? as Z'−456'?
3. Show the result of packing a field into itself if it originally contains three blanks. What would happen if you tried to do arithmetic with the packed field?
4. Show the value created by the assembler for each of the following definitions:
   a. `DC P'0'`
   b. `DC PL3'0'`
   c. `DC P'-38875'`
   d. `DC 2P'0'`
   e. `DC P'125'`
   f. `DC PL1'125'`
   g. `DC P'-388.75'`
   h. `DC 2P'125'`
5. Write instructions using packed decimal numbers to control a pretest loop that is to be performed no more than 50 times.
6. Write instructions to count the number of records read in that have codes 1, 2, or 3 in column 80 of the record.

7. Write definitions and instructions to edit a total in a five-byte packed decimal field that has two digits to the right of the assumed decimal place.
8. Assume that a five-byte field named ACCTNBR contains the zoned decimal digits 12345. Show the contents of this field after the instruction PACK ACCTNBR,ACCTNBR has been executed.
9. After the instruction in Exercise 8 has been executed, assume that the instruction UNPK ACCTNBR,ACCTNBR is executed. What will then be the contents of ACCTNBR?

PROGRAMMING PROBLEMS

1. Using Data Set 1 in Appendix D, write a program to print a report showing the name, department, job code, and hourly pay rate of all employees with pay type 'H' whose rate is less than $8.00. Count the number of such employees and print out the number two spaces below the last employee name in the report. Design your own headings. Edit the hourly rate to print with two decimal places.
2. Write a program using the same data set to count the number of employees in each pay class, 'A', 'W', and 'H', and add the total of the rates of each type. Do not print the detail records, but print three summary lines giving the count and total for each pay type.
3. Using Data Set 2 in Appendix D, write a program to create an Inventory Reorder Report. This report should list the item number, item description, and reorder quantity for each item in which the quantity on hand is less than the reorder point. Design your own headings. Edit all quantities.

5 More Decimal Operations and Modular Structure

OBJECTIVES

After studying this chapter, you should be able to:

- Explain and use packed decimal multiplication and division
- Correctly round results after multiplying and dividing
- Shift decimal data so as to drop excess digits
- Calculate averages and compound interest
- Divide programs into control and processing modules through use of subroutines
- Use standard modules for reading and writing records
- Use the ASA control character for controlling spacing and skipping on the printer

In this chapter we shall learn to perform packed decimal multiplication and division and to round the results. These operations are more complex than addition and subtraction and require more knowledge of machine operations and programming techniques. We shall employ a new method of controlling spacing and skipping on the printer by moving a special character to the first byte of the print line. We shall develop standard modules for reading and writing records. And we shall move further into the development and utilization of modular structure in our programs.

MULTIPLICATION

When we multiply two numbers together, there are rules that determine the size of their product. The number of digits in the product is equal to the number of digits in the multiplicand plus the number of digits in the multiplier. If a five-digit number is multiplied by a four-digit number, the product will contain nine digits. Some of the digits may be leading zeros, but the rule always applies. We can see this rule in the following examples:

```
    99999      12345
    *9999      *7682
---------  ---------
999890001  094834290
```

To determine the length of the product, we shall use the general form of having a 9 represent any digit. Thus we can readily calculate the length of the field without having to do the actual multiplication.

```
  999     9999     9999999
  *99     *999        *999
-----  -------  ----------
99999  9999999  9999999999
```

Aligning Decimal Points

Remember that decimal points are not actually present in packed decimal numbers. All numbers are processed as integers. The programmer must keep track of the location of the decimal point at all times and insert the decimal point through editing when numbers are printed.

The number of digits to the left of an assumed decimal point in the product is equal to the sum of the numbers of digits to the left of the decimal points in the two numbers being multiplied. Similarly, the number of digits to the right of the decimal in the product is equal to the sum of the numbers of digits to the right of the decimal points in the two numbers being multiplied.

```
  999.99       9999       99999.999
   *9.99      *99.9         *9.9999
---------  --------  --------------
9999.9999  999999.9  999999.9999999
```

Multiplication may be used to align decimal points before adding or subtracting packed decimal numbers. The number with fewer digits to the right of the decimal point should be multiplied by 1 followed by the number of zeros we need to make its value align with the number with more decimal places. Then the two numbers may be added or subtracted. The process of aligning decimal points and knowing the position of the decimal point after various calculations is often called *scaling*.

For example, suppose we have numbers defined as

```
OBJECT CODE    INSTRUCTION

00 34 56 7C    N1   DC PL4'345.67'
00 03 48 5C    N2   DC PL4'348.5'
01 0C          ONE  DC PL2'1.0'
```

It is obvious that N1 and N2 cannot be added correctly as they are. Multiplying N2 by ONE has the effect

```
 348.5
  *1.0
------
348.50
```

We may then add the new N2 correctly to N1.

The Multiply Packed (MP) Instruction

The MP instruction multiplies the first operand by the second operand and replaces the first operand with the product. The two operands may be of different lengths. The second operand cannot be longer than 15 digits plus sign (eight bytes), and the product cannot exceed 31 digits plus sign (16 bytes).

To ensure that there will be enough space for the product, the first operand must have at least one byte containing leading zeros for each byte in the second operand. In other words, if the second operand is three bytes long, the first operand must contain at least three bytes of leading zeros. Given these definitions

OBJECT CODE	NAME	INSTRUCTION
00 00 12 34 5C	NBR1	DC PL5'12345'
03 7C	NBR2	DC P'37'

we could execute MP NBR1,NBR2 because NBR1 has two bytes of leading zeros, equal to the length of NBR2. We could not execute MP NBR2,NBR1 because NBR2 has no bytes of leading zeros; it would require five bytes of leading zeros in NBR2 (the length of NBR1) to hold the product. The computer does not test whether the product will actually fit into the first operand. It merely tests that the required number of bytes of leading zeros is actually present. If not, the program is interrupted, and control is returned to the supervisor.

Rather than setting up fields of various lengths in working storage to hold the products of multiplication, I recommend the use of a standard eight-byte work area. This area will hold a 15-digit number with sign, long enough for almost all calculations in normal processing. This area could be defined as

```
PKWORK   DS  PL8
```

but I prefer to use this definition:

```
DOUBLE   DS  D
```

Type D defines a doubleword, an eight-byte area that is placed by the assembler to start on a doubleword boundary. This boundary is any storage address that can be evenly divided by eight. Such an area will be required later to convert packed decimal data to binary form. We may as well use it now.

Figure 5–1 shows packed decimal multiplication using a doubleword as a work area. The doubleword has enough bytes of leading zeros to contain any possible product of a four-byte field and a three-byte field. When we ZAP the product into PKAMOUNT, one byte of leading zeros will be truncated. Since the price had two digits to the right of the decimal point and the quantity had none, there will be two digits to the right of the decimal point in the product.

Rounding

The term *rounding* refers to using the value of a number accurate to the number of decimal places we require. We may round to the nearest whole number, or to the nearest one, two, three, or other decimal places. To round to a certain number of decimal places, we customarily add 5 to the place just to the right of the last place we wish to retain. Then we drop all excess digits that are to the right of the number we keep.

If the digit to which we add is 5 or greater, it causes a carry to the position we retain on the left, rounding it upward. If the digit to which we add is less than 5, there is no carry, and the digit we retain remains unchanged.

Suppose we wish to round to the nearest cent the pay of a person who worked 42.5 hours at $6.375 per hour. The rounding process works as shown in Figure 5–2.

Remember that all packed decimal numbers are regarded by the computer as integers. We are responsible as programmers for remembering the assumed location of the decimal point. We can add the 5 to the proper position by considering how many excess digits we wish to drop. In the example in Figure 5–2, we wish to drop two of the four digits. Figure 5–3 shows how we can generalize this procedure.

OBJECT CODE	NAME	DEFINITION
00 13 57 5C	PKPRICE	DC PL4'135.75'
00 24 5C	PKQUANT	DC PL3'245'
	PKAMOUNT	DS PL7
	DOUBLE	DS D

INSTRUCTIONS	DESTINATION FIELD	COMMENTS
ZAP DOUBLE,PKPRICE	00 00 00 00 00 13 57 5C	Two decimals assumed
MP DOUBLE,PKQUANT	00 00 00 00 33 25 87 5C	Two decimals assumed
ZAP PKAMOUNT,DOUBLE	00 00 00 33 25 87 5C	Truncated

Figure 5–1 Packed decimal multiplication

6.375	Rate to three decimals
* 42.5	Hours to one decimal
290.9375	Pay to four decimals
+ 0.0050	Add 5 to third decimal position
290.9425	Rounded result with four decimals
290.94	Drop excess digits

Figure 5–2 The rounding process

DIGITS TO BE DROPPED	VALUE TO BE ADDED
1	=P'5'
2	=P'50'
3	=P'500'
4	=P'5000'
5	=P'50000'
and so forth	

Figure 5–3 Determining the rounding factor

Dropping Excess Digits

After rounding the last digit we wish to retain in our result, we must drop all excess digits to its right. With packed decimal data, this means we must place a valid sign to the right of the last digit to be retained. The sign must always be in the rightmost four (numeric) bits of the last byte; therefore, the last digit must always be in the leftmost four (zone) bits of the last byte.

Move Numeric (MVN) Instruction If we wish to drop an *even* number of digits, the last digit we wish to retain in the packed field will still be in the leftmost (zone) bits of a byte. Therefore, we may simply move a sign next to that digit. The *Move Numeric* (MVN) instruction will do this operation. MVN works just like Move Characters (MVC) except that only the four numeric bits in each byte are moved (copied) to the destination field. The zone bits are unaffected. MVN moves the numeric bits of each byte from the second operand to the first, left to right. Only the length of the first operand is required. Since we are moving only the sign, we use a length of 1.

Examples in Figure 5–4 will clarify the use of the MVN instruction if the data item is in a field named DOUBLE.

After the sign is moved to the proper location, we may use the shortened result where it is, or ZAP it to another work area. Notice that in the first example, the result field is seven bytes long, the second is six bytes long, and the third is five bytes long.

VALUE BEFORE MVN	DIGITS TO BE DROPPED	INSTRUCTION	VALUE AFTER MVN
00 00 00 12 34 56 78 9C	2	MVN DOUBLE+6(1),DOUBLE+7	00 00 00 12 34 56 7C 9C
00 00 00 12 34 56 78 9C	4	MVN DOUBLE+5(1),DOUBLE+7	00 00 00 12 34 5C 78 9C
00 00 00 12 34 56 78 9C	6	MVN DOUBLE+4(1),DOUBLE+7	00 00 00 12 3C 56 78 9C

Figure 5–4 Dropping an even number of digits

	INSTRUCTION	DOUBLE AFTER INSTRUCTION
	ZAP DOUBLE,PKRATE	00 00 00 00 00 06 37 5C
	MP DOUBLE,PKHOURS	00 00 00 00 29 09 37 5C
	AP DOUBLE,=P'50'	00 00 00 00 29 09 42 5C
	MVN DOUBLE+6(1),DOUBLE+7	00 00 00 00 29 09 4C 5C
	ZAP PKPAY,DOUBLE(7)	00 00 00 00 29 09 4C 5C
	MVC PRLINE+50(10),PATTERN	
	ED PRLINE+50(10),PKPAY	
	.	
DOUBLE	DS D	
PKRATE	DC PL3'6.375'	
PKHOURS	DC PL2'42.5'	
PKPAY	DC PL4	
PATTERN	DC X'4020206B2020214B2020'	

Figure 5–5 Packed decimal multiplication, rounding, and editing

We can now write source statements to multiply the pay rate of 6.375 by 42.5 hours, round the result to two decimal places, and ZAP the result to PKPAY. The contents of DOUBLE after the instruction has been executed are shown to the right of each statement in Figure 5–5.

After the ZAP statement, PKPAY contains 00 29 09 4C, with two assumed decimal places (290.94). Even though the product of a three-byte rate and a two-byte hours field normally requires a five-byte product, we can safely assume that no pay amount will exceed $99,999.99 for one pay period. That seven-digit amount will fit into the four-byte PKPAY field.

The MVC and ED statements edit the result. We could have edited the final result from DOUBLE so long as we were careful to select the correct seven digits to match the edit pattern. The statement

```
ED  PRLINE+50(10),DOUBLE+3
```

will skip over the three bytes of leading zeros, edit the correct seven digits from the next four bytes, and ignore the last byte of DOUBLE.

Move with Offset (MVO) Instruction When we wish to drop an *odd* number of digits after rounding, the process is somewhat more complex. Whenever 1, 3, 5, 7, or any odd number of digits is dropped in a packed decimal field, the last digit we retain will always be in the rightmost four bits of a byte. Since the sign of a packed decimal number must also always be in the rightmost four bits of a byte, we must somehow shift the remaining digits one-half byte to the left so that the sign can occupy its normal place. The *Move with Offset* (MVO) instruction is designed for this purpose.

MVO moves the second operand to the first operand location byte by byte from right to left, at the same time offsetting it four bits to the left. If the first operand is longer than the second, it will be padded to the left with zeros. If the first operand is the shorter field, the data will be truncated to the size of the first operand. The rightmost four bits of the destination field will be unchanged by the move.

The examples in Figure 5–6 will help to illustrate the MVO instruction. Notice that the first example drops one digit of the source field, the second drops three digits, and the third drops five digits. Often, the MVO instruction is used to shift the digits within a single field. In other words, the source and destination fields overlap. This is especially useful when a doubleword is used as a work area for multiplication.

The last three examples of Figure 5–6 use the MVO instruction with overlapping fields.

Another possibility is to use MVO to lay the retained digits in their proper place in the result field and then use Move Numeric (MVN) to move in the proper sign. In this instance, the destination field could contain anything at all before the MVO and MVN instructions are used. For example:

INSTRUCTION	PKANS AFTER EXECUTION	PKANS BEFORE EXECUTION	SOURCE FIELD
MVO PKANS,SOURCE(5)	01 23 45 67 80	40 40 40 40 40	00 12 34 56 78 9C
MVN PKANS+4(1),=X'C'	01 23 45 67 8C	01 23 45 67 80	0C

MVO INSTRUCTION WITH SEPARATE FIELDS

INSTRUCTION	DEST AFTER MVO	DEST BEFORE MVO	SOURCE FIELD
MVO DEST,SOURCE(4)	00 00 01 23 45 6C	99 99 99 99 99 9C	00 12 34 56 7C
MVO DEST,SOURCE(3)	00 00 00 01 23 4C	99 99 99 99 99 9C	00 12 34 56 7C
MVO DEST,SOURCE(2)	00 00 00 00 01 2C	99 99 99 99 99 9C	00 12 34 56 7C

MVO INSTRUCTION WITH OVERLAPPING FIELDS

INSTRUCTION	DOUBLE AFTER MVO	DOUBLE BEFORE MVO
MVO DOUBLE,DOUBLE(7)	00 00 00 01 23 45 67 8C	00 00 00 12 34 56 78 9C
MVO DOUBLE,DOUBLE(6)	00 00 00 00 01 23 45 6C	00 00 00 12 34 56 78 9C
MVO DOUBLE,DOUBLE(5)	00 00 00 00 00 01 23 4C	00 00 00 12 34 56 78 9C

Figure 5–6 The Move with Offset instruction

In summary, to drop an *even* number of digits in a packed decimal field, use Move Numeric (MVN). To shift the digits one-half byte to drop an *odd* number of digits, use Move with Offset (MVO).

Rounding with the SRP Instruction

The Shift and Round Packed (SRP) instruction was not available on the System/360 computers, but has been added to later members of the family. It can be used to shift packed decimal digits to the right or left within a field. For right shifts, it can also round the result.

SRP has three operands. The first is the name of the packed field. The second is a *displacement* indicating the number of digits to be shifted. The third is a value from 0 to 9 that is used for filling or rounding the shifted data.

When the second operand is positive, a *left shift* is made. Vacated positions are filled in with the digit shown as the third operand. The effect can be the same as multiplying the number by a power of 10. Suppose DOUBLE contains the value 12345. Here are some examples of a left shift:

INSTRUCTION	DOUBLE AFTER SRP	DOUBLE BEFORE SRP
SRP DOUBLE,2,0	00 00 00 00 12 34 50 0C	00 00 00 00 00 12 34 5C
SRP DOUBLE,4,0	00 00 00 12 34 50 00 0C	00 00 00 00 00 12 34 5C

When the second operand is negative, a *right shift* is made. The digit shown as the third operand (usually 5) is added to the leftmost digit dropped to cause rounding. However, we cannot express the negative amount as −2 or −3. We must use *excess-64* notation; that is, subtract the negative amount from 64 and use the difference as the operand. Thus, −1 is expressed is expressed as 63, −2 as 62, and so forth. Here are some examples of right shift and rounding where DOUBLE contained the value 1234567:

INSTRUCTION	DOUBLE AFTER SRP	DOUBLE BEFORE SRP
SRP DOUBLE,63,5	00 00 00 00 01 23 45 7C	00 00 00 00 12 34 56 7C
SRP DOUBLE,61,5	00 00 00 00 00 01 23 5C	00 00 00 00 12 34 56 7C

In the first example, the rightmost 7 is dropped and the 6 is rounded upward. In the second example, the 5, 6, and 7 are dropped and the 4 is rounded upward. The rounding factor of 5 is added to the leftmost digit dropped (5), and the carry causes the 4 to be rounded upward to 5.

Programming Tips

- Be sure to allow one byte of leading zeros in the multiplicand field for each byte in the multiplier.
- A doubleword is a convenient work area for both multiplication and division to handle up to 15 decimal digits plus a sign.
- To round, add 5 to the leftmost digit to be dropped. Then drop that digit and all digits to its right.
- Use MVO to drop an odd number of digits by shifting the retained digits to a valid sign.
- Use MVN to drop an even number of digits by moving the sign to the right of the last digit retained.
- Use SRP to shift digits to the left and add trailing zeros, or to round a number and shift the retained digits to the right next to a sign.

DIVISION

The Divide Packed (DP) Instruction is used for packed decimal division. The first operand is divided by the second operand and is replaced by both the quotient and the remainder. The remainder always has the same length as the divisor, and it occupies the rightmost bytes of the first operand. The remaining leftmost bytes of the first operand hold the quotient.

Both the quotient and remainder have their own signs. The signs are determined by the following rules:

1. The quotient is positive if the dividend and divisor have the same signs.
2. The quotient is negative if the dividend and divisor have different signs.
3. The sign of the remainder is the same as that of the dividend.

Since the number of bytes required for the remainder is determined first, and the length of the remainder is the same as the length of the divisor, we must ensure that the first operand is long enough to hold a quotient of whatever length we require. For this reason, a doubleword is convenient to use as a work area for division, just as it is for multiplication. We rarely have a divisor of more than seven digits, which can be contained in a four-byte field. The remainder will therefore be four bytes long, leaving four bytes in the doubleword to hold a quotient of up to seven digits.

Suppose we are required to divide the sum of test scores by the number of students to get a class average score. The statements in Figure 5–7 illustrate the process. Note that in this example the quotient is to the nearest integer.

INSTRUCTION	DESTINATION FIELD AFTER EXECUTION	REMARKS
ZAP DOUBLE,TOTSCORE	00 00 00 00 00 01 77 3C	Padded left with zeros
DP DOUBLE,STUCOUNT	00 00 00 00 07 7C 00 2C	Remainder 2 bytes
ZAP AVERAGE,DOUBLE(6)	00 07 7C	Average = 77

Figure 5–7 Packed decimal division

INSTRUCTION	DESTINATION FIELD AFTER EXECUTION	REMARKS
ZAP DOUBLE,TOTSCORE	00 00 00 00 00 01 77 3C	
MP DOUBLE,=P'100'	00 00 00 00 01 77 30 0C	Get two extra zeros
DP DOUBLE,STUCOUNT	00 00 00 07 70 8C 01 6C	Quotient in 6 bytes
AP DOUBLE(6),=P'5'	00 00 00 07 71 3C 01 6C	Add 5 to quotient
MVO DOUBLE(6),DOUBLE(5)	00 00 00 00 77 1C 01 6C	Drop last digit
ZAP AVERAGE,DOUBLE(6)	00 77 1C	Average = 77.1

Figure 5–8 Packed decimal division and rounding

```
           ZAP   PKACCUM,PKPRIN          Move principal to accumulation
           ZAP   DOUBLE,PKDAYS           Set counter to number of days
           CVB   5,DOUBLE                *
REPEAT     EQU   *                       REPEAT
           ZAP   DOUBLE,PKACCUM            Multiply accumulation by rate
           MP    DOUBLE,PKRATE             * (six decimal places)
           DP    DOUBLE,=P'365'            Divide by 365 (Rem. 2 bytes)
           AP    DOUBLE(6),=P'5000'        Round quotient to two places
           MVN   DOUBLE+3(1),DOUBLE+5      Move sign to drop four digits
           ZAP   PKDAYINT,DOUBLE(4)        Zap to daily interest
           AP    PKACCUM,PKDAYINT          Add daily interest to accumulation
           BCT   5,REPEAT                  Subtract 1 from number of days
UNTIL      EQU   *                       UNTIL number of days = zero
           .
PKPRIN     DC    PL4'7483.57'
PKRATE     DC    PL3'.1075'
PKDAYS     DC    PL2'27'
PKDAYINT   DS    PL3
PKACCUM    DS    PL4
DOUBLE     DS    D
```

Figure 5–9 Routine for compounding interest daily

If we wish to carry the class average to one decimal place, we must multiply TOTSCORE by 10 before dividing. If we want the average *rounded* to one decimal place, we must multiply TOTSCORE by 100 before dividing, add 5 to the quotient, and drop the rightmost digit. Figure 5–8 shows the steps.

Notice that in referring to the quotient in DOUBLE, we must exclude the two bytes occupied by the remainder. The quotient is only six bytes long. To drop the last digit of the quotient after rounding, we retain only the first five bytes of the quotient and move them to an appropriate sign. We can then ZAP the quotient anywhere we wish for further processing.

The number of decimal places in the dividend must always equal or exceed the number of decimal places in the divisor. If they are equal, the quotient will be an integer. The number of decimal places in the quotient will be equal to the difference between the numbers of places in the dividend and in the divisor. For example, 3 divided by 7 will give a quotient of 0 and a remainder of 3. But 3.000 divided by 7 will give a quotient of 0.428 and a remainder of 4.

Let us now put together all of the foregoing instructions to show a rather common real-life example, daily compounding of interest. Although the data would normally be read from an external source, we will use constants to shorten the example. We will show how interest is compounded on $7,483.47 at an annual rate of 10.75 percent for 27 days.

We will first multiply $7,483.57 by 0.1075 to get the annual interest, with six decimal places. We then divide by 365 to get daily interest, still with six decimal places. We will then round the daily interest to two decimal places, add it to the principal amount, and repeat the cycle 27 times. In actual practice, we would print a line for each day, but in Figure 5–9 we will shorten the operation and show only the arithmetic steps and the control of repetition.

In Figure 5–9, rounding could be done by substituting

```
SRP  DOUBLE(6),62,5
```

for the AP and MVN instructions.

Programming Tips

- Recall that the quotient and remainder both replace the dividend. The remainder occupies the rightmost bytes and is the length of the divisor. The rest of the dividend field is available to hold the quotient.
- In referring to the quotient, use an explicit length to avoid including the remainder as part of the quotient field.

THE ASA CONTROL CHARACTER

Up to this point in the text, we have been using the Control (CNTRL) macro to space and skip the printer. An alternate method involves placing a special control character in the first byte of the printer record. ASA, for American Standards Association (since changed to American National Standards Institute), is the name assigned to this control character. This method of controlling spacing and skipping the printer is also used in other languages such as COBOL and FORTRAN.

To use the ASA control character we must make several changes in our program. In DOS under our DTFPR macro we use the statement CTLCHR=ASA instead of CONTROL=YES. The BLKSIZE operand must be increased by one to 133. In OS, under the DCB marco for the printer, we use MACRF=PMA instead of MACRF=PMC and change BLKSIZE to 133. In both DOS and OS, the size of our printer I/O area and of each of the printer work areas must be increased to 133. The data actually printed now begin in the second byte of our record.

To control spacing or skipping, we must move or define one of the ASA characters in the first byte of the output record. The characters are shown in Figure 5–10.

Printing Heading Lines

Use of ASA control characters with heading lines is simple. We define the proper character as a constant in the first byte of each line. When we print that line, the proper spacing or skipping will take place before the line is printed. For example, suppose we wish to print a heading with the title 'TRIAL BALANCE' exactly centered after skipping to a new page. We could use either definition shown in Figure 5–11. The first one shows the print control character as a separate constant, while the second one includes it with the first constant actually printed.

One advantage of using the ASA control character instead of the CNTRL macro is that the number of statements is reduced. For example, if HEAD1 is defined to skip to a new page, HEAD2 is defined for double spacing, and HEAD3 is defined for single spacing, we can print our complete heading in three statements:

```
PUT  PRINTER,HEAD1
PUT  PRINTER,HEAD2
PUT  PRINTER,HEAD3
```

CHARACTER	MEANING
1 (One)	Skip to the first line (channel 1) of a new page
b (Blank)	Singlespace before printing
0 (Zero)	Doublespace before printing
− (Minus)	Triplespace before printing
+ (Plus)	Suppress spacing

Figure 5–10 ASA control characters

CONTROL CHARACTER DEFINED SEPARATELY

```
HEAD1    DS    0CL133
         DC    CL1'1'                  This is the print control character.
         DC    CL59' '
         DC    CL73'TRIAL BALANCE'
```

CONTROL CHARACTER DEFINED WITH FIRST PRINTED CONSTANT

```
HEAD1    DS    0CL133
         DC    CL60'1'                 1 followed by 59 blanks
         DC    CL73'TRIAL BALANCE'
```

Figure 5–11 Defining heading lines with ASA control characters

```
PRDETAIL  EQU   *
IF        CP    LINECOUNT,=P'50'       IF LINECOUNT => 50
          BL    ENDIF                  *
THEN      PUT   PRINTER,HEAD1            THEN PRINT HEADING
          PUT   PRINTER,HEAD2            *
          PUT   PRINTER,HEAD3            *
          ZAP   LINECOUNT,=P'0'          SET LINECOUNT TO ZERO
          MVI   PRLINE,C'0'              MAKE DETAIL LINE DOUBLE SPACE
ENDIF     EQU   *                      ENDIF
          PUT   PRINTER,PRLINE         PRINT DETAIL LINE
          AP    LINECOUNT,=P'1'        ADD 1 TO LINECOUNT
CLEAR     MVI   PRLINE,C' '            CLEAR PRINT LINE
          MVC   PRLINE+1(132),PRLINE   *
          BR    10                     RETURN
```

Figure 5–12 Module to print detail lines

Printing Detail Lines

Up to this point, we have printed a heading to start the program and then again after printing each 50 lines. But if we had exactly 50 detail lines to print, we would have skipped to a new page, printed a heading, and then reached end of file. Nothing would be printed on the second page after the heading.

We can eliminate this problem by not printing a heading until we are ready to print a detail line. Before printing the detail line, we will check to see if a heading is needed and, if so, print it. The detail print module in Figure 5–12 will do this task.

The MVI instructions require some explanation. Good systems design dictates that the first detail line after a heading is double spaced. Other lines are normally single spaced. We have previously set up the line to be printed with a blank control character to cause single spacing. However, if the heading is printed, we must change the control character to a zero (0) so that the following detail line will be double spaced. If the linecount is less than 50, the program branches to ENDIF and prints the detail line with single spacing.

After printing the detail line and adding to the line count, we clear the entire line to prepare for setting up the next detail line. The first byte is a blank, which will cause single spacing of each line until we once again print a heading.

The last three lines in Figure 5–12 can be used as a separate module whenever we wish only to clear PRLINE by writing BAL 10,CLEAR.

In order to get a heading preceding the first detail line, the line counter must be equal to or greater than 50. In the initialization module, we will execute ZAP LINECOUNT,=P'51'. The linecount test for the first detail line will cause the heading to print, the linecount to be reset, and the first detail line to be double spaced.

Another option is to include the five statements at THEN in a separate heading subroutine that is entered with a BAL 11,HEADING. The PRINT subroutine as shown is sufficiently general to be usable as written for almost all situations.

Printing Total Lines

Another fairly common occurrence is to skip to a new page just before printing totals, leaving them stranded alone on the new page separated from the detail amounts. We can avoid this problem rather easily.

The solution is to have a separate module for printing total lines. This one does not test the line counter and therefore never skips to a new page before printing the totals. The total subroutine must, however, add to the line counter the number of lines, including extra spaces, that are included in the total.

If more than two or three total lines are to be printed, it will probably be necessary to reduce the number of detail lines per page to ensure space for the totals at the bottom of the page.

Total lines may be defined with constants for the ASA control characters, just as the heading lines are, or the ASA control character may be moved to the first byte of the total line with a MVI instruction just before printing takes place.

STANDARD MODULE TO READ RECORDS

Ordinarily the test for end of file is contained within the GET macro. As we have written our programs so far, any time that the end of file is reached in a GET macro, the program branches directly to the address specified in EOFADDR. In certain nested loops and selection structures this is awkward or impractical. Our program is clearer to understand if we read records in a

```
READRECD  EQU   *
          MVI   EOFFLAG,C'N'     SET END OF FILE FLAG OFF
          GET   INFILE,INRECD    READ RECORD
IFEOF     B     ENDIFEOF         IF END OF FILE
THENEOF   MVI   EOFFLAG,C'Y'       THEN SET END OF FILE FLAG ON
ENDIFEOF  EQU   *                ENDIF
          BR    10               RETURN
```

Figure 5–13 Module to read input records

module that sets an end-of-file flag that can be tested anywhere we wish. This method is normally used in COBOL programs.

The module in Figure 5–13 demonstrates this technique. To use this module, we must change the DTFCD entry to read

```
EOFADDR=THENEOF
```

Whenever we wish to read an input record, we use

```
BAL 10,READRECD
```

To test for end of file, we use the statements shown in Figure 5–14.

Upon entering the READRECD module, we set the EOFFLAG OFF by moving the character 'N' to it. The GET macro tests for end of file as always and branches to the EOFADDR (THENEOF) if the EOF record is read. At THENEOF the EOFFLAG is set ON by moving the character 'Y' to it. If the end of file is not reached, the instruction following the GET is executed, branching to ENDIFEOF and leaving the EOFFLAG set OFF. We will use this subroutine in our following program examples.

Programming Tips

- Add one byte to length of each printer record to use the ASA control character. The ASA control character eliminates the need for the separate CNTRL macro for spacing and skipping the printer.
- Use a module that prints headings only when a detail line is ready for printing. Have the heading routine set the ASA character for double spacing and reset the line counter to its initial value.
- Set an end-of-file flag in a standard module to read input records so that the flag can be tested wherever desired in the program.

```
DOWHILE    EQU    *
           CLI    EOFFLAG,C'Y'
           BE     ENDDO
           Processing instructions to be done if NOT end of file
           B      DOWHILE
ENDDO      EQU    *
```

Figure 5–14 DOWHILE loop testing end-of-file flag

PROGRAM 5: ACCUMULATING TOTALS AND AVERAGING

In this program we will incorporate the ASA control character and the standard modules for reading records and printing detail lines discussed in the preceding sections. We will also break the program into several levels of modules.

By definition, a module is a group of statements to perform some specific task. We can use the BAL instruction to branch to the module wherever logic dictates and, by use of a corresponding BR instruction at the end of the module, return to the proper point in the main program. We will tend to use the terms *module* and *subroutine* interchangeably.

Ideally, a module is no longer than a single page of coding. Each module has only a single entry and a single exit, so that each module usually reflects only a limited number of repetition or selection structures. Modular structure makes programs easier to design, code, debug, and modify.

Almost every program has three principal *first-level* modules: (1) initialization, (2) the main processing loop, and (3) final processing. The mainline of the program is a *control* module which uses three BAL instructions to execute the first-level modules. Each first-level module in turn can be a *processing module* that carries out a specific task, or a control module that links to second-level modules.

We can show the modular design through a structure chart. This type of chart contains a block to represent each module. At the top is the mainline control module. At the first level under it are the three principal modules. In some instances there may be more than three. Then at a still lower level are the processing modules that carry out more detailed functions. Ideally, no module would do more than one group of logically related tasks.

Our next program applies multiplication and division to data from the employee record we have used in previous problems. This time we are to calculate information about hourly-rated employees in Department 3477. We are to determine the number of such employees in the department and calculate their average hourly rate and average weekly earnings for a 40-hour week.

Pseudocode for the problem is shown in Figure 5–15.

```
START PROGRAM
Open files
Clear totals
Set line count > 50
Read first record
DOWHILE not end of file
   IF department = 3477
      THEN
      IF pay type = 'W'
         THEN add hourly rate to total
         Add 1 to employee count
         Set up print line
         If line count => 50
            THEN print heading
         ENDIF
         Print line
         Add 1 to line count
         Clear print line
      ENDIF
   ENDIF
   Read next record
ENDDO
Print total hourly rate
Calculate average rate
Calculate average weekly pay
Print averages
Close files
END PROGRAM
```

Figure 5–15 Pseudocode for Program 5

Because our programs are still relatively short, we will combine a few functions that might normally be separated, in order to avoid a large number of modules with only one or two instructions. We will establish our base register and open and close files in the mainline module.

We will employ the modules for reading a record and printing a line discussed in this chapter. Thus we will have a end-of-file flag that may be tested as needed, and will print no heading until we have a detail line ready for printing.

Our initialization includes one module to clear the totals and set the line count to force the first heading, and another to read the first record. The main processing loop determines whether the record is from the correct department and pay class, and it controls three second-level modules: one to add to the proper totals and set up the data for printing, a second to print it, and a third to read the next record. The print module in turn controls the third-level module to print headings when necessary. The final processing module prints accumulated totals, calculates averages, and prints the averages. Figure 5–16 shows the structure chart for this program.

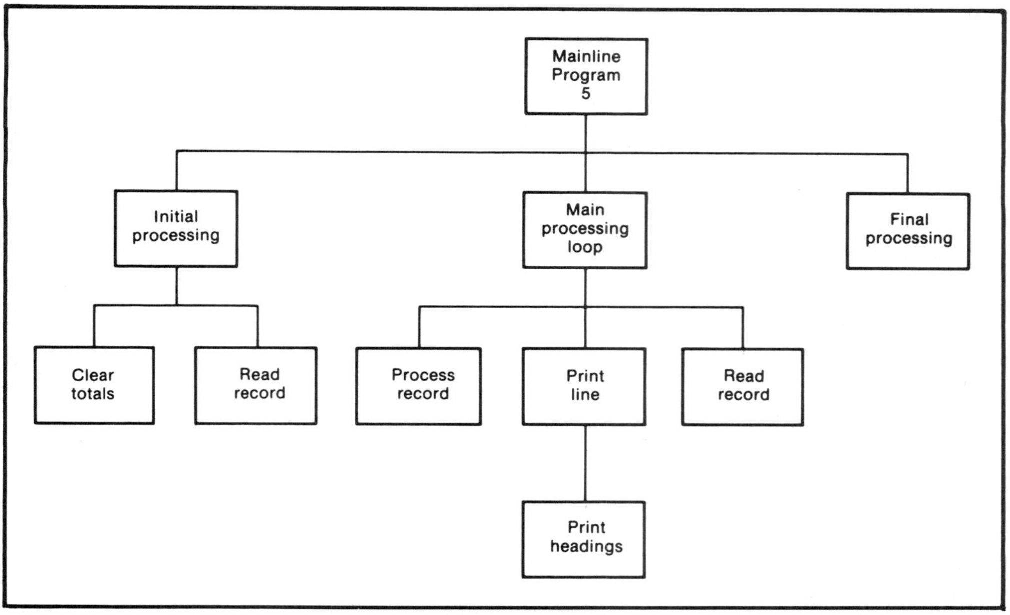

Figure 5–16 Structure chart for Program 5

```
  LOC  OBJECT CODE    A))R1 ADDR2  STMT   SOURCE STATEMENT                                      DOS/VSE ASSEMBLER 14.56 86-03-27

                                      1 ***********************************************************************
                                      2 *                ALTON R. KINDRED, PROGRAM 5
                                      3 * THIS PROGRAM PRINTS NAME, JOB CODE, AND RATE FOR ALL HOURLY-RATED
                                      4 * EMPLOYEES IN DEPARTMENT 5337.  IT ACCUMULATES THE NUMBER OF EMPLOYEES
                                      5 * AND THE TOTAL OF THE HOURLY RATES.  AT END OF FILE IT PRINTS THE
                                      6 * NUMBER OF EMPLOYEES, TOTAL HOURLY RATES, AVERAGE HOURLY RATE, AND
                                      7 * AVERAGE WEEKLY PAY OF THE HOURLY-RATED EMPLOYEES.
                                      8 *          REGISTERS USED:
                                      9 *                R9-11 - LINKS TO MODULES
                                     10 *                R12   - BASE REGISTER
                                     11 ***********************************************************************
                                     12          PRINT NOGEN
000000                               13 MAINLINE START 0                      SET LOCATION COUNTER
                                     14 *        STM   14,12,12(13)           SAVE REGISTEPS FOR OS        OS
000000 05C0                          15          BALR  12,0                   LOAD BASE REGISTER
                          00002      16          USING *,12                   DESIGNATE BASE REGISTER
                                     17 *        ST    13,SAVE+4              STORE REGISTER 13            OS
                                     18 *        LA    13,SAVE                LOAD SAVE AREA ADDRESS       OS
                                     19 *        OPEN  (INFILE,(INPUT),PRINTER,(OUTPUT))                   OS
                                     20          OPEN  INFILE,PRINTER         OPEN FILES                   DOS
000016 4590 C036          00038      29          BAL   9,INITIAL              DO INITIAL PROCESSING
00001A 4590 C040          00042      30          BAL   9,MAINLOOP             DO MAIN PROCESSING LOOP
00001E 4590 C06C          0006E      31          BAL   9,FINAL                DO FINAL PROCESSING
                                     32          CLOSE INFILE,PRINTER         CLOSE FILES                  DOS
                                     41          EOJ                          END PROGRAM                  DOS
                                     44 *        CLOSE (INFILE,,PRINTER)      CLOSE FILES                  OS
                                     45 *        L     13,SAVE+4              LOAD SAVE AREA ADDRESS       OS
                                     46 *        LM    14,12,12(13)           RESTORE REGISTERS            OS
                                     47 *        BR    14                     RETURN TO OS                 OS
                                     48 ***********************************************************************
                                     49 *                FIRST LEVEL MODULES
                                     50 ***********************************************************************
                                     51 *
                                     52 *                INITIALIZATION MODULE
                                     53 *
000038 45A0 C0EC          000EE      54 INITIAL  BAL   10,CLEARSET            SET INITIAL VALUES
00003C 45A0 C100          00102      55          BAL   10,READPECD            READ FIRST RECOPD
000040 07F9                          56          BR    9                      RETURN
                                     57 *
                                     58 *                MAIN PROCESSING LOOP
                                     59 *
                          00042      60 MAINLOOP EQU   *
000042 95E8 C67E    00680            61 DOWHILE  CLI   EOFFLAG,C'Y'           DOWHILE NOT END OF FILE
000046 4780 C06A    0006C            62          BE    ENDDO                    *
00004A D503 C31D C6A6 0031F C06A8    63 IF       CLC   INDEPT,=C'5337'          IF DEPT = 5337
000050 4770 C062    00064            64          BNE   ENDIF                      *
                          00054      65 THEN     EQU   *                          THEN
000054 95C8 C32C    0032E            66 IF2      CLI   INPAYTYP,C'H'              IF HOURLY PAY TYPE
```

Figure 5–17 Program 5 assembler listing

```
  LOC  OBJECT CODE     ADDR1 ADDR2  STMT   SOURCE STATEMENT                                  DOS/VSE ASSEMBLER 14.56 86-03-27

000058 4770 C062       00064          67              BNE    ENDIF2                          *
00005C 45A0 C11E             00120    68 THEN2        BAL    10,PROCESS                      PROCESS RECORD
000060 45A0 C154             00156    69              BAL    10,PRDETAIL                     PRINT LINE
                             00064    70 ENDIF2       EQU    *                              ENDIF
                             00064    71 ENDIF        EQU    *                             ENDIF
000064 45A0 C100             00102    72              BAL    10,READRECD                  READ NEXT RECORD
000068 47F0 C040       00042          73              B      DOWHILE                        *
                             0006C    74 ENDDO        EQU    *                           ENDDO
00006C 07F9                           75              BR     9                           RETURN
                                      76 *
                                      77 *                   FINAL PROCESSING MODULE
                                      78 *
00006E D203 C4E2 C686 004E4 00688     79 FINAL        MVC    PRTOTEMP,PATRN2             SET UP TOTAL LINE 1
000074 DE03 C4E2 C668 004E4 0066A     80              ED     PRTOTEMP,PKTOTEMP           *
00007A D209 C506 C68A 00508 0068C     81              MVC    PRTOTPAY,PATRN3             *
000080 DE09 C506 C664 00508 00666     82              ED     PRTOTPAY,PKTOTPAY           *
                                      83              PUT    PRINTER,TOTLINE1            PRINT TOTAL LINE 1
000096 F873 C676 C664 00678 00666     89              ZAP    DBL,PKTOTPAY                CALCULATE AVERAGE PAY
00009C FD71 C676 C668 00678 0066A     90              DP     DBL,PKTOTEMP                *
0000A2 F825 C66A C676 0066C 00678     91              ZAP    PKAVGPAY,DBL(6)             *
0000A8 D206 C58E C67F 00590 00681     92              MVC    PRAVGPAY,PATRN              SET UP AVERAGE PAY
0000AE DE06 C58E C66A 00590 0066C     93              ED     PRAVGPAY,PKAVGPAY           *
                                      94              PUT    PRINTER,TOTLINE2            PRINT AVERAGE PAY LINE
0000C4 F872 C676 C66A 00678 0066C    100              ZAP    DBL,PKAVGPAY                CALCULATE AVERAGE WEEKLY PAY
0000CA FC71 C676 C6CE 00678 006D0    101              MP     DBL,=P'40'                  *
0000D0 D206 C613 C67F 00615 00681    102              MVC    PRWKPAY,PATRN               SET UP WEEKLY PAY
0000D6 DE06 C613 C67B 00615 0067D    103              ED     PRWKPAY,DBL+5               *
                                     104              PUT    PRINTER,TOTLINE3            PRINT WEEKLY PAY LINE
0000EC 07F9                          110              BR     9                           RETURN
                                     111 ***********************************************************************
                                     112 *                   SECOND LEVEL MODULES
                                     113 ***********************************************************************
                                     114 *
                                     115 *                   CLEAR TOTALS AND SET INITIAL VALUES MODULE
                                     116 *
0000EE F830 C664 C6D4 00666 006D6    117 CLEARSET ZAP        PKTOTPAY,=P'0'              CLEAR TOTAL PAY
0000F4 F810 C668 C6D4 0066A 006D6    118              ZAP    PKTOTEMP,=P'0'              CLEAR EMPLOYEE COUNT
0000FA F811 C66D C6D0 0066F 006D2    119              ZAP    LINECNT,=P'51'              SET LINE COUNT > 50
000100 07FA                          120              BR     10                          RETURN
                                     121 *
                                     122 *                   READ RECORD MODULE
                                     123 *
000102 92D5 C67E       00680         124 READRECD MVI        EOFFLAG,C'N'                SET EOF FLAG OFF
                                     125              GET    INFILE,INRECD               READ RECORD
000116 47F0 C11C       0011E         131 IFEOF        B      ENDIFEOF                    IF END OF FILE
00011A 92E8 C67E       00680         132 THENEOF      MVI    EOFFLAG,C'Y'                  THEN SET EOF FLAG ON
                             0011E   133 ENDIFEOF EQU        *                           ENDIF
00011E 07FA                          134              BR     10                          RETURN
                                     135 *                   PROCESS RECORD MODULE
                                     136 *
000120 F227 C661 C32D 00663 0032F    137 PROCESS      PACK   PKRATE,INRATE                      ADD RATE TO TOTAL
000126 FA32 C664 C661 00666 00663    138              AP     PKTOTPAY,PKRATE                    *
00012C FA10 C668 C6D5 0066A 006D7    139              AP     PKTOTEMP,=P'1'                     ADD 1 TO EMPLOYEE COUNT
000132 9240 C343       00345         140              MVI    PRLINE,C' '                        CLEAR PRINT LINE
000136 D283 C344 C343 00346 00345    141              MVC    PRLINE+1(132),PRLINE        *
00013C D213 C34E C2FC 00350 002FE    142              MVC    PRNAME,INNAME                      SET UP PRINT LINE
000142 D203 C36C C328 0036E 0032A    143              MVC    PRJOBCD,INJOBCD                    *
000148 D206 C37A C67F 0037C 00681    144              MVC    PRRATE,PATRN                       *
00014E DE06 C37A C661 0037C 00663    145              ED     PRRATE,PKRATE                      *
000154 07FA                          146              BR     10                          RETURN
                                     148 *
                                     149 *                   PRINT DETAIL LINE MODULE
                                     150 *
                             00156   151 PRDETAIL EQU        *
000156 F911 C66D C6D2 0066F 006D4    152 IFEOP        CP     LINECNT,=P'50'              IF LINE COUNT => 50
00015C 4740 C162       00164         153              BL     ENDIFEOP                      *
000160 45B0 C184             00186   154 THENEOP      BAL    11,HEADING                    THEN PRINT HEADING
                             00164   155 ENDIFEOP EQU        *                           ENDIF
                                     156              PUT    PRINTER,PRLINE              PRINT DETAIL LINE
000174 FA10 C66D C6D5 0066F 006D7    162              AP     LINECNT,=P'1'               ADD 1 TO LINE COUNT
00017A 9240 C343       00345         163              MVI    PRLINE,C' '                 CLEAR PRINT LINE
00017E D283 C344 C343 00346 00345    164              MVC    PRLINE+1(132),PRLINE        *
000184 07FA                          165              BR     10                          RETURN
                                     166 ***********************************************************************
                                     167 *                   THIRD LEVEL HEADING MODULE
                                     168 ***********************************************************************
                                     169 HEADING      PUT    PRINTER,HEAD1               PRINT FIRST HEADING LINE
                                     175              PUT    PRINTER,HEAD2               PRINT SECOND HEADING LINE
0001A6 F810 C66D C6D4 0066F 006D6    181              ZAP    LINECNT,=P'0'               SET LINE COUNT TO ZERO
0001AC 92F0 C343       00345         182              MVI    PRLINE,C'0'                 SET LINE TO DOUBLE SPACE
0001B0 07FB                          183              BR     11                          RETURN
                                     184 *********************************************************************DOS
                                     185 *                   FILE DEFINITIONS AND I/O AREAS                  DOS
                                     186 *********************************************************************DOS
                                     187 INFILE   DTFCD BLKSIZE=80,IOAREA1=INAREA,DEVICE=2540,                DOSX
                                                        DEVADDR=SYSIPT,EOFADDR=THENEOF,WORKA=YES             DOS
                                     208 *                                                                   DOS
                                     209 PRINTER  DTFPR BLKSIZE=133,IOAREA1=PRTAREA,DEVICE=1403,              DOSX
                                                        CTLCHR=ASA,DEVADDR=SYS009,WORKA=YES                  DOS
                                     230 *                                                                   DOS
000220                               231 INAREA       DS     CL80                                            DOS
000270                               232 PRTAREA      DS     CL133                                           DOS
                                     233 *********************************************************************OS
                                     234 *                   DEVICE CONTROL BLOCKS AND SAVE AREA              OS
                                     235 *********************************************************************OS
                                     236 *INFILE      DCB    DDNAME=INFILE,BLKSIZE=80,LRECL=80,               OSX
                                     237 *                   MACRF=PM,DSORG=PS,EODAD=THENEOF                  OS
                                     238 *                                                                    OS
                                     239 *PRINTER DCB        DDNAME=PRINTER,BLKSIZE=133,LRECL=133,            OSX
                                     240 *                   MACRF=PMA,DSORG=PS                               OS
                                     241 *                                                                    OS
                                     242 *SAVE        DS     18F                                              OS
```

Figure 5–17 *(Continued)*

```
  LOC  OBJECT CODE    ADDR1 ADDR2  STMT   SOURCE STATEMENT                                     DOS/VSE ASSEMBLER 14.56 86-03-27

                                    244 ***********************************************************************
                                    245 *                DATA DEFINITIONS
                                    246 ***********************************************************************
0002F5                              247 INRECD   DS    0CL80
0002F5                              248          DS    CL9
0002FE                              249 INNAME   DS    CL20
000312                              250          DS    CL13
00031F                              251 INDEPT   DS    CL4
000323                              252          DS    CL7
00032A                              253 INJOBCD  DS    CL4
00032E                              254 INPAYTYP DS    CL1
00032F                              255 INRATE   DS    CL8
000337                              256          DS    CL14
                                    257 *
000345                              258 PRLINE   DS    0CL133
000345                              259          DS    CL11
000350                              260 PRNAME   DS    CL20
000364                              261          DS    CL10
00036E                              262 PRJOBCD  DS    CL4
000372                              263          DS    CL10
00037C                              264 PRRATE   DS    CL7
000383                              265          DS    CL71
                                    266 *
0003CA                              267 HEAD1    DS    0CL133
0003CA F140404040404040             268          DC    CL20'1'
0003DE C8D6E4D9D3E840C5             269          DC    CL113'HOURLY EMPLOYEES IN DEPARTMENT 5337'
                                    270 *
00044F                              271 HEAD2    DS    0CL133
00044F F040404040404040             272          DC    CL19'0'
000462 D5C1D4C540404040             273          DC    CL20'NAME'
000476 D1D6C240C3D6C4C5             274          DC    CL14'JOB CODE'
000484 C8D6E4D9D3E840D9             275          DC    CL80'HOURLY RATE'
                                    276 *
0004D4                              277 TOTLINE1 DS    0CL133
0004D4 F040404040404040             278          DC    CL16'0'
0004E4                              279 PRTOTEMP DS    CL4
0004E8 40C5D4D7D3D6E8C5             280          DC    CL21' EMPLOYEES'
0004FD E3D6E3C1D3404040             281          DC    CL11'TOTAL'
000508                              282 PRTOTPAY DS    CL10
000512 4040404040404040             283          DC    CL71' '
                                    284 *
000559                              285 TOTLINE2 DS    0CL133
000559 F040404040404040             286          DC    CL41'0'
000582 C1E5C5D9C1C7C540             287          DC    CL14'AVERAGE RATE'
000590                              288 PRAVGPAY DS    CL7
000597 4040404040404040             289          DC    CL71' '
                                    290 *
0005DE                              291 TOTLINE3 DS    0CL133
0005DE 4040404040404040             292          DC    CL35' '
000601 C1E5C5D9C1C7C540             293          DC    CL20'AVERAGE WEEKLY PAY'
000615                              294 PRWKPAY  DS    CL7
00061C 4040404040404040             295          DC    CL71' '
                                    296 *
000663                              297 PKRATE   DS    PL3
000666                              298 PKTOTPAY DS    PL4
00066A                              299 PKTOTEMP DS    PL2
00066C                              300 PKAVGPAY DS    PL3
00066F                              301 LINECNT  DS    PL2
000678                              302 DBL      DS    D
000680                              303 EOFFLAG  DS    CL1
                                    304 *
000681 402020214B2020               305 PATRN    DC    XL7'402020214B2020'
000688 40202120                     306 PATRN2   DC    XL4'40202120'
00068C 4020206B2020214B             307 PATRN3   DC    XL10'4020206B2020214B2020'
                                    308 *
                           00000    309          END   MAINLINE
000698 5B5BC2D6D7C5D540             310                =C'$$BOPEN '
0006A0 5B5BC2C3D3D6E2C5             311                =C'$$BCLOSE'
0006A8 F5F3F3F7                     312                =C'5337'
0006AC 000001F0                     313                =A(PRINTER)
0006B0 000004D4                     314                =A(TOTLINE1)
0006B4 00000559                     315                =A(TOTLINE2)
0006B8 000005DE                     316                =A(TOTLINE3)
0006BC 000001B8                     317                =A(INFILE)
0006C0 000002F5                     318                =A(INRECD)
0006C4 00000345                     319                =A(PRLINE)
0006C8 000003CA                     320                =A(HEAD1)
0006CC 0000044F                     321                =A(HEAD2)
0006D0 040C                         322                =P'40'
0006D2 051C                         323                =P'51'
0006D4 050C                         324                =P'50'
0006D6 0C                           325                =P'0'
0006D7 1C                           326                =P'1'
```

Figure 5–17 *(Concluded)*

We now must review our use of a link register. We may use the same register with several different BAL instructions, so long as we have returned from one module before we branch and link to the next one. But if we have used register 9 (R9) to BAL to the first-level initialization module, then that module cannot use the same register to link to a second-level module without destroying the return address to the mainline. To avoid this problem, we shall use R9 as a link to first-level modules, and they in turn will use R10 for second-level modules and R11 for the third-level heading routine.

Figure 5–17 is the assembler output, and Figure 5–18 is the output from the program.

SUMMARY

Multiplication may be done on two valid packed decimal fields by means of the Multiply Packed (MP) instruction. The first operand may be up to 16 bytes long and the second up to 8 bytes. Both lengths must be given implicitly or explicitly.

The first operand, which will be replaced by the product, must contain one byte of leading zeros for each byte in length of the second operand. The sign of the product follows normal arithmetic rules, positive if the signs of both operands are alike, and negative if they are different.

To determine the maximum number of digits in the product, add the total digits in the two operands. The number of digits to the left of the decimal point in the product is equal to the sum of the number of digits to the left of the decimal points in the two operands. The number of digits to the right of the decimal point in the product is equal to the sum of the numbers of digits to the right of the decimal point in the two operands. Determining the number of digits in the product is called scaling.

```
               HOURLY EMPLOYEES IN DEPARTMENT 5337

              NAME                JOB CODE       HOURLY RATE

        CONNIE SHURR                3245              8.75
        NEIL DOWNE                  3245              8.58
        HAMMOND RYE                 3245              8.49
        CANDY KANE                  3245              8.42
        CLEMENT SEE                 3245              8.37

              5 EMPLOYEES           TOTAL            42.61

                                    AVERAGE RATE      8.52
                                AVERAGE WEEKLY PAY  340.80
```

Figure 5–18 Output from Program 5

Values may be rounded by adding 5 to the digit to the right of the last digit to be retained, then dropping the excess digits. If the digit to which the 5 was added is 5 or greater, the last digit retained will be rounded up by 1; otherwise, it will be unchanged.

To drop an even number of digits, use the Move Numeric instruction to move the sign next to the last digit to be retained. To drop an odd number of digits, use the Move with Offset instruction to move the digits to be retained next to a sign. The Move with Offset instruction shifts the bits in the field four bits to the left during the move, leaving the sign position unchanged.

The Shift and Round Packed (SRP) instruction can shift decimal digits to the right or left within a field. On right shifts, it may also round the last digit retained.

Division is performed by the Divide Packed (DP) instruction on two valid packed decimal fields. The quotient and remainder both replace the first operand field. The remainder occupies the rightmost bytes of the first operand and has the same length as the divisor. The rest of the field holds the quotient. The quotient and remainder have their own signs.

The quotient is positive if the signs of the two operands are alike and negative if they are different. The remainder has the sign of the dividend (first operand).

Rounding may be done as with multiplication. Care must be taken in rounding and dropping excess digits to limit the length of the operands, since both quotient and remainder are in the field occupied by the dividend.

A doubleword consists of eight bytes that begin on an address evenly divisible by 8. It can hold 15 decimal digits plus sign, and is a convenient work area for doing multiplication and division.

The ASA control character is placed in the first byte of the print line to control skipping and spacing by the printer. The printer I/O area and work areas must be enlarged by one byte to accommodate this character.

A standard module to read records is described that sets a flag when end of file is reached. The flag may be tested at other points in the program to control loops and selection structures.

A standard detail line module tests to see if a heading should be printed only when a detail line is ready for printing, thus avoiding headings sitting alone on a page at end of file.

The use of modules makes structured programming easier. The mainline module controls overall logic by branching and linking to first-level modules to perform major tasks in the program. First-level modules in turn branch and link to second-level modules to perform specific smaller tasks.

A module which executes other modules is called a control module. One which performs a specific task is called a processing module. Each module should have only one entry point and only one exit.

TERMS FOR REVIEW

ASA control character
Control module
Doubleword
Excess-64 notation
Initialization
Move Numeric
Move with Offset
Processing module
Rounding
Scaling

REVIEW QUESTIONS

1. What are the longest packed decimal fields that can be multiplied together? How many digits does each contain?
2. Where does the product appear in packed decimal multiplication? What condition must be met to ensure that the product will have enough room?
3. Explain operation of the Move Numeric instruction. How is it used to supply the sign to certain packed decimal numbers?
4. Explain operation of the Move with Offset instruction. How is it normally used in packed decimal multiplication and division?
5. Where does the quotient appear in packed decimal division? Where is the remainder?
6. How is the length of the remainder determined? The length of the quotient?
7. Explain the difference between a control module and a processing module. Which type usually is the mainline module?
8. Why is it helpful to use a different link register for modules of different levels? Why can modules of the same level normally use the same link register?
9. Explain the concept of single entry, single exit for modules. Why is this good practice?
10. What activities usually are done in the initialization module?
11. Which of the modules normally requires a DOWHILE loop?
12. What activities are carried out after reaching end of file?
13. What changes must be made in a source statement to use the ASA control character rather than the CNTRL macro to control spacing and skipping?
14. What is an advantage of testing whether to print a heading line before printing the detail line rather than after printing the detail line? Can you think of any disadvantages?
15. How can we ensure that the first detail line after each heading is double spaced, even though all other detail lines are single spaced?
16. What technique is used to cause total lines to be printed on the same page as the detail amounts to which they refer?
17. Explain what spacing or skipping is caused by each of the following ASA control characters:
    a. (b) Blank b. 0 (Zero) c. 1 (One) d. + (Plus) e. − (Minus)
18. What is the advantage of setting an end-of-file flag instead of branching directly to the end of the mainline loop when end of file is reached?

19. Why is it better to test if a heading should be printed before a detail line is printed instead of after?

EXERCISES

1. Suppose A is a packed decimal field that has two decimal places and B is a packed decimal integer. Write instructions to add the two values together. How many decimal places will the sum contain?
2. Assume that each 9 below represents any decimal digit. Show how many digits will be to the left and right of the decimal point in the product after each of the following multiplications:

999.9	99.99	999.99
* 9	* 9.9	* 99.999

3. Write instructions to multiply hours by rate and get wages rounded to two decimal places, if you have the following definitions:

```
HOURS  DC  PL3'43.75'
RATE   DC  PL3'14.25'
WAGES  DS  PL5
```

4. Write instructions to calculate the class average on a test, rounded to one decimal place, with the AP and MVN or MVO instructions. Use the following data:

```
TOTSCORE  DC  PL3'2379'
STUCOUNT  DC  PL2'31'
TESTAVG   DS  PL3
```

5. Write instructions to calculate 30 days' interest, rounded to the nearest cent. Use the SRP instruction. Use the following principal amount and annual interest rate:

```
PRIN      DC  PL4'5678.95'
RATE      DC  PL3'.1185'     (11.85%)
MONTHINT  DS  PL4
```

6. Assume the value 123.45738 is in DOUBLE in packed decimal form. Write instructions with MVN or MVO to round the value to:
   a. 1 decimal place
   b. 2 decimal places
   c. 3 decimal places
   d. 4 decimal places

   In each case, ZAP the result to ANSWER.
7. Write instructions including the SRP to divide the value 43287 by 124.5, getting a quotient with four decimal places, and then rounding the result to two places.
8. Write DC statements to define three heading lines of your own choosing. Use ASA control characters to cause the first header to skip to a new page, the second to double space before printing, and the third to single space before printing.

PROGRAMMING PROBLEMS

NOTE: For these and all subsequent programming problems, use the standard read and print modules described in this chapter. Also use the ASA control character to control spacing and skipping of all print lines.

1. Using Data Set 2 in Appendix D, prepare an Inventory Valuation Report showing item number, item description, quantity on hand, unit price, and item value. The item value is the quantity on hand multiplied by the unit price. Design your own headings. Print 50 detail lines per page.
2. Modify Problem 1 to add the quantities on hand and the item values. At the end of the report, print out these totals and the average value for each item. The average value is computed by dividing the total of the item values by the total of the quantities on hand. Carry the average to three decimal places and round it to two places for printing. Use the SRP instruction for rounding.
3. Using Data Set 3 in Appendix D, prepare a Sales Analysis Report. Show the salesperson name, year-to-date sales, year-to-date returns, and percentage of sales returned. This percentage is computed by dividing the YTD sales into the YTD returns. Carry the quotient to four decimal places and round it to three places for printing. Use the AP, MVO, and MVN instructions for rounding.
4. Modify Problem 3 to add the total of all YTD sales and YTD returns and compute the percentage of sales returned for all salespersons. Print the totals and average at the end of the report.

6 Computer Architecture

OBJECTIVES

After studying this chapter, you should be able to:

- Explain what general registers are and how they are used
- Explain base-displacement addressing and give reasons why it is used
- Name the parts of the Program Status Word and explain their use
- Use explicit register notation to represent storage addresses
- Be able to load multiple base registers for programs
- Name the six instruction formats and the content of each byte in each format
- Explain use of the condition code and prepare a mask to test each possible setting of the code
- Name the types of input/output channels and how each is used

Before we can go further in our study of assembler language, we must learn something of the internal structure of the central processing unit and the form of the machine instructions. In assembler language we actually program in machine language, but take advantage of features in the assembler that allow us to use names for fields instead of specific addresses and to use decimal numbers for many operations instead of binary or hexadecimal numbers.

GENERAL REGISTERS

As mentioned earlier, there are 16 general registers that may be used for addressing or for binary arithmetic operations. The registers, numbered from 0 through 15, can be referenced in four bits 0000 through 1111 (hex digits X'0' through X'F').

Each register contains four bytes, or 32 bits, called a *fullword*. The maximum value that can be contained in the register is X'FFFFFFFF', or decimal number 4,294,967,295. However, only the rightmost 24 bits are used for addressing. The maximum address is therefore X'FFFFFF', or decimal 16,777,215. This normally means that IBM mainframes are limited to 16,777,216 bytes of storage, since only locations numbered 0 through 16,777,215 can be addressed.

Any register except register 0 (R0) can be used for addressing. The operating system uses certain of the registers for standard macros. Registers 0, 1, 14, and 15 are used for most input/output macros, such as OPEN, CLOSE, GET, PUT, and CNTRL. R1 and R2 are used by the machine instructions Edit and Mark (EDMK) and Translate and Test (TRT). R13 is used to contain the address of a save area when the registers are saved in connection with use of subroutines. We should normally avoid using these registers except for temporary purposes between I/O operations or machine instructions that might affect them.

BASE-DISPLACEMENT ADDRESSING

Many early mainframe computers and some present-day microcomputers use the address of each operand in machine instructions. To do so with the System 360/370 family would require three bytes for the address of each operand (X'FFFFFF'), plus the operation code and any length codes. Base-displacement addressing permits use of fewer bytes to represent addresses and also makes address modification easier.

At the start of each program, a *base address* is loaded into a register designated as the *base register*. We have consistently used R12 for this purpose, but any other can do just as well. The assembler can determine the distance, or *displacement*, between the base address and any location within the program. The assembler creates machine instructions with four bits (X'0' through X'F') to refer to the base register and 12 bits (X'000' through X'FFF'; decimal 0 through 4095) to refer to the displacement. Any address can therefore be expressed in only 16 bits, or two bytes. The displacement must always be a positive value.

When the object program is run, the control unit of the CPU constructs the *effective address* by adding together the contents of the base register and the displacement given in the instruction. For some types of instructions, an *index register* may also be used, and its contents are added to the base register and the displacement to make up the effective address.

Suppose we are using base register 12, which contains a base address of X'048400'. The address X'C124' in base-displacement form would mean to add the contents of register 12 (X'C') to the displacement of X'124'. The effective address would be X'048524'.

We must load the base register in our program before we use any instructions that refer to storage locations. Failure to do so will result in *addressability errors*, since we have not yet properly established the base register. Normally the BALR 12,0 instruction is the first executable instruction in the program. Since the START 0 assembler directive has set the location counter to zero, we might tend to think that zero is the base address. However, the BALR instruction puts the address of the *next* instruction into the specified register. The BALR instruction is two bytes long, and so the base address the assembler uses is X'000002'. On our assembler listings we will be able to confirm that the displacement in each machine instruction will always be *two less* than the actual address of any location within our program, since the base address of X'000002' added to the displacement will produce the effective address.

The BALR instruction is a close relative of the BAL instruction that we have used to branch and link to a subroutine. However, the BALR instruction is only two bytes long, while the BAL instruction is four. The hardware of the machine in carrying out the instruction BALR 12,0 works in this way:

1. An address two bytes higher than the BALR instruction is loaded into R12. This is normally the address to which the program will return after branching to a subroutine.
2. The program branches to the address contained in the second register named, in this case R0. However, R0 can never be used in addressing, so that the program does not branch but proceeds to the next instruction.

The USING *,12 assembler directive informs the assembler that register 12 is the base register that will contain the present value in the location counter (address X'000002') in all our examples.

We know that our program cannot actually be loaded at location X'000000' and that X'000002' will not be the base address at execution time. The supervisor occupies the lowest part of main storage of the computer. The linkage editor relocates the object module so that it will be loaded somewhere above the supervisor. If the program is loaded at, say, X'008400', the base address will be X'008402'. When the displacement is added to this new base address, every address in the program will be relocated to its position in main storage. The *relative* address of each instruction and data field within the program space is unchanged, but the *absolute* addresses have been changed because the entire program has been relocated.

Program Status Word

How does the computer get the proper address of the next instruction for use with BALR or BAL instructions? The *Program Status Word (PSW)* is a 64-bit (doubleword) area in the CPU control unit hardware that contains data needed as the program is executed. The bits, numbered from left to right, are:

0–7	System Mask
8–11	Storage Protection Key
12–15	AWMP Bits
16–31	Interrupt Code
32–33	Instruction Length Code
34–35	Condition Code
36–39	Program Mask
40–63	Address of Next Instruction

Bits 40–63 of the PSW are updated every time an instruction is executed so that the control unit can fetch the next instruction, decode it, and execute it. The BALR or BAL instruction places bits 32–63 of the PSW in the register specified as the first operand. The leftmost eight bits in the register (32–39 of the PSW) are ignored, and the rightmost 24 bits give the address of the next instruction.

Normally, as soon as the length of the instruction has been determined, the address in the PSW is set forward that many bytes. Branching instructions cause the branch address to replace the address of the next instruction in sequence.

The PSW is also used to service interrupts and for other management of the operating system. Most operations involving the PSW can be executed only when the computer is in the *supervisor state*. Instructions that can be executed only in this state are called *privileged instructions* and are not covered in this text.

Explicit Register Addressing

We are not limited to the use of the program base register. We can designate a separate base register for individual instructions. To do so, we use *explicit register notation*. Instead of giving the name of a field, we give the displacement to be used, usually as a decimal number, and the base register number (in parentheses). Some types of instructions also have a length operand or an index register in the parentheses with the base register.

We might execute the following instructions:

```
LA   6,INRECD          Put address of INRECD in register 6
MVC  PRNAME,9(6)       Move name to print line
MVC  PRDEPT,42(6)      Move department to print line
```

The address of the second operand in the second instruction is equivalent to INRECD+9, since the address of INRECD in R6 and the displacement of 9 are added together to make the effective address. Similarly, the third instruction refers to the field at INRECD+42. No length operand is needed for the second operand of a MVC instruction.

In the following examples we need an explicit length in the first operand but not in the second. The form of the operand where the length is required is D(L,B), where D, L, and B stand for displacement, length, and base respectively. Where no length is needed, as in the second operand in MVC instructions or the first operand in MVI instructions, the form is D(B).

```
LA   6,INRECD
LA   7,PRLINE
MVC  10(20,7),9(6)
MVC  35(4,7),42(6)
```

The third instruction moves 20 bytes from INRECD+9 to PRLINE+10. The fourth instruction moves four bytes from INRECD+42 to PRLINE+35.

We will use explicit register notation extensively in Chapter 10.

Multiple Base Registers

At times we have a program that occupies more than 4096 bytes. We therefore need to establish more than one base register. Several techniques are possible. In each case, we load the first base register as usual and then load the proper address in the remaining registers.

The address in each successive register is normally 4096 (X'1000') higher than the address in the previous register. The assembler will choose the base register that requires the smallest displacement in constructing the address.

If we use registers 10, 11, and 12 as base registers for our program, and R10 contains X'000002', then R11 should have X'001002' and R12 should have X'002002'. However, we cannot just load these values, because then our program would not be relocatable.

One way to solve this problem is by defining a new type of constant. The address constant (type A) will create the address of any number or name in the form of a four-byte hex number, of which only the rightmost three bytes contain the value. Consider the instructions in Figure 6–1.

The USING statement indicates that registers 10, 11, and 12 will be used as base registers. The current value in the location counter (*) will be the address the assembler expects to find in R10. This is also the address of the instruction named BASE. R11 should contain an address 4096 higher than that, and R12 should contain an address 8192 higher than the one in R10.

The DC statement creates two constants with the values we need. The linkage editor will relocate the address constants by adding the address at which the program will be loaded for execution. Wherever in storage the program is placed and whatever address BASE turns out to be, the constants will contain the proper values for the other two base registers. The Load Multiple (LM) instruction permits loading more than one register with successive fullwords from storage. The first address is therefore placed in R11 and the second address in R12.

You may wonder why we don't place the constants at the end of the program along with other data definitions. Because of our long program, those constants would be more than 4096 bytes away from the address in R10, and there would be no way to reach them. They must be placed within the part of the program covered by R10 until R11 and R12 are loaded.

We may also load multiple base registers with the Load Address (LA) instruction. We have used this instruction as LA 5,50 to load R5 with a line count of 50. We may also use explicit base-displacement addressing to load other values into the first operand register. The format of the second operand is actually D(X,B), where D, X, and B stand for displacement, index register, and base register respectively. LA 5,50 is equivalent to LA 5,50(0,0). When both the base and index register are specified as 0, then the displacement of 50 is the entire address.

Consider the sequence of instructions in Figure 6–2. The first two instructions load R10 and indicate what should be in each of the base registers. The first LA instruction takes the value in R10, adds a displacement of 4095 (the maximum allowable displacement, X'FFF'), and stores the result in R11. The second LA instruction adds 1 to the address in R11 and places it back into R11, making it exactly 4096 more than R10. The last two LA instructions repeat the process for R12, using the contents of R11.

LA instructions may seem to require more storage than using address constants, but they don't. Furthermore, they simplify our structure by not having to skip over the constants imbedded in our procedural instructions.

The multiple base registers need not be consecutive, but they must be named in the USING statement in ascending order of their addresses. For example, the sequence of instructions in Figure 6–3 will properly load registers 12, 3, and 7 for use as base registers.

```
MAINLINE    BALR     10,0
            USING    *,10,11,12
BASE        LM       11,12,ADDR
            B        START
ADDR        DC       A(BASE+4096,BASE+8192)
START       (Instructions here proceed as usual)
```

Figure 6–1 Using address constants with multiple base registers

```
BALR     10,0
USING    *,10,11,12
LA       11,4095(10)
LA       11,1(11)
LA       12,4095(11)
LA       12,1(12)
```

Figure 6–2 Using LA instructions with multiple base registers

```
BALR     12,0
USING    *,12,3,7
LA       7,2048
LA       3,2048(7,12)
LA       7,2048(7,3)
```

Figure 6–3 Another use of LA instructions with multiple base registers

The instruction LA 7,2048 places the address 2048 in R7 to be used as an index register. LA 3,2048(7,12) adds a displacement of 2048 and another 2048 from R7 to the address in R12, and stores the effective address in R3. That address is now exactly 4096 more than the one in R12. The LA 7,2048(7,3) makes the address in R7 exactly 4096 more than the one in R3.

INSTRUCTION FORMATS

There are six different machine instruction formats used with the System 360/370 family computers:

RR	(Register to Register)	2 bytes long
RX	(Register to Indexed Storage)	4 bytes long
RS	(Register to Storage)	4 bytes long
SI	(Storage Immediate)	4 bytes long
SS	(Storage to Storage)	6 bytes long
S	(Storage and Implied Operand)	4 bytes long

All formats except S have a single byte as the op code. Type S instructions have two bytes as the op code and another two bytes containing an address (or other operands) in base-displacement form. Type S instructions are used almost entirely in the supervisor state and will not be covered in this text.

Figure 6–4 shows the machine format for each of the types of instructions. Note that each of the first five types has the first byte as the op code. The second byte may refer to two general registers, a general register and an index register, a general register and a mask, one immediate operand, one length code, or two length codes. The third and fourth bytes, where present, always refer to a storage location in base-displacement form, with the first four bits of the third byte giving the base register (X'0' through X'F') and the next 12 bits giving the displacement (X'000' through X'FFF'). The fifth and sixth bytes, used only with SS format, always contain a storage address in base-displacement form.

RR Instructions

Type RR instructions transfer data or perform arithmetic operations between two registers. The first byte contains the op code, and the second byte contains the two register operands, each in a four-bit code. The RR format in assembler language is OP R1,R2. The operands appear in the same order as they do in the machine instructions in Figure 6–4.

In the examples in Figure 6–5, a space is left between bytes in the object code for clarity.

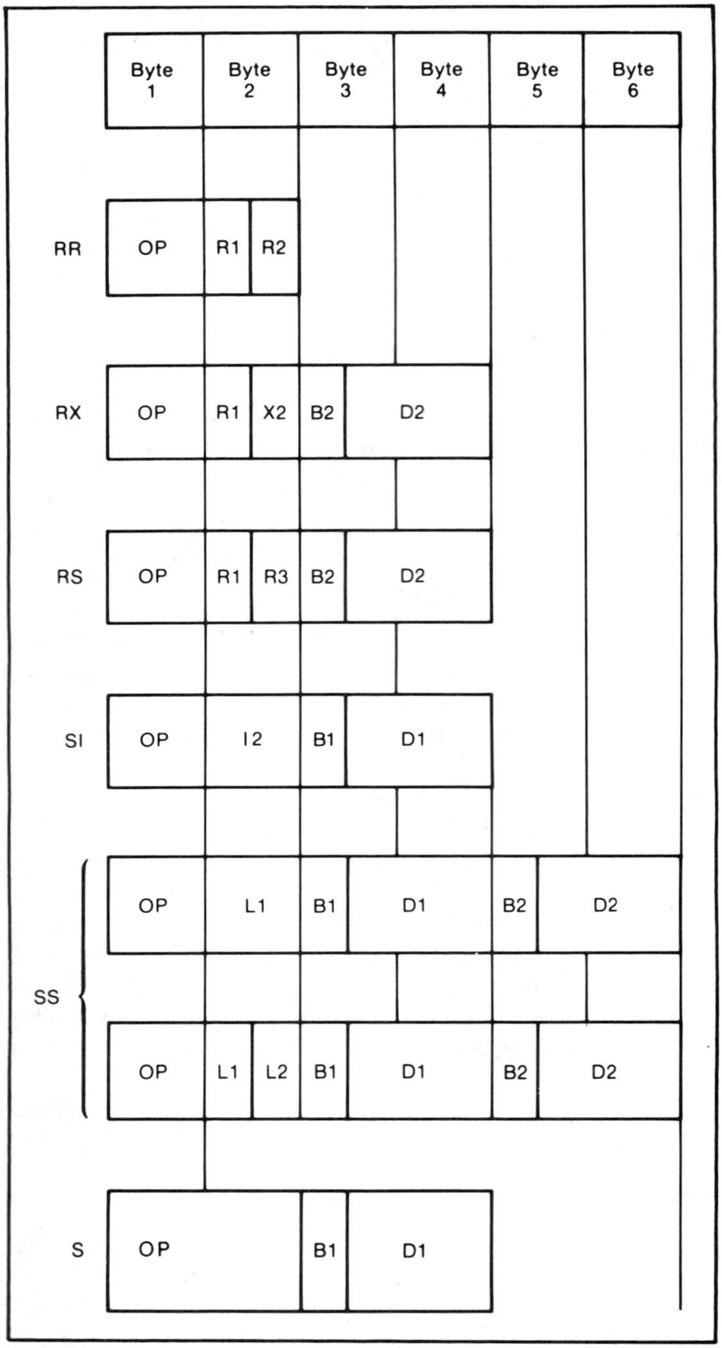

Figure 6–4 Formats for machine instructions. Legend: OP, operation code; R, general register; X, index register; B, base register; D, displacement; I, immediate data; L, length operand; 1, first operand; 2, second operand; 3, third operand.

OBJECT CODE	INSTRUCTION	REMARKS
05 C0	BALR 12,0	Load R12 as base register
1A 47	AR 4,7	Add contents of R7 to R4
19 B6	CR 11,6	Compare R11 with R6
18 98	LR 9,8	Load R8 into R9

Figure 6–5 Examples of RR-type instructions

OBJECT CODE	INSTRUCTION	FORMAT
58 80 C2 62	L 8,FULLWORD	OP R1,S2
58 80 C2 66	L 8,FULLWORD+4	OP R1,S2
5A 87 C2 62	A 8,FULLWORD(7)	OP R1,S2(X2)
59 80 C0 04	C 8,4(0,12)	OP R1,D2(X2,B2)

Figure 6–6 Examples of RX-type instructions

RX Instructions

The first operand in RX instructions is a general register. The second operand is a storage location in base-displacement form that may be indexed by an index register. The contents of the index register, if used, are added to the base register and the displacement to form the effective address of the second operand. As usual, the first byte of the machine instruction is the op code. The first operand register and the index register share the second byte, and the base-displacement of the second operand are in bytes 3 and 4.

Assembler language RX instructions may be written in any of the forms shown in Figure 6–6, where S2 refers to the name of a field in storage including relative addressing, and D2, X2, and B2 refer to displacement, index register, and base register of the second operand respectively. Notice in Figure 6–6 that the sequence of the operands in object code is different from those in assembler language.

If either the base or index register is omitted, it is assumed by the assembler to be 0. As we have seen, the statement LA 5,50 is equivalent to LA 5,50(0,0). If the index register is omitted, a comma must precede the base register within the parentheses to show the proper place. For example, LA 8,8(,12) is equivalent to LA 8,8(0,12), and LA 8,8(12) is equivalent to LA 8,8(12,0). If only one register is used in addressing, it makes no difference whether we consider it a base or an index register; the result is the same. The contents of that register added to the displacement form the effective address.

Branching instructions also use RX format, but the first four bits of the second byte are designated M1 for mask instead of R1 for register. The mask is used to test the condition code in conditional branching. We will consider this usage later in this chapter.

RS Instructions

Instructions in this group refer to two general registers and one storage address. The index register is not used. The two general registers occupy the second byte of the machine instruction, while the third and fourth bytes contain the storage address in base-displacement form.

The most commonly used RS instructions are Load Multiple (LM) and Store Multiple (STM). These instructions permit a sequence of fullwords in main storage to be loaded into a group of consecutively numbered registers. R1 indicates the first register and R3 the last register to be loaded or stored.

Allowable formats for RS instructions are shown in Figure 6–7. The third example shows *wraparound* use of the registers. Whenever R1 is higher than R3, the operation stores registers 14 and 15 and then continues with registers 0 through 2.

SI Instructions

We have used SI instructions rather extensively without knowing precisely how they were formatted. The op code as usual is in the first byte, the immediate operand (I2) is in the second byte, and the third and fourth bytes contain the storage address of the first operand in base-displacement form.

Allowable formats for SI instructions are shown in Figure 6–8. In the last example above, we used the decimal number 64 as the immediate operand. This is equivalent to X'40', which in turn is equivalent to the character blank (C' '). We may use decimal or hexadecimal numbers interchangeably in any of the operands for any instructions, so long as we identify the hex numbers with an X and put quotes around the hex value.

OBJECT CODE	INSTRUCTION	FORMAT
98 68 C4 40	LM 6,8,TABLE	OP R1,R3,S2
98 9A C4 48	LM 9,10,TABLE+8	OP R1,R3,S2
90 E2 C0 08	STM 14,2,8(12)	OP R1,R3,D2(B2)

Figure 6–7 Examples of RS-type instructions

OBJECT CODE	INSTRUCTION	FORMAT
95 F0 C1 24	CLI PRLINE,C'0'	OP S1,I2
92 60 C1 2B	MVI PRLINE+7,X'60'	OP S1,I2
92 6B 80 0C	MVI 12(8),X'6B'	OP D1(B1),I2
95 40 C1 24	CLI PRLINE,64	OP S1,I2

Figure 6–8 Examples of SI-type instructions

SS Instructions

Storage to Storage instructions all require six bytes. The first is the op code, the second contains one or two length codes, the third and fourth bytes contain the address of the first operand, and the fifth and sixth bytes contain the address of the second operand. As always, addresses are in base-displacement form.

Generally, SS instructions working with characters require only one length code, while those involving packed decimal operations require two. There are a few exceptions to this rule that will be discussed as they occur in the text.

Where only one length code is needed, it can use all eight bits and range from X'00' through X'FF' (0 through 255). Where two length codes are needed, only four bits are available for each, and the length of each operand is limited to X'0' through X'F' (0 through 15).

Since a length of zero has no meaning, the actual length of the operand is *one more* than the length code. In other words, a length code of X'FF', or 255, in a MVC instruction would actually cause 256 bytes to be moved. The length code of each operand in packed decimal instructions is limited to X'F', or 15, meaning an actual length of 16 bytes, or 31 decimal digits plus sign.

Recall from Chapter 3 that lengths do not need to be given explicitly when a name is used in procedural instructions. The length should, however, be given explicitly whenever relative addressing is used with type SS instructions. The assembler will use the implicit length given in the DS or DC statement that defined the field if no explicit length is stated. However, if the base and displacement are given explicitly for an operand, then its length must also be given explicitly. In showing the format of SS instructions in Figure 6–9, L1 indicates the length of the first operand and L2 that of the second. (Assume INNAME is 20 bytes long and PKAMT is four bytes long.)

S Instructions

Type S instructions are the only instructions that have two bytes as the op code. The third and fourth bytes contain an address (or other operands) in base-displacement form. Type S instructions are used almost entirely in the supervisor state and will not be covered in this text.

Instruction Length Codes

Op codes are assigned to machine instructions so that the first two bits always indicate the length of the instruction. The codes are summarized in Figure 6–10.

In fetching and decoding the machine instruction, the control unit can determine the number of bytes to access by referring to the first two bits of the op code. The address of the next instruction in the Program Status Word can then be increased by that same amount.

OBJECT CODE	INSTRUCTION	FORMAT
D2 13 C3 48 C2 E6	MVC PRNAME,INNAME	OP S1,S2
D2 13 C3 48 C2 E6	MVC PRLINE+9(20),INNAME	OP S1(L1),S2
F8 33 C2 27 C2 66	ZAP PKAMT,DOUBLE+2(4)	OP S1,S2(L2)
FA 32 C2 27 80 18	AP PKAMT,24(3,8)	OP S1,D2(L2,B2)
FB 42 60 04 40 1C	SP* 4(5,6),28(3,4)	OP D1(L1,B1),D2(L2,B2)

Figure 6–9 Examples of SS-type instructions

INSTRUCTION TYPE	LENGTH	FIRST TWO BITS	RANGE OF OP CODES
RR	2	00	00–3F
RX	4	01	40–7F
RX, SI, S	4	10	80–BF
SS	6	11	C0–FF

Figure 6–10 Instruction length codes

CONDITION CODE AND BRANCHING

We have seen previously that the condition code is set by Compare instructions and certain arithmetic operations. In Compare instructions, the code is based on whether the first operand is equal to, less than, or greater than the second operand. In arithmetic instructions, the code is based on whether the result is equal to, less than, or greater than zero. Overflow means that the result of an arithmetic operation is too large to fit into the space provided for it. In some computers, the bits representing different conditions are called *flags*.

Conditional branch instructions refer to the condition code, and branch or do not branch according to the type of test that is made. Let us see just how this works in the computer hardware.

The condition code is represented in two bits (bits 34 and 35) of the Program Status Word. For most instructions, the condition code has the meanings shown in Figure 6–11.

For certain instructions the same condition codes are used, but they have different meanings. These special cases will be discussed as we encounter the exceptions.

We test the condition code through use of a binary *mask*. A mask may be thought of as a four-bit screening device in which a 0 blocks out the corresponding bit position and a 1 allows it to pass. The four bits have place values of 8, 4, 2, and 1. We first arrange the various settings of the condition code in four columns and think of each possible setting as a binary number in which one and only one bit could be set at any one time. In our examples in Figure 6–12, we shall refer to A and B as the first and second operands being compared and R as the result to be compared with 0.

BINARY CODE	DECIMAL VALUE	MEANING
00	0	Both operands equal or result zero
01	1	First operand low or result negative
10	2	First operand high or result positive
11	3	Result overflows available space

Figure 6–11 Condition code meanings

CONDITIONS	EQUAL OR ZERO	LOW OR NEGATIVE	HIGH OR POSITIVE	OVERFLOW
Condition Code	0	1	2	3
Mask Bit Values	8	4	2	1
Settings:				
A=B or R=0	1	0	0	0
A<B or R<0	0	1	0	0
A>B or R>0	0	0	1	0
Overflow	0	0	0	1

Figure 6–12 Mask bit values for condition codes

Condition Code	1000	0100	0010	0001	1000	0100	0010	0001	1000
Condition Tested	A=B	A>B	A>B	0F	A=>B	A<>B	R>0	A<B	R>0
Mask	1000	0010	0010	0001	1010	0110	0001	0100	0010
Tested Bit	1xxx	xx0x	xx1x	xxx1	1x0x	x10x	xxx0	x0xx	xx0x
Condition True?	Yes	No	Yes	Yes	Yes	Yes	No	No	No

Figure 6–13 Testing the condition code

The mask allows us to test whether certain of these bits are 0 or 1. Wherever we place a 1 in the mask, we can test that setting of the condition code. Wherever we place a 0 in the mask, that setting is ignored. If the tested bit is a 1, the condition is true and the branch is made. If the tested bit is a 0, the condition is false and the program continues with the next instruction in sequence.

Consider the examples of testing various settings of the condition code in Figure 6–13. We do not actually have a different machine instruction for each of the conditional branches. The Branch on Condition (BC) instruction with the appropriate mask tests all conditions.

In the BC machine instruction, the mask occupies the first four bits of the second byte. This is the position normally occupied by R1 in an RX instruction.

Assembler language provides a set of *extended mnemonics* that we have used thus far in the text. The assembler converts each of the extended mnemonics, such as BE, BNE, BH, or BNL, into an op code and a mask in the object code.

We may explicitly use the Branch on Condition (BC) op code with a mask, which is normally given as a decimal number. The examples in Figure 6–14 all presume that the address of ENDIF is given by base register 12 (X'C') and displacement 256 (X'100'). The object code will be identical whether we use the extended mnemonics or the mask. In the format for these examples, M1 refers to the mask as the first operand.

Notice in the third example from the last how we make an unconditional branch by using a mask of 1111 (X'F' or decimal 15). This mask tests all four possible settings of the condition code and will always find one bit to cause a branch.

On the other hand, a mask of 0000 (X'0' or decimal 0) will never branch, and is therefore often called a No-Op (NOP), meaning No Operation. The NOP is useful in a few situations that will be discussed later in the text. Most assemblers require an operand for a NOP, even though it will never branch. Usually 0 is used as the operand.

It seems obvious that the extended mnemonics are easier to use and to understand than using the mask. This section is intended mainly to provide full understanding of the object code you must often examine in assembler language.

Programming Tips

- Use the LA instruction in format R1,D2(X2,B2) to add together the contents of two registers and a displacement in a single instruction.
- Review the object code of each assembler source listing to review the different instruction lengths, register operands, length codes, immediate bytes, condition code masks, and base-displacement forms of addresses.

INPUT/OUTPUT CHANNELS

Internal operations on any computer are much faster than input/output operations. Without some method of doing internal processing while I/O operations take place, the central processing unit would be sitting idle about 95 percent of the time. The ability to perform operations simultaneously is called *overlap*.

I/O channels are special-purpose computers that carry out the I/O operations under direction of the control unit. There are four major I/O instructions

OBJECT CODE	EXTENDED MNEMONIC	BC WITH MASK	FORMAT
47 80 C1 00	BE ENDIF	BC 8,ENDIF	OP M1,S2
47 70 C1 00	BNE ENDIF	BC 7,ENDIF	OP M1,S2
47 40 C1 00	BL 256(0,12)	BC 4,256(0,12)	OP M1,D2(X2,B2)
47 BC 01 00	BNL 256(12)	BC 11,256(12)	OP M1,D2(X2,B2)
47 20 C1 00	BP ENDIF	BC 2,ENDIF	OP M1,S2
47 D0 C1 00	BNP ENDIF	BC 13,ENDIF	OP M1,S2
47 10 C1 00	BO ENDIF	BC 1,ENDIF	OP M1,S2
47 EC 01 00	BNO 256(12)	BC 14,256(12)	OP M1,D2(X2,B2)
47 F0 C1 00	B ENDIF	BC 15,ENDIF	OP M1,S2
47 00 C1 00	NOP ENDIF	BC 0,ENDIF	OP M1,S2
47 00 00 00	NOP 0	BC 0,0(0)	OP M1,D2(X2,B2)

Figure 6–14 Extended mnemonics compared with mask bits

issued by the supervisor to the control unit: Start I/O, Halt I/O, TEST I/O, and Test Channel. All are type S privileged instructions not normally available to the application programmer.

The channel then carries out its program, which consists of *channel commands*, independently of the CPU. Meanwhile, the supervisor can transfer control to other programs in main storage. When the I/O operation is completed, the channel notifies the supervisor through the control unit, so that the program can continue.

There are two principal types of channels. The *byte-multiplexor* channel is normally used with relatively slow devices such as terminals, card readers, and printers. It has several subchannels that may be active concurrently. Thus messages to or from several devices may move along the channel at the same time. This method of operation is called *multiplex mode.*

The *block-multiplexor* channel is used with high-speed devices such as magnetic tapes and disks. It also has several subchannels to allow more than one channel program to be active at the same time. Usually blocks of data are transmitted rather than individual bytes at one time. This method of operation is called *burst mode*. Earlier IBM 360 and 370 computers had *selector* channels, similar to block-multiplexor channels but able to execute only one channel program at a time.

Channel programs are made up of one or more Channel Command Words (CCW). The CCW is a doubleword with bits assigned as shown in Figure 6–15.

The command code specifies such operations as Read, Write, Control, Sense, Read Backwards, or Transfer in Channel (Loop). The data address is that of the I/O area in main storage. The byte count is the number of bytes to be transmitted. The flags may be used for *chaining* data or commands. Data chaining permits one CCW to continue reading, for example, data from the same record into a different location in main storage from the location where the previous CCW was reading. Command chaining indicates that another CCW follows the present one.

BITS	USAGE
0–7	Command code
8–31	Data address
32–38	Flags
39	Zero
40–47	Ignored
48–63	Byte count

Figure 6–15 CCW format

COLUMNS	FIELD NAMES	PRINT POSITIONS
10–29	Employee name	11–30
58	Pay type	41
59–66	Pay rate 999999V99	45–57 bZ,ZZZ,ZZZ.99
	Annual pay	63–75 bZ,ZZZ,ZZZ.99
	Total employees	16–21 bZZZZZ
	Totals of annual pay	61–75 bZZZ,ZZZ,ZZZ.99

Figure 6–16 Input and output formats for Program 6

We can examine CCWs by using a PRINT GEN assembler directive preceding any DTF statement. One or more CCWs will appear near the end of the generated statements.

PROGRAM 6: ANNUAL TOTALS BY PAY TYPE

Our next program reads the employee records previously described; for each employee it prints name, pay type, pay rate, and annual pay. Fields needed in the employee record are shown in Figure 6–16, along with print positions and format for output.

Annual pay is the annual rate, the weekly rate times 52, or the hourly rate times 2080. We are to determine the total annual pay and number of employees in each type (A, W, and H) and the total annual pay and number of employees in the entire organization.

We have continued use of modular structure. Figure 6–17 shows the structure chart. We will omit pseudocode here, since the assembler listing in Figure 6–18 shows the program logic. The program is shown in Figure 6–19.

We have used explicit base-displacement addressing for our input records purely for illustrative purposes. We use R2 as a base register for IN-

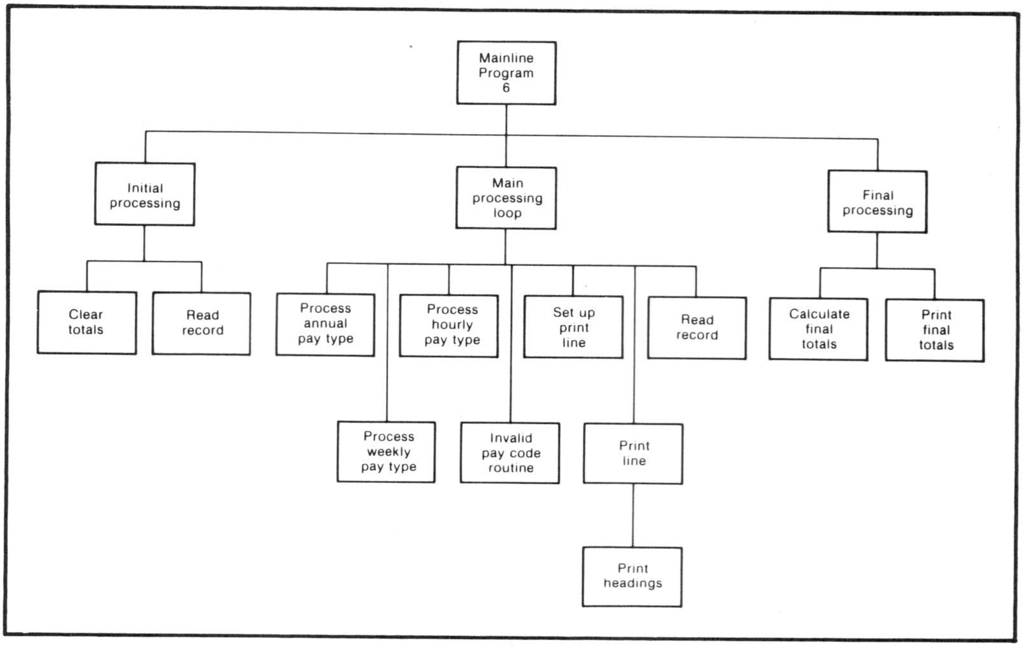

Figure 6–17 Structure chart for Program 6

RECD. The address is loaded immediately after the priming read in the initialization module. The displacement to the start of each field in that record is one less than the column number. Since we do not refer to INNAME, INPAYTYP, and INRATE by name, we do not divide INRECD into fields in the data definitions.

We have also used Branch on Condition instructions with a mask instead of extended mnemonics in several instances.

Look particularly at the object code on the assembler listing to identify the op code, type of each instruction, contents of the second byte, and the base-displacement form of the address in bytes 3 and 4 and in bytes 5 and 6. Note that in each instance the base register is 12 (X'C') and the displacement is two less than the address given under ADDR1 or ADDR2.

Also notice the second byte of each branch instruction. Identify the mask that tests the condition code for each conditional and unconditional branch.

SUMMARY

There are 16 general registers in the System 360/370 family of computers that are used for addressing and for binary arithmetic. Each register contains a 32-bit fullword. Addresses are limited to the rightmost 24 bits; the leftmost eight bits are ignored.

Addresses in machine instructions occupy two bytes (16 bits). The first four bits refer to a general register holding a base address. The next 12 bits

```
  LOC  OBJECT CODE    ADDR1 ADDR2  STMT   SOURCE STATEMENT                                   DOS/VSE ASSEMBLER 14.59 86-03-27

                                      1 ************************************************************************
                                      2 *                  ALTON R. KINDRED, PROGRAM 6
                                      3 * THIS PROGRAM READS THE EMPLOYEE FILE AND PRINTS EACH NAME, PAY TYPE,
                                      4 * PAY RATE, AND ANNUAL PAY.  THE ANNUAL PAY IS THE WEEKLY RATE TIMES
                                      5 * 52 OR THE HOURLY RATE TIMES 2080.  THE ANNUAL PAY FOR EACH PAY TYPE
                                      6 * IS ACCUMULATED AND PRINTED OUT AT END OF FILE ALONG WITH THE NUMBER
                                      7 * OF EMPLOYEES AND TOTAL ANNUAL PAYROLL.
                                      8 *         REGISTERS USED:
                                      9 *                  R2     - BASE FOR INPUT RECORD (INRECD)
                                     10 *                  R9-11  - LINKS TO MODULES
                                     11 *                  R12    - BASE REGISTER
                                     12 ************************************************************************
                                     13          PRINT NOGEN
000000                               14 MAINLINE START 0                         SET LOCATION COUNTER
                                     15 *        STM   14,12,12(13)               SAVE REGISTERS FOR OS          OS
000000 05C0                          16          BALR  12,0                       LOAD BASE REGISTER
                           00002     17          USING *,12                       DESIGNATE BASE REGISTER
                                     18 *        ST    13,SAVE+4                  STORE REGISTER 13              OS
                                     19 *        LA    13,SAVE                    LOAD SAVE AREA ADDRESS         OS
                                     20 *        OPEN  (INFILE,(INPUT),PRINTER,(OUTPUT))                         OS
                                     21          OPEN  INFILE,PRINTER             OPEN FILES                     DOS
000016 4590 C036           00038     30          BAL   9,INITIAL                  DO INITIAL PROCESSING
00001A 4590 C040           00042     31          BAL   9,MAINLOOP                 DO MAIN PROCESSING LOOP
00001E 4590 C092           00094     32          BAL   9,FINAL                    DO FINAL PROCESSING
                                     33          CLOSE INFILE,PRINTER             CLOSE FILES                    DOS
                                     42          EOJ                              END PROGRAM                    DOS
                                     45 *        CLOSE (INFILE,,PRINTER)          CLOSE FILES                    OS
                                     46 *        L     13,SAVE+4                  LOAD SAVE AREA ADDRESS         OS
                                     47 *        LM    14,12,12(13)               RESTORE REGISTERS              OS
                                     48 *        BR    14                         RETURN TO OS                   OS
                                     49 ************************************************************************
                                     50 *                  FIRST LEVEL MODULES
                                     51 ************************************************************************
                                     52 *
                                     53 *                  INITIALIZATION MODULE
                                     54 *
000038 45A0 C09C           0009E     55 INITIAL  BAL   10,CLEARSET                SET INITIAL VALUES
00003C 45A0 C0D8           000DA     56          BAL   10,READRECD                READ FIRST RECORD
000040 07F9                          57          BR    9                          RETURN
                                     58 *
                                     59 *                  MAIN PROCESSING LOOP
                                     60 *
                           00042     61 MAINLOOP EQU   *
000042 95E8 C73E     00740           62 DOWHILE  CLI   EOFFLAG,C'Y'               DOWHILE NOT END OF FILE
000046 4780 C090     00092           63          BE    ENDDO                        *
00004A 92D5 C73F     00741           64          MVI   INVALSW,C'N'                 SET INVALID SWITCH OFF
00004E 95C1 2039     00039           65 IF       CLI   57(2),C'A'                   IF ANNUAL PAY TYPE
000052 4770 C05C           0005E     66          BC    7,ELSE                         *
000056 45A0 C0F6           000F8     67 THEN     BAL   10,ANNUAL                      THEN DO ANNUAL SALARY
00005A 47F0 C080           00082     68          BC    15,ENDIF                       *
                           0005E     69 ELSE     EQU   *                            ELSE
00005E 95E6 2039     00039           70 IF2      CLI   57(2),C'W'                     IF WEEKLY PAY TYPE
000062 4770 C06C           0006E     71          BC    7,ELSE2                          *
000066 45A0 C110           00112     72 THEN2    BAL   10,WEEKLY                        THEN DO WEEKLY SALARY
00006A 47F0 C080           00082     73          BC    15,ENDIF2                        *
                           0006F     74 ELSE2    EQU   *                              ELSE
00006E 95C8 2039     00039           75 IF3      CLI   57(2),C'H'                       IF HOURLY PAY TYPE
000072 4770 C07C     0007E           76          BNE   ELSE3                              *
000076 45A0 C136           00138     77 THEN3    BAL   10,HOURLY                          THEN DO HOURLY SALARY
00007A 47F0 C080     00082           78          B     ENDIF3                             *
                           0007E     79 ELSE3    EQU   *                                ELSE
00007E 45A0 C15C           0015E     80          BAL   10,INVALID                         SET UP ERROR MESSAGE
                           00082     81 ENDIF3   EQU   *                                ENDIF
                           00082     82 ENDIF2   EQU   *                              ENDIF
                           00082     83 ENDIF    EQU   *                            ENDIF
000082 45A0 C168           0016A     84          BAL   10,SETUP                     SET UP PRINT LINE
000086 45A0 C1A0           001A2     85          BAL   10,PRDETAIL                  PRINT LINE
00008A 45A0 C0D8           000DA     86          BAL   10,READRECD                  READ NEXT RECORD
00008E 47F0 C040     00042           87          B     DOWHILE                      *
                           00092     88 ENDDO    EQU   *                          ENDDO
000092 07F9                          89          BR    9                          RETURN
                                     90 *
                                     91 *                  FINAL PROCESSING MODULE
                                     92 *
000094 45A0 C1D2           001D4     93 FINAL    BAL   10,FINALTOT                ACCUMULATE FINAL TOTALS
000098 45A0 C1F8           001FA     94          BAL   10,PRTOTAL                 PRINT TOTAL LINES
00009C 07F9                          95          BR    9                          RETURN
                                     96 ************************************************************************
                                     97 *                  SECOND LEVEL MODULES
                                     98 ************************************************************************
                                     99 *
                                    100 *                  CLEAR TOTALS AND SET INITIAL VALUES MODULE
                                    101 *
00009E F820 C726 C7AC 00728 007AE   102 CLEARSET ZAP   PKTOTEMP,=P'0'             CLEAR TOTALS
0000A4 F820 C70E C7AC 00710 007AE   103          ZAP   PKTOTA,=P'0'               *
0000AA F820 C711 C7AC 00713 007AE   104          ZAP   PKTOTH,=P'0'               *
0000B0 F820 C714 C7AC 00716 007AE   105          ZAP   PKTOTW,=P'0'               *
0000B6 F850 C729 C7AC 0072B 007AE   106          ZAP   PKTOTPAY,=P'0'             *
0000BC F840 C717 C7AC 00719 007AE   107          ZAP   PKTPA,=P'0'
0000C2 F840 C71C C7AC 0071E 007AE   108          ZAP   PKTPH,=P'0'                *
0000C8 F840 C721 C7AC 00723 007AE   109          ZAP   PKTPW,=P'0'                *
0000CE 4120 C41B           0041D    110          LA    2,INRECD                   USE R2 AS BASE FOR INRECD
0000D2 F821 C72F C7A6 00731 007A8   111          ZAP   LINECNT,=P'51'             SET LINE COUNT > 50
0000D8 07FA                         112          BR    10                         RETURN
                                    113 *
                                    114 *                  READ RECORD MODULE
                                    115 *
0000DA 92D5 C73F     00740          116 READRECD MVI   EOFFLAG,C'N'               SET EOF FLAG OFF
                                    117          GET   INFILE,INRECD              READ RECORD
0000EE 47F0 C0F4     000F6          123 IFEOF    B     ENDIFEOF                   IF END OF FILE
0000F2 92E8 C73E     00740          124 THENEOF  MVI   EOFFLAG,C'Y'                 THEN SET EOF FLAG ON
                           000F6    125 ENDIFEOF EQU   *                          ENDIF
0000F6 07FA                         126          BR    10                         RETURN
```

Figure 6–18 Program 6 assembler listing

```
   LOC  OBJECT CODE    ADDR1 ADDR2  STMT   SOURCE STATEMENT                                      DOS/VSE ASSEMBLER 14.59 86-03-27

                                     127 *
                                     128 *                 PROCESS ANNUAL PAY TYPE
                                     129 *
0000F8 F247 C704 203A 00706 0003A    130 ANNUAL    PACK   PKRATE,58(8,2)           GET ANNUAL PAY
0000FE F844 C709 C704 00708 00706    131           ZAP    PKANLPAY,PKRATE          *
000104 FA44 C717 C709 00719 0070B    132           AP     PKTPA,PKANLPAY           ADD TO TOTAL FOR ANN. EMPL.
00010A FA20 C70E C7AD 00710 007AF    133           AP     PKTOTA,=P'1'             ADD 1 TO ANNUAL EMPLOYEES
000110 07FA                          134           BR     10                       RETURN
                                     135 *
                                     136 *                 PROCESS WEEKLY PAY TYPE
                                     137 *
000112 F247 C704 203A 00706 0003A    138 WEEKLY    PACK   PKRATE,58(8,2)           CALC. ANL PAY * RATE * 2040
000118 F874 C736 C704 00738 00706    139           ZAP    DOUBLE,PKRATE            *
00011E FC71 C736 C7A8 00738 007AA    140           MP     DOUBLE,=P'52'            *
000124 F847 C709 C736 0070B 00738    141           ZAP    PKANLPAY,DOUBLE          *
00012A FA44 C721 C709 00723 0070B    142           AP     PKTPW,PKANLPAY           ADD TO TOTAL FOR WKLY. EMPL.
000130 FA20 C714 C7AD 00716 007AF    143           AP     PKTOTW,=P'1'             ADD 1 TO WKLY. EMPL.
000136 07FA                          144           BR     10                       RETURN
                                     145 *
                                     146 *                 PROCESS HOURLY PAY TYPE
                                     147 *
000138 F247 C704 203A 00706 0003A    148 HOURLY    PACK   PKRATE,58(8,2)           CALC. ANNUAL PAY = RATE * 2040
00013E F874 C736 C704 00738 00706    149           ZAP    DOUBLE,PKRATE            *
000144 FC72 C736 C7AE 00738 007B0    150           MP     DOUBLE,=P'2040'          *
00014A F847 C709 C736 0070B 00738    151           ZAP    PKANLPAY,DOUBLE          *
000150 FA44 C71C C709 0071E 0070B    152           AP     PKTPH,PKANLPAY           ADD TO TOTAL FOR HOURLY EMPL.
000156 FA20 C711 C7AD 00713 007AF    153           AP     PKTOTH,=P'1'             ADD 1 TO HOURLY EMPLOYEES
00015C 07FA                          154           BR     10                       RETURN
                                     155 *
                                     156 *                 INVALID PAY CODE MODULE
                                     157 *
00015E D20F C4BC C776 004BE 00778    158 INVALID   MVC    PRINVAL,=C'INVALID PAY CODE'
000164 92E8 C73F       00741         159           MVI    INVALSW,C'Y'             SET INVALID CODE SWITCH
000168 07FA                          160           BR     10                       RETURN
                                     161 *
                                     162 *                 SET UP PRINT LINE MODULE
                                     163 *
                             0016A   164 SETUP     EQU    *
00016A 9240 C46B       0046D         165           MVI    PRLINE,C' '              CLEAR PRINT LINE
00016E D282 C46C C46B 0046E 0046D    166           MVC    PRLINE+1(131),PRLINE     *
000174 D213 C476 2009 00478 00009    167           MVC    PRNAME,9(2)              SET UP NAME
00017A D200 C494 2039 00496 00039    168           MVC    PRPAYTYP,57(2)           SET UP PAY TYPE
000180 D20C C498 C740 0049A 00742    169           MVC    PRRATE,PATRN             SET UP RATE
000186 DE0C C498 C704 0049A 00706    170           ED     PRRATE,PKRATE            *
00018C 95E8 C73F       00741         171 IF4       CLI    INVALSW,C'Y'             IF INVALID SWITCH NOT = 'Y'
000190 4780 C19E       001A0         172           BE     ENDIF4                     *
000194 D20C C4AA C740 004AC 00742    173 THEN4     MVC    PRANLPAY,PATRN             THEN SET UP ANNUAL PAY
00019A DE0C C4AA C709 004AC 0070B    174           ED     PRANLPAY,PKANLPAY          *
                             001A0   175 ENDIF4    EQU    *                        ENDIF
0001A0 07FA                          176           BR     10                       RETURN
                                     177 *
                                     178 *                 PRINT DETAIL LINE MODULE
                                     179 *
                             001A2   180 PRDETAIL  EQU    *
0001A2 F921 C72F C7AA 00731 007AC    181 IFEOP     CP     LINECNT,=P'50'           IF LINE COUNT => 50
0001A8 4740 C1AE       001B0         182           BL     ENDIFEOP                   *
0001AC 45B0 C2AE             002B0   183 THENEOP   BAL    11,HEADING                 THEN PRINT HEADING
                             001B0   184 ENDIFEOP  EQU    *                        ENDIF
                                     185           PUT    PRINTER,PRLINE           PRINT LINE
0001C0 FA20 C72F C7AD 00731 007AF    191           AP     LINECNT,=P'1'            ADD 1 TO LINE COUNT
0001C6 9240 C46B       0046D         192           MVI    PRLINE,C' '              CLEAR PRINT LINE
0001CA D283 C46C C46B 0046E 0046D    193           MVC    PRLINE+1(132),PRLINE     *
0001D0 07FA                          194           BR     10                       RETURN
                             001D2   195 ENDIF5    EQU    *                        ENDIF
0001D2 07FA                          196           BR     10                       RETURN
                                     197 *
                                     198 *                 ACCUMULATE FINAL TOTALS MODULE
                                     199 *
0001D4 FA22 C726 C70E 00728 00710    200 FINALTOT  AP     PKTOTEMP,PKTOTA          ADD UP TOTAL EMPLOYEES
0001DA FA22 C726 C714 00728 00716    201           AP     PKTOTEMP,PKTOTW          *
0001E0 FA22 C726 C711 00728 00713    202           AP     PKTOTEMP,PKTOTH          *
0001E6 FA54 C729 C717 0072B 00719    203           AP     PKTOTPAY,PKTPA           ADD UP TOTAL ANNUAL PAY
0001EC FA54 C729 C721 0072B 00723    204           AP     PKTOTPAY,PKTPW           *
0001F2 FA54 C729 C71C 0072B 0071E    205           AP     PKTOTPAY,PKTPH           *
0001F8 07FA                          206           BR     10                       RETURN
                                     207 *
                                     208 *                 PRINT FINAL TOTALS MODULE
                                     209 *
0001FA D205 C60A C74D 0060C 0074F    210 PRTOTAL   MVC    PRTOTEMP,PATRN2          PRINT TOTALS FOR ANNUAL PAY CODE
000200 DE05 C60A C70E 0060C 00710    211           ED     PRTOTEMP,PKTOTA          *
000206 92C1 C62E       00630         212           MVI    PRTOTTYP,C'A'            *
00020A D20C C639 C740 0063B 00742    213           MVC    PRTOTPAY,PATRN           *
000210 DE0C C639 C717 0063B 00719    214           ED     PRTOTPAY,PKTPA           *
000216 92F0 C5FA       005FC         215           MVI    TOTLINE,C'0'             SET FOR DOUBLE SPACE
                                     216           PUT    PRINTER,TOTLINE          *
00022A D205 C60A C74D 0060C 0074F    222           MVC    PRTOTEMP,PATRN2          PRINT TOTALS FOR WEEKLY PAY CODE
000230 DE05 C60A C714 0060C 00716    223           ED     PRTOTEMP,PKTOTW          *
000236 92E6 C62E       00630         224           MVI    PRTOTTYP,C'W'            *
00023A D20C C639 C740 0063B 00742    225           MVC    PRTOTPAY,PATRN           *
000240 DE0C C639 C721 0063B 00723    226           ED     PRTOTPAY,PKTPW           *
000246 9240 C5FA       005FC         227           MVI    TOTLINE,C' '             SET FOR SINGLE SPACE
                                     228           PUT    PRINTER,TOTLINE          *
00025A D205 C60A C74D 0060C 0074F    234           MVC    PRTOTEMP,PATRN2          PRINT TOTALS FOR HOURLY PAY CODE
000260 DE05 C60A C711 0060C 00713    235           ED     PRTOTEMP,PKTOTH          *
000266 92C8 C62E       00630         236           MVI    PRTOTTYP,C'H'            *
00026A D20C C639 C740 0063B 00742    237           MVC    PRTOTPAY,PATRN           *
000270 DE0C C639 C71C 0063B 0071E    238           ED     PRTOTPAY,PKTPH           *
                                     239           PUT    PRINTER,TOTLINE          *
000286 D205 C68F C74D 00691 0074F    245           MVC    FTTOTEMP,PATRN2          PRINT OVERALL TOTALS
00028C DE05 C68F C726 00691 00728    246           ED     FTTOTEMP,PKTOTEMP        *
000292 D20E C6BC C753 006BE 00755    247           MVC    FTTOTPAY,PATRN3          *
000298 DE0E C6BC C729 006BE 0072B    248           ED     FTTOTPAY,PKTOTPAY        *
                                     249           PUT    PRINTER,FINTOTLN         *
```

Figure 6–18 *(Continued)*

```
  LOC  OBJECT CODE    ADDR1 ADDR2  STMT   SOURCE STATEMENT                                       DOS/VSE ASSEMBLER 14.59 86-03-27

0002AE 07FA                         255           BR    10                        RETURN
                                    256 ***********************************************************************
                                    257 *                 THIRD LEVEL HEADING MODULE
                                    258 ***********************************************************************
                                    259 HEADING  PUT    PRINTER,HEAD1             PRINT FIRST HEADING LINE
                                    265          PUT    PRINTER,HEAD2             PRINT SECOND HEADING LINE
0002D0 F820 C72F C7AC 00731 007AE   271          ZAP    LINECNT,=P'0'             SET LINE COUNT TO ZERO
0002D6 92F0 C46B       0046D        272          MVI    PRLINE,C'0'               SET LINE TO DOUBLE SPACE
0002DA 07FB                         273          BR     11                        RETURN
                                    275 *******************************************************************DOS
                                    276 *                 FILE DEFINITIONS AND I/O AREAS                   DOS
                                    277 *******************************************************************DOS
                                    278 INFILE   DTFCD BLKSIZE=80,IOAREA1=INAREA,DEVICE=2540,              DOSX
                                                       DEVADDR=SYSIPT,EOFADDR=THENEOF,WORKA=YES            DOS
                                    299 *                                                                  DOS
                                    300 PRINTER  DTFPR BLKSIZE=133,IOAREA1=PRTAREA,DEVICE=1403,            DOSX
                                                       CTLCHR=ASA,DEVADDR=SYS009,WORKA=YES                 DOS
                                    321 *                                                                  DOS
000348                              322 INAREA   DS    CL80                                                DOS
000398                              323 PRTAREA  DS    CL133                                               DOS
                                    324 ********************************************************************OS
                                    325 *                 DEVICE CONTROL BLOCKS AND SAVE AREA               OS
                                    326 ********************************************************************OS
                                    327 *INFILE  DCB   DDNAME=INFILE,BLKSIZE=80,LRECL=80,                   OSX
                                    328 *              MACRF=GM,DSORG=PS,EODAD=THENEOF                      OS
                                    329 *                                                                   OS
                                    330 *PRINTER DCB   DDNAME=PRINTER,BLKSIZE=133,LRECL=133,                OSX
                                    331 *              MACRF=PMA,DSORG=PS                                   OS
                                    332 *                                                                   OS
                                    333 *SAVE    DS    18F                                                  OS
                                    334 ***********************************************************************
                                    335 *                 DATA DEFINITIONS
                                    336 ***********************************************************************
00041D                              337 INRECD   DS    CL80
                                    338 *
00046D                              339 PRLINE   DS    0CL133
00046D                              340          DS    CL11
000478                              341 PRNAME   DS    CL20
00048C                              342          DS    CL10
000496                              343 PRPAYTYP DS    CL1
000497                              344          DS    CL3
00049A                              345 PRRATE   DS    CL13
0004A7                              346          DS    CL5
0004AC                              347 PRANLPAY DS    CL13
0004B9                              348          DS    CL5
0004BE                              349 PRINVAL  DS    CL16
0004CE                              350          DS    CL36
                                    351 *
0004F2                              352 HEAD1    DS    0CL133
0004F2 F140404040404040             353          DC    CL31'1'
000511 C1D5D5E4C1D340E2             354          DC    CL102'ANNUAL SALARIES BY PAY TYPE'
                                    355 *
000577                              356 HEAD2    DS    0CL133
000577 F040404040404040             357          DC    CL19'0'
00058A D5C1D4C540404040             358          DC    CL20'NAME'
00059E E3E8D7C540404040             359          DC    CL14'TYPE'
0005AC D9C1E3C540404040             360          DC    CL13'RATE'
0005B9 C1D5D5E4C1D340D7             361          DC    CL67'ANNUAL PAY'
                                    362 *
0005FC                              363 TOTLINE  DS    0CL133
0005FC 4040404040404040             364          DC    CL16' '
00060C                              365 PRTOTEMP DS    CL6
000612 40C5D4D7D3D6E8C5             366          DC    CL19' EMPLOYEES'
000625 E3D6E3C1D340E3E8             367          DC    CL11'TOTAL TYPE'
000630                              368 PRTOTTYP DS    CL1
000631 4040404040404040             369          DC    CL10' '
00063B                              370 PRTOTPAY DS    CL13
000648 4040404040404040             371          DC    CL57' '
                                    372 *
000681                              373 FINTOTLN DS    0CL133
000681 F040404040404040             374          DC    CL16'0'
000691                              375 FTTOTEMP DS    CL6
000697 40C5D4D7D3D6E8C5             376          DC    CL19' EMPLOYEES'
0006AA D6E5C5D9C1D3D340             377          DC    CL20'OVERALL TOTAL'
0006BE                              378 FTTOTPAY DS    CL15
0006CD 4040404040404040             379          DC    CL57' '
                                    380 *
000706                              381 PKRATE   DS    PL5
00070B                              382 PKANLPAY DS    PL5
000710                              383 PKTOTA   DS    PL3
000713                              384 PKTOTH   DS    PL3
000716                              385 PKTOTW   DS    PL3
000719                              386 PKTPA    DS    PL5
00071E                              387 PKTPH    DS    PL5
000723                              388 PKTPW    DS    PL5
000728                              389 PKTOTEMP DS    PL3
00072B                              390 PKTOTPAY DS    PL6
000731                              391 LINECNT  DS    PL3
000738                              392 DOUBLE   DS    D
000740                              393 EOFFLAG  DS    CL1
000741                              394 INVALSW  DS    CL1
000742 40206B2020206B20             395 PATRN    DC    XL13'40206B2020206B2020214B2020'
00074F 402020202120                 396 PATRN2   DC    XL6'402020202120'
000755 402020206B202020             397 PATRN3   DC    XL15'402020206B2020206B2020214B2020'
                                    398 *
                       00000        399          END   MAINLINE
000768 5B5BC2D6D7C5D540             400                =C'$$BOPEN '
000770 5B5BC2C3D3D6E2C5             401                =C'$$BCLOSE'
000778 C9D5E5C1D3C9C440             402                =C'INVALID PAY CODE'
000788 000002E0                     403                =A(INFILE)
00078C 0000041D                     404                =A(INRECD)
000790 00000318                     405                =A(PRINTER)
000794 0000046D                     406                =A(PRLINE)
```

Figure 6–18 *(Continued)*

```
  LOC  OBJECT CODE    ADDR1 ADDR2  STMT   SOURCE STATEMENT                          DOS/VSE ASSEMBLER 14.59 86-03-27

000798 000005FC                    407              =A(TOTLINE)
00079C 00000681                    408              =A(FINTOTLN)
0007A0 000004F2                    409              =A(HEAD1)
0007A4 00000577                    410              =A(HEAD2)
0007A8 051C                        411              =P'51'
0007AA 052C                        412              =P'52'
0007AC 050C                        413              =P'50'
0007AE 0C                          414              =P'0'
0007AF 1C                          415              =P'1'
0007B0 02040C                      416              =P'2040'
```

Figure 6–18 *(Concluded)*

```
                         ANNUAL SALARIES BY PAY TYPE

          NAME                 TYPE          RATE            ANNUAL PAY

MARK DOWN                       A         62,000.00          62,000.00
CLYDE S DALE                    A         51,750.00          51,750.00
CARRIE AHN                      W            415.00          21,580.00
CLAIRE VOYANT                   W            392.00          20,384.00
DUNNAN BRADSTREET               W            283.00          14,716.00
SALLY FORTH                     A         41,250.00          41,250.00
DELLA KATESSEN                  W            380.00          19,760.00
PETE MOSS                       W            275.00          14,300.00
BART ENDER                      A         38,000.00          38,000.00
JACK RABBETT                    W            352.00          18,304.00
BELLE TOWER                     H             10.75          21,930.00
BARRY MOORE                     H              9.83          20,053.20
LYON HART                       H              9.45          19,278.00
TOM KATZ                        H              9.37          19,114.80
SARAH MOANIE                    A         35,000.00          35,000.00
NORA GRETZ                      W            297.50          15,470.00
PEARL STRAND                    W            291.50          15,158.00
HEDDA HARE                      W            284.50          14,794.00
STEVE EDORE                     A         36,125.00          36,125.00
SUZY KEW                        W            317.50          16,510.00
CONNIE SHURR                    H              8.75          17,850.00
NEIL DOWNE                      H              8.58          17,503.20
HAMMOND RYE                     H              8.49          17,319.60
CANDY KANE                      H              8.42          17,176.80
CLEMENT SEE                     H              8.37          17,074.80
ABBY WESTMINSTER                A         31,785.00          31,785.00
LOTTA WAITE                     H              8.15          16,626.00
BETTA WAGER                     H              8.10          16,524.00
ROGER ANDOVER                   H              8.05          16,422.00
PERRY WINKLE                    H              8.02          16,360.80
ELLA MENTRY                     W            412.00          21,424.00
ANNE ARKIE                      H              7.62          15,544.80
BARBIE DAHL                     H              7.38          15,055.20
RICH PERSON                     W            395.00          20,540.00
SEYMOUR SEITZ                   H              6.75          13,770.00
OSCAR QUESTION                  H              6.66          13,586.40
BILL OLADING                    H              6.51          13,280.40
RICK SHAW                       H              6.38          13,015.20
BEN Z DREEN                     H              6.25          12,750.00
ARTHUR RYTUS                    H              6.10          12,444.00

              7 EMPLOYEES       TOTAL TYPE A                 295,910.00
             12 EMPLOYEES       TOTAL TYPE W                 212,940.00
             21 EMPLOYEES       TOTAL TYPE H                 342,679.20

             40 EMPLOYEES       OVERALL TOTAL                851,529.20
```

Figure 6–19 Output from Program 6

give a displacement to be added to the base to make the effective address. Some instructions use four bits to designate an index register, whose contents are added to those of the base register and the displacement to form the effective address.

The BALR instruction is used to load a base register for the program. It places the rightmost 32 bits of the Program Status Word in the base register. This gives the address of the next instruction following the BALR. The USING assembler instruction designates the base register and indicates what its contents are expected to be.

Base-displacement addressing is done implicitly by using field names that the assembler converts to the proper form. Alternatively, the programmer can give the explicit displacement as a decimal or hexadecimal number and show the base register for the instruction within parentheses. For some types of instruction the length operand or the index register is placed in parentheses with the base register.

For large programs more than one base register may be needed. The address in each additional register should be 4096 bytes more than the address in the preceding register.

Six instruction formats are provided. For RR instructions each operand is in a general register. RX instructions have one operand in a general register and the second in a storage location. An index register may be used with the second operand.

RS instructions refer to two general registers and one storage location. SI instructions have the first operand in storage and the second as a single byte located in the instruction itself. SS instructions refer to two different storage addresses. Some SS instructions use only a single length operand, which may be as large as 256 bytes. Others use two length operands, which are limited to 16 bytes each. Type S instructions have a two-byte op code and an address in base-displacement form. Type S instructions are used primarily in the supervisor state.

The condition code gives the result of comparing two values or of comparing the result of some arithmetic operations with zero. The condition code has four possible settings, which can be tested by the use of a four-bit binary mask. Conditional branch instructions test the condition code as specified by the mask, and branch if the tested condition is true.

Input/output channels carry out I/O operations independently of the CPU. They execute channel commands under direction of the control unit of the CPU. The supervisor must issue one of four I/O instructions to initiate the channel program.

TERMS FOR REVIEW

Addressability error
Base address
Base register
Base-displacement addressing
Block-multiplexor
Burst mode
Byte-multiplexor
Channel command word
Displacement
Effective address
Explicit register addressing
Extended mnemonics
Fullword
Index register
Input/output channel

Length code
Mask
Multiple base registers
NOP
Program Status Word (PSW)
RR instruction
RS instruction
RX instruction
S instruction
SI instruction
SS instruction
Wraparound

REVIEW QUESTIONS

1. How are base registers indicated in machine instructions? Why do you suppose the designers made exactly 16 of them?
2. What is the largest decimal value that can be placed in a general register? the largest address?
3. Give two reasons why base-displacement addressing is used. Explain how the effective address is formed.
4. What is meant by explicit register addressing?
5. What is the role of the Program Status Word in loading the base register for a program? What other useful information does the PSW contain?
6. Explain two methods of loading multiple base registers.
7. How is the condition code represented? Where does it appear? What do its different values mean?
8. What is the meaning of a 0 bit in a mask? of a 1 bit?
9. Distinguish between byte-multiplexor channels and block-multiplexor channels. Which kind of device is each used with?
10. What is meant by overlap in connection with I/O operations?
11. Where does the channel program for a file usually appear?

EXERCISES

1. Assume that register 12 contains X'8400' and register 7 contains X'80'. Give the effective address *in hex* for each of the following storage operands in an RX instruction:
   a. 22(0,12)
   b. 100(7,12)
   c. 5(7)
   d. 64(12,7)
2. Draw a diagram giving the contents of each of the bytes for each of the six formats of machine instructions.
3. Show examples of assembler language statements using implicit and explicit register addressing for each of the six formats of machine instructions.
4. Write Branch on Condition statements with a mask and also extended mnemonics for each of these conditions:
   a. Branch to ELSE if condition code is set to 0.

b. Branch to ENDIF if condition code is set to 3.
c. Branch to ENDDO if condition is not set to 2.
d. Branch unconditionally to DOWHILE.

5. Assume register 3 contains the address of INRECD and register 4 holds the address of PRLINE. Using explicit register notation, write instructions to perform each of the following actions:
   a. Move the first eight bytes of INRECD to eight bytes starting at PRLINE + 30.
   b. Compare the last three bytes of INRECD with the three bytes starting at PRLINE + 45.
   c. Pack the five-byte field starting at INRECD + 37 into itself.

PROGRAMMING PROBLEMS

1. Using Data Set 3 in Appendix D, write a program to produce a Salesperson Bonus Analysis Report. The report should list the name, net sales, and bonus for each employee. Net sales is computed by subtracting year-to-date returns from year-to-date sales. Bonus is four percent for net sales if not greater than $25,000, five percent if greater than $25,000 but not greater than $100,000, and six percent if greater than $100,000.
2. Modify Problem 1 to use two base registers and explicit base-displacement addressing for the detail print line.
3. Modify Problem 2 to use a Branch on Condition (BC or BCR) instruction with a four-bit mask to test the condition code for each branching instruction.

7

Diagnostics and Debugging

OBJECTIVES

After studying this chapter, you should be able to:

- Practice and explain methods of avoiding errors in programs
- Interpret output produced by the assembler
- Use assembler diagnostics to help in detecting and correcting errors that do occur
- Interpret the linkage editor map and the relocation of modules
- Choose sample data for use in testing the object program
- Detect and remove errors that occur at run time during testing of programs
- Utilize system macros and job control options that permit analysis of the contents of main storage
- Interpret object code displayed in a dump of main storage
- Cross reference assembler output with the contents of a core dump

Despite our best intentions and care in writing source programs, at some point errors are likely to occur. In this chapter we shall examine ways to avoid errors so far as possible, detect those that do occur, and correct those that are found.

In the first section we will examine ways to avoid errors in program design and coding. Then we will see how to remove errors detected by the assembler. Finally, we will see how to detect errors that occur when the program is being tested after assembly.

AVOIDING ERRORS IN PROGRAMS

In Chapter 1 we explored the five steps in developing programs:

1. Defining the problem
2. Planning the logical solution
3. Coding and assembling the program
4. Testing the program
5. Completing the documentation

We can write programs effectively only if, before starting these steps, we are thoroughly familiar with the applicable rules of assembler language, the architecture of the computer system, and the principles of structured programming.

Defining the problem usually involves design of output and input. Output is usually shown on a print chart or screen layout form. We must arrange headings, fields in detail lines, and total lines to conform to specifications. Output should be arranged to be easily read and understood and to follow accepted practice about spacing, editing, number of lines per page, and other details.

Input design is usually dictated by the record layout of existing files. We may show the various fields on a record form or simply list them with their starting and ending positions within the record. Additional specifications may be furnished giving processing formulas, maximum or minimum values for data elements, or other details that must be observed.

Planning the solution involves determining the programming logic. Structure charts, program flowcharts, pseudocode, and other tools are popular means for developing and documenting program logic. Logic should be completely clear before any coding is begun.

Coding is writing the source statements on the coding form. Here is the source of most syntax errors. The process of reviewing source statements before preparing them for entry to the assembler is called *desk checking*. The following list gives a number of ways to reduce the possibility of error in coding.

1. Write file definitions first. Where possible, use the same DTF entries that have been used before for similar files. Be sure that the name and size of each I/O area agrees with the DTF operands.
2. Write DS and DC statements to define record descriptions while referring to the print chart and record layout forms.
3. While writing procedural statements, refer to record descriptions to be sure that names of operands agree with names used to define the various files, records, and fields.
4. If a procedural statement refers to an item not yet defined, add the data definition immediately.
5. Proofread all operation codes. Keep the system reference book handy to look up any op codes in question.
6. Use only the structured programming names (IF, THEN, ELSE, ENDIF, DOWHILE, ENDDO, REPEAT, and UNTIL) as names of procedural statements. Verify that all branching statements refer to the proper statement.
7. Check all relative addresses. Be sure to include length operands when lengths differ from those defined in DS or DC statements.
8. Check the lengths of fields used in MVC instructions to be sure that they do not move extra bytes or truncate needed bytes.
9. Ensure that all total fields and counters are properly initialized.

10. Be sure that all arithmetic operations refer to packed decimal data fields.
11. Confirm that edit patterns contain an odd number of digit select codes.
12. Check that fields into which edit patterns are to be moved are long enough to hold the entire pattern.

After reviewing the source coding and finding that it appears to be correct, prepare the coding to submit to the assembler. Use a keypunch machine for batch processing or a terminal for online program development. During the keying operations, watch especially the spacing and shifting from upper- to lowercase. A misplaced space within a name or between operands may cause a number of errors to be flagged by the assembler. Proofread the entire source program after keying to be sure it agrees with the original coding forms.

The coding step includes assembling the program. Assembly requires correct use of statements in job control language (JCL). If assembling in batch, we normally keypunch or select from prepunched JCL sets the proper statements to insert before and after our source statements. If using online program development, we often use macros or other short codes that provide the proper JCL statements or options. Reference manuals are usually provided to give the proper JCL for assembly.

DETECTING ERRORS AT ASSEMBLY TIME

Assembly time refers to the time at which the assembler is translating source statements into machine language. This is contrasted with *run time*, or *execution time*, when the load module is being tested with sample data after assembly and linkage editing.

Most programs are assembled with the PRINT NOGEN option. This means that statements generated by macros are not printed, reducing the length of our assembler listing and focusing attention on the statements we have written. The assembler directive PRINT GEN can be used wherever we wish to examine the generated statements.

Figure 7–1 shows the DTFCD statements 8 through 27 suppressed as usual with the PRINT NOGEN directive and those for the DTFPR printed as statements 31 through 50. Each generated statement is designated with a plus sign (+) at the right of the statement number. These statements consist of constants showing codes, addresses, and channel command words needed by the printer module to send output lines to the line printer.

The assembler can detect certain errors when processing source statements. Most of these involve the syntax of the language. Examples include: a name longer than eight characters or not starting with a letter; an invalid op code; failure to use a comma to separate operands; placing a space between operands; use of a name as an operand that has not been defined in the name column; or omitting the value of a constant.

```
  LOC  OBJECT CODE     ADDR1 ADDR2  STMT   SOURCE STATEMENT                                   DOS/VSE ASSEMBLER 08.55 86-04-07

000000                                 1 MAINLINE START 0
                             00000     2          USING *,12
                                       3 ***********************************************************************
                                       4 *                 FILE DEFINITIONS AND I/O AREAS
                                       5 ***********************************************************************
                                       6          PRINT NOGEN
                                       7 INFILE   DTFCD BLKSIZE=80,IOAREA1=INAREA,DEVICE=2540,                  X
                                                        DEVADDR=SYS006,EOFADDR=THENEOF,WORKA=YES
                                      28 *                                        .
                                      29          PRINT GEN
                                      30 PRINTER  DTFPR BLKSIZE=133,IOAREA1=PRTAREA,DEVICE=1403,               X
                                                        CTLCHR=ASA,DEVADDR=SYS009,WORKA=YES
                                      31+* IOCS AND DEV INDEPENDENT I/O DTFPR  5745-SC-IOX(E24)        @D3CZDKH 02910000
000032 000000000000
000038                                32+         DC     0D'0'                                                 60000025
00003A 000080000000                   33+PRINTER  DC     X'000080000000'         RES. COUNT, COM. BYTES BTS  JJ 61510028
00003E 01                             34+         DC     AL1(1)                 LOGICAL UNIT CLASS                70000025
00003F 09                             35+         DC    AL1(9)                  LOGICAL UNIT                      70200028
000040 00000060                       36+         DC     A(*+32)                CCW  ADDR.                     JJ 71000028
000044 00000000                       37+         DC     4X'00'                 CCB-ST BYTE,CSW CCW ADDRESS    JJ 71200028
000048 00                             38+         DC     AL1(0)                 SWITCH 3                      4-0 71750027
000049 000000                         39+         DC     VL3(IJDFAZZW)                ADDR OF LOGIC MODUL3-8 76800025
00004C 08                             40+         DC     X'08'                  DTF TYPE  (PRINTER)            JJ 77580028
00004D 32                             41+         DC     AL1(50)                SWITCHES                          77600025
00004E 09                             42+         DC     AL1(9)                  NORMAL  COMM. CODE           4-0 78000027
00004F 09                             43+         DC     AL1(9)                  CONTROL COMM. CODE           4-0 78400027
000050 00000089                       44+          DC     A(PRTAREA+1)          ADDRESS OF DATA IN IOAREA1        78800025
000054 00000000                       45+         DC     4X'00'                  BUCKET                       3-5 84000025
000058 0700                           46+         NOPR   0                      PUT LENGTH IN REG12 (ONLY UNDEF. 84800025
00005A 4700 0000       00000          47+         NOP    0                      LOAD USER POINTER REG             86400025
00005E 0000                           48+         DC     2X'00'                  NOT USED                     3-5 89600025
000060 0900008920000084               49+          CCW   9,PRTAREA+1,X'20',133-1                              4-0 91200027
                             00068    50+IJJZ0002    EQU *                                                       92000025
                                      51 *
000068                                52 INAREA   DS     CL80
000088                                53 PRTAREA  DS     CL133
                                      54 ***********************************************************************
                                      55 *               DATA DEFINITIONS
000130                                56 THENEOF  DS     CL6
                             00000    57          END    MAINLINE
```

Figure 7–1 Effects of PRINT GEN and PRINT NOGEN

Whenever errors are detected and flagged by the assembler, we must systematically correct them. Sometimes a statement is flagged as a result of an error in some other statement. For example, an error in a DTF statement that prevents a file from being properly defined will cause each OPEN, CLOSE, GET, PUT, or CNTRL referring to that file to be flagged as well.

Addressability errors can be caused by an error such as omitting the USING statement that designates the base register. The assembler then cannot determine which register to use as the base and how to construct addresses in base-displacement form.

Program 7 reads the employee file used previously and prints each name, sex, department, job code, and rate for all hourly employees. It counts the number of men and women and the total of the hourly rates for each. At end of file it prints the number of men and women and the average hourly rate for each.

Figure 7–2 shows a version of Program 7 flagged by the assembler for a number of syntax errors that were deliberately introduced. After examining the various parts of the source listing, we will analyze each statement in error to determine what correction must be made.

Source Statement Listing

The principal part of the assembler output is the listing of *source statement and object code*. This shows us line-by-line exactly what machine language code was produced by the assembler from each source statement we wrote. Each line is assigned a statement number that appears near the center of the page.

```
  LOC  OBJECT CODE    ADDR1 ADDR2  STMT   SOURCE STATEMENT                                   DOS/VSE ASSEMBLER 09.06 86-04-10

                                      1 ***********************************************************************
                                      2 *                 ALTON R. KINDRED, PROGRAM 7
                                      3 * THIS PROGRAM READS THE EMPLOYEE FILE AND PRINTS EACH NAME, SEX,
                                      4 * DEPARTMENT, JOB CODE, AND RATE FOR ALL HOURLY EMPLOYEES.  IT COUNTS
                                      5 * THE NUMBER OF MEN AND WOMEN AND TOTAL OF THE HOURLY RATES FOR EACH.
                                      6 * AT END OF FILE IT PRINTS THE NUMBER OF MEN AND WOMEN AND AVERAGE
                                      7 * HOURLY RATE FOR EACH.
                                      8 *          REGISTERS USED:
                                      9 *                 R9-11   - LINKS TO MODULES
                                     10 *                 R12     - BASE REGISTER
                                     11 ***********************************************************************
                                     12          PRINT NOGEN
000000                               13 MAINLINE START 0                          SET LOCATION COUNTER
                                     14 *        STM   14,12,12(13)               SAVE REGISTERS FOR OS          OS
000000 05C0                          15          BALR  12,0                       LOAD BASE REGISTER
                              00002  16          USING *,12                       DESIGNATE BASE REGISTER
                                     17 *        ST    13,SAVE+4                  STORE REGISTER 13              OS
                                     18 *        LA    13,SAVE                    LOAD SAVE AREA ADDRESS         OS
                                     19 *        OPEN  (INFILE,(INPUT),PRINTER,(OUTPUT))                         OS
                                     20          OPEN  INFILE,PRINTER             OPEN FILES                     DOS
000016 4590 C036              00038  29          BAL   9,INITIAL                  DO INITIAL PROCESSING
00001A 4590 C040              00042  30          BAL   9,MAINLOOP                 DO MAIN PROCESSING LOOP
00001E 4590 C064              00066  31          BAL   9,TOTAL                    DO FINAL PROCESSING
                                     32          CLOSE INFILE,PRINTER             CLOSE FILES                    DOS
                                     41          EOJ                              END PROGRAM                    DOS
                                     44 *        CLOSE (INFILE,,PRINTER)          CLOSE FILES                    OS
                                     45 *        L     13,SAVE+4                  LOAD SAVE AREA ADDRESS         OS
                                     46 *        LM    14,12,12(13)               RESTORE REGISTERS              OS
                                     47 *        BR    14                         RETURN TO OS                   OS
                                     48 ***********************************************************************
                                     49 *                 FIRST LEVEL MODULES
                                     50 ***********************************************************************
                                     51 *
                                     52 *                 INITIALIZATION MODULE
                                     53 *
000038 45A0 C06E              00070  54 INITIAL  BAL   10,CLEARSET                SET INITIAL VALUES
00003C 45A0 C088              0008A  55          BAL   10,READRECD                READ FIRST RECORD
000040 07F9                          56          BR    9                          RETURN
                                     57 *
                                     58 *                 MAIN PROCESSING LOOP
                                     59 *
                              00042  60 MAINLOOP EQU   *
000042 0000 0000 0000                61 DOWHILE  CLC   EOFFLAG,C'Y'               DOWHILE NOT END OF FILE
        *** ERROR ***
                                     62          BEQ   ENDDO                        *
        *** ERROR ***
000048 95C8 C354        00356        63 IF       CLI   INRECD+57,C'H'               IF PAY CODE = 'H'
00004C 4770 C05A        0005C        64          BNE   ENDIF                          *
000050 45A0 C0A6              000A8  65 THEN     BAL   10,PROCESS                     THEN PROCESS RECORD
000054 0000 0000                     66          BAL   10,SETUPLN                     SET UP PRINT LINE
        *** ERROR ***
000058 45A0 C102              00104  67          BAL   10,PRDETAIL                    PRINT DETAIL LINE
                              0005C  68 ENDIF    EQU   *                            ENDIF
00005C 45A0 C088              0008A  69          BAL   10,READRECD                    READ NEXT RECORD
000060 47F0 C040        00042        70          B     DOWHILE                      *
                              00064  71 ENDDO    EQU   *                          ENDDO
000064 07F9                          72          BR    9                          RETURN
                                     73 *
                                     74 *                 TOTAL MODULE
                                     75 *
000066 45A0 C134              00136  76 TOTAL    BAL   10,CALCAVG                 CALCULATE AVERAGE RATES
00006A 45A0 C15A              0015C  77          BAL   10,PRTOTAL                 PRINT TOTAL LINES
00006E 0000                          78          BR    19                         RETURN
        *** ERROR ***
                                     79 ***********************************************************************
                                     80 *                 SECOND LEVEL MODULES
                                     81 ***********************************************************************
                                     82 *
                                     83 *                 CLEAR TOTALS AND SET INITIAL VALUES MODULE
                                     84 *
000070 0000 0000 0000                85 CLEARSET ZAP   PKTOTMEN,P'0'              CLEAR TOTALS
        *** ERROR ***
000076 F810 C4FA C542 004FC 00544    86          ZAP   PKTOTWOM,=P'0'             *
00007C F820 C4EC C542 004EE 00544    87          ZAP   PKTPMEN,=P'0'              *
000082 F821 C4F8 C53E 004FA 00540    88          ZAP   LINECNT,=P'51'             SET LINE COUNT > 50
000088 07FA                          89          BR    10                         RETURN
                                     90 *
                                     91 *                 READ RECORD MODULE
                                     92 *
00008A 0000 0000                     93 READRECD MVI   EOFFLAG,C'N'               SET EOF FLAG OFF
        *** ERROR ***
                                     94          GET   INFILE,INRECD              READ RECORD
00009E 47F0 C0A4        000A6       100 IFEOF    B     ENDIFEOF                   IF END OF FILE
0000A2 0000 0000                    101 THENEOF  MVI   EOFFLAG,C'Y'                 THEN SET EOF FLAG ON
        *** ERROR ***
                              000A6 102 ENDIFEOF EQU   *                          ENDIF
0000A6 07FA                         103          BR    10                         RETURN
                                    104 *
                                    105 *                 PROCESS DETAIL RECORD
                                    106 *
0000A8 0000 0000 0000               107 PROCESS  PACK  PKRATE,INRECD+58(8)        PACK HOURLY RATE
        *** ERROR ***
0000AE 9504 C338        0033A       108 IF2      CLI   INRECD+29,C'M'             IF MALE
0000B2 4770 C0BE        000C0       109          BNE   ELSE2                        *
                                    110 THEN2    ADD   PKTPMEN,PKRATE               ADD RATE TO TOTAL FOR MEN
        *** ERROR ***
0000B6 FA10 C4E8 C543 004FA 00545   111          AP    PKTOTMEN,=P'1'               ADD 1 TO TOTAL MEN
0000BC 47F0 C0CA        000CC       112          B     ENDIF2                       *
                              000C0 113 ELSE2    EQU   *                          ELSE
0000C0 0000 0000 0000               114          AP    PKTPWOM,PKRATE               ADD RATE TO TOTAL FOR WOMEN
        *** ERROR ***
0000C6 FA10 C4FA C543 004FC 00545   115          AP    PKTOTWOM,=P'1'               ADD 1 TO TOTAL WOMEN
                              000CC 116 ENDIF2   EQU   *
0000CC 07FA                         117          BR    10                         RETURN
                                    118 *
                                    119 *                 SET UP PRINT LINE MODULE
```

Figure 7–2 Program 7 source listing with errors

```
  LOC  OBJECT CODE    ADDR1 ADDR2  STMT   SOURCE STATEMENT                                      DOS/VSE ASSEMBLER 09.06 86-04-10

                                    120 *
                            000CE   121 SETUP     EQU   *
0000CE 0000 0000                    122           MVI   PRLINE,C' '                 CLEAR PRINT LINE
       *** ERROR ***
0000D2 0000 0000 0000               123           MVC   PRLINE+1(132),PRLINE        *
       *** ERROR ***
0000D8 D213 C376 C324 00378 00326   124           MVC   PRNAME,INRECD+9             SET UP NAME
0000DE 0000 0000 0000               125           MVC   PRSEX,INRECD+29(1)          SET UP SEX CODE
       *** ERROR ***
0000E4 D206 C3A0 C506 003A2 00508   126           MVC   PRRATE,PATRN                SET UP RATE
0000EA D203 C392 C345 00394 00347   127           MVC   PRDEPT,INRECD+42            SET UP DEPARTMENT
0000F0 D203 C39A C350 0039C 00352   128           MVC   PRJOB,INRECD+53             SET UP JOB CODE
0000F6 D206 C3A0 C506 003A2 00508   129           MVC   PRRATE,PATRN                SET UP RATE
0000FC CC00 0000 0000               130           ED    PRRATE,PKRATE               *
       *** ERROR ***
000102 07FA                         131           BR    10                          RETURN
                                    132 *
                                    133 *               PRINT DETAIL LINE MODULE
                                    134 *
                            00104   135 PRDETAIL EQU    *
000104 F921 C4F8 C540 004FA 00542   136 IFEOP    CP     LINECNT,=P'50'              IF LINE COUNT => 50
00010A 4740 C110       00112        137          BL     ENDIFEOP                      *
00010E 45B0 C1B0            001B2   138 THENEOP  BAL    11,HEADING                    THEN PRINT HEADING
                            00112   139 ENDIFEOP EQU    *                           ENDIF
                                    140          PUT    PRINTER,PRLINE              PRINT LINE
000122 FA20 C4F8 C543 004FA 00545   146          AP     LINECNT,=P'1'               ADD 1 TO LINE COUNT
000128 0000 0000                    147          MVI    PRLINE,C' '                 CLEAR PRINT LINE
       *** ERROR ***
00012C 0000 0000 0000               148          MVC    PRLINE+1(132),PRLINE        *
       *** ERROR ***
000132 07FA                         149          BR     10                          RETURN
                            00134   150 ENDIF5   EQU    *                           ENDIF
000134 07FA                         151          BR     10                          RETURN
                                    152 *
                                    153 *               CALCULATE AVERAGE PAY RATE MODULE
                                    154 *
000136 F872 C4FE C4EC 00500 004EE   155 CALCAVG  ZAP    DOUBLE,PKTPMEN              CALC. AVG. RATE FOR MEN
00013C FD71 C4FE C4E8 00500 004EA   156          DP     DOUBLE,PKTOTMEN             *
000142 F825 C4F2 C4FE 004F4 00500   157          ZAP    PKAVPMEN,DOUBLE(6)          *
000148 F872 C4FE C4EF 00500 004F1   158          ZAP    DOUBLE,PKTPWOM              CALC. AVG. RATE FOR WOMEN
00014E FD71 C4FF C4EA 00500 004EC   159          DP     DOUBLE,PKTOTWOM             *
000154 F825 C4F5 C4FE 004F7 00500   160          ZAP    PKAVPWOM,DOUBLE(6)          *
00015A 07FA                         161          BR     10                          RETURN
                                    162 *
                                    163 *               PRINT FINAL TOTALS MODULE
                                    164 *
00015C D203 C4C4 C50D 004C6 0050F   165 PRTOTAL  MVC    PRTOTEMP,PATRN2             PRINT AVERAGE RATE FOR MEN
000162 DE03 C4C4 C4E8 004C6 004EA   166          ED     PRTOTEMP,PKTOTMEN           *
000168 0000 0000                    167          MVI    PRMORW,=C'MEN  '            *
       *** ERROR ***
00016C D206 C4E1 C506 004E3 00508   168          MVC    PRAVGPAY,PATRN              *
000172 DE06 C4E1 C4F2 004E3 004F4   169          ED     PRAVGPAY,PKAVPMEN           *
                                    170          PUT    PRINTER,TOTLINE             *
000188 D203 C4C4 C50D 004C6 0050F   176          MVC    PRTOTEMP,PATRN2             PRINT AVERAGE RATE FOR WOMEN
                                    177          EDIT   PRTOTEMP,PKTOTWOM           *

       *** ERROR ***
00018E D204 C4C9 C544 004CB 00546   178          MVC    PRMORW,=C'WOMEN'            *
000194 D206 C4E1 C506 004E3 00508   179          MVC    PRAVGPAY,PATRN              *
00019A DE06 C4E1 C4F5 004E3 004F7   180          ED     PRAVGPAY,PKAVPWOM           *
                                    181          PUT    PRINTER,TOTLINE             *
0001B0 07FA                         187          BR     10                          RETURN
                                    188 **********************************************************************
                                    189 *               THIRD LEVEL HEADING MODULE
                                    190 **********************************************************************
                                    191 HEADING  PUT    PRINTER,HEAD1               PRINT FIRST HEADING LINE
                                    197          PUT    PRINTERHEAD2                PRINT SECOND HEADING LINE
0001CE F820 C4F8 C542 004FA 00544   202          ZAP    LINECNT,=P'0'               SET LINE COUNT TO ZERO
0001D4 0000 0000                    203          MVI    PRLINE,C'0'                 SET LINE TO DOUBLE SPACE
       *** ERROR ***
0001D8 07FB                         204          BR     11                          RETURN
                                    205 *******************************************************************DOS
                                    206 *               FILE DEFINITIONS AND I/O AREAS                     DOS
                                    207 *******************************************************************DOS
                                    208 INFILE   DTFCD BLKSIZE=80,IOAREA1=INAREA,DEVICE=2540,              DOS
                                                       DEVADDR=SYSIPT,EOFADDR=THENEOF,WORKA=YES            DOS
                                    229 *                                                                  DOS
                                    230 PPINTER  DTFPR BLKSIZE=133,IOAREA1=PRTAREA,DEVICE=1403,            DOS
                                                       CTLCHR=ASA,DEVADDR=SYS009,WORKA=YES                 DOS
                                    251 *                                                                  DOS
000248                              252 INAREA   DS    CL80                                                DOS
000298                              253 PRTAREA  DS    CL133                                               DOS
                                    254 ********************************************************************OS
                                    255 *               DEVICE CONTROL BLOCKS AND SAVE AREA                 OS
                                    256 ********************************************************************OS
                                    257 *INFILE  DCB    DDNAME=INFILE,BLKSIZE=80,LRECL=80,                 OSX
                                    258 *               MACRF=GM,DSORG=PS,EODAD=THENEOF                     OS
                                    259 *                                                                   OS
                                    260 *PRINTER DCB    DDNAME=PRINTER,BLKSIZE=133,LRECL=133,              OSX
                                    261 *               MACRF=PMA,DSORG=PS                                  OS
                                    262 *                                                                   OS
                                    263 *SAVE    DS     18F                                                 OS
                                    264 **********************************************************************
                                    265 *               DATA DEFINITIONS
                                    266 **********************************************************************
00031D                              267 INRECD   DS     CL80
                                    268 *
                                    269 PRLINE   DS     0CL133
       *** ERROR ***
00036D                              270          DS     CL11
000378                              271 PRNAME   DS     CL20
00038C                              272          DS     CL4
                                    273 PRSEX    DS     CL
```

Figure 7–2 *(Continued)*

```
   LOC  OBJECT CODE      ADDR1 ADDR2  STMT   SOURCE STATEMENT                                        DOS/VSE ASSEMBLER 09.06 86-04-10

         *** ERROR ***
000390                                 274           DS    CL4
000394                                 275 PRDEPT    DS    CL4
000398                                 276           DS    CL4
00039C                                 277 PRJOB     DS    CL4
0003A0                                 278           DS    CL2
0003A2                                 279 PRRATE    DS    CL7
                                       280           DS    L72
         *** ERROR ***
                                       281 *
0003A9                                 282 HEAD1     DS    0CL133
0003A9 F140404040404040                283           DC    CL18'1'
0003BB C1E5C5D9C1C7C540                284           DC    CL115'AVERAGE HOURLY RATES FOR MEN AND WOMEN'
                                       285 *
00042F                                 286 HEAD2     DS    0CL133
00042E F040404040404040                287           DC    CL18'0'
000440 D5C1D4C540404040                288           DC    CL16'NAME'
                                       289           DC    CL6'SEX
         *** ERROR ***
000450 C4C5D7E34B40                    290           DC    CL6'DEPT.'
000456 D1D6C240C3D6C4C5                291           DC    CL11'JOB CODE'
000461 D9C1E3C540404040                292           DC    CL76'RATE'
                                       293 *
0004AD                                 294 TOTLINE   DS    0CL133
0004AD F040404040404040                295           DC    CL25'0'
0004C6                                 296 PRTOTEMP  DS    CL4
0004CA 4C                              297           DC    CL1' '
0004CB                                 298 PRMORW    DS    CL5
0004D0 404040404040                    299           DC    CL6' '
0004D6 C1E5C5D9C1C7C540                300           DC    CL13'AVERAGE RATE'
0004E3                                 301 PRAVGPAY  DS    CL7
                                       302           DC    CL72
         *** ERROR ***
                                       303 *
                                       304 PKRATE    DC    PL3
         *** ERROR ***
0004EA                                 305 PKTOTMEN  DS    PL2
0004EC                                 306 PKTOTWOM  DS    PL2
0004EE                                 307 PKTPMEN   DS    PL3
0004F1                                 308 PKTPWOM   DS    PL3
0004F4                                 309 PKAVPMEN  DS    PL3
0004F7                                 310 PKAVPWOM  DS    PL3
0004FA                                 311 LINECNT   DS    PL3
000500                                 312 DOUBLE    DS    D
                                       313 EOFFLAG   DS    C1
         *** ERROR ***
000508 402020214B2020                  314 PATRN     DC    XL7'402020214B2020'
00050F 40202120                        315 PATRN2    DC    XL4'40202120'
000518                                 316                 LTORG
000518 5B5BC2D6D7C5D540                317                 =C'$$BOPEN '
000520 5B5BC2C3D3D6E2C5                318                 =C'$$BCLOSE'
000528 000001E0                        319                 =A(INFILE)
00052C 0000031D                        320                 =A(INRECD)
000530 00000218                        321                 =A(PRINTER)
000534 00000000                        322                 =A(PRLINE)
         *** ERROR ***
000538 000004AD                        323                 =A(TOTLINE)
00053C 000003A9                        324                 =A(HEAD1)
000540 051C                            325                 =P'51'
000542 050C                            326                 =P'50'
000544 0C                              327                 =P'0'
000545 1C                              328                 =P'1'
000546 E6D6D4C5D5                      329                 =C'WOMEN'
                         0054B         330 ENDLITRL  EQU   *
                         00000         331           END   MAINLINE
```

Figure 7–2 *(Concluded)*

The Location Counter Along the left side of the program listing is the *location counter*. This counter uses a six-digit hexadecimal number to show the location of each instruction, file description, and data definition used in the program. The location counter is normally set to zero by the statement START 0 at the beginning of the program, but it may be set to any other value if we wish. It is incremented by the number of bytes required for each machine instruction, DTF entry, or DS or DC statement. It tells us the relative location *within our program space* of every part of our object program.

Object Code Next to the location counter is the object code for each instruction or definition. All object code uses two hexadecimal digits to represent the contents of one byte. Machine instructions contain two, four, or six bytes, depending on the type of instruction. The first byte of the machine instruction is the *operation code*. The second byte may contain:

1. Length code of first operand only.
2. Length code of two operands.
3. One immediate operand.
4. Reference to two general registers.
5. Reference to one general register and one four-bit mask.

The third and fourth bytes of machine instructions contain a *storage address in base-displacement form*. The fifth and sixth bytes, when present, also contain a storage address in base-displacement form. Note that many of these statements are followed by the notation *** ERROR ***. In a later section, we will show how to detect and correct each statement flagged.

Only the first eight bytes of constants defined in DC statements are normally shown in object code. This option is controlled by the PRINT assembler directive. PRINT NODATA, which is the usual option by default, causes only eight bytes per constant to be shown in object code. PRINT DATA causes the entire constant to be shown in hexadecimal notation.

ADDR1 and ADDR2 To the right of the object code are two columns headed ADDR1 and ADDR2. These show the address (location counter value) of each operand that is located in main storage. Whenever the location counter is set to zero by START 0 and the following instructions are BALR and USING, the base address of the program in DOS is X'000002'. In OS, which requires a four-byte STM instruction to save the registers, the base address is X'000006'. The displacement portion of the address of each operand in object code will thus be 2 less than the address shown under ADDR1 or ADDR2 in DOS, or 6 less in OS.

The ADDR1 or ADDR2 column is blank when the corresponding operand refers to a general register rather than to a storage address. The ADDR2 column also shows the location counter address (X'00002') indicated by the USING statement that assigns the base register.

The Literal Pool Each literal used in the program is stored in a pool at the end of the program. Each literal is stored only once even though it may be used more than once in the program. The location counter value where the literal is stored is used by the assembler in the machine instruction.

In the literal pool, all doublewords are stored first, then all fullwords, then halfwords, and finally literals that do not have to be stored on specific boundaries. This method eliminates extra bytes in the literal pool that might be required for boundary alignment if the literals were stored in the order in which they are used.

Diagnostics and Statistics The assembler can detect syntax errors in form, spacing, punctuation, and use of names. It places the message *** ERROR *** following each line of source coding in which it finds an error. At the end of the assembler listing a more detailed list of diagnostics appears (Figure 7–3). It shows the number of the statement in error, an error code that may be looked up in an assembler reference manual, the position within the operand where the error was found, and a short message in English identifying the type of error. Let us now systematically find, analyze, and correct each error.

Statement 61 in Figure 7–3 indicates that the symbol 'EOFFLAG' is undefined. Scanning our source listing, we find that statement 313 defining 'EOFFLAG' was in error. The error message for statement 313 indicates an invalid operand. We change C1 to CL1. Looking further down our diagnostics, we find that we have also corrected the errors listed for statements 93 and 101.

Statement 62 indicates an undefined op code. We replace 'BEQ' with 'BE' to correct this error.

Statement 66 states that the symbol 'SETUPLN' is undefined. We find in our source listing that we used the name 'SETUP' for the module to set up the print line. We change the name in statement 66 to 'SETUP'.

Statement 78 shows that the first operand refers to an incorrect register number. We change R19 to R9.

Statement 85 shows an invalid operand. We insert an equal sign (=) in front of the literal.

Statements 93 and 101 were corrected as shown in statement 61.

```
                              DIAGNOSTICS AND STATISTICS

 STMNT ERROR NO.   MESSAGE

   61    IPK156    SYMBOL 'EOFFLAG' UNDEFINED
   62    IPK097    UNDEFINED OP CODE 'BEQ', OR MACRO NOT FOUND
   66    IPK156    SYMBOL 'SETUPLN' UNDEFINED
   78    IPK166    REGISTER VALUE IN OPERAND 1 OUT OF RANGE
   85    IPK116    INVALID SELF-DEFINING TERM, 'P'O''
   93    IPK156    SYMBOL 'EOFFLAG' UNDEFINED
  101    IPK156    SYMBOL 'EOFFLAG' UNDEFINED
  107    IPK156    SYMBOL 'PKRATE' UNDEFINED
  110    IPK097    UNDEFINED OP CODE 'ADD', OR MACRO NOT FOUND
  114    IPK156    SYMBOL 'PKRATE' UNDEFINED
  122    IPK156    SYMBOL 'PRLINE' UNDEFINED
  123    IPK156    SYMBOL 'PRLINE' UNDEFINED
  123    IPK156    SYMBOL 'PRLINE' UNDEFINED
  125    IPK173    DISPLACEMENT VALUE IN OPERAND 2 NOT ABSOLUTE
  125    IPK156    SYMBOL 'PRSEX' UNDEFINED
  130    IPK156    SYMBOL 'PKRATE' UNDEFINED
  147    IPK156    SYMBOL 'PRLINE' UNDEFINED
  148    IPK156    SYMBOL 'PRLINE' UNDEFINED
  148    IPK156    SYMBOL 'PRLINE' UNDEFINED
  167    IPK131    ILLEGAL USE OF LITERAL
  177    IPK097    UNDEFINED OP CODE 'EDIT', OR MACRO NOT FOUND
  199    IPK113    SYMBOL 'PRINTERH' TOO LONG
  203    IPK156    SYMBOL 'PRLINE' UNDEFINED
  269    IPK123    INVALID TYPE SPECIFICATION, 'OCL133'
  273    IPK129    INVALID DUPLICATION FACTOR OR MODIFIER, ' '
  280    IPK112    INVALID CHARACTER IN CONSTANT, '72'
  289    IPK115    UNPAIRED APOSTROPHE
  302    IPK128    CONSTANT FIELD MISSING OR PRECEDED BY INVALID FIELD, ' '
  304    IPK128    CONSTANT FIELD MISSING OR PRECEDED BY INVALID FIELD, ' '
  313    IPK112    INVALID CHARACTER IN CONSTANT, '1'
  322    IPK156    SYMBOL 'PRLINE' UNDEFINED

THE FOLLOWING MACRO NAMES HAVE BEEN FOUND IN MACRO INSTRUCTIONS
   OPEN      CLOSE      EOJ      BEQ      GET      ADD      PUT      EDIT      DTFCD      DTFPR

OPTIONS FOR THIS ASSEMBLY - ALIGN, LIST, NOXREF, NOLINK, NORLD, NODECK, NOEDECK

THE ASSEMBLER WAS RUN IN 130952 BYTES
END OF ASSEMBLY
```

Figure 7–3 Diagnostics and statistics

Statement 107 shows 'PKRATE' as undefined. We find that the definition of 'PKRATE' in statement 304 did not show a value for a constant. Since we did not intend this field to be a constant, we change the DC to a DS. This correction will also correct errors flagged in statements 114 and 130.

Statement 110 indicates an invalid op code. We change 'ADD' to 'AP'.

Statement 122 indicates that 'PRLINE' is undefined. Statement 252 defining 'PRLINE' is flagged for an invalid type specification. We find we used the letter 'O' instead of the zero for a duplication factor. By correcting this error, we correct also statements 123, 147, 148, 203, and 322.

Statement 125 shows that operand 2 has an incorrect displacement value. The assembler understood INRECD + 29 to be a displacement and R1 to be a base register. We actually used a length with the second operand in a MVC instruction. We remove the (1).

Statement 125 also shows that 'PRSEX' is undefined. We find in statement 273 that the length is omitted in the definition. We correct it to read CL1.

Statement 130 has already been corrected as in statement 107.

Statements 147 and 148 were corrected as discussed in statement 122.

Statement 167 shows an illegal use of a literal. Actually, the literal is correct. The op code MVI cannot use a literal. We change the op code to MVC.

Statement 177 shows that 'EDIT' is an invalid op code. We change it to 'ED'.

Statement 197 shows that the symbol 'PRINTERH' is too long. File names are limited to seven characters. We find that we actually omitted the comma between the operands 'PRINTER' and 'HEAD2'. We insert the comma.

Statement 203 has already been corrected as in statement 115.

Statement 269 indicates an invalid type specification. Again we find we have written a letter 'O' instead of a zero. We make this correction.

Statement 273 was corrected as indicated in statement 118.

Statement 280 is flagged for an invalid character in the constant '72'. We actually omitted the type for our DS statement. We correct the operand to CL72.

Statement 289 flags an unpaired apostrophe (single quote). We correct the operand to CL6'SEX'.

Statements 302 and 304 are flagged for having the constant field missing. We find that 302 should be changed to CL72' ', and 304 should have the op code changed from DC to DS.

Statement 313 was corrected as discussed under statement 61.

Statement 322 was corrected as discussed under statement 122.

After making these corrections, we resubmit our source program to the assembler. In the following section we examine each separate part of the assembler and linkage editor output.

OTHER ASSEMBLER OUTPUT

The assembler produces several outputs in addition to the source listing. The *External Symbol Dictionary* and the *Relocation Dictionary* provide information to the linkage editor. The *Cross-Reference Listing* is optional.

External Symbol Dictionary

Even for short programs, the assembler will produce four or five pages of output. The first page is the External Symbol Dictionary (ESD). This dictionary passes information to the linkage editor. It lists the name of each input/output module required to process the files described in DTF statements. It also gives the names of any other subprograms or modules that need to be linked to the main program we have written.

Figure 7–4 shows the ESD for Program 7. IJCFZIWO is a code name for the card module. IJDFAZZW names the printer module. The linkage editor must locate these two modules in the system library and link them to our object module to create a load module that can be executed.

Relocation Dictionary

The Relocation Dictionary (RLD) provides information to the linkage editor, giving the location of every address constant within the program that must be relocated. Figure 7–5 specifies the type of each constant, A for ordinary, V for an external address, and CCW for channel command word. Some address constants are four bytes long and some, used by the operating system, are only three, since addresses can be only 24 bits long.

When the linkage editor determines the load point of the program, it adds the relocation factor to each type A constant and CCW. The assembler assem-

```
                                                      EXTERNAL SYMBOL DICTIONARY

SYMBOL     TYPE          ID  ADDR   LENGTH LD-ID

MAINLINE   SD (CSECT)    001 000000 0005FC
IJCFZIWO   ER (EXTRN)    002
IJDFAZZW   ER (EXTRN)    003
```

Figure 7–4 External Symbol Dictionary

RELOCATION DICTIONARY

ESDID FOR ADDR CON	ESDID FOR REF SYMBOL	TYPE	LENGTH	ADDRESS
001	+001	A	4	00000C
001	+001	A	4	000010
001	+001	A	4	00002C
001	+001	A	4	000030
001	+001	A	4	0001F8
001	+002	V	3	000201
001	+001	A	4	000208
001	+001	A	3	00020D
001	+001	CCW	3	000211
001	+001	A	4	000230
001	+003	V	3	000239
001	+001	A	4	000240
001	+001	CCW	3	000251
001	+001	A	4	0005D0
001	+001	A	4	0005D4
001	+001	A	4	0005D8
001	+001	A	4	0005DC
001	+001	A	4	0005E0
001	+001	A	4	0005E4
001	+001	A	4	0005E8

Figure 7–5 Relocation Dictionary

CROSS-REFERENCE PAGE 8

86-04-07

SYMBOL	LEN	ID	VALUE	DEFN	REFERENCES							
CALCAVG	00006	001	00013E	00157	0077							
CLEARSET	00006	001	000072	00086	0054							
DOUBLE	00008	001	0005A8	00317	0157	0158	0159	0160	0161	0162		
DOWHILE	00004	001	000042	00061	0070							
ELSE2	00001	001	0000C8	00114	0110							
ENDDO	00001	001	000066	00071	0062							
ENDIF	00001	001	00005E	00068	0064							
ENDIFEOF	00001	001	0000A8	00103	0101							
ENDIFEOP	00001	001	00011A	00141	0139							
ENDIF2	00001	001	0000D4	00117	0113							
ENDIF5	00001	001	00013C	00152								
EOFFLAG	00001	001	0005B0	00318	0061	0094	0102					
HEADING	00004	001	0001C2	00195	0140							
HEAD1	00133	001	000402	00286	0330							
HEAD2	00133	001	000487	00290	0331							
IF	00004	001	00004A	00063								
IFEOF	00004	001	0000A0	00101								
IFEOP	00006	001	00010C	00138								
IF2	00004	001	0000B0	00109								
IJCX0C10	00008	001	000210	00229	0218							
IJJC0002	00004	001	000028	00037								
IJJ00001	00004	001	000008	00025								
IJJZ0010	00001	001	000222	00232								
IJJZ0011	00001	001	000258	00254								
INAREA	00080	001	000258	00256	0226	0229						
INFILE	00006	001	0001F0	00215	0026	0038	0325					
INITIAL	00004	001	000038	00054	0029							
INRECD	00080	001	00032D	00271	0063	0108	0109	0125	0126	0128	0129	0326
LINECNT	00003	001	0005A4	00316	0089	0138	0148	0205				
MAINLINE	00001	001	000000	00013	0322							
MAINLOOP	00001	001	000042	00060	0030							
PATRN	00007	001	0005B1	00319	0127	0130	0170	0181				
PATRN2	00004	001	0005B8	00320	0167	0178						
PKAVPMEN	00003	001	00059E	00314	0159	0171						
PKAVPWOM	00003	001	0005A1	00315	0162	0182						
PKRATE	00003	001	000591	00309	0108	0111	0115	0131				
PKTCTMEN	00002	001	000594	00310	0086	0112	0158	0168				
PKTOTWOM	00002	001	000596	00311	0087	0116	0161	0179				
PKTPMEN	00003	001	000598	00312	0088	0111	0157					
PKTPWOM	00003	001	000598	00313	0115	0160						
PRAVGPAY	00007	001	000542	00306	0170	0171	0181	0182				
PRDEPT	00004	001	0003A5	00279	0128							
PRDETAIL	00001	001	00010C	00137	0067							
PRINTER	00006	001	000228	00237	0027	0039	0327					
PRJOB	00004	001	0003AD	00281	0129							
PRLINE	00133	001	00037D	00273	0123	0124	0124	0149	0150	0150	0206	0328
PRMORW	00005	001	00052A	00303	0169	0180						
PRNAME	00020	001	000388	00275	0125							
PROCESS	00006	001	0000AA	00108	0065							
PRRATE	00007	001	0003B3	00283	0127	0130	0131					
PRSEX	00001	001	0003A0	00277	0126							
PRTAREA	00133	001	0002A8	00257	0248	0253						

Figure 7–6 Cross Reference Listing

```
                                                CROSS-REFERENCE                                          PAGE    9

PRTOTAL   00006 001 000164 00167  0078
PRTOTEMP  00004 001 000525 00301  0167  0168  0178  0179
READRECD  00004 001 00008C 00094  0055  0069
SYMBOL     LEN   ID VALUE  DEFN     REFERENCES                                                           86-04-07

SETUP     00001 001 0000D6 00122  0066
THEN      00004 001 000052 00065
THENEOF   00004 001 0000A4 00102  0228
THENEOP   00004 001 000116 00140
THEN2     00006 001 0000B8 00111
TOTAL     00004 001 000068 00077  0031
TOTLINE   00133 001 00050C 00299  0329
=A(HEAD1)
          00004 001 0005E4 00330  0196
=A(HEAD2)
          00004 001 0005E8 00331  0202
=A(INFILE)
          00004 001 0005D0 00325  0097
=A(INRECD)
          00004 001 0005D4 00326  0098
=A(PRINTER)
          00004 001 0005D8 00327  0144  0174  0185  0195  0201
=A(PRLINE)
          00004 001 0005DC 00328  0145
=A(TOTLINE)
          00004 001 0005E0 00329  0175  0186
=C'$$BOPEN '
          00008 001 0005C0 00323  0024
=C'$$BCLOSE'
          00008 001 0005C8 00324  0036
=C'MEN  '
          00005 001 0005F2 00336  0169
=C'WOMEN'
          00005 001 0005F7 00337  0180
=P'0'     00001 001 0005F0 00334  0086  0087  0088  0205
=P'1'     00001 001 0005F1 00335  0112  0116  0148
=P'50'    00002 001 0005EE 00333  0138
=P'51'    00002 001 0005EC 00332  0089
```

Figure 7–6 *(Concluded)*

bles each type V constant as X'000000', so the linkage editor must supply the actual address of the module in a type V constant.

The RLD is always produced by the assembler, but its listing is optional.

Cross-Reference Listing

An optional part of the assembler output that may prove useful is the Cross-Reference Listing (XREF). In Figure 7–6, this listing shows, in alphabetical order, each name (symbol) and literal used in the program. LEN specifies the length in decimal. The name of each DS and DC entry gives the length of the definition. Names of machine instructions show lengths of 2, 4, or 6. EQU instructions have a length of 1.

ID specifies a type code. VALUE gives the hex address of the name. DEFN is the statement number in decimal where the name is defined. The REFERENCES list in decimal all statement numbers that refer to the name as an operand.

PROGRAM RELOCATION AND LINKAGE

Once we have removed all errors detected by the assembler, we are ready to test our program. Figure 7–7 shows a version of Program 7 after assembler errors have been detected and removed.

Before any object program can be executed, it must first be processed by the linkage editor. The EXEC LNKEDT job control statement following the source program causes the linkage editor to be loaded and executed.

Programming Tips

- Use the PRINT GEN assembler statement in front of any macros where you wish to see the generated source statements. You can follow the macro with PRINT NOGEN to suppress generated statements from other macros.
- Remember that the assembler can find only syntax errors in source statements. You can test for logical errors only by running the program with sample data.
- Use test data that causes every part of the program to be executed at least once.

```
  LOC  OBJECT CODE    ADDR1 ADDR2  STMT   SOURCE STATEMENT                                    DOS/VSE ASSEMBLER 08.42 86-04-07

                                     1 ***********************************************************************
                                     2 *                  ALTON R. KINDRED, PROGRAM 7
                                     3 * THIS PROGRAM READS THE EMPLOYEE FILE AND PRINTS EACH NAME, SEX,
                                     4 * DEPARTMENT, JOB CODE, AND RATE FOR ALL HOURLY EMPLOYEES.  IT COUNTS
                                     5 * THE NUMBER OF MEN AND WOMEN AND TOTAL OF THE HOURLY RATES FOR EACH.
                                     6 * AT END OF FILE IT PRINTS THE NUMBER OF MEN AND WOMEN AND AVERAGE
                                     7 * HOURLY RATE FOR EACH.
                                     8 *           REGISTERS USED:
                                     9 *                  R9-11   - LINKS TO MODULES
                                    10 *                  R12     - BASE REGISTER
                                    11 ***********************************************************************
                                    12           PRINT NOGEN
000000                              13 MAINLINE START 0                             SET LOCATION COUNTER
                                    14 *         STM   14,12,12(13)                 SAVE REGISTERS FOR OS           OS
000000 05C0                         15           BALR  12,0                         LOAD BASE REGISTER
                           00002    16           USING *,12                         DESIGNATE BASE REGISTER
                                    17 *         ST    13,SAVE+4                    STORE REGISTER 13               OS
                                    18 *         LA    13,SAVE                      LOAD SAVE AREA ADDRESS          OS
                                    19 *         OPEN  (INFILE,(INPUT),PRINTER,(OUTPUT))                            OS
                                    20           OPEN  INFILE,PRINTER               OPEN FILES                      DOS
000016 4590 C036           00038    29           BAL   9,INITIAL                    DO INITIAL PROCESSING
00001A 4590 C040           00042    30           BAL   9,MAINLOOP                   DO MAIN PROCESSING LOOP
00001E 4590 C066           00068    31           BAL   9,TOTAL                      DO FINAL PROCESSING
                                    32           CLOSE INFILE,PRINTER               CLOSE FILES                     DOS
                                    41           EOJ                                END PROGRAM                     DOS
                                    44 *         CLOSE (INFILE,,PRINTER)            CLOSE FILES                     OS
                                    45 *         L     13,SAVE+4                    LOAD SAVE AREA ADDRESS          OS
                                    46 *         LM    14,12,12(13)                 RESTORE REGISTERS               OS
                                    47 *         BR    14                           RETURN TO OS                    OS
                                    48 ***********************************************************************
                                    49 *                  FIRST LEVEL MODULES
                                    50 ***********************************************************************
                                    51 *
                                    52 *                  INITIALIZATION MODULE
                                    53 *
000038 45A0 C070           00072    54 INITIAL  BAL   10,CLEARSET                   SET INITIAL VALUES
00003C 45A0 C08A           0008C    55          BAL   10,READRECD                   READ FIRST RECORD
000040 07F9                         56          BR    9                             RETURN
                                    57 *
                                    58 *                  MAIN PROCESSING LOOP
                                    59 *
                           00042    60 MAINLOOP EQU   *
000042 95E8 C5AE     005B0          61 DOWHILE  CLI   EOFFLAG,C'Y'                  DOWHILE NOT END OF FILE
000046 4780 C064     00066          62          BE    ENDDO                           *
00004A 95C8 C364     00366          63 IF       CLI   INRECD+57,C'H'                  IF PAY CODE = 'H'
00004E 4770 C05C     0005E          64          BNE   ENDIF                             *
000052 45A0 C0A8           000AA    65 THEN     BAL   10,PROCESS                        THEN PROCESS RECORD
000056 45A0 C0D4           000D6    66          BAL   10,SETUP                          SET UP PRINT LINE
00005A 45A0 C10A           0010C    67          BAL   10,PRDETAIL                       PRINT DETAIL LINE
                           0005E    68 ENDIF    EQU   *                               ENDIF
00005E 45A0 C08A           0008C    69          BAL   10,READRECD                       READ NEXT RECORD
000062 47F0 C040     00042          70          B     DOWHILE                         *
                           00066    71 ENDDO    EQU   *                             ENDDO
000066 07F9                         72          BR    9                             RETURN
```

Figure 7–7 Program 7 corrected source listing

```
LOC    OBJECT CODE      ADDR1 ADDR2  STMT   SOURCE STATEMENT                                      DOS/VSE ASSEMBLER 08.42 86-04-07

                                      74 *
                                      75 *                TOTAL MODULE
                                      76 *
000068 45A0 C130              0013E   77 TOTAL    BAL   10,CALCAVG                CALCULATE AVERAGE RATES
00006C 45A0 C162              00164   78          BAL   10,PRTOTAL                PRINT TOTAL LINES
000070 07F9                           79          BR    9                         RETURN
                                      80 ***********************************************************************
                                      81 *                SECOND LEVEL MODULES
                                      82 ***********************************************************************
                                      83 *
                                      84 *                CLEAR TOTALS AND SET INITIAL VALUES MODULE
                                      85 *
000072 F810 C592 C5EE 00594 005F0     86 CLEARSET ZAP   PKTOTMEN,=P'0'            CLEAR TOTALS
000078 F810 C594 C5EF 00596 005F0     87          ZAP   PKTOTWOM,=P'0'            *
00007E F820 C596 C5EE 00598 005F0     88          ZAP   PKTPMEN,=P'0'             *
000084 F821 C5A2 C5EA 005A4 005EC     89          ZAP   LINECNT,=P'51'            SET LINE COUNT > 50
00008A 07FA                           90          BR    10                        RETURN
                                      91 *
                                      92 *                READ RECORD MODULE
                                      93 *
00008C 9205 C5AE        005B0         94 READRECD MVI   EOFFLAG,C'N'              SET EOF FLAG OFF
                                      95          GET   INFILE,INRECD             READ RECORD
0000A0 47F0 C0A6        000A8        101 IFEOF    B     ENDIFEOF                  IF END OF FILE
0000A4 92E8 C5AE        005B0        102 THENEOF  MVI   EOFFLAG,C'Y'                THEN SET EOF FLAG ON
                              000A8  103 ENDIFEOF EQU   *                         ENDIF
0000A8 07FA                          104          BR    10                        RETURN
                                     105 *
                                     106 *                PROCESS DETAIL RECORD
                                     107 *
0000AA F227 C58F C365 00591 00367    108 PROCESS  PACK  PKRATE,INRECD+58(8)       PACK HOURLY RATE
0000B0 95D4 C348        0034A        109 IF2      CLI   INRECD+29,C'M'            IF MALE
0000B4 4770 C0C6        000C8        110          BNE   ELSE2                       *
0000B8 FA22 C596 C58F 00598 00591    111 THEN2    AP    PKTPMEN,PKRATE              ADD RATE TO TOTAL FOR MEN
0000BE FA10 C592 C5EF 00594 005F1    112          AP    PKTOTMEN,=P'1'              ADD 1 TO TOTAL MEN
0000C4 47F0 C0D2        000D4        113          B     ENDIF2                      *
                              000C8  114 ELSE2    EQU   *                         ELSE
0000C8 FA22 C599 C58F 0059B 00591    115          AP    PKTPWOM,PKRATE              ADD RATE TO TOTAL FOR WOMEN
0000CE FA10 C594 C5EF 00596 005F1    116          AP    PKTOTWOM,=P'1'              ADD 1 TO TOTAL WOMEN
                              000D4  117 ENDIF2   EQU   *
0000D4 07FA                          118          BR    10                        RETURN
                                     119 *
                                     120 *                SET UP PRINT LINE MODULE
                                     121 *
                              000D6  122 SETUP    EQU   *
0000D6 9240 C37B        0037D        123          MVI   PRLINE,C' '               CLEAR PRINT LINE
0000DA D283 C37C C37B 0037E 0037D    124          MVC   PRLINE+1(132),PRLINE      *
0000E0 D213 C386 C334 00388 00336    125          MVC   PRNAME,INRECD+9           SET UP NAME
0000E6 D200 C39E C348 003A0 0034A    126          MVC   PRSEX,INRECD+29           SET UP SEX CODE
0000EC D206 C3B1 C5AF 003B3 005B1    127          MVC   PRRATE,PATRN              SET UP RATE
0000F2 D203 C3A3 C355 003A5 00357    128          MVC   PRDEPT,INRECD+42          SET UP DEPARTMENT
0000F8 D203 C3AB C360 003AD 00362    129          MVC   PRJOB,INRECD+53           SET UP JOB CODE
0000FE D206 C3B1 C5AF 003B3 005B1    130          MVC   PRRATE,PATRN              SET UP RATE
000104 DE06 C3B1 C58F 003B3 00591    131          ED    PRRATE,PKRATE             *
00010A 07FA                          132          BR    10                        RETURN
                                     134 *
                                     135 *                PRINT DETAIL LINE MODULE
                                     136 *
                              0010C  137 PRDETAIL EQU   *
00010C F921 C5A2 C5EC 005A4 005EE    138 IFEOP    CP    LINECNT,=P'50'            IF LINE COUNT => 50
000112 4740 C118        0011A        139          BL    ENDIFEOP                    *
000116 45B0 C1C0              001C2  140 THENEOP  BAL   11,HEADING                  THEN PRINT HEADING
                              0011A  141 ENDIFEOP EQU   *                         ENDIF
                                     142          PUT   PRINTER,PRLINE            PRINT LINE
00012A FA20 C5A2 C5EF 005A4 005F1    148          AP    LINECNT,=P'1'             ADD 1 TO LINE COUNT
000130 9240 C37B        0037D        149          MVI   PRLINE,C' '               CLEAR PRINT LINE
000134 D283 C37C C37B 0037E 0037D    150          MVC   PRLINE+1(132),PRLINE      *
00013A 07FA                          151          BR    10                        RETURN
                              0013C  152 ENDIF5   EQU   *                         ENDIF
00013C 07FA                          153          BR    10                        RETURN
                                     154 *
                                     155 *                CALCULATE AVERAGE PAY RATE MODULE
                                     156 *
00013E F872 C5A6 C596 005A8 00598    157 CALCAVG  ZAP   DOUBLE,PKTPMEN            CALC. AVG. RATE FOR MEN
000144 FD71 C5A6 C592 005A8 00594    158          DP    DOUBLE,PKTOTMEN           *
00014A F825 C59C C5A6 0059E 005A8    159          ZAP   PKAVPMEN,DOUBLE(6)        *
000150 F872 C5A6 C599 005A8 0059B    160          ZAP   DOUBLE,PKTPWOM            CALC. AVG. RATE FOR WOMEN
000156 FD71 C5A6 C594 005A8 00596    161          DP    DOUBLE,PKTOTWOM           *
00015C F825 C59F C5A6 005A1 005A8    162          ZAP   PKAVPWOM,DOUBLE(6)        *
000162 07FA                          163          BR    10                        RETURN
                                     164 *
                                     165 *                PRINT FINAL TOTALS MODULE
                                     166 *
000164 D203 C523 C5B6 00525 005B8    167 PRTOTAL  MVC   PRTOTEMP,PATRN2           PRINT AVERAGE RATE FOR MEN
00016A DE03 C523 C592 00525 00594    168          ED    PRTOTEMP,PKTOTMEN         *
000170 D204 C528 C5F0 0052A 005F2    169          MVC   PRMORW,=C'MEN  '          *
000176 D206 C540 C5AF 00542 005B1    170          MVC   PRAVGPAY,PATRN            *
00017C DE06 C540 C59C 00542 0059E    171          ED    PRAVGPAY,PKAVPMEN         *
                                     172          PUT   PRINTER,TOTLINE           *
000192 D203 C523 C5B6 00525 005B8    178          MVC   PRTOTEMP,PATRN2           PRINT AVERAGE RATE FOR WOMEN
000198 DE03 C523 C594 00525 00596    179          ED    PRTOTEMP,PKTOTWOM         *
00019E D204 C528 C5F5 0052A 005F7    180          MVC   PRMORW,=C'WOMEN'          *
0001A4 D206 C540 C5AF 00542 005B1    181          MVC   PRAVGPAY,PATRN            *
0001AA DE06 C540 C59F 00542 005A1    182          ED    PRAVGPAY,PKAVPWOM         *
                                     183          PUT   PRINTER,TOTLINE           *
0001C0 07FA                          189          BR    10                        RETURN
                                     190 ***********************************************************************
                                     191 *                THIRD LEVEL HEADING MODULE
                                     192 ***********************************************************************
                                     193 HEADING  PUT   PRINTER,HEAD1             PRINT FIRST HEADING LINE
                                     199          PUT   PRINTER,HEAD2             PRINT SECOND HEADING LINE
0001E2 F820 C5A2 C5EE 005A4 005F0    205          ZAP   LINECNT,=P'0'             SET LINE COUNT TO ZERO
0001E8 92F0 C37B        0037D        206          MVI   PRLINE,C'0'               SET LINE TO DOUBLE SPACE
0001EC 07FB                          207          BR    11                        RETURN
```

Figure 7–7 *(Continued)*

```
  LOC  OBJECT CODE      ADDR1 ADDR2  STMT   SOURCE STATEMENT                                          DOS/VSE ASSEMBLER 08.42 86-04-07

                                      209 ***********************************************************************DOS
                                      210 *                   FILE DEFINITIONS AND I/O AREAS                     DOS
                                      211 ***********************************************************************DOS
                                      212 INFILE   DTFCD BLKSIZE=80,IOAREA1=INAREA,DEVICE=2540,                  DOSX
                                                         DEVADDR=SYSIPT,EOFADDR=THENEOF,WORKA=YES                DOS
                                      233 *                                                                      DOS
                                      234 PRINTER  DTFPR BLKSIZE=133,IOAREA1=PRTAREA,DEVICE=1403,                DOSX
                                                         CTLCHR=ASA,DEVADDR=SYS009,WORKA=YES                     DOS
                                      255 *                                                                      DOS
000258                                256 INAREA   DS    CL80                                                    DOS
0002A8                                257 PRTAREA  DS    CL133                                                   DOS
                                      258 ***********************************************************************OS
                                      259 *                   DEVICE CONTROL BLOCKS AND SAVE AREA                OS
                                      260 ***********************************************************************OS
                                      261 *INFILE  DCB     DDNAME=INFILE,BLKSIZE=80,LRECL=80,                    OSX
                                      262 *                MACRF=PM,DSORG=PS,EODAD=THENEOF                       OS
                                      263 *                                                                      OS
                                      264 *PRINTER DCB     DDNAME=PRINTER,BLKSIZE=133,LRECL=133,                 OSX
                                      265 *                MACRF=PMA,DSORG=PS                                    OS
                                      266 *                                                                      OS
                                      267 *SAVE     DS     18F                                                   OS
                                      268 ************************************************************************
                                      269 *                   DATA DEFINITIONS
                                      270 ************************************************************************
00032D                                271 INRECD   DS     CL80
                                      272 *
00037D                                273 PRLINE   DS     0CL133
00037D                                274          DS     CL11
000388                                275 PRNAME   DS     CL20
00039C                                276          DS     CL4
0003A0                                277 PRSEX    DS     CL1
0003A1                                278          DS     CL4
0003A5                                279 PRDEPT   DS     CL4
0003A9                                280          DS     CL4
0003AD                                281 PRJOB    DS     CL4
0003B1                                282          DS     CL2
0003B3                                283 PRRATE   DS     CL7
0003BA                                284          DS     CL72
                                      285 *
000402                                286 HEAD1    DS     0CL133
000402 F1404040404040404              287          DC     CL18'1'
000414 C1E5C5D9C1C7C540               288          DC     CL115'AVERAGE HOURLY RATES FOR MEN AND WOMEN'
                                      289 *
000487                                290 HEAD2    DS     0CL133
000487 F0404040404040 40              291          DC     CL18'0'
000499 D5C1D4C540404040               292          DC     CL16'NAME'
0004A9 E2C5E7404040                   293          DC     CL6'SEX'
0004AF C4C5D7E34B40                   294          DC     CL6'DEPT.'
0004B5 D1D6C240C3D6C4C5               295          DC     CL11'JOB CODE'
0004C0 D9C1E3C540404040               296          DC     CL76'RATE'
                                      297 *
00050C                                299 TOTLINE  DS     0CL133
00050C F040404040404040               300          DC     CL25'0'
000525                                301 PRTOTEMP DS     CL4
000529 40                             302          DC     CL1' '
00052A                                303 PRMORW   DS     CL5
00052F 404040404040                   304          DC     CL6' '
000535 C1E5C5D9C1C7C540               305          DC     CL13'AVERAGE RATE'
000542                                306 PRAVGPAY DS     CL7
000549 4040404040404040               307          DC     CL72' '
                                      308 *
000591                                309 PKRATE   DS     PL3
000594                                310 PKTOTMEN DS     PL2
000596                                311 PKTOTWOM DS     PL2
000598                                312 PKTPMEN  DS     PL3
00059B                                313 PKTPWOM  DS     PL3
00059E                                314 PKAVPMEN DS     PL3
0005A1                                315 PKAVPWOM DS     PL3
0005A4                                316 LINECNT  DS     PL3
0005A8                                317 DOUBLE   DS     D
0005B0                                318 EOFFLAG  DS     CL1
0005B1 40202021482020                 319 PATRN    DC     XL7'40202021482020'
0005B8 40202120                       320 PATRN2   DC     XL4'40202120'
                                      321 *
                          00000       322          END    MAINLINE
0005C0 5B5BC2D6D7C5D540               323                 =C'$$BOPEN '
0005C8 5B5BC2C3D3D6E2C5               324                 =C'$$BCLOSE'
0005D0 000001F0                       325                 =A(INFILE)
0005D4 0000032D                       326                 =A(INRECD)
0005D8 00000228                       327                 =A(PRINTER)
0005DC 0000037D                       328                 =A(PRLINE)
0005E0 0000050C                       329                 =A(TOTLINE)
0005E4 00000402                       330                 =A(HEAD1)
0005E8 00000487                       331                 =A(HEAD2)
0005EC 051C                           332                 =P'51'
0005EE 050C                           333                 =P'50'
0005F0 0C                             334                 =P'0'
0005F1 1C                             335                 =P'1'
0005F2 D4C5D54040                     336                 =C'MEN  '
0005F7 E6D6D4C5D5                     337                 =C'WOMEN'
```

Figure 7–7 *(Concluded)*

The linkage editor refers to two parts of the assembler output for information. From the External Symbol Dictionary, it determines other modules that must be linked to our program. These are primarily the modules for processing files for input or output. But they may be any other modules or subprograms needed by our program.

From the Relocation Dictionary the linkage editor determines each address constant within the program that must be relocated. It then adds to each ordinary address constant the relocation factor. The relocation factor is the difference between the address used by the assembler (usually location zero) and the address where the program will actually be loaded into main storage for execution.

The linkage editor must determine each external address and replace the address of all zeros that was created by the assembler.

The Linkage Editor Map

The linkage editor prints two outputs. The diagnosis of input lists the various modules with which it worked. This diagnosis gives little information of value to the programmer. On the other hand, the output map (Figure 7–8) is invaluable for diagnosing errors that cause program interrupts at execution time.

From this map, we can determine that the entire phase (program) has been loaded (LOCORE) at X'233078' and that the transfer address (XFR-AD) of the first instruction to be executed is also at X'233078'. The highest address in the phase (HICORE) is X'2337CD'. The phase is stored on disk starting at cylinder X'034', track X'06', record X'04'.

The MAINLINE control section (CSECT) is loaded starting at X'233078', offset X'000000' bytes from the start of the phase. Card module IJCFZIWO is loaded at X'233678', offset X'000600' bytes from start of the phase. Printer module IJDFAZZW is loaded at X'2336F8', offset X'000680' from the start of the phase.

In a later section of this chapter we will go through the process of detecting and correcting errors that happen when the program is running.

Input/Output Modules

Every program must have some form of output; otherwise, there would be no point in writing it. In addition, except for a few programs that generate all data internally, some input data is received. Each input and output file must be handled by special modules supplied with the operating system. The characteristics of the file specified in the DTF in DOS or the DCB in OS determine which module is to be linked to our program.

```
04/09/86 PHASE     XFR-AD  LOCORE  HICORE  DSK-AD     LABEL     LOADED  REL-FR OFFSET INPUT

         PHASE***  233078  233078  2337CD  034 06 04                                 RELOCATABLE
                                                      MAINLINE  233078  233078 000000 SYSLNK
                                                      IJCFZIWO  233678  233678 000600 IJCFZIWO
                                                      IJDFAZZW  2336F8  2336F8 000680 IJDFAZZW
```

Figure 7–8 Linkage Editor Map

Usually I/O modules are given specific names that indicate the type of device they handle and the characteristics of the file. For example, under DOS printer file modules have 8-byte names that start with the letters IJD, while the names of punched card files start with IJC. The remaining letters in the name indicate whether records are blocked or unblocked, fixed length or variable, input or output, and various other characteristics. Details about I/O modules can be obtained from manuals accompanying the operating system.

DETECTING ERRORS AT RUN TIME

Even though the assembler may have detected no errors in our program, they may still be present. For example, suppose you write BALR 3,0 followed by USING *,4. The assembler will use register 4 as the base, but R4 has not been loaded with the proper base address. All base-displacement addresses will therefore refer to the wrong locations.

Other errors that the assembler cannot detect include:

1. Referring to the wrong field, e.g., ININVAMT instead of PKINVAMT.
2. Omitting a field in a record description.
3. Omitting the name of the work area in a GET or PUT statement when WORKA=YES was used in the file definition.
4. Using an incorrect relative address or length operand.
5. Omitting an optional operand from a field definition.
6. Failing to initialize total fields.
7. Branching to the wrong instruction.
8. Using a BAL instruction without a corresponding BR at the end of the subroutine.
9. Using an invalid ASA print control character. This usually causes an interrupt in the printer module rather than in our program space.

In short, any statement written in the correct form but with the incorrect operands cannot be detected by the assembler. The assembler can tell only what the source statement says, not what we *intended* it to say.

Suppose we have corrected all errors detected by the assembler and link edited it. Then we attempt to execute it for testing. We are chagrined to get the error message from the operating system that there has been a program interrupt at location X'233140' because of a data exception (see Figure 7–9). The message also shows the content of the Program Status Word (PSW) at the time of interrupt. How do we find the problem? We follow the following steps:

1. Find the location of the instruction that was being executed when the interrupt occurred. In this case it is X'233140'.

2. Refer to the linkage editor map (Figure 7–8) to find the relocation factor for the mainline module. In this case it is X'233078'.
3. Subtract the relocation factor from the address of the interrupt. This gives X'0000C8', the address *within our program* of the instruction that caused the error.
4. On our program listing in Figure 7–7, read down the left-hand column to find location X'0000C8'. It is statement 115, which reads AP PKTPWOM,PKRATE. This statement could not be executed successfully, and therefore caused the program to be interrupted because of a data exception.
5. Most data exceptions are caused by attempting to operate on invalid packed decimal fields. In this case, either PKTPWOM or PKRATE was invalid. We should scan the program to see what happened to each field. We find in statement 108 the instruction PACK PKRATE,INRECD+58(8). We confirm that the eight-byte field starting in column 59 of INRECD does contain the rate of pay and that no other instructions have changed PKRATE. But we find that PKTPWOM was not defined in statement 313 with an initial value of zero, nor was it cleared with other totals in the CLEARSET module. We therefore conclude that PKTPWOM contained invalid data from some prior use of that part of storage. An attempt to add to that location produced the interrupt.
6. Insert a statement ZAP PKTPWOM,=P'0' following statement 88, reassemble, link edit again, and execute the program with test data.

Most of the time we can locate errors by carefully examining our source statements, once we know what statements or fields are at fault. But there are times when, just as a physician needs to look at an X-ray or perform exploratory surgery, we need to look inside the machine to find our problem.

System Diagnostic Aids

The operating system and the assembler provide ways in which we can examine the contents of main storage. In DOS, five methods are OPTION DUMP, OPTION PARTDUMP, DUMP, CANCEL, and PDUMP. We will see how each of the five operates, and then settle on the best for our purposes.

The first four methods provide a printout, usually called a *core dump*, of the general registers, the supervisor, and our program in main storage. The

```
0S03I PROGRAM CHECK INTERRUPTION - HEX LOCATION 233140 - CONDITION CODE 1 - DATA EXCEPTION
0S00I JOB LABAARK7 CANCELED
0S07I PROBLEM PROGRAM  PSW     034D100000233146
```

Figure 7–9 Execution time error message

supervisor on most modern computers is so large that the full core dump may run up to a hundred pages. We rarely need this much information.

OPTION DUMP is a DOS job control statement that may be used separately or combined with OPTION LINK after the JOB statement in the form OPTION LINK, DUMP. When OPTION DUMP is in effect, any abnormal termination of our program before reaching normal end of job (EOJ) will cause a core dump to be made. The abnormal termination is usually called an *ABEND*, short for abnormal end.

OPTION PARTDUMP is a DOS job control statement that gives a somewhat more limited, but still lengthy, dump of the registers, selected parts of the supervisor, and our program space. Figure 7–10 shows a selected portion of the PARTDUMP caused by the error in our program.

DUMP is a DOS macro that we may place in our program wherever we wish. Whenever it is reached in the program flow, it forces an ABEND and a core dump. It does not matter whether OPTION DUMP is in effect or not. DUMP can be used if we wish to examine a program that did not interrupt because of a data exception or other usual reason.

CANCEL is a DOS macro that may be placed anywhere in the source program. It causes an ABEND, but produces a core dump only if OPTION DUMP was in effect.

The most effective diagnostic tool is the DOS PDUMP macro (for partial dump). It causes only a limited printout of storage and does not interrupt the program. PDUMP is written in the op code field like any other macro. We may use two operands to indicate the points at which the dump is to begin and end. For example, PDUMP INRECD,OUTRECD would print out the contents of the general registers and storage locations starting at INRECD and ending at OUTRECD. Some additional bytes of storage may be printed out to cause the dump to begin and end on a doubleword boundary.

If the first executable instruction in our program is named BEGIN and the last field named is LINECNT, then the macro PDUMP BEGIN,LINECNT+100 would show our entire program, including the literal pool that follows the LINECNT.

The placement of the PDUMP statement is crucial to successful debugging. It is best not to use it at all unless we are unable to find our error by examining source code. Then, the best place to insert it is just in front of the statement that caused the program interrupt. The PDUMP will show the contents of storage just as they will be when the program interrupts on the next instruction.

Avoid placing a PDUMP in a loop. Since it does not interrupt the program, the partial dump will occur as many times as the loop is repeated, wasting time and paper. This can be avoided by placing an EOJ macro immediately after the PDUMP. After detecting and correcting the error, remove both the PDUMP and the EOJ macros before running the program again.

In OS, a snapshot of main storage may be taken at run time by the SNAP macro. Before SNAP can be executed, a SNAP data set must be defined and opened, and R13 must contain the address of the SAVE area.

```
LABAARK7                                   04/09/86   14.07.30    CPUID=0001163043410000

ENDING TASK REGISTERS

GR 0-F    002333A5 00233268 00286FFF 00000048    00286FFF 00000000 00000000 002330E0
          40E0B002 90233096 802330CE 00286FFF    4023307A 00287800 A0233118 00233678

FP REG    478030B6 F94BF4F9 41600000 00000000    BEC85800 00000000 00000000 00000000
CR 0-F    81400C60 00000000 FFFFFFFF 00000000    00000000 00000000 00000000 00000000
          00000800 00000000 00000000 00000000    00000000 00000000 8F000000 00000000

COMREG    F9 ADDR IS 004788
004788    F0F461F0 F961F8F6 00000000 00000000    00000000 00000000 D3C1C2C1 C1D9D2F7
0047A8    00286FFF 002337CD 002337CD 00000040    00FFFFFF FF7F4483 20A044C0 00000000
0047C8    37580000 00000000 10C810D5 1A7E3CF0    F4F0F9F8 F6F0F9F9 00000EF8 00000000
0047E8    4B480000 00000000 00000040 00000040    00007B18 00008038 00000BD0 0E28510C
004808    00000000 035011E1 00000000 40600F40    40404040 40404000 40404040 40404000
004828    000418C0 40000000 00F98FC0 2A048080    00000000 00000000 0003A924 01010000
004848    0F180007 00000000

SYSCOM    ADDRESS IS 000418
000418    0000D030 0000F00 0000DB42 00003AA8    00000000 00000000 00000000 000059B0
000438    0003E800 2A00AF40 00FF0034 000CC887    00000000 8300E660 00000000 00000000
000458    C0000CE8 00000000 00000000 000093B4    00000000 00000000 0000002A 0003D000
000478    00009F08 00009F40 00000000 0000E59C    00000558 00E142C8 00003F4A 00000AC0
000498    00000000 00000000 0000D800 00000000    0000D768 00006168 00000000 00000000
0004B8    00000000 00000000 00000000 00000000    00000000 00000000 00000000 00070000
0004D8    00000000 00000000 00000000 07F1000C    00000000 00000000 00000000 0000D0C0
0004F8    0000D0F4 001F0050 00000000 00000000    000092A8 E4E05000 00F6A800 00FA3800
000518    800139C4 00007996 02007228 00FEC800    00F48DE8 00E09000 00000000 B0009EA0
000538    00000000 0000D320 00024318 00F6C028

PUBTAB    ADDRESS IS 003758
003758    001FFF00 B00000F8 000CFF00 100002F8    000E3900 420080F8 000FFF00 430000F8
003778    001AFF00 230000F8 001EFF00 420000F8    002AFF00 100002F8 002CFF00 100002F8
003798    002DFF00 230000F8 002EFF00 420000F8    01200B00 B00080F8 01218000 B00080F8
0037B8    01227900 B00080F8 01234000 B00080F8    0124FF00 B00000F8 01257300 B00080F8
0037D8    01262500 B00080F8 01270800 B00080F8    01284500 B00080F8 01293000 B00080F8
0037F8    012A3E00 B00080F8 012B5600 B00080F8    012CFF00 B00000F8 012D5800 B00080F8
003818    012E1C00 B00080F8 012F1400 B00080F8    01303500 B00080F8 01316B00 B00080F8
003838    01324300 B00080F8 01337A00 B00080F8    01342F00 B00080F8 01356400 B00080F8
003858    01367400 B00080F8 01374E00 B00080F8    01388300 B00080F8 01391E00 B00080F8
003878    013A1900 B00080F8 013B3200 B00080F8    013C7200 B00080F8 013D8700 B00080F8
003898    013E2300 B00080F8 013F8600 B00080F8    01400300 B00080F8 01418500 B00080F8
0038B8    01420500 B00080F8 01437C00 B00080F8    01440E00 B00080F8 01456000 B00080F8
0038D8    01467E00 B00080F8 01478100 B00080F8    01486700 B00080F8 01495000 B00080F8
0038F8    014AFF00 B00000F8 014B4B00 B00080F8    014C6600 B00080F8 014D3700 B00080F8
003918    014E3100 B00080F8 014FFF00 B00000F8    01506800 B00080F8 01514100 B00080F8
003938    01521500 B00080F8 01531700 B00080F8    01548400 B00080F8 0155FF00 B00000F8
003958    01565500 B00080F8 01578B00 B00080F8    01582100 B00080F8 0159FF00 B00000F8
003978    015A2C00 B00080F8 015B1D00 B00080F8    015C0200 B00080F8 015D8C00 B00080F8
003998    015EFF00 B00000F8 015FFF00 B00000F8    01606900 B00080F8 01615C00 B00080F8
0039B8    01621000 B00080F8 01633400 B00080F8    01644800 B00080F8 0165FF00 B00000F8
0039D8    0166FF00 B00000F8 0167FF00 B00000F8    0168FF00 B00000F8 0169FF00 B00000F8
0039F8    016AFF00 B00000F8 016BFF00 B00000F8    016CFF00 B00000F8 016DFF00 B00000F8
003A18    016EFF00 B00000F8 016F2000 B00080F8    0170FF00 B00000F8 0171FF00 B00000F8
003A38    0172FF00 B00000F8 0173FF00 B00000F8    0174FF00 B00000F8 0175FF00 B00000F8
003A58    0176FF00 B00000F8 0177FF00 B00000F8    0178FF00 B00000F8 0179FF00 B00000F8
003A78    017AFF00 B00000F8 017BFF00 B00000F8    017CFF00 B00000F8 017DFF00 B00000F8
 233000  07C8C1E2 C55C5C5C 034D1000 00233146   90233096 802330CE 00286FFF 4023307A   *PHASE***                       *
 233020  00287800 A0233118 00233678 002333A5   00233268 00286FFF 00000048 00286FFF   *                               *
 233040  00000000 00000000 002330E0 40E0B002   00009AC0 8BB71D20 478030B6 F94BF4F9   *                           9.49*
 233060  41600000 00000000 BEC85800 00000000   00000000 00000000 05C00700 4110C5BE   * -        H                  E *
 233080  4500C012 00233268 002332A0 0A024590   C0364590 C0404590 C0660700 4110C5C6   *                             EF*
 2330A0  4500C032 00233268 002332A0 0A020A0E   45A0C070 45A0C08A 07F995E8 C5AE4780   *                        9 YE   *
 2330C0  C06495C8 C3644770 C05C45A0 C0A845A0   C0D445A0 C10A45A0 C08A47F0 C04007F9   *   HC     *      M  A      0  9*
 2330E0  45A0C13C 45A0C162 07F9F810 C592C5EE   F810C594 C5EEF820 C596C5EE F821C5A2   *  A   A  98 E E 8 E E 8 E E 8 E *
 233100  C5EA07FA 92D5C5AE 5810C5CE 5800C5D2   58F10010 45EF0008 47F0C0A6 92E8C5AE   *E     NE    E   EK 1       0  YE *
 233120  07FAF227 C58FC365 95D4C348 4770C0C6   FA22C596 C58FFA10 C592C5EF 47F0C0D2   *  2 E C  MC     F  E E   E E  0 K*
 233140  FA22C599 C58FFA10 C594C5EF 07FA9240   C37BD283 C37CC37B D213C386 C334D200   *  E E   E E    C K C C K C C K *
 233160  C39EC348 D206C3B1 C5AFD203 C3A3C355   D203C3AB C360D206 C3B1C5AF DE06C3B1   *C C K C E K C C K C C-K C E   C *
 233180  C58F07FA F921C5A2 C5EC4740 C11845B0   C1C05810 C5D65800 C5DA58F1 001045EF   *E   9 E E   A   A   E0  E  1    *
```

Figure 7–10 Storage dump

```
LABAARK7                              04/09/86  14.07.30   CPUID=000116304341000O                                        PAGE   13

2331A0   000CFA20 C5A2C5EF 9240C37B D283C37C   C37B07FA 07FAF872 C5A6C596 FD71C5A6   *    E E   C K C C     8 E E   E *
2331C0   C592F825 C59CC5A6 F872C5A6 C599FD71   C5A6C594 F825C59F C5A607FA D203C523   *E 8 E E 8 E E   E E 8 E E   K E *
2331E0   C5B6DE03 C523C592 D204C528 C5F0D206   C540C5AF DE06C540 C59C5810 C5D65800   *E   E E K E EOK E E   E E   EO  *
233200   C5DE58F1 001045EF 000CD203 C523C5B6   DE03C523 C594D204 C528C5F5 D206C540   *E  1      K E E   E E K E E5K E *
233220   C5AFDE06 C540C59F 5810C5D6 5800C5DE   58F10010 45EF000C 07FA5810 C5D65800   *E   E E   EC  E  1          EO  *
233240   C5E258F1 001045EF 000C5810 C5D65800   C5E658F1 001045EF 000CF820 C5A2C5EE   *ES 1         EO  EW 1      8 E E *
233260   92F0C37B 07FB0000 00008000 0C000001   00233288 00233290 00233678 02810202   * OC                             *
233280   002332D0 0023311C 022332D0 20000050   47000000 D24FD000 E0000000 00000000   *                  K             *
2332A0   00008000 0C000109 002332C8 00005D38   002336F8 08B20909 00233321 00000000   *            H        8          *
2332C0   07004700 00000000 09233321 20000084   F4F7F5F6 F1F2F0F3 F8C2C5D3 D3C540E3   *              475612038BELLE T*
2332E0   D6E6C5D9 40404040 40404040 40C6F0F7   F3F1F5F3 F1F2F0F1 F7F9F3F7 F5F6F0F1   *OWER           F07315312017937560l*
233300   F2F3F1F0 F7F5F6F2 F5C8F0F0 F0F0F1F0   F7F54040 40404040 40404040 40404040   *231075625H00001075              *
233320   00000000 --SAME--                                                          *                                *
2333A0   00000000 00F4F7F5 F6F1F2F0 F3F8C2C5   D3D3C540 E3D6E6C5 D9404040 40404040   *     475612038BELLE TOWER       *
2333C0   4040C6F0 F7F3F1F5 F3F1F2F0 F1F7F9F3   F7F5F6F0 F1F2F3F1 F0F7F5F6 F2F5C8F0   *  F07315312017937560123107562 5H0*
2333E0   F0F0F0F1 F0F7F540 40404040 40404040   40404040 40000000 00000000 00000000   *0001075                         *
233400   00000000 --SAME--                                                          *                                *
233420   00000000 00000000 00000000 00000000   00000000 40404040 40404040 00000004   *                                *
233440   00000000 00000000 00000000 40404040   40404040 F0F0F0F0 F0F0F0F0 40000000   *                     00000000   *
233460   10002000 30000000 04C10000 0000000C   1C4040F0 F1F0F1F1 0000F140 40404040   *         A          01011  1    *
233480   40404040 40404040 40404040 C1E5C5D9   C1C7C540 C8D6E4D9 D3E840D9 C1E3C5E2   *           AVERAGE HOURLY RATES*
2334A0   40C6D6D9 40D4C5D5 40C1D5C4 40E6D6D4   C5D54040 40404040 40404040 40404040   * FOR MEN AND WOMEN              *
2334C0   40404040 --SAME--                                                          *                                *
2334E0   40404040 40404040 40404040 40404040   40404040 40404040 40404040 404040F0   *                               0*
233500   40404040 40404040 40404040 40404040   40D5C1D4 C5404040 40404040 40404040   *                 NAME           *
233520   40E2C5E7 404040C4 C5D7E34B 40D1D6C2   40C3D6C4 C5404040 D9C1E3C5 40404040   * SEX   DEPT. JOB CODE   RATE    *
233540   40404040 --SAME--                                                          *                                *
233580   40404040 F0404040 40404040 40404040   40404040 40404040 40404040 40000000   *    0                           *
2335A0   00400000 00000040 40404040 40C1E5C5   D9C1C7C5 40D9C1E3 C5404720 D54ED204   *            AVERAGE RATE   N K *
2335C0   10404040 40404040 40404040 40404040   40404040 40404040 40404040 40404040   *                                *
2335E0   40404040 --SAME--                                                          *                                *
233600   40404040 40404040 4001075F 000C000C   00000C00 40000001 00000000 00051C00   *                                *
233620   00000000 00000000 D5402020 21482020   40202120 00000000 5B5BC2D6 D7C5D540   *       N    .           $$BOPEN *
233640   5B5BC2C3 D3D6E2C5 00233268 002333A5   002332A0 002333F5 00233584 0023347A   *$$BCLOSE               5        *
233660   002334FF 051C050C 0C1CD4C5 D54040E6   D6D4C5D5 00000000 0A320000 0A320000   *          MEN  WOMEN            *
233680   47F0F01A 0A320000 C9D1C3C6 E9C9E6F0   35300A00 91801002 4710F026 0A0750E0   * 00      IJCFZIWO         0     *
2336A0   F07858E0 10209101 10044780 F04C9140   10024710 F04658E0 F07847F0 F01A58E0   *0              0       0   0  00 *
2336C0   101C07FE D502F06A E0004770 F05A47F0   F04650D0 F07418D0 4400102C 98DEF074   *     N 0       0  00   0        0 *
2336E0   07FE615C 400C0010 22000000 00287800   A0233118 00000000 0A320000 0A320000   *   /*                           *
233700   0A320000 47F0F01A C9D1C4C6 C1E9E9E6   524090BE F0A09180 10024710 F0280A07   *      00 IJDFAZZW    0       0  *
233720   58E01018 06E018D0 D2001017 000048C0   102E44C0 F0B018CC 18DC43C0 101741E0   *        K            0          *
233740   001043DE F0B519DC 4780F05A 46E0F04A   0A3243DE F0C543C0 101619CD 4770F080   *    0      0    0    0E       0 *
233760   91801016 4780F080 920B1028 0A009180   10024710 F0800A07 42001016 42001028   *      0              0          *
233780   0A009180 10024710 F0940A07 92011028   98BEF0A0 0A0007FE 00000000 00000000   *        0        0              *
2337A0   00000000 00000000 D200E000 D000F2C2   C1F9F8F7 F6F5F4F3 C3F14E60 F04093DB   *        K     2BA9876543C1 -0   *
```

Figure 7–10 *(Concluded)*

A typical definition for the SNAP data set might be:

```
SNAPDCB DCB  DSORG=PS,RECFM=VBA,MACRF=(W),                  X
             BLKSIZE=133,RECSIZE=133,DDNAME=SNAPDD
```

At the point in the program where the dump is to be made, insert:

```
 LA      13,SAVE
 OPEN    (SNAPDCB,(OUTPUT))
 SNAP    DCB=SNAPDCB,ID=1,PDATA=(PSW,REGS),                X
         STORAGE=(BEGIN,LINECNT+100)
 CLOSE   (SNAPDCB)
```

In this example, ID may be any number between 0 and 127 to identify the SNAP, the PDATA operands indicate that the Program Status Word (PSW) and all registers will be shown, and the STORAGE operands indicate the start and end of the dump of main storage.

Verify the precise operands to be used in the DCB and SNAP macros for your computer installation.

Analyzing the Core Dump

The exact content of a core dump will vary between DOS and OS, and even between different versions of the same operating system. However, all follow generally the same format.

AVERAGE HOURLY RATES FOR MEN AND WOMEN

NAME	SEX	DEPT.	JOB CODE	RATE
BELLE TOWER	F	3756	5625	10.75
BARRY MOORE	M	3756	5625	9.83
LYON HART	M	3756	5625	9.45
TOM KATZ	M	3756	5625	9.37
CONNIE SHURR	F	5337	3245	8.75
NEIL DOWNE	M	5337	3245	8.58
HAMMOND RYE	M	5337	3245	8.49
CANDY KANE	F	5337	3245	8.42
CLEMENT SEE	M	5337	3245	8.37
LOTTA WAITE	F	6541	1250	8.15
BETTA WAGER	F	6541	1250	8.10
ROGER ANDOVER	M	6541	1250	8.05
PERRY WINKLE	M	6541	1250	8.02
ANNE ARKIE	F	7409	7735	7.62
BARBIE DAHL	F	7409	7735	7.38
SEYMOUR SEITZ	M	8823	8642	6.75
OSCAR QUESTION	M	8823	8642	6.66
BILL OLADING	M	8823	8642	6.51
RICK SHAW	M	8823	8642	6.38
BEN Z DREEN	M	8823	8642	6.25
ARTHUR RYTUS	M	8823	8642	6.10

14 MEN AVERAGE RATE 7.77

7 WOMEN AVERAGE RATE 8.45

Figure 7–11 Output from Program 7

In Figure 7–10, the contents of the general registers appear first. Registers 0 through 7 appear on the first line and registers 8 through 15 on the next. Each register is represented as eight hexadecimal digits standing for the 32 bits, or four bytes. The contents of R12, our base register, are X‘4023307A’. The leftmost eight bits (X‘40’) are not a part of the address and are ignored. The address X‘23307A’ is the value we get by adding the relocation factor (X‘233078’) stated on the linkage editor map to the address of the USING *,3 statement (X‘000002’) on our source statement listing.

We can also find other addresses in R9 and R10, our link registers. R9 contains X‘233096’. Subtracting the load address of X‘233078’, we get X‘00001E’. Referring to our source listing, we find that X‘00001E’ is the address following BAL 9,MAINLOOP. The interrupt occurred while executing MAINLOOP and its subordinate modules. R10 contains X‘2330CE’; after subtracting the load address of X‘233078’, this gives X‘000056’. We find that

X‘000056’ is the address following BAL 10,PROCESS. It was in the PROCESS module that our error occurred.

Following the 16 general registers, the core dump displays the contents of the four floating-point registers. Each register contains 64 bits (16 hex digits, or eight bytes). We have not used these registers. They might contain anything at all, depending upon what other programs might have been run recently.

Next on the core dump appear the 16 control registers, each four bytes long like the general registers. These registers are not covered in this text.

The dump of main storage follows the registers. We have omitted a number of pages showing parts of the supervisor. The dump of our program area starts on the line at X‘233060’. Down the left column is the address in hexadecimal of the first byte of storage displayed on that line. The contents of storage are presented in eight columns, each containing eight hexadecimal digits to represent four bytes. To the right of the eight columns are the contents of the 32 bytes in character format. Where the hexadecimal codes do not form a printable character, a blank is printed. The character format makes it easy to locate data such as headings and records in I/O areas and work areas.

With a little practice, we can quickly find any desired location in the dump. Each of the eight columns displays a fullword, properly aligned on an address evenly divisible by 4. For example, on the line starting at location X‘233060’ the first column contains the contents of locations X‘233060-63’, the second column X‘233064-67’, the third column X‘233068-6B’, and the fourth column X‘23306C-6F’. After the slightly wider space, the fifth column contains X‘233070-73’, the sixth X‘233074-77’, the seventh X‘233078-7B’, and the eighth X‘23307C-7F’. The leftmost four columns will contain sixteen bytes starting with the address in the location counter column, in this case X‘233060’. The rightmost four columns will contain sixteen bytes starting with an address containing the next higher digit in the next-to-last digit of the address, in this case X‘233070’. In other words, if the next-to-last digit of the address is even, we will find the data in the leftmost four columns; if the next-to-last digit of the address is odd, the data will be in the rightmost four columns.

The contents of any address ending in X‘F’ preceded by an even digit will be found in the last byte of column four. The contents of any address ending in X‘F’ preceded by an odd digit will be found in the last byte of column eight.

Now we are ready to see just why our program was interrupted by examining the fields that were being processed at the time of the interrupt. Recall that the instruction being executed was AP PKTPWOM,PKRATE at location X‘233140’. We can locate the instruction itself in the first six bytes on the line beginning with X‘233140’. However, finding that instruction in the core dump will not help us, because the instruction was written correctly. It was the *data* being processed that were invalid.

The address of PKTPWOM in our program was X‘00059B’. When we add the relocation factor of X‘233078’, we find that the address in the core dump should be X'233613'. PKTPWOM was three bytes long, so we examine the three bytes starting at X'233613'. We find that they contain X'004000'. This is an invalid packed decimal field, since it was not properly initialized at the start of our program. This invalid data item caused the program interrupt.

We can further verify that PKRATE contains valid data. Its address in the program (X'000591') plus the relocation factor of X'233078' gives the dump address of X'233609'. The three bytes starting at X'233609' contain X'01075F', which is valid packed decimal data for $10.75, the rate in the first input record.

We might wish to locate the literal pool in the core dump. The address of the first literal in our program is X'0005C0'. Adding the relocation factor gives X'233638'. We can compare the data starting at this location with the object code of the literal pool in our source statement listing and see that both contain the literal =C'$$BOPEN ' (X'5B5BC2D6D7C5D540').

Let us now examine the work of the linkage editor in relocating address constants. We will find that the third instruction in the literal pool is =A(INFILE). The object code is X'000001F0'. This address constant, as we can see, is stored at location X'0005D0'. Adding the relocation factor to both addresses, we see that the address of INFILE should be X'233268', and it should be stored at location X'233648'. When we examine the fullword starting at X'233648' in our core dump, we find that it does indeed contain X'00233268'. The linkage editor has done its duty.

We will normally find that all machine instructions and constants in our program appear to be identical with the core dump, but address constants, I/O areas, and work areas will be different. Address constants are increased by the relocation factor, and I/O areas and work areas contain whatever records were being worked on at the time the dump was made.

Programming Tips

- To find a statement that causes an interrupt, subtract the linkage editor relocation factor from the address of the interrupt. The difference is the location of the error statement in the assembler source listing.
- To find the location of any instruction or data in a core dump, add the relocation factor from the linkage editor map to the location shown on the assembler listing. The sum is the location of the field in the dump.
- If the program is interrupted, place a PDUMP macro immediately ahead of the point of interrupt and rerun the program. The PDUMP will give a snapshot of the contents of storage so that you can locate the source of error.

The character display at the right side of the core dump makes easier the job of finding input records and character constants. We can quickly spot the record with social security number 475612038 and name BELLE TOWER in the I/O area INAREA starting at X'2332D0' and also in the work area INRECD starting at X'2333A5'.

The core dump is a powerful diagnostic tool for analyzing programs as they actually appear in main storage at execution time.

SUMMARY

In this section we present a number of suggestions for avoiding errors in source programs. Attention to input and output formats and program specifications helps to ensure that data is correctly defined. Structure charts, program flowcharts, and pseudocode help in development of program logic.

Coding should be carefully desk checked to see that operands in procedural statements match record and field descriptions and that names, op codes, and operands are correctly spelled and punctuated. Source statements keyed from coding forms should be proofread.

The assembler will detect and flag errors in syntax. Each error must be analyzed and corrected. Often statements that are correct in themselves will be flagged because of errors in other related statements.

The assembler produces the External Symbol Dictionary and the Relocation Dictionary to provide information to the linkage editor. The assembler also produces an optional Cross-Reference Listing naming each field and literal in alphabetical order and showing its location, length, statement number in which defined, and statements that refer to it.

After removing errors detected by the assembler in source statements, we can test the program. The linkage editor produces a map showing the location where the program phase and each module will appear in main storage. It also shows the relocation factor to be added to each address shown by the assembler listing to determine where that address will be in main storage at execution time.

The operating system presents an error message showing the location in main storage where an interruption occurs and the cause of the interruption. By subtracting the relocation factor from the address of interruption, we can determine where in our program the interruption occurred. The location counter refers to the instruction at fault. We can then analyze source code and make corrections.

Where necessary, a core dump can be examined to see the actual contents of main storage when the program was interrupted. The core dump provides information about the contents of general registers and storage locations that can help with detailed debugging.

TERMS FOR REVIEW

ADDR1 and ADDR2
Assembly time
Core dump
Cross-Reference Listing
Desk checking
Diagnostics
Execution time
External address
External Symbol Dictionary
Linkage
Linkage editor map
Literal pool
Object code
PDUMP
PRINT GEN
Program relocation
Relocation Dictionary
Relocation factor
Run time

REVIEW QUESTIONS

1. What are the principal methods by which output and input formats are represented?
2. Name some of the methods by which program logic can be developed and documented.
3. What parts of source coding should be double checked to guard against syntax errors?
4. What is meant by desk checking? When and why is it done?
5. Identify the principal parts of the assembler source listing.
6. How does source code produced by the assembler when PRINT GEN is used differ from that when PRINT NOGEN is used?
7. Name the parts of the assembler output other than the source listing. What is the purpose of each part?
8. How does the assembler indicate source statements that are in error? How does it help you determine the nature of the error?
9. Explain the role of the linkage editor. What output does it produce?
10. Given the address furnished by the operating system to show where a program interrupt occurred, explain how to find the program statement that was being executed at the time.
11. What system macros or job control options are available to produce a core dump in the event of a program interrupt?

EXERCISES

1. Refer to the core dump in Figure 7–10. Give the hex address of each of the following records or fields when the program is being loaded and executed:
   a. INITIAL module
   b. HEAD1
   c. PRDETAIL module
   d. TOTLINE

2. Refer again to the core dump in Figure 7–10. Show the contents in hex of each of the following fields at the time the program was interrupted:
   a. INRECD+42(4)
   b. EOFFLAG
   c. LINECNT
   d. PRJOB
3. Find the starting address of the printer module in the core dump in Figure 7–10. At what location in the module does the name IJDFAZZW appear?
4. A two-byte field named LINECNT is defined at location X'0000457' on the assembler listing. The linkage editor map shows a relocation factor of X'273078'. Where does LINECNT appear in a core dump?
5. Your program has been interrupted at location X'232486'. The linkage editor map shows that the load point of your program was X'232058'. Where in your program did the interrupt occur?
6. A literal in your program is shown as A(INFILE) with object code of X'000248'. The address constant in the core dump shows this address as X'403878'. What is the relocation factor?

PROGRAMMING PROBLEMS

1. Using Data Set 3 in Appendix D, write a program to produce a report titled Average Rate of Sales Returns. It should show the salesperson name, YTD sales, YTD returns, and percentage rate of returns for each salesperson. Accumulate total sales and returns for all employees and compute the overall rate of returns by dividing the total returns by the total sales. Deliberately make at least three errors in writing op codes and three in writing operands. Systematically track down and eliminate the errors as explained in this chapter until the assembler indicates no errors are found.
2. Expand Problem 1 by failing to initialize one total to zeros. When an error occurs, find the instruction that caused the error, insert a PDUMP macro (if you use DOS, or SNAP macro for OS) immediately in front of the instruction in error. Examine the storage dump and locate both operands being processed by the instruction in error. Correct the error, remove the PDUMP (or SNAP), and continue until the program runs correctly.

8 Control Break Processing

OBJECTIVES

After studying this chapter, you should be able to:

- Check sequence on a series of records from a file
- Describe control break processing
- Produce reports with single-level totals and final totals
- Produce reports with multiple-level totals and final totals
- Describe both DOWHILE and IF-THEN-ELSE structures for control break processing
- Distinguish between detail-printed and group-printed reports
- Ensure that total lines will print on the same page as the amounts included in the total

CHECKING SEQUENCE

Most batch processing techniques require that input records be in a given sequence. This usually means that the keys to the records must be in ascending numerical or alphabetic order. Sorting routines provided by the operating system or the programmer may be used to place records in the desired sequence.

We can check the sequence of records during normal processing. However, if they are out of sequence, we may have to stop the program in the middle of the run, or else records out of sequence must be omitted, so that the report is incomplete. Where there is the possibility that records are out of sequence for any reason, it is well to check sequence before beginning other processing.

Suppose our records should be in ascending order by social security number. In master files, we normally would have only one record per person, so that every social security key field should be higher than the key in the preceding record. But in transaction files, we might have more than one transaction for the same person, so that each key field could be higher than or equal to the preceding field. In either instance, a key field that is lower than the key of the preceding record would indicate a sequence error.

The record containing the key lower than the preceding record is not necessarily the one that is out of sequence. In checking the sequence of keys 11, 12, 99, 14, 17, 18, the 14 would be flagged as being out of sequence, whereas the 99 is actually the record that is out of place.

The best approach is to print an error message indicating the key of the preceding record and the key that is lower. Then the file must be resorted or otherwise examined to correct the sequence.

Figure 8–1 shows a method of checking sequence and printing an error message if any key is equal to or lower than the previous key. This method would be appropriate for checking a master file to detect an out-of-sequence or duplicate key (key lower than or equal to preceding key). To check only out-of-sequence and allow duplicate keys for a transaction file, use the statements in Figure 8–2.

CONTROL BREAK PROCESSING

A popular method of processing sequential files is to sort the records on a control field such as zip code, state, student major, or inventory item number. The sorting not only puts the records in ascending order, but also groups together all records having the same control key. By recognizing when the con-

```
         BAL 10,READRECD       Read first record
         MVC PREVKEY,SSKEY     Save key
DOWHILE  CLI EOFFLAG,'Y'       DOWHILE NOT end of file
         BE  ENDDO                *
IF       CLC SSKEY,PREVKEY        IF key <= previous key
         BH  ENDIF                   *
THEN     BAL 10,ERRORRTN             THEN print error message
ENDIF    EQU *                    ENDIF
         MVC PREVKEY,SSKEY        Save key
         BAL 10,READRECD          Read next record
         B   DOWHILE              *
ENDDO    EQU *                 ENDDO
```

Figure 8–1 Checking sequence with unique keys

```
IF     CLC SSKEY,PREVKEY     If key < previous key
       BNL ENDIF                *
THEN   BAL 11,ERRORRTN          THEN print error message
ENDIF  EQU *                 ENDIF
```

Figure 8–2 Checking sequence with duplicate keys

trol key to a group changes as we read in the records, we can accumulate group totals and print the totals whenever the key changes. This is called *control break* processing.

Since we have already determined that the records are in sequence by key, any difference between the key to the current record and the previous key indicates that we have reached the first record of the next group. Before processing that record, we must print out any totals that relate to the previous group and clear the totals to begin accumulating the next group totals.

A familiar example of control break processing is to read student course records and add up the total credit hours the student is taking. When the student number changes, we print the total hours for the first student, clear the total, and continue with the next student. If we print each record for the student, we have a *detail-printed* report. If we print only the totals with identifying information for the student, we have a *group-printed* report.

Single-Level Totals

When we compare only one key per record for a control break, we are taking *single-level* totals. The records for each student are considered to be at the same level. We might also include a *final total*, which is an accumulation of all the records, but the final total is not necessary.

The pseudocode in Figure 8–3 shows logic for a single-level total with final total.

Note where we save the student number to compare with keys of the following records. For the first comparison in the inner loop, the keys will al-

```
START PROGRAM
Clear final total
Clear student total
Read first record
DOWHILE not end of file
   Print student identifying information
   Save student number
   DOWHILE not end of file AND same student number
      Print course information
      Add credit hours to student total
      Read next record
   ENDDO
   Print student total
   Add student total to final total
   Clear student total
ENDDO
Print final total
END PROGRAM
```

Figure 8–3 Pseudocode for single-level total

ways be equal. The student number is saved again only after each control break.

We see in the preceding example an important reason for setting an end-of-file flag to be tested in two different places. When the flag is set in the inner DOWHILE loop, that loop is terminated and the student total is printed and added to the final total.

When going back to the DOWHILE of the outer loop, we find the flag is set, so that loop is also terminated, printing the final total.

This logic would not be possible if we had gone directly to the ENDDO of the outer DOWHILE loop at end of file as we did in sample programs in the first four chapters.

Multiple-Level Totals

We may have more than one level of totals. For example, our file may have more than one record per student, each showing the credit hours for one course. Our student record has keys for department, field of study, and student number. The department code is considered the major key, field of study the intermediate key, and the student number the minor key. Our report calls for the total hours taken by each student having a given field of study, then the total hours within that major, then the total hours within the department, and the final total of all hours within the institution. This involves multiple-level totals.

For this logic we use nested DOWHILE loops with multiple conditions to test each level. We take a minor total whenever any of the keys change, an intermediate total whenever the major or intermediate key changes, and a major total only when the major key changes. Our pseudocode in Figure 8–4 concentrates on control break logic and omits references to line counts and headings.

The method shown for accumulating only one level of totals at a time is called *rolling totals*. In this method, detail records are added only to the minor total. When the minor total is printed, it is added to the intermediate total and then cleared. In turn, when the intermediate total is printed, it is added to the major total and then cleared. When a major total is printed, it is added to the final total and then cleared.

Another option is to add the credit hours to all four totals in the innermost loop while processing the detail record. The second method requires more actual additions, although the number of instructions written is the same.

PROGRAM 8: TOTAL MEN AND WOMEN BY JOB CODE WITHIN DEPARTMENT

Our next program is to show how many men and women there are within each job code in each department. We also show the total men and women in

```
START PROGRAM
Clear all totals
Read first record
Save student number, student major, and department keys
DOWHILE not end of file
   Print student identifying information
   DOWHILE not end of file AND same department
      DOWHILE not end of file AND same department and student major
         DOWHILE not end of file AND all keys the same
            Print course information
            Add credit hours to student total hours
            Read next record
         ENDDO
         Print student total hours
         Add student total hours to student major total hours
         Clear student total hours
         Save student number
      ENDDO
      Print student major total hours
      Add student major total hours to department total hours
      Clear student major total hours
      Save student major key
   ENDDO
   Print department total hours
   Add department total hours to institution total hours
   Clear department total hours
   Save department key
ENDDO
Print institution total hours
END PROGRAM
```

Figure 8–4 Pseudocode for multiple-level totals

Programming Tips

- Check sequence of data records before doing control break processing. It is better to find and correct sequence errors before the report is printed than to have to correct and rerun it later.
- For multiple-level control break processing, check the highest-level key first, then the next-highest, and on down to the lowest-level key. A control break at any level forces out all lower-level totals as well as the level where the break occurs.

each department and the totals for the entire organization. This task requires multiple-level control break processing as illustrated in this chapter.

The program uses the standard subroutines to read input records, print headings only when ready to print detail lines, and print total lines on the same page as the detail data they accumulate.

We use fully structured modular form. The module chart appears in Figure 8–5. There are three first-level modules and seven second-level modules.

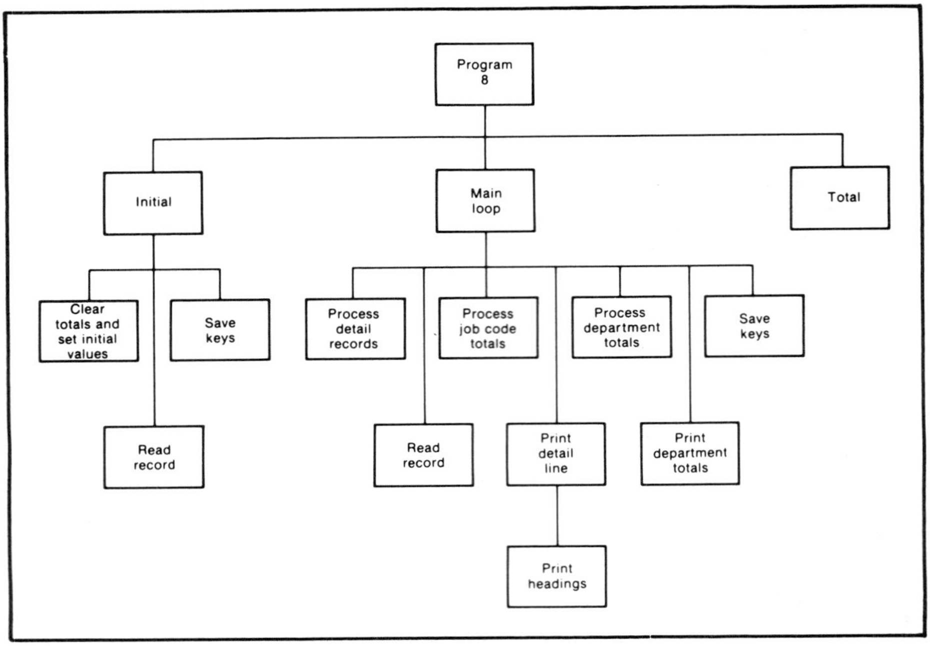

Figure 8–5 Structure chart for Program 8

Input records are arranged in order by department code. Within each department, they are in order by job code. Job code is our minor control field, department is the major field, and the entire organization (end of file) is the final total. With only two levels, there is no intermediate field.

This is a group-printed report. Individual records are not printed. So long as no control break occurs, we add to the totals for men or women for that job code. At the first control break, we print the totals for that job code and test to see if an intermediate control break occurs. If not, we continue with the next job code within the same department.

When an intermediate control break occurs, we take the minor total for the last job code within that department, then print the department total, and continue with the first job code within the next department.

We print the minor total single-spaced as a detail line, and space once after the department total to make our output attractive. We do not test the line counter before printing the department total so that it will always print on the same page with its job code totals.

We use nested compound DOWHILE loops to test for two levels of totals, plus final totals. The outer loop tests only for end of file (final total). The first nested loop tests end of file and department code (major control break). The innermost nested loop tests end of file, department code, and job code (minor break).

Careful analysis of this logic will reveal a general rule of control break processing. Whenever a control break occurs at any level, all lower-level totals are forced out before the current total is printed. In this case, whenever end of file is reached, the job code totals and department totals are printed before the final totals are.

Figure 8–6 shows the source statements with pseudocode for Program 8. Figure 8–7 shows the output from the program.

```
  LOC  OBJECT CODE     ADDR1 ADDR2  STMT   SOURCE STATEMENT                                     DOS/VSE ASSEMBLER 15.00 86-03-27

                                       1 ***********************************************************************
                                       2 *                  ALTON R. KINDRED, PROGRAM 8
                                       3 * THIS PROGRAM READS THE EMPLOYEE FILE AND PRINTS THE TOTAL MEN AND
                                       4 * WOMEN IN EACH JOB CODE WITHIN EACH DEPARTMENT.  THEN IT PRINTS THE
                                       5 * TOTAL OF EACH SEX WITHIN THE DEPARTMENT.  AT END OF FILE IT PRINTS
                                       6 * THE TOTAL MEN AND WOMEN WITHIN THE ENTIRE ORGANIZATION.
                                       7 *          REGISTERS USED:
                                       8 *                  R9-11  - LINKS TO MODULES
                                       9 *                  R12    - BASE REGISTER
                                      10 ***********************************************************************
                                      11          PRINT NOGEN
000000                                12 MAINLINE START 0                             SET LOCATION COUNTER
                                      13 *        STM   14,12,12(13)                   SAVE REGISTERS FOR OS          OS
000000 05C0                           14          BALR  12,0                           LOAD BASE REGISTER
                             00002    15          USING *,12                           DESIGNATE BASE REGISTER
                                      16 *        ST    13,SAVE+4                      STORE REGISTER 13              OS
                                      17 *        LA    13,SAVE                        LOAD SAVE AREA ADDRESS         OS
                                      18 *        OPEN  (INFILE,(INPUT),PRINTER,(OUTPUT))                             OS
                                      19          OPEN  INFILE,PRINTER                 OPEN FILES                     DOS
000016 4590 C036             00038    28          BAL   9,INITIAL                      DO INITIAL PROCESSING
00001A 4590 C044             00046    29          BAL   9,MAINLOOP                     DO MAIN PROCESSING LOOP
00001E 4590 C0AE             000B0    30          BAL   9,TOTAL                        DO TOTAL PROCESSING
                                      31          CLOSE INFILE,PRINTER                 CLOSE FILES                    DOS
                                      40          EOJ                                  END PROGRAM                    DOS
                                      43 *        CLOSE (INFILE,,PRINTER)              CLOSE FILES                    OS
                                      44 *        L     13,SAVE+4                      LOAD SAVE AREA ADDRESS         OS
                                      45 *        LM    14,12,12(13)                   RESTORE REGISTERS              OS
                                      46 *        BR    14                             RETURN TO OS                   OS
                                      47 ***********************************************************************
                                      48 *                  FIRST LEVEL MODULES
                                      49 ***********************************************************************
                                      50 *
                                      51 *                  INITIALIZATION MODULE
                                      52 *
000038 45A0 C0D8             000DA    53 INITIAL  BAL   10,CLEARSET                    SET INITIAL VALUES
00003C 45A0 C10E             00110    54          BAL   10,READRECD                    READ FIRST RECORD
000040 45A0 C12C             0012E    55          BAL   10,SAVEKEYS                    SAVE DEPT. AND JOB CODE KEYS
000044 07F9                           56          BR    9                              RETURN
                                      57 *
                                      58 *                  MAIN PROCESSING LOOP
                                      59 *
                             00046    60 MAINLOOP EQU   *
                             00046    61 DOWHILE  EQU   *                              DOWHILE NOT END OF FILE
000046 95E8 C6AD       006AF          62          CLI   EOFFLAG,C'Y'                     *
00004A 4780 C0AC       000AE          63          BE    ENDDO                            *
00004E 95E8 C6AD       006AF          64 DOWHILE2 CLI   EOFFLAG,C'Y'                     DOWHILE NOT END OF FILE
000052 4780 C098       0009A          65          BE    ENDDO2                             *
000056 D503 C3D5 C6A5  003D7 006A7    66 AND2     CLC   INDEPT,SAVEDEPT                  AND SAME DEPARTMENT
00005C 4770 C098       0009A          67          BNE   ENDDO2                             *
000060 95E8 C6AD       006AF          68 DOWHILE3 CLI   EOFFLAG,C'Y'                       DOWHILE NOT END OF FILE
000064 4780 C086       00088          69          BE    ENDDO3                               *
000068 D503 C3D5 C6A5  003D7 006A7    70 AND3     CLC   INDEPT,SAVEDEPT                    AND SAME DEPARTMENT
00006E 4770 C086       00088          71          BNE   ENDDO3                               *
000072 D503 C3E0 C6A9  003E2 006AB    72 AND3A    CLC   INJOB,SAVEJOB                      AND SAME JOB CODE
000078 4770 C086       00088          73          BNE   ENDDO3                               *
00007C 45A0 C13A             0013C    74          BAL   10,PROCESS                           PROCESS DETAIL RECORD
000080 45A0 C10E             00110    75          BAL   10,READRECD                          READ NEXT RECORD
000084 47F0 C05E       00060          76          B     DOWHILE3                             *
                             00088    77 ENDDO3   EQU   *                                  ENDDO
000088 45A0 C160             00162    78          BAL   10,JOBTOT                          PROCESS JOB CODE TOTALS
00008C 45A0 C1E2             001E4    79          BAL   10,PRDETAIL                        PRINT DETAIL LINE
000090 D203 C6A9 C3E0  006AB 003E2    80          MVC   SAVEJOB,INJOB                      SAVE JOB CODE KEY
000096 47F0 C04C       0004E          81          B     DOWHILE2                           *
                             0009A    82 ENDDO2   EQU   *                                ENDDO
00009A 45A0 C19E             001A0    83          BAL   10,DEPTOT                        PROCESS DEPARTMENT TOTALS
00009E 45A0 C212             00214    84          BAL   10,PRDEPTOT                      PRINT TOTAL LINE
0000A2 45A0 C12C             0012E    85          BAL   10,SAVEKEYS                      SAVE JOB CODE AND DEPT. KEYS
0000A6 92F0 C3FB       003FD          86          MVI   PRLINE,C'0'                      SET DOUBLE SPACE
0000AA 47F0 C044       00046          87          B     DOWHILE                          *
                             000AE    88 ENDDO    EQU   *                              ENDDO
0000AE 07F9                           89          BR    9                              RETURN
                                      90 *
                                      91 *                  FINAL TOTAL MODULE
                                      92 *
0000B0 D206 C633 C6B2  00635 006B4    93 TOTAL    MVC   PRTOTMEN,PATRN2                SET UP TOTAL MEN IN ORG.
0000B6 DE06 C633 C69D  00635 0069F    94          ED    PRTOTMEN,PKTOTMEN              *
0000BC D206 C641 C6B2  00643 006B4    95          MVC   PRTOTWOM,PATRN2                SET UP TOTAL WOMEN IN ORG.
0000C2 DE06 C641 C6A0  00643 006A2    96          ED    PRTOTWOM,PKTOTWOM              *
                                      97          PUT   PRINTER,TOTLINE                PRINT TOTAL LINE
0000D8 07F9                          103          BR    9                              RETURN
                                     104 ***********************************************************************
                                     105 *                  SECOND LEVEL MODULES
                                     106 ***********************************************************************
                                     107 *
                                     108 *                  CLEAR TOTALS MODULE
                                     109 *
0000DA F810 C695 C6F2  00697 006F4   110 CLEARSET ZAP   PKJOBMEN,=P'0'                 CLEAR TOTALS
0000E0 F810 C697 C6F2  00699 006F4   111          ZAP   PKJOBWOM,=P'0'                 *
```

Figure 8–6 Program 8 assembler listing

```
  LOC  OBJECT CODE    ADDR1 ADDR2  STMT   SOURCE STATEMENT                                     DOS/VSE ASSEMBLER 15.00 86-03-27

0000E6 F810 C699 C6F2 0069B 006F4   112          ZAP   PKDEPMEN,=P'0'           *
0000EC F810 C69B C6F2 0069D 006F4   113          ZAP   PKDEPWOM,=P'0'           *
0000F2 F820 C69D C6F2 0069F 006F4   114          ZAP   PKTOTMEN,=P'0'           *
0000F8 F820 C6A0 C6F2 006A2 006F4   115          ZAP   PKTOTWOM,=P'0'           *
0000FE F811 C6A3 C6EE 006A5 006F0   116          ZAP   LINECNT,=P'51'           SET LINE COUNT ABOVE MAX. LINES
000104 9240 C3FB      003FD         117          MVI   PRLINE,C' '              CLEAR PRINT LINE
000108 D283 C3FC C3FB 003FE 003FD   118          MVC   PRLINE+1(132),PRLINE     *
00010E 07FA                         119          BR    10                       RETURN
                                    120 *
                                    121 *              READ RECORD MODULE
                                    122 *
                            00110   123 READRECD EQU   *
000110 92D5 C6AD      006AF         124          MVI   EOFFLAG,C'N'             SET END OF FILE FLAG OFF
                                    125          GET   INFILE,INRECD            READ RECORD
000124 47F0 C12A      0012C         131 IFEOF    B     ENDIFEOF                 IF END OF FILE
000128 92E8 C6AD      006AF         132 THENEOF  MVI   EOFFLAG,C'Y'               THEN SET EOF FLAG ON
                            0012C   133 ENDIFEOF EQU   *                        ENDIF
00012C 07FA                         134          BR    10                       RETURN
                                    136 *
                                    137 *              SAVE KEYS MODULE
                                    138 *
00012E D203 C6A9 C3E0 006AB 003E2   139 SAVEKEYS MVC   SAVEJOB,INJOB            SAVE JOB CODE KEY
000134 D203 C6A5 C3D5 006A7 003D7   140          MVC   SAVEDEPT,INDEPT          SAVE DEPARTMENT KEY
00013A 07FA                         141          BR    10                       RETURN
                                    142 *
                                    143 *              PROCESS RECORD MODULE
                                    144 *
                            0013C   145 PROCESS  EQU   *
00013C 95D4 C3C8      003CA         146 IF       CLI   INSEX,C'M'               IF MALE
000140 4770 C152      00154         147          BNE   ELSE                       *
000144 FA10 C695 C6F3 00697 006F5   148 THEN     AP    PKJOBMEN,=P'1'             ADD 1 TO TOTAL MEN IN JOB
00014A FA10 C699 C6F3 0069B 006F5   149          AP    PKDEPMEN,=P'1'             ADD 1 TO TOTAL MEN IN DEPT.
000150 47F0 C15E      00160         150          B     ENDIF                      *
                            00154   151 ELSE     EQU   *                        ELSE
000154 FA10 C697 C6F3 00699 006F5   152          AP    PKJOBWOM,=P'1'             ADD 1 TO TOTAL WOMEN IN JOB
00015A FA10 C69B C6F3 0069D 006F5   153          AP    PKDEPWOM,=P'1'             ADD 1 TO TOTAL WOMEN IN DEPT
000160 07FA                         154 ENDIF    BR    10                       RETURN
                                    155 *
                                    156 *              JOB TOTAL MODULE
                                    157 *
                            00162   158 JOBTOT   EQU   *
000162 D204 C414 C6F4 00416 006F6   159          MVC   PRJOB(5),=C'     '       CLEAR MESSAGE AREA
000168 D203 C408 C6A5 0040A 006A7   160          MVC   PRDEPT,SAVEDEPT          SET UP IDENTIFIERS
00016E D203 C414 C6A9 00416 006AB   161          MVC   PRJOB,SAVEJOB            *
000174 D203 C421 C6AE 00423 006B0   162          MVC   PRMEN,PATRN              SET UP TOTALS FOR JOB CODE
00017A DE03 C421 C695 00423 00697   163          ED    PRMEN,PKJOBMEN           *
000180 D203 C42F C6AE 00431 006B0   164          MVC   PRWOM,PATRN              *
000186 DE03 C42F C697 00431 00699   165          ED    PRWOM,PKJOBWOM           *
00018C D203 C6A9 C3E0 006AB 003E2   166          MVC   SAVEJOB,INJOB            SAVE JOB CODE
000192 F810 C695 C6F2 00697 006F4   167          ZAP   PKJOBMEN,=P'0'           CLEAR JOB TOTALS
000198 F810 C697 C6F2 00699 006F4   168          ZAP   PKJOBWOM,=P'0'           *
00019E 07FA                         169          BR    10                       RETURN
                                    170 *
                                    171 *              DEPARTMENT TOTAL MODULE
                                    172 *
                            001A0   173 DEPTOT   EQU   *
0001A0 D203 C408 C6A5 0040A 006A7   174          MVC   PRDEPT,SAVEDEPT          SET UP DEPARTMENT CODE
0001A6 D204 C414 C6F9 00416 006FB   175          MVC   PRJOB(5),=C'TOTAL'       SET UP TOTAL MESSAGE
0001AC D203 C421 C6AE 00423 006B0   176          MVC   PRMEN,PATRN              SET UP TOTAL MEN IN DEPT.
0001B2 DE03 C421 C699 00423 0069B   177          ED    PRMEN,PKDEPMEN           *
0001B8 D203 C42F C6AE 00431 006B0   178          MVC   PRWOM,PATRN              SET UP TOTAL WOMEN IN DEPT.
0001BE DE03 C42F C69B 00431 0069D   179          ED    PRWOM,PKDEPWOM           *
0001C4 FA21 C69D C699 0069F 0069B   180          AP    PKTOTMEN,PKDEPMEN        ADD DEPT. TOTALS TO ORG. TOTALS
0001CA FA21 C6A0 C69B 006A2 0069D   181          AP    PKTOTWOM,PKDEPWOM        *
0001D0 D203 C6A5 C3D5 006A7 003D7   182          MVC   SAVEDEPT,INDEPT          *
0001D6 F810 C699 C6F2 0069B 006F4   183          ZAP   PKDEPMEN,=P'0'           CLEAR DEPT. TOTALS
0001DC F810 C69B C6F2 0069D 006F4   184          ZAP   PKDEPWOM,=P'0'           *
0001E2 07FA                         185          BR    10                       RETURN
                                    187 *
                                    188 *              PRINT DETAIL LINE MODULE
                                    189 *
                            001E4   190 PRDETAIL EQU   *
0001E4 F911 C6A3 C6F0 006A5 006F2   191 IFEOP    CP    LINECNT,=P'50'           IF LINE COUNT NOT < 50
0001EA 4740 C1F0      001F2         192          BL    ENDIFEOP                   *
0001EE 45B0 C22E            00230   193 THENEOP  BAL   11,HEADING                 THEN PRINT HEADINGS
                            001F2   194 ENDIFEOP EQU   *                        ENDIF
                                    195          PUT   PRINTER,PRLINE           PRINT DETAIL LINE
000202 FA10 C6A3 C6F3 006A5 006F5   201          AP    LINECNT,=P'1'            ADD 1 TO LINE COUNT
000208 9240 C3FB      003FD         202          MVI   PRLINE,C' '              CLEAR PRINT LINE
00020C D283 C3FC C3FB 003FE 003FD   203          MVC   PRLINE+1(132),PRLINE     *
000212 07FA                         204          BR    10                       RETURN
                                    205 *
                                    206 *              PRINT DEPT. TOTAL LINE
                                    207 *
                                    208 PRDEPTOT PUT   PRINTER,PRLINE           PRINT DEPT. TOTAL LINE
000224 92F0 C3FB      003FD         214          MVI   PRLINE,C'0'              SET FOR DOUBLE SPACE
000228 FA10 C6A3 C6FE 006A5 00700   215          AP    LINECNT,=P'2'            ADD 2 TO LINE COUNT
00022E 07FA                         216          BR    10                       RETURN
                                    217 *
                                    218 *              PRINT HEADING MODULE
                                    219 *
                                    220 HEADING  PUT   PRINTER,HEAD1            PRINT HEADINGS
                                    226          PUT   PRINTER,HEAD2            *
                                    232          PUT   PRINTER,HEAD3            *
000260 92F0 C3FB      003FD         238          MVI   PRLINE,C'0'              SET LINE TO DOUBLE SPACE
000264 F810 C6A3 C6F2 006A5 006F4   239          ZAP   LINECNT,=P'0'            CLEAR LINE COUNT
00026A 07FB                         240          BR    11                       RETURN
                                    241 ***********************************************************************DOS
                                    242 *              FILE DEFINITIONS AND I/O AREAS                          DOS
                                    243 ***********************************************************************DOS
                                    244 INFILE   DTFCD BLKSIZE=80,IOAREA1=INAREA,DEVICE=2540,                  DOSX
                                                       DEVADDR=SYSIPT,EOFADDR=THENEOF,WORKA=YES                DOS
                                    265 *                                                                      DOS
```

Figure 8–6 *(Continued)*

```
 LOC  OBJECT CODE     ADDR1 ADDR2  STMT   SOURCE STATEMENT                                     DOS/VSE ASSEMBLER 15.00 86-03-27

                                    266 PRINTER  DTFPR BLKSIZE=133,IOAREA1=PRTAREA,DEVICE=1403,          DOSX
                                                       CTLCHR=ASA,DEVADDR=SYS009,WORKA=YES               DOS
                                    287 *                                                                DOS
0002D8                              288 INAREA   DS    CL80                                              DOS
000328                              289 PRTAREA  DS    CL133                                             DOS
                                    290 *****************************************************************OS
                                    291 *                  DEVICE CONTROL BLOCKS AND SAVE AREA           OS
                                    292 *****************************************************************OS
                                    293 *INFILE  DCB   DDNAME=INFILE,BLKSIZE=80,LRECL=80,                OSX
                                    294 *              MACRF=GM,DSORG=PS,EODAD=THENEOF                   OS
                                    295 *                                                                OS
                                    296 *PRINTER DCB   DDNAME=PRINTER,BLKSIZE=133,LRECL=133,             OSX
                                    297 *              MACRF=PMA,DSORG=PS                                OS
                                    298 *                                                                OS
                                    299 *SAVE    DS    18F                                               OS
                                    301 ******************************************************************
                                    302 *                  DATA DEFINITIONS
                                    303 ******************************************************************
0003AD                              304 INRECD   DS    0CL80
0003AD                              305          DS    CL29
0003CA                              306 INSEX    DS    CL1
0003CB                              307          DS    CL12
0003D7                              308 INDEPT   DS    CL4
0003DB                              309          DS    CL7
0003E2                              310 INJOB    DS    CL4
0003E6                              311          DS    CL23
                                    312 *
0003FD                              313 PRLINE   DS    0CL133
0003FD                              314          DS    CL13
00040A                              315 PRDEPT   DS    CL4
00040E                              316          DS    CL8
000416                              317 PRJOB    DS    CL4
00041A                              318          DS    CL9
000423                              319 PRMEN    DS    CL4
000427                              320          DS    CL10
000431                              321 PRWOM    DS    CL4
000435                              322          DS    CL78
                                    323 *
000483                              324 HEAD1    DS    0CL133
000483 F140404040404040             325          DC    CL13'1'
000490 D5E4D4C2C5D940D6             326          DC    CL120'NUMBER OF EMPLOYEES BY DEPARTMENT AND JOB CODE'
                                    327 *
000508                              328 HEAD2    DS    0CL133
000508 F040404040404040             329          DC    CL26'0'
000522 D1D6C24040404040             330          DC    CL10'JOB'
00052C D5E4D4C2C5D940D6             331          DC    CL14'NUMBER OF'
00053A D5E4D4C2C5D940D6             332          DC    CL83'NUMBER OF'
                                    333 *
00058D                              334 HEAD3    DS    0CL133
00058D 4040404040404040             335          DC    CL11' '
000598 C4C5D7C1D9E3D4C5             336          DC    CL14'DEPARTMENT'
0005A6 C3D6C4C540404040             337          DC    CL14'CODE'
0005B4 D4C5D54040404040             338          DC    CL12'MEN'
0005C0 E6D6D4C5D5404040             339          DC    CL82'WOMEN'
                                    340 *
000612                              341 TOTLINE  DS    0CL133
000612 F040404040404040             342          DC    CL11'0'
00061D D6D9C7C1D5C9E9C1             343          DC    CL24'ORGANIZATION TOTALS'
000635                              344 PRTOTMEN DS    CL7
00063C 40404040404040               345          DC    CL7' '
000643                              346 PRTOTWOM DS    CL7
00064A 4040404040404040             347          DC    CL77' '
                                    348 *
000697                              349 PKJOBMEN DS    PL2
000699                              350 PKJOBWOM DS    PL2
00069B                              351 PKDEPMEN DS    PL2
00069D                              352 PKDEPWOM DS    PL2
00069F                              353 PKTOTMEN DS    PL3
0006A2                              354 PKTOTWOM DS    PL3
0006A5                              355 LINECNT  DS    PL2
0006A7                              356 SAVEDEPT DS    CL4
0006AB                              357 SAVEJOB  DS    CL4
0006AF                              358 EOFFLAG  DS    CL1
0006B0 40202120                     359 PATRN    DC    XL4'40202120'
0006B4 4020206B202120               360 PATRN2   DC    XL7'4020206B202120'
                                    361 *
                      00000         362          END   MAINLINE
0006C0 5B5BC2D6D7C5D540             363                =C'$$BOPEN '
0006C8 5B5BC2C3D3D6E2C5             364                =C'$$BCLOSE'
0006D0 000002A8                     365                =A(PRINTER)
0006D4 00000612                     366                =A(TOTLINE)
0006D8 00000270                     367                =A(INFILE)
0006DC 000003AD                     368                =A(INRECD)
0006E0 000003FD                     369                =A(PRLINE)
0006E4 00000483                     370                =A(HEAD1)
0006E8 00000508                     371                =A(HEAD2)
0006EC 0000058D                     372                =A(HEAD3)
0006F0 051C                         373                =P'51'
0006F2 050C                         374                =P'50'
0006F4 0C                           375                =P'0'
0006F5 1C                           376                =P'1'
0006F6 4040404040                   377                =C'     '
0006FB E3D6E3C1D3                   378                =C'TOTAL'
000700 2C                           379                =P'2'
```

Figure 8–6 *(Concluded)*

NUMBER OF EMPLOYEES BY DEPARTMENT AND JOB CODE

DEPARTMENT	JOB CODE	NUMBER OF MEN	NUMBER OF WOMEN
1234	0010	1	0
1234	0020	1	0
1234	1200	0	2
1234	4130	1	0
1234	TOTAL	3	2
2143	0050	0	1
2143	1200	0	1
2143	6715	1	0
2143	TOTAL	1	2
3756	0050	1	0
3756	1200	1	0
3756	5625	3	1
3756	TOTAL	5	1
4028	0050	0	1
4028	1200	0	3
4028	TOTAL	0	4
5337	0050	1	0
5337	1200	0	1
5337	3245	3	2
5337	TOTAL	4	3
6541	0050	0	1
6541	1250	2	2
6541	TOTAL	2	3
7409	0060	0	1
7409	7735	0	2
7409	TOTAL	0	3
8823	0060	1	0
8823	8642	6	0
8823	TOTAL	7	0
ORGANIZATION TOTALS		22	18

Figure 8–7 Output from Program 8

CONTROL BREAK PROCESSING WITH IF-THEN-ELSE STRUCTURE

Many programmers prefer to use IF-THEN-ELSE structures with control break processing. The pseudocode in Figure 8–8 shows single level totals with a final total.

The first time through the loop, the minor key in the input record will agree with the key that was just saved, so that no total will be taken. We need not save the minor key again until it changes and a minor total is taken.

At end of file, we must take a minor total for the last minor group and add that total to the final total before printing the final total. We could use a minor total subroutine, since the minor total is printed both when a control break occurs and at end of file.

Multiple-level totals using IF-THEN-ELSE structure are more complex. We must check first for the highest level control break. If it happens, all lower level totals must be printed out from lowest to highest. If the highest level has no control break, we then test the next highest level. If it changes, all lower level totals are forced out as well. After printing any totals that are necessary, we then process the detail record just read, read another record, and return to the start of our DOWHILE loop to test for end of file.

If no control break occurs at any level, we continue processing each detail record and read the next one until some change occurs.

The pseudocode in Figure 8–9 illustrates multiple-level totals with the IF-THEN-ELSE structure. Since each total except the final total must be printed under two or more conditions, each total routine is shown as a subroutine. Notice that when more than one total is taken, an extra space is taken only after the last total to improve the appearance of the report.

SUMMARY

Where records must be in a specified sequence, they may be checked by comparing the key of each record as it is read with the key of the preceding record. If records should be in ascending order, any key lower than the preceding key indicates a sequence error.

Control break processing requires that records be previously sorted into a sequence, placing all records with the same keys into groups. As each record is read, its key is compared to the key of the preceding record. If the keys are the same, counts or values are added to the group totals. When the keys differ, totals for that group must be printed out before processing for the first record of the new group is done.

Multiple-level totals may be taken by comparing more than one key from each record. Keys are called minor, intermediate, and major from lowest level to highest. In addition, final totals may be accumulated for all records. Major

```
START PROGRAM
Clear minor total and final total
Set line counter to 51
Read first record
Save minor key
DOWHILE NOT end of file
   IF minor key different
      THEN print minor total
      Add minor total to final total
      Clear minor total
      Take extra space
      Save minor key
   ENDIF
   Setup detail line
   IF line counter > 50
      THEN print headings
      Reset line counter to 0
      Set for double spacing
   ENDIF
   Print detail line
   Add amount to minor total
   Read next record
ENDDO
Print minor total
Add minor total to final total
Print final total
END PROGRAM
```

Figure 8–8 Pseudocode for single-level total with IF-THEN-ELSE structure

```
START PROGRAM
Clear all totals
Set line counter to 51
Read first record
Save major, intermediate, and minor keys
DOWHILE NOT end of file
   IF major key different
      THEN DO minor total routine
      DO intermediate total routine
      DO major total routine
      Take extra space
      Add 4 to line counter
   ELSE IF intermediate key different
         THEN DO minor total routine
         DO intermediate total routine
         Take extra space
         Add 3 to line counter
      ELSE IF minor key different
```

Figure 8–9 Pseudocode for multiple-level totals with IF-THEN-ELSE structure

```
            THEN DO minor total routine
            Take extra space
            Add 2 to line counter
         ENDIF
      ENDIF
   ENDIF
   Setup detail line
   DO print detail line routine
   Add amount to minor total
   Read next record
ENDDO
DO minor total routine
DO intermediate total routine
DO major total routine
Print final total
END PROGRAM

MINOR TOTAL ROUTINE
Print minor total
Add minor total to intermediate total
Clear minor total
Save minor key
RETURN

INTERMEDIATE TOTAL ROUTINE
Print intermediate total
Add intermediate total to major total
Clear intermediate total
Save intermediate key
RETURN

MAJOR TOTAL ROUTINE
Print major total
Add major total to final total
Clear major total
Save major key
RETURN

PRINT DETAIL LINE ROUTINE
IF line counter > 50
   THEN print heading
   Set print control for double space
   Reset line counter to 0

ENDIF
Print detail line
Add 1 to line counter
RETURN
```

Figure 8–9 *(Concluded)*

keys are compared first, then intermediate keys, and finally minor keys. Any change in a key forces out all lower level totals.

Nested DOWHILE structures or nested IF structures may be used for control break processing. Compound conditions are usually required to determine if a control break has occurred in any of the levels.

Detail-printed reports show each record that is processed, followed by totals whenever a control break occurs. Group-printed reports do not show individual records, but only totals. The minor total, being the lowest printed, appears to be a detail line and is usually single-spaced.

The method of rolling totals involves adding totals at one level to the next higher level after they have been printed and before they are cleared for use with the next group.

TERMS FOR REVIEW

Control break
Detail line
Detail-printed report
Group-printed report
Intermediate total
Key
Major total
Minor total
Multiple-level totals
Rolling totals
Sequence check
Single-level totals
Total line

REVIEW QUESTIONS

1. How are records checked to see if they are in sequence? In what kind of processing is correct sequence important?
2. What is meant by a control break? When does it occur?
3. Does it matter what sequence records are in for control break processing? Why?
4. Under what two conditions are single-level totals printed? What other total may be taken with single-level totals?
5. What two logical structures are described in this chapter for control break processing?
6. Why are compound conditions necessary when using nested loops with multiple-level totals?
7. What processing takes place in the innermost loop of nested loops with multiple-level totals?
8. What totals must be printed each time the major key changes in multiple-level totals? What ones are printed at end of file?
9. What problems would be encountered in multiple-level total processing if we merely let the GET macro branch to the end-of-file routine instead of setting a flag?

EXERCISES

1. Write statements to check sequence or a group of records where duplicate keys are not permitted. Make up your own names for data elements.
2. Modify the program you wrote for Exercise 1 to check sequence where duplicate keys are permitted.
3. Write in assembler language the main processing loop in the pseudocode showing nested IF structure for multiple-level totals at the end of this chapter. Make up meaningful names for the various keys and total fields. Use BAL statements to utilize processing modules to carry out the various total routines.
4. Write statements to add detail amounts to minor, intermediate, major, and final totals.
5. Rewrite the statements in Exercise 4 to add the detail amount only to the minor total and roll each to the next higher level total when a control break occurs.

PROGRAMMING PROBLEMS

1. Using Data Set 4 in Appendix D, write a program to create a Student Schedule Report. Print the schedules for four students per page. Omit column headings. On the first line for each student, print student number, name, and year and semester in form yy-2. Then double space and print the course abbreviation, course number and section in form nnnn.ss, and credit hours in form 3.0 on each detail line.

   Student number is the key. At the control break, skip four lines and start the schedule for the next student. Single space detail lines.
2. Modify Problem 1 to print a Student Grade Report. This report is similar to the Student Schedule Report, but adds one column for grade and one for grade points. Grade points for each course are calculated by multiplying the credit hours by 4 if the grade is an A, by 3 if grade is B, by 2 if C, or by 1 if D. All other grades receive no points.

   Add the credit hours and grade points for each student. At control break, calculate the grade point average by dividing total credit hours into total grade points. Carry the grade point average to one decimal place rounded. At end of file, print for all students the total hours, total grade points, and overall average.
3. Using Data Set 3 in Appendix D, write a Sales Analysis Report showing salesperson number, name, and net sales (year-to-date sales less year-to-date returns). Accumulate net sales for each region and overall net sales for the organization. The region code is the key. Show report headings and column headings. The region total should be identified with the region code.

9 Binary Operations

OBJECTIVES

After studying this chapter, you should be able to:

- Demonstrate formation of positive and negative binary numbers
- Define binary constants in different forms
- Use appropriate instructions to load and store data into and from registers
- Convert decimal numbers to binary and binary numbers to decimal
- Create and use signed binary numbers in arithmetic operations
- Explain causes of overflow in binary addition and subtraction
- Use comparison of binary numbers for control of program logic
- Use instructions to shift data left or right within registers
- Perform binary multiplication and division
- Perform rounding and truncation of binary numbers

Up to this point in the text, we have used only packed decimal instructions to perform all arithmetic operations. In this chapter we shall see how to perform operations on binary data in the general registers.

IBM mainframe computers provide a large set of instructions to manipulate data and to perform arithmetic operations on binary numbers in general registers. The assembler also allows us to define constants and storage areas to hold binary data.

BINARY NUMBER REPRESENTATION

The value of a number depends upon two factors:

1. the value of each digit used by the number system, and
2. the place in the number where each digit occurs. This is called the *place value*.

Since only the digits 0 and 1 are used in binary numbers, we must use more places to represent any given value than we need with decimal numbers. Let us explore the concept of place value in numbers.

We are already familiar with the place value of decimal numbers. The digit just left of the decimal point has a place value of 1. As we move left, the place values become 10, 100, 1000, and so forth. The number 325 has the value of (3 * 100) + (2 * 10) + (5 * 1) = 325.

Binary numbers are often called *fixed-point* numbers because they are normally treated as integers. Only the digits 0 and 1 are used. Any value larger than 1 requires more than one digit. We need two digits to represent the values 2 and 3, three digits to represent 4, 5, 6, and 7, and so forth. As we move left, the place value of each digit is double that of the preceding place.

Unsigned Binary Numbers

We can use a place value table to convert decimal numbers to binary or binary numbers to decimal. Unsigned numbers assign a place value to every digit in the number. Unsigned numbers of 4, 8, or 16 bits are often used by the operating system to represent lengths of operands, keys, or records in files. To represent the value of the numbers in Figure 9–1, we add the place value of the positions that contain 1 bits and ignore the 0 bits. The binary numbers at the left are equivalent to the decimal values at the right.

Signed Binary Numbers

The leftmost bit represents the sign of a binary number, 0 for positive and 1 for negative. A negative number is represented in *twos complement* form. The twos complement is formed in this way:

1. Write the number in positive form.
2. Reverse all the 0 bits to 1 and all 1 bits to 0. The result is called the *ones complement*.
3. Add 1 to the ones complement, forming the twos complement.

We can form the binary value −77 as shown in Figure 9–2.

The same principle applies with larger numbers, such as *halfwords* of 16 bits or *fullwords* of 32 bits. The leftmost bit is still the sign. We simply have more place values to represent larger values. We can expand any number to more bits by propagating the sign bit into the additional places. For example, the value −77 in eight-bit form is 1011 0011, equivalent to X'B3'. If we expand it to 16 bits, the binary value is 1111 1111 1011 0011, or X'FFB3'. Most negative halfwords or fullwords can be recognized as having one or more leading X'F' digits.

PLACE VALUES								
128	64	32	16	8	4	2	1	DECIMAL VALUE
0	1	0	0	1	1	0	1	77
0	0	1	0	1	0	1	1	43
1	1	0	0	1	0	0	0	200
0	1	1	1	1	1	1	1	127
1	1	1	1	1	1	1	1	255

Figure 9–1 Place values of unsigned binary numbers

PLACE VALUES									
SIGN	64	32	16	8	4	2	1	DECIMAL VALUE	
0	1	0	0	1	1	0	1	77	Positive number
1	0	1	1	0	0	1	0		Ones complement
							+1		Add 1
1	0	1	1	0	0	1	1	−77	Negative number

Figure 9–2 Forming the twos complement

It is somewhat lengthy to convert decimal numbers to binary or vice versa by going through all three steps shown. However, there are two shortcuts that can simplify the process. In the first method, once we know the number is negative from the sign bit of 1, we add the place value of each 0 rather than of each 1. Adding the place values of the 0 bits will give us *one less than* the value we seek. Then we add 1 and reverse the sign to get the correct value.

In Figure 9–2, the sign bit of 1 indicates that the number −77 is negative. Adding the place value of the 0 bits gives us 64 + 8 + 4, or 76. Adding 1 gives us 77. Reversing the sign gives −77.

As another example, the eight-bit number 1100 1101 has 0 bits in the 32, 16, and 2 place value positions. 32 + 16 + 2 = 50. Adding 1, we have 51. Reversing the sign gives −51. The binary number 1100 1101 = −51.

A second shortcut method for recognizing negative numbers is to assign the sign bit a negative value equal to the place value it would have if not used as a sign. Then add the values of the 1 bits as with positive numbers. Using this method with 1100 1101, we value the sign bit as −128. The values of the 1 bits are 64, 8, 4, and 1. Then −128 + 64 + 16 + 4 + 1 = −51.

DEFINING BINARY DATA

We may define binary fixed-point constants or storage in three types: binary (type B), fullword (type F), and halfword (type H). Recall that the term fixed-point refers to the fact that all values are considered to be integers.

Binary Constants

Type B constants are normally used for defining unsigned binary codes of only one or two bytes in length. We may use only 0 or 1 to specify value. If we use fewer than eight bits, or if we use a length operand longer than the value given, the assembler will pad leading zeros to the left to fill a complete byte. Object code is represented in hexadecimal, as usual. Figure 9–3 shows some examples.

Fullwords

Fullwords are 32-bit binary numbers. We may define them as type F with the value written as decimal numbers. We may include a sign, but normally not a decimal point. If we include a decimal point, the assembler will convert the value to a signed binary integer, rounded. If no length is specified, the assembler will use a standard length of four bytes, and will align the first byte on a fullword boundary, that is, an address evenly divisible by four.

Figure 9–4 shows some examples of fullword constants.

Halfwords

Halfwords are 16-bit binary numbers. A type H definition will produce an automatic length of two bytes, aligned on a halfword boundary, an even-numbered address. Some examples are shown in Figure 9–5.

Halfwords are often used for small binary numbers because they require less storage space than fullwords do. Special halfword instructions are available to process the 16-bit numbers.

OBJECT CODE	STATEMENT	DECIMAL VALUE	REMARKS
01	DC B'1'	1	Seven leading zeros added
07	DC B'0111'	7	Four leading zeros added
00 00 19	DC BL3'00011001'	25	Sixteen leading zeros added
00 01 FF	DC BL3'111111111'	511	Fifteen leading zeros added

Figure 9–3 Defining binary constants

OBJECT CODE	STATEMENT	REMARKS
00 00 00 64	DC F'100'	
00 00 00 0A	DC F'10'	
00 00 10 00	DC F'4096'	
7F FF FF FF	DC F'2147483647'	Largest possible positive fullword
80 00 00 00	DC F'-2147483648'	Largest negative fullword
FF FF FF FF	DC F'-1'	
00 00 64	DC FL3'100'	Explicit length rarely used
00 00 00 64	DC F'99.75'	Integer rounded to 100

Figure 9–4 Fullword constants

OBJECT CODE	STATEMENT	REMARKS
00 64	DC H'100'	
7F FF	DC H'32767'	Largest possible halfword
80 00	DC H'-32768'	Largest negative halfword
FF 9C	DC H'-100'	Twos complement of H'100'
00 0F	DC H'15'	

Figure 9–5 Halfword constants

Address Constants

An address constant (adcon) is a 24-bit binary value that gives the address of a field. The type is A, and the value is enclosed in parentheses, rather than the usual single quotation marks. The address is actually assembled as a 32-bit binary number, but only the rightmost 24 bits constitute the address. Each adcon is identified by the assembler in the relocation dictionary so that the linkage editor will add a relocation factor before the program is loaded for execution. Examples of adcons appear in Figure 9–6.

Address constants are usually produced by the operating system macros, such as OPEN, DTF, and CALL. They are normally loaded into general registers for use as base registers for certain operations. In application programs, we usually prefer to use Load Address (LA) instructions, since addresses created by LA do not require relocation.

MANIPULATING BINARY DATA

Three somewhat parallel sets of instructions allow us to manipulate binary data in three different forms (see Figure 9–7). We may use type RX in-

LOCATION	OBJECT CODE	STATEMENT
00 01 28		INRECD DS CL80
00 01 78		TABLE DS CL512
00 03 78		PRINTER DS CL133
00 04 58	00 00 01 28	ADCON DC A(INRECD)
00 04 5C	00 00 01 78	ADCON2 DC A(TABLE)
00 04 60	00 00 03 78	ACDON3 DC A(PRINTER)

Figure 9–6 Address constants

OPERATION	FULLWORDS	HALFWORDS	TWO REGISTERS
Load	L	LH	LR
Store	ST	STH	—
Add	A	AH	AR
Subtract	S	SH	SR
Multiply	M	MH	MR
Divide	D	—	DR
Compare	C	CH	CR

Figure 9–7 Instructions for binary data

structions to process fullwords or halfwords in main storage, or type RR instructions where both operands are in general registers.

For all of these instructions, operand 1 refers to a general register. Operations on a fullword in storage and one in another register are identical except for the location of operand 2. In most instances halfwords are expanded internally to 32 bits by propagating the sign bit into the additional 16 bits.

Loading and Storing Fullwords or Halfwords

Load instructions fill the general register specified as operand 1 with the 32-bit number taken from operand 2. Operand 2 is unchanged. Load (L) refers to a fullword in main storage. The fullword must be aligned on a fullword boundary, that is, an address evenly divisible by four. Load Register (LR) designates operand 2 as another general register. Load Halfword (LH) refers to operand 2 as a halfword aligned on an even-numbered address in main storage. The halfword is expanded internally in the arithmetic-logic unit to 32 bits by copying the sign bit into each of the 16 bit positions to its left.

Store instructions are just the converse of the load instructions. Operand 1 is the general register containing the source data. Operand 2 may be a fullword or halfword in storage. The instructions Store (ST) or Store

Halfword (STH) are used. When a halfword is stored, only the rightmost 16 bits in the operand 1 register are placed in the halfword. We should ensure that the value of the number to be stored does not exceed 16 bits.

There is no Store Register instruction. The Load Register (LR) is used for all data movement between registers. Note that the ST and STH instructions are two of the very few in which the movement of data is from operand 1 to operand 2.

Any type RX instruction may use relative addressing, indexing, or literals when referring to operand 2. In the examples in Figure 9–8, storage addresses in the object code use R3 as base register and some typical value as the displacement, unless explicit addressing is used.

Loading Addresses

Address constants may be loaded into registers by the Load (L) instruction. Address constants are normally aligned on fullword boundaries.

The Load Address (LA) instruction differs from Load (L) in that LA loads the *address* of operand 2 into the operand 1 register, while L loads the *contents* of operand 2. We have previously used LA to initialize a line counter. It is also widely used to initialize registers for loading and searching tables.

We often use LA with explicit operands. The format is OP R1,D2(X2,B2). If either X2 or B2 is omitted, the assembler supplies a 0 for the register. Recall that register 0 cannot be used as a base or index register. If both X2 and D2 are

OBJECT CODE	INSTRUCTION	FORMAT	REMARKS
58 80 32 62	L 8,FULLWORD	OP R1,S2	
50 87 32 62	ST 8,FULLWORD(7)	OP R1,S2(X2)	Indexed
40 87 40 00	STH 8,0(7,4)	OP R1,D2(X2,B2)	Explicit operands
48 80 34 46	LH 8,=H'5'	OP R1,S2	Literal
18 87	LR 8,7	OP R1,R2	
18 78	LR 7,8	OP R1,R2	

Figure 9–8 Loading and storing binary data

OBJECT CODE	INSTRUCTION	FORMAT	REMARKS
51 70 42 28	LA 7,TABLE	OP R1,S2	
51 60 42 2C	LA 6,TABLE+4	OP R1,S2	Relative address
51 50 40 00	LA 5,0(0,4)	OP R1,D2(X2,B2)	R0 not used
51 50 00 00	LA 5,0	OP R1,D2(X2,B2)	X2 and B2 omitted
51 50 00 0A	LA 5,10(0,0)	OP R2,D2(X2,B2)	
51 50 00 0A	LA 5,10	OP R1,D2(X2,B2)	X2 and B2 omitted

Figure 9–9 LA instructions with explicit operands

omitted, the displacement is the complete address that is loaded into the register. Figure 9–9 shows some examples.

We will discuss addition with Load Address later in this chapter.

Loading and Storing Multiple Registers

Load Multiple (LM) and Store Multiple (STM) are type RS instructions that refer to two general registers as operand 1 and operand 3, respectively, and a fullword in storage as operand 2. Indexing is not possible.

LM permits more than one register to be loaded with a single instruction. For example, LM 4,8,DATA causes registers 4 through 8 to be loaded with five successive fullwords starting at DATA. The format is OP R1,R3,S2 in this instance. If R1 is a higher-numbered register than R3, then *wraparound* takes place. For example, LM 14,2,DATA loads five successive fullwords starting at DATA into registers 14, 15, 0, 1, and 2. The registers may be regarded as a circle, in which registers 15 and 0 are adjacent.

Store Multiple (STM) is the counterpart of LM. Data moves from the registers R1 through R3 inclusive into successive fullwords starting at S2. Operand 2 may be a name or an explicit base-displacement address. Figure 9–10 shows some examples.

Other Load Instructions

None of the preceding load or store instructions sets the condition code. To test whether the value loaded into a register is positive, negative, or zero, a Compare instruction could compare the contents of a register with a fullword or a register containing zeros. However, it is often more convenient, and shorter, to use one of the following type RR instructions. All of them set the condition code.

Load and Test Register (LTR) loads the contents of the operand-2 register into the operand-1 register. The two operands may refer to the same register. The condition code may be set to zero, negative, or positive, but not to overflow.

Load Positive Register (LPR) loads the absolute value of operand 2 into operand 1. If operand 2 is negative, its twos complement is loaded into operand 1. The condition code may be set to zero, negative, or overflow. The max-

OBJECT CODE	INSTRUCTION	FORMAT	REMARKS
98 46 33 64	LM 4,6,TABLE	OP R1,R3,S2	
98 44 33 70	LM 4,4,TABLE+12	OP R1,R3,S2	Only Reg. 4 loaded
90 E3 40 00	STM 14,3,0(4)	OP R1,R3,D2(B2)	Wraparound 14 to 3
90 28 40 08	STM 2,8,8(4)	OP R1,R3,D2(B2)	

Figure 9–10 LM and STM instructions

imum negative number of −2,147,483,648 would cause overflow if set positive, since the maximum positive value in a register is 2,147,483,647.

Load Negative Register (LNR) makes the number in operand 2 negative and stores it in operand 1. The condition code may be set to zero or negative.

Load Complement Register (LCR) loads the twos complement of operand 2 into operand 1 and sets the condition code accordingly to any of its four possible settings.

CONVERSION TO AND FROM BINARY

A number normally is read into the computer from a card or keyboard in EBCDIC form. Two steps are necessary to convert the number to binary. First, it must be packed into a doubleword. In Chapter 5 we saw that a doubleword is defined as type D. The assembler reserves eight bytes and aligns the first byte on a doubleword boundary, an address evenly divisible by eight. Here is an example:

```
DOUBLE   DS  D
```

Next, we use the type RX instruction Convert to Binary (CVB). The packed decimal field in the operand-2 doubleword is converted to 32-bit binary form in the operand-1 general register. Operand 2 may be indexed. The proper sign will automatically be retained. In Figure 9–11, assume that INAMT contains the characters 0000125. The results are shown to the right of each statement. X‘0000007D’ is equivalent to decimal 125.

A doubleword may contain 15 decimal digits plus a sign. However, the largest positive number that can be held in a general register is X‘7FFFFFFF’,

```
                                    DESTINATION          SOURCE
         GET   INFILE,INRECD
         PACK  DOUBLE,INAMT         000000000000125C     F0F0F0F0F1F2F5
         CVB   4,DOUBLE             0000007D             000000000000125C
         A     4,=F'10'             00000087             0000000A
         CVD   4,DOUBLE             000000000000135C     00000087
         .
         .
         .
INRECD   DS    0CL80
         DS    CL28
INAMT    DS    CL7
         .
         .
         .
DOUBLE   DS    D
```

Figure 9–11 Decimal and binary conversions

equivalent to decimal 2,147,483,647. The largest negative number in the general register is X'80000000', or decimal −2,147,483,648. We should ensure that the number we expect to convert to binary does not exceed 32 bits, or approximately 10 decimal digits.

Convert to Decimal (CVD) is a type RX instruction that works opposite to CVB. The binary number in the operand-1 general register is converted to packed decimal form in the doubleword named as operand 2. The correct sign will be maintained in the decimal field.

Typically, we need to convert binary numbers to any other form only when we are ready to write them to some output file. After converting them to decimal, we may edit them directly from the doubleword or ZAP them to another packed decimal field for further processing.

BINARY ADDITION AND SUBTRACTION

Binary addition and subtraction are performed in any available general register. The register is always operand 1. Operand 2 may be a fullword or halfword in main storage or a fullword in another register. Binary addition follows the simple rules in Figure 9–12.

Subtraction is performed by adding the twos complement, which we have seen is the negative form of the number. The sign bits of the two numbers are added just like any other bits. If there is a carry out of the sign position, it is dropped. For clarity, we add some eight-bit signed binary numbers in Figure 9–13. The same principles apply to addition of binary numbers having more digits.

In the last example, carries resulted from adding place value positions 16, 32, 64, and the signs. The carry outside the sign position is dropped, since we are using only eight bits.

Figure 9–14 shows examples of adding two negative numbers.

Overflow in Binary Arithmetic

When a binary number is too large for the number of digits we are using to represent it, overflow occurs. The sign bit is set incorrectly as though it were one of the data bits.

0 + 0 = 0
0 + 1 = 1
1 + 0 = 1
1 + 1 = 10 (Zero with a carry)

Figure 9–12 Rules for binary addition

		PLACE VALUES								
		S	64	32	16	8	4	2	1	DECIMAL EQUIVALENT
(1)		0	0	1	1	0	0	1	0	50
		0	0	0	0	1	0	1	1	+ 11
		0	0	1	1	1	1	0	1	= 61
(2)		0	1	0	1	0	0	1	1	83
		0	0	1	0	1	0	1	0	+ 42
		0	1	1	1	1	1	0	1	=125
(3)		0	0	1	1	0	0	1	0	50
		1	1	1	1	0	1	0	1	+(−11)
	~~1~~	0	0	1	0	0	1	1	1	= 39

Figure 9–13 Signed binary addition

		PLACE VALUES								
		S	64	32	16	8	4	2	1	DECIMAL EQUIVALENT
(1)		1	1	1	1	0	1	0	1	−11
		1	1	0	1	0	1	0	0	+(−44)
	~~1~~	1	1	0	0	1	0	0	1	=(−55)
(2)		1	1	1	1	0	0	0	0	−16
		1	1	1	1	1	0	1	1	+(−5)
	~~1~~	1	1	1	0	1	0	1	1	=(−21)

Figure 9–14 Addition to negative binary numbers

In an eight-bit signed number, the maximum values are 127 and −128. Any result exceeding these values causes overflow. We have seen from preceding examples that a carry out of the sign position does not necessarily indicate overflow.

Figure 9–15 shows two examples of valid addition and two of overflow. Example 1 shows no carry into or out of the sign position, and the result is

		PLACE VALUES									
		S	64	32	16	8	4	2	1	DECIMAL EQUIVALENT	
(1)		0	1	1	0	0	1	0	1	101	
		0	0	0	1	0	1	1	1	+ 23	
		0	1	1	1	1	1	0	0	= 124	(Valid)
(2)		1	0	1	1	0	1	1	1	− 73	
		1	1	0	1	0	0	0	0	+ (−48)	
	~~1~~	1	0	0	0	0	1	1	1	=(−121)	(Valid)
(3)		0	1	1	0	0	1	0	1	101	
		0	1	0	0	1	0	0	1	+ 73	
		1	0	1	0	1	1	1	0	= 174	(Overflow)
(4)		1	0	0	0	0	1	1	0	−122	
		1	0	0	1	1	1	0	1	+(− 99)	
	~~1~~	0	0	1	0	0	0	1	1	+(−221)	(Overflow)

Figure 9–15 Overflow in binary addition

valid. Example 2 shows a carry into the sign position, but also out of the sign position (dropped), and the result is valid.

In Example 3, we recall that the maximum positive value in seven data bits plus sign is 127. A sum of 174 causes overflow. The carry into the sign position causes what should be a positive number to have a negative sign. If the sign bit had had a place value of 128, the result would have been correct, but since that position is reserved for the sign alone, the result is incorrect.

Example 4 also shows overflow. The maximum allowable value is −128. The sum of −221 causes overflow. We note that there was no carry into the sign position, but adding the two negative signs caused a carry out of that position. What should be a negative number appears to have a positive sign and is therefore incorrect.

The rules for determining overflow for addition and subtraction of signed binary numbers of any size are:

1. All corresponding bits, including sign bits, of both numbers are added together.

2. Subtraction is performed by adding the twos complement of the number to be subtracted.
3. A carry out of the sign position is dropped.
4. If there is no carry into the sign position and no carry out of it, the result is valid.
5. If there is a carry into the sign position and also a carry out of it, the result is valid.
6. If there is a carry into the sign position but no carry out of it, overflow occurs.
7. If there is no carry into the sign position but there is a carry out of it, overflow occurs.

   The condition code is set to reflect an overflow result.

Fullword Addition and Subtraction

Fullword addition is performed by the Add (A) and Add Register (AR) instructions. Subtract (S) and Subtract Register (SR) perform subtraction by adding the twos complement of the number to be subtracted. A and S are type RX instructions with operand 2 in a fullword in main storage. AR and SR are type RR instructions with operand 2 in a general register. In all other respects their operation is identical.

In each case, the 32-bit number in operand 2 is added to the contents of the operand-1 register. The sign is correctly set by the addition operation. The condition code is set to indicate a sum equal to, less than, or greater than zero, or an overflow result. Some examples are shown in Figure 9–16.

Halfword Addition and Subtraction

Add Halfword (AH) is a type RX instruction. Operand 1 is a general register to which the operand-2 halfword is to be added. The halfword is first expanded to 32 bits internally in the arithmetic-logic unit by propagating the leftmost (sign) bit to the left. Then the resulting fullword is added to the reg-

OBJECT CODE	STATEMENT	FORMAT
5A 80 34 18	A 8,=F'100'	OP R1,S2
5A 80 32 66	A 8,FULLWORD+4	OP R1,S2
5B 87 32 62	S 8,FULLWORD(7)	OP R1,S2(X2)
5A 87 40 0C	A 8,12(7,4)	OP R1,D2(X2,B2)
1A 87	AR 8,7	OP R1,R2
1B 87	SR 8,7	OP R1,R2

Figure 9–16 Formats for fullword addition and subtraction

ister specified as the first operand. The condition code is set, and overflow may occur.

Subtract Halfword (SH) converts operand-2 storage to twos complement form. Then it expands the number to 32 bits by propagating the sign bit to the left, and finally adds it to the operand-1 register. Some examples are shown in Figure 9–17.

Addition with Load Address Instruction

Load Address (LA), used previously to initialize a general register, may also be used to increment it. For example, the instruction LA 4,1(4) forms an address by adding the contents of register 4 and the displacement of 1 and loading that address back into register 4. Thus register 4 is incremented by 1.

The contents of one register may also be incremented by a displacement and loaded into another register, as in LA 5,1(4), but this technique is used infrequently. The maximum amount that may be added is X'FFF', or 4095, as that is the maximum displacement allowable in a machine instruction. Figure 9–18 shows some examples of addition with the LA instruction.

LA is used primarily in connection with address modification, as we shall see in the next chapter. It is preferable to other add instructions because it needs no fullword or halfword defined or stored to represent the amount added to the register.

OBJECT CODE	STATEMENT	FORMAT
4A 80 32 60	AH 8,HALFWORD	OP R1,S2
4A 87 32 60	AH 8,HALFWORD(7)	OP R1,S2(X2)
4B 87 40 00	SH 8,0(7,4)	OP R1,D2(X2,B2)
4B 87 40 0C	SH 8,12(7,4)	OP R1,D2(X2,B2)

Figure 9–17 Formats for halfword addition and subtraction

OBJECT CODE	STATEMENT	FORMAT	REMARKS
41 44 0004	LA 4,4(4,0)	OP R1,D2(X2,B2)	R0 ignored
41 44 0001	LA 4,1(4)	OP R1,D2(X2,B2)	B2 assumed zero
41 40 400A	LA 4,10(,4)	OP R1,D2(X2,B2)	X2 assumed zero
41 47 4000	LA 4,0(7,4)	OP R1,D2(X2,B2)	R4 = R4 + R7
47 47 500C	LA 4,12(7,5)	OP R1,D2(X2,B2)	R4 = R5 + R7 + 12

Figure 9–18 Formats for addition with LA instruction

Subtraction with Branch on Count Instruction

We have already seen how to use the Branch on Count (BCT) instruction to control a counter. It is a type RX instruction that subtracts 1 from the operand-1 register, tests if the result is 0, and branches to operand 2 if not 0. Its counterpart type RR instruction is Branch on Count Register (BCTR), in which the operand-2 branch address is in another general register. Both instructions work alike except for operand-2 location. For example, if register 8 contains the address of ENDIF, then BCTR 5,8 would have exactly the same effect as BCT 5,ENDIF.

When operand 2 in a BCTR instruction is register 0, the instruction merely subtracts from the operand-1 register and branches nowhere. Recall that R0 cannot be used for addressing. BCTR is especially useful for decrementing a register, since it requires only two bytes and needs no other data as an operand. The instruction BCTR 5,0 merely subtracts 1 from R5.

BINARY COMPARISON

A binary number in a general register named as operand 1 may be compared with a fullword in main storage, a fullword in another register, or a halfword in main storage as operand 2. Compare (C) and Compare Halfword (CH) are type RX instructions, while Compare Register (CR) is type RR. The first operand is compared with the second operand and the condition code is set accordingly. Compare Halfword (CH) expands the halfword internally to 32 bits by propagating the sign bit to the left before making the comparison. The compare instruction is normally followed by a conditional branch.

Figure 9–19 shows several ways to use binary arithmetic to control a loop to be executed 50 times.

SHIFTING BINARY NUMBERS

We may shift binary numbers to the left or right within a single register or an even-odd pair of registers. The sign bit does not move, but the remaining data bits move left or right the number of bits specified within the instruction. The four instructions within this group are type RX instructions in format OP R1,D2(B2). The data within operand 1 is shifted the number of bits specified in operand 2. Normally the B2 operand is omitted, and D2 indicates the number of bits to be shifted. The maximum shift is 32 bits for a single register and 64 bits for a register pair.

METHOD ONE, USING FULLWORD LITERALS:

```
         L      5,=F'0'        CLEAR COUNTER
REPEAT   EQU    *              REPEAT
         BAL    9,PROCESS        DO BODY OF LOOP
         A      5,=F'1'          ADD 1 TO COUNTER
         C      5,=F'50'         *
         BL     REPEAT           *
UNTIL    EQU    *              UNTIL COUNT => 50
```

METHOD TWO, USING LOAD ADDRESS INSTRUCTION WITH ADDITION:

```
         LA     5,0            CLEAR COUNTER
REPEAT   EQU    *              REPEAT
         BAL    9,PROCESS        DO BODY OF LOOP
         LA     5,1(5)           ADD 1 TO COUNTER
         C      5,=F'50'         *
         BL     REPEAT           *
UNTIL    EQU    *              UNTIL COUNT => 50
```

METHOD THREE, USING LOAD ADDRESS INSTRUCTION WITH BRANCH ON COUNT:

```
         LA     5,50           SET COUNTER TO 50
REPEAT   EQU    *              REPEAT
         BAL    9,PROCESS        DO BODY OF LOOP
         BCT    5,REPEAT         SUBTRACT 1 FROM COUNTER
UNTIL    EQU    *              UNTIL COUNT = 0
```

Figure 9–19 Controlling loops with binary arithmetic

Single Register Shifts

Shift Left Arithmetic (SLA) causes 31 data bits in the operand-1 register to be shifted left by the number of bits specified in operand 2. The sign bit does not move. The bit in the position to the right of the sign is shifted out of the register and dropped. If a bit unlike the sign is shifted out, overflow occurs. Positions at the right of the register vacated by the shift are filled in with zeros. The effect of the SLA instruction is to double the value of the binary number every time it is shifted one bit to the left.

Shift Right Arithmetic (SRA) causes the 31 data bits in the operand-1 register to be shifted right as specified by operand 2. The sign bit replaces vacated positions to its right. Bits shifted out of the right side of the register are dropped. The effect of SRA is to divide the number in the register by two (to the nearest integer) each time it is shifted one bit to the right.

Assume at the start of each of the following instructions that register 7 contains F'5' (B'0000 0101), and register 8 contains F' − 5' (B'11111011'). In Figure 9–20 we show the results as an eight-bit binary number, with the leftmost bit representing the sign.

Contents of registers at start of each instruction:
R7 = 0000 0101 (5)
R8 = 1111 1011 (−5)

OBJECT CODE	INSTRUCTION	REGISTER AFTER SHIFT	DECIMAL VALUE
8B 80 00 01	SLA 8,1	1111 0110	−10
8B 70 00 02	SLA 7,2	0001 0100	20
8A 80 00 04	SRA 8,4	1111 1111	− 1
8A 70 00 01	SRA 7,2	0000 0001	1
8B 70 00 04	SLA 7,4	0101 0000	80
8B 70 00 05	SLA 7,5	0010 0000 (Overflow)	

Figure 9–20 Single register shifts

Programming Tips

- Use binary arithmetic rather than decimal for fast, parallel operations.
- Use halfwords rather than fullwords for small operands with values between 32767 and −32768.
- Use LA to load addresses rather than loading address constants.
- Use LA to increment values in registers. The displacement of the second operand is the amount to be added to the register.
- Use BCTR with a second operand of 0 to subtract 1 from the specified register.
- Use LTR rather than Compare to test the value in a register and set the condition code.
- Remember that the maximum values that can be converted to binary are 2,147,483,647 and −2,147,483,648, even though a doubleword can hold values up to 15 decimal digits in length.

Double Register Shifts

Shift Left Double Arithmetic (SLDA) and Shift Right Double Arithmetic (SRDA) work on two registers as a pair containing a 64-bit number. The pair must have an even-numbered register on the left and an odd-numbered one on the right. Operand 1 refers to the even-numbered register. Operand 2 is the number of bits to be shifted, up to a maximum of 64.

Assume for discussion that we use registers 6 and 7 as our pair. The sign of the 64-bit number is the leftmost bit of R6. It does not shift. The remaining 63 bits shift right or left, subject to the same rules as for single register arithmetic shifts. The number is doubled each time it is shifted one bit to the left. It is divided by two for each shift of one bit to the right. If a bit that is shifted left out of R6 is different from the sign, overflow occurs. Bits shifted right out of R7 are dropped.

A right shift of 32 bits places the contents of R6 into R7. R6 contains all zeros or all ones, depending on its original sign. A right shift of 64 bits sets both registers to all zeros or all ones, depending on the original sign in R6.

A left shift of 32 bits sets R7 to zeros. The contents of R6 are unpredictable.

Assume in the examples in Figure 9–21 that each register can hold only eight bits. The register pair 6 and 7 contains 0011 0010 1000 1011 at the start of each instruction. We illustrate the effect of some shifts.

BINARY MULTIPLICATION

A binary number in a general register may be multiplied by a fullword or a halfword. Different instructions are required for fullwords and halfwords, and the results appear in different formats.

Fullword Multiplication

When a 32-bit binary number in a general register is multiplied by another 32-bit number, the product requires a maximum of 64 bits. We therefore use *two* general registers for multiplication. The multiplicand is loaded into the *odd-numbered* register of the pair. The multiplier may be either in main storage or in another general register. The product occupies both registers of the pair, and replaces the multiplicand.

Contents of registers at start of each instruction:
R6 = 0011 0010
R7 = 1000 1011

OBJECT CODE	INSTRUCTION	REGISTER 6	REGISTER 7
8F 60 00 01	SLDA 6,1	0110 0101	0001 0110
8F 60 00 02	SLDA 6,2	0100 1010	0010 1100 (Overflow)
8F 60 00 08	SLDA 6,8	0000 1011	0000 0000 (Overflow)
8E 60 00 04	SRDA 6,4	0000 0011	0010 1000
8E 60 00 08	SRDA 6,8	0000 0000	0011 0010
8E 60 00 10	SRDA 6,16	0000 0000	0000 0000

Figure 9–21 Double register shifts

Operand 1 in the Multiply instruction is always the *even-numbered* register of the pair. Operand 2 refers to the multiplier. If the multiplier is in main storage, we use the type RX Multiply (M) instruction. If the multiplier is in another register, we use the type RR Multiply Register (MR). In all other respects the operations are identical.

The 64-bit product occupies both registers. The leftmost bit of the even-numbered register is the sign. However, if the product contains no more than 32 significant bits, the even-numbered register will contain only zeros if positive and ones if negative. In such a case, the odd-numbered register contains the significant part of the product as a signed fullword.

We need not clear the even-numbered register before multiplying. The multiply instruction itself clears that register as it performs the repeated addition and shifting that produce the product. Figure 9–22 shows three examples of fullword multiplication.

Notice that each product is entirely contained within register 7 and that register 6 contains only leading zeros (or leading ones if negative). We could then add to this product in R7, convert it to decimal, or store it in another register or fullword in main storage.

The second example uses the Multiply Register (MR) instruction. The multiplier is placed in register 8. Then the pair R6–R7 is multiplied by R8.

Multiplier as a fullword literal:

INSTRUCTION	REG. HEX VALUE	DECIMAL VALUE
`L  7,=F'345'`	`???????? 00000159`	`F'345'`
`M  6,=F'12'`	`00000000 00001036`	`F'4140'`

Multiplier in another register:

INSTRUCTION	REG. HEX VALUE	DECIMAL VALUE
`L  8,=F'12'`	`0000000C`	`F'12'`
`L  7,=F'345'`	`???????? 00000159`	`F'345'`
`MR 6,8`	`00000000 00001036`	`F'4140'`

Multiplication with negative product:

INSTRUCTION	REG. HEX VALUE	DECIMAL VALUE
`L  8,=F'-12'`	`FFFFFFF4`	`F'-12'`
`L  7,=F'345'`	`???????? 00000159`	`F'345'`
`MR 6,8`	`FFFFFFFF FFFFEFCA`	`F'-4140'`

Figure 9–22 Binary multiplication

The third example of multiplication produces a negative product.

We do not need to concern ourselves with the binary or hexadecimal form of the data we are working with. If the product exceeds the decimal value 2,147,483,647, we know that some of the product will spill over into the even-numbered register. We can use 9s to represent the possible positions of significant decimal digits and a V to represent the assumed location of the decimal point as we consider more examples.

If we multiply a seven-digit number (9999999) by a five-digit number (99999), we know the product will require 12 digits (999999999999). The binary equivalent of a 12-digit decimal number will require more than 32 bits and will therefore occupy both registers of the even-odd pair. If the seven-digit number has three decimal places (9999V999) and the five-digit number has two decimals (999V99), then the 12-digit product will have five digits to the right of the decimal (9999999V99999).

Halfword Multiplication

Multiplication of halfwords differs from multiplication of fullwords in two respects. First, only one register is required for the product. Second, any general register may be used. The product replaces the multiplicand.

In the Multiply Halfword (MH) instruction, the contents of the general register specified as the first operand are multiplied by the contents of a halfword named as the second operand. The product thus could be 48 bits long, but only the rightmost 32 bits are retained. If the product exceeds 2,147,483,647 decimal, it will not be accurate. Overflow is not indicated. In general, the multiplicand should not exceed 16 significant bits so that the product will be limited to 32 bits.

Here is an example of halfword multiplication:

INSTRUCTION	REG. HEX VALUE	DECIMAL VALUE
`L  7,=H'255'`	`000000FF`	`H'255'`
`MH 7,=H'17'`	`000010EF`	`H'4335'`

Note that the product in register 7 can be stored either as a halfword or as a fullword, or converted to decimal. The maximum values a halfword can have are X‘7FFF’, or 32,767 if positive, and X‘8000’, or −32,768 if negative.

BINARY DIVISION

Binary division also requires an even-odd pair of registers. The dividend is in the pair of registers. The divisor may be in another register or in a fullword in storage. There is no halfword division instruction. The Divide (D) instruction is used when the divisor is in storage, and Divide Register (DR) when it is in another register. After division is completed, the quotient is in the odd-numbered register and the remainder is in the even-numbered register.

When dividing one fullword by another, we load the dividend into the even-numbered register and shift it into the odd-numbered one. This generates the correct sign in the 64-bit dividend. For example:

INSTRUCTION	REG. HEX VALUE	DECIMAL VALUE
`L 6,=F'4500'`	`00001194 ????????`	`F'4500'`
`SRDA 6,32`	`00000000 00001194`	`F'4500'`
`D 6,=F'7'`	`00000006 00000282`	`F'642' REM = 6`

If the divisor were in register 8, the last instruction would be written as DR 6,8, and the results would be identical.

After multiplication, the product occupies *both* registers of the pair, and we may divide directly into the 64-bit number.

If the portion of the dividend in the even-numbered register is equal to or larger than the divisor, *divide overflow* occurs and the program interrupts. Division by zero will also be detected by this condition.

We must be aware of the sign and number of digits in the quotient and remainder. The quotient is positive if the dividend and divisor have the same sign and negative if they have different signs. The sign of the remainder is always the same as the dividend.

The number of digits to the left of the decimal in the quotient is equal to the number of digits to the left of the decimal in the dividend *less* the number of digits to the *right* of the decimal in the divisor. We may put as many digits to the right of the decimal in the quotient as we wish to express its precision.

A few examples will illustrate these points. Suppose the sum of the test scores for a class of 18 students is 1523. We can calculate the class mean score as follows:

```
L     6,=F'1523'
SRDA  6,32
D     6,=F'18'
```

The quotient of 84 will be in register 7 and the remainder of 11 will be in register 6, since 1523/18 = 84 rem. 11.

If we wish to carry the quotient to two decimal places, we must multiply the total scores by 100 before dividing. The product is properly positioned in R6 and R7 for dividing.

INSTRUCTION	ASSUMED VALUE
`L 7,=F'1523'`	1523
`M 6,=F'100'`	1523.00
`D 6,=F'18'`	1523.00/18 = 84.61 rem. 2

Rounding Binary Numbers

To round binary numbers, we must first get at least one more decimal place in the result than we wish to retain. If the number is positive, we add 5 to the position just to the right of the last digit we will keep. If the number is negative, we subtract 5 from that position. If the digit in this position is 5 or greater, the last digit we retain will be rounded up to the next digit. If the digit in this position is less than 5, the retained digit will remain unchanged.

We cannot drop excess decimal digits by shifting bits within a register, because no binary digit has a place value of 10. We can, however, drop decimal digits by dividing by powers of 10. The remainder has the value of the digits dropped. For example, to drop one decimal digit we divide by 10, to drop two digits we divide by 100, and so forth. If we wish to round the class mean to one decimal place in the preceding example, we can use the approach shown in Figure 9–23.

Another important use of division is to reduce the number of digits in a product so it will fit into one register. Suppose we wish to calculate one year's interest, rounded to the nearest cent, on a principal amount of $256,479.18 at an annual rate of 14.375 percent (0.14375). The multiplication of the eight-digit principal by the five-digit rate produces a product of 13 digits, of which seven are to the right of the assumed decimal place. We use only

INSTRUCTION		ASSUMED VALUE
L	7,=F'1523'	1523
M	6,=F'100'	1523.00
D	6,=F'18'	84.61 Rem 2
A	7,=F'5'	84.66
LR	6,7	Clear previous remainder
SRDA	6,32	Shift back into position
D	6,=F'10'	84.6 Rem 6

The class mean rounded to one decimal place is 84.6.

Figure 9–23 Rounding binary quotient

INSTRUCTION		SIZE OF DATA
L	7,=F'25647918'	999999V99
M	6,=F'14375'	999999V9999999
A	7,=F'50000'	999999V9999999
D	6,=F'100000'	999999V99 REM 99999

Figure 9–24 Rounding to drop excess digits

9s and Vs to show the size of the decimal numbers we are working with at each stage of the routine in Figure 9–24.

The final result has eight digits, with two to the right of the assumed decimal point. This will fit into register 7. Actually, some of these eight digits will be leading zeros because of the data used. But the principle will still work, even if all the digits are 8s or 9s.

If we need to round a quotient that may be positive or negative, we can use the routine in Figure 9–25.

Programming Tips
• Use a left shift to multiply a binary number by a power of 2, or a right shift to divide it by a power of 2.   • To preserve the sign of the dividend and clear the even-numbered register for binary division, load the dividend into the even-numbered register and shift the register pair 32 bits to the right algebraically.   • To avoid divide overflow, the value of the divisor must be greater than the portion of the dividend in the even-numbered register of the register pair.

PROGRAM 9: AVERAGE SALARY BY DEPARTMENT AND ORGANIZATION

Our next program combines a number of features covered in this chapter. It reads the employee file, which is in sequence by department code. It produces a group-printed report, one line for each department, showing the number of employees within the department and the average annual salary. At end of file, it prints the total employees in the entire organization and the annual salary for all employees.

Program structure is fully modular. All arithmetic is done in binary, using the general registers. Standard modules for reading input records and printing detail lines have been included.

Figure 9–26 shows the program listing with pseudocode as comments, and Figure 9–27 shows program output.

SUMMARY

Binary numbers consist of 0s and 1s. Each digit in the number has a place value based on its position in the number. Each place value is twice as large

```
         L     6,DIVID        LOAD DIVIDEND
         SRDA  6,32           PRESERVE SIGN
         D     6,DIVIS        CREATE QUOTIENT IN R7
IF       LTR   7,7            IF QUOTIENT IS POSITIVE
         BNP   ELSE             *
THEN     A     7,=F'5'          ADD ROUNDING FACTOR
         B     ENDIF            *
ELSE     EQU   *              ELSE
         S     7,=F'5'          SUBTRACT ROUNDING
         LR    6,7            PREPARE TO DROP EXCESS
                              DIGITS
         SRDA  6,32           PRESERVE SIGN
         D     6,=F'10'       DROP EXCESS DIGITS
         ST    7,QUOTIENT     STORE ROUNDED QUOTIENT
```

Figure 9–25 Rounding positive or negative quotient

as the one to its right. Binary numbers may be signed or unsigned. Signed numbers reserve the leftmost bit for the sign, 0 for positive and 1 for negative. The negative of a number is in twos complement form.

Binary constants of one or two bytes may be defined as type B, with values of only 0 or 1. Zeros are padded to the left to make multiples of eight bits.

Halfwords contain 16 bits and fullwords contain 32 bits. Fullword operations always use a general register as operand 1 of an instruction. Operand 2 may be a fullword in main storage or in another register.

Fullword operations include loading, storing, adding, subtracting, multiplying, dividing, and comparing. Multiplying and dividing require use of an even-odd pair of registers. The product in multiplying is a 64-bit number, with the sign in the leftmost bit. After division, the quotient is in the odd-numbered register, and the remainder is in the even-numbered one.

Halfword operations have a general register as operand 1 and a halfword in main storage as operand 2. Halfwords are expanded internally to 32 bits by propagating the sign bit left through the additional 16 bits before loading, adding, subtracting, or comparing. Only the rightmost 16 bits of the operand-1 register are stored in a Store Halfword (STH) instruction. Halfword multiplication may be done in any single register. The product may not exceed 31 bits plus sign.

Signed binary numbers may be shifted left or right within a single register or within an even-odd register pair. On left shifts the sign does not move. If a bit unlike the sign is shifted out of the register, overflow occurs. Vacated bit positions on the right are filled with zeros. The effect of a left shift is to multiply by two for each bit position shifted.

On right shifts, the sign bit fills vacated positions, and bits shifted out of the register to the right are dropped. The effect of a right shift is to divide the number by two (to the nearest integer) for every bit position shifted.

The Load Address (LA) instruction may be used to add from 1 through 4095 to the contents of any register. The Branch on Count instructions (BCT or BCTR) can subtract 1 from the contents of any register. Load and Test Register, Load Positive, Load Negative, and Load Complement instructions may change the contents of a register in the same or a different register and also set the condition code.

```
  LOC  OBJECT CODE    ADDR1 ADDR2  STMT   SOURCE STATEMENT                                  DOS/VSE ASSEMBLER 14.45 86-04-02

                                     1 ***********************************************************************
                                     2 *                 ALTON R. KINDRED, PROGRAM 9
                                     3 * THIS PROGRAM USES CONTROL BREAK PROCESSING TO PRODUCE A GROUP-PRINTED
                                     4 * REPORT SHOWING NUMBER OF EMPLOYEES AND AVERAGE SALARY FOR EACH
                                     5 * DEPARTMENT AND FOR THE ENTIRE ORGANIZATION.  BINARY ARITHMETIC IS
                                     6 * USED FOR ALL CALCULATIONS.
                                     7 *           REGISTERS USED:
                                     8 *                 R0,R1       - WORK REGISTERS
                                     9 *                 R4          - DEPT. TOTAL ANNUAL PAY
                                    10 *                 R5          - LINE COUNTER
                                    11 *                 R6          - DEPT. TOTAL EMPLOYEES
                                    12 *                 R7          - OVERALL TOTAL EMPLOYEES
                                    13 *                 R8          - OVERALL ANNUAL PAY
                                    14 *                 R9,R10,R11  - LINKS TO MODULES
                                    15 *                 R12         - BASE REGISTER
                                    16 ***********************************************************************
                                    17          PRINT NOGEN
000000                              18 MAINLINE START 0                         SET LOCATION COUNTER
                                    19 *        STM   14,12,12(13)              SAVE REGISTERS FOR OS       OS
000000 05C0                         20          BALR  12,0                      LOAD BASE REGISTER
                            00002   21          USING *,12                      DESIGNATE BASE REGISTER
                                    22 *        ST    13,SAVE+4                 STORE REGISTER 13           OS
                                    23 *        LA    13,SAVE                   LOAD SAVE AREA ADDRESS      OS
                                    24 *        OPEN  (INFILE,(INPUT),PRINTER,(OUTPUT))                     OS
                                    25          OPEN  INFILE,PRINTER            OPEN FILES                  DOS
000016 4590 C036            00038   34          BAL   9,INITIAL                 DO INITIAL PROCESSING
00001A 4590 C046            00048   35          BAL   9,MAINLOOP                DO MAIN PROCESSING LOOP
00001E 4590 C07A            0007C   36          BAL   9,FINAL                   DO FINAL TOTAL PROCESSING
                                    37          CLOSE INFILE,PRINTER            CLOSE FILES                 DOS
                                    46          EOJ                             END PROGRAM                 DOS
                                    49 *        CLOSE (INFILE,,PRINTER)         CLOSE FILES                 OS
                                    50 *        L     13,SAVE+4                 LOAD SAVE AREA ADDRESS      OS
                                    51 *        LM    14,12,12(13)              RESTORE REGISTERS           OS
                                    52 *        BR    14                        RETURN TO OS                OS
                                    53 ***********************************************************************
                                    54 *              FIRST LEVEL MODULES
                                    55 ***********************************************************************
                                    56 *
                                    57 *              INITIALIZATION MODULE
                                    58 *
000038 45A0 C0C2            000C4   59 INITIAL  BAL   10,CLEARSET               SET INITIAL VALUES
00003C 45A0 C0DA            000DC   60          BAL   10,READRECD               READ FIRST RECORD
000040 D203 C60E C33D 00610 0033F   61          MVC   SAVEDEPT,INDEPT           SAVE DEPARTMENT CODE
000046 07F9                         62          BR    9                         RETURN
                                    63 *
                                    64 *              MAIN PROCESSING LOOP
                                    65 *
                            00048   66 MAINLOOP EQU   *
                            00048   67 DOWHILE  EQU   *                         DOWHILE NOT END OF FILE
000048 95E8 C612      00614         68          CLI   EOFFLAG,C'Y'                *
00004C 4780 C078      0007A         69          BE    ENDDO                       *
000050 95E8 C612      00614         70 DOWHILE2 CLI   EOFFLAG,C'Y'                DOWHILE NOT END OF FILE
000054 4780 C06C      0006E         71          BE    ENDDO2                        *
000058 D503 C33D C60F 0033F 00610   72 AND2     CLC   INDEPT,SAVEDEPT             AND SAME DEPARTMENT
00005E 4770 C06C      0006E         73          BNE   ENDDO2                        *
000062 45A0 C0F8            000FA   74          BAL   10,PROCESS                     DO DETAIL PROCESSING
000066 45A0 C0DA            000DC   75          BAL   10,READRECD                    READ NEXT RECORD
00006A 47F0 C04E      00050         76          B     DOWHILE2                       *
                            0006E   77 ENDDO2   EQU   *                           ENDDO
00006E 45A0 C126            00128   78          BAL   10,DEPTOT                   CALCULATE DEPT. TOTALS
000072 45A0 C172            00174   79          BAL   10,PRDETAIL               PRINT DEPT. TOTAL LINE
000076 47F0 C046      00048         80          B     DOWHILE                     *
                            0007A   81 ENDDO    EQU   *                         ENDDO
00007A 07F9                         82          BR    9                         RETURN
                                    83 *
                                    84 *              FINAL TOTAL ROUTINE
                                    85 *
00007C 1808                         86 FINAL    LR    0,8                       LOAD TOTAL ORG. SALARIES
00007E 8E00 0020            00020   87          SRDA  0,32                      *
000082 1D07                         88          DR    0,7                       DIVIDE BY TOTAL EMPLOYEES
000084 5A10 C62E            00630   89          A     1,=F'50'                  ROUND TO NEAREST DOLLAR
000088 1801                         90          LR    0,1                       *
00008A 8E00 0020            00020   91          SRDA  0,32                      *
00008E 5D00 C632            00634   92          D     0,=F'100'                 *
000092 4E70 C606            00608   93          CVD   7,DOUBLE                  SET UP TOTAL EMPLOYEES
000096 D206 C406 C617 00408 00619   94          MVC   PRTOTEMP,PATRN2           *
00009C DE06 C406 C60B 00408 0060D   95          ED    PRTOTEMP,DOUBLE+5         *
0000A2 4E10 C606            00608   96          CVD   1,DOUBLE                  SET UP AVERAGE SALARIES
0000A6 D206 C41B C617 0041D 00619   97          MVC   PRTOTAVG,PATRN2           *
0000AC DE06 C41B C60B 0041D 0060D   98          ED    PRTOTAVG,DOUBLE+5         *
                                    99          PUT   PRINTER,TOTLINE           PRINT TOTAL LINE
0000C2 07F9                        105          BR    9                         RETURN
                                   106 ***********************************************************************
                                   107 *              SECOND LEVEL MODULES
                                   108 ***********************************************************************
                                   109 *
                                   110 *              CLEAR TOTALS AND SET INITIAL VALUES MODULE
                                   111 *
0000C4 1B44                        112 CLEARSET SR    4,4                       CLEAR DEPT. TOTAL ANNUAL PAY
```

Figure 9–26 Program 9 assembler listing

```
  LOC  OBJECT CODE      ADDR1 ADDR2  STMT    SOURCE STATEMENT                                    DOS/VSE ASSEMBLER 14.45 86-04-02

0000C6 1B66                           113           SR    6,6                        CLEAR DEPT. TOTAL EMPLOYEES
0000C8 1B77                           114           SR    7,7                        CLEAR OVERALL TOTAL EMPLOYEES
0000CA 1B88                           115           SR    8,8                        CLEAR OVERALL TOTAL ANNUAL PAY
0000CC 4150 0033              00033   116           LA    5,51                       SET LINE COUNT > 50
0000D0 9240 C363        00365         117           MVI   PRLINE,C' '                CLEAR PRINT LINE
0000D4 D283 C364 C363 00366 00365     118           MVC   PRLINE+1(132),PRLINE       *
0000DA 07FA                           119           BR    10                         RETURN
                                      120 *
                                      121 *               READ RECORD MODULE
                                      122 *
0000DC 9205 C612        00614         123 READRECD MVI   EOFFLAG,C'N'               SET EOF FLAG OFF
                                      124          GET   INFILE,INRECD              READ READ RECORD
                              000F0   130 IFEOF    EQU   *                          IF END OF FILE
0000F0 47F0 C0F6        000F8         131          B     ENDIFEOF                     *
0000F4 92E8 C612        00614         132 THENEOF  MVI   EOFFLAG,C'Y'                 THEN SET EOF FLAG UN
                              000F8   133 ENDIFEOF EQU   *                          ENDIF
0000F8 07FA                           134          BR    10                         RETURN
                                      136 *
                                      137 *               PROCESS RECORD MODULE
                                      138 *
0000FA F277 C606 C34D 00608 0034F     139 PROCESS  PACK  DOUBLE,INRATE              CONVERT RATE TO BINARY
000100 4F10 C606              00608   140          CVB   1,DOUBLE                   *
000104 95E6 C34C        0034E         141 IF       CLI   INPAYTYP,C'W'              IF PAY IS WEEKLY
000108 4770 C112        00114         142          BNE   ELSE                         *
00010C 5C00 C646              00648   143 THEN     M     0,=F'52'                     THEN MULT. RATE BY 52
000110 47F0 C11E        00120         144          B     ENDIF                        *
                              00114   145 ELSE     EQU   *                          ELSE
000114 95C8 C34C        0034E         146 IF2      CLI   INPAYTYP,C'H'                IF PAY IS HOURLY
000118 4770 C11E        00120         147          BNE   ENDIF2                         *
00011C 5C00 C64A              0064C   148 THEN2    M     0,=F'2040'                     THEN MULT. RATE BY 2080
                              00120   149 ENDIF2   EQU   *                            ENDIF
                              00120   150 ENDIF    EQU   *                          ENDIF
000120 1A41                           151          AR    4,1                        ADD ANNUAL PAY TO DEPT. TOTAL
000122 4166 0001              00001   152          LA    6,1(6)                     ADD 1 TO DEPT. EMPLOYEES
000126 07FA                           153          BR    10                         RETURN
                                      154 *
                                      155 *               CALCULATE AND SET UP DEPARTMENT TOTALS
                                      156 *
000128 1804                           157 DEPTOT   LR    0,4                        CALC. DEPT. AVG. ANNUAL PAY
00012A 8E00 0020              00020   158          SRDA  0,32                       *
00012E 1D06                           159          DR    0,6                        *
000130 5A10 C62E              00630   160          A     1,=F'50'                   ROUND TO NEAREST DOLLAR
000134 1801                           161          LR    0,1                        *
000136 8E00 0020              00020   162          SRDA  0,32                       *
00013A 5D00 C632              00634   163          D     0,=F'100'                  *
00013E D203 C371 C60E 00373 00610     164          MVC   PRDEPT,SAVEDEPT            SET UP DEPT. CODE
000144 4E60 C606              00608   165          CVD   6,DOUBLE                   SET UP DEPT. EMPLOYEES
000148 D203 C384 C613 00386 00615     166          MVC   PRDEPEMP,PATRN             *
00014E DE03 C384 C60C 00386 0060E     167          ED    PRDEPEMP,DOUBLE+6          *
000154 4E10 C606              00608   168          CVD   1,DOUBLE                   SET UP DEPT. AVG. ANNUAL PAY
000158 D206 C396 C617 00398 00619     169          MVC   PRDEPAVG,PATRN2            *
00015E DE06 C396 C60B 00398 0060D     170          ED    PRDEPAVG,DOUBLE+5          *
000164 1A76                           171          AR    7,6                        ADD DEPT. EMPLOYEES TO TOTAL
000166 1A84                           172          AR    8,4                        ADD DEPT. ANNUAL PAY TO TOTAL
000168 1B66                           173          SR    6,6                        CLEAR DEPT. EMPOLOYEES
00016A 1B44                           174          SR    4,4                        CLEAR DEPT. ANNUAL PAY
00016C D203 C60E C33D 00610 0033F     175          MVC   SAVEDEPT,INDEPT            SAVE DEPT. CODE
000172 07FA                           176          BR    10                         RETURN
                                      177 *
                                      178 *               PRINT DEPARTMENT TOTAL LINE MODULE
                                      179 *
                              00174   180 PRDETAIL EQU   *
000174 5950 C62E              00630   181 IFEOP    C     5,=F'50'                   IF LINE COUNT => 50
000178 4740 C17E        00180         182          BL    ENDIFEOP                     *
00017C 45B0 C19E              001A0   183 THENEOP  BAL   11,HEADING                   THEN PRINT HEADINGS
                              00180   184 ENDIFEOP EQU   *                          ENDIF
                                      185          PUT   PRINTER,PRLINE             PRINT DEPT. TOTAL LINE
000190 4155 0001              00001   191          LA    5,1(5)                     ADD 1 TO LINE COUNT
000194 9240 C363        00365         192          MVI   PRLINE,C' '                CLEAR PRINT LINE
000198 D283 C364 C363 00366 00365     193          MVC   PRLINE+1(132),PRLINE       *
00019E 07FA                           194          BR    10                         RETURN
                                      196 *******************************************************************
                                      197 *               THIRD LEVEL HEADING MODULE
                                      198 *******************************************************************
                                      199 HEADING  PUT   PRINTER,HEAD1                THEN PRINT HEADINGS
                                      205          PUT   PRINTER,HEAD2                *
                                      211          PUT   PRINTER,HEAD3                *
0001D0 92F0 C363        00365         217          MVI   PRLINE,C'0'                  SET DOUBLE SPACE
0001D4 1B55                           218          SR    5,5                          CLEAR LINE COUNT
0001D6 07FB                           219          BR    11                         RETURN
                                      220 ****************************************************************DOS
                                      221 *               FILE DEFINITIONS AND I/O AREAS                    DOS
                                      222 ****************************************************************DOS
                                      223 INFILE   DTFCD BLKSIZE=80,IOAREA1=INAREA,DEVICE=2540,              DOSX
                                                       DEVADDR=SYSIPT,EOFADDR=THENEOF,WORKA=YES           DOS
                                      244 *                                                               DOS
                                      245 PRINTER  DTFPR BLKSIZE=133,IOAREA1=PRTAREA,DEVICE=1403,            DOSX
                                                       CTLCHR=ASA,DEVADDR=SYS009,WORKA=YES                DOS
                                      266 *                                                               DOS
000240                                267 INAREA   DS    CL80                                             DOS
000290                                268 PRTAREA  DS    CL133                                            DOS
                                      269 ****************************************************************OS
                                      270 *               DEVICE CONTROL BLOCKS AND SAVE AREA               OS
                                      271 ****************************************************************OS
                                      272 *INFILE  DCB   DDNAME=INFILE,BLKSIZE=80,LRECL=80,                 OSX
                                      273 *              MACRF=PM,DSORG=PS,EODAD=THENEOF                    OS
                                      274 *                                                               OS
                                      275 *PRINTER DCB   DDNAME=PRINTER,BLKSIZE=133,LRECL=133,              OSX
                                      276 *              MACRF=PMA,DSORG=PS                                 OS
                                      277 *                                                               OS
                                      278 *SAVE    DS    18F                                                OS
                                      279 ****************************************************************
                                      280 *               DATA DEFINITIONS
                                      281 *******************************************************************
```

Figure 9–26 *(Continued)*

```
000315                           INRECD   DS    0CL80
000315                                    DS    CL42
00033F                           INDEPT   DS    CL4
000343                                    DS    CL11
00034E                           INPAYTYP DS    CL1
00034F                           INRATE   DS    CL8
000357                                    DS    CL14
                                 *
000365                           PRLINE   DS    0CL133
000365                                    DS    CL14
000373                           PRDEPT   DS    CL4
000377                                    DS    CL15
000386                           PRDEPEMP DS    CL4
00038A                                    DS    CL14
000398                           PRDEPAVG DS    CL7
00039F                                    DS    CL75
                                 *
0003EA                           TOTLINE  DS    0CL133
0003EA F040404040404040                   DC    CL11'0'
0003F5 D6D9C74B40E3D6E3                   DC    CL19'ORG. TOTALS'
000408                           PRTOTEMP DS    CL7
00040F 4040404040404040                   DC    CL14' '
00041D                           PRTOTAVG DS    CL7
000424 4040404040404040                   DC    CL75' '
                                 *
00046F                           HEAD1    DS    0CL133
00046F F140404040404040                   DC    CL11'1'
00047A C1E5C5D9C1C7C540                   DC    CL18'AVERAGE SALARY BY'
00048C C4C5D7C1D9E3D4C5                   DC    CL18'DEPARTMENT AND BY'
00049E D6D9C7C1D5C9E9C1                   DC    CL96'ORGANIZATION'
                                 *
0004FE                           HEAD2    DS    0CL133
0004FE F040404040404040                   DC    CL31'0'
00051D D5E4D4C2C5D94006                   DC    CL20'NUMBER OF'
000531 C1E5C5D9C1C7C540                   DC    CL82'AVERAGE'
                                 *
000583                           HEAD3    DS    0CL133
000583 4040404040404040                   DC    CL11' '
00058E C4C5D7C1D9E3D4C5                   DC    CL20'DEPARTMENT'
0005A2 C5D4D7D3D6E8C5C5                   DC    CL21'EMPLOYEES'
0005B7 E2C1D3C1D9E84040                   DC    CL81'SALARY'
                                 *
000608                           DOUBLE   DS    D
000610                           SAVEDEPT DS    CL4
000614                           EOFFLAG  DS    CL1
000615 40202120                  PATRN    DC    XL4'40202120'
000619 4020206B202120            PATRN2   DC    XL7'4020206B202120'
                                 *
                        00000             END   MAINLINE
000620 5B5BC2D6D7C5D540                         =C'$$BOPEN '
000628 5B5BC2C3D3D6E2C5                         =C'$$BCLOSE'
000630 00000032                                 =F'50'
000634 00000064                                 =F'100'
000638 00000210                                 =A(PRINTER)
00063C 000003EA                                 =A(TOTLINE)
000640 000001D8                                 =A(INFILE)
000644 00000315                                 =A(INRECD)
000648 00000034                                 =F'52'
00064C 000007F8                                 =F'2040'
000650 00000365                                 =A(PRLINE)
000654 0000046F                                 =A(HEAD1)
000658 000004FE                                 =A(HEAD2)
00065C 00000583                                 =A(HEAD3)
```

Figure 9–26 *(Concluded)*

Load and Store Multiple instructions permit more than one consecutive fullword to be loaded into consecutively numbered registers or to be stored from them.

Packed decimal data placed in a doubleword may be converted to binary form and placed in any general register specified. The contents of a register may be converted back to packed decimal form and placed in a doubleword.

Overflow occurs in binary addition or subtraction whenever the carry into the sign does not agree with the carry out of it. The effect is to give the result an incorrect sign and an incorrect value.

Rounding is done in registers by adding a fullword with a value of 5 followed by enough zeros to add to the correct digit. Then the result is divided by a power of 10 containing one zero for each digit to be dropped. The quotient is the correct rounded value. The dropped digits are the remainder.

AVERAGE SALARY BY DEPARTMENT AND BY ORGANIZATION		
DEPARTMENT	NUMBER OF EMPLOYEES	AVERAGE SALARY
1234	5	34,086
2143	3	25,103
3756	6	22,780
4028	4	20,106
5337	7	19,937
6541	5	19,544
7409	3	17,341
8823	7	14,198
ORG. TOTALS	40	21,288

Figure 9–27 Output from Program 9

TERMS FOR REVIEW

Address constant
Binary constant
Double-register shift
Even-odd register pair
Fixed-point number
Halfword
Ones complement
Place value
Shift
Single-register shift
Twos complement

REVIEW QUESTIONS

1. State which carries are valid and which cause overflow in binary addition and subtraction.
2. Explain what happens to halfwords when they are loaded, added, subtracted, or compared with contents of a general register.
3. How many bits are there in an address constant, and how many actually represent the address?
4. Explain wraparound in using the Load Multiple or Store Multiple instruction.
5. How many registers are loaded by the instruction LM 2,8,FULLWORD? How many are stored by STM 14,6,FULLWORD?
6. Explain how the instructions L 6,DIVIDEND followed by SRDA 6,32 preserves the correct sign of DIVIDEND, while L 7,DIVIDEND followed by SR 6,6 might or might not.

EXERCISES

1. On a place value table for eight-bit unsigned binary numbers, show the binary equivalent of each of these decimal numbers:
   17 29 48 63 99 128 254

2. Convert each of these eight-bit unsigned binary numbers to decimal (bits are grouped in fours for readability):
   0000 1111   0011 1110   0101 0101   1000 0101   1001 0010
3. On a place value table for eight-bit signed binary numbers, show the binary equivalent of each of these decimal numbers:
   7   32   79   127   −1   −32   −100
4. Convert each of these eight-bit signed binary numbers to decimal:
   0001 0101   0111 1000   1000 0000   1000 0101   1111 1011
5. Add the following pairs of eight-bit signed binary numbers. To the right of each number, show the decimal equivalent. Mark any that cause overflow.

0001 0001	0011 1110	0110 1100	1000 0100	1111 1000
0001 0010	0100 0001	0110 0000	1011 1001	1110 1000

6. Show object code (in hex) created by the assembler for each of the following constants:

DC B'101'	DC B'11110000'	DC H'255'	DC H'1000'
DC H'−7'	DC F'127'	DC F'65535'	DC F'−4096'

7. The definition WORD DC F'428' appears at location X'428' in your program. Show the contents (in hex) of R7 after L 7,WORD is executed. What (in hex) is in R7 after LA 7,WORD is executed?
8. What are the largest positive and negative values that can be contained in a halfword? Show them in decimal and hex form.
9. What are the largest positive and negative values that can be contained in a fullword? Show them in decimal and hex form.
10. Write instructions to add 5 to contents of R7 using:
    a. A halfword literal
    b. A fullword constant in main storage
    c. Another register
    d. A Load Address instruction
11. Write instructions to multiply 12345.678 by 4.739, round the result to two decimal places, and edit the answer to a field called PRANSWER.
12. Write instructions to calculate one day's interest, rounded to the nearest cent, on $42,387.29 at 11.75 percent per year.

PROGRAMMING PROBLEMS

1. Using Date Set 1 in Appendix D, write a program to print an Analysis of Weekly Salaries. This report shows the name, department, and weekly rate for each employee whose pay type is 'W'. When the department number changes, print out the average weekly rate for the department. Print your own headings, and doublespace between departments. Do all arithmetic operations, including counting lines, in binary. Print only 40 detail lines per page to allow space for department averages.

2. Modify Problem 1 to convert annual salaries to a weekly rate by dividing by 52 and hourly rate to weekly rate by multiplying by 40. Print the weekly rate for all employees and the average weekly rate for all employees in each department. Do all arithmetic in binary.
3. Using Date Set 3 in Appendix D, prepare a Sales Analysis Report showing region, name, and net sales for each salesperson. Net sales are computed by subtracting year-to-date returns from year-to-date sales. At the end of the report, print the region, name, and net sales for the salesperson having the highest net sales and the same data for the person having the lowest net sales. Do all arithmetic in binary.

10 Address Modification and Table Handling

OBJECTIVES

After studying this chapter, you should be able to:

- Explain reasons for and uses of address modification
- Initialize and modify addresses by several different methods
- Use either explicit addressing or dummy sections to apply address modification
- Set up tables by defining constants
- Load tables by reading in records from external files
- Describe searching by factor matching and address calculation and explain which method to employ in a given situation
- Define, load, and process single- and multiple-level tables

The term *data structure* is applied to the way in which we arrange data in storage or in a record. Where different values of one type of data, such as test scores or daily temperatures, are placed in consecutive fields of the same size, the structure is called an *array*. The different values of the data are called *array elements*.

If the repeated data may contain more than one field, the structure is a *table*. In our daily life, we are familiar with many tables, such as income tax rates, price lists, and directories. A table is made up of *table entries*, with each entry corresponding generally to one row of a printed table. Each table entry normally contains one field, called the *key*, that identifies the subject of the entry, and other fields that describe characteristics of the entry.

Many persons use the terms "array" and "table" interchangeably. For efficient processing, each element in an array or each entry in a table must be of the same size. We will use "array" or "list" to refer to the recurrence of a single type of data, and "table" to refer to a recurring structure with more than one field.

If only two or three items are repeated in the array or table, it is efficient to process them as separate items. But if more than three are to be processed, they are best handled with a loop by initializing an address within a register to the first item and modifying the address from item to item during successive iterations of the loop.

In this chapter, we shall explore a number of methods for organizing data into tables, for processing data so arranged, and for searching and retrieving essential data from tables.

INITIALIZING ADDRESSES

We have previously initialized loops by setting some initial value such as a counter. Then we have continued the loop until the counter has been decremented to zero. To initialize a loop to process arrays or tables, we must also place the address of the first element or table entry into a base register or, in some instances, an index register. Then we modify that address by adding the size of the element or entry to that register each time we repeat the loop. The loop may be terminated by a counter, by reaching the ending address of the data, or by testing for some other condition.

The Load Address (LA) instruction is well suited for initializing addresses. If a table starts at a location named TABLE, then

```
LA 7,TABLE
```

places the address of TABLE into R7. We can then use R7 explicitly to refer to the first entry in the table.

The Load (L) instruction also can place an address constant or literal into a register for initialization:

```
         L  7,TABADDR or L 7,=A(TABLE)
            .
TABADDR  DC A(TABLE)
```

MODIFYING ADDRESSES

To modify the address in a register we may use the Load Address (LA) or any of the binary fullword or halfword instructions. For example, any of these instructions will add 5 to the contents of R7:

```
LA   7,5(7)
LA   7,5(0,7)
A    7,=F'5'
AH   7,=H'5'
```

In the LA instructions, the 5 is considered a displacement added to the address contained in R7 (within parentheses). The address thus formed is then loaded back into R7 (operand 1), incrementing it by 5.

If data is to be processed from the end of the list or table back toward the start, addresses may be modified by subtraction. Subtract (S) or Subtract Halfword (SH) may be used.

Later in the chapter we will see how Branch on Index High (BXH) and Branch on Index Low or Equal (BXLE) instructions can both modify and test addresses.

EXPLICIT OPERANDS

We cannot use ordinary names for fields in address modification. The assembler makes each name equivalent to a fixed address that is a certain displacement from the base address for the program. Each time we use the name, the assembler uses the base register and the proper displacement.

To modify addresses, we must use our own base registers and displacements. We have used explicit operands in earlier programs by loading a base register with the address of an input work area and writing a displacement to refer to the specific columns in the record.

Each type of instruction has its own format. We must be certain whether an explicit operand is the displacement, length, base register, or index register.

For our first example, assume we wish to get the total hours worked by an employee. The record (Figure 10–1) contains seven fields, one for each day, starting at INRECD+26 (column 27). Each field is three bytes wide, so that the fields start at positions 27, 30, 33, 36, 39, 42, and 45 respectively. We assume the data is in the form 99V9, representing hours to the nearest tenth. We will initialize our address at INRECD+26 and add 3 to that address each time we repeat the loop, as shown in Figure 10–2.

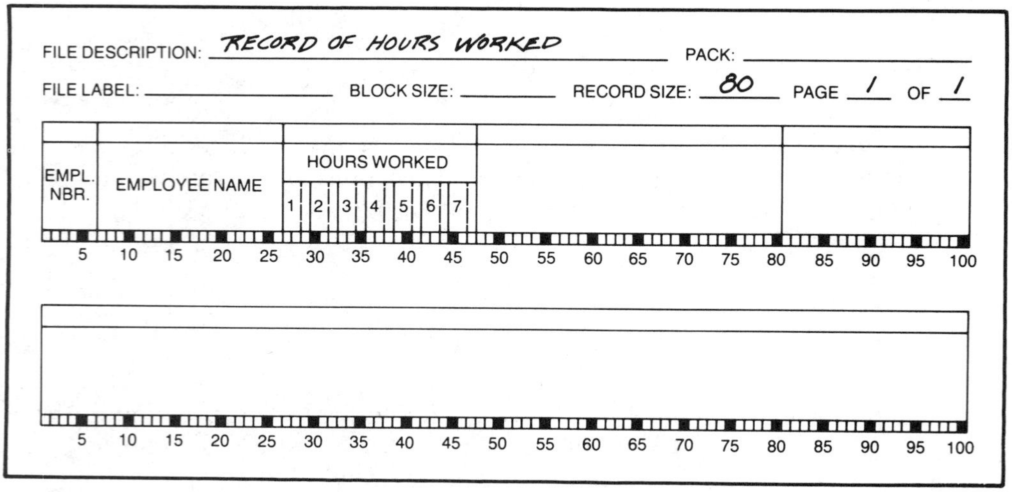

Figure 10–1 Record containing hours worked each day

```
         ZAP   PKTOTAL,=P'0'       Clear total
         LA    7,INRECD+26         Set starting address to first day
         LA    5,7                 Set day counter to 7
REPEAT   EQU   *                   REPEAT
         PACK  PKHOURS,0(3,7)        Pack 3 bytes at specified address
         AP    PKTOTAL,PKHOURS       Add hours to total
         LA    7,3(7)                Add 3 to address
         BCT   5,REPEAT              Subtract 1 from day counter
UNTIL    EQU   *                   UNTIL day counter = 0
```

Figure 10–2 Loop to add total hours worked per week

In the second operand in the PACK instruction in Figure 10–2, 0 is the displacement added to the address in R7 to make the effective address, and 3 is the length. In the second operand of the LA instruction, 3 is the displacement added to the previous contents of R7 to form a new address to load into R7.

As another example of address modification, suppose we wish to know the number of blank bytes in an input record. For variety, we shall use binary arithmetic in Figure 10–3.

We can modify two or more addresses within the same loop. Suppose, from our earlier example in Figure 10–2, that we wish to print the hours worked spaced eight bytes apart in the print line. The first day's hours might start in PRLINE + 32 (column 32 after print control byte) and the others in 40, 48, 56, 64, 72, and 80 respectively. Figure 10–4 shows a possible solution.

INDEX REGISTERS

Index registers may be used only with type RX instructions. They do not apply to type SS instructions that move characters, edit, and do decimal arithmetic. However, they are useful where data is stored in the form of fullwords or halfwords.

Suppose we have 20 halfwords in an array. We wish to get their sum. The first halfword is at ARRAY + 0, the second at ARRAY + 2, and so on until the last is added at ARRAY + 38. Figure 10–5 shows this routine.

Index register 7 contains the exact amount to be added to the address of ARRAY to designate the proper halfword.

We do not always have to use a counter to control our loop. In the preceding example, we could have tested the value of the index register. When the index register exceeded 38, we would terminate the loop. In this instance, we could replace the BCT instruction with these instructions:

```
         C     7,=F'38'      *
         BNH   REPEAT        *
UNTIL    EQU   *             Until index register > 38
```

```
         SR    6,6          Clear R6 as total
         LA    7,INRECD     Set starting column address
         LA    5,80         Set count to 80
REPEAT   EQU   *            REPEAT
IF       CLI   0(7),C' '      IF specified column is blank
         BNE   ENDIF             *
THEN     LA    6,1(6)            THEN add 1 to total
ENDIF    EQU   *              ENDIF
         LA    7,1(7)         Add 1 to column address
         BCT   5,REPEAT     Subtract 1 from count
UNTIL    EQU   *            UNTIL count = 0
         ST    6,TOTBLANK   Store total of blank columns
```

Figure 10–3 Loop to count blank columns in an input record

```
         LA     7,INRECD+26        Set input address
         LA     8,PRLINE+32        Set print line address
         LA     5,7                Set count to 7
REPEAT   EQU    *                  REPEAT
         PACK   PKHOURS,0(3,7)       Pack hours for first day
         MVC    0(5,8),PATRN         Move edit pattern to print line
         ED     0(5,8),PKHOURS       Edit hours
         LA     7,3(7)               Add 3 to input address
         LA     8,8(8)               Add 8 to print address
         BCT    5,REPEAT             Subtract 1 from count
UNTIL    EQU    *                  UNTIL count = 0
         .
PKHOURS  DS     PL3
PATRN    DC     XL5'4020214B20'
```

Figure 10–4 Modifying two addresses in one loop

```
         LA    7,0          Set index register to zero
         SR    6,6          Clear R6 as total
         LA    5,20         Set count to 20
REPEAT   EQU   *            REPEAT
         AH    6,ARRAY(7)     Add first halfword to total
         LA    7,2(7)         Add 2 to index register
         BCT   5,REPEAT       Subtract 1 from count
UNTIL    EQU   *            UNTIL count = 0
         .
ARRAY    DS    20H
```

Figure 10–5 Adding 20 halfwords in an array

Branch on Index High Instruction

The Branch on Index High (BXH) instruction can perform several necessary functions with index registers. It is most valuable to decrement the index register to process the array of data from last to first. BXH is a type RS instruction with two general register operands and one storage operand.

Examples are:

INSTRUCTION	FORMAT
BXH 7,8,REPEAT	OP R1,R3,S2
BXH 7,9,0(3)	OP R2,R3,D2(B2)

In the first example, the contents of R8 are added to R7. Then R7 is compared with R9 (implied). If the contents of R7 are higher than R9, a branch is made to REPEAT. Whenever the R3 operand is *even-numbered*, the comparison is made with the next adjacent *odd-numbered* register. In the second example, the contents of R9 are added to R7 and then compared with R9. When the R3 operand is *odd-numbered*, the index register is compared with that register itself, rather than the next-higher numbered register.

To illustrate BXH, let us repeat the example of adding the 20 halfwords, starting with the last and ending with the first. The index register must first be set to 38. It is decremented by 2 for each iteration of the loop. The loop is executed the last time when the index is zero, and terminates when the index reaches −2. Since both the increment and the final test value of the index are −2, we can put that value in the R3 operand. Figure 10–6 is an example.

Note that it was not possible to initialize the increment with a LA instruction. The LA uses a displacement, which can never be negative. We used the LH instruction, rather than L, to load the halfword literal.

Branch on Index Low or Equal Instruction

Branch on Index Low or Equal (BXLE) works like BXH, except that the branch is made if the index is *lower than or equal to* the test value. BXLE normally is used to increment the register to process the array from first to last. It is normally not possible to have the same value as both the index and

```
         LA    7,38           Set index for last halfword
         LH    9,=H'-2'       Set increment and test value
         SR    6,6            Clear R6 as total
REPEAT   EQU   *              REPEAT
         AH    6,ARRAY(7)       Add halfword to total
         BXH   7,9,REPEAT       Subtract 2 from index
UNTIL    EQU   *              UNTIL index = -2
```

Figure 10–6 Branch on Index High (BXH) instruction to add 20 halfwords

the test value. Figure 10–7 shows an example of adding the 20 halfwords with BXLE.

Note that INITVAL is defined as four separate fullwords, with values of 0, 0, 2, and 38 respectively. These are loaded with the LM instruction into R6 through R9 to set the total and index to zero, the increment to 2, and the test value to 38. The BXLE instruction continues to add the contents of R8 to index register R7 until it exceeds R9. R9 is the implied operand since R8 is even-numbered.

DUMMY SECTIONS

We often have records or tables in which a group of several different data elements is repeated in a list. For example, a four-byte item number, three-byte quantity, and five-byte price might be repeated six times within an input record. Explicit addressing in such a case can become confusing. It is often difficult to remember which instructions require one or two length codes and

```
         LM    6,9,INITVAL      Clear total (R6)
*                               Set index (R7) to zero
*                               Set increment (R8) to 2
*                               Set test value (R0) to 38
REPEAT   EQU   *                REPEAT
         AH    6,ARRAY(7)         Add halfword to total
         BXLE  7,8,REPEAT         Add 2 to index
UNTIL    EQU   *                UNTIL index > 38
         .
INITVAL  DC    F'0,0,2,38'
```

Figure 10–7 Branch on Index Low or Equal (BXLE) instruction to add 20 halfwords

```
         LA    7,INRECD           Set address of first group
         LA    5,6                Set count
REPEAT   EQU   *                  REPEAT
         MVC   PRITEM,0(7)          Move item number to print line
         PACK  PKQTY,4(3,7)         Pack quantity
         PACK  PKPRICE,7(5,7)       Pack price
         ZAP   DOUBLE,PKQTY         Multiply quantity by price
         MP    DOUBLE,PKPRICE       *
         and so forth.
```

Figure 10–8 Explicit register addressing

which part of an operand is the base or index register. Suppose we are required to move the item number to a print line and multiply the quantity by the price. The coding (in part) might look like Figure 10–8.

We can simplify this problem by defining and using a *dummy section*. A dummy section describes the *format* of data that is repeated, but does not actually reserve space within our program area for it. Figure 10–9 illustrates use of a dummy section for the problem in Figure 10–8.

The DSECT op code designates the start of a dummy section. Each DSECT statement requires an entry in the name field. The assembler leaves the MAINLINE control section (CSECT) which was defined by the START statement at the beginning of the program. The location counter is reset to zero and then advances as each field is defined to show the relative position of that field *within the dummy section*. In Figure 10–9 we have defined the three fields that will be repeated six times throughout the input record. The definition shows two of the three things we need to define any field, the displacement (location) and the length. The dummy section must be followed by another DSECT or by a CSECT giving the same name (if any) used in the START statement.

To refer to names of fields within the dummy section, we must define a base register that applies only to the dummy section. We do this near the start of our program with the statement

```
USING INDUMMY,7
```

```
LOCATION    NAME        INSTRUCTION
000000      MAINLINE    START 0
000000                  BALR  12,0
000002                  USING *,12
000002                  USING 7,INDUMMY
.                       Other instructions in MAINLINE
                        LA    7,INRECD
                        LA    5,6
            REPEAT      EQU   *
                        MVC   PRITEM,INITEM
                        PACK  PKQTY,INQTY
                        PACK  PKPRICE,INPRICE
                        ZAP   DOUBLE,PKQTY
                        MP    DOUBLE,PKPRICE
                        and so forth
.
000486      Last location reached in MAINLINE
000000      INDUMMY     DSECT
000000      INITEM      DS    CL4
000004      INQTY       DS    CL3
000007      INPRICE     DS    CL5
000486      MAINLINE    CSECT
```

Figure 10–9 Using a dummy section

to tell the assembler to use R7 as the base register for any names that appear in INDUMMY dummy section. Now after loading the correct address into R7, we can refer to INITEM instead of 0(4,7). The assembler will supply base register 7, displacement 0, length 4, exactly as we need. We can refer to INQTY instead of 4(3,7) and INPRICE instead of 7(5,7).

Use of a dummy section relieves us of the burden of remembering which type of instruction requires which explicit operand. We think of each field only by its name in the dummy section, just as we think of any other field by its name within a record. We are still responsible for designating the base register to be used with the dummy section and for initializing and modifying the address within that register.

We will use dummy sections extensively in future examples.

Programming Tips

- Use the LA instruction to initialize a register with the address of the first item in a table. Use another LA instruction to modify that address to the next item in the table. The displacement of the second LA instruction gives the amount to be added.
- An index register can be used only with RX instructions. It is usually set to zero for the first time through the loop and incremented by the displacement between items in the table.
- The BXH instruction is convenient to process items in a table from last to first. A negative value equal to the distance between items in the table can be placed in an odd-numbered register to be both the increment and the test value.
- The BXLE instruction is designed to process items from first to last. The test value should be set at least one higher than the relative position of the last item from the start of the table.
- To define a dummy section, write a named DSECT followed by the fields that are repeated. Designate a base register to refer to the name of the DSECT. Load the proper address into that base register to refer to the first item in a table, and increment it to refer to the next successive entry each time the loop is repeated.

DEFINITION OF A TABLE

A table consists of *table entries*, each of which consists of one field called a *table key* or *table argument*, and one or more additional fields called *func-*

tions. The functions generally give characteristics related to the key. For example, if the table key is an inventory item number, the function fields might contain item description, quantity on hand, cost, selling price, reorder point, reorder quantity, and other relevant items.

Each table entry must be of the same length, and each key must be of the same type and the same length. Corresponding functions, such as item description, must also be of the same type and length in each entry.

Thus a table resembles a file, with each table entry a fixed-length record, except that it normally resides in main storage rather than on an external device.

TABLE ELEMENTS

A table might be in any sequence by key, although the common sequence is in ascending order. Having the keys in sequence simplifies searching the table and shortens search time.

The keys to a table might be consecutive, sequential with some missing keys, or sequential to indicate a range of values. Here is an example of a table of each type:

A consecutive table has no missing keys within the prescribed range. A table of the names of the days of the week is an example:

KEY	FUNCTION
1	Sunday
2	Monday
.	
7	Saturday

A chart of accounts is an example of a sequential table with some numbers missing:

KEY	FUNCTION
101	Cash in Office
105	Cash in Bank
110	Notes Receivable

A sales tax table indicates a range of values for each function:

KEYS	FUNCTION
0.00 through 0.09	0.00
0.10 through 0.19	0.01
0.20 through 0.39	0.02

CREATING THE TABLE

There are two ways to create a table:

1. Define the table entries as constants.
2. Load the table by reading records from some external device at run time.

Constants may be employed when the table has little or no change over a period of time. A table of days of the week, months of the year, or state abbreviations with the full state names could well be created by defining constants.

Tables that change frequently can be maintained on tape or disk and updated like any other file as changes are made. Then the records are read into main storage and loaded into the table entries when needed for reference.

Defining Constants

Any type of constants may be used in tables. Table keys may be different types of constants from the functions. The keys might be characters (type C) while the functions might be packed decimal (type P).

We might define a table of month numbers and names as follows:

```
MONTABLE   DS   0CL132
           DC   C'01JANUARY  '
           DC   C'02FEBRUARY '
           .
           DC   C'12DECEMBER '
```

Here, each table entry is 11 bytes long, two for the month number and 9 for the longest month name, SEPTEMBER. Each entry must be the same length. The entire table occupies 132 bytes (12 entries of 11 bytes each).

We might have a table of 10 items, in which item numbers consist of three characters while prices are three bytes of packed decimal. We might define such a table in either of these ways and still have identical data:

```
INVTABLE  DS   0CL60             DS   0CL60
          DC   C'101'            DC   X'F1F0F100438C'
          DC   PL3'4.38'         DC   X'F1F0F501250C'
          DC   C'105'            .
          DC   PL3'12.50'        .
          etc.
```

Reading Table Records

To load the table of months and names, we know that there are exactly 12 months. If the table data appears with one entry per input record in the first 11 bytes, we could load the table with the routine shown in Figure 10–10.

To illustrate a somewhat more complex loading routine, suppose the inventory table records are all in character form, with the item number occupy-

```
         LA    7,MONTABLE          Set address of first table entry
         LA    5,12                Set count to 12
REPEAT   EQU   *                   REPEAT
         GET   INFILE,INRECD         Read table record
         MVC   0(11,7),INRECD        Move to table entry
         LA    7,11(7)               Set address to next entry
         BCT   5,REPEAT              Subtract 1 from count
UNTIL    EQU   *                   UNTIL count = 0
```

Figure 10–10 Routine to load table of month numbers and names

ing three bytes followed by the price in five bytes. Suppose further that to conserve space, we have arranged ten inventory items per record. The maximum number of inventory items is 600, but there may be fewer. Following the last item is an entry of 99999999. We must move 9s to the end of the table and also count the number of entries loaded into the table.

We will need two loops, the outer one to read the table records and the inner one to load the 10 entries in each record. We will use R7 to hold the table address and R8 for the address of each entry within the input record. R5 will count total items placed in the table, and R6 will count the 10 entries in each record. Figure 10–11 shows this routine.

The ORG Statement

Often we read input records to load a table from the same file from which data is read to be processed against that table. The table records usually have a different format from the processing records. We may redefine the fields within any area by means of the ORG (originate) statement. ORG is an assembler directive that resets the location counter to the value given as the operand. The name field for the statement must be blank.

Figure 10–12 shows an example of a table record and a data record sharing the same work area. Notice the effect of ORG on the location counter.

The ORG statement without an operand resets the location counter to the maximum value it had before the ORG with an operand was used.

SEARCHING TECHNIQUES

Searching a table involves comparing some value, called the *search argument*, with the key of each entry in the table until the matching key is found or determined not to be present in the table. We must either know the total number of table entries or place some value that can be recognized as terminating the table. Usually a value of X'FFFF's or 9999s indicates the end of the table.

There are two ways of terminating the search: (1) finding the desired key, or (2) not finding it. Many programmers have two comparisons within the loop, one of which branches to FOUND and the other to NOTFOUND. The

```
         LA    7,INVTABLE          Set address of first table entry
         SR    5,5                 Clear R5 as entry count
         GET   INFILE,INRECD       Read first table record
         LA    8,INRECD            Set record address
DOWHILE  CLC   0(8,8),=C'99999999' DOWHILE NOT end of table input
         BE    ENDDO                 *
AND      CH    5,=H'600'           AND record count <= 600
         BH    ENDDO                 *
         LA    6,10                  Set loop count to 10
DOWHILE2 CLC   0(8,8),=C'99999999'   DOWHILE NOT end of table input
         BE    ENDDO2                  *
AND2     LTR   6,6                   AND loop count > 0
         BZ    ENDDO2                  *
         MVC   0(3,7),0(8)               Move key to table
         PACK  3(3,7),3(5,8)             Pack price into table
         BCTR  6,0                       Subtract 1 from loop count
         LA    7,6(7)                    Add 6 to table address
         LA    8,8(8)                    Add 8 to record address
         LA    5,1(5)                    Add 1 to entry count
         B     DOWHILE2                  *
ENDDO2   EQU   *                     ENDDO
         GET   INFILE,INRECD         Read next table record
         LA    8,INRECD              Set record address
         B     DOWHILE               *
ENDDO    EQU   *                   ENDDO
         MVC   0(3,7),=C'999'      Put 999 as key at end of table
         ZAP   3(3,7),=P'99999'    Put 999 as price at end of table
         ST    5,ENTRYCNT          Store entry count
```

Figure 10–11 Routine to load table from records with multiple entries

```
LOCATION             STATEMENT

000420   TABRECD     DS    0CL80
000420   TABKEY      DS    CL5
000425   TABPRICE    DS    CL8
00042D               DS    CL67
000420               ORG   TABRECD
000420   INRECD      DS    0CL80
000420   INKEY       DS    CL5
000425   INDESCR     DS    CL20
000439   INQTY       DS    CL5
00043D               DS    CL50
000470               ORG
```

Figure 10–12 Use of ORG statement to redefine input record

use of two exits violates good structured programming principles. We can avoid this violation by the use of a compound DOWHILE loop to search the table and an IF structure to test the condition that terminated the search. Pseudocode in Figure 10–13 shows the technique.

```
Set address of first table entry
DOWHILE key argument NOT = search argument
AND NOT end of table
  Set address to next table entry
ENDDO
IF key argument = search argument
  THEN process table functions
ELSE
  Print 'INVALID KEY'
ENDIF
```

Figure 10–13 Pseudocode of table search technique

Factor Matching

The term *factor matching* is applied to any search in which we try to find a key argument that matches our search argument. In limited instances the factor to be matched is one of the functions in the table entry rather than the key. For example, we might search for an item having a price greater than $1,000.

Figure 10–14 shows a search to find the name of the day of the week that matches a day number. In this first example, we put an end-of-table value, called a *sentinel*, of X'FF' at the end of the table. This code will be higher than the EBCDIC codes for the numbers 1 through 7. We will terminate the search when we find a value higher than or equal to the search argument.

Another approach is to determine that the day number is between 1 and 7 before attempting the search. Then we know that we will always find an equal key. Figure 10–15 shows the technique.

Address Calculation

A *positional table* is one in which the number of the entry is the same as its relative position within the table. Where this occurs, we can omit the key to the table and calculate the position of the desired entry.

Using the day of the week table as an example, we can now construct the table to contain only the names of the days and omit their numbers. The first day, Sunday, is in the first table entry, while the seventh day, Saturday, is in the seventh. We will require nine bytes for each to accommodate the longest name, Wednesday. Our table will then contain 63 bytes for the seven names. We will find that the first name is displaced by 0 bytes from the start of the table, the second by 9, the third by 18, until the seventh is displaced by 56 bytes. A generalized formula for calculating this displacement is

$$(n - 1) * l$$

where n = the number of the entry and l = the length of each entry.

We can now directly calculate the address of the day name with the routine in Figure 10–16.

```
          LA   7,DAYTABLE                    Set address to first entry
DOWHILE   CLC  0(1,7),DAYNBR                 DOWHILE key < search argument
          BNL  ENDDO                           *
          LA   7,10(7)                         Set address to next entry
          B    DOWHILE                         *
ENDDO     EQU  *                             ENDDO
IF        BNE  ELSE                          IF key = search argument
THEN      MVC  PRDAY,1(7)                      THEN move day from table
          B    ENDIF                           *
ELSE      EQU  *                             ELSE
          MVC  PRMESG,=C'INVALID CODE'         Move invalid message
ENDIF     EQU  *                             ENDIF
          .
DAYTABLE  DS   0CL70
          DC   C'1SUNDAY   '
          DC   C'2MONDAY   '
          .
          DC   C'7SATURDAY '
          DC   X'FF'
```

Figure 10–14 Factor matching, key high or equal

```
IF        CLI  DAYNBR,C'1'                   IF day number => 1
          BL   ELSE                            *
AND       CLI  DAYNBR,C'7'                   AND day number <= 7
          BH   ELSE                            *
THEN      LA   7,DAYTABLE                      THEN set address to first entry
DOWHILE   CLI  0(1,7),DAYNBR                   DOWHILE key <> search argument
          BE   ENDDO                             *
          LA   7,10(7)                           Set address to next entry
          B    DOWHILE                           *
ENDDO     EQU  *                               ENDDO
          MVC  PRDAY,1(7)                      Move day to print line
          B    ENDIF                           *
ELSE      EQU  *                             ELSE
          MVC  PRMESG,=C'INVALID CODE'         Move invalid message
ENDIF     EQU  *                             ENDIF
```

Figure 10–15 Factor matching, key tested for validity

SINGLE-LEVEL TABLES

A *single-level table* is one that has one key and one or more functions in each table entry. Searching a single-level table requires only one loop or direct calculation to find the proper table entry. Using the location of the entry as a base, any of the functions can be retrieved by using their displacements from the start of the entry. Where there are several functions, a dummy section may also be used to refer to the various fields in the entry.

Suppose we have an inventory table, in which each entry has the following fields:

```
IF      CLI  DAYNBR,C'1'           IF day number => 1
        BL   ELSE                    *
AND     CLI  DAYNBR,C'7'           AND day number <=7
        BH   ELSE                    *
THEN    PACK DOUBLE,DAYNBR           THEN convert number to binary
        CVB  7,DOUBLE                *
        BCTR 7,0                     Subtract 1
        MH   7,=H'9'                 Multiply by 9 (entry length)
        LA   8,DAYTABLE              Set base of table
        AR   7,8                     Add to displacement
        MVC  PRDAY,0(7)              Move day to print line
        B    ENDIF                   *
ELSE    EQU  *                     ELSE
        MVC  PRMESG,=C'INVALID CODE'  Move invalid message
ENDIF   EQU  *                     ENDIF
```

Figure 10–16 Table address calculation

RECORD POSITIONS	ITEM
1–5	Item number (key)
6–25	Item description
26–28	Price 999V99 packed

Following the last table entry is a sentinel consisting of 99999 in the item number location..

Our input record has the following fields:

RECORD POSITIONS	ITEM
1–5	Item number
6–9	Quantity ordered
10–80	Unused

Our problem is to find the item number in the table, move the description to the print line, multiply the price by the quantity ordered, and move the quantity, price, and cost to the print line. Finding a key higher than the search argument will indicate the item is not in the table. Figure 10–17 shows the search routine.

MULTIPLE-LEVEL TABLES

A *multiple-level table* has one or more tables located in each table entry. An example is an income tax table having one entry for each pay range, with another table showing tax for each number of exemptions. In this example, the outer table requires factor matching while the inner table is a positional table that could be directly addressed.

```
         LA    7,INVTABLE                     Set address to first entry
DOWHILE  CLC   0(5,7),INITEM                  DOWHILE key < search argument
         BNL   ENDDO                            *
         LA    7,28(7)                          Set address to next entry
         B     DOWHILE
ENDDO    EQU   *                              ENDDO
IF       BNE   ELSE                           IF key = search argument
THEN     MVC   PRDESCR,5(20,7)                  Move description to print line
         PACK  DOUBLE,INQTY                     Pack quantity ordered
         MVC   PRQTY,PATRN                      Set up quantity
         ED    PRQTY,DOUBLE+5                   *
         MP    DOUBLE,25(3,7)                   Multiply by price
         MVC   PRPRICE,PATRN2                   Set up price
         ED    PRPICE,25(3,7)                   *
         MVC   PRCOST,PATRN3                    Set up cost
         ED    PRCOST,DOUBLE+3                  *
         B     ENDIF                            *
ELSE     EQU   *                              ELSE
         MVC   PRMESG,=C'INVALID ITEM'          Move invalid message
ENDIF    EQU   *                              ENDIF
```

Figure 10–17 Searching key high or equal

```
IF       CLC   INAGE,=C'18'                   IF age => 18
         BL    ELSE                             *
AND      CLC   INAGE,=C'65'                   AND age <= 65
         BH    ELSE                             *
ANDB     CLC   INCLASS,=C'1'                  AND class => 1
         BL    ELSE                             *
ANDC     CLC   INCLASS,=C'4'                  AND class <= 4
         BH    ELSE                             *
THEN     LA    7,RATETBL                        THEN set address of first entry
DOWHILE  CLC   0(2,7),INAGE                     DOWHILE age < table key
         BNL   ENDDO                              *
         LA    7,10(7)                            Set address of next entry
         B     DOWHILE                            *
ENDDO    EQU   *                                ENDDO
         PACK  DOUBLE,INCLASS                   Convert class to binary
         CVB   8,DOUBLE                         *
         BCTR  8,0                              Subtract 1
         MH    8,=H'2'                          Multiply by 2 (entry length)
         LA    7,2(8,7)                         Add displacement+2 to entry addr.
         ZAP   PKRATE,0(2,7)                    Zap rate to work area
         B     ENDIF                            *
ELSE     EQU   *                              ELSE
         MVC   PRMESG,=C'INVALID DATA'          Move error message
ENDIF    EQU   *                              ENDIF
```

Figure 10–18 Searching multiple-level table

Another example could be an inventory table that lists the item number, description, and cost of each item and then has an imbedded table in each entry giving the quantity on hand at each of 10 warehouses.

Suppose we have a table giving premium rates for an employee insurance plan. Eligible ages are 18 through 65. Table entries are based on age groups, with first age from 18 through 24. We need not show the low age for each group in the table, but only the high age. Wherever we find a table key higher than or equal to the search argument, we have the right entry. There is an imbedded table showing the premium rate for each of four classes of coverage. The layout of each table entry is this:

ENTRY POSITIONS	ITEM
1–2	High age for range
3–4	Rate for class 1 coverage 9V99 packed
5–6	Rate for class 2 coverage
7–8	Rate for class 3 coverage
9–10	Rate for class 4 coverage

We must verify that the age is between 18 and 65 and that the class is between 1 and 4. We will get the address of the age group in R7 and the displacement for the correct class in R8, add the two together, and zap the rate at the resulting location to a work area. Assume the table has entries for 15 groups and thus occupies 150 bytes. Figure 10–18 shows the search routine.

Programming Tips

- When factor matching with keys in ascending order, terminate the search when you find a key higher than the key argument.
- When factor matching with keys representing a range of values, terminate the search when you find a key higher than or equal to the key argument.
- Use the formula $(n - 1) * l$ to calculate the relative location of the nth item in a positional table if the first item in the table has a key of 1 and the length of each table entry is l.
- For proper program structure, use one or more conditions to terminate a table search. Then, after leaving the loop, make an IF-THEN-ELSE structure to determine whether the item was found.

PROGRAM 10: LOCATING DELIVERY RATES

Program 10 processes multiple-level tables to determine delivery rates on materials. The larger table shows the maximum weight for each class of shipment. Each entry of this table contains an inner table giving the delivery charges for each of the five regions served by the transportation company.

The data for the two tables is shown in Figure 10–19.

The table is loaded from seven input records, each containing the data for one entry in the format shown in Figure 10–20.

We do not require the minimum weight for each class in each table. Our logic will be to search each table entry unit we find a weight that is equal to or greater than the weight of the item to be delivered. Then we will retrieve the applicable rate for the region from the inner table.

Each outer table entry will then be arranged:

01–14 Maximum weight for class (characters)

05–14 Rate for regions 1–5, each two bytes packed, form 9V99

Our transaction records contain three fields:

01–05 Order number

06–09 Weight

10 Region number

WEIGHT		**REGION**				
OVER	NOT OVER	1	2	3	4	5
01–04	05–08	09–11	12–14	15–17	18–20	21–23
0000	0050	.050	.053	.056	.059	.062
0050	0100	.047	.049	.051	.053	.055
0100	0200	.045	.047	.049	.051	.053
0200	0400	.042	.044	.046	.048	.050
0400	0800	.038	.040	.042	.044	.046
0800	1600	.033	.035	.037	.039	.041
1600	9999	.027	.029	.031	.033	.035

Figure 10–19 Data for table of delivery rates

01–04	Minimum weight for class
05–08	Maximum weight for class
09–11	Rate for Region 1
12–14	Rate for Region 2
15–17	Rate for Region 3
18–20	Rate for Region 4
21–23	Rate for Region 5

Figure 10–20 Format for table input records

The maximum weight for any shipment is 9999 pounds, also the maximum weight in our table. We therefore need no test for end of table, since any weight that can be represented within four columns will be found in the table. Our table search module first verifies that the region is not less than 1 and not greater than 5. The loop at DOWHILE2 locates the correct weight class and places the address of that table entry in R7.

Steps to calculate the address of the rate for the applicable region are:

1. Pack the region code.
2. Convert to binary in R8.
3. Subtract 1 with BCTR 8,0.
4. Multiply by 2 (length of each rate) with the SLA 8,1 instruction.
5. Add together the address of the table entry in R7, a displacement of 4 to move over the weight field in that entry, and the address of the rate for the specified region in R8. The one instruction LA 7,4(8,7) combines these three factors into a single address and places it in R7.
6. Zap the resulting two bytes to PKRATE.

If the region code is invalid, we print an error message by the transaction data.

Figure 10–21 shows the assembler listing, and Figure 10–22 shows the output.

SUMMARY

Data is often arranged so that a series of data elements of the same type appears in an array or table. Address modification involves changing the address in a base or index register so as to refer to each of the elements in turn. The register is initialized to hold the address of the first element. Each time we go through a loop, we modify the address to refer to the next element. Only the address is changed to move from one element to the next.

Explicit operands are often used to refer to the specific base register, index register, displacement, and length of the data element. Any binary arithmetic operation may be used to modify the address within a general register. The Load Address (LA) instruction is especially useful for both initializing and modifying addresses.

The dummy section is a description of one or more data elements that occur in a repeated fashion. The DSECT statement designates the start of the dummy section and resets the location counter to zero. As each field is described, the location counter indicates its displacement from the start of the dummy section. The USING statement relates a dummy section to a specific base register. The dummy section is effectively positioned to start at whatever address is in the base register. A field may be called by its name in the dummy section rather than by use of explicit operands.

```
  LOC  OBJECT CODE    ADDR1 ADDR2 STMT   SOURCE STATEMENT                                     DOS/VSE ASSEMBLER 15.15 86-03-27

                                     1 ***********************************************************************
                                     2 *                 ALTON R. KINDRED, PROGRAM 10
                                     3 * THIS PROGRAM READS IN RECORDS TO LOAD A TABLE OF DELIVERY RATES.
                                     4 * EACH TABLE ENTRY CONTAINS THE MAXIMUM WEIGHT FOR THAT CLASS AND THE
                                     5 * APPLICABLE RATE FOR EACH OF FIVE REGIONS.  THEN IT READS ORDER
                                     6 * RECORDS GIVING ORDER NUMBER, WEIGHT, AND REGION.  IT LOOKS UP THE
                                     7 * CORRECT WEIGHT CLASS IN THE TABLE AND RETRIEVES THE APPLICABLE
                                     8 * CHARGES FOR THE REGION GIVEN.  IT USES FACTOR MATCHING TO FIND THE
                                     9 * WEIGHT CLASS AND DIRECT CALCULATION TO FIND THE REGION IN THE TABLE.
                                    10 *          REGISTERS USED:
                                    11 *                 R0-1  - WORK REGISTERS
                                    12 *                 R5-6  - COUNTERS
                                    13 *                 R7-8  - ADDRESS REGISTERS
                                    14 *                 R9-11 - LINKS TO MODULES
                                    15 *                 R12   - PROGRAM BASE REGISTER
                                    16 ***********************************************************************
                                    17          PRINT NOGEN
000000                              18 MAINLINE START 0                       SET LOCATION COUNTER
                                    19 *        STM   14,12,12(13)            SAVE REGISTERS FOR OS         OS
000000 05C0                         20          BALR  12,0                    LOAD BASE REGISTER
                          00002     21          USING *,12                    DESIGNATE BASE REGISTER
                                    22 *        ST    13,SAVE+4               STORE REGISTER 13             OS
                                    23 *        LA    13,SAVE                 LOAD SAVE AREA ADDRESS        OS
                                    24 *        OPEN  (INFILE,(INPUT),PRINTER,(OUTPUT))                     OS
                                    25          OPEN  INFILE,PRINTER          OPEN FILES                    DOS
000016 4590 C03A          0003C     34          BAL   9,LOADTBL               LOAD TABLE
00001A 4590 C070          00072     35          BAL   9,INITIAL               SET INITIAL VALUES
00001E 4590 C080          00082     36          BAL   9,MAINLOOP              DO MAIN PROCESSING LOOP
000022 4590 C0AA          000AC     37          BAL   9,FINAL                 DO FINAL PROCESSING
                                    38          CLOSE INFILE,PRINTER          CLOSE FILES                   DOS
                                    47          EOJ                                                         DOS
                                    50 *        CLOSE (INFILE,,PRINTER)       CLOSE FILES                   OS
                                    51 *        L     13,SAVE+4               LOAD SAVE AREA ADDRESS        OS
                                    52 *        LM    14,12,12(13)            RESTORE REGISTERS             OS
                                    53 *        BR    14                      RETURN TO OS                  OS
                                    54 ***********************************************************************
                                    55 *                 FIRST LEVEL MODULES
                                    56 ***********************************************************************
                                    57 *
                                    58 *                 LOAD TABLE MODULE
                                    59 *
00003C 4170 C5C0          005C2     60 LOADTBL  LA    7,TABLE                 SET ADDRESS TO FIRST ENTRY
000040 4160 0007          00007     61          LA    6,7                     SET TABLE RECORD COUNT
                          00044     62 REPEAT   EQU   *                       REPEAT
000044 45A0 C0AC          000AE     63          BAL   10,READRECD               READ TABLE RECORD
000048 D203 7000 C32F 00000 00331   64          MVC   0(4,7),TABMAXWT           MOVE MAX. WT. TO TABLE
00004E 4177 0004          00004     65          LA    7,4(7)                    SET TABLE ADDR. TO REGION 1
000052 4180 C333          00335     66          LA    8,TABRATES                SET RECORD ADDR. TO REGION 1
000056 4150 0005          00005     67          LA    5,5                       SET REGION COUNTER TO 5
                          0005A     68 REPEAT1  EQU   *                         REPEAT
00005A F212 7000 8000 00000 00000   69          PACK  0(2,7),0(3,8)                 PACK RATE INTO TABLE
000060 4177 0002          00002     70          LA    7,2(7)                        SET TO NEXT REGION ADDR.
000064 4188 0003          00003     71          LA    8,3(8)                        SET TO NEXT INPUT ADDR.
000068 4650 C058          0005A     72          BCT   5,REPEAT1                     SUBTRACT 1 FROM REGION COUNT
                          0006C     73 UNTIL1   EQU   *                         UNTIL REGION COUNT = 0
00006C 4660 C042          00044     74          BCT   6,REPEAT                  SUBTRACT 1 FROM TAB. REC. CNT.
                          00070     75 UNTIL    EQU   *                       UNTIL TABLE RECORD COUNT = 0
000070 07F9                         76          BR    9                       RETURN
                                    77 *
                                    78 *                 SET INITIAL VALUES MODULE
                                    79 *
000072 F811 C5A6 C652 005A8 00654   80 INITIAL  ZAP   LINECNT,=P'51'          SET LINE COUNT > 50
000078 45A0 C0AC          000AE     81          BAL   10,READRECD             READ FIRST RECORD
00007C 45A0 C1A0          001A2     82          BAL   10,CLEAR                CLEAR PRING LINE
000080 07F9                         83          BR    9                       RETURN
                                    84 *
                                    85 *                 MAIN PROCESSING LOOP
                                    86 *
                          00082     87 MAINLOOP EQU   *
000082 95E8 C58F    00591           88 DOWHILE  CLI   EOFFLAG,C'Y'            DOWHILE NOT END OF FILE
000086 4780 C0A8    000AA           89          BE    ENDDO                     *
00008A 45A0 C0CA          000CC     90          BAL   10,TBSEARCH               SEARCH TABLE
00008E 95D5 C590    00592           91 IF       CLI   INVALFLG,C'N'             IF VALID REGION
000092 4770 C098    0009A           92          BNE   ENDIF                       *
000096 45A0 C118          0011A     93 THEN     BAL   10,CALC                     THEN CALCULATE CHARGES
                          0009A     94 ENDIF    EQU   *                         ENDIF
00009A 45A0 C138          0013A     95          BAL   10,SETUP                  SET UP PRINT LINE
00009E 45A0 C17C          0017E     96          BAL   10,PRDETAIL               PRINT LINE
0000A2 45A0 C0AC          000AE     97          BAL   10,READRECD               READ NEXT RECORD
0000A6 47F0 C080    00082           98          B     DOWHILE                   *
                          000AA     99 ENDDO    EQU   *                       ENDDO
0000AA 07F9                        100          BR    9                       RETURN
                                   101 *
                                   102 *                 FINAL PROCESSING MODULE
                                   103 *
0000AC 07F9                        104 FINAL    BR    9                       RETURN
                                   105 ***********************************************************************
                                   106 *                 SECOND LEVEL MODULES
                                   107 ***********************************************************************
                                   108 *
                                   109 *                  READ RECORD MODULE
                                   110 *
0000AE 9205 C58F    00591          111 READRECD MVI   EOFFLAG,C'N'            SET EOF FLAG OFF
                                   112          GET   INFILE,INRECD           READ RECORD
0000C2 47F0 C0C8    000CA          118 IFEOF    B     ENDIFEOF                IF END OF FILE
0000C6 92E8 C58F    00591          119 THENEOF  MVI   EOFFLAG,C'Y'              THEN SET EOF FLAG ON
                          000CA    120 ENDIFEOF EQU   *                       ENDIF
0000CA 07FA                        121          BR    10                      RETURN
                                   122 *
                                   123 *                 TABLE SEARCH MODULE
                                   124 *
0000CC 4170 C5C0          005C2    125 TBSEARCH LA    7,TABLE                 SET INITIAL TABLE ADDRESS
0000D0 95F1 C334    00336          126 IF2      CLI   INREGION,C'1'           IF REGION => 1
```

Figure 10–21 Assembler listing of Program 10

```
  LOC  OBJECT CODE    ADDR1 ADDR2  STMT   SOURCE STATEMENT                                       DOS/VSE ASSEMBLER 15.15 86-03-27

0000D4 4740 C112      00114         127          BL    ELSE2                              *
0000D8 95F5 C334      00336         128 AND2     CLI   INREGION,C'5'                    AND REGION <= 5
0000DC 4720 C112      00114         129          BH    ELSE2                              *
                            000E0   130 THEN2    EQU   *                                   THEN
0000E0 D503 7000 C330 00000 00332   131 DOWHILE2 CLC   0(4,7),INWEIGHT                     DOWHILE TABLE WT. < REC. WT.
0000E6 4780 C0F0      000F2         132          BNL   ENDDO2                                *
0000EA 4177 000E            0000E   133          LA    7,14(7)                               SET ADDRESS TO NEXT ENTRY
0000EE 47F0 C0DF      000E0         134          B     DOWHILE2                              *
                            000F2   135 ENDDO2   EQU   *                                   ENDDO
0000F2 F270 C59E C334 005A0 00336   136          PACK  DOUBLE,INREGION                     CONVERT REGION TO BINARY
0000F8 4F80 C59E            005A0   137          CVB   8,DOUBLE                            *
0000FC 0680                         138          BCTR  8,0                                 SUBTRACT 1
0000FE 8B80 0001            00001   139          SLA   8,1                                 MULTIPLY BY 2 BY SHIFTING
000102 4178 7004            00004   140          LA    7,4(8,7)                            COMBINE TABLE ADDRESSES
000106 F821 C591 7000 00593 00000   141          ZAP   PKRATE,0(2,7)                       ZAP RATE FROM TABLE
00010C 92D5 C590      00592         142          MVI   INVALFLG,C'N'                       SET INVALID FLAG OFF
000110 47F0 C116      00118         143          B     ENDIF2                              *
                            00114   144 ELSE2    EQU   *                                 ELSE
000114 92E8 C590      00592         145          MVI   INVALFLG,C'Y'                       SET INVALID FLAG ON
                            00118   146 ENDIF2   EQU   *                                 ENDIF
000118 07FA                         147          BR    10                                RETURN
                                    148 *
                                    149 *              CALCULATIONS MODULE
                                    150 *
00011A F223 C599 C330 0059B 00332   151 CALC     PACK  PKWEIGHT,INWEIGHT                   PACK WEIGHT
000120 F872 C59E C599 005A0 0059B   152          ZAP   DOUBLE,PKWEIGHT                     MULTIPLY RATE BY WEIGHT
000126 FC72 C59E C591 005A0 00593   153          MP    DOUBLE,PKRATE                       *
00012C F075 C59E 003F 005A0 0003F   154          SRP   DOUBLE,63,5                         ROUND TO NEAREST CENT
000132 F837 C595 C59E 00597 005A0   155          ZAP   PKCHARGE,DOUBLE                     *
000138 07FA                         156          BR    10                                RETURN
                                    157 *
                                    158 *              SET UP PRINT LINE MODULE
                                    159 *
00013A D204 C386 C32B 00388 0032D   160 SETUP    MVC   PRORDER,INORDER                   SET UP INPUT DATA
000140 D206 C390 C5A8 00392 005AA   161          MVC   PRWEIGHT,PATRN                    *
000146 DE06 C390 C599 00392 0059B   162          ED    PRWEIGHT,PKWEIGHT                 *
00014C D200 C39C C334 0039E 00336   163          MVC   PRREGION,INREGION                 *
000152 95D5 C590      00592         164 IF3      CLI   INVALFLG,C'N'                     IF INVALID SWITCH OFF
000156 4770 C174      00176         165          BNE   ELSE3                               *
00015A D206 C3A2 C5AF 003A4 005B1   166 THEN3    MVC   PRRATE,PATRN2                       SET UP RATE AND CHARGES
000160 DE06 C3A2 C591 003A4 00593   167          ED    PRRATE,PKRATE                       *
000166 D209 C3AE C5B6 003B0 005B8   168          MVC   PRCHARGE,PATRN3                     *
00016C DE09 C3AE C595 003B0 00597   169          ED    PRCHARGE,PKCHARGE                   *
000172 47F0 C17A      0017C         170          B     ENDIF3                              *
                            00176   171 ELSE3    EQU   *                                 ELSE
000176 D20D C3A2 C654 003A4 00656   172          MVC   PRINVAL,=C'INVALID REGION'  SET UP ERROR MESSAGE
                            0017C   173 ENDIF3   EQU   *                                 ENDIF
00017C 07FA                         174          BR    10                                RETURN
                                    175 *
                                    176 *              PRINT DETAIL LINE MODULE
                                    177 *
                            0017E   178 PRDETAIL EQU   *
00017E F911 C5A6 C662 005A8 00664   179 IFEOP    CP    LINECNT,=P'50'                    IF LINE COUNT => 50
000184 4740 C18A      0018C         180          BL    ENDIFEOP                            *
000188 45B0 C1AC            001AE   181 THENEOP  BAL   11,HEADING                          THEN PRINT HEADING
                            0018C   182 ENDIFEOP EQU   *                                 ENDIF
                                    183          PUT   PRINTER,PRLINE                    PRINT LINE
00019C FA10 C5A6 C664 005A8 00666   189          AP    LINECNT,=P'1'                     ADD 1 TO LINE COUNT
0001A2 9240 C37B      0037D         190 CLEAR    MVI   PRLINE,C' '                       CLEAR PRINT LINE
0001A6 D283 C37C C37B 0037E 0037D   191          MVC   PRLINE+1(132),PRLINE              *
0001AC 07FA                         192          BR    10                                RETURN
                                    194 ***********************************************************************
                                    195 *              THIRD LEVEL HEADING MODULE
                                    196 ***********************************************************************
                                    197 HEADING  PUT   PRINTER,HEAD1                       THEN PRINT HEADINGS
                                    203          PUT   PRINTER,HEAD2                       *
                                    209          PUT   PRINTER,HEAD3                       *
0001DE 92F0 C37B      0037D         215          MVI   PRLINE,C'0'                         SET DOUBLE SPACE
0001E2 F810 C5A6 C665 005A8 00667   216          ZAP   LINECNT,=P'0'                       CLEAR LINE COUNT
0001E8 07FB                         217          BR    11                                RETURN
                                    218 ********************************************************************DOS
                                    219 *              FILE DEFINITIONS AND I/O AREAS                       DOS
                                    220 ********************************************************************DOS
                                    221 INFILE   DTFCD BLKSIZE=80,IOAREA1=INAREA,DEVICE=2540,               DOSX
                                                       DEVADDR=SYSIPT,EOFADDR=THENEOF,WORKA=YES             DOS
                                    242 *                                                                   DOS
                                    243 PRINTER  DTFPR BLKSIZE=133,IOAREA1=PRTAREA,DEVICE=1403,             DOSX
                                                       CTLCHR=ASA,DEVADDR=SYS009,WORKA=YES                  DOS
                                    264 *                                                                   DOS
000258                              265 INAREA   DS    CL80                                                 DOS
0002A8                              266 PRTAREA  DS    CL133                                                DOS
                                    267 ********************************************************************OS
                                    268 *              DEVICE CONTROL BLOCKS AND SAVE AREA                  OS
                                    269 ********************************************************************OS
                                    270 *INFILE  DCB   DDNAME=INFILE,BLKSIZE=80,LRECL=80,                   OSX
                                    271 *              MACRF=GM,DSORG=PS,EODAD=THENEOF                      OS
                                    272 *                                                                   OS
                                    273 *PRINTER DCB   DDNAME=PRINTER,BLKSIZE=133,LRECL=133,                OSX
                                    274 *              MACRF=GMA,DSORG=PS                                   OS
                                    275 *                                                                   OS
                                    276 *SAVE    DS    18F                                                  OS
                                    277 ***********************************************************************
                                    278 *              DATA DEFINITIONS
                                    279 ***********************************************************************
00032D                              280 INRECD   DS    0CL80
00032D                              281 INORDER  DS    CL5
000332                              282 INWEIGHT DS    CL4
000336                              283 INREGION DS    CL1
000337                              284          DS    CL70
                                    285 *
00037D                      0032D   286          ORG   INRECD
00032D                              287 TABRECD  DS    0CL80
00032D                              288 TABMINWT DS    CL4
```

Figure 10–21 *(Continued)*

```
  LOC  OBJECT CODE     ADDR1 ADDR2  STMT   SOURCE STATEMENT                                     DOS/VSE ASSEMBLER 15.15 86-03-27

000331                               289 TABMAXWT DS    CL4
000335                               290 TABRATES DS    CL15
000344                               291          DS    CL57
00037D                   0037D       292          ORG
                                     293 *
00037D                               294 PRLINE   DS    0CL133
00037D                               295          DS    CL11
000388                               296 PRORDER  DS    CL5
00038D                               297          DS    CL5
000392                               298 PRWEIGHT DS    CL7
000399                               299          DS    CL5
00039E                               300 PRREGION DS    CL1
00039F                               301          DS    CL5
0003A4                               302 PRINVAL  DS    0CL14
0003A4                               303 PRRATE   DS    CL7
0003AB                               304          DS    CL5
0003B0                               305 PRCHARGE DS    CL10
0003BA                               306          DS    CL72
                                     307 *
000402                               308 HEAD1    DS    0CL133
000402 F140404040404040              309          DC    CL23'1'
000419 C4C5D3C9E5C5D9E8              310          DC    CL110'DELIVERY CHARGES ON ORDERS'
                                     311 *
000487                               312 HEAD2    DS    0CL133
000487 F040404040404040              313          DC    CL11'0'
000492 D6D9C4C5D9404040              314          DC    CL42'ORDER'
0004BC C4C5D3C9E5C5D9E8              315          DC    CL80'DELIVERY'
                                     316 *
00050C                               317 HEAD3    DS    0CL133
00050C 4040404040404040              318          DC    CL11' '
000517 D5E4D4C2C5D94040              319          DC    CL11'NUMBER'
000522 E6C5C9C7C8E34040              320          DC    CL8'WEIGHT'
00052A D9C5C7C9D6D54040              321          DC    CL12'REGION'
000536 D9C1E3C540404040              322          DC    CL12'RATE'
000542 C3C8C1D9C7C5E240              323          DC    CL79'CHARGES'
                                     324 *
000591                               325 EOFFLAG  DS    CL1
000592                               326 INVALFLG DS    CL1
000593                               327 PKRATE   DS    PL3
000596                               328 PKREGION DS    PL1
000597                               329 PKCHARGE DS    PL4
00059B                               330 PKWEIGHT DS    PL3
0005A0                               331 DOUBLE   DS    D
0005A8                               332 LINECNT  DS    PL2
0005AA 4020206B202120                333 PATRN    DC    XL7'4020206B202120'
0005B1 4020214B202020                334 PATRN2   DC    XL7'4020214B202020'
0005B8 4020206B2020214B              335 PATRN3   DC    XL10'4020206B2020214B2020'
0005C2                               336 TABLE    DS    7CL14
                         00000       337          END   MAINLINE
000628 5B5BC2D6D7C5D540              338                =C'$$BOPEN '
000630 5B5BC2C3D3D6E2C5              339                =C'$$BCLOSE'
000638 000001F0                      340                =A(INFILE)
00063C 0000032D                      341                =A(INRECD)
000640 00000228                      342                =A(PRINTER)
000644 0000037D                      343                =A(PRLINE)
000648 00000402                      344                =A(HEAD1)
00064C 00000487                      345                =A(HEAD2)
000650 0000050C                      346                =A(HEAD3)
000654 051C                          347                =P'51'
000656 C9D5E5C1D3C9C440              348                =C'INVALID REGION'
000664 050C                          349                =P'50'
000666 1C                            350                =P'1'
000667 0C                            351                =P'0'
```

A table consists of entries containing a table key, or table argument, and one or more functions giving characteristics related to the key. Factor matching involves comparing a search argument with the table key until the corresponding key is found or determined not to be in the table.

Direct addressing may be used to locate elements in a positional table. This is a table in which the key has a direct relationship to its position within the table.

Tables may be created by defining constants or by reading in data from an input device. The ORG statement permits the same area to be defined in more than one format.

Single-level tables have functions relating to a specific key in each entry. Multiple-level tables have entries containing one or more additional tables.

DELIVERY CHARGES ON ORDERS

ORDER NUMBER	WEIGHT	REGION	RATE	DELIVERY CHARGES
40327	175	3	.049	8.58
40328	2,850	5	.035	99.75
40329	27	4	.059	1.59
40330	769	2	.040	30.76
40331	100	1	.047	4.70
40332	100	7	INVALID REGION	
40333	1,000	3	.037	37.00
40334	4,500	2	.029	130.50
40335	92	5	.055	5.06

Figure 10–22 Output from Program 10

TERMS FOR REVIEW

Address calculation
Address modification
Array
DSECT
Dummy section
Factor matching
Multiple-level table
ORG
Positional table
Search argument
Sentinel
Single-level table
Table
Table argument
Table entry
Table function
Table key

REVIEW QUESTIONS

1. What is the difference between an array and a table? Give an example of each.
2. What instructions may be used to initialize addresses? What ones to modify addresses?
3. What is meant by explicit operands? When are they used? What is their major disadvantage?
4. What are the differences between modifying a base register and modifying an index register?
5. Explain operation of the BXH and BXLE instructions. Under what conditions does each have an implied operand?
6. What are advantages of using a dummy section over using explicit operands in processing tables? Can you think of any disadvantages?

7. What different technique would you use to search a table if the keys were in sequence from that used if the keys were in random order? Why?
8. Explain how the formula $(n - 1) * l$ will correctly locate the desired item in a positional table.

EXERCISES

1. Write a dummy section to describe each entry in a table of college courses. Each entry contains course number (seven bytes), course description (20 bytes), and semester hour value (two bytes packed, one decimal place). Write a USING statement to relate a base register to the dummy section.
2. Write character constants to define five entries of a table with the following key and functions:

1–4	Salesperson code (key)
5–6	Branch number
7–12	Sales in dollars
13–18	Sales returns in dollars

   How long would the table entry be if each field were in packed decimal? How long if each were a halfword or fullword?
3. Write a loading routine to read in 10 table cards, each containing 22 bytes of data representing one table entry.
4. Each table record contains a five-byte key and six three-byte scores. Write nested loops to load the table, packing each of the six scores into one table entry. Continue until the key is 99999. Count how many entries are loaded.
5. Assume you have a positional table of 43 entries representing ages from 18 through 60. Each entry contains 15 bytes. Write a routine to verify the correct age and calculate the position within the table for any given age. (Hint: Use $(n - 18) * l$ as the formula.)

PROGRAMMING PROBLEMS

1. Using Data Set 5 in Appendix D, write a program to print a Test Average Report. Show each student's number and name, the five test scores, and the average of the five scores on a single line. Use address modification to process the five scores and to set them up in the detail print line. Add the student averages and divide by the number of students to determine the overall test score average and print it out at the end of the report. Do all arithmetic in binary, with all averages rounded to one decimal place.
2. Modify Problem 1 to determine each student's final average. The test average counts 75 percent and the final exam 25 percent of the final average. For each student, print the student number, name, test average, final exam grade, and final average. At the end of the report, print the overall test average, the final exam

average, and the final average for all students. Do all arithmetic in binary, with all averages rounded to one decimal place.

3. Read Data Set 2 in Appendix D into an inventory table, with all quantities and prices in packed decimal form. Compare item numbers and do not put an item in the table if its item number is equal to or less than the preceding number. Put a sentinel with an item number of X'FF's at the end of the table. Then read records from Data Set 6 in Appendix D and create a Sales Report. Search the inventory table for each item number read from Data Set 6.

   If it is found, check whether the quantity sold is greater than the quantity on hand; if so, print the item number, both quantities, and the message 'INSUFFICIENT QUANTITY'. If the quantity sold is less than the quantity on hand, subtract the quantity sold from the quantity on hand and compute the sales amount by multiplying the quantity sold by the unit price in the table. Print the item number, item description, quantity sold, unit price, and amount of sale on a single line.

   If the item number is not in the table, print the item with the message 'INVALID ITEM NUMBER'. Accumulate the total sales amount and print it out at the end of the report.

11

System Macros, Subroutines, and Subprograms

OBJECTIVES

After studying this chapter, you should be able to:

- Describe and use the COMRG, GETIME, and TIME macros
- Explain methods of subroutine linkage
- Define calling sequence and explain methods of supplying addresses of data to subroutines
- Explain differences between subroutines and subprograms
- Give differences between EXTRN and ENTRY statements and give examples of each
- Relate standard uses of registers in processing subprograms
- Explain the use of a save area with subprograms
- Describe and use the CALL, SAVE, and RETURN system macros
- Illustrate multiple-level CALL statements
- Explain how assembler language subprograms can be used with other languages

SYSTEM MACROS

We have already used a number of macros provided by DOS or OS in connection with files. The OPEN, CLOSE, GET, PUT, and CNTRL macros fall in this group. We have also used the EOJ macro in DOS to return control to the supervisor at the end of each program.

Two additional system macros enable us to retrieve the current date and time stored in areas of the supervisor.

COMRG Macro

The *communication region* is an area in the DOS supervisor that contains information about a job currently being executed. Each job has its own communication region. The COMRG macro in DOS, used without a name or operand, causes the address of the communication region to be placed in register 1. This address may be used explicitly to retrieve data from the communication region.

Fields within the communication region are identified in Figure 11–1.

The following statements would allow us to retrieve and print the current date and job name from the communication region. PRDATE and PRJOB must be eight-byte fields.

```
COMRG
MVC     PRDATE,0(1)
MVC     PRJOB,24(1)1
```

The user area between bytes 12 and 22 is the only part of the communication region that can be changed by the user. One program may leave data in the user area to be picked up by another program if it is in the same job. The user area is set to zeros by the JOB statement.

```
COMRG                       First program saves data
ZAP    12(11,1),PKCTLTOT    Save control total
.
COMRG                       Second program retrieves data
ZAP    PKPROOF,12(11,1)     Retrieve control total
```

GETIME Macro

The GETIME macro in DOS retrieves the current time of day in any of three forms. GETIME STANDARD places the time in register 1 as a packed decimal number in the form

OH HM MS S+

where 0 is a leading zero, HH is hours, MM is minutes, SS is seconds, and + is the sign.

00–07	Current date in form MM/DD/YY or DD/MM/YY.
08–11	Reserved.
12–22	User area: set to zero by JOB statement. May be used for communication within or between job steps.
23	UPSI program switches.
24–31	Job name, from job statement.
32–35	Address of uppermost byte of problem program area.
36–39	Address of uppermost byte of current problem program phase.
40–43	Address of uppermost byte of phase with highest ending address.
43–45	Length of problem program label area.

Figure 11–1 Fields in the communication region

Hours are represented as a 24-hour clock, from 00 through 23. The time 7:25:00 p.m. would be represented as 01 92 50 OC.

GETIME BINARY presents the time in R1 as a binary number representing the number of seconds from midnight to the current time. 7:25:00 p.m. would be the binary equivalent of F‘69900’, computed as follows:

Hours:	19 * 3600 seconds	=	68400
Minutes:	25 * 60 seconds	=	1500
Seconds:	0 * 1 second	=	0
Total		=	69900

GETIME TU presents the time in R1 as a binary number having the number of units of 1/300 second since midnight. This would be 300 times the number of seconds, or the equivalent of F‘20970000’ at 7:25:00 p.m. This third option is useful where time must be determined to the nearest 1/100 or 1/10 of a second. We get a starting time, save it, get an ending time, get the difference, and divide by 3 to get the elapsed time to the nearest 1/100 of a second.

Program 11 will show examples of working with time of day in several forms.

TIME Macro

In OS, the TIME macro with no operand returns the date at run time in R1 and the time of day in R0. Both are in packed decimal form. The date is in Julian form (year and day of year) with seven digits and sign. The form is

00 YY DD D+

where 00 is two leading zeros, YY is the two-digit year, DDD is the day of the year between 001 and 366, and + represents the sign.

The time in R0 has eight decimal digits *without* a sign in the form

HH MM SS th

where HH is hours (00–23), MM is minutes (00–59), SS is seconds (00–59), t is one-tenths of a second (0–9), and h is one-hundredths of a second (0–9). To attach a sign to the time of day, the following statements could be used, where FULL is a fullword and PKTIME is a five-byte packed decimal field:

```
ST    0,FULL
MVO   PKTIME,FULL
MVN   PKTIME+4(1),=X'0C'
```

SUBROUTINES

Since our first program, we have used subroutines for heading routines performed from different places in our program and for program modules. Typically, we have used the Branch and Link (BAL) instruction to place a return address in a general register and branch to the subroutine. A separate register has linked each module of a different level, R9 for first level, R10 for second level, and R11 for third level.

The act of branching to the subroutine is often called *invoking* or *calling* the subroutine. A program or module that calls or invokes a subroutine is the *calling* module. The subroutine to which the branch is made is the *called* module. This terminology is convenient when there are several levels of modules.

Linkage

The *linkage* to a subroutine refers to the means of returning to the calling module after execution of the subroutine. It may not always be possible to dedicate a separate register to each module level. We may use the same link register for different levels if each called module saves the contents of the link register and restores the register just before returning to the calling module. Consider the example in Figure 11–2.

By saving the contents of the link register immediately upon entering the subroutine, we can use that register for any purpose so long as we restore it with the correct return address before returning to the calling module.

Calling Sequence

The term *calling sequence* applies to any address or actual data that is supplied to the subroutine when the branch and link is made. For example, if our subroutine is to calculate the area of a circle, the calling module might place the diameter as a fullword in R1, and the subroutine would place the

MAINLINE MODULE	FIRST LEVEL MODULE	SECOND LEVEL MODULE
`MAINLINE BAL 9,SUB1`	`SUB1  ST  9,SAVE1`	`SUB2  ST  9,SAVE2`
`         BAL 9,SUB2`	`      BAL 9,SUB2`	`      .`
`         BAL 9,SUB1`	`      .`	`      L   9,SAVE2`
`         .   .`	`      L   9,SAVE1`	`      BR  9`
`         .   .`	`      BR  9`	`SAVE2 DS  F`
`         .   .`	`SAVE1 DS  F`	

Figure 11–2 Use of one link register for different levels of modules

fullword area in R2. So long as these register conventions are observed, the same subroutine could be placed without change in any program where it is needed. Where the data is in binary form, we can place the *data itself* in a register so that the subroutine can work on it.

Address in Register Often we want subroutines to work on packed decimal or character data rather than binary. For example, our subroutine might have to receive a four-byte packed decimal number and return the area as an eight-byte packed decimal number in a doubleword. In this case R1 would contain the *address* of the packed decimal number, and R2 the address where the area should be placed. The calling sequence would thus be:

```
LA     1,PKDIAMTR
LA     2,PKAREA
BAL    9,AREACIRC
```

The subroutine could then be self-contained, with any work areas or constants needed to compute the area. For an example, let us assume each number has one decimal place. We will recall that the formula is

$$A = PI * R * R$$

where PI is 3.1416 and R (radius) is one-half the diameter. Figure 11–3 shows a possible subroutine.

Note that the work area (WORKS) must be 10 bytes long, instead of the usual doubleword for multiplication and division. The repeated multiplication produces a maximum of 19 digits as shown in Figure 11–3. The final 14-digit result will fit into an eight-byte field.

Parameter List Rather than have the calling module put specific addresses into registers, we may prefer to construct a list of addresses, called a *parameter list*. We then put into R1 the *address of the list* rather than the address of specific data elements. The calling module looks like this:

```
          LA     1,PARAMLST
          BAL    9,AREACIRC
          .
PARAMLST  DC     A(PKDIAMTR,PKAREA)
```

For this approach, the AREACIRC subroutine in Figure 11–3 must add one instruction that refers to R1 to load the addresses into two registers. We may use R1 and R2 as before:

```
AREACIRC LM    1,2,0(1)        Load addresses into R1 and R2
                               Use remaining instructions as before
```

Another option is to put the parameter list immediately after the BAL instruction. The link register can now be used as a pointer to the parameter list, so long as the parameter list starts on the exact byte where the following instruction would normally be.

```
AREACIRC ZAP   WORKX,0(4,1)        ZAP diameter to work area
         DP    WORKX,=P'2'         Divide by 2 to make radius
         ZAP   WORKX,WORKX(9)      Remove the remainder
         MP    WORKX,WORKX         Square the radius
         MP    WORKX,=P'31416'     Multiply by pi
         AP    WORKX,=P'50000'     Round to nearest tenth
         MVO   WORKX,WORKX(7)      Drop excess 5 digits
         ZAP   0(8,2),WORKX        Send area to calling module
         BR    9                   Return
WORKX    DS    PL10
```

CALCULATION OF SCALING

Original diameter	999999.9	
Radius	999999.9	
Radius squared	999999999999.99	
R**2 * PI	9999999999999.999999	(19 digits)
After MVO	9999999999999.9	(14 digits)

Figure 11–3 Subroutine for area of a circle

The problem is that BAL, being a machine instruction four bytes in length, can start on any even-numbered address. If BAL happens to start two bytes past a fullword boundary, the address placed into R9 will be two bytes past a fullword boundary. But the assembler will move the location counter to the next fullword boundary to place the address constants. The address in R9 could be two bytes less than the address of the parameter list.

The *CNOP (conditional No-op)* is an assembler directive that produces one, two, or three NOP (no-operation) instructions as necessary to move the location counter to the desired boundary. The object code for each NOP is X'0700', a two-byte legal instruction that branches only to the next instruction.

There are six valid operands for CNOP instructions. Their effects are shown in Figure 11–4.

Our calling sequence could now be:

```
CNOP    0,4                   Align on fullword boundary
BAL     9,AREACIRC            Address in R9 now is that of parameter
                                list
DC      A(PKDIAMTR,PKAREA)
(Return here from subroutine)
```

We *cannot* now use BR 9 in the subroutine to return to the calling module. To do so would branch to the first address constant following the BAL in the calling module. We must skip eight bytes to return to the first instruction after the parameter list. We change the first and last instructions to:

OPERAND	EFFECT
0,4	Align on fullword boundary
2,4	Align 2 bytes past fullword boundary
0,8	Align on doubleword boundary
2,8	Align 2 bytes past doubleword boundary
4,8	Align 4 bytes past doubleword boundary
6,8	Align 6 bytes past doubleword boundary

Figure 11–4 Effect of CNOP operands

```
AREACIRC    LM  1,2,0(9)        Load addresses into R1 and R2
   .
   B        8(9)                Return 8 bytes past address in R9
```

Programming Tips

- To print the current date for headings, use the DOS COMRG macro followed by MVC PRDATE,0(1), where PRDATE is the eight-byte field to show the date in form MM/DD/YY.
- The DOS GETIME macro provides the time of day in R1 in any of three forms. TU or BINARY permits calculation of elapsed time. STANDARD permits time to be edited and printed in form HH:MM:SS.
- Store the address in a link register into a fullword immediately upon entering a subroutine. The register can then be used for any other purpose. Load the address back into the register before the return to the calling module.
- Use a CNOP assembler instruction to ensure that the location is on a specific halfword, fullword, or doubleword boundary.

SUBPROGRAMS

A subprogram differs from a subroutine in that it is assembled in a different control (CSECT) from the calling program. The subprogram therefore cannot refer by name to any of the files, records, or fields defined in the calling program. The only means of passing data between the calling program and the subprogram is through addresses in registers.

The subprogram is normally assembled, and the object module is stored in the system library. When it is to be called, the linkage editor must attach the subprogram to the object code of the calling program.

EXTRN and ENTRY Statements

An EXTRN (for External Symbol) is an assembler declarative that identifies a name used in this program (CSECT) that is defined in another CSECT. The assembler cannot assign an address to the name defined as an EXTRN. It therefore places the name of the EXTRN in the External Symbol Dictionary to notify the linkage editor to supply the address at link edit time.

A type V constant is an address constant that is automatically designated as an EXTRN. The assembler places an address of X'00000000' in each type V constant. At link edit time the linkage editor replaces the zeros with the correct address.

An ENTRY is an assembler declarative that identifies a name defined in this program (CSECT) that may be used as an EXTRN in another CSECT. The name used on any START or CSECT statement is automatically defined as an ENTRY. Each ENTRY is shown on the External Symbol Dictionary and on the linkage editor map. Correct use of EXTRNs and ENTRYs is essential to communication between calling programs and subprograms. Figure 11–5 shows some examples.

Register Conventions

Five of the 16 general registers are consistently used for special purposes in connection with input/output macros and with linkage to and from subprograms. Figure 11–6 shows these conventions.

```
         CALLING PROGRAM            REMARKS

MAINLINE START 0                    MAINLINE is automatically an ENTRY
         EXTRN SUBDATA              SUBDATA is defined as an EXTRN
         ENTRY RESULT               RESULT is defined as an ENTRY
         L     15,=V(SUBP1)         SUBP1 is automatically an EXTRN
         .
         L     1,ADDRDATA           ADDRDATA holds external address
         .
ADDRDATA DC    A(SUBDATA)           Object code for ADDRDATA is X'00000000'
RESULT   DS    PL5


         SUBPROGRAM

SUBP1    CSECT                      SUBP1 is automatically an ENTRY
         ENTRY SUBDATA              SUBDATA is defined as an ENTRY
         EXTRN RESULT               RESULT is defined as an EXTRN
         L     2,ADCON              ADCON holds external address
SUBDATA  DS    CL80
ADCON    DC    A(RESULT)            Object code for ADCON is X'00000000'
```

Figure 11–5 Examples of EXTRN and ENTRY statements

R15	Contains the address of the subprogram.
R14	Contains the address of the return point in the calling program.
R13	Contains the address of a 72-byte save area to hold the contents of the general registers.
R1	Contains the address of the parameter list.
R0	May contain another address required by the subprogram.

Figure 11–6 Subprogram register conventions

```
LA      13,SAVE        Load address of save area into R13
L       15,=V(SUBP)    Load address of subprogram into R15
LA      1,PARAMLST     Load address of parameter list into R1
BALR    14,15          Set return address in R14; branch to SUBP
EQU     *              This is return point
```

Figure 11–7 Calling sequence loading registers individually

It is the responsibility of the calling program to define a 72-byte save area and to put the address of the save area into R13. It is not the calling program, but the *subprogram*, that saves the registers even though the save area is in the calling program area. The remaining registers may be loaded individually as in Figure 11–7.

The most common means of linking to a subprogram is through the CALL macro, which properly places the correct addresses into R15, R14, and R1 and also constructs the parameter list.

The CALL Macro

CALL is a system macro in the form

```
NAME CALL SUBP,(PARAM1,PARAM2,PARAM3)
```

where NAME is optional, SUBP is the name of the subprogram to which to branch, and the items enclosed in the parentheses are names of fields whose addresses are to be placed in the parameter list. Statements generated by the CALL macro are shown in Figure 11–8. Each statement is explained as follows:

1. CNOP creates a two-byte NOP if necessary to set the location counter two bytes past a fullword boundary. This will ensure that the BALR instruction nestles against the first address in the parameter list.
2. L 15,=V(SUBP) loads the external address of the subprogram into R15.

```
1.   CNOP   2,4
2.   L      15,=V(SUBP)
3.   LA     14,*+6+4*3
4.   BALR   1,15
5.   DC     A(PARAM1,PARAM2,PARAM3)
6.   ORG    *-4
7.   DC     X'80'
8.   ORG
```

Figure 11–8 Statements generated by the CALL macro

3. LA 14,* +6+4*3 loads the return address into R14. The first asterisk (*) refers to the current location where LA begins. The LA is four bytes long, and the BALR is two bytes long. Then we must skip over the three four-byte address constants in the parameter list. The general calculation is $* + 6 + 4 * n$, where n is the number of addresses in the parameter list.
4. BALR 1,15 puts the address of the next instruction (the parameter list) into R1 and then branches to the address in R15 (the subprogram).
5. The DC creates address constants for all names appearing in parentheses in the CALL macro. Each constant is four bytes long.

6–8. The first ORG sets the location counter back three bytes to the first byte of the last address constant in the parameter list. The DC defines an X'80' in the leftmost byte of the last address in the list. The ORG without an operand sets the location counter back to the address immediately following the last address in the list.

The purpose of the last three instructions is to place a 1 in the leftmost (sign) bit of the last address in the list. This 1 bit can distinguish the last item from other items in the list. The 1 sign bit makes this address a negative binary number, while the other addresses are all positive. Only the rightmost 24 bits of the constant are used for the actual address. This technique is useful when our subroutine must be able to handle a variable number of parameters. We will see an example of this usage later in the chapter.

The SAVE and RETURN MACROS

It is a standard convention that the contents of all general registers be saved in an area in the *calling* program. The SAVE macro permits the subprogram to store the registers in the address specified by R13. The calling program is responsible for placing the save area address in R13.

The save area is 72 bytes long, usually defined as nine doublewords or 18 fullwords. The displacement from the start of the save area is four bytes for each fullword. The fullwords are used as follows:

WORD	DISPLACEMENT	CONTENTS
1	0	Used only by PL/I
2	4	Address of previous save area
3	8	Address of next save area
4–18	12–68	Registers 14 through 12

The previous save area refers to the save area in the program that calls this subprogram. The next save area is the save area (if any) in the called subprogram. Thus, if one subprogram calls another, which in turn calls still another, words 2 and 3 provide a path to return eventually to the original calling program.

The usual form of the SAVE macro is

```
SAVE (14,12)
```

which generates the equivalent of STM 14,12,12(13). This instruction places R14 in word 4 of the save area, R15 in word 5, and so on until R12 is in word 18. The SAVE macro is constructed so that it automatically adjusts the displacement and the register numbers to be stored. For example, SAVE (5,9) would generate STM 5,9,40(13) to place R5 through R9 in their assigned positions in words 11 through 15 of the save area.

When the subprogram is entered, R13 contains the address of the previous save area in the calling program. The instruction ST 13,SAVESUB+4 places this address in word 2 in the subprogram save area. To place the address of SAVESUB in word 3 of the calling program save area, we may write:

```
LA    2,SAVESUB
ST    2,8(13)
L     2,28(13)
```

The first two instructions destroy the contents of R2. The third one then restores the original contents of R2 from word 8 of the previous save area for possible use by the subprogram.

The RETURN macro first restores the general registers with the contents they had upon entering the subprogram, and then returns to the calling program. Before RETURN is issued, R13 must be reloaded with the address of the preceding save area, which was stored in word 3 of the subprogram save area. These instructions are typical:

```
L      13,SAVESUB+4
RETURN (14,12)
```

The RETURN macro in this instance generates these two instructions:

```
LM   14,12,12(13)
BR   14
```

The Load Multiple is the exact counterpart of the Store Multiple generated by the SAVE macro. The same two registers should be used in both the SAVE and the RETURN. R14 is always assumed to have the return address to the calling program.

Base Registers for Subprograms

There are two ways to use base registers for subprograms. The first is merely to use R15 as the base. Recall that the calling program loaded R15 with the address of the subprogram, so that we need only to designate R15 as the base as follows:

```
SUBPROG    CSECT
           USING *,15
           SAVE (14,12)
```

If R15 is to be the base register, the USING statement must precede any other instructions so that the asterisk in the USING statement refers to the first byte of SUBPROG.

The second method is to load the base register as usual *after* issuing the SAVE macro. This ensures that any contents of the register designated as the base will still be available in the save area if needed by the subprogram. The SAVE macro uses R13 as its base and does not depend on any base address within the subprogram.

```
SUBPROG    CSECT
           SAVE (14,12)           Save registers
           BALR 12,0              Load R12 as base
           USING *,12             Designate base register
```

If we later need the original contents of R12 in the subprogram, we could recover them from word 18 of the save area by using L 5,68(13).

Subprogram Examples

Now that we have covered the essential features of subprograms, let us show a couple of examples. In the first, the subprogram will look up a two-character state abbreviation and return the full name of the state. The calling program will provide the address of the state abbreviation and the address of a 14-byte field where the full name is to be placed. If the abbreviation is not valid, the name field will be filled with Xs.

The calling program will contain:

```
LA      13,SAVE
CALL    SUBPROG,(INABBREV,PRSTATE)
```

```
SUBPROG  CSECT
         USING   *,15                  Designate R15 as base
         SAVE    (14,12)               Save registers
         LM      2,3,0(1)              Get addresses of abbreviation and name
         LA      7,TABLE               Get address of first entry
DOWHILE  CLC     0(2,7),0(2)           DOWHILE table abbreviation < abbreviation
         BNL     ENDDO                   *
         LA      7,16(7)                 Set address to next entry
         B       DOWHILE                 *
ENDDO    EQU     *                     ENDDO
IF       CLC     0(2,7),0(2)           IF table abbreviation = abbreviation
         BNE     ELSE                    *
THEN     MVC     0(14,3),2(7)            Move name to print area
         B       ENDIF                   *
ELSE     EQU     *                     ELSE
         MVC     0(14,3),=14C'X'         Move Xs to print area
ENDIF    EQU     *                     ENDIF
         RETURN  (14,12)               RETURN
TABLE    DS      0CL832
         DC      'AKALASKA         '
         DC      'ALALABAMA        '
         .
         DC      14C'Z'
         END
```

Figure 11–9 Subprogram to look up state name in table

The complete subprogram is shown in Figure 11–9.

In this example, this subprogram does not call another, so we use R15 as the base register and leave R13 unchanged. There are 52 table entries to accommodate the 50 states, the District of Columbia, and the end sentinel. Each table entry is 16 bytes long, allowing two bytes to hold the abbreviation and 14 bytes to accommodate the longest state names. (The District of Columbia's name is given as D.C. to keep the table within this size.) The table is arranged in alphabetic order by state abbreviation. We leave the search upon finding a key higher than or equal to the search argument. We then check to see if the keys were equal. If so, we move the state name from the table back to the calling program. If not equal, we move 14 Xs to the state name.

In our second complete subprogram we add all fullwords named in the parameter list (except the last) and store the sum in the fullword named last in the list. Thus we must add a variable number of words. Each fullword named can be anywhere in the calling program. They need not be in sequence. The X'80' in the leftmost byte of the last address in the list will be tested to determine when to stop adding the fullwords.

The main program calling sequence is:

```
LA      13,SAVE
CALL    SUBPROG,(FULL7,BINARY,FULL2,ZZFULL,SUM)
```

The complete subprogram is shown in Figure 11–10. Each time an address from the parameter list is placed into R2, we test whether it is positive. If so, we add the number at that address to our sum. If the address is negative,

```
SUBPROG  CSECT
         SAVE    (14,12)      Save registers
         BALR    12,0         Load base register
         USING   *,12         Designate base register
         L       2,0(1)       Load R2 with first parameter address
         SR      6,6          Clear R6 as total
DOWHILE  LTR     2,2          DOWHILE R2 is positive
         BM      ENDDO          *
         A       6,0(2)         Add Parameter to total
         LA      1,4(1)         Set R1 to next parameter address
         L       2,0(1)         Load R2 with next parameter address
         B       DOWHILE        *
ENDDO    EQU     *            ENDDO
         ST      6,0(2)       Store total at last parameter address
         RETURN  (14,12)      RETURN
         END                  End of subprogram
```

Figure 11–10 Subprogram to add a variable number of fullwords

R2 contains a 1 bit in its leftmost position (X'80' in the leftmost byte), indicating the last address. We terminate the loop and store the total at this address in the calling program.

Multiple-Level Calls

If the main program calls Subprogram 1, which in turns calls Subprogram 2, which then might call Subprogram 3, the register conventions we have discussed ensure an orderly return back through the subprograms to the main program. In each subprogram, we must define its own save area of 18 fullwords and follow these steps:

1. Use the SAVE macro to save in the calling program all registers that will be used in the subprogram.
2. Establish the subprogram base register.
3. Store the address of the previous save area in word 2 of the subprogram save area.
4. Store the address of the subprogram save area in word 3 of the previous save area.
5. Load R13 with the address of the subprogram save area.
6. Issue the CALL macro to the next level subprogram.
7. Upon return from the next subprogram, load R13 with the address of the previous save area from word 2 of the subprogram save area.
8. Issue the RETURN macro.

Using Files in Subprograms

Files may be defined and used in subprograms just as in mainline programs. A special problem occurs when we may wish to leave a file in the subprogram open so that it can be processed each time the subprogram is called. We cannot open a file that is already open; further, when a sequential file is closed and then reopened, processing resumes at the start of the file instead of with the last record processed.

Assume that WORKFLE is defined in the subprogram with a DTF. Figure 11–11 shows one way of coping with the problem.

The first time SUBPROG is called OPENSW is set to 'N', and the file is opened. Each subsequent call will find OPENSW = 'Y', and the OPEN statement will be bypassed.

To refer to a file in the calling program, the subprogram must receive the address of the DTF and (usually) its work area. Figure 11–12 has the subprogram receive the address of the printer DTF and its work area and send a 20-byte error message to bytes 101–120 of the print line.

```
SUBPROG  CSECT
         SAVE   (14,12)         Save registers
         BALR   12,0            Load base register
         USING  *,12            Designate base register
IF       CLI    OPENSW,C'Y'     IF file is not open
         BE     ENDIF             *
THEN     OPEN   WORKFLE           THEN open it
         MVI    OPENSW,C'Y'       Set open switch on
ENDIF    EQU    *               ENDIF
         .
OPENSW   DC     CL1'N'
WORKFLE  DTFSD  (Disk file operands)
```

Figure 11–11 Subprogram to open work file on disk

CALLING PROGRAM:

```
CALL   SUBP,(PRINTER,PRLINE)
```

SUBPROGRAM:

```
LM     2,3,0(1)                 Load file and work area addresses
MVC    100(20,3),ERRMSG         Move error message to print line
PUT    (2),(3)                  Print line
```

Figure 11–12 Subprogram using file defined in calling program

This illustrates register notation for I/O operations. R2 has the address of the PRINTER DTFPR and R3 has the address of PRLINE when the MVC and PUT instructions are executed.

Assembler Subprograms with Other Languages

The major high-level programming languages use the same register conventions when calling subprograms that assembler language does. The CALL statement in COBOL is in the form

```
CALL SUBPROG, USING PARAM-1, PARAM-2, PARAM-3
```

where SUBPROG is the name of the subprogram and the three parameters refer to items described in a LINKAGE SECTION of the PROCEDURE DIVISION. The parameters are usually records, or group items, so that passing a single address makes it possible to refer to all the fields within that record.

The CALL in FORTRAN is in exactly the same form as used in assembler language, with the first operand being the name of the subprogram and with the parameters enclosed in parentheses.

The subprogram must know the form and length of each parameter whose address is furnished by a calling program, whether in assembler language or any other. Then it can refer to that record or field to obtain data from or send results back to the calling program.

Programming Tips

- Write the SAVE macro as the first executable instruction upon entering a subprogram. Write the RETURN macro as the last executable instruction to return to the calling module.
- Define the 18-fullword save area in the calling program, and load its address into R13 before calling the subprogram.
- Store R13 into the second word of a save area in the subprogram. Store the address of the subprogram save area into the third word of the save area in the calling program.

PROGRAM 11: TIMING OPERATIONS

Program 11 has a main program that calculates elapsed time for loops to perform four different operations. It calls a subprogram to obtain time of day in two different forms. The first is a fullword containing time in units of

1/300 second. The second is a 20-byte area showing time in the form TIME = 11:37:25 A.M. (or P.M.).

The events timed are these:

1. Call TIMESUB 1,500 times.
2. Subtract 1,000,000 times from a counter using BCT instruction.
3. Add the decimal numbers from 1 to 1,000,000 to a total field.
4. Multiply each of the decimal numbers from 1 to 1,000,000 by 99.

Figure 11–13 shows the calling program. To remain consistent with our earlier program structure, we use a mainline module and first, second, and third level modules. Nothing is done after reaching end of file, so that no final processing module is necessary.

Each of the four timed operations is identical except for three items:

1. the number of iterations
2. the address of the module that performs the loop
3. the constant that identifies the loop being performed.

```
  LOC  OBJECT CODE    ADDR1 ADDR2  STMT   SOURCE STATEMENT                                        DOS/VSE ASSEMBLER 11.11 86-03-28

                                      1 ***********************************************************************
                                      2 *                  ALTON R. KINDRED, PROGRAM 11
                                      3 * THIS PROGRAM CALLS A SUBPROGRAM THAT RETURNS THE TIME OF DAY IN
                                      4 * UNITS OF 1/300 SECOND AND ALSO IN FORM TIME = HH:MM:SS A.M.
                                      5 * (OR P.M.).  THE PROGRAM TIMES FOUR DIFFERENT OPERATIONS AND PRINTS
                                      6 * THE STARTING, ENDING, AND ELAPSED TIMES FOR EACH.
                                      7 *          REGISTERS USED:
                                      8 *                  R1 - WORK REGISTER
                                      9 *                  R2 - COUNTER FOR ITERATIONS
                                     10 *                  R3 - ADDRESS OF TIMING ROUTINES
                                     11 *                  R5 - COUNTER FOR OPERATIONS
                                     12 *                  R6 - POINTER TO ROUTINE ADDRESSES
                                     13 *                  R7 - POINTER TO MESSAGES
                                     14 *                  R9-R11 - LINK REGISTERS
                                     15 *                  R12 - BASE REGISTER
                                     16 *                  R13 - ADDRESS OF SAVE AREA
                                     17 *                  R14-R15 - SUBPROGRAM LINKAGE
                                     18 ***********************************************************************
                                     19          PRINT NOGEN
000000                               20 MAINLINE START 0                          SET LOCATION COUNTER
                                     21 *        STM   14,12,12(13)               SAVE REGISTERS FOR OS          OS
000000 05C0                          22          BALR  12,0                       LOAD BASE REGISTER
                           00002     23          USING *,12                       DESIGNATE BASE REGISTER
                                     24 *        ST    13,SAVE+4                  STORE REGISTER 13              OS
                                     25 *        LA    13,SAVE                    LOAD SAVE AREA ADDRESS         OS
                                     26 *        OPEN  (PRINTER,(OUTPUT))         OPEN FILE                      OS
                                     27          OPEN  PRINTER                    OPEN FILE                      DOS
000012 4590 C02A           0002C     35          BAL   9,INITIAL                  DO INITIAL PROCESSING
000016 4590 C042           00044     36          BAL   9,MAINLOOP                 DO MAIN PROCESSING LOOP
                                     37          CLOSE PRINTER                    CLOSE FILES                    DOS
                                     45          EOJ                              END PROGRAM                    DOS
                                     48 *        CLOSE (PRINTER)                  CLOSE FILES                    OS
                                     49 *        L     13,SAVE+4                  LOAD SAVE AREA ADDRESS         OS
                                     50 *        LM    14,12,12(13)               RESTORE REGISTERS              OS
                                     51 *        BR    14                         RETURN TO OS                   OS
                                     52 ***********************************************************************
                                     53 *                  FIRST LEVEL MODULES
                                     54 ***********************************************************************
                                     55 *
                                     56 *                  SET INITIAL VALUES MODULE
                                     57 *
00002C F811 C456 C516 00458 00518    58 INITIAL  ZAP   LINECNT,=P'51'             SET LINE COUNT > 50
000032 4150 0004           00004     59          LA    5,4                        SET LOOP COUNTER TO 4
000036 4160 C3CE           003D0     60          LA    6,TIMES                    SET START OF TIMING LIST
00003A 4170 C45F           00461     61          LA    7,CONST1                   SET ADDRESS OF MESSAGE
00003E 45A0 C120           00122     62          BAL   10,CLEAR                   CLEAR PRINT LINE
000042 07F9                          63          BR    9                          RETURN
                                     64 *
                                     65 *                  MAIN PROCESSING LOOP
                                     66 *
                           00044     67 MAINLOOP EQU   *
                           00044     68 REPEAT   EQU   *                          REPEAT
000044 45A0 C066           00068     69          BAL   10,STARTIME                  GET STARTING TIME
000048 5826 0000           00000     70          L     2,0(6)                       SET ITERATIONS
00004C 5836 0010           00010     71          L     3,16(6)                      SET ADDRESS OF ROUTINE
```

Figure 11–13 Program 11 calling program for timing operations

```
  LOC  OBJECT CODE    ADDR1 ADDR2  STMT   SOURCE STATEMENT                                     DOS/VSE ASSEMBLER 11.11 86-03-28

000050 05A3                          72          BALR  10,3                         BAL TO ROUTINE
000052 45A0 C0CC              000CE  73          BAL   10,ENDTIME                   GET ENDING TIME
000056 45A0 C0FC              000FE  74          BAL   10,PRDETAIL                  PRINT LINE
00005A 4166 0004              00004  75          LA    6,4(6)                       ADD 4 TO ADDR. OF TIMING LIST
00005E 4177 0023              00023  76          LA    7,35(7)                      ADD 35 TO ADDR. OF MESG. LIST
000062 4650 C042              00044  77          BCT   5,REPEAT                     SUBTRACT 1 FROM CONTROL LOOP
                              00066  78 UNTIL    EQU   *                          UNTIL CONTROL LOOP = 0
000066 07F9                          79          BR    9                          RETURN
                                     80 ***********************************************************************
                                     81 *                SECOND LEVEL MODULES
                                     82 ***********************************************************************
                                     83 *
                                     84 *                GET STARTING TIME MODULE
                                     85 *
000068 45B0 C12C              0012E  86 STARTIME BAL   11,CALLIT                  CALL TIME SUBR.
00006C 5810 C3CA              003CC  87          L     1,TIME300                  SAVE START TIME UNITS
000070 5010 C3C6              003C8  88          ST    1,STTIME                   *
000074 D213 C254 C436 00256 00438    89          MVC   PRSTART,TIMEDIT            SET UP START TIME (PRINT)
00007A D222 C22C 7000 0022E 00000    90          MVC   PRMESG,0(7)                SET UP NAME OF OPERATION
000080 07FA                          91          BR    10                         RETURN
                                     92 *
                                     93 *                CALL 1500 TIMES MODULE
                                     94 *
                              00082  95 CALLSUB  EQU   *
000082 45B0 C12C              0012E  96 REPEAT2  BAL   11,CALLIT                  CALL TIME SUBR.
000086 4620 C080              00082  97          BCT   2,REPEAT2                  SUBTRACT 1 FROM ITERATIONS
                              0008A  98 UNTIL2   EQU   *                          UNTIL ITERATIONS = 0
00008A 07FA                          99          BR    10                         RETURN
                                    100 *
                                    101 *                COUNT 1 MILLION IN BINARY MODULE
                                    102 *
                              0008C 103 CNTBIN   EQU   *
                              0008C 104 REPEAT3  EQU   *                          REPEAT
00008C 4620 C08A              0008C 105          BCT   2,REPEAT3                  SUBTRACT 1 FROM ITERATIONS
                              00090 106 UNTIL3   EQU   *                          UNTIL ITERATIONS = 0
000090 07FA                         107          BR    10                         RETURN
                                    108 *
                                    109 *                ADD 1 MILLION DECIMAL NUMBERS MODULE
                                    110 *
                              00092 111 ADDDEC   EQU   *
000092 F870 C44A C51C 0044C 0051E   112          ZAP   PKTOTAL,=P'0'              CLEAR TOTAL
000098 F830 C452 C51D 00454 0051F   113          ZAP   PKNUMBER,=P'1'             SET NUMBER AT 1
                              0009E 114 REPEAT4  EQU   *                          REPEAT
00009E FA73 C44A C452 0044C 00454   115          AP    PKTOTAL,PKNUMBER             ADD NUMBER TO TOTAL
0000A4 FA30 C452 C51D 00454 0051F   116          AP    PKNUMBER,=P'1'               ADD 1 TO NUMBER
0000AA 4620 C09C              0009E 117          BCT   2,REPEAT4                    SUBTRACT 1 FROM ITERATIONS
                              000AE 118 UNTIL4   EQU   *                          UNTIL ITERATIONS = 0
0000AE 07FA                         119          BR    10                         RETURN
                                    120 *
                                    121 *                MULTIPLY 1 MILLION NUMBERS BY 99
                                    122 *
                              000B0 123 MULTDEC  EQU   *
0000B0 F830 C452 C51D 00454 0051F   124          ZAP   PKNUMBER,=P'1'             SET NUMBER TO 1
                              000B6 125 REPEAT5  EQU   *                          REPEAT
0000B6 F873 C3BE C452 003C0 00454   126          ZAP   DOUBLE,PKNUMBER              MULTIPLY NUMBER
0000BC FC71 C3BE C518 003C0 0051A   127          MP    DOUBLE,=P'99'                BY 99
0000C2 FA30 C452 C51D 00454 0051F   128          AP    PKNUMBER,=P'1'               ADD 1 TO NUMBER
0000C8 4620 C0B4              000B6 129          BCT   2,REPEAT5                    SUBTRACT 1 FROM ITERATIONS
                              000CC 130 UNTIL5   EQU   *                          UNTIL ITERATIONS = 0
0000CC 07FA                         131          BR    10                         RETURN
                                    132 *
                                    133 *                GET ENDING TIME MODULE
                                    134 *
                              000CE 135 ENDTIME  EQU   *
0000CE 45B0 C12C              0012E 136          BAL   11,CALLIT                  GET TIME
0000D2 5810 C3CA              003CC 137          L     1,TIME300                  CALCULATE ELAPSED TIME IN UNITS
0000D6 5B10 C3C6              003C8 138          S     1,STTIME                   *
0000DA 1B00                         139          SR    0,0                        *
0000DC 5D00 C4FF              00500 140          D     0,=F'3'                    CHANGE TIME TO 1/100 SECOND
0000E0 4E10 C3BE              003C0 141          CVD   1,DOUBLE                   CONVERT TO DECIMAL
0000E4 D213 C26D C436 0026F 00438   142          MVC   PREND,TIMEDIT              SET UP ENDING TIME
0000EA D206 C286 C458 00288 0045A   143          MVC   PRELAPSE,PATRN             SET UP ELAPSED TIME
0000F0 DE06 C286 C3C3 00288 003C5   144          ED    PRELAPSE,DOUBLE+5          *
0000F6 D206 C28E C51E 00290 00520   145          MVC   PRSECOND,=C'SECONDS'       *
0000FC 07FA                         146          BR    10                         RETURN
                                    147 *
                                    148 *                PRINT DETAIL LINE MODULE
                                    149 *
                              000FE 150 PRDETAIL EQU   *
0000FE F911 C456 C51A 00458 0051C   151 IFEOP    CP    LINECNT,=P'50'             IF LINE COUNT => 50
000104 4740 C10A        0010C       152          BL    ENDIFEOP                     *
000108 45B0 C144              00146 153 THENEOP  BAL   11,HEADING                   THEN PRINT HEADING
                              0010C 154 ENDIFEOP EQU   *                          ENDIF
                                    155          PUT   PRINTER,PRLINE             PRINT LINE
00011C FA10 C456 C51D 00458 0051F   161          AP    LINECNT,=P'1'              ADD 1 TO LINE COUNT
000122 9240 C22B        0022D       162 CLEAR    MVI   PRLINE,C' '                CLEAR PRINT LINE
000126 D283 C22C C22B 0022E 0022D   163          MVC   PRLINE+1(132),PRLINE       *
00012C 07FA                         164          BR    10                         RETURN
                                    165 ***********************************************************************
                                    166 *                THIRD LEVEL MODULES
                                    167 ***********************************************************************
                                    168 *
                                    169 *                CALL TIME SUBPROGRAM MODULE
                                    170 *
                                    171          PRINT GEN
00012E 41D0 C3EE              003F0 172 CALLIT   LA    13,SAVE                    GET ADDR. OF SAVE AREA
                                    173          CALL  TIMESUB,(TIME300,TIMEDIT)  CALL SUBPROGRAM
                                    174+* SUPVR COMMN MACROS - CALL - 5745-SC-SUP - REL. 28.0                       12000028
000132                              175+        CNOP  2,4                                                          40000025
000132 58F0 C50A              0050C 176+        L     15,=V(TIMESUB)                                               42000025
000136 41E0 C142              00144 177+        LA    14,*+6+4*2                                                   44000025
00013A 051F                         178+        BALR  1,15                                                         46000025
00013C 000003CC00000438             179+        DC    A(TIME300,TIMEDIT)                                           58000025
```

Figure 11–13 *(Continued)*

```
  LOC  OBJECT CODE    ADDR1 ADDR2 STMT   SOURCE STATEMENT                                          DOS/VSE ASSEMBLER 11.11 86-03-28

000144                      00140  180+          ORG   *-4                                                    3-7 60000025
000140 80                          181+          DC    X'80'                                                  3-7 62000025
000141                      00144  182+          ORG   *+3                                                    3-9 64000025
                                   183           PRINT NOGEN
000144 07FB                        184           BR    11                          RETURN
                                   186 *
                                   187 *               PRINT HEADING MODULE
                                   188 *
                                   189 HEADING  PUT   PRINTEP,HEAD1               PRINT HEADINGS
                                   195          PUT   PRINTER,HEAD2               *
000166 92F0 C22B       0022D       201          MVI   PRLINE,C'0'                 SET DOUBLE SPACE
00016A F810 C456 C51C 00458 0051E  202          ZAP   LINECNT,=P'0'               CLEAR LINE COUNT
000170 07FB                        203          BR    11                          RETURN
                                   204 ******************************************************************DOS
                                   205 *               FILE DEFINITION AND I/O AREA                      DOS
                                   206 ******************************************************************DOS
                                   207 PRINTER  DTFPR BLKSIZE=133,IOAREA1=PRTAREA,DEVICE=1403,           DOSX
                                                      CTLCHR=ASA,DEVADDR=SYS009,WORKA=YES                DOS
                                   228 *                                                                 DOS
0001A8                             229 PRTAREA  DS    CL133                                              DOS
                                   230 ******************************************************************OS
                                   231 *               DEVICE CONTROL BLOCKS AND SAVE AREA               OS
                                   232 ******************************************************************OS
                                   233 *PRINTER DCB   DDNAME=PRINTER,BLKSIZE=133,LRECL=133,              OSX
                                   234 *              MACRF=PMA,DSORG=PS                                 OS
                                   235 *                                                                 OS
                                   236 *SAVE    DS    18F                                                OS
                                   237 ***********************************************************************
                                   238 *               DATA DEFINITIONS
                                   239 ***********************************************************************
00022D                             240 PRLINE   DS    0CL133
00022D                             241          DS    CL1
00022E                             242 PRMESG   DS    CL35
000251                             243          DS    CL5
000256                             244 PRSTART  DS    CL20
00026A                             245          DS    CL5
00026F                             246 PREND    DS    CL20
000283                             247          DS    CL5
000288                             248 PRELAPSE DS    CL7
00028F                             249          DS    CL1
000290                             250 PRSECOND DS    CL7
000297                             251          DS    CL27
                                   252 *
0002B2                             253 HEAD1    DS    0CL133
0002B2 F140404040404040            254          DC    CL44'1'
0002DE E3C9D4C9D5C740D6            255          DC    CL89'TIMING OPERATIONS'
                                   256 *
000337                             257 HEAD2    DS    0CL133
000337 F040404040404040            258          DC    CL14'0'
000345 D6D7C5D9C1E3C9D6            259          DC    CL30'OPERATION'
000363 E2E3C1D9E3C9D5C7            260          DC    CL26'STARTING TIME'
00037D C5D5C4C9D5C740E3            261          DC    CL22'ENDING TIME'
000393 C5D3C1D7E2C5C440            262          DC    CL41'ELAPSED TIME'
                                   263 *
0003C0                             264 DOUBLE   DS    D
0003C8                             265 STTIME   DS    F
0003CC                             266 TIME300  DS    F
0003D0 000005DC000F4240            267 TIMES    DC    F'1500,1000000,1000000,1000000'
0003E0 000000820000008C            268 ADDRSS   DC    A(CALLSUB,CNTBIN,ADDDEC,MULTDEC)
0003F0                             269 SAVE     DS    18F
000438                             270 TIMEDIT  DS    CL20
00044C                             271 PKTOTAL  DS    PL8
000454                             272 PKNUMBER DS    PL4
000458                             273 LINECNT  DS    PL2
00045A 402020214B2020              274 PATRN    DC    XL7'402020214B2020'
000461 C3C1D3D340E2E4C2            275 CONST1   DC    CL35'CALL SUBPROGRAM 1500 TIMES'
000484 C3D6E4D5E340E3D6            276 CONST2   DC    CL35'COUNT TO 1 MILLION IN BINARY'
0004A7 C1C4C440F14004C9            277 CONST3   DC    CL35'ADD 1 MILLION DECIMAL NUMBERS'
0004CA D4E4D3E3C9D7D3E8            278 CONST4   DC    CL35'MULTIPLY 1 TO 1 MILLION BY 99'
                            00000  279          END   MAINLINE
0004F0 5B5BC2D6D7C5D540            280                =C'$$BOPEN '
0004F8 5B5BC2C3D3D6E2C5            281                =C'$$BCLOSE'
000500 00000003                    282                =F'3'
000504 00000178                    283                =A(PRINTER)
000508 0000022D                    284                =A(PRLINE)
00050C 00000000                    285                =V(TIMESUB)
000510 000002B2                    286                =A(HEAD1)
000514 00000337                    287                =A(HEAD2)
000518 051C                        288                =P'51'
00051A 099C                        289                =P'99'
00051C 050C                        290                =P'50'
00051E 0C                          291                =P'0'
00051F 1C                          292                =P'1'
000520 E2C5C3D6D5C4E2              293                =C'SECONDS'
```

Figure 11–13 *(Concluded)*

We therefore set up a loop repeated four times using data from three tables. Table 1, called TIMES, has four fullwords with the number of iterations for the four operations. Table 2, ADDRSS, has the addresses of the four modules. Table 3, starting at CONST1, contains the three identifiers for the operations.

The initial values module sets R5 to 4 as a counter for operations to be performed. It initializes R6 with the address of the TIMES table, and R7 with the address of CONST1. R6 also is used as a pointer to the ADDRSS table, since each element in ADDRSS is exactly 16 bytes from the corresponding element in TIMES.

The main processing loop gets the starting for each event, initializes R2 with the number of iterations and R3 with the address of the module, and uses BALR to perform the module. Upon return from the module, the main loop gets the ending time, calculates the elapsed time to the nearest 1/100 second, and prints the results. Then it modifies addresses in R6 and R7 to set up for the next event. After four events, the program terminates.

The CALL macro generates 10 statements. Rather than repeat it a number of times throughout the program, it is obtained in the CALLIT module. Whenever time of day is needed, the instruction BAL 11,CALLIT requires only four bytes.

The subprogram (Figure 11–14) first saves R14–12, loads the base register, saves addresses of the respective save areas, and gets the addresses of the parameters in R2 and R3. It then gets the time in units of 1/300 second and stores in the first parameter address given in R2.

The subprogram then gets the time in decimal in form HH:MM:SS, where HH is hours on a 24-hour basis. If the hour is less than 12, it is considered A.M.; if equal to or greater than 12, it is P.M. If the hour is greater than 13, then 12 is subtracted. If the hour is less than 1, then 12 is added. The 20-byte constant showing time of day is returned to the address in the calling program specified in R3.

Figure 11–15 shows output from Program 11.

SUMMARY

The operating system supplies a number of useful macros in addition to those that perform I/O operations. COMRG in DOS puts into R1 the address of the communication region. This permits access to the current date, job name, and a user area, among other things. GETIME in DOS supplies the current time of day in R1 in either of three different forms: seconds in binary, 1/300 second in binary, or hours, minutes, and seconds in packed decimal form. The TIME macro in OS puts the Julian date in R1 and the time of day to the nearest hundredth of a second in R0.

Subroutines are assembled with the main line of a program. They perform tasks that may be repeated several times during a program, or permit the program to be divided into modules. The BAL and BALR instructions provide linkage by placing the main line return address into a register than can be referenced in the subroutine.

The calling sequence is the means of furnishing data or addresses needed by the subroutine. The data itself may be placed in registers before the BAL or BALR to the subroutine is executed. Or the data may be placed in main storage as a parameter list, and the address of the list loaded into a register.

```
  LOC  OBJECT CODE     ADDR1 ADDR2  STMT   SOURCE STATEMENT                                 DOS/VSE ASSEMBLER 11.11 86-03-28

                                       1 ************************************************************************
                                       2 *                 ALTON R. KINDRED, TIME SUBPROGRAM
                                       3 * THIS SUBPROGRAM GETS TIME OF DAY IN UNITS OF 1/300 OF A SECOND AND
                                       4 * RETURNS IT AS A FULLWORD TO THE CALLING PROGRAM.  IT ALSO EDITS TIME
                                       5 * OF DAY IN FORM TIME = 11:14:25 A.M. AND RETURNS TO CALLING PROGRAM
                                       6 * IN 20-BYTE AREA.
                                       7 *          REGISTERS USED:
                                       8 *                   R01:  ADDRESS OF PARAMETER LIST
                                       9 *                   R02:  ADDRESS OF FIRST PARAMETER (TIME300)
                                      10 *                   R03:  ADDRESS OF SECOND PARAMETER (TIMEDIT)
                                      11 *                   R12:  BASE REGISTER
                                      12 *                   R13:  ADDRESS OF SAVE AREA
                                      13 ************************************************************************
                                      14          PRINT NOGEN
000000                                15 TIMESUB  CSECT
                                      16          SAVE  (14,12)                 SAVE REGISTERS
000004 05C0                           19          BALR 12,0                     LOAD BASE REGISTER
                            00006     20          USING *,12                    DESIGNATE BASE REGISTER
000006 4120 C0D6            000DC     21          LA    2,SAVE                  GET ADDRESS OF SUBP. SAVE AREA
00000A 50D2 0004            00004     22          ST    13,4(2)                 SAVE ADDR. OF PREV. SAVE AREA
00000E 502D 0008            00008     23          ST    2,8(13)                 STORE THIS SAVE AREA ADDR.
000012 582D 001C            0001C     24          L     2,28(13)                RESTORE R2 CONTENTS
000016 41D0 C0D6            000DC     25          LA    13,SAVE                 LOAD THIS SAVE AREA ADDR IN R13
00001A 9823 1000            00000     26          LM    2,3,0(1)                LOAD PARAM. ADDR INTO R2 AND R3
                                      27          GETIME TU                     GET TIME IN 1/300 SECONDS
000022 5012 0000            00000     34          ST    1,0(2)                  STORE IN CALLING PROGRAM
                                      35          GETIME STANDARD               GET TIME IN DECIMAL
00007C 5010 C11E            00124     62          ST    1,TIME                  STORE FOR EDITING
000080 F933 C11E C152 00124 00158     63 IF       CP    TIME,=P'120000'         IF TIME < NOON
000086 47B0 C08E      00094           64          BNL   ELSE                      *
00008A D203 C132 C156 00138 0015C     65 THEN     MVC   AMPM,=C'A.M.'             THEN INDICATE A.M.
000090 47F0 C094      0009A           66          B     ENDIF                     *
000094 D203 C132 C15A 00138 00160     67 ELSE     MVC   AMPM,=C'P.M.'         ELSE INDICATE P.M.
                            0009A     68 ENDIF    EQU   *                       ENDIF
00009A F933 C11E C15E 00124 00164     69 IF1      CP    TIME,=P'130000'         IF TIME => 12 HOURS
0000A0 47B0 C0A4      000AA           70          BNL   ENDIF1                    *
0000A4 FB33 C11E C152 00124 00158     71 THEN1    SP    TIME,=P'120000'           THEN SUBTRACT 12 HOURS
                            000AA     72 ENDIF1   EQU   *                       ENDIF
0000AA F932 C11E C162 00124 00168     73 IF2      CP    TIME,=P'10000'          IF TIME < 1 HOUR
0000B0 47B0 C0B4      000BA           74          BNL   ENDIF2                    *
0000B4 FA33 C11E C152 00124 00158     75 THEN2    AP    TIME,=P'120000'           THEN ADD 12 HOURS
                            000BA     76 ENDIF2   EQU   *                       ENDIF
0000BA D209 C136 C140 0013C 00146     77          MVC   WORK,PATRN              EDIT TIME
0000C0 DE09 C136 C11E 0013C 00124     78          ED    WORK,TIME               *
0000C6 D207 C129 C138 0012F 0013E     79          MVC   EDITIME,WORK+2          *
0000CC D213 3000 C122 00000 00128     80          MVC   0(20,3),TIMEAREA        MOVE 20-BYTES TO CALLING PROG.
0000D2 58D0 C0DA            000E0     81          L     13,SAVE+4               LOAD PREV. SAVE AREA ADDR.
                                      82          RETURN (14,12)                RETURN TO CALLING PROG.
                                      86 *
0000DC                                88 SAVE     DS    18F
000124                                89 TIME     DS    F
000128                                90 TIMEAREA DS    0CL20
000128 E3C9D4C5407E40                 91          DC    C'TIME = '
00012F                                92 EDITIME  DS    CL8
000137 40                             93          DC    C' '
000138                                94 AMPM     DS    CL4
00013C                                95 WORK     DS    CL10
000146 40202120 7A20207A              96 PATRN    DC    XL10'402021207A20207A2020'
                                      97          END
000150 0000012C                       98                =F'300'
000154 0000003C                       99                =F'60'
000158 0120000C                      100                =P'120000'
00015C C14BD44B                      101                =C'A.M.'
000160 D74BD44B                      102                =C'P.M.'
000164 0130000C                      103                =P'130000'
000168 10000C                        104                =P'10000'
```

Figure 11–14 Program 11 subprogram to return time of day

```
                                        TIMING OPERATIONS

          OPERATION                     STARTING TIME             ENDING TIME             ELAPSED TIME

CALL SUBPROGRAM 1500 TIMES         TIME = 11:12:07 A.M.      TIME = 11:12:09 A.M.         1.85 SECONDS
COUNT TO 1 MILLION IN BINARY       TIME = 11:12:09 A.M.      TIME = 11:12:10 A.M.         1.71 SECONDS
ADD 1 MILLION DECIMAL NUMBERS      TIME = 11:12:10 A.M.      TIME = 11:12:15 A.M.         4.84 SECONDS
MULTIPLY 1 TO 1 MILLION BY 99      TIME = 11:12:15 A.M.      TIME = 11:12:35 A.M.        20.20 SECONDS
```

Figure 11–15 Program 11 output

Subprograms differ from subroutines in that they are assembled separately from the main line modules. Certain registers are assigned standard usages with subprograms. The CALL macro is convenient to utilize these conventions. R15 contains the address of the subprogram, R14 the address of the return point, and R13 the address of a save area to hold the contents of all registers. R1 holds the address of a parameter list. The list contains other addresses (and occasionally data) needed by the subprogram.

The program (or module) that issues the CALL macro is the calling module. The subprogram to which it transfers is the called program (or module). An address needed by one module but defined in another is called an EXTRN. An address defined in one module but referenced in another is an ENTRY. The name of any control section is automatically an ENTRY. A type V address constant is automatically an EXTRN.

The SAVE macro is used in subprograms to store the registers in the save area in the calling program. The RETURN macro restores the registers and returns to the calling program.

Subprograms may open and use their own files. Or they may process files in the calling program if they are given the address of the DTF of each file to be used. Assembler subprograms may also be called by other languages, and assembler programs may call subprograms written in other languages if both observe the same register conventions.

TERMS FOR REVIEW

CALL
Called module
Calling module
Calling sequence
CNOP (Conditional No-op)
Communication region
ENTRY
EXTRN
Parameter list
Register conventions
RETURN
SAVE
Save area
Subprogram
Subroutine
Type V constant

REVIEW QUESTIONS

1. Name system macros used in previous chapters.
2. What is contained in the communication region? What is its purpose?
3. What areas of the communication region are most useful to the applications programmer?
4. What is the difference between the linkage and the calling sequence to a subroutine?
5. What is the difference between a subroutine and a subprogram? Which does not need to be assembled each time it is used with a different program?
6. Distinguish between an EXTRN and an ENTRY.
7. What is a conditional no-op (CNOP) and why is it used?
8. Explain the standard register conventions for subprograms.

9. What is the first operand in a CALL macro? What are the operands in parentheses called?
10. Why is a X'80' placed in the last address in the parameter list in a CALL macro?
11. How are the addresses from the parameter list usually made available for processing in the subprogram?
12. Describe the format of a standard save area. How is a subprogram notified where it should save any registers it will use?
13. Explain instructions generated by the macro SAVE (14,12). What would be generated by SAVE (6,7)?

EXERCISES

1. Write instructions to move the current date to a field called PRDATE and the current time (24-hour basis) to a field called PRTIME.
2. Write a subroutine that will compare a fullword in R2 with one in R3 and put the larger of the two in R4. Then write the mainline calling sequence so that the number 375 will be compared with 248.
3. Modify the subroutine in Exercise 2 so that R2 and R3 will contain the addresses of two three-byte packed decimal fields to be compared and R4 will contain the address where the larger of the two will be placed. Write a mainline calling sequence with field names of your own choice.
4. Write two examples of an ENTRY and two of an EXTRN.
5. PRINTER is a file opened in a calling program. Write the necessary statements to allow the subprogram to write a record to PRINTER.
6. Write statements to open a PRINTER file within a subprogram the first time it is called and keep it open for each subsequent CALL.

PROGRAMMING PROBLEMS

1. Rewrite the program of Problem 1 from Chapter 10 to use a subprogram to calculate the student average from the five test scores. The calling program issues the macro as CALL CALCAVG,(SCORES,AVERAGE), where CALCAVG is the name of the subprogram, SCORES is the address of the first score in the input record, and AVERAGE is the field where the rounded average is to be placed. Do all calculations and return the average in binary form. Calculate only the average in the subprogram; have the calling program set up the five scores in the detail line for printing.
2. Write a subprogram that will return the current date, time of day, and name of the job into locations specified in the calling program. The subprogram is called with the statement CALL HEADDATA,(DATE,TIME,JOB). All three parameters name eight-byte fields. DATE is in form MM/DD/YY, TIME is in form HH/MM/SS, and JOB is a type C field.

3. Define a table in a subprogram giving bonus rates on net year-to-date sales as follows:

AT LEAST	BUT LESS THAN	RATE
0	10,000	3.0%
10,000	20,000	3.5%
20,000	30,000	4.0%
30,000	40,000	4.4%
40,000	50,000	4.7%
50,000	999,999	5.0%

Write a calling program to read Data Set 3 in Appendix D and produce a Bonus Report showing salesperson name, net year-to-date sales, and bonus. The net year-to-date sales is computed by subtracting YTD returns from YTD sales. Call the subprogram in the form CALL BONUSCLC,(NETYTD,BONUS). The subprogram must look up the correct rate in the table, multiply the net YTD sales by the bonus rate, and return the rate to the calling program. Add the bonus amounts and show the average bonus at the end of the report.

12 Macro Definitions and Conditional Assemblies

OBJECTIVES

After studying this chapter, you should be able to:

- Distinguish between defining a macro and invoking a macro
- Name the four parts of a macro definition and give their functions
- Distinguish between insertion, modification, and manipulation of source statements by macro definitions
- Distinguish between positional operands and keyword operands in prototype statements
- Name the different kinds of variable symbols used in macro definitions
- Explain the kinds of attributes and how to use each kind
- Use SET symbols to represent variables in macro definitions
- Distinguish between local and global definitions of symbols
- Use conditional assembly statements to generate source statements under different conditions encountered at assembly time
- Explain how macros are defined for use by one program or by many different programs
- Name and explain the system variable symbols

A macro is a statement in assembler language that can generate one or more source statements. We *define* a macro by writing its name and operands followed by the statements it is to generate. We *invoke*, or *call*, the macro by writing its name as an op code with appropriate operands in our source program.

The assembler reads through the source code for macro definitions and macro instructions before it begins the usual assembly process of translating source statements into object code. This preliminary phase is called *pre-assembly time*. During pre-assembly, the assembler generates source statements as specified in the macro definitions and inserts them into the source module.

Since our first program in this text, we have used macros provided by DOS or OS for input/output operations. OPEN, CLOSE, GET, PUT, and CNTRL are system macros that generate machine instructions. DTFCD and DTFPR are macros that generate data definitions, channel commands, and in some instances machine instructions. The EOJ macro (in DOS) generates an instruction that transfers control to the supervisor at the end of the program.

INVOKING MACROS

To invoke (or call) a macro at pre-assembly time, the programmer writes the name of the macro in the op code field and the appropriate operands in the operand field. The name must not be the same as any machine instruction mnemonic, assembler statement, or macro previously defined. The macro normally allows a name to be written in columns 1 to 8, and allows one or more operands to be specified. The assembler must then find the statements that define the macro to generate the correct source statements. A macro may be called anywhere within a source program except before or between macro definitions.

Macros are used for a number of reasons:

1. They reduce coding. A single macro may produce dozens, even hundreds, of source statements.
2. They improve accuracy. Complex machine instructions can be reduced to a single macro, with the operands providing the data or *parameters* on which the instructions will work.
3. They make standard processing techniques available to all programmers.
4. They allow experienced programmers to write macros for special purposes that less experienced partners can use.

DEFINING MACROS

Every macro must be defined before it can be invoked. The definition follows a prescribed form. It may be placed at the beginning of the source program if the macro applies to that program alone. The macro definition statements must precede all statements except comments or assembler statements such as TITLE, EJECT, PRINT, SPACE, ICTL, OPSYN, or ISEQ.

If the macro is to be made available to many programs, the macro definition is catalogued into the system library. Upon encountering a macro instruction in the source code, the assembler retrieves the source statements from the library and places them into the source code. The statements thus generated are translated just like any written by the programmer.

Source statements outside of and after any macro definitions are called *open code*.

Macro definitions generate statements in three different ways discussed in this chapter:

1. Text insertion
2. Text modification
3. Text manipulation

Up to this point in the text, all names of files, records, fields, or procedural instructions have been of the type called *ordinary symbols*. An ordinary symbol must begin with an alphabetic character and contain up to eight alphabetic characters or digits. For this purpose, not only the letters but also the characters @, #, and $ are considered alphabetic.

Symbols in macro definitions fall into three categories:

1. Ordinary symbols
2. Variable symbols
   a. Symbolic parameters
   b. SET symbols
   c. System variable symbols
3. Sequence symbols

We will discuss each category in the following sections.

FORM OF THE MACRO DEFINITION

Every macro definition has four parts: (1) a header; (2) a prototype statement; (3) the body of the definition; and (4) a trailer statement. These statements define the bounds of the definition, give it a name, declare the parameters to be used, and provide the statements the macro contains.

The MACRO Header

Every definition begins with a header, consisting of the word MACRO in the op code field. The name field must not be used and no operands are required.

The Prototype Statement

The prototype statement shows the form in which the macro will appear when it is invoked. The op code contains the name of the macro definition. This is the name that calls, or invokes, the macro. It must not duplicate the name of any other machine instruction, assembler instruction, system macro, or any other macro catalogued in the system library.

The name field may contain a parameter or be left blank.

The operand field contains zero or more *symbolic parameters* separated by commas. Symbolic parameters represent names or other values that you may pass to the macro definition when you invoke the macro. Names of symbolic parameters begin with an ampersand (&) followed by a letter and one to seven alphanumeric characters.

Symbolic parameters may be *positional* or *keyword* parameters. Positional parameters must always occur in a prescribed sequence. Keyword parameters are identified by a word such as &BLKSIZE=. The programmer writes the keyword followed by the value to be assigned. Keyword operands may appear in any order.

The Body

The body of the macro definition may contain (1) model statements; (2) processing statements, and (3) comments.

Model statements become the generated source statements, either as written or as modified by the definition at pre-assembly time. They may be machine instructions, assembler directives, assembler declaratives, or other macros.

Processing statements determine what statements are to be generated and what values they will have. Most processing statements are *conditional assembly* statements, which can generate different statements depending upon conditions encountered at pre-assembly time.

Comments are of two kinds, internal and ordinary. Internal comments have a period in column 1 and an asterisk in column 2. They are included in the macro definition, but not in the generated statements. Ordinary comments contain an asterisk in column 1 and do appear in the generated statements.

The MEND Statement

The MEND (Macro End) statement terminates the macro definition. It may have a sequence symbol in the name field, but this name never appears in the generated code. A sequence symbol is used in conditional assembly statements, to be discussed later. No operands are required.

TEXT INSERTION

We may use a prototype statement with no operands to insert procedural statements directly into the source module. For example, the definition in Figure 12–1 causes all statements between INIT and MEND to be inserted into the text when we use the macro INIT. Notice that the generated statements include assembler directives (PRINT, START, and USING), one machine instruction (BALR), and the OPEN macro.

Another popular use of direct text insertion is to produce record descriptions or other data definitions. For example, we could write the macro definition in Figure 12–2 to insert the complete description of INRECD by using the macro INRECD. There is no conflict between using the same word as an op code for a macro and as the name of a declarative, as they appear in different fields of the source statement.

TEXT MODIFICATION

Straight text insertion has limited application. Often we wish to change the names we use or generate in macro definitions. We may supply variable information to the macro definitions through variable symbols appearing in the name field or operands of the prototype statement.

Variable Symbols

A variable symbol consists of an ampersand (&) followed by up to eight letters or digits, the first of which must be alphabetic. When used in a prototype

```
          MACRO
          INIT
          PRINT   NOGEN
MAINLINE  START   0
          BALR    12,0
          USING   *,12
          OPEN    INFILE,PRINTER
          MEND
```

Figure 12–1 INIT macro definition

```
          MACRO
          INRECD
INRECD    DS      0CL80
INSOCSEC  DS      CL9
INNAME    DS      CL20
INADDR    DS      CL20
INCITY    DS      CL14
INSTATE   DS      CL2
INZIP     DS      CL5
          DS      CL10
          MEND
```

Figure 12–2 Macro definition for INRECD record description

Programming Tips

- Write macro definitions to generate source statements that are frequently used or especially complex in nature.
- If the macro applies to only a single program, write its definition at the start of the program.
- If the macro will be used in many programs, catalog the definition into the system macro library.

statement, the variable symbol is called a *symbolic parameter.* It gives us a way to pass names to the macro definition to be used in the model statements. The variable symbol takes on the value of the ordinary symbol that is used when the macro is invoked. For example, in our INIT macro, we might wish to vary the name of the CSECT used in the START statement, the base register, and the names of the two files that are opened. If we change our definition to include four variable symbols and invoke the macro by writing

```
PROG1 INIT 3,TAPEIN,PRINTER
```

statements are generated as shown in Figure 12–3.

Wherever a variable symbol is replaced in the prototype statement, it is also replaced wherever it appears in the body of the definition. In this example &NAME = PROG1, &R = 3, &FILEIN = TAPEIN, and &FILEOUT = PRINTER wherever they occur. We now have flexibility to insert our own names when we invoke the macro and have them appear in the model statements that are generated.

Positional Parameters The foregoing example used *positional parameters.* A positional parameter is a symbolic parameter that must appear in a specific position among the operands. The position within the prototype statement indicates the purpose of the operand. In our example, the name field referred to the name of the control section, the first operand specified the base regis-

```
                                              GENERATED STATEMENTS
         MACRO
&NAME    INIT   &R,&FILEIN,&FILEOUT           PROG1    INIT   3,TAPEIN,PRINTER
         PRINT  NOGEN                                  PRINT  NOGEN
&NAME    START  0                             PROG1    START  0
         BALR   &R,0                                   BALR   3,0
         USING  *,&R                                   USING  *,3
         OPEN   &FILEIN,&FILEOUT                       OPEN   TAPEIN,PRINTER
         MEND
```

Figure 12–3 Symbolic parameters in a macro definition

ter, the second named the input file, and the third gave the output file. We must always enter the names in exactly this sequence when we invoke the macro.

Keyword Parameters A *keyword parameter* is a type of symbolic parameter that may be written in any sequence. The keyword is preceded by an ampersand (&) and followed by an equal sign (=). We may specify default values, which are names or numbers to be used if the keyword is omitted. We might write the prototype statement as follows to name R12 as the default base register without changing the body of the definition at all:

```
&NAME INIT &FILEIN=,&R=12,&FILEOUT=
```

To invoke the macro, we must use the keyword and then the name we wish associated with it. If we make no entry for keyword &R=, register 12 will be used by default. Keyword parameters are used extensively in DTF macros.

Concatenation

The word *concatenation* means *joining together*. We may concatenate ordinary symbols, variable symbols, numbers, and special characters to make meaningful operands. A period must be used before a letter, digit, or left parenthesis joined to a variable symbol. Figure 12–4 shows some examples of concatenation.

Note in the last example that concatenation has produced an invalid operand. It is obviously our responsibility to use features of the macro definitions correctly to generate valid instructions.

A useful macro to fill any given field with any character we wish is defined and illustrated in Figure 12–5. The first example fills PRLINE with 133 hyphens. The second fills PRMESG with 20 spaces (X'40').

Attributes

Attributes are qualities or characteristics that describe data or instructions in programs. The assembler assigns attributes to each symbol (name) appearing

STATEMENT	VALUES	RESULT
&FLD.A	&FLD=PKAMT	PKAMTA
A&FLD	&FLD=PKAMT	APKAMT
&FLD.(&L)	&FLD=DOUBLE,&L=3	DOUBLE(3)
&FLD+&DISP	&FLD=PRLINE,&DISP=20	PRLINE+20
&DISP+&FLD	&FLD=PRLINE,&DISP=20	20+PRLINE

Figure 12–4 Examples of concatenation

```
         MACRO
&NAME    FILL     &DEST,&CHAR,&LEN
&NAME    MVI      &DEST,&CHAR
         MVC      &DEST+1.(&LEN-1),&DEST
         MEND
```

GENERATED STATEMENTS FROM TWO DIFFERENT USES OF THE MACRO

```
THEN     FILL     PRLINE,C'-',133               FILL  PRMESG,X'40',20
THEN     MVI      PRLINE,C'-'                   MVI   PRMESG,X'40'
         MVC      PRLINE+1(133-1),PRLINE        MVC   PRMESG+1(20-1),PRMESG
```

Figure 12–5 The FILL macro

in columns 1 to 8 of the source statement. In earlier chapters, we have used the location and length attributes implicitly and explicitly in operands referring to fields and records. Figure 12–6 shows six attributes useful in macro definitions.

We can obtain the attributes of any symbol from the assembler by using the appropriate letter followed by a single quote and the name of the symbol.

Length The length attribute is obtained in the form L'&PARAM, where &PARAM is any variable symbol. Length is always numeric. If &DEST is a symbolic parameter having the value of PRLINE, which was defined as PRLINE DS CL133 (or 0CL133), then we may refer to the length of &DEST as L'&DEST in the body of the macro definition. By using the length attribute, we can shorten our FILL macro definition above. The assembler will supply the length of whatever field replaces &DEST so that the programmer need not specify that length when invoking the macro.

```
         MACRO
&NAME    FILL     &DEST,&CHAR
&NAME    MVI      &DEST,&CHAR
         MVC      &DEST+1.(L'&DEST-1),&DEST
         MEND
```

Names of machine instructions will have lengths of two, four, or six depending upon the type of instruction. Names of EQU statements have a length of one.

Type The type attribute is obtained in the form T'&PARAM, where &PARAM is any variable symbol. The type is always a single alphabetic character referring to the type of an ordinary symbol or a macro instruction operand.

Figure 12–7 shows the type attributes for names used with DS and DC statements, with procedural statements, control section names, external symbols, self-defining terms, and omitted operands.

Notice that these types apply to the way data was defined, not necessarily to the content of the data within the field. For example, if &FLD refers to

L—length
T—type
K—count
N—number
I—integer
S—scaling

Figure 12–6 Attributes of symbols

TYPE	DATA CHARACTERIZED
	LABELS FOR DC AND DS STATEMENTS
A	A-type address constant, implicit length, aligned
B	Binary constant
C	Character constant
D	Doubleword; long floating-point constant, implicit length, aligned
E	Short floating-point constant, implicit length, aligned
F	Fullword, implicit length, aligned
G	Fixed-point constant, explicit length
H	Halfword, implicit length, aligned
K	Floating-point constant, explicit length
L	Extended floating-point constant, implicit length, aligned
P	Packed decimal constant
Q	Q-type address constant, implicit length, alligned (OS only)
R	A-, S-, Q-, V-, or Y-type address constant, explicit length
S	S-type address constant, implicit length, aligned
V	External V-type address constant, implicit length, aligned
X	Hexadecimal constant
Y	Y-type address constant, implicit length, aligned
Z	Zoned decimal constant
	LABELS FOR ASSEMBLER LANGUAGE STATEMENTS
I	Machine instruction
M	Macro instruction
W	Channel command word (CCW)
	OTHER LABELS
J	Control section name
T	External symbol (EXTRN)
$	External symbol (WXTRN)
N	Self-defining term
O	Omitted operand (value: null character string)
N	Value of SETA or SETB variable (OS only)

Figure 12–7 Type attributes

DOUBLE defined as a doubleword, the type is 'D' even though the field may contain packed decimal data.

The type of a name used with an EQU statement is 'U'.

The type attribute is used in conditional assembly statements to verify that two fields are of the same data type or that the op code refers to the correct data type.

Count The count refers to the number of characters in the name itself. The count attribute is referenced as K'&PARAM. If &PARAM = PRLINE, then K'&PARAM = 6 for the six letters in the name PRLINE. The count attribute can be used only in arithmetic expressions.

Number A symbolic parameter enclosed in parentheses is called a *sublist*. The sublist has zero or more operands separated by commas. The number attribute N'&PARAM refers to the number of items inside the parentheses. It is always one more than the number of commas. The number attribute may be used only with operands in macro instructions.

The prototype statement for the CALL macro is

```
&NAME CALL &SUBP,&PARAM
```

If we write the statement

```
REPEAT CALL TIMESUB,(TIME300,TIMEDIT)
```

then &PARAM = (TIME300,TIMEDIT), and N'&PARAM = 2 for the two items within the sublist.

Integer The integer attribute refers to the number of digits to the left of the decimal point in binary or decimal numbers. The integer attribute is obtained by I'&PARAM, where &PARAM is a variable symbol. The binary numbers may be fixed-point or floating-point, and the decimal numbers may be zoned or packed. With the following definitions:

```
PACK   DC   PL4'1234.56'
ZONE   DC   ZL6'1234.56'
```

and &PACK = PACK and &ZONE = ZONE, then I'&PACK = 5 (a leading zero was supplied to fill the four bytes). I'&ZONE = 4 since no leading zero was supplied.

The integer attribute of binary data is based on a formula relating to the type of data, length, and scaling attributes. Scaling of binary data is not covered in this text.

Scaling The scaling attribute is obtained by S'&PARAM. This attribute refers to the number of digits to the right of the decimal point. Zoned decimal data can have a scaling value of 0 through 16, while packed decimal data has a value of 0 through 31. In the preceding examples, S'&PACK = 2 and S'&ZONE = 2. This attribute can be used only in arithmetic expressions.

Sublists

Sublists are symbolic parameters that contain zero or more operands enclosed within parentheses and separated by commas. We have seen how the number attribute N'&PARAM can supply the number of items.

To refer to the specific item within the sublist, a subscript is used. The subscript is a number, variable symbol, or expression enclosed within parentheses. Figure 12–8 shows the values of certain attributes of the sublist when A, B, and C are fullwords, and D is a halfword. The prototype for the CALL macro is

```
&NAME CALL &SUB,&PARAM
```

and the statement to invoke the macro is

```
REPEAT CALL SUBP5,(A,B,C,D)
```

TEXT MANIPULATION

By *text manipulation* we mean the ability to program the macro definition so that at pre-assembly time we can generate one group of statements under one condition and different statements under another condition. We can also vary the content of operands within statements.

PROTOTYPE STATEMENT	STATEMENT TO INVOKE MACRO
&NAME CALL &SUB,&PARAM	REPEAT CALL SUBP5,(A,B,C,D)

NOTE: A, B, and C are fullwords and D is a halfword.

PARAMETER	VALUE GENERATED	REMARKS
&PARAM	(A,B,C,D)	Entire sublist if not subscripted
&PARAM(3)	C	Third item in sublist
&PARAM(2)	B	Second item in sublist
&PARAM(5)	Null character string	Subscript refers beyond end of list
L'&PARAM(1)	4	A is a fullword
K'&PARAM	9	9 characters in the string (A,B,C,D)
T'&PARAM(4)	H	D is a halfword
K'&PARAM(3)	1	C is a 1-character name

Figure 12–8 Attributes of sublists

Conditional Assembly Language

The *conditional assembly language* is a relatively high-level language that permits text manipulation at pre-assembly time. The conditional assembly language consists of

1. SET symbols that represent data.
2. Sequence symbols that identify statements for branching at pre-assembly time.
3. Expressions as values for substitution, subscripts, or condition tests.
4. Selection of character strings for substitution, concatenation, or condition tests.
5. Branching for repetition and selection within the macro definition.

SET Symbols

SET symbols are variable symbols that may contain arithmetic, binary, or character values that can be modified at pre-assembly time. They may be used as subscripts, values for substitution, terms in expressions, counters, switches, and character strings.

SET symbols allow great flexibility in controlling conditional assembly logic and generating different source statements from the same model statements.

SET symbols may be *local* or *global* in scope. A local SET symbol is defined as used only in the macro definition in which it appears or in open code. A global SET symbol may be recognized and used within the assembly in any macro definition and in open code. The global symbol must be declared in each macro definition that will refer to it.

The three kinds of SET symbols are SETA, SETB, and SETC. SET symbols of the different kinds should not have the same names within a single macro definition. They should not begin with the characters &SYS. These characters are reserved for system variable symbols, to be explained later.

SETA Symbols SETA symbols are arithmetic symbols that may contain a 32-bit signed binary value. When used as subscripts they may not be zero or negative. SETA symbols must be defined as global with a GBLA statement or local with an LCLA statement. The definition assigns an initial value of zero to the symbol. The GBLA and LCLA statements require that the name field be blank. Operands are one or more variable symbols separated by commas.

Once defined, a SETA symbol may be assigned other values from decimal constants, other SETA symbols, or arithmetic expressions. The SETA symbol appears in the name field, and the values to be assigned are in the operand field. Some examples of SETA symbols are shown in Figure 12–9.

SETA symbols may be subscripted if they are defined in the GBLA or LCLA statement with the maximum subscript value in parentheses. The highest allowable subscript is 32767. For example:

	STATEMENTS	REMARKS
	GBLA &ALL	&ALL is global, value now 0
	LCLA &A,&B	&A, &B are local, with values of 0
&ALL	SETA 66	&ALL now has value of 66 in other definitions or in open code
&A	SETA 4	&A=4
&B	SETA &A+4	&B=8
&A	SETA (&B-1)*3	&A=21

Figure 12–9 Examples of SETA symbols

```
         LCLA &X(50)      Defines 50 elements named &X
&X(1)    SETA 10          First element of &X has value of 10
```

SETB Symbols SETB symbols are variable symbols that may contain single bit values of only 0 or 1. They are defined as global with the GBLB statement or local with the LCLB statement. The initial value assigned is 0. SETB symbols are used as switches. SETB symbols may be subscripted if defined with the maximum subscript to be used.

SETB symbols are given values in SETB statements. The SETB symbol appears in the name field. The values to be assigned may be a binary value 0 or 1, a 0 or 1 enclosed within parentheses, or a logical expression enclosed within parentheses. If the logical expression is true, the value assigned is 1; if the expression is false, the value is 0. Valid logical operators for comparison and examples of SETB symbols are shown in Figure 12–10.

SETC Symbols SETC symbols are variable symbols that contain character strings. They are defined as global with the GBLC statement and local with the LCLC statement. They are initially assigned a value of null, represented by two consecutive single quotes (''). We may assign single characters, complete strings, or concatenated strings to the SETC symbol by means of the SETC statement. The SETC symbol in the name field takes on the value of the string appearing in the operand field.

Operands may include a type attribute, a concatenated string, a character expression, or a substring. A *character expression* consists of any combination of characters enclosed in single quotes. A *substring* is a string of characters contained within another string. A substring is referenced by following a string with two subscripts enclosed in parentheses and separated by a comma. The first subscript indicates the starting position of the substring and the second subscript its length. Figure 12–11 shows some examples of SETC symbols.

Sequence Symbols

Sequence symbols must begin with a period followed by an alphabetic character and zero to six alphanumeric characters. They are used for branching to

VALID LOGICAL OPERATORS

EQ	Equal	NE	Not equal
GT	Greater than	LT	Less than
GE	Greater than or equal to	LE	Less than or equal to

	STATEMENT	REMARKS
	GBLB &SW	&SW is global and set to 0
	LCLB &LSW	&LSW is local and set to 0
&SW	SETB 0	Set to 0
&LSW	SETB (1)	Set to 1
&SW	SETB (8 GT 5)	True; set to 1
&SW	SETB (5 EQ 8)	False; set to 0
&SW	SETB (L'&PAR GT 6)	True, if &PARAM has length of 8

Figure 12–10 Examples of logical operators and SETB symbols

	STATEMENT	REMARKS
	GBLC &STRING	&STRING is global and set to null
	LCLC &C,&D	&C and &D are local and set to null
&STRING	SETC 'SYS'	&STRING has value 'SYS'
&C	SETC '&STRING'.'LST'	&C has value 'SYSLST' (concatenation)
&D	SETC '&C'(3,3)	&D has value 'SLS' (substring)
&C	SETC T'&PACK	&C has value 'P' if &PACK was type P

Figure 12–11 Examples of SETC symbols

a specified statement in macro definitions. They appear in the name field of the statement to which the branch is to be made.

They must not be used as name entries for any of these assembler instructions: COPY, EQU, GBLA, GBLB, GBLC, ICTL, ISEQ, LCLA, LCLB, LCLC, MACRO, or OPSYN. Sequence symbols are never shown in the generated source statements. They will be demonstrated in the section that follows.

Branching Statements

Four statements control branching within macro definitions: AIF, AGO, ACTR, and ANOP.

AIF The AIF permits branching based upon a condition test. The condition must be enclosed in parentheses in the operand field and followed by a sequence symbol. If the condition is true, a branch is made to the specified sequence symbol. If false, the next statement in sequence is executed. The name field of the AIF statement may be blank or contain a sequence symbol.

AIF permits control of selection and repetition. It also allows a check for error conditions and display of error messages. Some typical AIF statements follow:

```
AIF   (&A GT 4).THEN
AIF   (T'&FLD NE 'P').ELSE
AIF   ('&RSP' EQ 'YES').ENDDO
```

AGO The AGO statement causes an unconditional branch to the sequence symbol named in the operand field. The name field may be blank or contain a sequence symbol. The AGO statement is written in the form:

```
AGO    .ENDIF
```

ACTR The ACTR statement sets a conditional assembly loop counter within a macro definition or in open code. Each AIF or AGO processed subtracts 1 from the loop counter. If the number of iterations exceeds the value assigned to the loop counter, the assembler exits from the macro definition or stops processing statements in open code.

If no ACTR statement is used, the assembler maintains a standard loop counter with a value of 4096 for each macro definition and for open code. To prevent more than 20 executions of AIF and AGO to occur in any conditional assembly, we would write:

```
ACTR   20
```

ANOP The ANOP allows branching to a location that has some other entry in the name field. The ANOP instruction has no operand but has a sequence symbol in the name field. For example, if you wish to branch to a SETA statement, which requires a SETA symbol in the name field, you could use:

```
           AIF    (&A GT 20).ENDIF
           .
.ENDIF     ANOP
&A         SETA   0
```

System Variable Symbols

Six variable symbols are assigned values by the assembler according to specific rules. They are &SYSLIST, &SYSNDX, &SYSECT, &SYSPARM, &SYSTIME, and &SYSDATE. These symbols may be used for text substitution. They must not be used in prototype statements or declared as SET symbols.

&SYSLIST This symbol may be used only within macro definitions. It refers to the entire list of positional parameters used in the prototype statement. It does not refer to keyword parameters. With a subscript, it refers to a positional operand. When the position operand is a sublist, a second subscript refers to the specific positional operand within the sublist. A subscript of zero refers to the entry in the name field. A subscript greater than the number of parameters produces a null value. Figure 12–12 shows some examples of &SYSLIST for a macro instruction.

&SYSNDX This is a counter maintained by the assembler. It contains a four-digit number that may be concatenated to a symbol containing four characters or less. &SYSNDX is set to 0001 by the first macro called in the program and incremented by one for each subsequent macro call. It may be used only within macro definitions.

If a macro appears in more than one place in the program, &SYSNDX will have different values. The symbol to which it is concatenated will thus not be flagged as a duplicate symbol.

The type attribute of &SYSNDX is always N (for numeric), and the count attribute is always 4 (T'&SYSNDX = 'N', K'SYSNDX = 4).

Even though the concatenation of &SYSNDX and the symbol may exceed eight bytes, the resulting name field should not exceed eight.

Here is an example of a loop within model statements that might occur more than once within a program:

```
RPT&SYSNDX EQU *
           Other statements
           BCT 5,RPT&SYSNDX
```

If the macro containing the &SYSNDX reference is the fifth and eleventh macro appearing in the program, source code would appear as follows:

IN FIFTH MACRO	IN ELEVENTH MACRO
RPT0005 EQU * Other statements BCT 5,RPT0005	RPT0011 EQU * Other statements BCT 5,RPT0011

&SYSECT This statement may be used within a macro definition only to generate the name of the current control section. This is the name used with the CSECT or START statement in the source module being assembled.

```
NAME     SUMUP FIRST,SECOND,(X,Y,Z),,FIVE
```

STATEMENT	VALUE SUBSTITUTED
&SYSLIST(0)	NAME
&SYSLIST(5)	FIVE
&SYSLIST(4)	Null (Fourth parameter omitted)
&SYSLIST(3)	(X,Y,Z)
&SYSLIST(3,2)	Y (Second item in sublist)
&SYSLIST(7)	Null (Only 5 parameters)

Figure 12–12 Examples of &SYSLIST

&SYSECT would most commonly be used to generate the address of the current control section:

```
DC A(&SYSECT)
```

&SYSPARM &SYSPARM allows communication with the assembler source module through the job control language. It is a global variable symbol valid within macro definitions or in open code. It is treated as a SETC symbol whose value cannot be changed. The value is assigned by a job control statement and compared or used as a string within the source module. Statements such as

```
         AIF ('&SYSPARM' NE 'DEBUG').OMIT
         .
.OMIT    ANOP
```

would allow a section of source code to be skipped. The value of &SYSPARM is null if no entry is made in job control statements. Further details are available in appropriate system manuals.

&SYSTIME This system variable symbol is available in OS only. It may appear either in macro definitions or in open code. It produces the time of day at assembly time as a five-character string in the form

HH.MM

where HH represents hours on 24-hour basis and MM gives the minutes. Its value cannot be changed within the source module.

&SYSDATE This system variable symbol is available only in OS. It may appear in macro definitions or in open code. It presents the data at assembly time as an eight-character string in the form

MM/DD/YY

where MM is the month, DD the day, and YY the year. Its value cannot be changed within the source module.

SEVERAL USEFUL MACROS

We will now define several macros that may prove useful in a number of different applications.

A common problem in working with packed decimal numbers is a data exception because of an invalid sign. The following macro ORs the rightmost four bits of the last byte of the field with X‘C’. This will correct a sign of X‘0’

Programming Tips

- You cannot do arithmetic on a symbolic parameter in a prototype statement. Assign its value to a SETA symbol for use in arithmetic operations.
- Both symbolic parameters and SET symbols can generate operands in model statements.
- Be careful to distinguish between conditional assembly AIF and AGO statements and branching instructions generated in the source statements. AIF, AGO, and ANOP statements never appear in generated source code.
- Concatenate &SYSNDX to the name used as the target of a branch statement. Then if the macro is used more than once in a program, the name will not be duplicated.

or the X'4' sign that results from packing a blank field, and will not change any valid sign X'C', X'D', or X'F'.

```
        MACRO
&NAME   FXSGN &PKFLD
&NAME   OI    &PKFLD+L'&PKFLD-1,X'0C'
        MEND
```

If PKAMOUNT were a five-byte field, the statement to invoke the macro and its generated code would be:

```
        FXSGN PKAMOUNT
+       OI    PKAMOUNT+5-1,X'0C'
```

correctly adjusting the sign position.

We often need to move a string of identical characters to some field, such as moving blanks or asterisks to a print line. We can define a macro to do this as follows:

```
        MACRO
&NAME   SPRED &DEST,&CHAR
        MVI   &DEST,&CHAR
        MVC   &DEST+1.(L'&DEST-1),&DEST
        MEND
```

The statement to invoke this macro to spread 133 asterisks through a print line, and its generated statements, are as follows:

```
        SPRED PRLINE,C'*'
+       MVI   PRLINE,C'*'
+       MVC   PRLINE+1(133-1),PRLINE
```

We may need to add the contents of a 64-bit binary integer in main storage to another 64-bit integer in an even-odd register pair. The approach is to add the rightmost 32 bits of the integer *logically* to the odd register. If the condition code indicates a carry, then 1 is added logically to the even register before the 32 high order bits are added to it arithmetically. The logical additions work correctly regardless of the sign in either register.

We could write our macro in the form

```
THEN  ADDBL 6,BIT64
```

where the register would have to be even-numbered, and the second operand must be two fullwords or a doubleword in main storage. Figure 12–13 shows the macro definition.

Macro definitions often use relative addressing in branching instructions. The asterisk (*) refers to the current location while the number added to or subtracted from the asterisk indicates the distance forward or backward to the branch address. This eliminates the need for names of the locations to which we branch. In the preceding example, the branch from the BC instruction to the Add (A) is eight bytes, since BC and AL are both four-byte type RX instructions. The definition could be written as shown in Figure 12–14.

```
              MACRO
&NAME         ADDBL  &R,&DOUBLE
              LCLA   &R2
&R2           SETA   &R+1
&NAME         AL     &R2,&DOUBLE+4        Add rightmost 32 bits
IF&SYSNDX     BC     12,ENDF&SYSNDX       IF carry
THEN&SYSNDX   AL     &R,=F'1'               THEN add 1 to leftmost 32 bits
ENDF&SYSNDX   A      &R,&DOUBLE           Add leftmost 32 bits
              MEND
```

Figure 12–13 Macro definition to add 64-bit integers

```
        MACRO
&NAME   ADDBL  &R,&DOUBLE
        LCLA   &R2
&R2     SETA   &R+1
&NAME   AL     &R2,&DOUBLE+4
        BC     12,*+8
        AL     &R,=F'1'
        A      &R,&DOUBLE
        MEND
```

Figure 12–14 Macro definition with asterisk addressing

Figure 12–15 shows the definition for the GET macro. While the branching is not formally structured, it presents an excellent example of many different conditional assembly language features for individual study and analysis.

The GET macro may be written with or without a work area. The first operand filename is required. The filename address may be preloaded into R1 or any other general register except R0, R14, or R15. The work area address may be preloaded into other R0 or any other general register except R1, R14, or R15.

The macro definition will generate two, three, or four source statements. The last two will always put the address of the I/O module into R15 and the return address into R14. The first two, if needed, get the filename address into R1 and the work area address into R0.

PROGRAM 12: SAV13 and RET13 MACROS

Program 12 uses a calling program and subprogram to do a table lookup operation. The calling program in Figure 12–16 creates its entire mainline

```
         BKEND   A.GET
          MACRO                                                        S4530001
&LABEL    GET     &FILEN,&PARAM                                        S4530002
.* IBM SYSTEM/360 DISK OPERATING SYSTEM                                S4530003
* 360N-CL-453 GET       CHANGE LEVEL 3-0                               S4530004
          AIF    (T'&FILEN NE '0').ONE                                 S4530005
          MNOTE 0,'NO FILENAME SPECIFIED.SET TO ''*'''                 S4530006
&LABEL    L      1.=A(*)              *****ERROR-PATCH DTF TABLE ADDRESS S4530007
          AGO    .THREE                                                S4530008
.ONE      AIF    ('&FILEN'(1,1) NE '(').TWO                            S4530009
          AIF    ('&FILEN(1)' EQ '1').FOUR                             S4530010
&LABEL    LR     1,&FILEN(1)                GET DTF TABLE ADDRESS      S4530011
          AGO    .THREE                                                S4530012
.TWO      ANOP                                                         S4530013
&LABEL    L      1,+A(&FILEN)               GET DTF TABLE ADDRESS      S4530014
.THREE    AIF    (T'&PARAM EQ '0').EIGHT                               S4530015
          AIF    ('&PARAM'(1,1) EQ '(').SIX                            S4530016
          L      0,=A(&PARAM)               GET WORK AREA ADDRESS      S4530017
          AGO    .EIGHT                                                S4530018
.SIX      AIF    ('&PARAM(1)' NE '1').SEVEN                            S4530019
          MNOTE 0,'INVALID REGISTER SPECIFICATION FOR WORKAREA'        S4530020
          LR     0,0                  *****ERROR-PATCH REGISTER NUMBER S4530021
          AGO    .EIGHT                                                S4530022
.SEVEN    AIF    ('&PARAM(1)' EQ '0').EIGHT                            S4530023
          LR     0,&PARAM(1)                GET WORK AREA ADDRESS      S4530024
.EIGHT    L      15,16(1)                   GET LOGIC MODULE ADDRESS   S4530025
          BAL    14,8(15)                   BRANCH TO GET ROUTINE      S4530026
          MEXIT                                                        S4530027
.FOUR     ANOP                                                         S4530028
&LABEL    DC   OH'0'                                                   S4530029
          AGO    .THREE                                                S4530030
          MEND                                                         S4530031

         BKEND
```

Figure 12–15 GET macro definition

```
LOC    OBJECT CODE    ADDR1 ADDR2  STMT  SOURCE STATEMENT                                 DOS/VSE ASSEMBLER 14.04 86-03-28

                                       1 ***********************************************************************
                                       2 *                ALTON R. KINDRED, PROGRAM 12
                                       3 * THIS PROGRAM READS A RECORD CONTAINING A DATE IN FORM MM/DD/YY AND
                                       4 * CALLS A SUBPROGRAM THAT CONVERTS IT TO FORM SEPTEMBER 27, 1985.
                                       5 * MONTH NAME IS LEFT JUSTIFIED TO BE NEXT TO THE DAY OF THE MONTH.
                                       6 * IF MONTH NUMBER IS NOT BETWEEN 1 AND 12, THE SUBPROGRAM RETURNS
                                       7 * NINE XS IN MONTH NAME FIELD.  BOTH THE CALLING PROGRAM AND THE
                                       8 * SUBPROGRAM MAKE USE OF SEVERAL USER-DEFINED MACROS.  RESULTS ARE
                                       9 * PRINTED OUT SIDE BY SIDE FOR COMPARISON.
                                      10 *        REGISTERS USED:
                                      11 *                R09-R11:  LINK REGISTERS
                                      12 *                R12:      BASE REGISTER
                                      13 *                R13:      ADDRESS OF SAVE AREA
                                      14 *                R14-R15:  SUBPROGRAM LINKAGE
                                      15 ***********************************************************************
                                      16 *                MACRO DEFINITIONS
                                      17 ***********************************************************************
                                      18          MACRO
                                      19 &NAME    MNLN  &BASEREG=12,&INFILE=INFILE,&OUTFILE=PRINTER
                                      20 &NAME    START 0
                                      21 *        STM   14,12,12.(13)                                            OS
                                      22          BALR  &BASEREG,0
                                      23          USING *,&BASEREG
                                      24 *        ST    13,SAVE+4                                                OS
                                      25 *        LA    13,SAVE                                                  OS
                                      26 *        OPEN  (&INFILE.(INPUT),&OUTFILE.(OUTPUT))                      OS
                                      27          OPEN  &INFILE,&OUTFILE                                        DOS
                                      28          BAL   9,INITIAL
                                      29          BAL   9,MAINLOOP
                                      30          BAL   9,FINAL
                                      31          CLOSE &INFILE,&OUTFILE                                        DOS
                                      32          EOJ                                                           DOS
                                      33 *        CLOSE (&INFILE,,&OUTFILE)                                      OS
                                      34 *        L     13,SAVE+4                                                OS
                                      35 *        LM    14,12,12.(13)                                            OS
                                      36 *        BR    14                                                       OS
                                      37          MEND
                                      38 *
                                      39          MACRO
                                      40 &NAME    GETDATE &PRDATE
                                      41 &NAME    COMRG
                                      42          MVC   &PRDATE.(8),0(1)
                                      43          MEND
                                      44 ***********************************************************************
                                      45 *                MAINLINE MODULE
                                      46 ***********************************************************************
                                      47          PRINT GEN                      PRINT GENERATED MAINLINE MODULE
                                      48 MAINLINE MNLN  GENERATE MAINLINE MODULE
000000                                49+MAINLINE START 0
                                      50+*        STM   14,12,12.(13)                                           OS
000000 05C0                           51+         BALR  12,0
                         00002        52+         USING *,12
                                      53+*        ST    13,SAVE+4                                               OS
                                      54+*        LA    13,SAVE                                                 OS
                                      55+*        OPEN  (&INFILE.(INPUT),&OUTFILE.(OUTPUT))                     OS
                                      56+* IOCS - OPEN - 5745-SC-IOX - REL 28.0                                       12000028
000002 0700                           57+         CNOP  0,4                                                          20000025
000004                                58+         DC    0F'0'                                                        22000025
000004 4110 C3CE         003D0        59+         LA    1,=C'$$BOPEN '                                               46000025
000008 4500 C012         00014        60+IJJ00002    BAL 0,*+4+4*(3-1)                                               54000025
00000C 000000F8                       61+         DC    A(INFILE)                                                    64000025
000010 00000130                       62+         DC    A(PRINTER)                                                   64000025
000014 0A02                           63+         SVC   2                                                            74000025
000016 4590 C036         00038        64+         BAL   9,INITIAL
00001A 4590 C046         00048        65+         BAL   9,MAINLOOP
00001E 4590 C060         00062        66+         BAL   9,FINAL
                                      67+* IOCS AND DEVICE INDEPENDANT I/O - CLOSE - 5745-SC-IOX - REL. 28.0        08100028
000022 0700                           68+         CNOP  0,4                                                          20000025
000024                                69+         DC    0F'0'                                                        22000025
000024 4110 C3D6         003D8        70+         LA    1,=C'$$BCLOSE'                                               46000025
000028 4500 C032         00034        71+IJJC0003    BAL 0,*+4+4*(3-1)                                               54000025
00002C 000000F8                       72+         DC    A(INFILE)                                                    64000025
000030 00000130                       73+         DC    A(PRINTER)                                                   64000025
000034 0A02                           74+         SVC   2                                                            74000025
                                      75+* SUPVR COMMN MACROS - EOJ - 5745-SC-SUP - REL. 28.0                         40000028
000036 0A0E                           76+         SVC   14                                                           50000025
                                      77+*        CLOSE (&INFILE,,&OUTFILE)                                     OS
                                      78+*        L     13,SAVE+4                                               OS
                                      79+*        LM    14,12,12.(13)                                           OS
                                      80+*        BR    14                                                      OS
                                      81          PRINT NOGEN                    PRINT NO GENERATED STATEMENTS
                                      82 ***********************************************************************
                                      83 *                FIRST LEVEL MODULES
                                      84 ***********************************************************************
                                      85 *
                                      86 *                SET INITIAL VALUES MODULE
                                      87 *
000038 F811 C384 C3F6 00386 003F8     88 INITIAL  ZAP   LINECNT,=P'51'           SET LINE COUNT >50
00003E 45A0 C0C2            000C4     89          BAL   10,CLEAR                 CLEAR PRINT LINE
000042 45A0 C062            00064     90          BAL   10,READRECD              READ FIRST RECORD
000046 07F9                           91          BR    9                        RETURN
                                      92 *
                                      93 *                MAIN PROCESSING LOOP
                                      94 *
                            00048     95 MAINLOOP EQU   *
000048 95E8 C383      00385           96 DOWHILE  CLI   EOFFLAG,C'Y'             DOWHILE NOT END OF FILE
00004C 4780 C05E      00060           97          BE    ENDDO                      *
000050 45A0 C080            00082     98          BAL   10,SETUP                   SET UP PRINT LINE
000054 45A0 C09E            000A0     99          BAL   10,PRDETAIL                PRINT THE LINE
000058 45A0 C062            00064    100          BAL   10,READRECD                READ NEXT RECORD
00005C 47F0 C046      00048          101          B     DOWHILE                    *
                            00060    102 ENDDO    EQU   *                        ENDDO
00006C 07F9                          103          BR    9                        RETURN
```

Figure 12–16 Calling program for Program 12

```
  LOC  OBJECT CODE    ADDR1 ADDR2  STMT   SOURCE STATEMENT                                    DOS/VSE ASSEMBLER 14.04 86-03-28

                                   104 *
                                   105 *                  FINAL PROCESSING MODULE
                                   106 *
000062 07F9                        107 FINAL    BR    9                       RETURN
                                   109 ***********************************************************************
                                   110 *                  SECOND LEVEL MODULES
                                   111 ***********************************************************************
                                   112 *
                                   113 *                  READ RECORD MODULE
                                   114 *
000064 92D5 C383        00385      115 READRECD MVI   EOFFLAG,C'N'            SET EOF FLAG OFF
                                   116          GET   INFILE,INRECD           READ RECORD
000078 47F0 C07E        00080      122 IFEOF    B     ENDIFEOF                IF END OF FILE
00007C 92E8 C383        00385      123 THENEOF  MVI   EOFFLAG,C'Y'              THEN SET EOF FLAG ON
                              00080 124 ENDIFEOF EQU   *                       ENDIF
000080 07FA                        125          BR    10                      RETURN
                                   126 *
                                   127 *                  SET UP PRINT LINE MODULE
                                   128 *
000082 41D0 C386              00388 129 SETUP    LA    13,SAVEAREA             GET SAVE AREA ADDRESS INTO R13
                                   130          CALL  MONTHSUB,(INDATE,PRDATE2)
000098 D207 C288 C233 0028A 00235  140          MVC   PRDATE1,INDATE          SET UP NUMERIC DATE
00009E 07FA                        141          BR    10                      RETURN
                                   142 *
                                   143 *                  PRINT DETAIL LINE MODULE
                                   144 *
                              000A0 145 PRDETAIL EQU   *
0000A0 F911 C384 C3F8 00386 003FA  146 IFEOP    CP    LINECNT,=P'50'          IF LINE COUNT => 50
0000A6 4740 C0AC        000AE      147          BL    ENDIFEOP                  *
0000AA 45B0 C0CE              000D0 148 THENEOP  BAL   11,HEADING                THEN PRINT HEADINGS
                              000AE 149 ENDIFEOP EQU   *                       ENDIF
                                   150          PUT   PRINTER,PRLINE          PRINT LINE
0000BE FA10 C384 C3FA 00386 003FC  156          AP    LINECNT,=P'1'           ADD 1 TO LINE COUNT
0000C4 9240 C283        00285      157 CLEAR    MVI   PRLINE,C' '             CLEAR PRINT LINE
0000C8 D283 C284 C283 00286 00285  158          MVC   PRLINE+1(132),PRLINE    *
0000CE 07FA                        159          BR    10                      RETURN
                                   160 ***********************************************************************
                                   161 *                  THIRD LEVEL HEADING MODULE
                                   162 ***********************************************************************
                              000D0 163 HEADING  EQU   *
                                   164          PRINT GEN
                                   165          GETDATE HDDATE                SET UP CURRENT DATE
                                   166+* SUPERVISOR - COMRG - 5745-SC-SUP - REL. 35.0                    @D359DEM 30050035
0000D0 5810 0014              00014 167+         L     1,20               POINT TO PARTITION COM.REGION@D359DEM 30150035
0000D4 0A21                        168+         SVC   33                                                        70000035
0000D6 D207 C336 1000 00338 00000  169+         MVC   HDDATE(8),0(1)
                                   170          PRINT NOGEN
                                   171          PUT   PRINTER,HEAD1           PRINT HEADING LINE
0000EC 92F0 C283        00285      177          MVI   PRLINE,C'0'             SET FOR DOUBLE SPACE
0000FC F810 C384 C3FB 00386 003FD  178          ZAP   LINECNT,=P'0'           SET LINE COUNT TO ZERO
0000F6 07FB                        179          BR    11                      RETURN
                                   181 ********************************************************************DOS
                                   182 *                  FILE DEFINITIONS AND I/O AREAS                  DOS
                                   183 ********************************************************************DOS
                                   184 INFILE   DTFCD BLKSIZE=80,IOAREA1=INAREA,DEVICE=2540,                DOSX
                                                      DEVADDP=SYSIPT,EOFADDR=THENEOF,WORKA=YES              DOS
                                   205 *                                                                    DOS
                                   206 PRINTER  DTFPR BLKSIZE=133,IOAREA1=PRTAREA,DEVICE=1403,              DOSX
                                                      CTLCHR=ASA,DEVADDR=SYS009,WORKA=YES                   DOS
                                   227 *                                                                    DOS
000160                             228 INAREA   DS    CL80                                                  DOS
000180                             229 PRTAREA  DS    CL133                                                 DOS
                                   230 *********************************************************************OS
                                   231 *                  DEVICE CONTROL BLOCKS AND SAVE AREA              OS
                                   232 *********************************************************************OS
                                   233 *INFILE  DCB   DDNAME=INFILE,BLKSIZE=80,LRECL=80,                     OSX
                                   234 *              MACRF=PM,DSORG=PS,EODAD=THENEOF                       OS
                                   235 *                                                                    OS
                                   236 *PRINTER DCB   DDNAME=PRINTER,BLKSIZE=133,LRECL=133,                  OSX
                                   237 *              MACRF=PMA,DSORG=PS                                    OS
                                   238 *                                                                    OS
                                   239 *SAVE    DS    18F                                                   OS
                                   240 ***********************************************************************
                                   241 *                  DATA DEFINITIONS
                                   242 ***********************************************************************
000235                             243 INRECD   DS    0CL80
000235                             244 INDATE   DS    CL8
00023D                             245          DS    CL72
                                   246 *
000285                             247 PRLINE   DS    0CL133
000285                             248          DS    CL5
00028A                             249 PRDATE1  DS    CL8
000292                             250          DS    CL10
00029C                             251 PRDATE2  DS    CL18
0002AE                             252          DS    CL92
                                   253 *
00030A                             254 HEAD1    DS    0CL133
00030A F14040                      255          DC    CL3'1'
00030D D5E4D4C5D9C9C340            256          DC    CL20'NUMERIC DATE'
000321 C4C1E3C540E6C9E3            257          DC    CL23'DATE WITH MONTH NAME'
000338                             258 HDDATE   DS    CL8
000340 4040404040404040            259          DC    CL69' '
                                   260 *
000385                             261 EOFFLAG  DS    CL1
000386                             262 LINECNT  DS    PL2
000388                             263 SAVEAREA DS    18F
                                   264 *
                              00000 265          END   MAINLINE
0003D0 5B5BC2D6D7C5D540            266                =C'$$BOPEN '
0003D8 5B5BC2C3D3D6E2C5            267                =C'$$BCLOSE'
0003E0 000000F8                    268                =A(INFILE)
0003E4 00000235                    269                =A(INRECD)
0003E8 00000000                    270                =V(MONTHSUB)
0003EC 00000130                    271                =A(PRINTER)
```

Figure 12–16 *(Continued)*

```
  LOC  OBJECT CODE     ADDR1 ADDR2  STMT   SOURCE STATEMENT                        DOS/VSE ASSEMBLER 14.04 86-03-28

0003F0 00000285                      272              =A(PRLINE)
0003F4 0000030A                      273              =A(HEAD1)
0003F8 051C                          274              =P'51'
0003FA 050C                          275              =P'50'
0003FC 1C                            276              =P'1'
0003FD 0C                            277              =P'0'
```

Figure 12–16 *(Concluded)*

module by means of a macro defined at the start of the program. It also defines another macro to get the current date from the communication region and move it to a specified eight-byte field.

The calling program reads input records with the date in the first eight columns in the form

MM/DD/YY

It sends the subprogram the address of the date and that of an 18-byte field in which to receive the date in the form

```
SEPTEMBER 22, 1987
```

The subprogram in Figure 12–17 defines the SAV13 and RET13 macros. The SAV13 macro stores the save area addresses in the proper words of the respective save areas. Register R13, containing the address of the calling program save area, is stored in word 2 of the subprogram save area. Then the address of the subprogram save area is stored in word 3 of the calling program save area.

The SAV13 macro should be placed immediately after the SAVE macro if R15 is used for the base register of the subprogram. Otherwise, SAV13 should follow the BALR and USING statements.

The RET13 macro is used just before the system RETURN macro to restore the address of the calling program save area into R13 so that the RETURN macro will refer to the correct address.

The subprogram receives the current data in form MM/DD/YY and returns it as an 18-byte character field in the form SEPTEMBER 22, 1987. The month name will be right-justified to appear next to the day as, for example,

```
bbbbbbMAY 17, 1987
```

Figure 12–18 shows output from Program 12.

SUMMARY

Macros permit generation of a number of source statements by writing only a single statement. Macros save time, ensure accuracy, and permit

```
  LOC  OBJECT CODE     ADDR1 ADDR2  STMT   SOURCE STATEMENT                                       DOS/VSE ASSEMBLER 14.05 86-03-28

                                       1 ***********************************************************************
                                       2 *                  ALTON R. KINDRED, MONTH SUBPROGRAM
                                       3 * THIS SUBPROGRAM TAKES THE DATE FROM THE MAIN PROGRAM IN FORM MM/DD/YY
                                       4 * AND CONVERTS IT TO FORM SEPTEMBER 25, 1987.  IF MONTH NUMBER IS LESS
                                       5 * THAN 1 OR GREATER THAN 12, MONTH NAME IS FILLED WITH XS.  THE SUB-
                                       6 * PROGRAM DEFINES AND USES THE SAV13 AND RET13 MACROS FOR PROPER
                                       7 * STORAGE AND RECOVERY OF SAVE AREA ADDRESSES.
                                       8 *          REGISTERS USED:
                                       9 *                  R01:       ADDRESS OF PARAMETER LIST
                                      10 *                  R02-R03:   ADDRESSES OF PARAMETERS
                                      11 *                  R07:       INDEX FOR TABLE SEARCH
                                      12 *                  R12:       BASE REGISTER
                                      13 *                  R13:       ADDRESS OF SAVE AREA
                                      14 ***********************************************************************
                                      15 *                  MACRO DEFINITIONS
                                      16 ***********************************************************************
                                      17          MACRO
                                      18 &NAME    SAV13 &SAVE
                                      19 &NAME    ST    13,&SAVE+4
                                      20          LA    2,&SAVE
                                      21          ST    2,8(13)
                                      22          L     2,28(13)
                                      23          L     13,&SAVE
                                      24          MEND
                                      25 *
                                      26          MACRO
                                      27 &NAME    RET13 &SAVE
                                      28 &NAME    L     13,&SAVE+4
                                      29          MEND
                                      30 ***********************************************************************
                                      31          PRINT GEN
000000                                32 MONTHSUB CSECT
                                      33          SAVE  (14,12)                  SAVE REGISTERS
                                      34+* SUPERVISOR - SAVE - 5745-SC-SUP - REL. 28.0                          12000028
000000 90EC D00C             0000C    35+         STM   14,12,12+4*(14+2-(14+2)/16*16)(13)                     70000025
000004 05C0                           36          BALR  12,0                     LOAD BASE REGISTER
                             00006    37          USING *,12                     DESIGNATE BASE REGISTER
                                      38          SAV13 SAVESUB                  SAVE ADDRESSES OF SAVE AREAS
000006 50D0 C07E             00084    39+         ST    13,SAVESUB+4
00000A 4120 C07A             00080    40+         LA    2,SAVESUB
00000E 502D 0008             00008    41+         ST    2,8(13)
000012 582D 001C             0001C    42+         L     2,28(13)
000016 58D0 C07A             00080    43+         L     13,SAVESUB
00001A 9823 1000             00000    44          LM    2,3,0(1)                 GET PARAMETER ADDRESSES
00001E F271 C072 2000 00078 00000     45          PACK  DOUBLE,0(2,2)            PACK MONTH NUMBER
000024 F970 C072 C146 00078 0014C     46 IF       CP    DOUBLE,=P'1'             IF MONTH NUMBER < 1
00002A 4740 C032       00038          47          BL    THEN                       *
00002E F971 C072 C142 00078 00148     48 OR       CP    DOUBLE,=P'12'            OR MONTH NUMBER > 12
000034 4700 C03C       00042          49          BNH   ELSE                       *
000038 D208 C0C2 C147 000C8 0014D     50 THEN     MVC   MNTHNAME,=C'XXXXXXXXX'     THEN MOVE XS TO MONTH NAME
00003E 47F0 C050       00056          51          B     ENDIF                      *
                             00042    52 ELSE     EQU   *                        ELSE
000042 4F70 C072             00078    53          CVB   7,DOUBLE                   CONVERT TO BINARY
000046 0670                           54          BCTR  7,0                        SUBTRACT 1
000048 4C70 C144             0014A    55          MH    7,=H'9'                    MULT. BY 9 (LNGTH. TBL. ENTRY)
00004C 4177 C0D4             000DA    56          LA    7,TABLE(7)                 ADD MONTH LOC. TO TBL. ADDR
000050 D208 C0C2 7000 000C8 00000     57          MVC   MNTHNAME,0(7)              MOVE NAME TO WORK AREA
                             00056    58 ENDIF    EQU   *                        ENDIF
000056 D201 C0CC 2003 000D2 00003     59          MVC   DAY,3(2)                 MOVE DAY TO WORK AREA
00005C D201 C0D2 2006 000D8 00006     60          MVC   YEAR,6(2)                MOVE YEAR TO WORK AREA
000062 D211 3000 C0C2 00000 000C8     61          MVC   0(18,3),WORK             MOVE WORK AREA TO MAIN PROG.
                                      62          RET13 SAVESUB                  RESTORE R13
000068 58D0 C07E             00084    63+         L     13,SAVESUB+4
                                      64          RETURN (14,12)                 RESTORE REGS. AND RETURN
                                      65+* SUPERVISOR - RETURN - 5745-SC-SUP - REL. 28.0                        12000028
00006C 98EC D00C             0000C    66+         LM    14,12,12+4*(14+2-(14+2)/16*16)(13)                     72000025
000070 07FE                           67+       BR    14                                                      74000025
                                      68 ***********************************************************************
                                      69 *                  DATA DEFINITIONS
                                      70 ***********************************************************************
000078                                71 DOUBLE   DS    D
000080                                72 SAVESUB  DS    18F
0000C8                                73 WORK     DS    0CL18
0000C8                                74 MNTHNAME DS    CL9
0000D1 40                             75          DC    CL1' '
0000D2                                76 DAY      DS    CL2
0000D4 6B40F1F9                       77          DC    CL4', 19'
0000D8                                78 YEAR     DS    CL2
0000DA                                79 TABLE    DS    0CL108
0000DA 4040D1C1D5E4C1D9               80          DC    CL9'  JANUARY'
0000E3 40C6C5C2D9E4C1D9               81          DC    CL9' FEBRUARY'
0000EC 404040D4C1D9C3                 82          DC    CL9'    MARCH'
0000F5 404040C1D7D9C9                 83          DC    CL9'    APRIL'
0000FE 40404040404D4C1                84          DC    CL9'      MAY'
000107 4040404040D1E4D5               85          DC    CL9'     JUNE'
000110 4040404040D1E4D3               86          DC    CL9'     JULY'
000119 404040C1E4C7E4E2               87          DC    CL9'   AUGUST'
000122 E2C5D7E3C5D4C2C5               88          DC    CL9'SEPTEMBER'
00012B 4040D6C3E3D6C2C5               89          DC    CL9'  OCTOBER'
000134 40D5D6E5C5D4C2C5               90          DC    CL9' NOVEMBER'
00013D 40C4C5C3C5D4C2C5               91          DC    CL9' DECEMBER'
                                      92          END
000148 012C                           93                =P'12'
00014A 0009                           94                =H'9'
00014C 1C                             95                =P'1'
00014D E7E7E7E7E7E7E7E7               96                =C'XXXXXXXXX'
```

Figure 12–17 Subprogram for Program 12

```
NUMERIC DATE          DATE WITH MONTH NAME   03/28/86

  01/01/00              JANUARY 01, 1900
  12/25/87             DECEMBER 25, 1987
  07/04/76                 JULY 04, 1976
  01/08/22              JANUARY 08, 1922
  12/23/76             DECEMBER 23, 1976
  15/04/99            XXXXXXXXX 04, 1999
  11/11/88             NOVEMBER 11, 1988
```

Figure 12–18 Output from Program 12

standardization among program and programmers. Macros are called, or invoked, by using the name of the macro as an op code along with parameters. The parameters may be positional or keyword.

Macro definitions determine what statements will be generated when the macro is called. They have a MACRO header, a prototype statement giving the format of the macro statement, a body giving model statements and processing statements, and a MEND trailer.

Source statements may be produced by text insertion, text modification, and text manipulation. Variable symbols are identified with an ampersand preceding the name. They are replaced by whatever symbols are used when the macro is called. The operands and source statements may be modified each time the macro is invoked.

Each name is given attributes by the assembler that may be utilized in macro definitions. The attributes are length, type, count, number, integer, and scaling. All attributes are numeric except for type, which is a single alphabetic character.

A sublist is a series of symbols enclosed in parentheses and separated by commas. The individual items in the sublist may be referenced by use of a subscript following the name of the sublist.

Text manipulation is performed by the conditional assembly language. This language uses SET symbols, sequence symbols, and branching statements to create loops and selection structures to choose and modify source statements at pre-assembly time. Character strings may be concatenated or substrings extracted to form new names and operands for the source statements that are generated.

Six system variable symbols are provided for use in macro definitions or, in some instances, in open code.

TERMS FOR REVIEW

Attributes	Concatenation	Global
Body	Conditional assembly	Header statement

Invoke
Keyword parameter
Local
Macro definition
Model statement
Parameter
Positional parameter
Prototype statement
Sequence symbol
SET symbol
Sublist
Substring
Symbolic parameter
Text insertion
Text manipulation
Text modification
Trailer statement
Variable symbol

REVIEW QUESTIONS

1. Distinguish between defining a macro and invoking it.
2. Name the chief advantages of using macros. Can you think of any disadvantages?
3. Name the four parts of each macro definition and state the purpose of each.
4. Distinguish between text insertion, modification, and manipulation.
5. What is meant by variable symbols? How many different kinds of variable symbols are there?
6. Distinguish between positional parameters and keyword parameters. Which allows use of default values?
7. What is meant by concatenation? What is the concatenation character? When is it required?
8. Name the six kinds of attributes. Which kind is a single alphabetic character?
9. Which attribute refers to the number of characters in the name? to the number of bytes in the field defined?
10. What is a sublist? How does one refer to a single element within the sublist?
11. Name the principal parts of the conditional assembly language.
12. What are sequence symbols and where may they be used?
13. What is the purpose of the ANOP instruction? What name field and operands does it have?
14. Distinguish between global and local as they relate to SET symbols. What initial values are given to SET symbols when they are defined?
15. What are system variable symbols? Which one is incremented by 1 by the assembler each time a macro is invoked in the source program?

EXERCISES

1. Write a macro definition for a heading line of 133 bytes titled HEAD1, with the words SOFTWARE ENTERPRISES, INC centered and with a four-byte field to hold an edited page number in print positions 125–128. Provide an ASA print control character to skip to a new page.
2. Write a macro definition using SETA symbols to permit a value in a fullword in main storage to be added to four consecutive registers that are to be specified when the macro is called.

3. Write a macro definition to add two binary words together in a register to be specified and store the result in a third word. If type for any of the three words is 'H' (for halfword), concatenate an 'H' to the op code of the instruction that handles that field.

4. **Write a macro definition to add five consecutive three-byte packed decimal fields to another packed decimal field that is first set to zeros. Use SETA symbols to modify the displacement in this fashion:**

```
ZAP    SUM,=P'0'
AP     SUM,PKFLD+0(3)
AP     SUM,PKFLD+3(3)
```

etc.

5. Write an instruction to concatenate the first three bytes of &P1 to bytes five through seven of &P2 and assign the resulting string to a SETC symbol.

6. Write a macro definition to interchange the contents of any two general registers. Verify that both operands are within the range 0 through 15. Define a four-byte hold area within the macro definition to perform the interchange.

PROGRAMMING PROBLEMS

1. Write macro definitions to generate the READRECD module as shown in Program 12. Use keyword parameters and let EOFFLAG, INFILE, and INRECD be the default values. Concatenate &SYSNDX to the instruction names IF, THEN, and ENDF. Invoke this macro in a program to read Data Set 5 in Appendix D and print out student number, name, and test average in three columns.

2. Modify the macro of Problem 1 to include a macro definition for the PRDETAIL module shown in Program 12. Provide LINECNT, HEADING, PRINTER, and PRLINE as default values. Concatenate &SYSNDX to the instruction names IF, THEN, and ENDF.

3. Modify the macro of Problems 1 and 2 to include a macro definition that will add the five test scores using register notation. The prototype for the macro should be

```
&NAME ADDP &SCORE1,&SUM,&N
```

where &SCORE1 is the name of the first unpacked score, &SUM is the name of the field to hold the sum, and &N is the number of scores. Your macro should set the initial address of &SCORE1 in R1, ZAP zeros to &SUM, and perform a loop &N times. Each time through the loop, pack the score, add it to the sum, and increment the address of the score by L'&SCORE1. You may use R0 as a loop counter.

13 Advanced Logical Operations

OBJECTIVES

After studying this chapter, you should be able to:

- Distinguish between logical and arithmetic operations
- Explain and use OR, AND, EXCLUSIVE OR, and Test Under Mask instructions
- Define and use editing patterns for check protection, signed fields, date editing, and multiple fields
- Explain and use single and double register shifts of logical data
- Explain and use logical addition, subtraction, and comparing in registers
- Construct a table to translate any 8-bit code to any other 8-bit code
- Explain operation of the Translate (TR), Translate and Test (TRT) and Execute (EX) instructions
- Scan character strings for delimiters and separate the strings into fields

BIT MANIPULATION

All instructions used so far in the text have worked on complete fields, binary numbers, full bytes, or (in a few cases) four bits at a time. Now we will explore a group of logical instructions that permit us to set individual bits to 0 or 1 or to test whether individual bits are 0 or 1.

The term *logical* in this context is contrasted with *arithmetic* or *algebraic* operations, in which certain bits indicate the sign of a number. Logical data has no sign. Bits are processed individually without considering whether the data is intended to be character, packed decimal, binary, or machine instruction in format.

Logical instructions work on corresponding bits in two different registers or fields. A bit in the first operand might be changed by the operation, but there is never any carry into or borrow from another bit position.

Logical instructions derive from a Boolean logic developed by George Boole, an English mathematician who worked around the middle of the nineteenth century. They form the basis for electrical circuit design and also for the development of *truth tables*, which provide a formal way to evaluate compound conditional statements. We will see examples in the next section.

Three logical instructions widely used are available in four different instruction formats. The mnemonic code is shown under each instruction type:

INSTRUCTION	RR	RX	SI	SS
OR	OR	O	OI	OC
AND	NR	N	NI	NC
EXCLUSIVE OR	XR	X	XI	XC

OR Instructions

OR is a logical operation that somewhat resembles binary addition. Its effects are shown in the following truth table:

```
0 OR 0 = 0
0 OR 1 = 1
1 OR 0 = 1
1 OR 1 = 1
```

This is like binary addition, except that 1 + 1 = 10 whereas 1 OR 1 = 1. In truth tables, a 1 indicates a true condition and 0 a false one. OR operates just as it does in ordinary conversation, where we say we will take some action if one condition is true OR another is true. So long as *either* condition is true or *both* are, we will take the action.

Here are some examples of OR operations:

First operand before OR	1010	1100	1001
Second operand	1100	0001	0011
First operand after OR	1110	1101	1011

Note from these examples that wherever we have a 1 bit in the second operand, the corresponding bit in the first operand is set to 1. Wherever there is a 0 in the second operand, the corresponding bit in the first operand is unchanged. We thus say that we can use the OR operation to set a bit ON, that is, to 1.

AND Instructions

AND has this effect:

```
0 AND 0 = 0
0 AND 1 = 0
1 AND 0 = 0
1 AND 1 = 1
```

This is identical to binary multiplication. The result is 1 only if *both* corresponding bits are 1. We might say we will hire a person who has a degree AND knowledge of COBOL. Both conditions must be true for the result to be true. Here are some examples of AND operations:

First operand before AND	1010	1100	1001
Second operand	1100	0001	0011
First operand after AND	1000	0000	0001

Wherever there is a 0 bit in the second operand, the corresponding bit in the first operand is set to 0. Wherever there is a 1 bit in the second operand, the corresponding bit in the first operand is unchanged. Thus, AND can be used to set any selected bit OFF, that is, to 0.

EXCLUSIVE OR Instructions

EXCLUSIVE OR uses this table:

```
0 XOR 0 = 0
0 XOR 1 = 1
1 XOR 0 = 1
1 XOR 1 = 0
```

Like bits become 0 and unlike bits become 1. Bits are exclusive when they differ. This is similar to hiring either of two qualified people but not both.

Here are some examples of EXCLUSIVE OR:

First operand before XOR	1010	1100	1001
Second operand	1100	0001	0011
First operand after XOR	0110	1101	1010

EXCLUSIVE OR has three principal uses. When all bits in the second operand are 1, all bits in the first operand are reversed, forming the ones complement:

First operand before XOR	1010	1100	1001
Second operand	1111	1111	1111
First operand after XOR	0101	0011	0110

A second use is to set the first operand to zeros by using the same bits to form the second operand. No such bits can be exclusive.

First operand before XOR	1010	1100	1001
Second operand	1010	1100	1001
First operand after XOR	0000	0000	0000

A third use is to interchange the contents of two fields without moving either to a separate save area. Assume that two bytes named A and B are to be interchanged, where A contains 10101010 and B contains 11110000. We use XOR three times, alternating first and second operands:

Instruction	XC A,B	XC B,A	XC A,B
First operand before XOR	10101010	11110000	01011010
Second operand	11110000	01011010	10101010
First operand after XOR	01011010	10101010	11110000

The first column shows A changed to 01011010, the second shows B changed to 10101010, and the third shows A changed to 11110000. At the end of the three instructions, A and B are interchanged.

Test Under Mask Instruction

Test Under Mask (TM) is a type SI instruction to test individual bits within a single byte. Each 1 bit in the eight-bit mask tests the corresponding bit position for 0 or 1. Any position having a 0 bit in the mask is ignored. The condition code is set as shown in Figure 13–1.

The condition code settings have been chosen to permit the same mnemonics used in other conditional branch statements. For example:

MNEMONIC	MEANING AFTER TM	MEANING AFTER OTHER COMPARISONS
BZ	Branch if all zeros	Branch if zero
BM	Branch if mixed bits	Branch if minus
BO	Branch if all ones	Branch on overflow

Byte to be tested:	01010101	01010101	01010101
Mask:	11000011	10100010	01010000
Result of bits tested:	01xxxx01	0x0xxx0x	x1x1xxxx
Condition:	Mixed	All 0	All 1
Condition code setting:	1 or <	0 or =	3 or overflow

Figure 13–1 Condition code settings by Test Under Mask (TM)

POSITION	MEANING
0	U.S. citizen
1	Florida resident
2	College graduate
3	Registered voter
4	Automobile owner
5	Over 65
6	Home owner
7	Property tax paid

Figure 13–2 Values of bits in the STATUS byte

Example 1: Send letter to Florida resident home owners whose property tax is unpaid:

```
IF       TM    STATUS,B'01000010'   IF Fla. resident and home owner
         BNO   ENDIF                  *
AND      TM    STATUS,B'00000001'   AND tax not paid
         BO    ENDIF                  *
THEN     BAL   10,SENDLTR             THEN send letter
ENDIF    EQU   *                    ENDIF
```

Example 2: Hire U.S. citizen who is college graduate not over 65:

```
IF       TM    STATUS,B'10100000'   IF citizen and graduate
         BNO   ENDIF                  *
AND      TM    STATUS,B'00000100'   AND NOT over 65
         BO    ENDIF                  *
THEN     BAL   10,HIRE                THEN hire
ENDIF    EQU   *                    ENDIF
```

Example 3: Call anyone who is home owner or registered voter but not both:

```
IF       TM    STATUS,B'00010010'   IF either home owner or voter
         BNM   ENDIF                  But not both
THEN     BAL   10,CALL                THEN call
ENDIF    EQU   *                    ENDIF
```

Figure 13–3 Examples of TM instruction to select characteristics from STATUS byte

To illustrate TM instructions, assume that STATUS is a byte in which each 1 bit indicates the presence of a characteristic and a 0 bit its absence. Figure 13–2 shows the meanings of the bits. Figure 13–3 shows three examples of using the TM instruction to select characteristics from the STATUS byte.

We can tell whether bits are mixed with a single Test Under Mask, but we cannot tell which bit is the 0 and which the 1 without a second test. Sometimes three or more tests are necessary to determine the setting of each group or individual bit.

Programming Tips

- Use AND instructions to set selected bits to zero; use OR instructions to set selected bits to one.
- Use XOR instructions to reverse selected bits, to set all bits in a field to zeros, or to interchange contents of two registers or fields.
- Use the TM instruction to analyze the setting of any individual bit within a byte.

ADVANCED EDITING

As we have seen earlier, the Edit (ED) instruction is one of the more powerful in the entire instruction set. Now we will explore more advanced editing features.

Multiple Field Editing

Sometimes we have several similar fields close together in main storage that we wish to print close together in a print line. Rather than use several consecutive MVC and ED instructions to set up each pattern and edit the data, we can edit more than one field with the same pattern.

A special code, X'22', is called the *field separator*. When it is encountered in the edit pattern, it turns off the significance indicator and then is replaced by the fill character. This causes leading zeros in the next field to be suppressed.

The sign position at the end of the first packed field will be bypassed. Any valid sign in the rightmost four bits of a packed decimal field will not be selected. Any four bits with values 0 through 9 will be selected and expanded to character form.

As an example, we have four two-byte fields representing three-digit test scores. We wish to print them on the print line, edited, with two spaces between fields. The results are:

Packed decimal fields:	082C091C100C088C
Editing pattern:	40202120222220212022222021202222202120
Data after editing (hex):	4040F8F2404040F9F14040F1F0F0404040F8F8
Prints as:	b b 8 2 b b b 9 1 b b 1 0 0 b b b 8 8

If we have at least two blank spaces after the last field in the print line, we can make our edit pattern more readable by defining it as follows:

```
PATRN    DS    0CL21
         DC    X'40'
         DC    4XL5'2021202222'
```

Check Protection

When printing dollar amounts on checks, certificates, or anything of value, it is good practice to fill in the high order positions to prevent someone from writing in a higher value. This is called *check protection*. The most common symbols to replace the leading zeros are dollar signs ($) and asterisks (*). We make the fill character the dollar sign (X'5B') or the asterisk (X'5C') instead of the space (X'40'). Here are two examples:

Packed decimal field:	0000875C	1234567C
Editing pattern:	5B20206B2020 214C2020	5C20206B2020 214C2020
Data after editing (hex):	5B5B5B5B5B5B F84CF7F5	5CF1F26BF3F4 F54CF6F7
Prints as:	$ $ $ $ $ $ 8 . 7 5	* 1 2 , 3 4 5 . 6 7

Editing Negative Amounts

As a carryover from punched card days, negative amounts have often been indicated by placing the CR symbol to the right of the amount. We may place any message characters we wish to the right of the last digit select character in the edit pattern. If the sign of the packed field is positive (X'C'), the significance indicator is turned off and the message characters are blanked out. If the sign is negative (X'D'), the indicator remains on, and remaining message characters print.

Thus we could indicate negative amounts by the symbols CR or DB, a minus sign (−), one or more asterisks (* or ***), or a word (OVERDRAFT). Here are two examples:

Packed decimal field:	00875D	12345C
Editing pattern:	402020214C20 20C3D9	402020214C20 20C3D9
Data after editing (hex):	404040F84CF7 F5C3D9	40F1F2F34CF4 F54040
Prints as:	b b b 8 . 7 5 C R	b 1 2 3 . 4 5 b b

The negative sign in the first example left the significance indicator ON so that the CR symbol printed. The positive sign in the second example turned the indicator OFF, blanking out the CR message characters.

Edit and Mark Instruction

We may wish to print a single dollar sign or minus sign immediately to the left of the first significant digit. The Edit and Mark (EDMK) instruction inserts into R1 the address of the point where the first significant digit is inserted in the editing pattern. We can then subtract 1 from R1 and use it for explicit addressing to move in the desired character.

Figure 13–4 shows a routine to do this operation, together with results from two different sets of data.

```
MVC     PRAMOUNT,PATTERN        Move in edit pattern
EDMK    PRAMOUNT,PKAMOUNT       Edit and put address in R1
BCTR    1,0                     Subtract 1 from R1
MVI     0(1),C'$'               Move in dollar sign
```

RESULTS WITH TWO DIFFERENT SETS OF DATA

Packed decimal field:	00875C	12345C
Editing pattern:	402020214C2020	402020214C2020
Data after EDMK:	404040F84CF7F5	40F1F2F34CF4F5
Address in R1:	PRAMOUNT+3	PRAMOUNT+1
Data after MVI:	40405BF84CF7F5	5BF1F2F34CF4F5
Prints as:	b b $ 8 . 7 5	$ 1 2 3 . 4 5

Figure 13–4 Examples of Edit and Mark (EDMK) instruction

```
MVC     PRAMOUNT,PATRN          Move in edit pattern
LA      1,PRAMOUNT+4            Preload R1 with address of decimal point
EDMK    PRAMOUNT,PKAMOUNT       Edit and mark
BCTR    1,0                     Subtract 1 from R1
MVI     0(1),C'$'               Move in dollar sign
```

Packed decimal field:	00008C
Edit pattern:	402020214C2020
Data after EDMK	404040404CF0F8
Address in R1:	PRAMOUNT+4 Significance forced before digit found
Data after MVI	4040405B4CF0F8
Prints as	b b b $. 0 8

Figure 13–5 EDMK instruction with address preloaded into R1

```
         LA      1,PRAMOUNT+4
         MVC     PRAMOUNT,PATRN
         ED      PRAMOUNT,PKAMOUNT
IF       CP      PKAMOUNT,=P'0'        IF amount is negative
         BNM     ENDIF                   *
THEN     BCTR    1,0                     THEN insert minus sign
         MVI     0(1),C'-'               *
ENDIF    EQU     *                     ENDIF
```

Figure 13–6 EDMK instruction to insert minus sign

A problem occurs when no significant digit is found, and significance is forced ON by an X'21' character. In this case, no address is placed in R1, and the results of the BCTR and MVI instructions are unpredictable. To avoid this problem, we preload the address of the decimal point (or other limit on zero suppression) into R1 before the EDMK. Figure 13–5 shows an example.

To print a minus sign in front of a possibly negative amount requires testing to see whether the minus sign should be inserted or left blank. Figure 13–6 shows a possible approach.

LOGICAL SHIFT INSTRUCTIONS

We may shift bits right or left within single registers or register pairs as logical data. Unlike the arithmetic shift instructions, the logical shifts do not regard the leftmost bit as a sign. It moves just like any other bit. Bits shifted out of the register are lost. Vacated positions in either direction are filled with 0 bits. The condition code is not set by any of the logical shifts.

Single Register Shifts

Shift Left Logical (SLL) and Shift Right Logical (SRL) affect a single register only. They are type RX instructions, but only the rightmost six bits of the address indicate the number of bits to shift. Bits 12 to 15 (index register) of the machine instruction are ignored. Usually only the displacement is used with the second operand. Operand 1 names the register to be shifted.

In the following examples we shall use only an eight-bit register for illustration. Figure 13–7 shows the results after each instruction is executed in sequence.

Double Register Shifts

Shift Left Double Logical (SLDL) and Shift Right Double Logical (SRDL) affect even-odd register pairs. The even-numbered register is the first operand of this type RX instruction. As with SLL and SRL, bits 12 to 15 (index register)

OBJECT CODE	INSTRUCTION	REGISTER 5
(Original contents of R5)		1001 0101
89 50 00 01	SLL 5,1	0010 1010
88 50 00 02	SRL 5,2	0000 1010
89 50 00 04	SLL 5,4	1010 0000
88 50 00 06	SRL 5,6	0000 0010

Figure 13–7 Single register logical shifts

OBJECT CODE	INSTRUCTION	REGISTER 6	REGISTER 7
(Original contents of R6 and R7)		1001 0101	1111 0001
8D 60 00 03	SLDL 6,3	1010 1111	1000 1000
8C 60 00 04	SRDL 6,4	0000 1010	1111 1000
8D 60 00 08	SLDL 6,8	1111 1000	0000 0000
8C 60 00 05	SRDL 6,5	0000 0111	1100 0000
8D 60 00 02	SLDL 6,2	0001 1111	0000 0000

Figure 13–8 Double register logical shifts

are ignored in the machine instruction, and only the rightmost six bits of the address indicate the number of bits to be shifted.

The examples in Figure 13–8 show R6 and R7 as a pair after execution of some SLDL and SRDL instructions. Only eight bits are used in each register.

OTHER LOGICAL OPERATIONS

There are many instructions to move, add, subtract, and compare logical data in addition to those already treated in the text. Here we shall identify and explain some of them.

Data Movement

Move Characters Long (MVCL) is a type RR instruction that permits movement of fields longer than 256 bytes in main storage. Each operand R1 and R2 refers to an even-odd register pair. Four registers therefore contain data needed to carry out the instruction. To illustrate the function of each register, we write:

```
MVCL 6,8
```

R6, R7, R8, and R9 are all used. The leftmost eight bits in R6, R7, and R8 are ignored. The rightmost 24 bits of each register specify an address or a length. R6 indicates the address of the first operand, that is, the receiving field in main storage. R7 gives the length of the receiving field. R8 gives the address of the sending field. R9 gives the length of the sending field.

If the sending field is longer than the receiving field, the excess bytes are truncated. If the receiving field is the longer, the excess bytes are padded with the *pad* character specified in the leftmost eight bits of R9.

If the fields overlap so that part of the receiving field becomes the source of data, no movement takes place, and the condition code is set.

Possible settings of the condition code are:

```
LA      6,DEST             Set destination address
LA      7,600              Set destination length
LA      8,SOURCE           Set source address
LA      9,500              Set source length
O       9,=X'40000000'     Set pad char. in leftmost byte of R9
MVCL    6,8
```

Figure 13–9 Move Characters Long (MVCL) instruction

0 (equal)	Fields are the same length
1 (low)	Receiving field is shorter
2 (high)	Receiving field is longer
3	Destructive overlap; no movement performed

The instructions in Figure 13–9 move a 500-byte source field into a 600-byte destination field and pad the last 100 bytes with spaces.

Move Inverse (MVCIN) is a type SS instruction. Length is specified for the first operand only. Data is moved from the second operand and placed in the first operand with the left-to-right sequence of the bytes inverted. When fields overlap, results may be unpredictable. The instruction

```
MVCIN PRLINE(80),INRECD
```

puts the contents of INRECD into PRLINE in inverse order of columns.

Insert Character (IC) and Store Character (STC) are type RX instructions that move a single byte between main storage and the rightmost eight bits of a general register. The leftmost 24 bits of the register are unaffected. The condition code is not set. IC moves the byte from storage to the register, and STC moves in the opposite direction.

Insert Characters under Mask (ICM) and Store Characters under Mask (STCM) are type RS instructions with format

```
OP R1,M3,S2 or OP R1,M3,D2(B2)
```

M3 is a four-bit mask corresponding to the four byte positions in R1. The second operand refers to the address of one to four consecutive bytes in main storage. ICM inserts a byte from the storage field into R1 in each byte corresponding to a 1 bit in the mask. The STCM selects bytes from the register corresponding to 1 bits in the mask and stores them in consecutive positions in storage. Each 0 bit causes the corresponding byte to be ignored. If we give the instructions

```
ICM  7,B'1101',FULLWORD
STCM 7,B'0011',FULLWORD
```

the results would be as follows:

	REGISTER 7	FULLWORD
Contents before ICM	00000000	C1C2C3C4
Contents after ICM	C1C200C3	C1C2C3C4
Contents after STCM	C1C200C4	00C4C3C4

The condition code after STCM is unchanged. After ICM it is set as follows:

0 All inserted bits are zeros, or the mask is zero
1 Leftmost bit inserted is one
2 Leftmost bit inserted is zero, but some other bits are 1
3 Not used

Addition and Subtraction

Logical addition is performed by the Add Logical (AL) and Add Logical Register (ALR) instructions. AL is of type RX, while ALR is type RR. They are identical except for the location of the second operand. Each operand is considered to be a 32-bit unsigned binary number. After they are added, the condition code is set as follows:

0 Sum is zero, with no carry
1 Sum is not zero, with no carry
2 Sum is zero, with carry
3 Sum is not zero, with carry

We can add a 64-bit integer in storage to an even-odd register pair with the following routine:

```
         AL    7,DOUBLE+4    Add rightmost 32 bits to odd register
IF       BC    12,ENDIF      IF carry
THEN     AL    6,=F'1'         THEN add 1 to even register
ENDIF    EQU   *             ENDIF
         A     6,DOUBLE      Add leftmost 32 bits to even register
```

Logical subtraction is done with the Subtract Logical (SL) and Subtract Logical Register (SLR) instructions. SL is of type RX, while SLR is type RR. They operate identically except for the location of the second operand. The ones complement of the second operand is added to the first operand and then 1 is added. (This assures a carry when subtracting zero.)

The condition code is set as follows:

0 Not used
1 Difference is not zero, with no carry

2 Difference is zero, with carry
3 Difference is not zero, with carry

Comparison

Compare Logical (CL) and Compare Logical Register (CLR) work exactly like Compare Logical Characters (CLC) except in the length and location of the operands. Both CL and CLR compare 32 bits in the operand-1 general register with 32 bits in operand 2. CL is a type RX instruction, with operand 2 in a fullword in main storage. CLR has operand 2 in another register.

The condition code is set to 0, 1, or 2 respectively if the first operand is equal to, lower than, or higher than the second operand. There is no overflow.

Compare Logical Characters Under Mask (CLM) has the format

`OP R1,M3,S2` or `OP R1,M3,D2(B2)`

and constructs the values to be compared in a manner similar to ICM and STCM. The bytes in R1 corresponding to 1 bits in the mask are compared with consecutive bytes in the operand 2 field in storage. Bytes corresponding to 0 bits in the mask are not compared.

The condition code is set as follows:

0 Selected bytes are equal, or the mask is zero
1 Selected field of first operand is low
2 Selected field of first operand is high
3 Not used

Compare Logical Long (CLCL) is a type RR instruction using two even-odd register pairs in the same way that MVCL does. In the instruction

```
CLCL 6,8
```

R6 contains the address of the first operand, R7 its length, R8 the address of operand 2, and R9 its length. Each address or length uses only the rightmost 24 bits of the register. The leftmost eight bits of R9 contains the pad byte, which is used to extend the length of operand 2 before the comparison if it is shorter than operand 1.

The comparison proceeds left to right and ends as soon as an inequality is found or the end of the longer operand is reached. The condition code is set as follows:

0 Operands are equal, or both lengths are zero
1 First operand is low
2 First operand is high

Compare and Swap (CS) and Compare Double and Swap (CDS) are both type RS instructions that compare two values and replace one of the two. The format is

```
OP R1,R3,S2 or OP R1,R3,D2(B2)
```

CS compares 32 bits in R1 with a fullword in main storage. CDS compares 64 bits in the even-odd register pair specified in R1 with a doubleword in main storage. If the two operands are equal, the contents of R3 are stored at the operand 2 location. If they are different, the contents of operand 2 replace operand 1. The condition code is set as follows:

0 First two operands are equal; second operand replaced by third
1 First two operands are unequal; first operand replaced by second
2 Not used
3 Not used

If we give the instruction

```
CS 6,7,FULLWORD
```

the results from two sets of data would be as follows:

	REGISTER 6	REGISTER 7	FULLWORD	OP-1 = OP-2?
Operands before CS	00043857	00039286	00043857	Yes
Operands after CS	00043857	00039286	00039286	OP-3 => OP-2
Operands before CS	00043857	00055555	0002AD36	No
Operands after CS	0002AD36	00055555	0002AD36	OP-2 => OP-1

Supervisor Call

The Supervisor Call (SVC) is a type RR instruction with format

```
OP I
```

where I is an eight-bit code specifying the code for the interruption. This instruction interrupts the problem program and transfers control to the supervisor. The interruption code is stored, with eight leading zero bits, in bits 16 to 31 of the Program Status Word. Supervisor calls are made for input/output operations, normal end of job, and abnormal terminations.

Programming Tips

- Use a single edit pattern with field separators to edit several packed decimal fields that are adjacent to one another in the same sequence in which they are to be printed.
- When using EDMK, be sure to preload R1 with the address of the byte in which significance will be forced if no significant digit is found previously.
- Logical add, subtract, and compare instructions operate on all 32 bits of a number as unsigned binary data.

TRANSLATE INSTRUCTION

The Translate (TR) instruction permits any eight-bit code in a byte to be changed to any other eight-bit code. TR is a type SS instruction. The first operand is the field in storage to be translated. The second operand is a 256-byte table containing the codes to which translation is made. The length code applies to the first operand only.

Translation proceeds left to right through the first operand field. As each byte is processed, its value becomes a displacement added to the address of the table (second operand). The byte at that position in the table replaces the byte in the first operand. For example, if the first byte in the source field contains the letter A, its value (X'C1' or decimal 193) is added to the address of the table. Whatever byte is at location TABLE + 193 replaces the letter A.

If certain bytes are not to be translated, the table must contain the original byte in its assigned location. In other words, if the letter A is not to be changed, TABLE + 193 must contain C'A' or X'C1'.

Where many bytes in a record are to be translated, it is easier to construct the table with constants. Where only a few are to be changed, as for example changing blanks to zeros or semicolons to commas, the table can first be constructed with original values, and then the bytes that are to be changed can be inserted.

The routine in Figure 13–10 is useful to put original values into a table. In this routine, R3 serves three purposes. It contains the byte to be stored, beginning with the last byte in the table (X'FF'). It is the index register containing the address to be added to that of TABLE. Finally, it is the counter to control the loop.

Once the table is constructed, if we wish to translate blank to zero and semicolon to comma, we would modify the table with these entries:

```
MVI   TABLE+64,C'0'          Move zero to blank location in table
MVI   TABLE+X'5E',X'6B'      Move comma to semicolon location
```

```
         LA    3,255          Put byte value X'FF' into R3
REPEAT   EQU   *              REPEAT
         STC   3,TABLE(3)       Store byte in TABLE + byte value
         BCT   3,REPEAT         Subtract 1 from byte value
UNTIL    EQU   *              UNTIL byte value = zero
         STC   3,TABLE        Store X'00' at first byte in table
```

Figure 13–10 Routine to load table for Translate (TR) instruction

CHARACTERS	EBCDIC	ASCII
A–I	X'C1'–X'C9'	X'41'–X'49'
J–R	X'D1'–X'D9'	X'4A'–X'52'
S–Z	X'E2'–X'E9'	X'53'–X'5A'
0–9	X'F0'–X'F9'	X'30'–X'39'
Space	X'40'	X'20'

```
TABLE    DS    0CL256
         DC    32X'00'
         DC    X'40'                          Translate ASCII space
         DC    15X'00'
         DC    X'F0F1F2F3F4F5F6F7F8F9'        Translate ASCII digits
         DC    7X'00'
         DC    X'C1C2C3C4C5C6C7C8C9'          Translate ASCII A–I
         DC    X'D1D2D3D4D5D6D7D8D9'          Translate ASCII J–R
         DC    X'E2E3E4E5E6E7E8E9'            Translate ASCII S–Z
         DC    165X'00'
```

Figure 13–11 Translation from ASCII to EBCDIC codes

The assembler recognizes operands in character, decimal, or hexadecimal form.

A common translation is to change ASCII code to EBCDIC or vice versa. Figure 13–11 shows the comparable codes for letters and decimal digits and a table to translate these characters from ASCII to EBCDIC. Any other codes will be changed to X'00'.

TRANSLATE AND TEST INSTRUCTION

Like Translate, the Translate and Test (TRT) instruction makes use of a 256-byte table as operand 2. TRT is used to scan a string of characters until it finds one of special interest. All bytes in the table are set to X'00' except the characters we wish to find in the string. In the table positions for those characters, we may place any nonzero hex code.

For example, if we wish to scan a string of numbers for a comma used as a delimiter between numbers, we would create the table with all X'00' except TABLE + 107 (the comma position), where we might place a X'6B' or X'01'. Low hex numbers are normally used.

As the TRT instruction is executed, each byte in the first operand becomes a displacement to refer to a byte in the table. However, the bytes in the first operand are not changed. When a nonzero byte is found in the table, three things happen:

1. The address of the byte in the first operand that found the nonzero table entry is placed into register 1.
2. The nonzero byte from the table is placed in register 2.
3. The condition code is set.

If no nonzero byte is found, R1 and R2 are unchanged.

There are three possible settings of the condition code by TRT:

0 No nonzero byte was found
1 Incomplete (nonzero byte was found before reaching last byte)
2 Complete (nonzero byte was found by last byte of first operand)
3 Not used

The TRT instruction is used primarily to scan an input string of characters for delimiters separating the various fields. This permits processing of variable-length fields and eliminates the use of blank spaces to pad out the fields. The address of the first byte to be scanned is loaded into one register. That address is subtracted from R1, which contains the address of the delimiter between fields. The difference between the two is the length of the field.

EXECUTE INSTRUCTION

Before we give examples of TRT, we must explain the Execute (EX) instruction, which normally is used with TRT. EX is a type RX instruction that operates somewhat like the Branch and Link (BAL). Its format is

```
OP R1,S2 or OP R1,S2(X2) or OP R1,D2(X2,B2)
```

The second operand is the name (or address) of a single instruction out of the main path of the program. EX causes the rightmost byte in the operand-1 register to be ORed with the second byte of the operand-2 instruction. Then that instruction is executed, and control returns to the instruction following EX.

EX permits moving or packing a variable number of bytes. The length code for the number of bytes to be processed is placed into the operand-1 register. The second operand then effectively moves or packs that number of bytes. A TRT instruction can also be the second operand of an EX instruction to translate a specified number of bytes.

The second byte of the instruction executed is not actually changed in main storage. The ORing takes place in the internal circuitry of the control unit.

For example, let R5 contain X'00000004' as the length code for a five-byte field. (Recall that the length code is always one less than the actual length.) We issue the instruction

```
EX 5,MOVEINST
```

MOVEINST is defined as:

OBJECT CODE	NAME	INSTRUCTION
D20040003000	MOVEINST	MVC 0(0,4),0(3)

EX causes the length code in the second byte of MOVEINST to be treated as X'04' instead of X'00'. Five bytes are moved from the location specified in R3 to that stated in R4.

To illustrate TRT and EX, suppose we have two integers separated by a comma and followed by a space. Either integer can be up to 15 digits in length. Our job is to scan the string, find the comma, determine the length of the first number, pack it into a doubleword, scan the rest of the string for the blank, pack the second number into another doubleword, and add the two doublewords together. Figure 13–12 shows the routine.

In Figure 13–12, the table is set so that X'01' is placed in R2 when a comma is found and X'02' when a space is found. We go through the loop twice, processing one field each time. R2 is cleared so that only the value 1 or 2 will be in the register. R3 points to the start of each field in STRING. R5 counts a loop to process the two fields. R6 points in turn to each doubleword into which we pack. R7 is loaded with 1 or 2 to compare that the correct delimiter for each field is found. The TRT instruction has a length of 16 to test for a maximum of 15 bytes plus the delimiter.

The first time through the loop, R3 has the address of STRING and R1 will contain the address of the comma, STRING+7. The difference between R1 and R3 is the length of 7. The BCTR changes this to the correct length code of 6. The EX instruction has this effect:

Contents of rightmost byte of R1	0000 0110	(Length code 6)
Second byte of PACKINST	0111 0000	(OP-1 length code 7)
Result after ORing second byte	0111 0110	(Length codes 7 and 6)

When PACKINST is executed the first time, it packs the seven-byte string into the eight-byte doubleword.

The instruction LA 3,2(1,3) places the starting address of the next field into R3 in this way:

```
         MVI   TABLE+64,X'02'      Identify blank with X'02'
         MVI   TABLE+107,X'01'     Identify comma with X'01'
         SR    2,2                 Clear R2
         LA    3,STRING            Set string address
         LA    5,2                 Set R5 to count 2 fields
         LA    6,DOUBLE1           Set R6 to first doubleword
         LA    7,1                 Put code for comma in R7
REPEAT   EQU   *                   REPEAT
         TRT   0(16,3),TABLE         TRT up to 15 bytes at string
IF       BZ    ELSE                  IF delimiter found
AND      CR    2,7                   AND delimiter is correct code
         BNE   ELSE                  *
THEN     SR    1,3                     Get length of field
         BCTR  1,0                     Set length code (L-1)
         EX    1,PACKINST              Pack field into doubleword
         B     ENDIF                   *
ELSE     BAL   10,ERROR              ELSE process error routine
ENDIF    EQU   *                     ENDIF
         LA    3,2(1,3)              Set R3 to start of next field
         LA    6,8(6)                Set R6 to next doubleword
         LA    7,2                   Put code for space in R7
         BCT   5,REPEAT              Subtract 1 from loop count
UNTIL    EQU   *                   UNTIL loop count = 0
         AP    DOUBLE1,DOUBLE2     Add numbers together
         .
TABLE    DC    256X'00'
STRING   DC    C'4328794,12579'
         DC    C' '
PACKINST PACK  0(8,6),0(0,3)       Object code: F2 70 60 00 30 00
DOUBLE1  DS    D
DOUBLE2  DS    D
```

Figure 13–12 TRT routine to add two variable-length integers

Previous contents of R3	A(STRING)
Length code in R1	6
Displacement	2
New address placed in R3	A(STRING + 8)

We do not illustrate the error routine. An error could occur in two ways: a condition code of zero could appear, indicating that no delimiter was found in 16 bytes; or the wrong delimiter could be found and placed in R2, not agreeing with R7. The error routine could simply terminate processing, print a general error message, or determine which specific error occurred and print either of two messages.

Programming Tips

- To construct a translate table, find the relative location (X'00' to X'FF') of the byte to be translated. In that location put the hex code for the byte to which you wish to translate.
- For use with TRT, the 256-byte table must contain X'00' in each position except the relative locations representing the bytes for which you are scanning. Those usually contain a low hexadecimal value.
- The length code in a register used as the first operand in an EX instruction must be one less than the actual length of the field to be processed.

PROGRAM 13: SCANNING CHARACTER STRINGS

Program 13 involves preparation of mailing labels. Each field of the name and address is variable in length, with a maximum of 30 bytes per field. If the field is longer than 30 bytes, only the first 30 are printed. Each label may contain up to six lines. Each line in the record is ended with a slash (/) and the record is terminated with two consecutive slashes (//). The end of data is indicated by /*.

Normally, data for such a program would come from tape or disk files. However, we shall define constants to be better able to compare the input data with the labels produced.

Ordinarily, when printing labels, we would use a carriage control tape with a punch in channel 1 at the start of each label. Instead, we will skip to channel 1 for the first label and then count eight lines for each label. If the record has fewer than eight fields, we will print blank lines to complete the eight for each label.

If the input data does not contain a slash or asterisk within 100 bytes, we cancel the program.

Figure 13–13 shows the assembler listing, and Figure 13–14 shows the program output.

SUMMARY

Logical instructions permit individual bits within bytes to be manipulated in a number of ways. OR, AND, and EXCLUSIVE OR instructions are available in RR, RX, SI, and SS formats. OR may be used to set selected bits to

```
  LOC  OBJECT CODE    ADDR1 ADDR2  STMT   SOURCE STATEMENT                                     DOS/VSE ASSEMBLER 14.09 86-03-28

                                      1 ***********************************************************************
                                      2 *                    ALTON R. KINDRED, PROGRAM 13
                                      3 * THIS PROGRAM READS AN INPUT CHARACTER STRING AND PRODUCES MAILING
                                      4 * LABELS CONTAINING UP TO SIX LINES FOR NAME AND ADDRESS.  EACH FIELD
                                      5 * IN THE STRING MAY BE UP TO 30 BYTES LONG AND IS TERMINATED WITH A
                                      6 * SLASH.  EACH RECORD ENDS WITH TWO CONSECUTIVE SLASHES, EXCEPT THAT
                                      7 * /* FOLLOWS THE LAST RECORD.
                                      8 *        REGISTERS USED:
                                      9 *                R1 - ADDRESS OF DELIMITER IN TRANSLATE AND TEST
                                     10 *                R2 - DELIMITER CODE IN TRT TABLE
                                     11 *                R3 - STARTING FIELD ADDRESS
                                     12 *                R9-R10 - LINK REGISTERS
                                     13 *                R12 - BASE REGISTER
                                     14 ***********************************************************************
                                     15          PRINT NOGEN
000000                               16 MAINLINE START 0                          SET LOCATION COUNTER
                                     17 *        STM   14,12,12(13)               SAVE REGISTERS FOR OS          OS
000000 05C0                          18          BALR  12,0                       LOAD BASE REGISTER
                         00002       19          USING *,12                       DESIGNATE BASE REGISTER
                                     20 *        ST    13,SAVE+4                  STORE REGISTER 13              OS
                                     21 *        LA    13,SAVE                    LOAD SAVE AREA ADDRESS         OS
                                     22 *        OPEN  (PRINTER,(OUTPUT))         OPEN FILE                      OS
                                     23          OPEN  PRINTER                    OPEN FILE                      DOS
000012 4590 C02A               0002C 31          BAL   9,INITIAL                  DO INITIAL PROCESSING
000016 4590 C048               0004A 32          BAL   9,MAINLOOP                 DO MAIN PROCESSING LOOP
                                     33          CLOSE PRINTER                    CLOSE FILE                     DOS
                                     41          EOJ                                                             DOS
                                     44 *        CLOSE (PRINTER)                  CLOSE FILE                     OS
                                     45 *        L     13,SAVE+4                  LOAD SAVE AREA ADDRESS         OS
                                     46 *        LM    14,12,12(13)               RESTORE REGISTERS              OS
                                     47 *        BR    14                         RETURN TO OS                   OS
                                     48 ***********************************************************************
                                     49 *                FIRST LEVEL MODULES
                                     50 ***********************************************************************
                                     51 *
                                     52 *                SET INITIAL VALUES MODULE
                                     53 *
00002C D7FF C2E4 C2E4 002E6 002E6    54 INITIAL  XC    TABLE,TABLE                SET TABLE TO BINARY ZEROS
000032 9201 C345      00347          55          MVI   TABLE+97,X'01'             SET CODE 1 FOR SLASH
000036 9202 C340      00342          56          MVI   TABLE+92,X'02'             SET CODE 2 FOR ASTERISK
00003A 1822                          57          SR    2,2                        CLEAR R2
00003C 45A0 C0C8            000CA    58          BAL   10,CLEAR                   CLEAR PRINT LINE
000040 92F1 C1AB      001AD          59          MVI   PRLINE,C'1'                SET TO SKIP TO NEW PAGE
000044 4130 C230            00232    60          LA    3,INPUT                    SET STARTING STRING ADDRESS
000048 07F9                          61          BR    9                          RETURN
                                     62 *
                                     63 *                MAIN PROCESSING LOOP
                                     64 *
                            0004A    65 MAINLOOP EQU   *
00004A 955C 3000      00000          66 DOWHILE  CLI   0(3),C'*'                  DOWHILE CHARACTER IS NOT *
00004E 4780 C0A2      000A4          67          BE    ENDDO                        *
000052 F810 C2E2 C406 002E4 00408    68          ZAP   LINECNT,=P'0'                SET LINE COUNT TO ZERO
                            00058    69 REPEAT   EQU   *                            REPEAT
000058 DD1E 3000 C2E4 00000 002E6    70          TRT   0(31,3),TABLE                  TRANSLATE 31 BYTES
00005E 4780 C06C      0006E          71 IF       BZ    ELSE                           IF SLASH FOUND
000062 45A0 C0A4            000A6    72 THEN     BAL   10,PROCESS                       PROCESS FIELD
000066 45A0 C0B2            000B4    73          BAL   10,PRDETAIL                      PRINT THE LINE
00006A 47F0 C070      00072          74          B     ENDIF                            *
                            0006E    75 ELSE     EQU   *                              ELSE
00006E 45A0 C0D4            000D6    76          BAL   10,TOOLONG                       DO TOO LONG ROUTINE
                            00072    77 ENDIF    EQU   *                              ENDIF
000072 955C 3000      00000          78          CLI   0(3),C'*'                      *
000076 4780 C080      00082          79          BE    UNTIL                          *
00007A 9561 3000      00000          80          CLI   0(3),C'/'                      *
00007E 4770 C056      00058          81          BNE   REPEAT                         *
                            00082    82 UNTIL    EQU   *                            UNTIL NEXT BYTE IS / OR *
000082 F910 C2E2 C407 002E4 00409    83 DOWHILE2 CP    LINECNT,=P'8'                DOWHILE LINECOUNT <= 8
000088 4780 C092      00094          84          BNL   ENDDO2                         *
00008C 45A0 C0B2            000B4    85          BAL   10,PRDETAIL                    PRINT BLANK LINE
000090 47F0 C080      00082          86          B     DOWHILE2                       *
                            00094    87 ENDDO2   EQU   *                            ENDDO
000094 9561 3000      00000          88 IF2      CLI   0(3),C'/'                    IF NEXT BYTE IS /
000098 4770 C09E      000A0          89          BNE   ENDIF2                       *
00009C 4133 0001            00001    90 THEN2    LA    3,1(3)                         THEN ADJUST ADDRESS
                            000A0    91 ENDIF2   EQU   *                            ENDIF
0000A0 47F0 C048      0004A          92          B     DOWHILE                        *
                            000A4    93 ENDDO    EQU   *                          ENDDO
0000A4 07F9                          94          BR    9                          RETURN
                                     95 ***********************************************************************
                                     96 *                SECOND LEVEL MODULES
                                     97 ***********************************************************************
                                     98 *
                                     99 *                PROCESS FIELD MODULE
                                    100 *
0000A6 1813                         101 PROCESS  SR    1,3                        CALCULATE LENGTH
0000A8 0610                         102          BCTR  1,0                        COMPUTE LENGTH CODE
0000AA 4410 C3E4            003E6   103          EX    1,MOVEINST                 MOVE FIELD TO PRINT LINE
0000AE 4131 3002            00002   104          LA    3,2(1,3)                   ADJ. ADDR. TO NEXT FIELD
0000B2 07FA                         105          BR    10                         RETURN
                                    106 *
                                    107 *                PRINT DETAIL LINE MODULE
                                    108 *
                                    109 PRDETAIL PUT   PRINTER,PRLINE             PRINT LINE
0000C4 FA10 C2E2 C408 002E4 0040A   115          AP    LINECNT,=P'1'              ADD 1 TO LINE COUNT
0000CA 9240 C1AB      001AD         116 CLEAR    MVI   PRLINE,C' '                CLEAR PRINT LINE
0000CE D283 C1AC C1AB 001AE 001AD   117          MVC   PRLINE+1(132),PRLINE       *
```

Figure 13–13 Assembler listing of Program 13

```
  LOC  OBJECT CODE    ADDR1 ADDR2  STMT   SOURCE STATEMENT                                   DOS/VSE ASSEMBLER 14.09 86-03-28

0000D4 07FA                         118            BR    10                      RETURN
                                    119 *
                                    120 *                STRING TOO LONG MODULE
                                    121 *
0000D6 D21D C1AC 3000 001AE 00000   122 TOOLONG    MVC   PRLINE+1(30),0(3)       MOVE 30 BYTES TO PRINT LINE
0000DC 4133 001E            0001E   123            LA    3,30(3)                 SET STRING UP BY 30
0000E0 DD63 3000 C2E4 00000 002E6   124            TRT   0(100,3),TABLE          SCAN 100 BYTES FOR DELIMITER
0000E6 4770 C0EC      000EE         125 IF3        BNZ   ELSE3                   IF NOT FOUND
                                    126 THEN3      CANCEL ,                        THEN CANCEL
                            000EE   131 ELSE3      EQU   *                       ELSE
0000EE 4131 0001            00001   132            LA    3,1(1)                    SET TO NEXT FIELD
                            000F2   133 ENDIF3     EQU   *                       ENDIF
0000F2 07FA                         134            BR    10                      RETURN

                                    136 ********************************************************************DOS
                                    137 *                FILE DEFINITIONS AND I/O AREAS                      DOS
                                    138 ********************************************************************DOS
                                    139 PRINTER    DTFPR BLKSIZE=133,IOAREA1=PRTAREA,DEVICE=1403,            DOSX
                                                         CTLCHR=ASA,DEVADDR=SYS009,WORKA=YES                 DOS
                                    160 *                                                                    DOS
000128                              161 PRTAREA    DS    CL133                                               DOS
                                    162 *********************************************************************OS
                                    163 *                DEVICE CONTROL BLOCKS AND SAVE AREA                  OS
                                    164 *********************************************************************OS
                                    165 *PRINTER DCB     DDNAME=PRINTER,BLKSIZE=133,LRECL=133,                OSX
                                    166 *                MACRF=PMA,DSORG=PS                                   OS
                                    167 *                                                                     OS
                                    168 *SAVE      DS    18F                                                  OS
                                    169 ***********************************************************************
                                    170 *                DATA DEFINITIONS
                                    171 ***********************************************************************
0001AD                              172 PRLINE     DS    CL133
000232 C5C1D9D340C540C2             173 INPUT      DC    C'EARL E BYRD/P O BOX 244/RURAL FL 30599//'
00025A D9D6D3C1D5C440E3             174            DC    C'ROLAND TOSS/284 MAIN ST/APT 17/OLD WESTERN CA 91603//'
00028F C2C5D540C5E5C1D3             175            DC    C'BEN EVALENT/2 SEASIDE MANSION/HEATHCLIFF HEIGHTS/'
0002C0 C1E3D3C1D5E3C9C3             176            DC    C'ATLANTIC HIGHWAY/WESTPORT CT 06880/*'
0002E4                              177 LINECNT    DS    PL2
0002E6                              178 TABLE      DS    XL256
0003E6 D200 C1AC 3000 001AE 00000   179 MOVEINST   MVC   PRLINE+1(0),0(3)
                            00000   180            END   MAINLINE
0003F0 5B5BC2D6D7C5D540             181                  =C'$$BOPEN '
0003F8 5B5BC2C3D3D6E2C5             182                  =C'$$BCLOSE'
000400 000000F8                     183                  =A(PRINTER)
000404 000001AD                     184                  =A(PRLINE)
000408 0C                           185                  =P'0'
000409 8C                           186                  =P'8'
00040A 1C                           187                  =P'1'
```

Figure 13–13 *(Concluded)*

1. AND can set selected bits to 0. EXCLUSIVE OR can set an entire field to zeros, form the ones complement of a field, or interchange two fields. Test Under Mask can test any or all of eight bits and set the condition code to indicate whether they are all zeros, all ones, or mixed.

Editing can be performed to supply check protection symbols, usually dollar signs or asterisks, in place of leading zeros. Negative amounts can be designated with message characters, such as CR symbols or minus signs, to the right of the edited field. Field separator characters in the editing pattern turn off the significance indicator and permit more than one field to be edited with a single instruction.

Bits may be shifted left or right within a single register or register pair. All bits participate; data is considered to be unsigned.

A variety of instructions permit logical data to be moved between fields in storage or between general registers and storage. MVCL utilizes two register pairs for addresses and lengths to move more than 256 bytes and to pad the first field with a specified character if it is longer than the second field. A single byte may be inserted into the rightmost byte of a register with the IC instruction, or stored from there with the STC instruction. ICM and STCM instructions utilize a mask to specify which bytes in a register are to be inserted from or stored in contiguous bytes in storage.

```
EARL E BYRD
P O BOX 244
RURAL FL 30599




ROLAND TOSS
284 MAIN ST
APT 17
OLD WESTERN CA 91603




BEN EVALENT
2 SEASIDE MANSION
HEATHCLIFF HEIGHTS
ATLANTIC HIGHWAY
WESTPORT CT 06880
```

Figure 13–14 Output from Program 13

The contents of a general register may be added to or subtracted from logically, using the AL, ALR, SL, and SLR instructions. The main difference between these operations and other Add and Subtract instructions is their setting of the condition code.

Logical data may be compared between two registers with the CLR instruction and between a register and storage with CL. A mask may be used in the CLM instruction to select one to four bytes in the register to be compared with contiguous bytes in storage. Two fields in storage of more than 256 bytes may be compared with the CLCL instruction, which uses two register pairs to hold addresses, lengths, and pad character. Contents of one register or a register pair may be compared with a fullword or doubleword in storage with the CS or CDS instructions, and one of the operands is replaced by a third operand.

The SVC transfers control from the application program to the supervisor and transmits a one-byte code giving the reason for the interruption.

The Translate (TR) instruction permits any eight-bit code to be changed to any other within each byte in a field. A 256-byte table contains the function byte in the position in the table corresponding to the argument byte.

The Translate and Test (TRT) instruction uses a 256-byte table to scan a string of characters for codes of special interest. When a character references a nonzero byte in the table, the character address is placed into R1 and the byte from the table in R2. The condition code is set to determine whether a nonzero byte was found before the end of the character string, by the last byte in the string, or not found at all.

The Execute (EX) instruction ORs the rightmost byte of the operand-1 general register with the second byte of an instruction named as the second operand. Then it executes the modified instruction and returns immediately to the instruction following EX.

TERMS FOR REVIEW

AND
Boolean logic
Check protection symbol
Compare Logical (CL)
EXCLUSIVE OR
Execute (EX)
Insert Character (IC)
Logical instructions
Move Inverse (MVCIN)
Multiple field editing
OR
Pad character
Scan
Store Character (STC)
Test Under Mask (TM)
Translate (TR)
Translate and Test (TRT)
Truth tables

REVIEW QUESTIONS

1. Distinguish between arithmetic operations and logical operations.
2. Explain the main uses of OR and AND instructions in setting switches or status bytes.
3. Describe three uses of the EXCLUSIVE OR instruction.
4. How is logical subtraction performed in the SL and SLR instructions? How does the final result differ from ordinary subtraction?
5. Explain operation of the Translate instruction.
6. Explain how Translate differs from the Translate and Test instruction. What is the chief use of the latter?
7. Explain operation of the Execute instruction. Where is the field named as its second operand usually found?
8. Explain how to determine the length of a field once a delimiter has been found in a TRT instruction.

EXERCISES

1. Write one or more instructions to test a byte named STATUS and branch to THEN if bits 2 and 3 are set to 0 and bit 6 is set to 1.

2. You have five two-byte packed decimal fields in an area named SCORES. You wish to print them as edited integers three bytes apart on a print line. Write data definitions and instructions to do this using a single edit pattern.
3. You have a table of ten temperature readings, each in a two-byte packed decimal field. Write a loop to edit each field separately to print four bytes apart on a print line. If the temperature is less than zero, insert a minus sign (−) in front of the first significant digit in the temperature.
4. Write single or double logical shift instructions to do each of these:
   a. Shift the leftmost four bits of R7 into the rightmost four bit positions.
   b. Shift all bits from R7 into R6.
   c. Shift the rightmost eight bits of R7 and the leftmost eight bits of R6 until they occupy the rightmost 16 bits of R6 and all other bit positions are zeros.
5. Write instructions to move 800 bytes from SOURCE to 1000 bytes at DEST, padding the extra 200 bytes with character zeros.
6. Use IC and STC instructions to move a byte from BYTE1 to BYTE2.
7. Write instructions to insert the first two bytes of INRECD into the first and fourth bytes of R7.
8. Write instructions to compare the first, third, and fourth bytes of R7 with three consecutive bytes at CHECK.
9. Construct a table to translate the codes for the decimal digits from X'F0' through X'F9' to X'00' through X'09'.
10. A series of integers is separated by commas. Write instructions to examine the string for the first comma and pack the first number into DOUBLE. Then initialize addresses to the start of the next field.

PROGRAMMING PROBLEMS

1. A student file uses a byte called STATUS to indicate eight different characteristics of each student. A 1 bit indicates YES to the characteristic, and a 0 indicates NO. The characteristics are indicated in the following bits:

0	Citizen	4	Financial aid
1	Resident	5	Graduate
2	Full-time	6	Honors
3	Veteran	7	Auto permit

   Write a program to define the following data in a table and print a report showing the student name and the word YES or NO under a column heading for each of the eight characteristics. Use the Test Under Mask instruction.

NAME (01–20)	STATUS (21)
JAY BIRD	X'C7'
JUNE BUGG	X'2E'

```
HORACE KOLLAR    X'91'
MARSHALL ARTS    X'BA'
```

2. Write a program to read in Data Set 5 in Appendix D. Using the AND, OR, and Test Under Mask instructions, verify that each byte of the five test scores is numeric, that is, has X'F' as zone bits. If any byte in the score is not numeric, set a bit indicating a field error. For each record, print the student name, the five scores, and the number of field errors (0–5).
3. Write a program to read variable-length records in Data Set 7 in Appendix D. The first field is the name, the second is the account number, and the third is the balance due, with two assumed decimal places. Each field ends with a slash. Using the TRT and EX instructions, scan the three fields for a slash. Print the input data as received in positions 1–40 of the print line. Print the name left justified in positions 50–69, the account number right justified in positions 75–80, and the balance due right justified in 85–94.

   Maximum field sizes are 20 for the name, six for the account number, and seven for the balance due. If any field is longer than maximum, print only the input data and the message 'INVALID DATA' in positions 50–61.

14 Magnetic Tape Files

OBJECTIVES

After studying this chapter, you should be able to:

- Describe the physical characteristics of magnetic tape devices and records
- Calculate the number of records and space required for files under different blocking factors
- Explain characteristics of variable-length records and reasons for using them
- Describe tape labels and give reasons for using them
- Write file definitions for magnetic tape files
- Explain operation of I/O macros when processing magnetic tape files
- Compare record processing when using a work area and when processing within the I/O area
- Create, retrieve records from, and update magnetic tape files

TAPE CHARACTERISTICS

Magnetic tape is made of Mylar material coated on one side with an iron oxide. The tape is one-half inch wide and comes in lengths of 300, 800, 1200, or 2400 feet. It is capable of being magnetized in small areas, each of which represents one bit. Bits are recorded in nine channels running the length of the tape. The nine bits make up one byte.

The tape to be read or written is placed on one reel. A second reel is used as a take-up reel. Near each end of the tape is a reflective aluminum strip that can be sensed by a photoelectric device on the tape drive. The *load point marker* is from four to ten feet from the start of the tape. This allows some leader tape that can be wrapped around the take-up reel. Reading or writing starts at the load point marker.

Between the two reels is the *read-write head*. This head writes by erasing previous bits and recording the new bits over the nine channels. Then the head rereads the bits to ensure validity. On read operations, the head reads the bits twice to ensure validity.

Near the end of the reel is an *end-of-tape marker*. When this is sensed, the record being written is finished, leaving some winding space at the end of the data.

Parity Bit

Each byte is made up of nine bits, eight of them representing data and one acting as a *parity bit*. (Some older tape units have seven channels, holding six data bits and a parity bit.) When an even number of the data bits are set to 1, the parity bit is set to 1 to make an odd number of 1 bits in the byte. If an odd number of data bits already contain 1, the parity bit is set to 0. The machine is thus said to use *odd parity*.

The hardware verifies parity on every byte. An even number of 1 bits on the byte is an indication of machine or tape failure.

Longitudinal Check Byte

At the end of each record on the tape is a *longitudinal check byte*. This is made up of nine parity bits, one on each channel of the tape. If the total number of 1 bits in any channel is even, the parity bit for that channel is set to 1. If the channel contains an odd number of 1 bits, that channel's parity bit is set to 0.

Interrecord Gap

An *interrecord*, or *interblock, gap* is left between records on the tape. The gap is 0.6 inch long on present equipment. The gap allows time for the tape to start and stop between read or write operations.

Tape Density

The bits are recorded on the tape in a *density* of 800, 1600, or 6250 bits per inch, depending upon the specific tape drive. Because each byte is recorded across the nine channels, the tape density is the same for bits per inch as for bytes per inch.

Tape Speed

The tape moves past the read-write heads at speeds of 75, 125, or 200 inches per second. The rate at which data is read or written, called the *tape transfer rate*, is a function of tape speed and density. A density of 800 bpi (bytes per inch) at 75 inches per second (ips) gives a transfer rate of 60 KB (kilobytes, or 1000 bytes, per second). A density of 6250 bpi with a speed of 200 ips gives a transfer rate of 1250 KB.

BLOCKED RECORDS

We have been working largely with 80-byte records thus far in the course. If we record 80-byte records on tape having density of 800 bpi, each record requires only 0.1 inch. But the gap between records is 0.6 inch long. In this case we would be using only 1/7 of the tape space for data. Futhermore, we would have to start and stop the tape for each record that we read or write.

A solution is to build a *block* of records in main storage consisting of, say, 20 records and then write the entire block as a unit to the tape. A block is often called a *physical record*, while the *logical record* is the unit relating to a single person or subject. A block of 20 records in the preceding example would use 1600 bytes, or 2 inches, for data for each 0.6 inch gap.

There is no physical limit on the length a block can be. In practice, the space available for the I/O area in main storage usually limits block length to several thousand bytes. Figure 14–1 shows blocked and unblocked tape records.

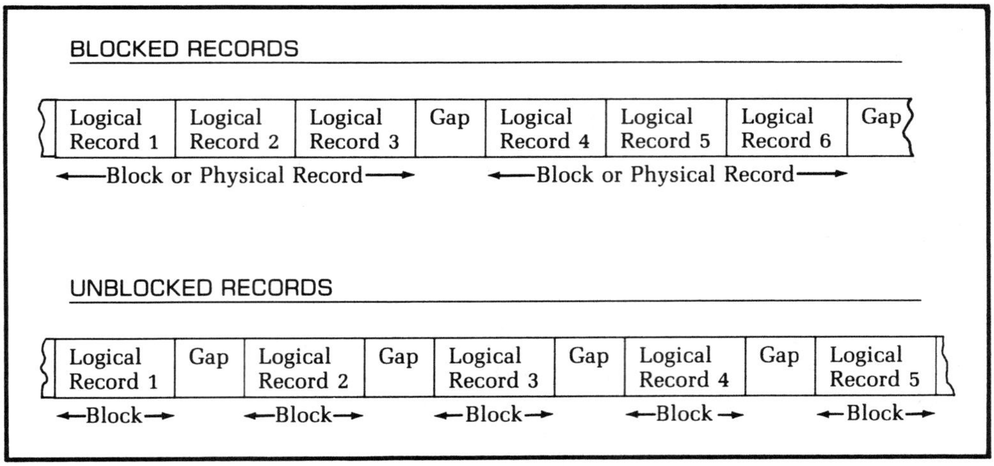

Figure 14–1 Blocked and unblocked tape records

VARIABLE-LENGTH RECORDS

When using fixed-length records and blocks, we specify the record and block size in our magnetic tape file definition. Often it is desirable to use *variable-length records* to avoid the blank spaces often found in fixed length fields.

The I/O modules of the operating system can handle variable length records if we place a four-byte *record length field* preceding each logical record and a four-byte *block length field* at the beginning of each block. These fields must themselves be counted in the record and block lengths.

In each field the first two bytes are a halfword containing the length as a 16-bit unsigned binary integer. The maximum block or record length is thus 65,535 bytes. The second two bytes in each four-byte field are not used by the operating system and are set to blanks (X'4040').

Many variable-length records are made up of a fixed-length segment, called the *root*, and a variable number of additional fixed-length segments, each representing one transaction or item related to the root. For example, a student record might have a 100-byte root giving basic information about each student and from one to eight 20-byte segments representing courses taken in one semester. Including the record length field, the minimum record length would thus be

$$4 + 100 + (1 * 20) = 124$$

while the maximum would be

$$4 + 100 + (8 * 20) = 264$$

The programmer is responsible for computing and recording the record length field when the record is created. The operating system refers to it when reading back from tape to determine how many bytes to read. Figure 14–2 shows blocked and unblocked variable-length records.

TAPE LABELS

Tape files are identified in two ways. An *exterior label* is a sticker or tag placed on the reel that can be read by the personnel who handle it. An *interior label* is recorded magnetically on the tape itself and read by the operating system to verify that the correct tape is being used.

Standard labels are normally used with tape files. However, the operating system allows nonstandard labels, for which the programmer is responsible. Labels may also be omitted, especially where data if transported on a tape reel to some other location or organization.

Each reel of tape is called a *volume*. There are two types of standard interior labels, both 80 bytes long. The *volume label* is recorded once after the load point marker and normally not changed unless the entire tape is erased. A utility program initializes a new tape reel with the volume label in this format:

POSITIONS	NAME	DESCRIPTION
01–03	Type of label	VOL identifies volume label.
04	Volume label number	Normally 1; some systems allow more than one volume label.

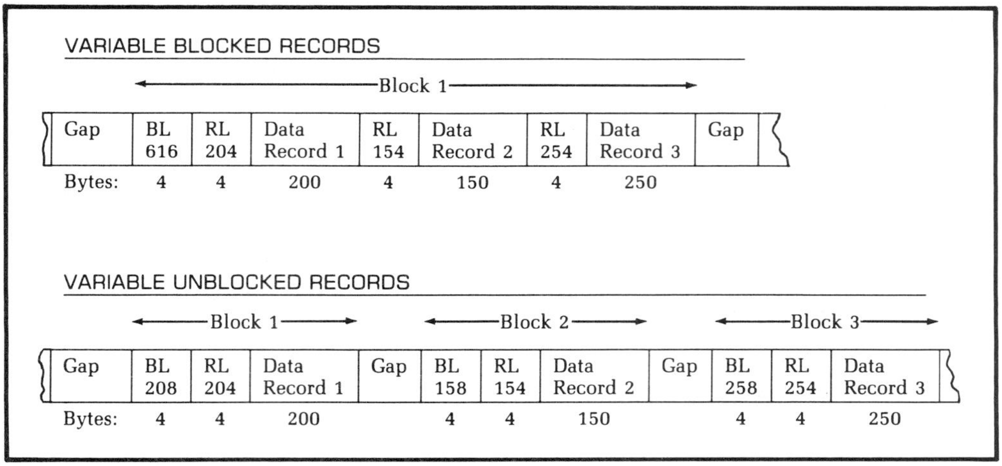

Figure 14–2 Blocked and unblocked variable-length records

05–10	Volume serial number	A six-digit permanent unique number identifying this volume.
11	Volume security	A special code used by OS.
12–41		Unused.
42–51	Owner name and address	Used by OS to identify owner of reel.
52–80		Unused.

Each file is identified by a *header label* preceding the data and a *trailer label* following the data. The label uniquely identifies the file and contains, among other things, an expiration date to ensure that the file will not be written over. DOS supports one standard header and trailer label. OS requires two header and two trailer labels.

There is a header label at the start of the file. The header label contains HDR in the first three bytes. If the file extends for more than one volume (multivolume file), there is another header label at the start of each volume containing the file.

There is a trailer label at the end of the entire file with EOF in its first three bytes. For a multivolume file, there is a trailer label at the end of each volume with EOV (end of volume) in its first three bytes. Figure 14–3 shows magnetic tape volume and file labels.

Standard file labels have this format:

POSITIONS	NAME	DESCRIPTION
01–03	Label identifier	HDR for header; EOF or EOV for trailer.
04	File label number	Usually 1; some systems allow more than one.
05–21	Flie identifier	A unique name to identify the file.

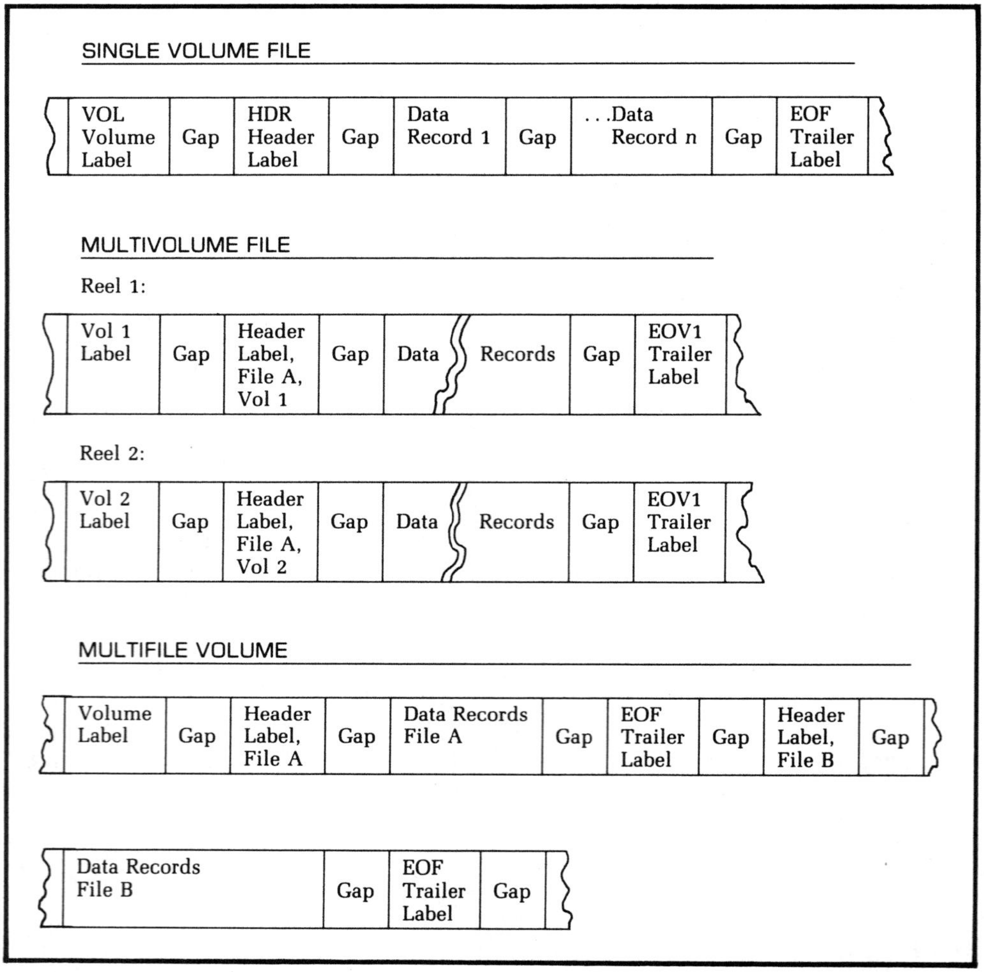

Figure 14–3 Magnetic tape volume and file labels

22–27	File serial number	Same as serial number of first or only volume.
28–31	Volume sequence number	0001 for single volume files; numbered consecutively for multivolume files.
32–35	File sequence number	Number of the file on this volume.
36–39	Generation number	Consecutive number updated each time the file is rewritten.
40–41	Version number of generation	Version number of generation.
42–47	Creation date	Date file was first written. Uses form bYYDDD, where b = blank, YY = year, and DDD = day of year.

48–53	Expiration date	Year and day when file may be overwritten. Same form as creation date.
54	File security	Special security code used by OS.
55–60	Block count	Count of physical records in the file, shown in trailer labels only.
61–73	System code	Identifier for operating system.
74–80		Reserved.

The label for output files is created from data supplied on a TLBL job control statement. On input the label is checked against the TLBL statement. The format for TLBL under DOS is:

// TLBL filename,'file-id',date,file-number,volume-sequence-number, file-sequence-number,generation-number,version-number

where filename is required and is the name used in the DTFMT macro;
'file-ID' is 1 to 17 characters identifying the file;
date is the expiration date in form YYDDD or DDDD for numbers of days to be retained for output files;
file-serial-number is 1 to 6 characters agreeing with the volume serial number;
volume-sequence-number is 1 to 4 digits showing volume in a multivolume file;
file-sequence-number is 1 to 4 digits showing file in a multifile volume;
generation-number is 1 to 4 digits for generation number;
version-number is 1 to 2 digits for version number.

No spaces are allowed within or between operands in the TLBL statement. On output files, the system assumes a default value of 1 if any of the last four operands is omitted. On input labels, omitted operands are not checked.

Some versions of DOS require use of a // LBLTYP TAPE job control statement when executing programs containing tape files with standard labels. This statement is positioned as follows:

```
// LBLTYP TAPE
// EXEC LNKEDT
// TLBL etc.
// EXEC
```

The // LBLTYP TAPE statement notifies the linkage editor to reserve an extra 80 bytes at the start of the program area for creating or verifying labels. If this is not done, the labels will be read over the first 80 bytes of the program, destroying instructions and data and usually causing a program interrupt.

Later versions of DOS process labels differently and do not require the // LBLTYP TAPE statement.

MAGNETIC TAPE FILE DEFINITIONS

Magnetic tape files are defined in DOS with the DTFMT (Define the File for Magnetic Tape) macro. OS uses the DCB (Define Control Block) macro with different operands. In both systems the name field is required and is one to seven characters, the first of which must be alphabetic. The name is used in OPEN, CLOSE, GET, PUT, and CNTRL macros for the file.

DOS

The most common operands under DOS are:

BLKSIZE Give length of I/O area in bytes.

DEVADDR Use SYS*nnn* (where *nnn* can be 000 through 244). This is a symbolic name used in job control statements to assign the file to a specific tape device.

EOFADDR Give name of instruction to which program is to branch upon reaching end of input file.

FILABL Use STD if standard labels, NSTD if nonstandard, and NO if unlabeled tape.

IOAREA1 Give name of I/O area.

IOAREA2 Give name of second I/O area if used.

IOREG Use (r) where r is a register number between 2 and 12. Use only if no work area is used. Omit WORKA.

RECFORM Use FIXUNB, FIXBLK, VARUNB, or VARBLK, to indicate fixed or variable-length records and whether blocked or unblocked.

RECSIZE If RECFORM=FIXBLK, give number of bytes per record.

REWIND Specify UNLOAD or NORWND to cause tape to unload or prevent rewinding upon CLOSE. If omitted, tape will rewind.

TYPEFLE Specify INPUT or OUTPUT. If omitted, INPUT is assumed.

VARBLD Use (r) where r is a register number between 2 and 12. Use only for output files with variable-length records where records are built in the I/O area. Omit WORKA.

WORKA Specify YES if separate work area is used to GET or PUT statements. Omit IOREG and VARBLD.

There are additional entries that are not required for the scope of this book. Consult an I/O macro manual for further information.

OS

Typical OS entries for the DCB are:

DDNAME Write name for the DD (Data Definition) job control statement.

DSORG Write PS to indicate that data set organization is physical sequential.

EODAD Write name of routine to which to branch upon reaching end of an input file.

MACRF Indicate macro format with G for GET, GM for GET and move to a work area, P for PUT, and PM for PUT with move to work area.

DEN Write DEN=2 of density of 800 bytes per inch or DEN=3 for 1600 bpi.

BLKSIZE Write length of I/O area in bytes.

LRECL Write length of each logical record, if fixed length.

RECFM To indicate record format write F for fixed-length unblocked, FB for fixed blocked, V for variable-length unblocked or VB for variable blocked.

The BLKSIZE, RECFM, and DEN entries may be enclosed within parentheses and placed in the DD operands in job control statements instead of in the DCB within the program. This permits these items to be changed without reassembling the entire program.

OPEN, CLOSE, GET, PUT MACROS

All of the I/O macros must carry out more complex operations with magnetic tape files than they did with card or printer files. Writing and verifying labels, blocking and unblocking records, and backspacing and rereading records are some of the additional duties performed by these macros.

The OPEN macro makes a tape file available for processing. A maximum of 16 files may be opened with a single OPEN statement. The filename may be spelled out, or its address may be preloaded into a general register and the register number specified within parentheses. For example, we might use

```
OPEN INTAPE,INFILE,PRINTER
```

or we could use

```
LA    1,INTAPE
LA    2,INFILE
LA    3,PRINTER
OPEN  (1),(2),(3)
```

or a combination of names and register notation.

On output files OPEN verifies that a volume label is present. It also verifies that there is no unexpired file on the tape to be written. It then creates the header label from data supplied in the TLBL statement.

On input files OPEN compares data on the label with fields given in the TLBL statement and notifies the operator of any discrepancies.

On output files, the CLOSE macro writes out any records still remaining in the I/O area. Then it writes an end-of-file record and the trailer label, including a count of blocks written to the file, and deactivates the file.

On input files, CLOSE merely deactivates the file. CLOSE may be written in register notation as OPEN is.

The GET macro has as its first operand the name of the file given in DTFMT macro. If a work area is specified with WORKA=YES, the second operand gives the name of the work area. Each GET makes the next sequential logical record available for processing by moving it to the work area or by putting its address into the I/O register specified in the IOREG entry. The I/O module handling does all deblocking of records and alternating between I/O areas if more than one is specified.

The PUT macro is used to output logical records. They can be built in a separate work area, or directly in the I/O area if IOREG is specified. Only when a block of records is filled is the block actually written out to the tape drive.

The GET or PUT macros may be written in any of these forms:

```
GET filename                PUT filename
GET filename,workarea       PUT filename,workarea
GET (1),(0)                 PUT (1),(0)
GET (r1),(r2)               PUT (r1),(r2)
```

The first is used when records are to be processed in the I/O area and no work area is used. The second is the form we have used with card and printer files with a work area. The third is used where the address of the DTFMT is preloaded into R1 and the address of the work area into R0. In the fourth, any other general registers may be used for r1 and r2 to specify address of DTFMT and work area, respectively.

The CNTRL macro permits operations such as rewinding tape, writing tapemarks, backspacing or forward spacing, or writing blank tape. We will not cover these operations in this text.

RECORD PROCESSING

As mentioned in the foregoing sections, tape records may be used for both output and input. They may be blocked or unblocked, and fixed or variable in length. They may be processed in a work area or directly in the I/O area.

Using a Work Area

Where a work area is specified, it should be the size of *one logical record*. If the record is variable-length, the work area should be the size of the largest record and include the four-byte record length field.

For output files, the record is built in the work area. Data may be in any format, character, binary, or packed decimal. Halfwords and fullwords may present alignment problems. There may be gaps left between fields to align binary data on the proper boundary.

When a PUT is issued, the logical record is transferred to the I/O area. If there are ten records per block, there will be ten PUTs before the block is finally written out to the tape. The CLOSE macro will write any remaining records in the block.

On input files, GET causes a record to be moved from the I/O area to the work area. The next GET moves the next logical record from the I/O area to the work area. Only after the last record in the block has been presented for processing is another block read from the tape unit.

Figure 14–4 shows processing blocked records using a work area.

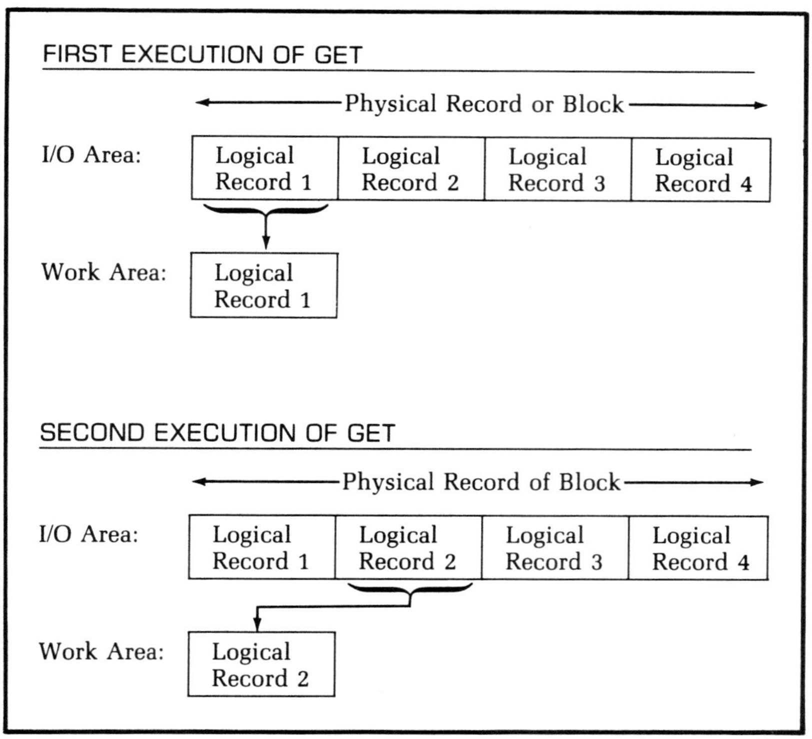

Figure 14–4 Processing blocked records using a work area

Processing in the Input/Output Area

If we specify IOREG=(r) in the DTFMT macro, we omit WORKA=YES and no work area is used. Instead, the operating system places the address of the next logical record into the I/O register we have specified. We can then use explicit register addressing to process the fields within the record.

It is usually convenient to define a dummy section such as

```
TPDUMMY DSECT
```

matching the format of the logical record so that we can process each field by name. If we have used IOREG=(4), then near the start of our program we can write USING TPDUMMY,4 to identify R4 with the dummy section. The operating system handles initializing and modifying the addresses in R4.

While variable-length records may be processed in the I/O area, it is usually easier to work with them in a separate work area.

Figure 14–5 shows processing blocked records in the I/O area.

PROGRAM 14A: CREATING A TAPE FILE

Program 14A creates a magnetic tape file of year-to-date sales records. Input records are checked to be sure that keys are in ascending order and that

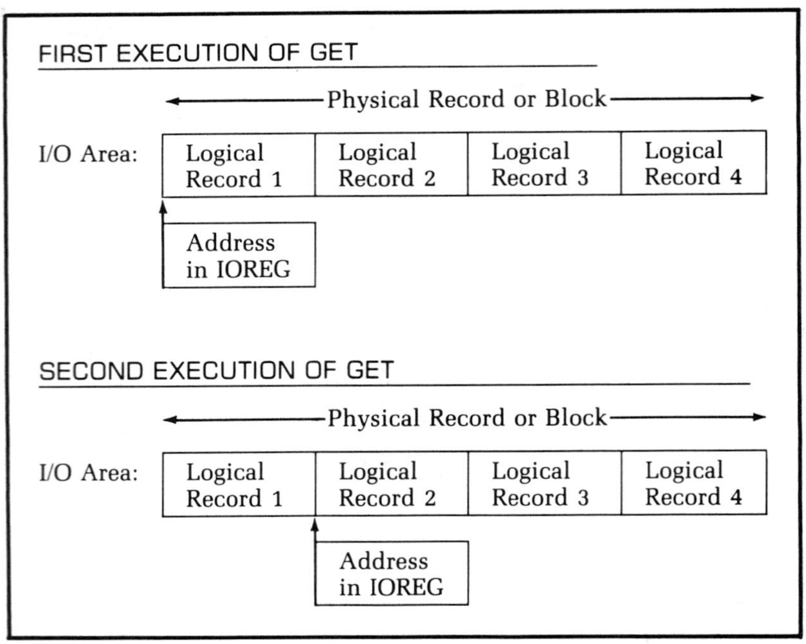

Figure 14–5 Processing blocked records in the I/O area

INPUT	FIELD NAME	TAPE
01–02	Region	01–02
03–07	Employee number	03–07
08–27	Employee name	08–27
28–36	Year-to-date sales	28–32 (packed) 9999999V99
37–43	Year-to-date returns	33–36 (packed) 99999V99
44–80	Unused	

Figure 14–6 Formats for records for Program 14A

there are no duplicate keys. Formats for the input records and tape records are shown in Figure 14–6.

The key to each record consists of the first seven bytes, with region as the two high order characters and employee number as the seven low order characters. Any record with a key that is out of sequence or a duplicate of the previous record is not written to the file. An unformatted listing of each input record is printed. An error message is printed next to each record not written to the file.

The two year-to-date fields are packed to conserve space on the tape and simplify processing when tape records are read back into main storage.

Each tape record is 36 bytes long, with 20 records per block.

Figure 14–7 shows the program listing, and Figure 14–8 shows the output.

PROGRAM 14B: RETRIEVING A TAPE FILE

Program 14B retrieves records from the file created in Program 14A and prints a report. It calculates the net sales for each employee by subtracting the year-to-date returns from the year-to-date sales. It also shows total net sales for each region and for the entire organization.

This logic uses the IF-THEN structure to test for control breaks rather than the nested DOWHILE structure used in Chapter 8. Before processing each record, the region code is checked with the previous code. If a change occurs, region totals are printed and added to the final total. Then the region totals are cleared, the new region key is saved, and processing continues with the first record of the new region.

At end of file, the totals for the last region must be printed and added to the final totals before the final totals can be printed.

Figure 14–9 shows the program listing, and Figure 14–10 shows the output.

```
LOC    OBJECT CODE     ADDR1 ADDR2 STMT SOURCE STATEMENT                         DOS/VSE ASSEMBLER 11.34 86-03-28

                                     1 ***********************************************************************
                                     2 *                 ALTON R. KINDRED, PROGRAM 14A
                                     3 * THIS PROGRAM READS YEAR-TO-DATE SALES RECORDS AND CREATES A MAGNETIC
                                     4 * TAPE FILE. TAPE RECORDS ARE 36 BYTES LONG, WITH 20 RECORDS PER
                                     5 * BLOCK. AS THE FILE IS CREATED, RECORDS ARE CHECK THAT THEY ARE IN
                                     6 * SEQUENCE BY REGION AND EMPLOYEE NUMBER. EACH RECORD IS LISTED ON
                                     7 * THE PRINTER AS IT IS WRITTEN TO TAPE.
                                     8 *          REGISTERS USED:
                                     9                 R9-R11 - LINK REGISTERS
                                    10 *                R12    - BASE REGISTER
                                    11 ***********************************************************************
                                    12          PRINT  NOGEN
000000                              13 MAINLINE START  0                            SET LOCATION COUNTER
                                    14 *        STM    14,12,12(13)                 SAVE REGISTERS FOR OS              OS
00000  0500                         15          BALR   12,0                         LOAD BASE REGISTER
                              00002 16          USING  *,12                         DESIGNATE BASE REGISTER
                                    17 *        ST     13,SAVE+4                    STORE REGISTER 13                  OS
                                    18 *        LA     13,SAVE                      LOAD SAVE AREA ADDRESS             OS
                                    19 *        OPEN   (INFILE,(INPUT))             OPEN FILES                         OS
                                    20 *        OPEN   (OUTTAPE,(OUTPUT))           *                                  OS
                                    21 *        OPEN   (PRINTER,(OUTPUT))           *                                  OS
                                    22          OPEN   INFILE,OUTTAPE,PRINTER       OPEN FILES                         DOS
00001A 4590 C03A             0003C  32          BAL    9,INITIAL                    DO INITIAL PROCESSING
00001E 4590 C056             00058  33          BAL    9,MAINLOOP                   DO MAIN PROCESSING LOOP
                                    34          CLOSE  INFILE,OUTTAPE,PRINTER       CLOSE FILES                        DOS
                                    44          EOJ                                 END PROGRAM                        DOS
                                    47 *        CLOSE  (INFILE,OUTTAPE,PRINTER)     CLOSE FILES                        OS
                                    48 *        L      13,SAVE+4                    LOAD SAVE AREA ADDRESS             OS
                                    49 *        LM     14,12,12(13)                 RESTORE REGISTERS                  OS
                                    50 *        BR     14                           RETURN TO OS                       OS
                                    51 ***********************************************************************
                                    52 *               FIRST LEVEL MODULES
                                    53 ***********************************************************************
                                    54 *
                                    55 *               SET INITIAL VALUES MODULE
                                    56 *
00003C F811 C738 C772 0073D 00774   57 INITIAL  ZAP    LINECNT,=P'51'               SET LINE COUNT > 50
000042 F810 C739 C776 00738 00778   58          ZAP    ERRCNT,=P'0'                 SET ERROR COUNT TO 0
000048 45A0 C096             00098  59          BAL    10,READRECD                  READ FIRST RECORD
00004C D206 C73F C777 00740 00779   60          MVC    SAVEKEY,=7C'0'               SET PRIOR KEY TO ZEROS
000052 45A0 C11E             00120  61          BAL    10,CLEAR                     CLEAR PRINT LINE
000056 07F9                         62          BR     9                            RETURN
                                    63 *
                                    64 *               MAIN PROCESSING LOOP
                                    65 *
                             00058  66 MAINLOOP EQU    *
000058 95E8 C73D      0073F         67 DOWHILE  CLI    EOFFLAG,C'Y'                 DOWHILE NOT END OF FILE
00005C 4780 C094      00096         68          BE     ENDDO                        *
000060 F910 C739 C77E 0073B 00780   69 AND      CP     ERRCNT,=P'5'                 AND ERROR COUNT < 5
000066 47B0 C094      00096         70          BNL    ENDDO                           *
00006A D506 C5BB C73E 005BD 00740   71 IF       CLC    INKEY,SAVEKEY                   IF KEY > PREVIOUS KEY
000070 47D0 C07E      00080         72          BNH    ELSE                            *
000074 45A0 C0B4             000B6  73 THEN     BAL    10,SETTAPE                         THEN SET UP TAPE RECORD
000078 45A0 C0E8             000EA  74          BAL    10,WRITTAPE                        WRITE TAPE RECORD
00007C 47F0 C082      00084         75          B      ENDIF                              *
                             00080  76 ELSE     EQU    *                            ELSE
000080 4540 C0D4             000D6  77          BAL    10,OUTSEQ                          SET UP ERROR MESSAGE
                             00084  78 ENDIF    EQU    *                               ENDIF
000084 45A0 C0FA             000FC  79          BAL    10,PRDETAIL                     PRINT LINE
000088 D206 C73E C5BB 00740 005BD   80          MVC    SAVEKEY,INKEY                   SAVE KEY
00008E 45A0 C096             00098  81          BAL    10,READRECD                     READ NEXT RECORD
000092 47F0 C056      00058         82          B      DOWHILE                         *
                             00096  83 ENDDO    EQU    *                            ENDDO
000096 07F9                         84          BR     9                            RETURN
                                    85 ***********************************************************************
                                    86 *               SECOND LEVEL MODULES
                                    87 ***********************************************************************
                                    88 *
                                    89 *               READ RECORD MODULE
                                    90 *
000098 92D5 C73D      0073F         91 READRECD MVI    EOFFLAG,C'N'                 SET EOF FLAG OFF
                                    92          GET    INFILE,INRECD                READ RECORD
0000AC 47F0 C0B2      000B4         98 IFEOF    B      ENDIFEOF                     IF END OF FILE
0000B0 92E8 C73D      0073F         99 THENEOF  MVI    EOFFLAG,C'Y'                   THEN SET EOF FLAG ON
                             000B4 100 ENDIFEOF EQU    *                            ENDIF
000084 07FA                        101          BR     10                           RETURN
                                   102 *
                                   103 *               SETUP TAPE MODULE
                                   104 *
0000B6 D206 C60B C5BB 0060D 005BD  105 SETTAPE  MVC    TPKEY,INKEY                  MOVE INPUT FIELDS TO TAPE RECORD
0000BC D213 C612 C5C2 00614 005C4  106          MVC    TPNAME,INNAME                *
0000C2 F248 C626 C5D6 00628 005D8  107          PACK   TPYTDSAL,INYTDSAL            *
0000C8 F236 C62B C5DF 0062D 005E1  108          PACK   TPYTDRET,INYTDRET            *
0000CE D22A C630 C5BB 00632 005BD  109          MVC    PRRECD,INRECD                MOVE INPUT RECORD TO PRINT LINE
0000D4 07FA                        110          BR     10                           RETURN
                                   111 *
                                   112 *               OUT OF SEQUENCE MODULE
                                   113 *
0000D6 D22A C630 C5BB 00632 005BD  114 OUTSEQ   MVC    PRRECD,INRECD                MOVE INPUT RECORD TO PRINT LINE
0000DC D21A C660 C77F 00662 00781  115          MVC    PRERROR,=C'SEQUENCE ERROR OR DUPLICATE' MOVE ERR. MSG.
0000E2 FA10 C739 C79A 0073B 0079C  116          AP     ERRCNT,=P'1'                 ADD 1 TO ERROR COUNT
0000E8 07FA                        117          BR     10                           RETURN
                                   118 *
                                   119 *               WRITE TAPE MODULE
                                   120 *
                             000EA 121 WRITTAPE EQU    *
                                   122          PUT    OUTTAPE,TAPERECD             WRITE TO TAPE
0000FA 07FA                        128          BR     10                           RETURN
                                   129 *
                                   130 *               PRINT DETAIL LINE MODULE
                                   131 *
                             000FC 132 PRDFTAIL EQU    *
0000FC F911 C73B C774 0073D 00776  133 IFEOP    CP     LINECNT,=P'50'               If LINE COUNT => 50
000102 4740 C108      0010A        134          BL     ENDIFEOP                       *
000106 45B0 C12A             0012C 135 THENEOP  BAL    11,HEADING                     THEN PRINT HEADINGS
                             0010A 136 ENDIFEOP EQU    *                            ENDIF
                                   137          PUT    PRINTER,PRLINE               PRINT LINE
00011A FA10 C73B C79A 0073D 0079C  143          AP     LINECNT,=P'1'                ADD 1 TO LINE COUNT
000120 9240 C62F      00631        144 CLEAR    MVI    PRLINE,C' '                  CLEAR PRINT LINE
000124 D283 C630 C62F 00632 00631  145          MVC    PRLINE+1(132),PRLINE         *
00012A 07FA                        146          BR     10                           RETURN
```

Figure 14–7 Assembler listing of Program 14A

```
LOC    OBJECT CODE     ADDR1 ADDR2 STMT SOURCE STATEMENT                                    DOS/VSE ASSEMBLER 11.34 86-03-28

                                    147 ***********************************************************************
                                    148 *                       THIRD LEVEL MODULE
                                    149 ***********************************************************************
                             0012C  150 HEADING  EQU    *
                                    151          PUT    PRINTER,HEAD1               PRINT HEADING LINE
00013C 92F0 C62F       00631        157          MVI    PRLINE,C'0'                 SET FOR DOUBLE SPACE
000140 F810 C73B C776 0073D 00778   158          ZAP    LINFCNT,=P'0'               SET LINE COUNT TO ZERO
000146 07FB                         159          BR     11                          RETURN
                                    160 *********************************************************************DOS
                                    161 *                       FILE DEFINITIONS                            DOS
                                    162 *********************************************************************DOS
                                    163 INFILE   DTFCD  BLKSIZE=80,IOAREA1=INAREA,DEVICE=2540,              DOSX
                                                        DEVADDR=SYS006,EOFADDR=THENEOF,WORKA=YES            DOS
                                    184 *                                                                   DOS
                                    185 PRINTER  DTFPR  BLKSIZE=133,IDAREA1=PRTAREA,DEVICE=1403,            DOSX
                                                        CTLCHR=ASA,DEVADDR=SYS009,WORKA=YES                 DOS
                                    206 *                                                                   DOS
                                    207 OUTTAPE  DTFMT  BLKSIZE=720,RECSIZE=36,IOAREA1=TAPEAREA,            DOSX
                                                        RECFORM=FIXBLK,DEVADDR=SYS011,TYPEFLE=OUTPUT,       DOSX
                                                        WORKA=YES,FILABL=STD                                DOS
                                    243 *                                                                   DOS
000218                              244 TAPEAREA DS     CL720                                               DOS
0004E8                              245 INAREA   DS     CL80                                                DOS
000538                              246 PRTAREA  DS     CL133                                               DOS
                                    247 **********************************************************************OS
                                    248 *                DEVICE CONTROL BLOCKS AND SAVE AREA                 OS
                                    249 **********************************************************************OS
                                    250 *INFILE  DCB    DDNAME=INFILE,BLKSIZE=80,LRECL=80,                   OSX
                                    251 *               MACRF=GM,DSORG=PS,EODAD=THENEOF                      OS
                                    252 *                                                                    OS
                                    253 *PRINTER DCB    DDNAME=PRINTER,BLKSIZE=133,LRECL=133,                OSX
                                    254 *               MACRF=PMA.DSORG=PS                                   OS
                                    255 *                                                                    OS
                                    256 *OUTTAPE DCB    DDNAME=OUTTAPE,BLKSIZE=720,LRECL=36,                 OSX
                                    257 *               MACRF=PM,DSORG=PS,RECFM=FB                           OS
                                    258 *                                                                    OS
                                    259 *SAVE    DS     18F                                                  OS
                                    260 ***********************************************************************
                                    261 *                       DATA DEFINITIONS
                                    262 ***********************************************************************
00058D                              263 INRECD   DS     0CL80
0005BD                              264 INKEY    DS     0CL7
0005BD                              265 INREGION DS     CL2
0005BF                              266 INEMPNBR DS     CL5
0005C4                              267 INNAME   DS     CL20
0005D8                              268 INYTDSAL DS     CL9
0005E1                              269 INYTDRET DS     CL7
0005E8                              270          DS     CL37
                                    271 *
000600                              272 TAPERECD DS     0CL36
00060D                              273 TPKEY    DS     CL7
000614                              274 TPNAME   DS     CL20
000628                              275 TPYTDSAL DS     PL5
00062D                              276 TPYTDRET DS     PL4
                                    277 *
000631                              278 PRLINE   DS     0CL133
000631                              279          DS     CL1
000632                              280 PRRECD   DS     CL43
00065D                              281          DS     CL5
000662                              282 PRERROR  DS     CL27
00067D                              283          DS     CL57
                                    284 *
0006B6                              285 HEAD1    DS     0CL133
0006B6 F140404040404040             286          DC     CL25'1'
0006CF E8C5C1D960E3D660             287          DC     CL108'YEAR-TO-DATE SALES FILE'
                                    288 *
00073B                              289 ERRCNT   DS     PL2
00073D                              290 LINECNT  DS     PL2
00073F                              291 EOFFLAG  DS     CL1
000740                              292 SAVEKEY  DS     CL7
                             00000  293          END    MAINLINE
000748 5B5BC2D6D7C5D540             294                 =C'$$BOPEN'
000750 5B5BC2C3D3D6E2C5             295                 =C'$$BCLOSE'
000758 00000148                     296                 =A(INFILE)
00075C 000005BD                     297                 =A(INRECD)
000760 000001B0                     298                 =A(OUTTAPE)
000764 0000060D                     299                 =A(TAPERECD)
000768 00000180                     300                 =A(PRINTER)
00076C 00000631                     301                 =A(PRLINE)
000770 000006B6                     302                 =A(HEAD1)
000774 051C                         303                 =P'51'
000776 050C                         304                 =P'50'
000778 0C                           305                 =P'0'
000779 F0F0F0F0F0F0F0               306                 =7C'0'
000780 5C                           307                 =P'5'
000781 E2C5D8E4C5D5C3C5             308                 =C'SEQUENCE ERROR OR DUPLICATE'
000790 1C                           309                 =P'1'
```

Figure 14–7 *(Concluded)*

PROGRAM 14C: UPDATING A MASTER TAPE FILE

Program 14C shows updating of a sequential tape file. This is usually called *father-son* processing. Transaction records are in the same format as the input file for Program 14A. This program requires two tape files, an old

```
                    YEAR-TO-DATE SALES FILE

0112345BORDEN RHEUM       002172822012441 7
0123456CANDICE PARAGUS    004739100031620 9
0137928MAE B KNOTT        001791412009140 5
0145913JEANIE ALOGY       004328916032295 0
0177402DUSTIN DE CORNER   003197548024168 1
0213579LETTA SPRAY        006042231047228 9
0224680FULLER BOLOGNIE    002751560013700 2
0247036MIKE ROE FISH      003237781018991 1
0277602OTTO KNOWBETTER    004125918031728 0
0325814JUSTIN CASE        003621415028282 8
0333369SOL FEGGIO         002990456025916 2
0355001FERRIN WARNER      003760738027794 0
0372727PHIL A MIGNON      001925516014918 3
0389115ADAM ZAPPEL        002837270022142 2
0428115CORA SPOND         003551708028272 6
0419006DONIA LOVETT       002263941016335 7  SEQUENCE ERROR OR DUPLICATE
0432714IRA SCHEIZ         004089106031407 9
0446333ARCH BISHOP        003636363029943 3
```

Figure 14–8 Output from Program 14A

master input file and a new master output file. Both input files will be in ascending sequence by key. The transaction input file has been presorted to be in the same sequence as the master file. A year-to-date sales report shows the status of each record after updating takes place.

Program logic calls for reading one record from the old master and one from the transaction file. If the master key is lower than the transaction key, the master record is written to the new master tape file, and the next record is read from the old master file. If the two keys are equal, the year-to-date amounts in the transaction record are added to those in the master record, and a new transaction record is read. If the transaction key is lower than the master key, the transaction is unmatched, and an error message is written.

Whenever either the master or transaction file reaches end of file, its key is set to all 9s. This step permits the remaining records in the other file to be flushed out, since they will have lower keys than the 9s. When both files have keys of 9s, processing is finished.

Notice that the new master file is not written immediately after the old record is updated, but is delayed to see if there are additional transactions to be applied. Only after all equal keys have been updated and the next transaction has a higher key is the new master record written.

```
LOC     OBJECT CODE      ADDR1 ADDR2 STMT SOURCE STATEMENT                                   DOS/VSE ASSEMBLER 11.34 86-03-28
                                        1 ***********************************************************************
                                        2 *                    ALTON R. KINDRED, PROGRAM 14B
                                        3 * THIS PROGRAM RETRIEVES RECORDS FROM THE SALES REPORT MASTER FILE ON
                                        4 * MAGNETIC TAPE AND PRINTS A LISTING OF YEAR-TO-DATE FIGURES FOR SALES
                                        5 * SALES RETURNS, AND NET SALES FOR EACH EMPLOYEE, EACH REGION, AND THE
                                        6 * ENTIRE ORGANIZATION.
                                        7 *          REGISTERS USED:
                                        8 *                  R09-R11:   LINK REGISTERS
                                        9 *                  R12:       BASE REGISTER
                                       10 ***********************************************************************
                                       11          PRINT  NOGEN
000000                                 12 MAINLINE START  0                          SET LOCATION COUNTER
                                       13 *        STM    14,12,12(13)               SAVE REGISTERS FOR OS       OS
000000 0500                            14          BALR   12,0                       LOAD BASE REGISTER
```

Figure 14–9 Assembler listing of Program 14B

```
LOC      OBJECT CODE        ADDR1 ADDR2 STMT SOURCE STATEMENT                           DOS/VSE ASSEMBLER 11.34 86-03-28
                                  00002   15           USING *,12                       DESIGNATE BASE REGISTER
                                          16 *         ST    13,SAVE+4                  STORE REGISTER 13            OS
                                          17 *         LA    13,SAVE                    LOAD SAVE AREA ADDRESS       OS
                                          18 *         OPEN  (INTAPE,(INPUT),PRINTER,(OUTPUT) OPEN FILES           OS
                                          19           OPEN  INTAPE,PRINTER             OPEN FILES                   DOS
000016 4590 C036                  00038   28           BAL   9,INITIAL                  DO INITIAL PROCESSING
00001A 4590 C04A                  0004C   29           BAL   9,MAINLOOP                 DO MAIN PROCESSING LOOP
00001E 4590 C07A                  0007C   30           BAL   9,FINAL                    DO FINAL PROCESSING
                                          31           CLOSE INTAPE,PRINTER             CLOSE FILES                  DOS
                                          40           EOJ                              END PROGRAM                  DOS
                                          43 *         CLOSE (INTAPE,,PRINTER)          CLOSE FILES                  OS
                                          44 *         L     13,SAVE+4                  LOAD SAVE AREA ADDRESS       OS
                                          45 *         LM    14,12,12(13)               RESTORE REGISTERS            OS
                                          46 *         BR    14                         RETURN TO OS                 OS
                                          47 ***********************************************************************
                                          48 *               FIRST LEVEL MODULES
                                          49 ***********************************************************************
                                          50 *
                                          51 *               SET INITIAL VALUES MODULE
                                          52 *
000038 45A0 C084                  00086   53 INITIAL   BAL   10,CLEARSET                CLEAR AND SET INITIAL VALUES
00003C 45A0 C0B0                  000B2   54           BAL   10,READTAPE                READ FIRST RECORD
000040 D201 C8E8 C676       008EA 00678   55           MVC   SAVEREG,TPREGION           SAVE REGION CODE
000046 45A0 C1AE                  001B0   56           BAL   10,CLEAR                   CLEAR PRINT LINE
00004A 07F9                               57           BR    9                          RETURN
                                          58 *
                                          59 *               MAIN PROCESSING LOOP
                                          60 *
                                  0004C   61 MAINLOOP EQU    *
00004C 95E8 C8EA            008EC         62 DOWHILE  CLI    EOTFLAG,C'Y'               DOWHILE NOT END OF TAPE
000050 4780 C078            0007A         63          BE     ENDDO                        *
000054 D501 C676 C8E8       00678 008EA   64 IF       CLC    TPREGION,SAVEREG             IF DIFFERENT REGION
00005A 4780 C068            0006A         65          BE     ENDIF                          *
00005E 45A0 C0CE                  000D0   66 THEN     BAL    10,REGTOT                      THEN PRINT REGION TOTALS
000062 45A0 C1AE                  001B0   67          BAL    10,CLEAR                       CLEAR PRINT LINE
000066 92F0 C69A            0069C         68          MVI    PRLINE,C'0'                    SET FOR DOUBLE SPACE
                                  0006A   69 ENDIF    EQU    *                            ENDIF
00006A 45A0 C134                  00136   70          BAL    10,PROCESS                   PROCESS INPUT RECORD
00006E 45A0 C18A                  0018C   71          BAL    10,PRDETAIL                  PRINT RECORD
000072 45A0 C0B0                  000B2   72          BAL    10,READTAPE                  READ NEXT RECORD
000076 47F0 C04A            0004C         73          B      DOWHILE                      *
                                  0007A   74 ENDDO    EQU    *                          ENDDO
00007A 07F9                               75          BR     9                          RETURN
                                          76 *
                                          77 *               FINAL PROCESSING MODULE
                                          78 *
00007C 45A0 C0CE                  000D0   79 FINAL    BAL    10,REGTOT                  PRINT REGION TOTALS
000080 45A0 C1BA                  001BC   80          BAL    10,PRTOTAL                 PRINT FINAL TOTALS
000084 07F9                               81          BR     9                          RETURN
                                          82 ***********************************************************************
                                          83 *               SECOND LEVEL MODULES
                                          84 ***********************************************************************
                                          85 *
                                          86 *               CLEAR AND SET INITIAL VALUES MODULE
                                          87 *
000086 F840 C8AE C930 00880 00932         88 CLEARSET ZAP    PKREGSAL,=P'0'             CLEAR REGION TOTALS
00008C F830 C8B3 C930 008B5 00932         89          ZAP    PKREGRET,=P'0'             *
000092 F840 C8B7 C930 008B9 00932         90          ZAP    PKREGNET,=P'0'             *
000098 F840 C8BC C930 008BE 00932         91          ZAP    PKTOTSAL,=P'0'             CLEAR TOTALS
00009E F830 C8C1 C930 008C3 00932         92          ZAP    PKTOTRET,=P'0'             *
0000A4 F840 C8C5 C930 008C7 00932         93          ZAP    PKTOTNET,=P'0'             *
0000AA F811 C8E6 C926 008E8 00928         94          ZAP    LINECNT,=P'51'             SET LINE COUNT > 50
0000B0 07FA                               95          BR     10                         RETURN
                                          96 *
                                          97 *               READ TAPE MODULE
                                          98 *
0000B2 92D5 C8EA            008EC         99 READTAPE MVI    EOTFLAG,C'N'               SET END OF TAPE FLAG OFF
                                         100          GET    INTAPE,TAPERECD            READ TAPE RECORD
0000C6 47F0 C0CC            000CE        106 IFEOT    B      ENDIFEOT                   IF END OF TAPE
0000CA 92E8 C8EA            008EC        107 THENEOT  MVI    EOTFLAG,C'Y'                 THEN SET EOT FLAG ON
                                  000CE  108 ENDIFEOT EQU    *                          ENDIF
0000CE 07FA                              109          BR     10                         RETURN
                                         110 *
                                         111 *               PRINT REGION TOTALS MODULE
                                         112 *
0000D0 D205 C6AB C928 006AD 0092A        113 REGTOT   MVC    PRNAME(6),=C'TOTALS'       SET UP TOTAL LINE
0000D6 D20C C6C2 C8CF 006C4 008D1        114          MVC    PRYTDSAL,PATRN             *
0000DC DE0C C6C2 C8AE 006C4 008B0        115          ED     PRYTDSAL,PKREGSAL          *
0000E2 D209 C6D2 C8DC 006D4 008DE        116          MVC    PRYTDRET,PATRN2            *
0000E8 DE09 C6D2 C8B3 006D4 008B5        117          ED     PRYTDRET,PKREGRET          *
0000EE D20C C6DF C8CF 006E1 008D1        118          MVC    PRYTDNET,PATRN             *
0000F4 DE0C C6DF C8B7 006E1 008B9        119          ED     PRYTDNET,PKREGNET          *
                                         120          PUT    PRINTER,PRLINE             PRINT TOTAL LINE
00010A FA44 C8BC C8AE 008BE 008B0        126          AP     PKTOTSAL,PKREGSAL          ADD TO FINAL TOTALS
000110 FA33 C8C1 C8B3 008C3 008B5        127          AP     PKTOTRET,PKREGRET          *
000116 FA44 C8C5 C8B7 008C7 008B9        128          AP     PKTOTNET,PKREGNET          *
00011C F840 C8AE C930 008B0 00932        129          ZAP    PKREGSAL,=P'0'             CLEAR REGION TOTALS
000122 F830 C8B3 C930 008B5 00932        130          ZAP    PKREGRET,=P'0'             *
000128 F840 C8B7 C930 008B9 00932        131          ZAP    PKREGNET,=P'0'             *
00012E D201 C8E8 C676 008EA 00678        132          MVC    SAVEREG,TPREGION           SAVE REGION CODE
000134 07FA                              133          BR     10                         RETURN
                                         135 *
                                         136 *               PROCESS TAPE RECORD MODULE
                                         137 *
000136 D201 C69D C676 0069F 00678        138 PROCESS  MVC    PPREGION,TPREGION          SET UP REGION, NUMBER, AND NAME
00013C D204 C6A3 C678 006A5 0067A        139          MVC    PRNUMBER,TPNUMBER          *
000142 D213 C6AB C67D 006AD 0067F        140          MVC    PRNAME,TPNAME              *
000148 D20C C6C2 C8CF 006C4 008D1        141          MVC    PRYTDSAL,PATRN             *
00014E DE0C C6C2 C691 006C4 00693        142          ED     PRYTDSAL,TPYTDSAL          *
000154 D209 C6D2 C8DC 006D4 008DE        143          MVC    PRYTDRET,PATRN2            *
00015A DE09 C6D2 C696 006D4 00698        144          ED     PRYTDRET,TPYTDRET          *
000160 F844 C8CA C691 008CC 00693        145          ZAP    PKYTDNET,TPYTDSAL          CALCULATE NET SALES
000166 FB43 C8CA C696 008CC 00698        146          SP     PKYTDNET,TPYTDRET          *
00016C D20C C6DF C8CF 006E1 008D1        147          MVC    PRYTDNET,PATRN             SET UP NET SALES
000172 DE0C C6DF C8CA 006E1 008CC        148          ED     PRYTDNET,PKYTDNET          *
000178 FA44 C8AE C691 008B0 00693        149          AP     PKREGSAL,TPYTDSAL          ADD TO REGION TOTALS
00017E FA33 C8B3 C696 008B5 00698        150          AP     PKREGRET,TPYTDRET          *
000184 FA44 C8B7 C8CA 008B9 008CC        151          AP     PKREGNET,PKYTDNET          *
00018A 07FA                              152          BR     10                         RETURN
                                         153 *
                                         154 *               PRINT DETAIL LINE MODULE
                                         155 *
                                  0018C  156 PRDETAIL EQU    *
00018C F911 C8E6 C92E 008E8 00930        157 IFEOP    CP     LINECNT,=P'50'             IF LINE COUNT =>50
000192 4740 C198            0019A        158          BL     ENDIFEOP                     *
000196 45B0 C1FA                  001FC  159 THENEOP  BAL    11,HEADING                   THEN PRINT HEADING
                                  0019A  160 ENDIFEOP EQU    *                          ENDIF
```

Figure 14–9 *(Continued)*

```
LOC     OBJECT CODE       ADDR1  ADDR2  STMT SOURCE STATEMENT                                DOS/VSE ASSEMBLER 11.34 86-03-28

                                         161           PUT    PRINTER,PRLINE               PRINT LINE
0001AA  FA10  C8E6 C931  008E8  00933   167           AP     LINECNT,=P'1'                ADD 1 TO LINE COUNT
0001B0  9240  C69A        0069C          168 CLEAR     MVI    PRLINE,C' '                  CLEAR PRINT LINE
0001B4  D283  C69B C69A  0069D  0069C   169           MVC    PRLINE+1(132),PRLINE         *
0001BA  07FA                             170           BR     10                           RETURN
                                         171 *
                                         172 *                PRINT FINAL TOTALS MODULE
                                         173 *
0001BC  92F0  C69A        0069C          174 PRTOTAL   MVI    PRLINE,C'0'                  SET FOR DOUBLE SPACE
0001C0  D20B  C6AB C90E  006AD  00910   175           MVC    PRNAME(12),=C'FINAL TOTALS'  SET UP TOTAL LINE
0001C6  D20C  C6C2 C8CF  006C4  008D1   176           MVC    PRYTDSAL,PATRN               *
0001CC  DE0C  C6C2 C8BC  006C4  008BE   177           ED     PRYTDSAL,PKTOTSAL            *
0001D2  D209  C6D2 C8DC  006D4  008DE   178           MVC    PRYTDRET,PATRN2              *
0001D8  DE09  C6D2 C8C1  006D4  008C3   179           ED     PRYTDRET,PKTOTRET            *
0001DF  D20C  C6DF C8CF  006E1  008D1   180           MVC    PRYTDNET,PATRN               *
0001E4  DE0C  C6DF C8C5  006E1  008C7   181           ED     PRYTDNET,PKTOTNET            *
                                         182           PUT    PRINTER,PRLINE               PRINT TOTAL LINE
0001FA  07FA                             188           BR     10                           RETURN
                                         189 ***********************************************************************
                                         190 *                THIRD LEVEL HEADING MODULE
                                         191 ***********************************************************************
                                 001FC   192 HEADING   EQU    *
                                         193           PUT    PRINTER,HEAD1                PRINT FIRST HEADING LINE
                                         199           PUT    PRINTER,HEAD2                PRINT SECOND HEADING LINE
                                         205           PUT    PRINTER,HEAD3                PRINT THIRD HEADING LINE
00022C  92F0  C69A        0069C          211           MVI    PRLINE,C'0'                  SET FOR DOUBLE SPACE
000230  F810  C8E6 C930  008E8  00932   212           ZAP    LINECNT,=P'0'                SET LINE COUNT TO ZERO
000236  07FB                             213           BR     11                           RETURN
                                         215 **********************************************************************DOS
                                         216 *                FILE DEFINITIONS AND I/O AREAS                       DOS
                                         217 **********************************************************************DOS
                                         218 INTAPE    DTFMT  BLKSIZE=720,RECSIZE=36,IOAREA1=TAPEAREA,             DOSX
                                                              RECFORM=FIXBLK,DEVADDR=SYS011,TYPEFLE=INPUT,         DOSX
                                                              WORKA=YES,EOFADDR=THENEOT,FILABL=STD                 DOS
                                                                                                                   DOS
                                         256 *                                                                     DOSX
                                         257 PRINTER   DTFPR  BLKSIZE=133,IOAREA1=PRTAREA,DEVICE=1403,             DOS
                                                              CTLCHR=ASA,DEVADDR=SYS009,WORKA=YES                  DOS
                                                                                                                   DOS
                                         278 *                                                                     DOS
0002D8                                   279 TAPEAREA DS      CL720                                                DOS
0005A8                                   280 PRTAREA  DS      CL133
                                         281 ***********************************************************************OS
                                         282 *                DEVICE CONTROL BLOCKS AND SAVE AREA                   OS
                                         283 ***********************************************************************OS
                                         284 *INTAPE   DCB    DDNAME=INTAPE,BLKSIZE=720,LRECL=36,                   OSX
                                         285 *                MACRF=GM,DSORG=PS,RECFM=FB                            OS
                                         286 *                                                                      OS
                                         287 *PRINTER DCB     DDNAME=PRINTER,BLKSIZE=133,LRECL=133,                 OSX
                                         288 *                MACRF=PMA,DSORG=PS                                    OS
                                         289 *                                                                      OS
000630                                   290 SAVE      DS     18F
                                         291 ***********************************************************************
                                         292 *                DATA DEFINITIONS
                                         293 ***********************************************************************
000678                                   294 TAPERECD DS      0CL36
000678                                   295 TPREGION DS      CL2
00067A                                   296 TPNUMBER DS      CL5
00067F                                   297 TPNAME   DS      CL20
000693                                   298 TPYTDSAL DS      PL5
000698                                   299 TPYTDRET DS      PL4
                                         300 *
00069C                                   301 PRLINE   DS      0CL133
00069C                                   302          DS      CL3
00069F                                   303 PRREGION DS      CL2
0006A1                                   304          DS      CL4
0006A5                                   305 PRNUMBER DS      CL5
0006AA                                   306          DS      CL3
0006AD                                   307 PRNAME   DS      CL20
0006C1                                   308          DS      CL3
0006C4                                   309 PRYTDSAL DS      CL13
0006D1                                   310          DS      CL3
0006D4                                   311 PRYTDRET DS      CL10
0006DE                                   312          DS      CL3
0006E1                                   313 PRYTDNET DS      CL13
0006EE                                   314          DS      CL51
                                         315 *
000721                                   316 HEAD1    DS      0CL133
000721  F140404040404040                 317          DC      CL35'1'
000744  E2C1D3C5E240D9C5                 318          DC      CL98'SALES REPORT'
                                         319 *
0007A6                                   321 HEAD2    DS      0CL133
0007A6  F040404040404040                 322          DC      CL8'0'
0007AE  C5D4D7D3D6E8C5C5                 323          DC      CL34'EMPLOYEE'
0007D0  E8C5C1D960E3D660                 324          DC      CL14'YEAR-TO-DATE'
0007DE  E8C5C1D960E3D660                 325          DC      CL16'YEAR-TO-DATE'
0007EE  E8C5C1D960E3D660                 326          DC      CL61'YEAR-TO-DATE'
                                         327 *
00082B                                   328 HEAD3    DS      0CL133
00082B  40                               329          DC      CL1' '
00082C  D9C5C7C9D6D54040                 330          DC      CL24'REGION NUMBER'
000844  D5C1D4C540404040                 331          DC      CL21'NAME'
000859  E2C1D3C5E2404040                 332          DC      CL13'SALES'
000866  D9C5E3E4D9D5E240                 333          DC      CL14'RETURNS'
000874  D5C5E340E2C1D3C5                 334          DC      CL60'NET SALES'
                                         335 *
0008B0                                   336 PKREGSAL DS      PL5
0008B5                                   337 PKREGRET DS      PL4
0008B9                                   338 PKREGNET DS      PL5
0008BE                                   339 PKTOTSAL DS      PL5
0008C3                                   340 PKTOTRET DS      PL4
0008C7                                   341 PKTOTNET DS      PL5
0008CC                                   342 PKYTDNET DS      PL5
0008D1  40206B2020206B20                 343 PATRN    DC      XL13'40206B2020206B2020214B2020'
0008DE  4020206B2020214B                 344 PATRN2   DC      XL10'4020206B2020214B2020'
0008E8                                   345 LINECNT  DS      PL2
0008EA                                   346 SAVEREG  DS      CL2
0008EC                                   347 EOTFLAG  DS      CL1
                                 00000   348          END     MAINLINE
0008F0  5B5BC2D6D7C5D540                 349                  =C'$$BOPEN '
0008F8  5B5BC2C3D3D6E2C5                 350                  =C'$$BCLOSE'
000900  00000238                         351                  =A(INTAPE)
000904  00000678                         352                  =A(TAPERECD)
000908  000002A8                         353                  =A(PRINTER)
```

Figure 14–9 *(Continued)*

```
LOC      OBJECT CODE       ADDR1 ADDR2 STMT SOURCE STATEMENT                      DOS/VSE ASSEMBLER 11.34 86-03-28

  00090C 0000069C                      354               =A(PRLINE)
  000910 C6C9D5C1D340E3D6              355               =C'FINAL TOTALS'
  00091C 00000721                      356               =A(HEAD1)
  000920 000007A6                      357               =A(HEAD2)
  000924 0000082B                      358               =A(HEAD3)
  000928 051C                          359               =P'51'
  00092A E3D6E3C1D3E2                  360               =C'TOTALS'
  000930 050C                          361               =P'50'
  000932 0C                            362               =P'0'
  000933 1C                            363               =P'1'
```

Figure 14–9 *(Concluded)*

```
                              SALES REPORT

        EMPLOYEE                       YEAR-TO-DATE YEAR-TO-DATE YEAR-TO-DATE
REGION   NUMBER   NAME                    SALES        RETURNS     NET SALES

  01     12345    BORDEN RHEUM          21,728.22     1,244.17     20,484.05
  01     23456    CANDICE PARAGUS       47,391.00     3,162.09     44,228.91
  01     37928    MAE B KNOTT           17,914.12       914.05     17,000.07
  01     45913    JEANIE ALOGY          43,289.16     3,229.50     40,059.66
  01     77402    DUSTIN DE CORNER      31,975.48     2,416.81     29,558.67
                  TOTALS               162,297.98    10,966.62    151,331.36

  02     13579    LETTA SPRAY           60,422.31     4,722.89     55,699.42
  02     24680    FULLER BOLOGNIE       27,515.60     1,370.02     26,145.58
  02     47036    MIKE ROE FISH         32,377.81     1,899.11     30,478.70
  02     77602    OTTO KNOWBETTER       41,259.18     3,172.80     38,086.38
                  TOTALS               161,574.90    11,164.82    150,410.08

  03     25814    JUSTIN CASE           36,214.15     2,828.28     33,385.87
  03     33369    SOL FEGGIO            29,904.56     2,591.62     27,312.94
  03     55001    FERRIN WARNER         37,607.38     2,779.40     34,827.98
  03     72727    PHIL A MIGNON         19,255.16     1,491.83     17,763.33
  03     89115    ADAM ZAPPEL           28,372.70     2,214.22     26.158.48
                  TOTALS               151,353.95    11,905.35    139,448.60

  04     28115    CORA SPOND            35,517.08     2,827.26     32,689.82
  04     32714    IRA SCHEIZ            40,891.06     3,140.79     37,750.27
  04     46333    ARCH BISHOP           36,363.63     2,994.33     33,369.30
                  TOTALS               112,771.77     8,962.38    103,809.39

                  FINAL TOTALS         587,998.60    42,999.17    544,999.43
```

Figure 14–10 Output from Program 14B

Figure 14–11 shows the program listing, and Figure 14–12 shows the output.

SUMMARY

Data is recorded on tape in the form of magnetic spots in nine channels along the tape. The channels provide for the eight data bits and one parity bit. The parity bit is set to either 0 or 1 to cause the number of 1 bits for each byte always to be odd. The longitudinal check byte at the end of each record provides a parity check for each channel on the tape.

```
LOC    OBJECT CODE    ADDR  ADDR2 STMT SOURCE STATEMENT                          DOS/VSE ASSEMBLER 15.01 86-04-02
                       1

                                         1 ************************************************************************
                                         2 *                  ALTON R. KINDRED, PROGRAM 14C
                                         3 * THIS PROGRAM PERFORMS A SEQUENTIAL TAPE FILE UPDATE ON THE MASTER
                                         4 * YEAR-TO-DATE SALES FILE AND PRINTS A SALES UPDATE REPORT. TRANS-
                                         5 * ACTION RECORDS CONTAIN SALES AND SALES RETURNS FOR THE CURRENT
                                         6 * MONTH. WHEN THE MASTER RECORD KEY IS LOWER THAN THE TRANSACTION
                                         7 * KEY, THE MASTER RECORD IS WRITTEN TO THE NEW MASTER FILE. WHEN
                                         8 * KEYS ARE EQUAL, THE MASTER RECORD IS UPDATED. LOW TRANSACTION KEYS
                                         9 * ARE LISTED AS ERRORS.
                                        10 *         REGISTERS USED:
                                        11 *                R09=R11:  LINK REGISTERS
                                        12 *                R12:      BASE REGISTER
                                        13 ************************************************************************
                                        14          PRINT  NOGEN
000000                                  15 MAINLINE START  0                         SET LOCATION COUNTER
                                        16 *        STM    14,12,12(13)              SAVE REGISTERS FOR OS        OS
000000 05C0                             17          BALR   12,0                      LOAD BASE REGISTER
                                 00002  18          USING  *,12                      DESIGNATE BASE REGISTER
                                        19          OPEN   OLDMAST,INTRANS,NEWMAST,PRINTER  OPEN FILES            DOS
                                        30 *        OPEN   (OLDMAST),(INPUT),INTRANS,(INPUT))                     OS
                                        31 *        OPEN   (NEWMAST,(OUTPUT),PRINTER,(OUTPUT))                    OS
00001E 4590    C046              00048  32          BAL    9,INITIAL                 DO INITIAL PROCESSING
000022 4590    C058              0005A  33          BAL    9,MAINLOOP                DO MAIN PROCESSING LOOP
000026 4590    C0A3              000B0  34          BAL    9,FINAL                   DO FINAL PROCESSING
                                        35          CLOSE  OLDMAST,INTRANS,NEWMAST,PRINTER  CLOSE FILES           DOS
                                        46          EOJ                              END PROGRAM                  DOS
                                        49 *        CLOSE  (OLDMAST,,INTRANS)        CLOSE FILES                  OS
                                        50 *        CLOSE  (NEWMAST,,PRINTER)        CLOSE FILES                  OS
                                        51 *        L      13,SAVE+4                 LOAD SAVE AREA ADDRESS       OS
                                        52 *        LM     14,12,12(13)              RESTORE REGISTERS            OS
                                        53 *        BR     14                        RETURN TO OS                 OS
                                        54 ************************************************************************
                                        55 *               FIRST LEVEL MODULES
                                        56 ************************************************************************
                                        57 *
                                        58 *               SET INITIAL VALUES MODULE
                                        59 *
000048 45A0    C0B4              000B6  60 INITIAL  BAL    10,CLEARSET               CLEAR AND SET INITIAL VALUES
00004C 45A0    C0C8              000CA  61          BAL    10,RDTRANS                READ FIRST TRANSACTION RECORD
000050 45A0    C0E4              000E6  62          BAL    10,RDMAST                 READ FIRST MASTER RECORD
000054 45A0    C162              00164  63          BAL    10,CLEAR                  CLEAR PRINT LINE
000058 07F9                             64          BR     9                         RETURN
                                        65 *
                                        66 *               MAIN PROCESSING LOOP
                                        67 *
                                 0005A  68 MAINLOOP EQU    *
00005A D506    C9EB CCE8 009ED   00CEA  69 DOWHILE  CLC    MASTKEY,=7C'9'            DOWHILE MASTER KEY NOT = 9S
000060 4770    C06C      0006E          70          BNE    DO                          *
000064 D506    CA0F CCE8 00A11   00CEA  71 AND      CLC    TRANKEY,=7C'9'            AND TRANS. KEY NOT = 9S
00006A 4780    C0AC      000AE          72          BE     ENDDO                       *
                                 0006E  73 DO       EQU    *                           *
00006E D506    C9EB CA0F 009ED   00A11  74 IF       CLC    MASTKEY,TRANKEY             IF MASTER KEY LOW
000074 47B0    C0BA      000BC          75          BNL    ELSE                          *
000078 45A0    C100              00102  76 THEN     BAL    10,WRMAST                     THEN WRITE MASTER RECORD
00007C 45A0    C112              00114  77          BAL    10,SETUP                      SET UP PRINT LINE
000080 45A0    C13E              00140  78          BAL    10,PRDETAIL                   PRINT LINE
000084 45A0    C0E4              000E6  79          BAL    10,RDMAST                     READ NEXT MASTER
000088 47F0    C0A8      000AA          80          B      ENDIF                         *
                                 0008C  81 ELSE     EQU    *                           ELSE
00008C D506    C9EB CA0F 009ED   00A11  82 IF2      CLC    MASTKEY,TRANKEY               IF KEYS EQUAL
000092 4770    C09C      0009E          83          BNE    ELSE2                           *
000096 45A0    C16E              00170  84 THEN2    BAL    10,UPDATE                       THEN UPDATE RECORD
00009A 47F0    C0A4      000A6          85          B      ENDIF2                          *
                                 0009E  86 ELSE2    EQU    *                             ELSE
00009E 45A0    C1AC              001AE  87          BAL    10,SETERROR                     SET UP ERROR MESSAGE
0000A2 45A0    C13E              00140  88          BAL    10,PRDETAIL                     PRINT LINE
                                 000A6  89 ENDIF2   EQU    *                             ENDIF
0000A6 45A0    C0C8              000CA  90          BAL    10,RDTRANS                    READ NEXT TRANSACTION
                                 000AA  91 ENDIF    EQU    *                           ENDIF
0000AA 47F0    C058      0005A          92          B      DOWHILE                     *
                                 000AE  93 ENDDO    EQU    *                         ENDDO
0000AE 07F9                             94          BR     9                         RETURN
                                        95 *
                                        96 *               FINAL PROCESSING MODULE
                                        97 *
0000B0 45A0    C1C6              001C8  98 FINAL    BAL    10,PRTOTAL                PRINT TOTALS
0000B4 07F9                             99          BR     9                         RETURN
                                       100 ************************************************************************
                                       101 *               SECOND LEVEL MODULES
                                       102 ************************************************************************
                                       103 *
                                       104 *               CLEAR AND SET INITIAL VALUES MODULE
                                       105 *
0000B6 F840    CC7D CCEF 00C7F   00CF1 106 CLEARSET ZAP    PKYTDTOT,=P'0'            CLEAR TOTALS
0000BC F840    CC82 CCEF 00C84   00CF1 107          ZAP    PKCURTOT,=P'0'            *
0000C2 F811    CC9E CCDE 00CA0   00CE0 108          ZAP    LINECNT,=P'51'            SET LINE COUNT > 50
0000C8 07FA                            109          BR     10                        RETURN
                                       110 *
                                       111 *               READ TRANSACTION MODULE
                                       112 *
                                       113 RDTRANS  GET    INTRANS,TRANRECD          READ TRANSACTION RECORD
0000DA 47F0    C0E2      000E4         119 IFEOT    B      ENDIFEOT                  IF END OF TRANS. FILE
0000DE D206    CA0F CCE8 00A11   00CEA 120 THENEOT  MVC    TRANKEY,=7C'9'              THEN MOVE 9S TO TRANS. KEY
                                 000E4 121 ENDIFEOT EQU    *                         ENDIF
0000E4 07FA                            122          BR     10                        RETURN
                                       123 *
                                       124 *               READ OLD MASTER MODULE
                                       125 *
                                       126 RDMAST   GET    OLDMAST,OMRECD            READ OLD MASTER RECORD
0000F6 47F0    C0FE      00100         132 IFEOM    B      ENDIFEOM                  IF END OF OLD MASTER FILE
0000FA D206    C9EB CCE8 009ED   00CEA 133 THENEOM  MVC    MASTKEY,=7C'9'              THEN MOVE 9S TO MAST. KEY
                                 00100 134 ENDIFEOM EQU    *                         ENDIF
000100 07FA                            135          BR     10                        RETURN
                                       137 *
                                       138 *               WRITE NEW MASTER MODULE
                                       139 *
                                       140 WRMAST   PUT    NEWMAST,OMRECD            WRITE OLD MASTER TO NEW MASTER
000112 07FA                            146          BR     10                        RETURN
                                       147 *
                                       148 *               SET UP PRINT LINE
                                       149 *
000114 D201    CA62 C9EB 00A64   009ED 150 SETUP    MVC    PRREGION,OMREGION         SET UP PRINT FIELDS
00011A D204    CA68 C9ED 00A6A   009EF 151          MVC    PRNUMBER,OMNUMBER         *
```

Figure 14–11 Assembler listing of Program 14C

```
LOC    OBJECT CODE      ADDR  ADDR2 STMT SOURCE STATEMENT                                    DOS/VSE ASSEMBLER 15.01 86-04-02
                        1
000120 D213 CA70 C9F2 00A72 009F4  152          MVC   PRNAME,OMNAME                *
000126 D20C CA87 CC91 00A89 00C93  153          MVC   PRCURNET,PATRN               *
00012C DE0C CA87 CC8C 00A89 00C8E  154          ED    PRCURNET,PKCURNET            *
000132 D20C CA97 CC91 00A99 00C93  155          MVC   PRYTDNET,PATRN               *
000138 DE0C CA97 CC87 00A99 00C89  156          ED    PRYTDNET,PKYTDNET            *
00013E 07FA                        157          BR    10                           RETURN
                                   158 *
                                   159 *              PRINT DETAIL LINE MODULE
                                   160 *
                             00140 161 PRDETAIL EQU   *
000140 F911 CC9E CCE0 00CA0 00CE2  162 IFEDP    CP    LINECNT,=P'50'               IF LINE COUNT => 50
000146 4740 C14C       0014E       163          BL    ENDIFEOP                       *
00014A 45B0 C1FA             001FC 164 THENEOP  BAL   11,HEADING                     THEN PRINT HEADING
                             0014E 165 ENDIFEOP EQU   *                            ENDIF
                                   166          PUT   PRINTER,PRLINE               PRINT LINE
00015E FA10 CC9E CCF0 00CA0 00CF2  172          AP    LINECNT,=P'1'                ADD 1 TO LINE COUNT
000164 9240 CA5F       00A61       173 CLEAR    MVI   PRLINE,C' '                  CLEAR PRINT LINE
000168 D283 CA60 CA5F 00A62 00A61  174          MVC   PRLINE+1(132),PRLINE         *
00016E 07FA                        175          BR    10                           RETURN
                                   176 *
                                   177 *              UPDATE MODULE
                                   178 *
000170 F248 CC73 CA2A 00C75 00A2C  179 UPDATE   PACK  PKCURSAL,TRCURSAL            PACK TRANSACTION AMOUNTS
000176 F246 CC78 CA33 00C7A 00A35  180          PACK  PKCURRET,TRCURRET            *
00017C FA44 CA06 CC73 00A08 00C75  181          AP    OMYTDSAL,PKCURSAL            ADD TO MASTER FILE TOTALS
000182 FA34 CA0B CC78 00A0D 00C7A  182          AP    OMYTDRET,PKCURRET            *
000188 F844 CC8C CC73 00C8E 00C75  183          ZAP   PKCURNET,PKCURSAL            CALC. CURRENT MONTH NET SALES
00018E FB44 CC8C CC78 00C8E 00C7A  184          SP    PKCURNET,PKCURRET            *
000194 F844 CC87 CA06 00C89 00A08  185          ZAP   PKYTDNET,OMYTDSAL            CALC. YEAR-TO-DATE NET SALES
00019A FB43 CC87 CA0B 00C89 00A0D  186          SP    PKYTDNET,OMYTDRET            *
0001A0 FA44 CC82 CC8C 00C84 00C8E  187          AP    PKCURTOT,PKCURNET            ADD TO REPORT TOTALS
0001A6 FA44 CC7D CC87 00C7F 00C89  188          AP    PKYTDTOT,PKYTDNET            *
0001AC 07FA                        189          BR    10                           RETURN
                                   190 *
                                   191 *              SET UP ERROR LINE MODULE
                                   192 *
0001AE D201 CA62 CA0F 00A64 00A11  193 SETERROR MVC   PRREGION,TRREGION            SET UP REGION, NUMBER, NAME
0001B4 D204 CA68 CA11 00A64 00A13  194          MVC   PRNUMBER,TRNUMBER            *
0001BA D213 CA70 CA16 00A72 00A18  195          MVC   PRNAME,TRNAME                *
0001C0 D214 CA87 CCF1 00A89 00CF3  196          MVC   PRCURNET(21),=C'UNMATCHED TRANSACTION' SET ERR. MSG.
0001C6 07FA                        197          BR    10                           RETURN
                                   199 *
                                   200 *              PRINT TOTALS MODULE
                                   201 *
0001C8 92F0 CA5F       00A61       202 PRTOTAL  MVI   PRLINE,C'0'                  SET FOR DOUBLE SPACE
0001CC D205 CA70 CCE2 00A72 00CE4  203          MVC   PRNAME(6),=C'TOTALS'         SET UP TOTAL LINE
0001D2 D20C CA87 CC91 00A89 00C93  204          MVC   PRCURNET,PATRN               *
0001D8 DE0C CA87 CC82 00A89 00C84  205          ED    PRCURNET,PKCURTOT            *
0001DE D20C CA97 CC91 00A99 00C93  206          MVC   PRYTDNET,PATRN               *
0001E4 DE0C CA97 CC7D 00A99 00C7F  207          ED    PRYTDNET,PKYTDTOT            *
                                   208          PUT   PRINTER,PRLINE               PRINT TOTAL LINE
0001FA 07FA                        214          BR    10                           RETURN
                                   215 ***********************************************************************
                                   216 *              THIRD LEVEL HEADING MODULE
                                   217 ***********************************************************************
                                   218 HEADING  PUT   PRINTER,HEAD1                PRINT FIRST HEADING LINE
                                   224          PUT   PRINTER,HEAD2                PRINT SECOND HEADING LINE
                                   230          PUT   PRINTER,HEAD3                PRINT THIRD HEADING LINE
00022C 92F0 CA5F       00A61       236          MVI   PRLINE,C'0'                  SET FOR DOUBLE SPACE
000230 F810 CC9E CCBF 00CA0 00CF1  237          ZAP   LINECNT,=P'0'                SET LINE COUNT TO ZERO
000236 07FB                        238          BR    11                           RETURN
                                   239 *********************************************************************DOS
                                   240 *              FILE DEFINITIONS AND I/O AREAS                        DOS
                                   241 *********************************************************************DOS
                                   242 INTRANS  DTFCD BLKSIZE=80,IOAREA1=TRANAREA,DEVICE=2540,              DOSX
                                                      DEVADDR=SYS006,EOFADDR=THENEOT,WORKA=YES              DOS
                                   263 *                                                                    DOS
                                   264 OLDMAST  DTFMT BLKSIZE=720,RECSIZE=36,IOAREA1=OLDMAREA,              DOSX
                                                      RECFORM=FIXBLK,DEVADDR=SYS011,TYPEFLE=INPUT,          DOSX
                                                      WORKA=YES,EOFADDR=THENEOM,FILABL=STD                  DOS
                                   302 *                                                                    DOS
                                   303 NEWMAST  DTFMT BLKSIZE=720,RECSIZE=36,IOAREA1=NEWMAREA,              DOSX
                                                      RECFORM=FIXBLK,DEVADDR=SYS012,TYPEFLE=OUTPUT,         DOSX
                                                      WORKA=YES,FILABL=STD                                  DOS
                                   339 *                                                                    DOS
                                   340 PRINTER  DTFPR BLKSIZE=133,IOAREA1=PRTAREA,DEVICE=1403,              DOSX
                                                      CTLCHR=ASA,DEVADDR=SYS009,WORKA=YES                   DOS
                                   361 *                                                                    DOS
000378                             362 OLDMAREA DS    CL720                                                 DOS
000648                             363 TRANAREA DS    CL80                                                  DOS
000698                             364 NEWMAREA DS    CL720                                                 DOS
000968                             365 PRTAREA  DS    CL133                                                 DOS
                                   367 **********************************************************************OS
                                   368 *              DEVICE CONTROL BLOCKS AND SAVE AREA                    OS
                                   369 **********************************************************************OS
                                   370 *INTRANS DCB   DDNAME=INTRANS,BLKSIZE=80,LRECL=80                     OSX
                                   371 *              MACRF=GM,DSORG=PS,EODAD=THENEOT                        OS
                                   372 *                                                                     OS
                                   373 *PRINTER DCB   DDNAME=PRINTER,BLKSIZE=133,LRECL=133,                  OSX
                                   374 *              MACRF=PMA,DSORG=PS                                     OS
                                   375 *                                                                     OS
                                   376 *OLDMAST DCB   DDNAME=OLDMAST,BLKSIZE=720,LRECL=36,                   OSX
                                   377 *              MACRF=GM,DSORG=PS,RECFM=FB,EODAD=THENEOM               OS
                                   378 *                                                                     OS
                                   379 *NEWMAST DCB   DDNAME=NEWMAST,BLKSIZE=720,LRECL=36,                   OSX
                                   380 *              MACRF=PM,DSORG=PS,RECFM=FB                             OS
                                   381 *                                                                     OS
                                   382 *SAVE    DS    18F                                                    OS
                                   383 ***********************************************************************
                                   384 *              DATA DEFINITIONS
                                   385 ***********************************************************************
0009ED                             386 OMRECD   DS    0CL36
0009ED                             387 MASTKEY  DS    0CL7
0009ED                             388 OMREGION DS    CL2
0009EF                             389 OMNUMBER DS    CL5
0009F4                             390 OMNAME   DS    CL20
000A08                             391 OMYTDSAL DS    PL5
000A0D                             392 OMYTDRET DS    PL4
                                   393 *
000A11                             394 TRANRECD DS    0CL80
000A11                             395 TRANKEY  DS    0CL7
000A11                             396 TRREGION DS    CL2
000A13                             397 TRNUMBER DS    CL5
```

Figure 14–11 *(Continued)*

```
LOC     OBJECT CODE       ADDR  ADDR2 STMT SOURCE STATEMENT                              DOS/VSE ASSEMBLER 15.01 86-04-02
                          1

000A18                                 398 TRNAME   DS     CL20
000A2C                                 399 TRCURSAL DS     CL9
000A35                                 400 TRCURRET DS     CL7
000A3C                                 401          DS     CL37
                                       402 *
000A61                                 403 PRLINE   DS     0CL133
000A61                                 404          DS     CL3
000A64                                 405 PRREGION DS     CL2
000A66                                 406          DS     CL4
000A6A                                 407 PRNUMBER DS     CL5
000A6F                                 408          DS     CL3
000A72                                 409 PRNAME   DS     CL20
000A86                                 410          DS     CL3
000A89                                 411 PRCURNET DS     CL13
000A96                                 412          DS     CL3
000A99                                 413 PRYTDNET DS     CL13
000AA6                                 414          DS     CL64
                                       415 *
000AE6                                 416 HEAD1    DS     0CL133
000AE6  F140404040404040               417          DC     CL25'1'
000AFF  E2C1D3C5E240E4D7               418          DC     CL108'SALES UPDATE REPORT'
                                       419 *
000B6B                                 421 HEAD2    DS     0CL133
000B6B  F040404040404040               422          DC     CL8'0'
000B73  C5D4D7D3D6E8C5C5               423          DC     CL34'EMPLOYEE'
000B95  C3E4D9D9C5D5E340               424          DC     CL17'CURRENT MONTH'
000BA6  E8C5C1D960E3D660               425          DC     CL74'YEAR-TO-DATE'
                                       426 *
000BF0                                 427 HEAD3    DS     0CL133
000BF0  40                             428          DC     CL1' '
000BF1  D9C5C7C9D6D54040               429          DC     CL24'REGION NUMBER'
000C09  D5C1D4C540404040               430          DC     CL19'NAME'
000C1C  D5C5E340E2C1D3C5               431          DC     CL16'NET SALES'
000C2C  D5C5E340E2C1D3C5               432          DC     CL73'NET SALES'
                                       433 *
000C75                                 434 PKCURSAL DS     PL5
000C7A                                 435 PKCURRET DS     PL5
000C7F                                 436 PKYTDTOT DS     PL5
000C84                                 437 PKCURTOT DS     PL5
000C89                                 438 PKYTDNET DS     PL5
000C8E                                 439 PKCURNET DS     PL5
000C93  40206B202020206B20             440 PATRN    DC     XL13'40206B2020206B2020214B2020'
000CA0                                 441 LINECNT  DS     PL2
                                00000  442              END MAINLINE
000CA8  5B5BC2D6D7C5D540               443                 =C'$$BOPEN '
000CB0  5B5BC2C3D3D6E2C5               444                 =C'$$BCLOSE'
000CB8  0000238                        445                 =A(INTRANS)
000CBC  00000A11                       446                 =A(TRANRECD)
000CC0  00000270                       447                 =A(OLDMAST)
000CC4  000009ED                       448                 =A(OMRECD)
000CC8  000002E0                       449                 =A(NEWMAST)
000CCC  00000348                       450                 =A(PRINTER)
000CD0  00000A61                       451                 =A(PRLINE)
000CD4  00000AE6                       452                 =A(HEAD1)
000CD8  00000B6B                       453                 =A(HEAD2)
000CDC  00000BF0                       454                 =A(HEAD3)
000CE0  051C                           455                 =P'51'
000CE2  050C                           456                 =P'50'
000CE4  E3D6E3C1D3E2                   457                 =C'TOTALS'
000CEA  F9F9F9F9F9F9F9                 458                 =7C'9'
000CF1  0C                             459                 =P'0'
000CF2  1C                             460                 =P'1'
000CF3  E4D5D4C1E3C3C85                461                 =C'UNMATCHED TRANSACTION'
```

Figure 14–11 *(Concluded)*

A gap of 0.6 inch is left between tape records to allow the tape to start and stop between read/write operations. The density at which bits are recorded is 800, 1600, or 6250 bits per inch. The tap moves at speeds of 75, 125, or 200 inches per second.

The read/write heads are between the data reel and the takeup reel on the tape drive unit. They deposit magnetic spots during the write operation and sense the spots during the read operation.

Several logical records are normally blocked together to create one physical record, or block, before they are written on tape. Blocking reduces the number of read/write operations necessary to retrieve the records as well as the number of gaps between records.

Physical records may be blocked or unblocked and of fixed or variable length. Variable length records are preceded by a four-byte record length field giving the total length of the record, including the four-byte field. Each block of variable length records is also preceded by a four-byte block length field. The length is expressed as an unsigned binary halfword.

SALES UPDATE REPORT

REGION	EMPLOYEE NUMBER	NAME	CURRENT MONTH NET SALES	YEAR-TO-DATE NET SALES
01	12345	BORDEN RHEUM	7,277.76	27,761.81
01	23456	CANDICE PARAGUS	14,896.36	59,125.27
01	37928	MAE B KNOTT	14,896.36	59,125.27
01	45913	JEANIE ALOGY	13,641.82	53,701.48
01	77402	DUSTIN DE CORNER	9,736.73	39,295.40
02	13579	LETTA SPRAY	20,269.23	75,968.65
02	24680	FULLER BOLOGNIE	20,269.23	75,968.65
02	47036	MIKE ROE FISH	20,269.23	75,968.65
02	77602	OTTO KNOWBETTER	12,669.19	50,755.57
03	25814	JUSTIN CASE	11,114.62	44,500.49
03	33369	SOL FEGGIO	9,563.87	36,876.81
03	55001	FERRIN WARNER	12,508.85	47,336.83
03	72727	PHIL A MIGNON	12,508.85	47,336.83
03	89115	ADAM ZAPPEL	9,135.02	35,293.50
04	19006	DONIA LOVETT	UNMATCHED TRANSACTION	
04	28115	CORA SPOND	10,214.11	42,903.93
04	32714	IRA SCHEIZ	12,463.48	50,213.75
04	46333	ARCH BISHOP	11,825.56	45,194.86
		TOTALS	155,316.60	608,928.35

Figure 14–12 Output from Program 14C

Exterior labels are placed on the outside of each reel (volume) for identification. Optional interior labels are recorded magnetically on the tape itself. The volume label is an 80-byte record at the start of the tape that uniquely identifies the reel. File labels are 80-byte records that precede and follow each file on the tape.

Header labels start with the letters HDR in the first three columns. Trailer labels contain EOV (end of volume) at the end of each reel of a multivolume file and EOF (end of file) at the end of the entire file. A single-file volume contains only one file. A multifile volume contains more than one file per reel.

Magnetic tape files are defined in DOS with the DTFMT macro and in OS with a DCB. Entries specify the block size, type of file (input or output), whether fixed or variable in length, whether labels are used, end-of-file address for input files, and other details.

The I/O macros (OPEN, CLOSE, GET, and PUT) perform more complex tasks with tape files than they do with printers or cards. OPEN checks to ensure that output files are not written over unexpired files and writes header labels. CLOSE writes any unfilled blocks from the I/O area to the tape and writes the trailer labels.

GET alternates between I/O areas if more than one is specified, unblocks the logical records, and either moves the next logical record to a work area or presents its address in an I/O register. PUT also alternates between I/O areas and permits building records either in a work area or directly in the I/O area. Records are moved to the tape only after each block is filled.

Tape records are normally kept in sequential order by one field designated as the key to the record. Master files are created by reading in records from some input file and writing them to tape. Transaction records must be in the same sequence as master records. To update a master file, a record is read from each file and their keys are compared. A master record with a low key is written to the new master file. If keys are equal, the transaction is added to the master record. If the transaction key is low, it signifies an error.

TERMS FOR REVIEW

Block
Block length field
DTFMT
End-of-tape marker
Exterior label
File label
Header label
Interior label
Interrecord gap
IOREG
LBLTYP
Load point marker
Logical record
Longitudinal check byte
Multifile volume
Multivolume file
Parity bit
Physical record
Read-write head
Record length field
Root
Tape density
Tape transfer rate
TLBL
Trailer label
Variable-length record
Volume
Volume label

REVIEW QUESTIONS

1. Describe how data is recorded on magnetic tape.
2. Where are the load point marker and the end-of-tape marker and what is their purpose?
3. What is the purpose of the parity bit for each byte?
4. What is the longitudinal check byte and why is it used?
5. Distinguish between volume labels and file labels. Which is described in the TLBL statement?
6. Distinguish between the two types of trailer labels. Which type might occur more than once for a single file and under what conditions?
7. In what ways do trailer labels differ from header labels?
8. What is the purpose of the LBLTYP statement? Where does it appear in the job control statements?
9. Describe what is done by the OPEN statement with output files, and with input files?
10. What functions are carried out by the CLOSE statement on magnetic tape files besides deactivating the files?
11. What is the relationship between the size of the I/O area and the work area for magnetic tape files?

12. Explain the procedure for processing output records in the I/O area.
13. Can packed decimal data be stored on magnetic tape files? Why would one want to do so?
14. What problems are encountered in storing binary data on tape files? How can they be overcome?
15. Explain the procedure for updating tape files using father-son processing. What is done when either input file reaches end of file?

EXERCISES

1. With a gap of 0.6 inch, calculate how many inches of tape are required to hold the following amounts of data:

	NUMBER OF RECORDS	RECORD LENGTH	BLOCKING FACTOR	TAPE DENSITY
a.	10,000	100	1	800
b.	10,000	100	100	800
c.	5,000	250	10	1,600
d.	5,000	125	40	1,600

2. Assume you have variable-length records with a root segment of 120 bytes and from one to 15 additional segments of 18 bytes each. What is the minimum length record? the maximum length record?
3. Write statements to open two magnetic tape files and one printer file using register notation.
4. Write a DTF and a DCB to describe a magnetic tape file with records 120 bytes long, blocked 8, to be processed in the I/O area with register 5 as the pointer.
5. Write a mainline control module to perform father-son processing with four magnetic tape files. Refer to modules already defined to carry out these operations:

READTRAN	Read transaction tape
READMAST	Read old master tape
WRITMAST	Write new master tape
WRITERR	Write invalid transaction tape
UPDATE	Update old master with transaction

PROGRAMMING PROBLEMS

1. Write a program to read in Data Set 2 in Appendix D and create a magnetic tape Inventory Master File. Compare each key with that of the preceding record, and do not write any record to the tape file with a key that is out of sequence or a

duplicate of the preceding record. Print each input record, showing 'OUT OF SEQUENCE' or 'DUPLICATE KEY' where appropriate. Count the number of records and print the record count at the bottom of the printed listing. Records are 49 bytes long, with 10 records per block.

2. Write a program to read the Inventory Master File created in Problem 1 and perform a father-son update using Data Set 2A in Appendix D. Add purchases (transaction code 'P') and subtract sales ('S') from the quantity on hand in the master record. Print out each transaction record. Print error messages to the right of the transaction if the transaction key is unmatched, or if the transaction code is not 'P' or 'S'.

3. Write a program to read the Inventory Master File that was updated in Problem 2 and add or delete records according to Data Set 2B in Appendix D. Add transactions with a code of 'A' if the transaction key is lower than the master key, and delete those with a code of 'D' if the transaction and master keys are equal. Print out each transaction with a message indicating the action taken, 'ADDED', 'DELETED', 'NOT FOUND', 'DUPLICATE KEY', or 'INVALID CODE'.

15 Sequential Disk Files

OBJECTIVES

After studying this chapter, you should be able to:

- Describe the physical characteristics of disk devices
- Describe the organization of data on each track
- Describe the concept of cylinders and their function in disk input/output operations
- Calculate track capacity for records of different sizes and blocking factors
- Write file definitions for sequential disk files for both DOS and OS.
- Describe the function of each of the processing macros used with sequential disk files
- Write programs to create, retrieve, and update disk records with both fixed-length and variable-length records

As we saw in Chapter 14, magnetic tape can be used only for sequential processing of files. All modern computer systems need to be able to go directly to specified records without searching the entire file. The term *direct access storage device* (DASD) is applied to any device with this capability.

With IBM mainframe computers there are several classes of DASD devices, including magnetic disks, drums, and mass storage devices. However, the vast majority of systems use disks principally or exclusively. We shall limit our discussion to disk devices and processing.

DISK CHARACTERISTICS

Magnetic disk drives for present-day mainframes include those with removable disk packs and those with nonremovable storage. The more common models for removable disks (called *disk packs*) include the 2314, 3330, and 3340. Models for nonremovable storage are the 3344, 3350, 3375, and 3380.

While the density, number of surfaces, number of tracks per surface, and number of bytes per track vary from one device to another, programming for all is the same.

All disks mentioned are rigid platters coated with a metallic oxide that can readily be magnetized with tiny spots to represent 0 and 1 bits. The bits are deposited around concentric tracks. Even though the outer tracks on the disk are larger than the inner tracks, all tracks on the same model disk contain the same number of bytes.

Most surfaces have several *alternate tracks*, so that if a track is defective, the operating system will assign an alternate track for the defective one.

Cylinders

Data is normally read on both sides of each disk, except the top and bottom surfaces of removable disk packs. The disks are separated, allowing *read-write heads* to be inserted between them. The heads are part of a *read-write assembly* that moves all heads as a unit.

Tracks are numbered from the outside in, with the outside track on each surface being track 0. Tracks directly above one another are said to be in the same *cylinder*. The cylinder is a primary factor in disk processing, since all the records on the cylinder can be read or written without moving the read-write assembly.

Records in a disk file are customarily written from top to bottom on a cylinder before moving to the next cylinder. This minimizes movement of the read-write assembly and speeds operations. The top surface of each cylinder is called head (or surface) 0. The number of heads per cylinder varies with the disk unit.

Figure 15–1 shows the arrangement of a cylinder on a disk pack.

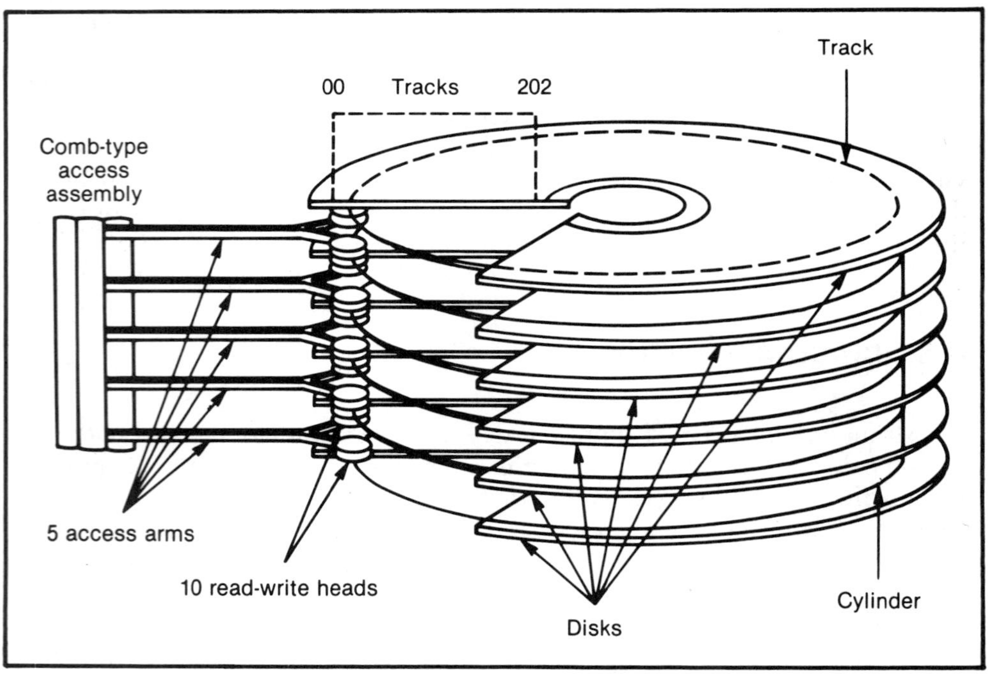

Figure 15–1 Cylinder arrangement on disk pack

Access Timing

The time required to complete a read or write operation is called *access time* This is a combination of four factors that vary with the individual disk drives:

1. *Seek time* is the time required to move the read-write head to the correct cylinder. This is the longest part of access time, since it involves starting and stopping a physical unit.
2. *Head selection* is choosing which surface within the cylinder is to be read or written. This is done electronically, and is so fast that it is usually not a part of the timing calculation.
3. *Rotational delay* is the wait until the proper record on the track appears beneath the read-write head. On the average, this time is half of one rotation. Disks typically rotate at 40 revolutions per second, 2400 per minute.
4. *Data transfer rate* is the time needed to write the bits on the track or to read those already there and to send them back to main storage. This depends on the density of recording and length of the record.

Track Format

Each track has an *index point* that identifies the beginning point for reading or writing data. Following a gap is the *home address* field, giving the cylinder number, head or surface number, and whether the track is a primary or alternate track, or a defective track.

Next comes *Record Zero*, used by the operating system to describe characteristics of the track. Record Zero is used in different ways in different methods of file organization.

Data records are written around the track starting with record 1. Between records is a gap, the exact size of which varies from one device to another. Records are often blocked as they are on tape, to lengthen record size and reduce the number of gaps, increasing storage capacity.

As with tape, data is actually written as a block, or *physical record*, that may contain several *logical records*. Figure 15–2 shows the track format.

Count, Key, Data Organization

Each physical record on a track consists of a count area, an optional key area, and a data area. There is a gap between the areas. The count area contains eight bytes of interest to the programmer. These bytes contain unsigned binary data.

BYTES	CONTENT
0–1	Cylinder number (16 bits)
2–3	Head (surface) number (16 bits)
4	Record number (8 bits)
5	Length of key area (8 bits)
6–7	Length of data area (block length, 16 bits)

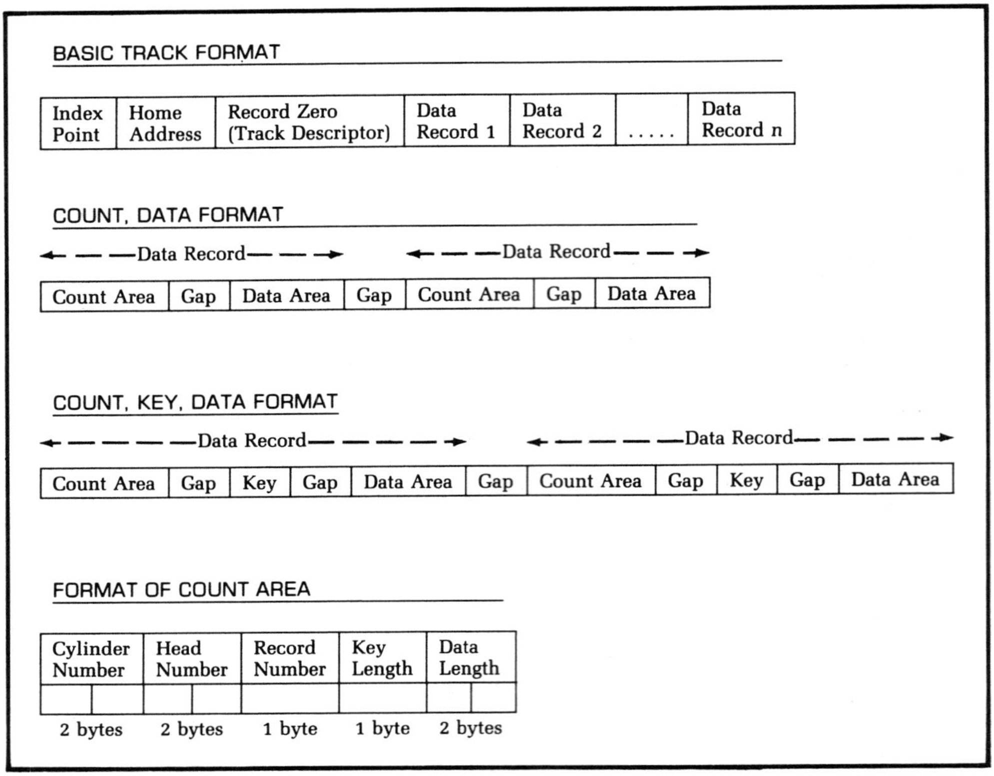

Figure 15–2 Disk track format

The maximum value for each 8-bit field is 255, and for each 16-bit field it is 65,535.

Sequential files do not use the key field. The key length would thus always be zero for the count area in sequential file records.

The end-of-file marker on disk files consists of a count area showing a key length of zero and data length of zero.

Cyclic Check Bytes

Bits are written serially on each track, not in parallel across several channels as they are on tape. If parity bits were deposited with each byte, they would occupy 1/9 (about 11 percent) of the usable track space.

To conserve space, the disk control unit strips off the parity bit from each byte, recording only eight data bits per byte. A count of parity bits is recorded at the end of each separate area on disk in the form of two *cyclic check bytes*. On any area longer than 16 bytes, the cyclic check bytes conserve space.

The cyclic check bytes are attached to every disk area: the count area, the key area (if used), and the data area of each record. They are not counted in key length or record length nor in track capacity tables.

TRACK CAPACITY TABLES

Unlike magnetic tapes, on which records can be virtually any length, disk tracks have finite lengths. The manufacturer supplies track capacity tables from which we can compute the number of physical records of different sizes that will fit on one track. Separate calculations are necessary if the key area is used with the record.

Figure 15–3 shows capacity for the 3340 disk as an example. There are two tables, one for records without keys and one for records with keys. The largest record without the key area that can fit on a single track is 8,368 bytes long. If a separate key field is used, the longest record (key and data portion together) is only 8,293 bytes long. The extra gap for the key field accounts for the difference in bytes.

We are most concerned with the track capacity tables when determining the most efficient blocking factor. Suppose we have a sequential file with records 100 bytes long and a maximum block length of 2,000 bytes. For a block of 2,000 bytes we can get only three physical records per track. At twenty 100-byte records per block, we have 60 logical records per track. By reducing the block length to 1,500, we can get five physical records per track. Five blocks times 15 records per block yields 75 logical records per track. The shorter block size gives more records per track.

We should always aim for a block size equal to or just less than the maximum number of bytes per record shown in one of the table entries. A block size of 899 bytes gives eight blocks per track, but a block size just one byte larger, 900 bytes, gives only seven blocks per track.

VOLUME TABLE OF CONTENTS

Unlike magnetic tapes, which have labels as optional features, magnetic disks require labels for all files. The labels are not associated physically with the files, as they are with tape, but are placed in a *disk directory*, called a *volume table of contents* (VTOC).

The VTOC is usually placed on cylinder 0, head 0 of each volume (pack or fixed unit). The first record on the track, as always, is Record Zero, the track descriptor record. The next two records are used for the initial program load (IPL) routine on the system residence pack (SYSRES) containing the operating system. On other volumes, these two records contain zeros.

Record 3 in the VTOC is the volume label. Its format is similar to the volume label on magnetic tape except that bytes 12 to 21 contain the address of the starting address of the VTOC. It is called a Format-4 label.

Record 4 and subsequent records contain the file labels, which have several formats.

MAXIMUM NUMBER OF BYTES PER RECORD		NUMBER OF RECORDS	
WITHOUT KEYS	WITH KEYS	PER TRACK	PER CYLINDER
8368	8293	1	12
4100	4025	2	24
2678	2603	3	36
1966	1891	4	48
1540	1465	5	60
1255	1180	6	72
1052	977	7	84
899	824	8	96
781	706	9	108
686	611	10	120
608	533	11	132
544	469	12	144
489	414	13	156
442	367	14	168
402	327	15	180
366	291	16	192
335	260	17	204
307	232	18	216
282	207	19	228
259	184	20	240
239	164	21	252
220	145	22	264
204	129	23	276
188	113	24	288
174	99	25	300
161	86	26	312
149	74	27	324
137	62	28	336
127	52	29	348
117	42	30	360
108	33	31	372
99	24	32	384
91	16	33	396
84	9	34	408
76		35	420
70		36	432
63		37	444
57		38	456
46		39	468
41		40	480

Figure 15–3 Track capacity table

DISK LABELS AND EXTENTS

All magnetic disk files require labels. The Format-1 file label has 140 bytes. It is used with most disk files. The Format-2 label identifies indexes of indexed sequential files. The Format-3 label is used if the file requires more than three extents (contiguous disk tracks). The Format-4 label identifies the VTOC.

Fields in the Format-1 file label are:

POSITIONS	NAME	DESCRIPTION
01–44	File identification	A unique identification name. This is written as the key area preceding the data portion of the record.
45	Format identifier	1 for Format 1.
46–51	File serial number	Same as volume serial number.
52–53	Volume sequence number	For multivolume files, the sequence number of this volume.
54–56	Creation date	Binary: 8 bits for year (00–99); 16 bits for day (1–366).
57–59	Expiration date	Same format as creation date.
60	Extent count	Number of extents on this volume for this file.
61	Bytes used in last block of directory	Used by OS only.
62		Reserved.
63–75	System code	Name of the operating system.
76–82		Reserved.
83–84	File type	SD for sequential disk; IS for indexed sequential; DA for direct organization.
85	Record format	Used by OS only.
86	Option codes	IS only; options for master index and type of overflow area.
87–88	Block length	IS only; length of each block.
89–90	Record length	IS only; length of each record.
91	Key length	IS only; length of key area.
92–93	Key location	IS only; position of first byte of key within record.
94	Data set indicators	SD only; indicates if this is the last volume.
95–98		OS only.
99–103	Last record pointer	OS only.
104–105		Reserved.
106–115	First extent data	106 Extent type. 107 Extent sequence number. 108–111 Extent lower limit. 112–115 Extent upper limit.
116–125	Second extent data	Same format as first extent.
126–135	Third extent data	Same format as first two extents.
136–140	Pointer	Address of next label: Format-2 for IS; Format-3, if any, for SD and DA.

Data for disk labels is provided through DLBL and EXTENT job control statements. The format for DLBL is shown in Figure 15–4.

The *extent* of a file is determined by the number of its first track on the volume and the number of tracks it occupies. Sequential disk files may have more than one extent, each representing a number of consecutive tracks that hold a portion of the file. The first track is expressed as a *relative track* giving its number relative to the start of the volume. The first track on the volume is track 0.

The format of the EXTENT statement is shown in Figure 15–5.

```
Format:     // DLBL filename,'file-ID',date,codes
Example:    // DLBL DKFILE,'INVENTORY MASTER',99/365,SD
```

OPERAND	DESCRIPTION
filename	Name of the DTFSD, 1–7 characters.
'file-ID'	1–44 characters within single quotes identifying the file.
date	Retention date or time in either format: (1) dddd = days to be retained; (2) yy/ddd = last year and day to be retained.
codes	Type of file label: SD for sequential disk; ISC for indexed sequential file create; ISE for IS file extend (or process); DA for direct organization. Default is SD.

Figure 15–4 Format of DLBL statement

```
Format:     // EXTENT symbolic-unit,serial#,type,sequence#,
                      rel-track,#tracks,split-cyl-trk
Example:    // EXTENT SYS011,VOL123,1,1,2244,48
```

OPERAND	DESCRIPTION
symbolic-unit	The system code SYSnnn. May be omitted for EXTENT statements after the first for the file.
serial#	Volume serial number for the volume. May be omitted from second or additional EXTENT statements.
type	Type of extent: 1 for normal data area; 2 for independent IS overflow area; 4 for IS index area; 8 for data area if split cylinder. Default is 1.
sequence#	Sequence number (0–255) of this extent if more than one per file. 0 is first extent number for SD and DA files and IS files with master index.
rel-track	Relative track where extent begins (1–5 digits). The relative track formula = tracks per cylinder * cylinder number + track number.
#tracks	Number of tracks in this extent (1–5 digits).
split-cyl-trk	Used only with SD files using only part of each cylinder for the file. Digits 0–19 specify upper track of each cylinder within this file.

Figure 15–5 Format of EXTENT statement

Some versions of DOS require a LBLTYP job control statement for *nonsequential* disk files. The operand is NSD followed by the number of extents enclosed in parentheses. The LBLTYP statement precedes the EXEC LNKEDT statement:

```
// LBLTYP NSD(2)  (two extents required for each indexed sequential file)
// EXEC LNKEDT
```

SEQUENTIAL DISK FILE DEFINITIONS

Each sequential disk file must be defined with a DTFSD macro in DOS or a DCB macro in OS. As with tape, printer, and card files, these macros give characteristics of the file. The assembler constructs a table containing various constants and addresses used by the I/O modules in processing the disk files.

DOS

The DTFSD (Define the File, Sequential Disk) macro contains a name of one to seven characters in the name field, and the keyword operands separated by commas in the operand field. The BLKSIZE, DEVADDR, IOAREA1, IOAREA2, RECFORM, RECSIZE, TYPEFLE, VERIFY, WORKA, and IOREG operands are used exactly like those in the DTFMT entry for magnetic tape.

DEVICE operands include the disk devices such as 3310, 3330, 3340, 3350, or 3370. No FILABL operand is required, since file labels are always required with sequential disk files.

The UPDATE=YES operand permits records read from sequential disk files to be rewritten to the same position. This operand is not available on magnetic tape files.

Sample programs later in the chapter will demonstrate various DTFSD entries.

OS

The DCB macro in OS supplies some information about the sequential disk file, and the DD entry in the job command supplies other entries. The entries DDNAME, DSORG, EODAD, MACRF, LRECL, BLKSIZE, and RECFM are similar to those on magnetic tape. OS statements for each type of file will be shown with each of the sample programs.

OPEN, CLOSE, GET, PUT MACROS

The OPEN macro for output sequential disk files verifies that the extents specified in the EXTENT statements do not contain unexpired files. Then it records the label and extent information in the VTOC and makes the file available for processing.

On input files OPEN verifies label and extent information with the file labels in the VTOC and then makes the file available for processing.

The CLOSE macro with output files writes the last unfilled block of records and deactivates the file. With input files, CLOSE merely deactivates the file.

The first GET macro reads in a block of records and either positions the address in the IOREG to the first logical record in the block, or moves the first record to the work area. Subsequent GET macros make the next logical record available for processing. When the last record in the block has been processed, new block is read in, and the cycle is repeated.

If two I/O areas are specified, GET alternates between the two areas as it reads in blocks of records and always makes the next logical record available for processing.

The PUT macro moves a record from the work area (if one is used) to the I/O area. If output records are built in the I/O area, PUT writes out each block as the I/O area is filled and keeps track of the proper address when two I/O areas are specified.

PUT also causes a record that has been read from a file to be rewritten to the same place if the operand UPDATE=YES has been specified within the DTFSD macro.

PROCESSING SEQUENTIAL DISK FILES

Processing of sequential disk files is similar to processing tape files, even though their physical structures differ widely. Almost any program that processes tape files can be run on magnetic tapes with only minor changes. Even the entries in the DTFSD are almost identical to those in the DTFMT.

To adapt a magnetic tape file for processing on disk, make these changes:

1. Change the name of the file definition macro from DTFMT to DTFSD.
2. Add eight bytes (for the count area) to the BLKSIZE operand and to the I/O area of any output disk file.
3. Change the TLBL job control statement to DLBL and EXTENT statements.
4. Change the DEVICE entries to reflect the correct disk drive numbers.
5. Remove the FILABL statement (if any) from the DTFMT.

Sequential disk files may be used for father-son processing with an old master file, a transaction file, and a new master file. However, disk files have the ability to update the original master file in place. Tapes cannot be processed in this fashion.

If the entry UPDATE=YES appears in the DTFSD macro, then changes may be made to any record obtained with a GET macro. The ensuing PUT causes the updated record to be written back to its original location on the disk. Only the records that are changed need to be rewritten, so that disk updating is considerably faster than tape updating.

Figure 15–6 shows pseudocode for updating a sequential disk master file in place. The logic involves comparing the key of a record from the master file. If the master key is low and the record has been updated, the master record is rewritten to the disk before the next master record is read.

If the keys are equal, the master record is updated and the update switch is set ON. If the transaction key is low, the unmatched transaction is written to an error file. In either event, the next transaction is read and the keys are again compared.

```
START PROGRAM
Open files
Read transaction record
Read master record
Set update switch OFF
DOWHILE transaction key is NOT equal to 9s
AND master key is NOT equal to 9s
  IF master key < transaction key
    THEN
    IF update switch is ON
      THEN rewrite master record
      Set update switch OFF
    ENDIF
    Read master record
    IF end of master file
    OR transaction key = 9s
      THEN move 9s to master key
    ENDIF
  ELSE
    IF master key = transaction key
      THEN update record
      Set update switch ON
    ELSE
      Write transaction to error file
    ENDIF
    Read transaction record
    IF end of transaction file
      THEN move 9s to transaction key
    ENDIF
  ENDIF
ENDDO
Close files
END PROGRAM
```

Figure 15–6 Pseudocode for sequential master file update in place

If end of file is reached for either file, the corresponding key is set to 9s. Once the transaction file has reached end of file, processing is finished.

Records can be added to sequential disk files only by creating a new file. Any attempt to add records to an existing file in place would overlay other records already present in the file.

PROGRAM 15A: CREATING VARIABLE-LENGTH RECORDS

To illustrate sequential disk file creation, we will build variable-length records containing student courses. The root segment contains the student number, name, year and semester, total credit hours, and total courses. Each variable segment contains course abbreviation, course number and section, credit hours, and grade. Each record may contain from 1 to 10 courses.

The root contains 35 bytes, while each course segment contains 10. Record length therefore can range from a minimum of 49 bytes (35 + 10 + 4 for record length field) to a maximum of 139 bytes (35 + (10 * 10) + 4). The average record size for five courses is 89 bytes (35 + (5 * 10) + 4).

A block size of 1,204 bytes was chosen. The 1,200 bytes (exclusive of block length field) can hold 24 minimum sized records, 13 of average size, and eight of maximum size. The operating system will place as many records as will fit in the I/O area before writing them to disk.

Input is in the form of course records. Their format is as shown in Figure 15–7. The format of the variable-length disk records is shown in Figure 15–8.

We use R5 to develop the record length and R6 to point to the next segment as the records are built. As the root segment is processed, totals for credit hours and courses are cleared, and R5 is set to 39 (root length + record length field). As each segment is processed, credit hours are added to the total, total courses are incremented by one, and R5 and R6 are incremented by 10. At the control break, R5 is stored in the record length field at the start of the record.

COLUMNS	DESCRIPTION	
01–09	Student number	
10–29	Student name	
30–32	Year and term	99V9
33–35	Course abbreviation	
36–41	Course number and section	9999V99
42–43	Credit hours	9V9
44	Grade	

Figure 15–7 Input record format for Program 15A

As each record is written to disk, a printed log is kept showing information from the root segment. Figure 15–9 shows the assembler listing for Program 15A, and Figure 15–10 shows the output.

For OS, the DCB entries for the output disk file are:

```
DKFILE  DCB  DDNAME=DISKOUT,BLKSIZE=1204,                         X
             RECFM=VB,DSORG=PS,LRECL=139,MACRF=(PM)
```

ROOT SEGMENT

01–09	Student number		
10–29	Student name		
30–31	Year and term	99V9	Packed
32–33	Total credit hours	99V9	Packed
34–35	Total courses	099	Packed

COURSE SEGMENT (1 TO 10 SEGMENTS)

01–03	Course abbreviation		
04–07	Course number and section	09999V99	Packed
08–09	Credit hours	99V9	Packed
10	Grade		

Figure 15–8 Format of variable-length disk records for Program 15A

```
  LOC  OBJECT CODE    ADDR1 ADDR2  STMT   SOURCE STATEMENT                                    DOS/VSE ASSEMBLER 15.04 86-04-02

                                      1 ***********************************************************************
                                      2 *                  ALTON P. KINDRED, PROGRAM 15A
                                      3 * THIS PROGRAM READS IN CLASS RECORDS AND CREATES VARIABLE-LENGTH
                                      4 * STUDENT SCHEDULE RECORDS ON MAGNETIC DISK.  THE ROOT SEGMENT OF THE
                                      5 * RECORD CONTAINS STUDENT NUMBER, NAME, YEAR AND SEMESTER, TOTAL
                                      6 * CREDIT HOURS, AND TOTAL COURSES.  THE VARIABLE SEGMENT CONTAINS FROM
                                      7 * 1 TO 10 COURSES SHOWING COURSE ABBREVIATION, COURSE NUMBER AND SEC-
                                      8 * TION, CREDIT HOURS, AND GRADE.
                                      9 *            REGISTERS USED:
                                     10 *                  R05:       RECORD LENGTH
                                     11 *                  R06:       SEGMENT ADDRESS
                                     12 *                  R09-R11:   LINK REGISTERS
                                     13 *                  R12:       BASE REGISTER
                                     14 ***********************************************************************
                                     15          PRINT NOGEN
000000                               16 MAINLINE START 0                            SET LOCATION COUNTER
                                     17 *        STM   14,12,12(13)                 SAVE REGISTERS FOR OS        OS
000000 05C0                          18          BALR  12,0                         LOAD BASE REGISTER
                           00002     19          USING *,12                         DESIGNATE BASE REGISTER
                           00000     20          USING DKDUMMY,6                    BASE REG. FOR COURSE SEGMENT
                                     21 *        ST    13,SAVE+4                    STORE REGISTER 13            OS
                                     22 *        LA    13,SAVE                      LOAD SAVE AREA ADDRESS       OS
                                     23 *        OPEN  (INFILE,(INPUT),DKFILE,(OUTPUT),PRINTER,(OUTPUT))    OS
                                     24          OPEN  INFILE,DKFILE,PRINTER        OPEN FILES                   DOS
00001A 4590 C03A           0003C     34          BAL   9,INITIAL                    DO INITIAL PROCESSING
00001E 4590 C04A           0004C     35          BAL   9,MAINLOOP                   DO MAIN PROCESSING LOOP
                                     36          CLOSE INFILE,DKFILE,PRINTER        CLOSE FILES                  DOS
                                     46          EOJ                                END PROGRAM                  DOS
                                     49 *        CLOSE (INFILE)                     CLOSE FILES                  OS
                                     50 *        CLOSE (DKFILE,,PRINTER)                                         OS
                                     51 *        L     13,SAVE+4                    LOAD SAVE AREA ADDRESS       OS
                                     52 *        LM    14,12,12(13)                 RESTORE REGISTERS            OS
                                     53 *        BR    14                           RETURN TO OS                 OS
                                     54 ***********************************************************************
                                     55 *                  FIRST LEVEL MODULES
                                     56 ***********************************************************************
                                     57 *
                                     58 *                  SET INITIAL VALUES MODULE
```

Figure 15–9 Assembler listing of Program 15A

```
  LOC  OBJECT CODE    ADDR1 ADDR2  STMT   SOURCE STATEMENT                                     DOS/VSE ASSEMBLER 15.04 86-04-02

00006E 45A0 C086            00088    76               BAL   10,READRECD                  READ NEXT RECORD
000072 47F0 C056      00058          77               B     DOWHILE2                       *
                            00076    78 ENDDO2        EQU   *                            ENDDO
000076 45A0 C100            00102    79               BAL   10,WRDISK                    WRITE DISK RECORD
00007A 45A0 C11C            0011E    80               BAL   10,SETUP                     SET UP PRINT LINE
00007E 45A0 C15A            0015C    81               BAL   10,PRDETAIL                  PRINT LINE
000082 47F0 C04A      0004C          82               B     DOWHILE                        *
                            00086    83 ENDDO         EQU   *                          ENDDO
000086 07F9                          84               BR    9                          RETURN
                                     85 ***********************************************************************
                                     86 *                   SECOND LEVEL MODULES
                                     87 ***********************************************************************
                                     88 *
                                     89 *                   READ RECORD MODULE
                                     90 *
000088 92D5 CB79      00B7B          91 READRECD MVI   EOFFLAG,C'N'               SET END OF FILE FLAG OFF
                                     92          GET   INFILE,INRECD              READ RECORD
00009C 47F0 C0A2      000A4          98 IFEOF    B     ENDIFEOF                   IF END OF FILE
0000A0 92E8 CB79      00B7B          99 THENEOF  MVI   EOFFLAG,C'Y'                 THEN SET EOF FLAG ON
                            000A4   100 ENDIFEOF EQU   *                          ENDIF
0000A4 07FA                         101          BR    10                         RETURN
                                    102 *
                                    103 *              SET UP ROOT MODULE
                                    104 *
0000A6 F810 C8FB CBE0 008FD 00BE2   105 SETROOT  ZAP   DKTOTHRS,=P'0'             CLEAR TOTAL HOURS AND COURSES
0000AC F810 C8FD CBE0 008FF 00BE2   106          ZAP   DKTOTCRS,=P'0'             *
0000B2 D208 C8DC C887 008DE 00889   107          MVC   DKNUMBER,INNUMBER          SET UP NUMBER AND NAME
0000B8 D213 C8E5 C890 008E7 00892   108          MVC   DKNAME,INNAME              *
0000BE F212 C8F9 C8A4 008FB 008A6   109          PACK  DKYRSEM,INYRSEM            SET UP YEAR AND SEMESTER
0000C4 4150 0027            00027   110          LA    5,39                       SET UP ROOT LENGTH + 4
0000C8 D208 CB7A C887 00B7C 00889   111          MVC   SAVENBR,INNUMBER           SAVE STUDENT NUMBER
0000CE 4160 C8FF            00901   112          LA    6,SEGADDR                  SET ADDR. OF FIRST SEGMENT
0000D2 07FA                         113          BR    10                         RETURN
                                    114 *
                                    115 *              BUILD SEGMENT MODULE
                                    116 *
0000D4 D202 6000 C8A7 00000 008A9   117 BLDSEG   MVC   DKABBREV,INABBREV          SET UP COURSE ABBREVIATION
0000DA F235 6003 C8AA 00003 008AC   118          PACK  DKNBRSEC,INNBRSEC          PACK COURSE NUMBER & SECTION
0000E0 F211 6007 C8B0 00007 008B2   119          PACK  DKCRHRS,INCRHRS            PACK CREDIT HOURS
0000E6 D200 6009 C8B2 00009 008B4   120          MVC   DKGRADE,INGRADE            SET UP GRADE
0000EC FA11 C8FB 6007 008FD 00007   121          AP    DKTOTHRS,DKCRHRS           ADD TO TOTAL HOURS
0000F2 FA10 C8FD CBE1 008FF 00BE3   122          AP    DKTOTCRS,=P'1'             ADD 1 TO TOTAL COURSES
0000F8 4166 000A            0000A   123          LA    6,10(6)                    SET ADDR. TO NEXT SEGMENT
0000FC 4155 000A            0000A   124          LA    5,10(5)                    INCREMENT RECORD LENGTH
000100 07FA                         125          BR    10                         RETURN
                                    126 *
                                    127 *              WRITE DISK MODULE
                                    128 *
000102 4050 C8D8            008DA   129 WRDISK   STH   5,DKRECLEN                 STORE RECORD LENGTH
000106 D201 C8DA CBDC 008DC 00BDE   130          MVC   DKRECLEN+2(2),=X'4040'     BLANK REST OF REC.LEN FIELD
                                    131          PUT   DKFILE,DKRECD              WRITE DISK RECORD
00011C 07FA                         137          BR    10                         RETURN
                                    139 *
                                    140 *              SET UP LINE MODULE
                                    141 *
00011E F248 CB83 C8DC 00B85 008DE   142 SETUP    PACK  PKNUMBER,DKNUMBER          SET UP STUDENT NUMBER
000124 D20B C963 CB88 00965 00B8A   143          MVC   PRNUMBER,PATRN             *
00012A DE0B C963 CB83 00965 00B85   144          ED    PRNUMBER,PKNUMBER          *
000130 D213 C972 C8E5 00974 008E7   145          MVC   PRNAME,DKNAME              SET UP NAME
000136 D204 C989 CB94 0098B 00B96   146          MVC   PRYRSEM,PATRN2             SET UP YEAR AND SEMESTER
00013C DE04 C989 C8F9 0098B 008FB   147          ED    PRYRSEM,DKYRSEM            *
000142 D204 C991 CB99 00993 00B9B   148          MVC   PRTOTHRS,PATRN3            SET UP TOTAL CREDIT HOURS
000148 DE04 C991 C8FB 00993 008FD   149          ED    PRTOTHRS,DKTOTHRS          *
00014E D203 C99B CB9E 0099D 00BA0   150          MVC   PRTOTCRS,PATRN4            SET UP TOTAL COURSES
000154 DE03 C99B C8FD 0099D 008FF   151          ED    PRTOTCRS,DKTOTCRS          *
00015A 07FA                         152          BR    10                         RETURN
                                    153 *
                                    154 *              PRINT DETAIL LINE MODULE
                                    155 *
                            0015C   156 PRDETAIL EQU   *
00015C F911 CB77 CBDE 00B79 00BE0   157 IFEOP    CP    LINECNT,=P'50'             IF LINE COUNT => 50
000162 4740 C168      0016A         158          BL    ENDIFEOP                     *
000166 45B0 C18A            0018C   159 THENEOP  BAL   11,HEADING                   THEN PRINT HEADING
                            0016A   160 ENDIFEOP EQU   *                          ENDIF
                                    161          PUT   PRINTER,PRLINE             PRINT LINE
00017A FA10 CB77 CBE1 00B79 00BE3   167          AP    LINECNT,=P'1'              ADD 1 TO LINE COUNT
000180 9240 C963      00965         168 CLEAR    MVI   PRLINE,C' '                CLEAR PRINT LINE
000184 D283 C964 C963 00966 00965   169          MVC   PRLINE+1(132),PRLINE       *
00018A 07FA                         170          BR    10                         RETURN
                                    171 ***********************************************************************
                                    172 *              THIRD LEVEL HEADING MODULE
                                    173 ***********************************************************************
                                    174 HEADING  PUT   PRINTER,HEAD1              PRINT FIRST HEADING LINE
                                    180          PUT   PRINTER,HEAD2              PRINT SECOND HEADING LINE
                                    186          PUT   PRINTER,HEAD3              PRINT THIRD HEADING LINE
0001BC 92F0 C963      00965         192          MVI   PRLINE,C'0'                SET FOR DOUBLE SPACE
0001C0 F810 CB77 CBE0 00B79 00BE2   193          ZAP   LINECNT,=P'0'              SET LINE COUNT TO ZERO
0001C6 07FB                         194          BR    11                         RETURN
                                    195 *********************************************************************DOS
                                    196 *              FILE DEFINITIONS AND I/O AREAS                        DOS
                                    197 *********************************************************************DOS
                                    198 INFILE   DTFCD BLKSIZE=80,IOAREA1=INAREA,DEVICE=2540,                DOSX
                                                       DEVADDR=SYS006,EOFADDR=THENEOF,WORKA=YES              DOS
                                    219 *                                                                    DOS
                                    220 DKFILE   DTFSD BLKSIZE=1212,IOAREA1=DKAREA,DEVADDR=SYS011,           DOSX
                                                       DEVICE=3340,RECFORM=VARBLK,TYPEFLE=OUTPUT,            DOSX
                                                       VERIFY=YES,WORKA=YES                                  DOS
                                    288 *                                                                    DOS
                                    289 PRINTER  DTFPR BLKSIZE=133,IOAREA1=PRTAREA,DEVICE=1403,              DOSX
                                                       CTLCHR=ASA,DEVADDR=SYS009,WORKA=YES                   DOS
                                    310 *                                                                    DOS
0002F8                              311 INAREA   DS    CL80                                                  DOS
000348                              312 DKAREA   DS    CL1212                                                DOS
000804                              313 PRTAREA  DS    CL133                                                 DOS
```

Figure 15–9 *(Continued)*

```
 LOC  OBJECT CODE      ADDR1 ADDR2  STMT   SOURCE STATEMENT                          DOS/VSE ASSEMBLER 15.04 86-04-02

                                     315 ************************************************************************OS
                                     316 *                  DEVICE CONTROL BLOCKS AND SAVE AREA                  OS
                                     317 ************************************************************************OS
                                     318 *INFILE  DCB   DDNAME=INFILE,BLKSIZE=80,LRECL=80,                        OSX
                                     319 *              MACRF=PM,DSORG=PS,EODAD=THENEOF                          OS
                                     320 *                                                                       OS
                                     321 *PRINTER DCB   DDNAME=PRINTER,BLKSIZE=133,LRECL=133,                     OSX
                                     322 *              MACRF=PMA,DSORG=PS                                       OS
                                     323 *                                                                       OS
                                     324 *DKFILE  DCB   DDNAME=DISKOUT,BLKSIZE=1204,LRECL=139                     OSX
                                     325 *              MACRF=PM,DSORG=PS,RECFM=VB                               OS
                                     326 *                                                                       OS
                                     327 *SAVE    DS    18F                                                      OS
                                     328 ***************************************************************************
                                     329 *                  DATA DEFINITIONS
                                     330 ***************************************************************************
000889                               331 INRECD   DS    0CL80
000889                               332 INNUMBER DS    CL9
000892                               333 INNAME   DS    CL20
0008A6                               334 INYRSEM  DS    CL3
0008A9                               335 INABBREV DS    CL3
0008AC                               336 INNBRSEC DS    CL6
0008B2                               337 INCRHRS  DS    CL2
0008B4                               338 INGRADE  DS    CL1
0008B5                               339          DS    CL36
                                     340 *
0008DA                               341          DS    0H                     TO FORCE HALFWORD ALIGNMENT
0008DA                               342 DKRECD   DS    0CL139
0008DA                               343 DKRECLEN DS    H
0008DC                               344          DS    CL2
0008DE                               345 DKNUMBER DS    CL9
0008E7                               346 DKNAME   DS    CL20
0008FB                               347 DKYRSEM  DS    PL2
0008FD                               348 DKTOTHRS DS    PL2
0008FF                               349 DKTOTCRS DS    PL2
000901                               350 SEGADDR  DS    CL100
                                     351 *
000000                               352 DKDUMMY  DSECT
000000                               353 DKABBREV DS    CL3
000003                               354 DKNBRSEC DS    PL4
000007                               355 DKCRHRS  DS    PL2
000009                               356 DKGRADE  DS    CL1
000965                               357 MAINLINE CSECT
                                     358 *
000965                               359 PRLINE   DS    0CL133
000965                               360 PRNUMBER DS    CL12
000971                               361          DS    CL3
000974                               362 PRNAME   DS    CL20
000988                               363          DS    CL3
00098B                               364 PRYRSEM  DS    CL5
000990                               365          DS    CL3
000993                               366 PRTOTHRS DS    CL5
000998                               367          DS    CL5
00099D                               368 PRTOTCRS DS    CL4
0009A1                               369          DS    CL73
                                     370 *
0009EA                               371 HEAD1    DS    0CL133
0009EA F140404040404040              372          DC    CL17'1'
0009FB E2E3E4C4C5D5E340              373          DC    CL116'STUDENT DISK FILE CREATION'
                                     374 *
000A6F                               375 HEAD2    DS    0CL133
000A6F F0404040E2E3E4C4              376          DC    CL39'0   STUDENT'
000A96 E8C5C1D940404040              377          DC    CL94'YEAR     TOTAL     NUMBER'
                                     378 *
000AF4                               379 HEAD3    DS    0CL133
000AF4 40404040D5E4D4C2              380          DC    CL23'     NUMBER'
000B0B D5C1D4C540404040              381          DC    CL16'NAME'
000B1B E2C5D44B404040C3              382          DC    CL94'SEM.   CR.HRS.  COURSES'
                                     383 *
000B79                               384 LINECNT  DS    PL2
000B7B                               385 EOFFLAG  DS    CL1
000B7C                               386 SAVENBR  DS    CL9
000B85                               387 PKNUMBER DS    PL5
000B8A 4020202060202060              388 PATRN    DC    XL12'402020206020206020202020'
000B96 4020206020                    389 PATRN2   DC    XL5'4020206020'
000B9B 4020214B20                    390 PATRN3   DC    XL5'4020214B20'
000BA0 40202120                      391 PATRN4   DC    XL4'40202120'
                                     392 *
                         00000       393          END MAINLINE
000BA8 5B5BC2D6D7C5D540              394                =C'$$BOPEN '
000BB0 5B5BC2C3D3D6E2C5              395                =C'$$BCLOSE'
000BB8 000001C8                      396                =A(INFILE)
000BBC 00000889                      397                =A(INRECD)
000BC0 00000208                      398                =A(DKFILE)
000BC4 000008DA                      399                =A(DKRECD)
000BC8 000002C8                      400                =A(PRINTER)
000BCC 00000965                      401                =A(PRLINE)
000BD0 000009EA                      402                =A(HEAD1)
000BD4 00000A6F                      403                =A(HEAD2)
000BD8 00000AF4                      404                =A(HEAD3)
000BDC 051C                          405                =P'51'
000BDE 4040                          406                =X'4040'
000BE0 050C                          407                =P'50'
000BE2 0C                            408                =P'0'
000BE3 1C                            409                =P'1'
```

Figure 15–9 *(Concluded)*

```
                  STUDENT DISK FILE CREATION

  STUDENT                                  YEAR     TOTAL      NUMBER
  NUMBER               NAME                SEM.    CR.HRS.    COURSES

135-79-2468   PETER ABBOTT                 87-2     16.0          5
375-98-6420   MERCEDES BENNS               87-2      9.0          3
654-32-1987   WARREN PEACE                 87-2     13.0          4
```

Figure 15–10 Output from Program 15A

PROGRAM 15B: PROCESSING VARIABLE-LENGTH RECORDS

The next program reads back the variable-length records created in Program 15A and prints student schedules. In this example, up to four schedules are printed on each page. In actual practice, specially printed schedule reports would be used, and each report would begin on a new page.

The program requires two loops. The first continues reading and processing the records until end of file is reached. Data from the root segment is printed, and 39 is subtracted from the record length field.

The inner loop processes each segment, subtracts 10 from the record length field, and continues until the record length reaches zero.

Three heading lines are provided, one for each page and two printed with the root segment data. The usual treatment of line counters and heading control is modified to cause double spacing before the first course listed and single spacing for all other courses.

Figure 15–11 shows the assembler listing, and Figure 15–12 shows the output.

```
  LOC  OBJECT CODE    ADDR1 ADDR2  STMT   SOURCE STATEMENT                                DOS/VSE ASSEMBLER 15.08 86-04-02

                                      1 **********************************************************************
                                      2 *                    ALTON R. KINDRED, PROGRAM 15B
                                      3 * THIS PROGRAM READS IN VARIABLE=LENGTH STUDENT SCHEDULE RECORDS FROM
                                      4 * MAGNETIC DISK AND CREATES A STUDENT SCHEDULE REPORT.  THE ROOT SEG-
                                      5 * MENT OF THE RECORD CONTAINS STUDENT NUMBER, NAME, YEAR AND SEMESTER,
                                      6 * TOTAL CREDIT HOURS, AND TOTAL COURSES.  THE VARIABLE SEGMENT CONTAINS
                                      7 * FROM 1 TO 10 COURSES SHOWING COURSE ABBREVIATION, COURSE NUMBER AND
                                      8 * SECTION, CREDIT HOURS, AND GRADE.
                                      9 *          REGISTERS USED:
                                     10 *                    R05:      RECORD LENGTH
                                     11 *                    R06:      SEGMENT ADDRESS
                                     12 *                    R09-R11:  LINK REGISTERS
                                     13 *                    R12:      BASE REGISTER
                                     14 **********************************************************************
                                     15          PRINT NOGEN
000000                               16 MAINLINE START 0                          SET LOCATION COUNTER
                                     17 *        STM   14,12,12(13)               SAVE REGISTERS FOR OS        OS
000000 05C0                          18          BALR  12,0                       LOAD BASE REGISTER
                         00002       19          USING *,12                       DESIGNATE BASE REGISTER
                         00000       20          USING DKDUMMY,6                  BASE REG. FOR COURSE SEGMENT
                                     21 *        ST    13,SAVE+4                  STORE REGISTER 13            OS
                                     22 *        LA    13,SAVE                    LOAD SAVE AREA ADDRESS       OS
                                     23 *        OPEN  (DKFILE,(INPUT),PRINTER,(OUTPUT))                       OS
                                     24          OPEN  DKFILE,PRINTER             OPEN FILES                   DOS
000016 4590 C032         00034       33          BAL   9,INITIAL                  DO INITIAL PROCESSING
00001A 4590 C042         00044       34          BAL   9,MAINLOOP                 DO MAIN PROCESSING LOOP
                                     35          CLOSE DKFILE,PRINTER             CLOSE FILES                  DOS
                                     44          EOJ                              END PROGRAM                  DOS
```

Figure 15–11 Assembler listing of Program 15B

```
  LOC  OBJECT CODE    ADDR1 ADDR2  STMT   SOURCE STATEMENT                                 DOS/VSE ASSEMBLER 15.08 86-04-02

                                     47 *         CLOSE (DKFILE,,PRINTER)                                             OS
                                     48 *         L      13,SAVE+4               LOAD SAVE AREA ADDRESS               OS
                                     49 *         LM     14,12,12(13)            RESTORE REGISTERS                    OS
                                     50 *         BR     14                      RETURN TO OS                         OS
                                     51 ***********************************************************************
                                     52 *                FIRST LEVEL MODULES
                                     53 ***********************************************************************
                                     54 *
                                     55 *                SET INITIAL VALUES MODULE
                                     56 *
000034 F810 CA54 CAB6 00A56 00AB8    57 INITIAL   ZAP    STUCOUNT,=P'5'          SET STUDENT COUNT => 4
00003A 45A0 C182            00184    58           BAL    10,CLEAR                CLEAR PRINT LINE
00003E 45A0 C07A            0007C    59           BAL    10,READDISK             READ FIRST RECORD
000042 07F9                          60           BR     9                       RETURN
                                     61 *
                                     62 *                MAIN PROCESSING LOOP
                                     63 *
                            00044    64 MAINLOOP  EQU    *
000044 95E8 CA56      00A58          65 DOWHILE   CLI    EODFLAG,C'Y'            DOWHILE NOT END OF FILE
000048 4780 C078      0007A          66           BE     ENDDO                     *
00004C 45A0 C098            0009A    67           BAL    10,SETROOT                SET UP ROOT SEGMENT
000050 45A0 C0CA            000CC    68           BAL    10,PRROOT                 PRINT ROOT SEGMENT
000054 1255                          69 DOWHILE2  LTR    5,5                       DOWHILE REC. LEN. > 0
000056 47D0 C064      00066          70           BNP    ENDDO2                      *
00005A 45A0 C134            00136    71           BAL    10,SETSEG                   SET UP COURSE SEGMENT
00005E 45A0 C162            00164    72           BAL    10,PRDETAIL                 PRINT THE COURSE
000062 47F0 C052      00054          73           B      DOWHILE2                    *
                            00066    74 ENDDO2    EQU    *                         ENDDO
000066 45A0 C182            00184    75           BAL    10,CLEAR                  TRIPLE SPACE BETWEEN STUDENTS
00006A 9260 C83B      0083D          76           MVI    PRLINE,C'-'               *
00006E 45A0 C162            00164    77           BAL    10,PRDETAIL               *
000072 45A0 C07A            0007C    78           BAL    10,READDISK               READ NEXT RECORD
000076 47F0 C042      00044          79           B      DOWHILE                   *
                            0007A    80 ENDDO     EQU    *                       ENDDO
00007A 07F9                          81           BR     9                       RETURN
                                     82 ***********************************************************************
                                     83 *                SECOND LEVEL MODULES
                                     84 ***********************************************************************
                                     85 *
                                     86 *                READ RECORD MODULE
                                     87 *
00007C 92D5 CA56      00A58          88 READDISK  MVI    EODFLAG,C'N'            SET END OF FILE FLAG OFF
                                     89           GET    DKFILE,DKRECD           READ RECORD
000090 47F0 C096      00098          95 IFEOD     B      ENDIFEOD                IF END OF FILE
000094 92E8 CA56      00A58          96 THENEOD   MVI    EODFLAG,C'Y'              SET END OF FILE FLAG ON
                            00098    97 ENDIFEOD  EQU    *                       ENDIF
000098 07FA                          98           BR     10                      RETURN
                                     99 *
                                    100 *                SET UP ROOT MODULE
                                    101 *
00009A D20B C83B CA61 0083D 00A63   102 SETROOT   MVC    PRNUMBER,PATRN          SET UP NUMBER AND NAME
0000A0 F248 CA4F C7B4 00A51 007B6   103           PACK   PKNUMBER,DKNUMBER       *
0000A6 DE0B C83B CA4F 0083D 00A51   104           ED     PRNUMBER,PKNUMBER       *
0000AC D213 C84A C7BD 0084C 007BF   105           MVC    PRNAME,DKNAME           *
0000B2 D204 C861 CA6D 00863 00A6F   106           MVC    PRYRSEM,PATRN2          SET UP YEAR AND SEMESTER
0000B8 DE04 C861 C7D1 00863 007D3   107           ED     PRYRSEM,DKYRSEM         *
0000BE 4850 C7B0            007B2   108           LH     5,DKRECLEN              SET RECORD LENGTH IN R5
0000C2 4B50 CAB2            00AB4   109           SH     5,=H'39'                SUBT. ROOT LEN. FROM REC. LEN.
0000C6 4160 C7D7            007D9   110           LA     6,SEGADDR               SET ADDR. OF FIRST SEGMENT
0000CA 07FA                         111           BR     10                      RETURN
                                    112 *
                                    113 *                PRINT ROOT MODULE
                                    114 *
                            000CC   115 PRROOT    EQU    *
0000CC F910 CA54 CAB7 00A56 00AB9   116 IFEOP     CP     STUCOUNT,=P'4'          IF STUDENT COUNT => 4
0000D2 4740 C0EA      000EC         117           BL     ENDIFEOP                  *
                                    118 THENEOP   PUT    PRINTER,HEAD1             THEN PRINT REPORT HEADING
0000E6 F810 CA54 CAB8 00A56 00ABA   124           ZAP    STUCOUNT,=P'0'            SET STU. COUNT TO ZERO
                            000EC   125 ENDIFEOP  EQU    *                       ENDIF
                                    126           PUT    PRINTER,HEAD2           PRINT COLUMN HEADINGS
                                    132           PUT    PRINTER,HEAD3           *
00010C 92F0 C83B      0083D         138           MVI    PRLINE,C'0'             SET FOR DOUBLE SPACE
                                    139           PUT    PRINTER,PRLINE          PRINT ROOT LINE
000120 FA10 CA54 CAB9 00A56 00ABB   145           AP     STUCOUNT,=P'1'          ADD 1 TO STUDENT COUNT
000126 92E8 CA57      00A59         146           MVI    FSTFLAG,C'Y'            SET FIRST COURSE FLAG ON
00012A 9240 C83B      0083D         147           MVI    PRLINE,C' '             CLEAR PRINT LINE
00012E D283 C83C C83B 0083E 0083D   148           MVC    PRLINE+1(132),PRLINE    *
000134 07FA                         149           BR     10                      RETURN
                                    151 *
                                    152 *                SET UP SEGMENT MODULE
                                    153 *
000136 D202 C842 6000 00844 00000   154 SETSEG    MVC    PRABBREV,DKABBREV       SET UP COURSE ABBREVIATION
00013C D208 C84A CA72 0084C 00A74   155           MVC    PRNBRSEC,PATRN3         SET UP COURSE NUMBER & SECTION
000142 DE08 C84A 6003 0084C 00003   156           ED     PRNBRSEC,DKNBRSEC       *
000148 D204 C859 CA7B 0085B 00A7D   157           MVC    PRCRHRS,PATRN4          SET UP CREDIT HOURS
00014E DE04 C859 6007 0085B 00007   158           ED     PRCRHRS,DKCRHRS         *
000154 D200 C864 6009 00866 00009   159           MVC    PRGRADE,DKGRADE         SET UP GRADE
00015A 4166 000A            0000A   160           LA     6,10(6)                 SET ADDR. TO NEXT SEGMENT
00015E 4B50 CAB4            00AB6   161           SH     5,=H'10'                SUBT. SEG. LEN FROM REC. LEN.
000162 07FA                         162           BR     10                      RETURN
                                    163 *
                                    164 *                PRINT DETAIL LINE MODULE
                                    165 *
                            00164   166 PRDETAIL  EQU    *
000164 95E8 CA57      00A59         167 IFFST     CLI    FSTFLAG,C'Y'            IF FIRST COURSE
000168 4770 C16E      00170         168           BNE    ENDIFFST                  *
00016C 92F0 C83B      0083D         169 THENFST   MVI    PRLINE,C'0'               THEN SET FOR DOUBLE SPACE
                            00170   170 ENDIFFST  EQU    *                       ENDIF
                                    171           PUT    PRINTER,PRLINE          PRINT LINE
000180 92D5 CA57      00A59         177           MVI    FSTFLAG,C'N'            SET FIRST COURSE FLAG OFF
000184 9240 C83B      0083D         178 CLEAR     MVI    PRLINE,C' '             CLEAR PRINT LINE
000188 D283 C83C C83B 0083E 0083D   179           MVC    PRLINE+1(132),PRLINE    *
00018E 07FA                         180           BR     10                      RETURN
                                    181 ***********************************************************************
                                    182 *                FILE DEFINITIONS AND I/O AREAS
                                    183 ***********************************************************************
```

Figure 15–11 *(Continued)*

```
  LOC  OBJECT CODE    ADDR1 ADDR2  STMT   SOURCE STATEMENT                                DOS/VSE ASSEMBLER 15.08 86-04-02

                                    184 DKFILE    DTFSD BLKSIZE=1204,IOAREA1=DKAREA,DEVADDR=SYS011,          DOSX
                                                        DEVICE=3340,RECFORM=VARBLK,TYPEFLE=INPUT,            DOSX
                                                        WORKA=YES,EOFADDR=THENEOD                            DOS
                                                                                                             DOS
                                    246 *                                                                    DOSX
                                    247 PRINTER   DTFPR BLKSIZE=133,IOAREA1=PRTAREA,DEVICE=1403,             DOS
                                                        CTLCHR=ASA,DEVADDR=SYS009,WORKA=YES                  DOS
                                                                                                             DOS
                                    268 *                                                                    DOS
000278                              269 DKAREA    DS    CL1204                                               DOS
00072C                              270 PRTAREA   DS    CL133                                                DOS
                                    271 *****************************************************************OS
                                    272 *                   DEVICE CONTROL BLOCKS AND SAVE AREA              OS
                                    273 *****************************************************************OS
                                    274 *DKFILE   DCB   DDNAME=DKFILE,BLKSIZE=1204,LRECL=139,                OSX
                                    275 *               MACRF=GM,DSORG=PS,RECFM=VB,EODAD=THENEOD             OS
                                    276 *                                                                    OS
                                    277 *PRINTER DCB    DDNAME=PRINTER,BLKSIZE=133,LRECL=133,                OSX
                                    278 *               MACRF=PMA,DSORG=PS                                   OS
                                    279 *                                                                    OS
                                    280 *SAVE     DS    18F                                                  OS
                                    282 *******************************************************************
                                    283 *               DATA DEFINITIONS
                                    284 *******************************************************************
0007B2                              285           DS    0H
0007B2                              286 DKRECD    DS    0CL139
0007B2                              287 DKRECLEN  DS    H
0007B4                              288           DS    CL2
0007B6                              289 DKNUMBER  DS    CL9
0007BF                              290 DKNAME    DS    CL20
0007D3                              291 DKYRSEM   DS    PL2
0007D5                              292 DKTOTHRS  DS    PL2
0007D7                              293 DKTOTCRS  DS    PL2
0007D9                              294 SEGADDR   DS    CL100
                                    295 *
000000                              296 DKDUMMY   DSECT
000000                              297 DKABBREV  DS    CL3
000003                              298 DKNBRSEC  DS    PL4
000007                              299 DKCRHRS   DS    PL2
000009                              300 DKGRADE   DS    CL1
00083D                              301 MAINLINE  CSECT
                                    302 *
00083D                              303 PRLINE    DS    0CL133
00083D                              304 PRNUMBER  DS    CL12
000849                              305           DS    CL3
00084C                              306 PRNAME    DS    CL20
000860                              307           DS    CL3
000863                              308 PRYRSEM   DS    CL5
000868                              309           DS    CL90
                                    310 *
0008C2                      0083D   311           ORG   PRLINE
00083D                              312 PRLINE2   DS    0CL133
00083D                              313           DS    CL7
000844                              314 PRABBREV  DS    CL3
000847                              315           DS    CL5
00084C                              316 PRNBRSEC  DS    CL9
000855                              317           DS    CL6
00085B                              318 PRCRHRS   DS    CL5
000860                              319           DS    CL6
000866                              320 PRGRADE   DS    CL1
000867                              321           DS    CL91
0008C2                      008C2   322           ORG
                                    323 *
0008C2                              324 HEAD1     DS    0CL133
0008C2 F140404040404040             325           DC    CL14'1'
0008D0 E2E3E4C4C5D5E340             326           DC    CL119'STUDENT SCHEDULE'
                                    327 *
000947                              328 HEAD2     DS    0CL133
000947 F0404040E2E3E4C4             329           DC    CL39'0   STUDENT'
00096E E8C5C1D940404040             330           DC    CL94'YEAR'
                                    331 *
0009CC                              332 HEAD3     DS    0CL133
0009CC 40404040D5E4D4C2             333           DC    CL21'     NUMBER'
0009E1 D5C1D4C540404040             334           DC    CL18'NAME'
0009F3 E2C5D44B40404040             335           DC    CL94'SEM.'
                                    336 *
000A51                              337 PKNUMBER  DS    PL5
000A56                              338 STUCOUNT  DS    PL2
000A58                              339 EODFLAG   DS    CL1
000A59                              340 FSTFLAG   DS    CL1
000A5A                              341 SAVENBR   DS    CL9
000A63 4020202060202060             342 PATRN     DC    XL12'402020206020206020202020'
000A6F 4020206020                   343 PATRN2    DC    XL5'4020206020'
000A74 4021202020204B20             344 PATRN3    DC    XL9'40212020202048 2020'
000A7D 4020214B20                   345 PATRN4    DC    XL5'4020214B20'
                                    346 *
                            00000   347           END   MAINLINE
000A88 5B5BC2D6D7C5D540             348                 =C'$$BOPEN '
000A90 5B5BC2C3D3D6E2C5             349                 =C'$$BCLOSE'
000A98 00000198                     350                 =A(DKFILE)
000A9C 000007B2                     351                 =A(DKRECD)
000AA0 00000248                     352                 =A(PRINTER)
000AA4 000008C2                     353                 =A(HEAD1)
000AA8 00000947                     354                 =A(HEAD2)
000AAC 000009CC                     355                 =A(HEAD3)
000AB0 0000083D                     356                 =A(PRLINE)
000AB4 0027                         357                 =H'39'
000AB6 000A                         358                 =H'10'
000AB8 5C                           359                 =P'5'
000AB9 4C                           360                 =P'4'
000ABA 0C                           361                 =P'0'
000ABB 1C                           362                 =P'1'
```

Figure 15–11 *(Concluded)*

Programming Tips

- With DOS, the I/O area for each output disk file must include an extra eight bytes for the count field. OS does not require the extra eight bytes.
- With variable-length records, be sure to put a four-byte record length field at the start of each logical record and include it in the total record length. Allow four bytes for the block length field at the start of each block. DOS or OS will calculate the correct block length.
- Make the work area for variable-length records the length of the maximum record, including the record length field.
- Align the first byte of a variable-length record on a halfword boundary to facilitate creating or using the record length field.

SUMMARY

Data is recorded on concentric tracks on the surface of a disk. Often both sides of the disk may be used. Tracks are numbered from 00 upward, from the outside of the disk toward the center. The collection of tracks directly above one another is called a cylinder. All the tracks on a cylinder can be read or written without moving the read/write heads.

Access time for disk records is based on four factors:

1. seek time
2. head selection
3. rotational delay
4. data transfer rate

Data transfer rate depends upon rotational speed and density of recording.

Each track has an index point, a home address, a Record Zero used by the operating system, and one or more data records depending upon block length and other factors.

Each record has an eight-byte count field, an optional key field, and a data field. Interrecord gaps appear between fields and between records. Each field has a two-byte cyclic check byte field containing a parity check. The parity bit is stripped off each byte as it is recorded serially on the track.

Track capacity tables are available for each different disk model giving the number of physical records of various sizes that can be placed upon one track. Records with separate key fields require more space than those without key fields.

```
                    STUDENT SCHEDULE

    STUDENT                                             YEAR
    NUMBER                NAME                          SEM.

135-79-2468         PETER ABBOTT                        87-2

        ACG         2001.03                3.0           B
        BOT         2010.01                4.0           A
        LIT         2124.01                3.0           B
        MAC         2233.02                3.0           C
        PSY         2012.04                3.0           A



    STUDENT                                             YEAR
    NUMBER                NAME                          SEM.

375-98-6420         MERCEDES BENNS                      87-2

        COC         1300.03                3.0           B
        COP         1510.01                3.0           C
        MAC         1102.02                3.0           C



    STUDENT                                             YEAR
    NUMBER                NAME                          SEM.

654-32-1987         WARREN PEACE                        87-2

        AMH         1020.04                3.0           B
        MAC         1104.07                3.0           C
        PHY         2049.01                4.0           D
        REL         2000.03                3.0           B
```

Figure 15–12 Output from Program 15B

The Volume Table of Contents holds the volume labels and file labels for all files on each disk pack or unit. Each volume label is 80 bytes long. File labels have several different formats. The most common Format 1 label has a count area, a 44-byte key field, and a 96-byte data field.

When a disk file is created, the label information for DOS is obtained from DLBL and EXTENT job control statements. When the file is later processed, label information from DLBL and EXTENT statements is compared with the label in the VTOC to ensure that the correct file is being handled. Label information for OS is provided in DD statements.

Disk files may be processed using father-son processing just like tape files. They may also be updated in place by rewriting a modified record back into its original location on disk.

TERMS FOR REVIEW

Access time
Alternate track
Count-key-data organization
Cyclic check bytes
Cylinder
Data transfer rate
Direct-access storage device (DASD)
Disk label
DLBL
DTFSD
EXTENT
Head selection
Home address field
Index point
Nonsequential disk file
Read-write assembly
Record Zero
Relative track
Rotational delay
Seek time
Track capacity table
Volume Table of Contents (VTOC)

REVIEW QUESTIONS

1. What is meant by a DASD? How does it differ from a magnetic tape unit?
2. What are alternate tracks and why are they used?
3. What are cylinders? Why are they important in the way in which data is recorded on disk files?
4. What four factors make up access time for disk files? Explain what is meant by each.
5. Describe the physical organization of each track on a disk file.
6. What is meant by count-key-organization? How is the key field used with sequential disk files?
7. What are cyclic check bytes and why are they used?
8. What is the Volume Table of Contents? How is it organized?
9. Summarize the purpose of each of the four formats for disk file labels.
10. What is the largest number of extents that can be listed in a Format 1 label? What happens if the file requires more extents?
11. Explain the role of the GET and PUT macros when updating blocked records in place on sequential disk files.
12. What entry must be placed in the DTFSD macro to permit updating in place?

EXERCISES

1. Refer to the track capacity table for the 3340 disk drive in this chapter. Calculate how many *logical records* can be placed on one track for the following data:

	LOGICAL RECORD LENGTH	RECORDS PER BLOCK	SEPARATE KEY?
a.	120	10	No
b.	120	10	Yes
c.	500	3	No
d.	500	6	No
e.	94	20	Yes

2. Write DLBL and EXTENT statements to describe a Student Course File named STUCRSE to be retained permanently on relative tracks 50 through 69 of a disk file.
3. Write DTFSD entries for an output file named OUTDISK on a 3340 disk having logical records 160 bytes long, blocked five, to be processed in a single I/O area.
4. Write DTFSD entries to read in the file described in Exercise 3 and process the records in a separate work area.
5. Write a mainline control module to update a master sequential disk file by rewriting the updated records back to their original locations. Refer to any processing modules with BAL instructions. Do not write the processing modules.

PROGRAMMING PROBLEMS

1. Write a program to read Data Set 6 in Appendix D and create a sequential disk Checking Account File with variable-length records. The root segment is 100 bytes (plus 4 for record length field). Provide for a maximum of fifty 12-byte segments to reflect transactions. Make the work area 704 bytes long and the I/O area 716 bytes long (8-byte count area plus 708 block length).

   When you create the file, there will be no transactions. Fill each packed field with zeros, put the current date in both date fields, and put spaces in the unused part of the root segment.

   The format of the root segment is as follows:

01–09	Customer number	71–75	Previous balance, packed
10–29	Customer name	76–81	Date of last statement
30–49	Street address	82–83	Number of transactions, packed
50–63	City	84–88	Current balance, packed
64–65	State abbreviation	89–94	Current date
66–70	Zip code	95–100	Unused

   Print a log of input records, with an error message if any customer numbers are out of sequence or duplicate keys. Do not write error records to the file.

2. Write a program to read Data Set 6A in Appendix D and add one variable-length segment for each transaction to the master record in the Checking Account File of Problem 1. The format for each segment is:

01–06	Date of transaction
07	Transaction code (C–check; D–deposit; S–service charge; I–interest)
08–12	Transaction amount (packed)

Add 1 to bytes 82–83 in the root segment for each transaction processed for the master record. Add deposits and interest to the current balance, and subtract checks and service charges from the current balance. Put the current date in bytes 89–94 of the root segment for each record having transactions.

Print a log giving customer number, name, previous balance (zero in each case), number of transactions (if any), and current balance. For any unmatched transactions, print customer number, name, and the message 'INVALID KEY'.

3. Write a program to read the records from the Checking Account File processed in Problem 2. Print a Checking Account Statement for each customer on a separate page. Omit report title and column headings. The top line should show the customer name, number, and current date from the root segment. The second line shows the street address, and the third line shows the city, state, and zip, with three columns between fields.

Triple space after the heading and print a summary line showing previous balance, date of last statement, number of transactions, and current balance. Triple space after the summary line, and list transactions single-spaced showing separate columns for transaction code, check or service charge, deposit or interest, date of transaction, and running balance after recording the transaction. At the end of each statement, verify that the running balance agrees with the current balance showing on the top line.

16

Indexed Sequential Files

OBJECTIVES

After studying this chapter, you should be able to:

- Describe the organization of indexed sequential files
- Explain the purpose of and give examples of each of the indexes
- Explain the content and use of the overflow areas
- Explain and write DTFIS and DCB macros for file creation, sequential retrieval, random retrieval, and reorganization
- Explain the process by which records are retrieved randomly or sequentially
- Explain the process of adding and deleting records from an indexed sequential file
- Write instructions to test the error and status byte for results of read or write operations
- Write routines to create, extend, retrieve, update, add to or delete from, and reorganize indexed sequential files

The Indexed Sequential Access Method (ISAM) has been one of the most popular types of file organization for direct access storage devices (DASD). ISAM makes use of two or more indexes to locate records quickly. The files may be processed either sequentially or randomly (directly). ISAM is supported by IBM and many other manufacturers on computers of all sizes. Many installations today are turning to the Virtual Storage Access Method (VSAM), which offers the ability to process alternate keys, variable-length records, and other features not available in ISAM.

The most common operations on ISAM files are to:

1. Load or extend the file. Loading is the original creation of the file. Extending it is adding records, all having keys higher than the last one previously in the file.
2. Retrieve records sequentially. Sequential processing is useful for listing records from the file or for updating a large proportion of records within the file. Records may be rewritten to their original locations.
3. Retrieve records randomly (directly). Direct retrieval is widely used for online applications or for processing transaction records that are not in sequence.

4. Add or delete records. Adding records requires one or more overflow areas. Records are deleted by inserting a code that can cause them to be bypassed during processing.
5. Reorganize the file. To enlarge a file or remove records from overflow areas, the file is copied into a new file.

FILE ORGANIZATION

An indexed sequential file consists of a prime data area, two or more indexes, and one or two types of optional overflow areas.

Prime Data Area

When the file is created, records are placed in key sequence in the *prime data area*. Each key must be unique; no duplicate keys are permitted. Count-key-data format is used on the disk tracks. Records may be blocked or unblocked. If blocked, the key area contains the key of the last record within the block.

Under DOS, all records in the prime data area must be of the same length. OS permits variable-length records. Under both operating systems, keys must be of the same length, and all must start in the same relative location within the record.

Track Index

The first track (track 0) of each cylinder contains the *track index*. This index contains the key to the last record on each track on the cylinder. Each entry is in count-key-data format. The data portion is a pointer to the first record of the track.

The track index has a *normal entry* and an *overflow entry* for each track. When the file is first created, both entries are alike. As records are added to the overflow area, the normal entry contains the key to the last record currently on the track, while the overflow entry points to the next record belonging to that track that is now in the overflow area.

The first record (record 0) of the track index contains the *cylinder overflow control record* (COCR). It is in count-data format. The data portion of this record contains a pointer to the last record in the cylinder overflow area and the number of remaining tracks available in that area.

The track index ends with one or more *dummy entries* having a key of all 1 bits (X'FF's).

Cylinder Index

The *cylinder index* is in a disk extent separate from the prime data area. It has one entry for each cylinder of the file in count-key-data format. The key refers to the last key on the cylinder. The data area is a pointer to track 0 of that cylinder. The cylinder index is always required for ISAM files. It ends with a dummy entry with key of X'FF's. Figure 16–1 shows a portion of the cylinder index, track indexes, and prime data area.

Master Index

The *master index* is optional and useful only with larger ISAM files. Each entry is in count-key-data format. The key field contains the highest (last) key on each *track of the cylinder index*, and the data field is a pointer to that track.

When used, the master index must immediately precede the cylinder index in an extent separate from the prime data area. It ends with a dummy entry with key of X'FF's.

Overflow Areas

Two optional overflow areas are provided: a *cylinder overflow area* and an *independent overflow area*. Unless records are to be added to the file, no overflow area needs to be provided.

Cylinder Overflow Area We may specify a number of tracks at the end of each cylinder to be reserved as a cylinder overflow area. No records are placed in this area when the file is first created. As a record is added to any track on the cylinder, the last record currently on that track is pushed down to the overflow area, and other records are shifted to permit the new record to be added to the proper position in key sequence.

When this happens, the normal entry in the track index is adjusted to show the new last record currently on the prime track, and the overflow entry is adjusted to point to the record now in the overflow area.

Records in the overflow area are in count-key-data format but *always unblocked*. Attached to the end of the data portion of the record is a 10-byte *sequence link field* that points to the next record in sequence belonging to the same track.

Records in the overflow area are not in key sequence. For both sequential and direct retrieval, ISAM depends upon the sequence link fields to locate each record belonging to the same track.

Independent Overflow Area An independent overflow area may be specified instead of or in addition to the cylinder overflow area. It is in a separate disk extent and receives overflow records from any cylinders within the file. If both cylinder and independent overflow areas are specified, the independent overflow area receives records from any cylinder only after its cylinder overflow area is full.

The independent overflow area may be on a separate volume from the prime data area.

INDEXED SEQUENTIAL FILE DEFINITIONS

Because of their complex nature, ISAM files require more file definition entries than other types of files. These entries are written with the DTFIS macro under DOS and the DCB under OS. These macros differ widely between the two operating systems. Processing macros also show numerous differences between DOS and OS.

Cylinder Index:

KEY	CYL.	HEAD
125	12	00
348	13	00
561	14	00
723	15	00
995	16	00

Track Index, Cylinder 12:

NORMAL ENTRY				OVERFLOW ENTRY			
KEY	CYL.	HEAD	REC.	KEY	CYL.	HEAD	REC.
013	12	01	00	019	12	06	03
038	12	02	00	038	12	02	00
056	12	03	00	059	12	06	02
097	12	04	00	097	12	04	00
125	12	05	00	125	12	05	00

Prime Data Area, Cylinder 12:

CYL.	HEAD	RECORD 0	RECORD 1	RECORD 2	RECORD 3	RECORD 4	RECORD 5
12	01	xxx	004	008	009	012	013
12	02	xxx	023	026	030	035	038
12	03	xxx	041	044	049	052	056
12	04	xxx	066	072	078	090	097
12	05	xxx	103	110	115	120	125

Overflow Area, Cylinder 12:

CYL.	HEAD	RECORD 0	RECORD 1		RECORD 2		RECORD 3	
12	06	xxx	019	C12,H1,R255	059	C12,H3,R255	016	C12,H6,R1
12	07	xxx						

Summary of Changes:

RECORD ADDED	PLACED ON HEAD NUMBER	RECORD SHIFTED TO OVERFLOW AREA	RECORD NUMBER IN OVERFLOW AREA	LAST RECORD NOW ON PRIME TRACK
13	01	19	1	16
52	03	59	2	56
09	01	16	3	13

Figure 16–1 Indexed sequential file indexes and prime data area

DOS

A file is defined under DOS with the DTFIS macro. The name field contains the name of the file, which must contain one to seven alphanumeric characters, with the first being alphabetic. Some of the most commonly used operands in DOS for defining ISAM files are:

DSKXTNT Give the maximum number of extents required for this file. There are always two, one for the prime data area and one for the cylinder index. There will be others if a master index and independent overflow area are used. Extents of prime data areas must always begin on track 0 of a cylinder and occupy complete cylinders.

IOROUT Specify LOAD, ADD, RETRVE, or ADDRTR to indicate the type of processing to be done with the file.

KEYLEN Specify number of bytes in key (1–255).

NRECDS Specify number of logical records in each block. May be omitted for unblocked, and 1 is assumed.

RECFORM Specify FIXBLK if fixed-length blocks or FIXUNB if unblocked.

RECSIZE State number of bytes in each logical record.

CYLOFL Give number of tracks (if any) to be reserved on each cylinder for overflow area. Maximum number depends upon the specific disk device.

DEVICE Show type of disk drive. 3330, 3340, and 3350 are most common.

HINDEX Show type of disk drive containing the cylinder and (if used) the master index.

INDAREA Give name of main storage area to hold cylinder index. Placing all or a part of this index in core eliminates a seek operation and speeds record retrieval.

INDSKIP Use to indicate index skip feature. If INDAREA will not hold the entire cylinder index and records to be processed are in sequence, this entry will eliminate searching cylinder indexes sequentially.

INDSIZE Give size of cylinder index area in main storage. The minimum number of bytes is

$$(m + 3) * (\text{keylength} + 6)$$

where m is the number of entries to be read into main storage at a time. If m is set equal to the number of prime data cylinders plus 1, the entire cylinder index is read into INDAREA at one time.

IOAREAL Give name of first I/O area for file to be loaded or added.

IOAREAR Give name of first I/O area if file is processed randomly.

IOAREAS Give name of first I/O area if file is processed sequentially.

IOAREA2 Give name of second I/O area if used.

IOREG Use to specify a register (2–12) to point to the current record if records are to be processed in the I/O area. Omit WORKR or WORKS.

KEYARG Give name of a field in main storage in which to place the key of a record to be searched for in the file. This field is used for direct retrieval or to specify a beginning key for sequential retrieval.

KEYLOC For blocked records, give location of leftmost byte of key within the record.

MSTIND Write YES if master index is used.

TYPEFLE Indicate RANDOM for random processing, SEQNTL for sequential processing, or RANSEQ for both types.

VERIFY Write YES to check disk records after they are written.

WORKL Give name of work area for loading or adding records to the file.

WORKR Give name of work area for random retrieval. Omit IOREG.

WORKS Write YES if GET or PUT will name a work area for sequential retrieval. Omit IOREG.

OS

DCB entries for indexed sequential files include the following items. The BLKSIZE, CYLOFL, KEYLEN, LRECL, NTM, OPTCD, RECFM, and RKP entries are used *only* when the IS data set is *created*.

BLKSIZE Give number of bytes in the block, including four bytes for block length field for variable-length records. The extra eight bytes for count area are not required in OS.

CYLOFL Specify number of tracks for cylinder overflow area.

DDNAME Give name of the DD statement that describes the data set.

DSORG Use IS for indexed sequential file.

KEYLEN Specify number of bytes in key.

LRECL Give length of each logical record. Should be 4 + maximum record length for variable-length record.

MACRF Write PM for PUT macro with move to work area; PL for PUT in locate mode; PU for PUT to update a record. Write GM for GET with move or GL for GET in locate mode. Write SK when sequential retrieval begins at a specified key.

NTM Write number of tracks in cylinder index at which to create master index, if OPTCD=M. If the master index reaches this number, then a higher level index is created. Up to three levels of indexes may be created in this fashion.

OPTCD Specify I for independent overflow area, L for delete flag option, M for master index to be created, Y for cylinder overflow areas.

RECFM Write FB for fixed-length blocked records or VB for variable-length blocked records.

RKP Write relative position of the first byte of the key field. Use 0 if key starts in the first byte of the record. For RECFM = VL, RKP must be 4 or higher.

ERROR AND STATUS BYTE

Under DOS, the input/output control system (IOCS) uses one byte in the DTFIS table to report the results of each read or write operation to an ISAM file. This byte is called *filenameC* because the letter C is concatenated to the file name and that name is generated at the thirty-first byte of the DTFIS table (filename + 30).

Bits within this byte are numbered 0 to 7, as usual. The bits have one meaning when loading the file (IOROUT=LOAD) and other meanings when adding or retrieving records (IOROUT=ADD, RETRVE, or ADDRTR). The meanings during the load process are shown in Figure 16–2.

Meanings of filenameC during ADD, RETRVE, or ADDRTR are shown in Figure 16–3.

Following each read or write operation, the user should check filenameC with a Test Under Mask (TM) operation and branch to the appropriate routine to process the error or status indicated.

Under OS, byte 24 of the data event control block (DECB) contains error and status bits. This byte is used only during direct retrieval or update, and will be discussed in that section later in the chapter.

BIT	CAUSE	EXPLANATION
0	DASD error	Any uncorrectable DASD error other than wrong length record has occurred.
1	Wrong length record	Record length is not as stated in count area.
2	Prime data area full	The next-to-last track of the prime data area has been filled during load or extend. The programmer should issue ENDFL macro and then extend the file with a larger extent.
3	Cylinder index full	User must extend size of cylinder index.
4	Master index full	User must extend size of master index.
5	Duplicate record	Key of current record is the same as that of a previous record.
6	Sequence check	Key of current record is not in sequence.
7	Prime data area overflow	There is not enough space to write an EOF record.

Figure 16–2 Meanings of filenameC during the load process

BIT	CAUSE	EXPLANATION
0	DASD error	Any uncorrectable DASD error other than wrong length record has occurred.
1	Wrong length record	Record length is not as stated in count area.
2	End of file	EOF occurred during sequential retrieval.
3	No record found	The record to be retrieved has not been found.
4	Illegal ID specified	The value specified to begin sequential retrieval is outside file limits.
5	Duplicate record	The key to the record being added duplicates that of another record in the file.
6	Overflow area full	No space remains in which to add a record. User should assign an independent overflow area or extend the existing one.
7	Overflow	The record retrieved has come from the overflow area.

Figure 16–3 Meanings of filenameC during ADD, RETRVE, or ADDRTR

MACROS FOR FILE CREATION AND EXTENSION

To *create* an indexed sequential file, we should first sort the input records so that they are in sequence with no duplicate keys. We may later *extend* the file if all keys are in sequence and higher than the last key previously in the file. The same program that creates a file may later be used to extend it. The last operand in the // DLBL statement must be changed from ISC to ISE for file extension.

DTFIS

The DTFIS (Define the File, Indexed Sequential) macro in DOS gives specifications for all IS files. The name of the file appears in the name field. Operands of special interest for creating or extending an IS file are:

IOROUT=LOAD

IOAREAL=buffer-name

WORKL=work-area-name

The I/O area, named in IOAREAL, must be large enough to contain the count field, the key, and the block of data. The work area named in WORKL must be large enough to hold the key and one logical record.

DCB

The DCB entries in OS used to create an indexed sequential data set include BLKSIZE, CYLOFL, KEYLEN, LRECL, NTM, OPTCD, and RKP, as described in an earlier section. Each of these entries may be used *only* to create the file. They do not appear in DCBs for other types of processing. In addition, the following entries are typical:

DSORG=IS
DDNAME=name-of-DD-statement
MACRF=(PM) or (PL)

OPEN

The OPEN macro with IS files checks the file specifications and DLBL and EXTENT records to ensure that:

1. Prime data area extents are contiguous.
2. Master and cylinder index extents are continuous on the same device.
3. No extents overlap.
4. Extent types are valid.
5. Extent sequence numbers are in the correct sequence.
6. No unexpired file will be overwritten by the new file.

OPEN then makes the file available for processing.

SETFL

The Set File Load (SETFL) is used in DOS only after the OPEN macro for the indexed sequential file and before the first write to the file. The SETFL macro may be given a name and uses as its only operand the name of the IS file.

The SETFL macro causes ISAM to set up the file for loading (or extending). It preformats the track index so that, if there is room, some prime data records may be written on the same track as the index. This is called a *shared track*.

WRITE or PUT

Records to be written to the file under DOS must first be set up in the field named in the WORKL operand of the DTFIS. The key must precede the data of the logical record in this area. Records are written to the new or extended file with the WRITE macro in the form

```
WRITE filename,NEWKEY
```

where filename is the name of the DTFIS macro. This macro causes the data from the work area to be moved to the I/O area. When the I/O area is filled, the count, key, and data portion of the block are written to the disk. ISAM checks records and writes them to disk only if their keys are in sequence and unduplicated.

As tracks and cylinders are filled on the disk, WRITE updates the respective indexes.

OS uses the PUT macro to create an IS data set. PUT may be used with or without a work area.

ENDFL

After all records have been written to the file, the End File Load (ENDFL) macro is used in DOS before the CLOSE. ENDFL may be given a name. Its only operand is the file name. It writes out any unfilled blocks of records, writes an end-of-file record, and completes the indexes.

CLOSE

The CLOSE macro deactivates the file from further processing. Failure to close a file after loading or extending will cause labels to be written incorrectly in the Volume Table of Contents (VTOC) and may cause trouble in later processing.

PROGRAM 16A: CREATING AN INVENTORY MASTER FILE

Our first program with indexed sequential files creates an inventory master file. Record formats are as shown in Figure 16–4.

Disk records contain 50 bytes, with 10 records per block. The key field contains five bytes. The work area must be 50 bytes long to hold one logical record. The I/O area must be 513 bytes long to hold the count area of eight bytes, the key of five bytes, and the block of 500 bytes.

INPUT RECORDS

01	Delete code	
02–06	Item number (key)	
07–26	Item description	
27–33	Unit price	99999V99
34–38	Quantity on hand	99999
39–43	Reorder point	99999
34–48	Reorder quantity	99999
49	Transaction code: A = add; D = delete; C = change; P = purchase; S = sale	
50–80	Unused	

DISK RECORDS

01	Delete code
02–06	Item number (key)
07–26	Item description
27–30	Unit price (packed)
31–33	Quantity on hand (packed)
34–36	Reorder point (packed)
37–39	Reorder quantity (packed)
40–50	Available for expansion

Figure 16–4 Record formats for creating IS inventory master file

As each record is written to disk, a log is printed. The log also indicates any records out of sequence or having duplicate keys. Any other type of disk error causes a dump of storage and cancellation of the program. Note that the files are closed before the program is cancelled.

The LTORG statement and the statement ENDLITRL EQU * provide a name at the end of the literal pool that can serve as the last byte to be shown on the PDUMP.

Figure 16–5 shows the assembler listing from Program 16A, and Figure 16–6 shows the output.

For OS, the DCB entries for this program would be:

```
ISFILEN  DCB  BLKSIZE=500,CYLOFL=2,DSORG=IS,                    X
              DDNAME=ISFILEN,KEYLEN=5,LRECL=50,                 X
              MACRF=(PM),OPTCD=YW,RECFM=FB,RKP=2
```

```
  LOC  OBJECT CODE    ADDR1 ADDR2  STMT   SOURCE STATEMENT                                          DOS/VSE ASSEMBLER 15.03 86-04-08

                                     1 ************************************************************************
                                     2 *                   ALTON R. KINDRED, PROGRAM 16A
                                     3 * THIS PROGRAM READS IN INVENTORY MASTER RECORDS AND CREATES AN
                                     4 * INDEXED SEQUENTIAL FILE.  AT THE SAME TIME, IT PRINTS A LOG OF
                                     5 * RECORDS AS WRITTEN.  IF ANY RECORD HAS A DUPLICATE KEY OR SEQUENCE
                                     6 * ERROR, IT IS FLAGGED ON THE LOG AND NOT WRITTEN TO THE DISK.
                                     7 *          REGISTERS USED:
                                     8 *                   R09-R11:  LINK REGISTERS
                                     9 *                   R12:      BASE REGISTER
                                    10 ************************************************************************
                                    11          PRINT NOGEN
000000                              12 MAINLINE START 0                          SET LOCATION COUNTER
                                    13 *        STM   14,12,12(13)               SAVE REGISTERS FOR OS       OS
000000 05C0                         14          BALR  12,0                       LOAD BASE REGISTER
                             00002  15          USING *,12                       DESIGNATE BASE REGISTER
                                    16 *        ST    13,SAVE+4                  STORE REGISTER 3            OS
                                    17 *        LA    13,SAVE                    LOAD SAVE AREA ADDRESS      OS
                                    18 *        OPEN  (INFILE,(INPUT),ISFILEN,(OUTPUT),PRINTER,(OUTPUT))     OS
                                    19          OPEN  INFILE,ISFILEN,PRINTER  OPEN FILES                     DOS
00001A 4590 C03E             00040  29          BAL   9,INITIAL               DO INITIAL PROCESSING
00001E 4590 C05F             00060  30          BAL   9,MAINLOOP              DO MAIN PROCESSING LOOP
000022 4590 C094             00096  31          BAL   9,FINAL                 DO FINAL PROCESSING
                                    32          CLOSE INFILE,ISFILEN,PRINTER  CLOSE FILES                    DOS
                                    42          EOJ                           END PROGRAM                    DOS
                                    45 *        CLOSE (INFILE)                CLOSE FILES                    OS
                                    46 *        CLOSE (ISFILEN,,PRINTER)      *                              OS
                                    47 *        L     13,SAVF+4               LOAD SAVE AREA ADDRESS         OS
                                    48 *        LM    14,12,12(13)            RESTORE REGISTERS              OS
                                    49 *        BR    14                      RETURN TO OS                   OS
                                    50 ************************************************************************
                                    51 *                  FIRST LEVEL MODULES
                                    52 ************************************************************************
                                    53 *
                                    54 *                  SET INITIAL VALUES MODULES
                                    55 *
000040 F811 C8AA C926 008AC 00928   56 INITIAL  ZAP   LINECNT,=P'51'          SET LINE COUNT => 50
000046 92D5 C8AD      008AF         57          MVI   ERRFLAG,C'N'            SET FATAL ERROR FLAG OFF
00004A 45A0 C184             00186  58          BAL   10,CLEAR                CLEAR PRINT LINE
00004E 45A0 C0C8             000CA  59          BAL   10,READRECD             READ FIRST RECORD
                                    60          SETFL ISFILEN                 SET FILE LOAD MODE             DOS
00005E 07F9                         66          BR    9                       RETURN
                                    67 *
                                    68 *                  MAIN PROCESSING LOOP
                                    69 *
                             0006C  70 MAINLOOP EQU   *
000060 95E8 C8AC      008AE         71 DOWHILE  CLI   EOFFLAG,C'Y'            DOWHILE NOT END OF FILE
000064 4780 C092      00094         72          BE    ENDDO                     *
000068 95E8 C8AD      008AF         73 AND      CLI   ERRFLAG,C'Y'            AND ERROR FLAG NOT SET
00006C 4780 C092      00094         74          BE    ENDDO                     *
000070 45A0 C0E6             000E8  75          BAL   10,SETDISK                SET UP DISK RECORD
000074 45A0 C106             00108  76          BAL   10,WRDISK                 WRITE DISK RECORD
000078 45A0 C114             00116  77          BAL   10,PROCERR                TEST FOR ERRORS
00007C 95E8 C8AD      008AF         78 IF       CLI   ERRFLAG,C'Y'              IF NO FATAL ERROR
000080 4780 C08E      00090         79          BE    ENDIF                       *
000084 45A0 C146             00148  80 THEN     BAL   10,SETLOG                   THEN SET UP LOG
000088 45A0 C160             00162  81          BAL   10,PRDETAIL                 PRINT LOG
00008C 45A0 C0C8             000CA  82          BAL   10,READRECD                 READ NEXT RECORD
000090 47F0 C05E      00060         83 ENDIF    B     DOWHILE                   ENDIF
                             00094  84 ENDDO    EQU   *                       ENDDO
000094 07F9                         85          BR    9                       RETURN
                                    86 *
                                    87 *                  FINAL PROCESSING MODULE
                                    88 *
                             00096  89 FINAL    EQU   *
```

Figure 16–5 Assembler listing of Program 16A

```
  LOC  OBJECT CODE    ADDR1 ADDR2  STMT   SOURCE STATEMENT                                        DOS/VSE ASSEMBLER 15.03 86-04-08
000096 95E8 C8AD      008AF          90 IFERR     CLI   ERRFLAG,C'Y'           IF FATAL ERROR
00009A 4770 C0A6      000A8          91           BNE   ENDIFERR                 *
                                     92 THENERR   PDUMP MAINLINE,ENDLITRL        THEN DUMP STORAGE          DOS
                                     98 *         OPEN  (SNAPDCB,(OUTPUT))       *                          OS
                                     99 *         SNAP  DCB=SNAPDCB,ID=1,PDATA=(PSW,REGS),                  OSX
                                    100 *               STORAGE=(MAINLINE,ENDLITRL)                         OS
                                    101 *         CLOSE (SNAPDCB)                *                          OS
                            000A8   102 ENDIFERR  EQU   *                      ENDIF
                                    103           ENDFL ISFILEN                END FILE LOAD MODE           DOS
0000C8 07F9                         115           BR    9                      RETURN
                                    116 *****************************************************************
                                    117 *               SECOND LEVEL MODULES
                                    118 *****************************************************************
                                    119 *
                                    120 *               READ RECORD MODULE
                                    121 *
0000CA 92D5 C8AC      008AE         122 READRECD  MVI   EOFFLAG,C'N'           SET END OF FILE FLAG OFF
                                    123           GET   INFILE,INRECD          READ RECORD
0000DE 47F0 C0E4      000E6         129 IFEOF     B     ENDIFEOF               IF ENDOF FILE
0000E2 92E8 C8AC      008AE         130 THENEOF   MVI   EOFFLAG,C'Y'             THEN SET EOF FLAG ON
                            000E6   131 ENDIFEOF  EQU   *                      ENDIF
0000E6 07FA                         132           BR    10                     RETURN
                                    133 *
                                    134 *               SET UP DISK RECORD MODULE
                                    135 *
0000E8 D219 C664 C614 00666 00616   136 SETDISK   MVC   INVRECD(26),INRECD     SET UP CODE, ITEM NO, DESCR.
0000EE F236 C67E C62E 00680 00630   137           PACK  INVPRICE,INPRICE       PACK AMOUNTS
0000F4 F224 C682 C635 00684 00637   138           PACK  INVQOH,INQOH           *
0000FA F224 C685 C63A 00687 0063C   139           PACK  INVREOP,INREOP         *
000100 F224 C688 C63F 0068A 00641   140           PACK  INVREOQ,INREOQ         *
000106 07FA                         141           BR    10                     RETURN
                                    142 *
                                    143 *               WRITE DISK RECORD MODULE
                                    144 *
                                    145 WRDISK    WRITE ISFILEN,NEWKEY         WRITE DISK RECORD            DOS
                                    150 *         PUT   ISFILEN,INVRECD        *                            OS
000114 07FA                         151           BR    10                     RETURN
                                    152 *
                                    153 *               PROCESS ERROR MODULE
                                    154 *
                            00116   155 PROCERR   EQU   *
000116 91FF C224      00226         156 IF1       TM    ISFILENC,B'11111111'   IF ANY ERRORS                DOS
                                    157 *         TM    ISFILE+81,B'11111111'  *                            OS
00011A 4780 C144      00146         158           BZ    ENDIF1                 *
                            0011E   159 THEN1     EQU   *                      THEN
00011E 9104 C224      00226         160 IF2       TM    ISFILENC,B'00000100'     IF DUPLICATE RECORD        DOS
                                    161 *         TM    ISFILE+81,B'10000000"    *                          OS
000122 4780 C12E      00130         162           BZ    ELSE2                    *
000126 D209 C6DC C928 006DE 0092A   163 THEN2     MVC   PRMESG,=CL10'DUPL.RECD.'   THEN SO INDICATE
00012C 47F0 C144      00146         164           B     ENDIF2                   *
                            00130   165 ELSE2     EQU   *                        ELSE
000130 9102 C224      00226         166 IF3       TM    ISFILENC,B'00000010'       IF OUT OF SEQUENCE       DOS
                                    167 *         TM    ISFILE+81,B'01000000'      *                        OS
000134 4780 C140      00142         168           BZ    ELSE3                      *
000138 D209 C6DC C932 006DE 00934   169 THEN3     MVC   PRMESG,=CL10'OUT SEQU.'      THEN SO INDICATE
00013E 47F0 C144      00146         170           B     ENDIF3                     *
                            00142   171 ELSE3     EQU   *                          ELSE
000142 92E8 C8AD      008AF         172           MVI   ERRFLAG,C'Y'                 SET FATAL ERROR FLAG            PRINT
                            00146   173 ENDIF3    EQU   *                          ENDIF
                            00146   174 ENDIF2    EQU   *                        ENDIF
                            00146   175 ENDIF1    EQU   *                      ENDIF
000146 07FA                         176           BR    10                     RETURN
                                    177 *
                                    178 *               SET UP LOG MODULE
                                    179 *
000148 D204 C697 C615 00699 00617   180 SETLOG    MVC   PRITEM,INITEM          SET UP ITEM NUMBER AND DESCRIP.
00014E D213 C69E C61A 006A0 0061C   181           MVC   PRDESCR,INDESCR        *
000154 D224 C6B4 C8AE 006B6 008B0   182           MVC   PRPRICE,PATRN          EDIT 4 AMOUNTS WITH 1 PATTERN
00015A DE24 C6B4 C67E 006B6 00680   183           ED    PRPRICE,INVPRICE       *
000160 07FA                         184           BR    10                     RETURN
                                    185 *
                                    186 *               PRINT DETAIL LINE MODULE
                                    187 *
                            00162   188 PRDETAIL  EQU   *
000162 F911 C8AA C93C 008AC 0093E   189 IFEOP     CP    LINECNT,=P'50'         IF LINE COUNT => 50
000168 4740 C16E      00170         190           BL    ENDIFEOP                 *
00016C 45B0 C190            00192   191 THENEOP   BAL   11,HEADING               THEN PRINT HEADING
                            00170   192 ENDIFEOP  EQU   *                      ENDIF
                                    193           PUT   PRINTER,PRLINE         PRINT LINE
000180 FA10 C8AA C93E 008AC 00940   199           AP    LINECNT,=P'1'          ADD 1 TO LINE COUNT
000186 9240 C696      00698         200 CLEAR     MVI   PRLINE,C' '            CLEAR PRINT LINE
00018A D283 C697 C696 00699 00698   201           MVC   PRLINE+1(132),PRLINE   *
000190 07FA                         202           BR    10                     RETURN
                                    203 *****************************************************************
                                    204 *               THIRD LEVEL HEADING MODULE
                                    205 *****************************************************************
                            00192   206 HEADING   EQU   *
                                    207           PUT   PRINTER,HEAD1          PRINT FIRST HEADING LINE
                                    213           PUT   PRINTER,HEAD2          PRINT SECOND HEADING LINE
                                    219           PUT   PRINTER,HEAD3          PRINT THIRD HEADING LINE
0001C2 92F0 C696      00698         225           MVI   PRLINE,C'0'            SET FOR DOUBLE SPACE
0001C6 F810 C8AA C93F 008AC 00941   226           ZAP   LINECNT,=P'0'          SET LINE COUNT TO ZERO
0001CC 07FB                         227           BR    11                     RETURN
                                    228 ****************************************************************DOS
                                    229 *               FILE DEFINITIONS AND I/O AREAS                  DOS
                                    230 ****************************************************************DOS
                                    231 INFILE    DTFCD BLKSIZE=80,IOAREA1=INAREA,DEVICE=2540,              DOSX
                                                        DEVADDR=SYS006,EOFADDR=THENEOF,WORKA=YES            DOS
                                    252 *                                                                   DOS
                                    253 ISFILEN   DTFIS DSKXTNT=2,IOROUT=LOAD,KEYLEN=5,NRECDS=10,           DOSX
                                                        RECFORM=FIXBLK,RECSIZE=50,CYLOFL=2,                 DOSX
                                                        DEVICE=3340,HINDEX=3340,IOAREAL=INVAREA,            DOSX
                                                        KEYLOC=2,VERIFY=YES,WORKL=INVRECD                   DOS
```

Figure 16–5 *(Continued)*

```
  LOC  OBJECT CODE     ADDR1 ADDR2  STMT   SOURCE STATEMENT                                              DOS/VSE ASSEMBLER 15.03 86-04-08

                                     302 *                                                                   DOS
                                     303 PRINTER  DTFPR BLKSIZE=133,IOAREA1=PRTAREA,DEVICE=1403,             DOSX
                                                        CTLCHR=ASA,DEVADDR=SYS009,WORKA=YES                  DOS
                                     324 *                                                                   DOS
000340                               325 INAREA   DS    CL80                                                 DOS
000390                               326 INVAREA  DS    CL513                                                DOS
000591                               327 PRTAREA  DS    CL133                                                DOS
                                     328 ********************************************************************OS
                                     329 *              DEVICE CONTROL BLOCKS AND SAVE AREA                  OS
                                     330 ********************************************************************OS
                                     331 *INFILE  DCB   DDNAME=INFILE,BLKSIZE=80,LRECL=80,                   OSX
                                     332 *              MACRF=GM,DSORG=PS,EODAD=THENEOF                      OS
                                     333 *                                                                   OS
                                     334 *PRINTER DCB   DDNAME=PRINTER,BLKSIZE=133,LRECL=133,                OSX
                                     335 *              MACRF=PMA,DSORG=PS                                   OS
                                     336 *                                                                   OS
                                     337 *ISFILEN DCB   DDNAME=ISFILEN,BLKSIZE=500,LRECL=50,CYLOFL=2,        OSX
                                     338 *              MACRF=PM,DSORG=IS,RECFM=FB,KEYLEN=5,OPTCD=YW,RKP=2   OS
                                     339 *                                                                   OS
                                     340 *SNAPDCB DCB   DSORG=PS,RECFM=VBA,MACRF=(W),BLKSIZE=1320,           OSX
                                     341 *              LRECL=132,DDNAME=SNAPDD                              OS
                                     342 *                                                                   OS
                                     343 *SAVE    DS    18F                                                  OS
                                     344 ***********************************************************************
                                     345 *              DATA DEFINITIONS
                                     346 ***********************************************************************
000616                               347 INRECD   DS    0CL80
000616                               348 INDELET  DS    CL1
000617                               349 INITEM   DS    CL5
00061C                               350 INDESCR  DS    CL20
000630                               351 INPRICE  DS    CL7
000637                               352 INQOH    DS    CL5
00063C                               353 INREOP   DS    CL5
000641                               354 INREOQ   DS    CL5
000646                               355 INTRCODE DS    CL1
000647                               356          DS    CL31
                                     357 *
000666                               358 INVRECD  DS    0CL50
000666                               359 INVDELET DS    CL1
000667                               360 INVITEM  DS    CL5
00066C                               361 INVDESCR DS    CL20
000680                               362 INVPRICE DS    PL4
000684                               363 INVQOH   DS    PL3
000687                               364 INVREOP  DS    PL3
00068A                               365 INVREOQ  DS    PL3
00068D 4040404040404040              366          DC    11C' '
                                     367 *
000698                               368 PRLINE   DS    0CL133
000698                               369          DS    CL1
000699                               370 PRITEM   DS    CL5
00069E                               371          DS    CL2
0006A0                               372 PRDESCR  DS    CL20
0006B4                               373          DS    CL2
0006B6                               374 PRPRICE  DS    CL37
0006DB                               375          DS    CL3
0006DE                               376 PRMESG   DS    CL10
0006E8                               377          DS    CL53
                                     378 *
00071D                               379 HEAD1    DS    0CL133
00071D F140404040404040              380          DC    CL31'1'
00073C C9D5E5C5D5E3D6D9              381          DC    CL102'INVENTORY LISTING'
                                     382 *
0007A2                               383 HEAD2    DS    0CL133
0007A2 F040C9E3C5D44040              384          DC    CL36'0 ITEM'
0007C6 E4D5C9E34040D8E4              385          DC    CL16'UNIT  QUANTITY'
0007D6 D9C5D6D9C4C5D940              386          DC    CL81'REORDER  REORDER'
                                     387 *
000827                               388 HEAD3    DS    0CL133
000827 40D5E4D4C2C5D940              389          DC    CL12' NUMBER'
000833 C4C5E2C3D9C9D7E3              390          DC    CL23'DESCRIPTION'
00084A D7D9C9C3C54040D6              391          DC    CL18'PRICE  ON HAND'
00085C D7D6C9D5E34040D8              392          DC    CL80'POINT  QUANTITY'
                                     393 *
0008AC                               394 LINECNT  DS    PL2
0008AE                               395 EOFFLAG  DS    CL1
0008AF                               396 ERRFLAG  DS    CL1
0008B0                               397 PATRN    DS    0CL37
0008B0 4020206B2020214B              398          DC    XL10'4020206B2020214B2020'
0008BA 22222220206B2020              399          DC    3XL9'22222220206B202020'
0008D8                               400          LTORG
0008D8 5B5BC2D6D7C5D540              401                =C'$$BOPEN '
0008E0 5B5BC2C3D3D6E2C5              402                =C'$$BCLOSE'
0008E8 5B5BC2E2C5E3C6D3              403                =C'$$BSETFL'
0008F0 5B5BC2D7C4E4D4D7              404                =CL8'$$BPDUMP'
0008F8 0000000000000942              405                =A(MAINLINE,ENDLITRL)
000900 5B5BC2C5D5C4C6D3              406                =C'$$BENDFL'
000908 00000208                      407                =A(ISFILEN)
00090C 000001D0                      408                =A(INFILE)
000910 00000616                      409                =A(INRECD)
000914 00000310                      410                =A(PRINTER)
000918 00000698                      411                =A(PRLINE)
00091C 0000071D                      412                =A(HEAD1)
000920 000007A2                      413                =A(HEAD2)
000924 00000827                      414                =A(HEAD3)
000928 051C                          415                =P'51'
00092A C4E4D7D34BD9C5C3              416                =CL10'DUPL.RECD.'
000934 D6E4E340E2C5D8E4              417                =CL10'OUT SEQU.'
00093E 050C                          418                =P'50'
000940 1C                            419                =P'1'
000941 0C                            420                =P'0'
                       00942         421 ENDLITRL EQU   *
                       00000         422          END MAINLINE
```

Figure 16–5 *(Concluded)*

INVENTORY LISTING

ITEM NUMBER	DESCRIPTION	UNIT PRICE	QUANTITY ON HAND	REORDER POINT	REORDER QUANTITY	
11357	PASCAL-Z COMPILER	159.50	28	20	15	
17890	QUICK-DOS	219.75	13	15	10	
26774	FILEX MANAGER	395.00	15	12	10	
32209	PERSONAL FILER	118.95	11	12	12	
44332	HI-RES GRAPHICS	225.00	21	15	15	
48105	FLEXI-UTILITY	179.95	35	20	20	
49681	QUICK FINGERS WP	348.95	19	15	12	
51234	SPACE EXPLORER	59.75	87	100	50	
57699	PLANETARY JAUNT	63.50	114	100	50	
65003	GHOSTS AND WITCHES	48.25	133	150	60	
68838	FILEIT UTILITY	219.60	28	20	15	
71225	ZZ ASSEMBLER	79.50	30	25	25	
71225	TOP DOG INTEG PKG	1,234.50	4	5	5	DUPL.RECD.
80217	MAGIC SPREADSHEET	648.00	9	8	8	
74746	INDEX BUILDER	458.25	14	10	10	OUT SEQU.
87938	DATA BASE SUPERB	759.50	10	8	8	
94631	KIDDIES MATH	29.95	3	5	5	

Figure 16–6 Output from Program 16A

Programming Tips

- Be sure to test the error and status byte after each I/O operation with an IS file in DOS. If any bits are set to 1, branch and link to a module that analyzes individual bits to determine the condition that occurred.
- The same program that created an IS file can be used to extend it. Only disk label information needs to be changed to indicate that the file is already in existence.
- Avoid placing the key in the first byte of a record in an IS file. If a delete code is placed in this byte, the key is regarded as out of sequence.

MACROS FOR SEQUENTIAL RETRIEVAL

An indexed sequential file may be retrieved sequentially to list all or part of the records to update the file. Retrieval may begin at the beginning of the file or at a specified record.

If a specified record is given, ISAM searches each index for a key higher than or equal to the record given. Then it searches the track for the specified record. If found, it delivers the record to the problem program. If the record is not found, under DOS bit 3 of filenameC is set to 1.

DTFIS

DTFIS entries most common under DOS for sequential retrieval and updating are:

IOROUT=RETRVE
IOAREAS=I/O-area-name
WORKS=YES or IOREG=(2–12)
TYPEFLE=SEQNTL
KEYARG=search-argument-field

The size of the I/O area must be key length plus block length for unblocked records, or block length only for blocked records. The work area must be large enough for one logical record.

DCB

DCB entries under OS for sequential retrieval and updating are:

DSORG=IS
EODAD=end-of-data address
MACRF=(GL) or (GM), and (PU) for update

OPEN and CLOSE

The OPEN macro verifies labels in the VTOC with those supplied in job control statements and then activates the file. The CLOSE macro deactivates the file.

SETL

The Set Limits (SETL) macro is used after the OPEN and before the first GET macro in both DOS and OS. It may be given a name and uses one of these operands:

DOS	OS
`SETL filename,BOF`	`SETL datasetname,B`
`SETL filename,KEY`	`SETL datasetname,K`
`SETL filename,GKEY`	`SETL datasetname,KH`

BOF in DOS or B in OS causes retrieval to start at the beginning of the file. Retrieval then will continue until end of file is reached or until terminated by the program.

KEY in DOS or K in OS indicates that retrieval will begin exactly with the specified key. The desired key must be placed into the field named in the KEYARG operand in the DTFIS macro before the SETL macro is given. If that key is not found in the file, filenameC will indicate no record found.

GKEY in DOS stands for *generic key*, or *group key*. A generic (or group) key is a code that begins with one or more of the leftmost (high-order) digits or characters of the key to be processed. It indicates that retrieval will begin with the first key having the high order digits or characters specified. The rest of the key must be filled in with zeros, spaces, or other characters lower in collating sequence than the lower order digits in the file. The key must be placed in the KEYARG field before SETL is given.

In OS, the KH operand specifies that retrieval will begin with the first key higher than or equal to the one specified.

For example, if our keys range from 00001 to 10000, we could begin retrieval with the first key above 04000 by placing 04000 in the KEYARG field. FilenameC will indicate no record found only if there is no key in the file higher than 04000. As another example, if keys are alphabetic and five characters long and we wish to begin retrieval with the letter K, we would supply the generic key of Kbbbb (where b = blank).

If the generic key is higher than any key in the file, filenameC will indicate no record found.

GET

The GET macro has the same form as GET with other files already used. It may have a name and one or two operands. The first operand refers to the file name and the second, if used, to the work area. If no work area is specified, records are processed in the I/O area. Under DOS, IOREG must be specified if blocked records are to be processed in the I/O area.

The GET macro delivers a block of records to the I/O area and presents the next record in sequence to the application program. Where necessary, GET follows the indexes and sequence link fields through the overflow area to get the next record in sequence.

In sequential file updating, GET also can cause a block of records to be rewritten to the disk. This feature is discussed in the next section.

PUT or PUTX

The PUT macro in DOS or PUTX in OS is used to write updated records back to an indexed sequential file. The PUT, like GET, may refer to data in the I/O area or in the work area. There must be a GET issued before each PUT. The record obtained by the GET can be updated, and the PUT causes it to be rewritten to the same place in the IS file.

If records are unblocked, the PUT causes the updated record to be rewritten.

If records are blocked, the PUT does *not* cause rewriting. Instead, it sets an indicator that the block has been changed and needs rewriting. The GET macro actually causes the block to be rewritten before reading in the next block of records.

ESETL

The End Set Limit (ESETL) macro is used in both DOS and OS to end the sequential mode that was begun with the SETL macro. If records were blocked, ESETL causes any unfilled block remaining in the I/O area to be written to disk.

PROGRAM 16B: INVENTORY LISTING BY SEQUENTIAL RETRIEVAL

Our next program reads the newly created inventory master file sequentially and prints a reorder report. This report lists all items on which the quantity on hand is less than the reorder point.

Notice in our DOWHILE loop that the operating system does not provide an automatic branch to a specified end-of-file address. We must test filenameC for the end-of-file bit and provide our own instructions to discontinue sequential retrieval.

The TM statement at IF requires explanation. We have just tested bit 2 of filenameC to see if it indicated the end of file. Now we test all other bits except bit 7, which is set to 1 if that record came from the overflow area. It is not an error if a record comes from the overflow area, and we do not wish to alter our processing. However, any other 1 bit in filenameC following our GET statement will cause the abnormal end processing.

We have chosen to process disk records in I/O area. Accordingly, we have used IOREG = (4) in the DTFIS macro, defined a dummy section to refer to the disk record, and written the statement USING INVDUMMY,4 to associate R4 with the dummy section.

Figure 16–7 shows the assembler listing, and Figure 16–8 shows the program output.

DCB entries under OS are as follows for this program:

```
ISFILE  DCB  DDNAME=ISFILE,DSORG=IS,EODAD=THENEOF,        X
             MACRF=(GL),SYNAD=THENERR
```

MACROS FOR DIRECT RETRIEVAL AND UPDATE

Direct (random) retrieval and update are probably the most common applications for indexed sequential files. A transaction record is read from some input file, and its key becomes the search argument for retrieval. ISAM first searches each index for a key that is higher than or equal to the search argument. Then it searches each record on the track and returns the corresponding record if it is found. If not found, ISAM sets the "no record found" bit in filenameC.

```
LOC    OBJECT CODE    ADDR1 ADDR2 STMT   SOURCE STATEMENT                                    DOS/VSE ASSEMBLER 15.13 86-04-14

                                     1 ************************************************************************
                                     2 *                  ALTON R. KINDRED, PROGRAM 16B
                                     3 * THIS PROGRAM READS THE INDEXED SEQUENTIAL INVENTORY MASTER FILE FROM
                                     4 * DISK AND CREATES THE INVENTORY REORDER REPORT.  THIS REPORT LISTS ALL
                                     5 * INVENTORY ITEMS FOR WHICH THE QUANTITY ON HAND IS LESS THAN THE
                                     6 * REORDER POINT.  THIS PROGRAM PROCESSES DISK RECORDS IN THE I/O AREA
                                     7 * INSTEAD OF USING A WORK AREA.
                                     8 *
                                     9 *         REGISTERS USED:
                                    10 *                R04:      BASE FOR DUMMY SECTION
                                    11 *                R09-R11:  LINK REGISTERS
                                    12 *                R12:      BASE REGISTER
                                    13 *************************************************************************
                                    14          PRINT NOGEN
000000                              15 MAINLINE START 0                      SET LOCATION COUNTER
                                    16 *        STM   14,12,12(13)           SAVE REGISTERS FOR OS          OS
000000 05C0                         17          BALR  12,0                   LOAD BASE REGISTER
                              00002 18          USING *,12                   DESIGNATE BASE REGISTER
                              00000 19          USING INVDUMMY,4             DESIGNATE DUMMY SECT. BASE REG.
                                    20 *        ST    13,SAVE+4              STORE REGISTER 3               OS
                                    21 *        LA    13,SAVE                LOAD SAVE AREA ADDRESS         OS
                                    22 *        OPEN  (INFILE,(INPUT),ISFILEN,(OUTPUT),PRINTER,(OUTPUT))    OS
                                    23          OPEN  ISFILE,PRINTER         OPEN FILES                     DOS
000016 4590 C036              00038 32          BAL   9,INITIAL              DO INITIAL PROCESSING
00001A 4590 C066              00068 33          BAL   9,MAINLOOP             DO MAIN PROCESSING LOOP
00001E 4590 C092              00094 34          BAL   9,FINAL                DO FINAL PROCESSING
                                    35          CLOSE ISFILE,PRINTER         CLOSE FILES                    DOS
                                    44          EOJ                          END PROGRAM                    DOS
                                    47 *        CLOSE (ISFILE,,PRINTER)                                     OS
                                    48 *        L     13,SAVE+4              LOAD SAVE AREA ADDRESS         OS
                                    49 *        LM    14,12,12(13)           RESTORE REGISTERS              OS
                                    50 *        BR    14                     RETURN TO OS                   OS
                                    51 *************************************************************************
                                    52 *              FIRST LEVEL MODULES
                                    53 *************************************************************************
                                    54 *
                                    55 *              SET INITIAL VALUES MODULE
                                    56 *
000038 F811 C74D C7B6 0074F 007B8   57 INITIAL  ZAP   LINECNT,=P'51'         SET LINE COUNT => 50
00003E 92D5 C74B      0074D         58          MVI   EOFFLAG,C'N'           SET EOF FLAG OFF
000042 92D5 C74C      0074E         59          MVI   ERRFLAG,C'N'           SET ERROR FLAG OFF
000046 45A0 C11A            0011C   60          BAL   10,CLEAR               CLEAR PRINT LINE
                                    61          SETL  ISFILE,BOF             START AT BEGINNING OF FILE     DOS
                                    70 *        SETL  ISFILE,B                 *                            OS
000062 45A0 C0B2            000B4   71          BAL   10,RDMAST              READ INVENTORY MASTER RECORD
000066 07F9                         72          BR    9                      RETURN
                                    73 *
                                    74 *              MAIN PROCESSING LOOP
                                    75 *
                            00068   76 MAINLOOP EQU   *
000068 95E8 C74B      0074D         77 DOWHILE  CLI   EOFFLAG,C'Y'           DOWHILE NOT END OF INV. MASTER
00006C 4780 C090      00092         78          BE    ENDDO                    *
000070 95E8 C74C      0074E         79 AND      CLI   ERRFLAG,C'Y'           AND NO ERRORS
000074 4780 C090      00092         80          BE    ENDDO                    *
000078 F922 401E 4021 0001E 00021   81 IF2      CP    INVQOH,INVREOP           IF QUANTITY < REORDER POINT
00007E 47B0 C088      0008A         82          BNL   ENDIF2                     *
000082 45A0 C0DC            000DE   83 THEN2    BAL   10,SETUP                     THEN SET UP REPORT
000086 45A0 C0F6            000F8   84          BAL   10,PRDETAIL                  PRINT LINE
                            0008A   85 ENDIF2   EQU   *                          ENDIF
00008A 45A0 C0B2            000B4   86          BAL   10,RDMAST                  READ NEXT RECORD
00008E 47F0 C066      00068         87          B     DOWHILE                    *
                            00092   88 ENDDO    EQU   *                      ENDDO
000092 07F9                         89          BR    9                      RETURN
                                    90 *
                                    91 *              FINAL PROCESSING MODULE
                                    92 *
                            00094   93 FINAL    EQU   *
000094 95E8 C74C      0074E         94 IFERR2   CLI   ERRFLAG,C'Y'           IF FATAL ERROR
000098 4770 C0A4      000A6         95          BNE   ENDERR2                  *
                                    96 THENERR2 PDUMP MAINLINE,ENDLITRL        THEN DUMP STORAGE            DOS
                                   102 *        OPEN  (SNAPDCB,(OUTPUT))       *                            OS
                                   103 *        SNAP  DCB=SNAPDCB,ID=1,PDATA=(PSW,REGS),                    OSX
                                   104 *              STORAGE=(MAINLINE,ENDLITRL)                           OS
                                   105 *        CLOSE (SNAPDCB)                *                            OS
                            000A6  106 ENDERR2  EQU   *                      ENDIF
                                   107          ESETL ISFILE                 END SEQUENTIAL RETRIEVAL
0000B2 07F9                        112          BR    9                      RETURN
                                   113 ************************************************************************
                                   114 *              SECOND LEVEL MODULES
                                   115 ************************************************************************
                                   116 *
                                   117 *              READ INVENTORY MASTER MODULE
                                   118 *
                                   119 RDMAST   GET   ISFILE                 READ MASTER RECORD
                                   124 *        LR    4,1                    PUT RECORD ADDR. IN R4         OS
0000C0 9120 C184      00186        125 IFEOF    TM    ISFILEC,B'00100000'    IF END OF FILE                 DOS
0000C4 4780 C0CE      000D0        126          BZ    ELSEEOF                  *                            DOS
0000C8 92E8 C74B      0074D        127 THENEOF  MVI   EOFFLAG,C'Y'             THEN SET EOF FLAG ON
0000CC 47F0 C0DA      000DC        128          B     ENDIFEOF                 *
                            000D0  129 ELSEEOF  EQU   *                      ELSE
0000D0 91DE C184      00186        130 IFERR    TM    ISFILEC,B'11011110'      IF OTHER ERRORS              DOS
0000D4 4780 C0DA      000DC        131          BZ    ENDIFERR                   *                          DOS
0000D8 92E8 C74C      0074E        132 THENERR  MVI   ERRFLAG,C'Y'               THEN SET ERROR FLAG ON
                            000DC  133 ENDIFERR EQU   *                        ENDIF
                            000DC  134 ENDIFEOF EQU   *                      ENDIF
0000DC 07FA                        135          BR    10                     RETURN
                                   136 *
                                   137 *              SET UP PRINT LINE MODULE
                                   138 *
0000DE D204 C538 4001 0053A 00001  139 SETUP    MVC   PRITEM,INVITEM         SET UP ITEM NUMBER AND DESCR.
0000E4 D213 C53F 4006 00541 00006  140          MVC   PRDESCR,INVDESCR       *
0000EA D224 C555 C74F 00557 00751  141          MVC   PRPRICE(37),PATRN      EDIT 4 FIELDS WITH 1 PATTERN
0000F0 DE24 C555 401A 00557 0001A  142          ED    PRPRICE,INVPRICE       *
```

Figure 16–7 Assembler listing of Program 16B

```
  LOC  OBJECT CODE      ADDR1 ADDR2  STMT    SOURCE STATEMENT                                      DOS/VSE ASSEMBLER 15.13 86-04-14

0000F6 07FA                          143              BR    10                        RETURN
                                     144 *
                                     145 *                    PRINT DETAIL LINE MODULE
                                     146 *
                              000F8  147 PRDETAIL EQU   *
0000F8 F911 C74D C7B8 0074F 007BA    148 IFEOP    CP    LINECNT,=P'50'            IF LINE COUNT => 50
0000FE 4740 C104      00106          149          BL    ENDIFEOP                    *
000102 45B0 C126            00128    150 THENEOP  BAL   11,HEADING                  THEN PRINT HEADINGS
                            00106    151 ENDIFEOP EQU   *                         ENDIF
                                     152          PUT   PRINTER,PRLINE            PRINT LINE
000116 FA10 C74D C7BA 0074F 007BC    158          AP    LINECNT,=P'1'             ADD 1 TO LINE COUNT
00011C 9240 C537      00539          159 CLEAR    MVI   PRLINE,C' '               CLEAR PRINT LINE
000120 D283 C538 C537 0053A 00539    160          MVC   PRLINE+1(132),PRLINE      *
000126 07FA                          161          BR    10                        RETURN
                                     162 ************************************************************************
                                     163 *                    THIRD LEVEL HEADING MODULE
                                     164 ************************************************************************
                                     165 HEADING  PUT   PRINTER,HEAD1             PRINT FIRST HEADING LINE
                                     171          PUT   PRINTER,HEAD2             PRINT SECOND HEADING LINE
                                     177          PUT   PRINTER,HEAD3             PRINT THIRD HEADING LINE
000158 92F0 C537      00539          183          MVI   PRLINE,C'0'               SET FOR DOUBLE SPACE
00015C F810 C74D C7BB 0074F 007BD    184          ZAP   LINECNT,=P'0'             SET LINE COUNT TO ZERO
000162 07FB                          185          BR    11                        RETURN
                                     186 ************************************************************************
                                     187 *                    FILE DEFINITIONS AND I/O AREAS
                                     188 ************************************************************************
                                     189 ISFILE   DTFIS DSKXTNT=2,IOROUT=RETRVE,KEYLEN=5,                          DOSX
                                                        NRECDS=10,RECFORM=FIXBLK,RECSIZE=50,                       DOSX
                                                        CYLOFL=2,DEVICF=3340,HINDEX=3340,                          DOSX
                                                        IOAREAS=INVAREA,IOREG=4,KEYLOC=2,                          DOSX
                                                        TYPEFLE=SEQNTL                                             DOS
                                     267 *                                                                         DOS
                                     268 PRINTER  DTFPR BLKSIZE=133,IOAREA1=PRTAREA,DEVICE=1403,                   DOSX
                                                        CTLCHR=ASA,DEVADDR=SYS009,WORKA=YES                        DOS
                                     289 *                                                                         DOS
0002C0                               290 INVAREA  DS    CL500                                                      DOS
0004B4                               291 PRTAREA  DS    CL133                                                      DOS
                                     292 **********************************************************************OS
                                     293 *                    DEVICE CONTROL BLOCKS AND SAVE AREA                  OS
                                     294 **********************************************************************OS
                                     295 *PRINTER DCB   DDNAME=PRINTER,BLKSIZE=133,LRECL=133,                      OSX
                                     296 *              MACRF=PMA,DSORG=PS                                         OS
                                     297 *                                                                         OS
                                     298 *ISFILE  DCB   DDNAME=ISFILE,DSORG=IS,MACRF=GL,EODAD=THENEOF,             OSX
                                     299 *              SYNAD=THENERR                                              OS
                                     300 *                                                                         OS
                                     301 *SNAPDCB DCB   DSORG=PS,RECFM=VBA,MACRF=(W),BLKSIZE=1320,                 OSX
                                     302 *              LRECL=132,DDNAME=SNAPDD                                    OS
                                     303 *                                                                         OS
                                     304 *SAVE    DS    18F                                                        OS
                                     305 ************************************************************************
                                     306 *                    DATA DEFINITIONS
                                     307 ************************************************************************
000000                               308 INVDUMMY DSECT
000000                               309 INVRECD  DS    0CL50
000000                               310 INVDELET DS    CL1
000001                               311 INVITEM  DS    CL5
000006                               312 INVDESCR DS    CL20
00001A                               313 INVPRICE DS    PL4
00001E                               314 INVQOH   DS    PL3
000021                               315 INVREOP  DS    PL3
000024                               316 INVREOQ  DS    PL3
000027                               317          DS    CL11
000539                               318 MAINLINE CSECT
                                     319 *
000539                               320 PRLINE   DS    0CL133
000539                               321          DS    CL1
00053A                               322 PRITEM   DS    CL5
00053F                               323          DS    CL2
000541                               324 PRDESCR  DS    CL20
000555                               325          DS    CL2
000557                               326 PRPRICE  DS    CL37
00057C                               327          DS    CL66
                                     328 *
0005BE                               329 HEAD1    DS    0CL133
0005BE F140404040404040              330          DC    CL28'1'
0005DA C9D5E5C5D5E3D6D9              331          DC    CL105'INVENTORY REORDER REPORT'
                                     332 *
000643                               333 HEAD2    DS    0CL133
000643 F040C9E3C5D44040              334          DC    CL35'0 ITEM'
000666 E4D5C9E34040D8E4              335          DC    CL16'UNIT  QUANTITY'
000676 D9C5D6D9C4C5D940              336          DC    CL82'REORDER  REORDER'
                                     337 *
0006C8                               338 HEAD3    DS    0CL133
0006C8 40D5E4D4C2C5D940              339          DC    CL12' NUMBER'
0006D4 C4C5E2C3D9C9D7E3              340          DC    CL23'DESCRIPTION'
0006E8 D7D9C9C3C54040D6              341          DC    CL17'PRICE  ON HAND'
0006FC D7D6C9D5E34040D8              342          DC    CL81'POINT  QUANTITY'
                                     343 *
00074D                               344 EOFFLAG  DS    CL1
00074E                               345 ERRFLAG  DS    CL1
00074F                               346 LINECNT  DS    PL2
000751                               347 PATRN    DS    0CL37
000751 4020206B2020214B              348          DC    XL10'4020206B2020214B2020'
00075B 222222202068B2021             349          DC    3XL9'2222222020682O2120'
000778                               350          LTORG
000778 5B5BC2D6D7C5D540              351                =C'$$BOPEN '
000780 5B5BC2C3D3D6E2C5              352                =C'$$BCLOSE'
000788 5B5BC2E2C5E3D340              353                =C'$$BSETL '
000790 5B5BC2D7C4E4D4D7              354                =CL8'$$BPDUMP'
000798 00000000000007BE              355                =A(MAINLINE,ENDLITRL)
0007A0 00000168                      356                =A(ISFILE)
0007A4 00000290                      357                =A(PRINTER)
```

Figure 16–7 *(Continued)*

```
  LOC  OBJECT CODE     ADDR1 ADDR2  STMT    SOURCE STATEMENT                          DOS/VSE ASSEMBLER 15.13 86-04-14

0007A8 00000539                      358                =A(PRLINE)
0007AC 000005BE                      359                =A(HEAD1)
0007B0 00000643                      360                =A(HEAD2)
0007B4 000006C8                      361                =A(HEAD3)
0007B8 051C                          362                =P'51'
0007BA 050C                          363                =P'50'
0007BC 1C                            364                =P'1'
0007BD 0C                            365                =P'0'
                           007BE     366 ENDLITRL EQU   *
                           00000     367          END   MAINLINE
```

Figure 16–7 *(Concluded)*

```
                                   INVENTORY REORDER REPORT

 ITEM                                   UNIT   QUANTITY   REORDER   REORDER
NUMBER         DESCRIPTION              PRICE   ON HAND    POINT   QUANTITY

17890   QUICK-DOS                      219.75        13        15         10
32209   PERSONAL FILER                 118.95        11        12         12
51234   SPACE EXPLORER                  59.75        87       100         50
65003   GHOSTS AND WITCHES              48.25       133       150         60
94631   KIDDIES MATH                    29.95         3         5          5
```

Figure 16–8 Output from Program 16B

Programming Tips

- Sequential retrieval of an IS file can begin at the start of the file, at a specified key, or at the first key higher than or equal to a generic key.
- The SETL and ESETL macros can be reused in a program to permit sequential retrieval to begin and end at various places as the program continues. A form of direct retrieval can be executed in this fashion.
- In DOS, filenameC must be tested for end of file; in OS, a branch is made to the instruction named in the EODAD operand in the DCB.

If found, the record may be updated if desired and written back to the same location on disk.

OPEN and CLOSE have their normal functions and are not discussed especially in the following sections.

DTFIS

DTFIS entries especially useful for direct retrieval are:

IOROUT = RETRVE
IOAREAR = I/O-area-name
WORKR = work-area-name or IOREG = (2–12)
TYPEFLE = RANDOM
KEYARG = search-argument-field

DCB

The DCB entries under OS differ greatly from the DTFIS entries under DOS. OS normally uses *dynamic buffering*, meaning that buffer space is allocated as needed by the operating system. For direct retrieval only one buffer is needed. The entry BUFNO = 1 specifies only one buffer.

The MACRF entry specifies the type of reading or writing to be done with the data set. R and W indicate that the READ and/or WRITE macros will be used. U indicates that the record read will be updated. In this case, RU and WU must be specified.

As always, the DSORG = IS and the DDNAME entries are required.

READ

Under DOS, before records can be read by direct retrieval, the desired key must first be obtained from an input record and placed in the search argument field specified by KEYARG. Then the READ macro is issued in the form:

```
READ filename,KEY
```

The KEY operand causes ISAM to search the indexes for an exact matching key and to return the record to the problem program. If the record is not found, bit 3 of filenameC is set to 1.

OS uses a *data event control block* (DECB) in conjunction with READ and WRITE macros. This block contains 28 bytes containing the following data:

DISPLACEMENTS	DESCRIPTION
00	I/O status byte
01–03	Unused
04–05	Macro type code from READ or WRITE statement
06–07	Buffer length from READ or WRITE statement
08–11	DCB address from READ or WRITE statement
12–15	Buffer address from READ or WRITE statement
16–19	Address in buffer of record with matching key
20–23	Key address from READ or WRITE statement

24–25	Exception code giving cause of unsuccessful I/O
26–27	Unused

Byte 24 of the DECB is similar to filenameC under DOS and has the following meanings. Byte 25 is used only by OS.

BITS	MEANING
0	Record not found
1	Invalid record length
2	Overflow area full on adding record
3	Invalid dynamic buffering request or update WRITE
4	Uncorrectable I/O transfer error
5	Unreachable block
6	Record just read came from overflow area
7	Duplicate key on record to be added

Under OS, the READ macro has *execute* and *list* forms. The execute form is identified with the parameter MF=E and appears among the procedural statements where the READ is to be performed. The list form is identified with MF=L and appears among the data definitions to define the data event control block of 28 bytes.

A typical list form is

```
READ  ISAMDECB,KU,ISFILE,'S','S',KEYAREA,MF=L
```

The name ISAMDECB is the name of the 28-byte DECB area. KU indicates that retrieval will be by key and that updating will be used. The first 'S' indicates that dynamic buffering will be used. The second 'S' indicates that the block length is to be taken from the count field of the disk record. KEYAREA is the name of the field where the key to be retrieved is placed, corresponding to the KEYARG field in DOS.

A typical execute form is

```
READ  ISAMDECB,KU,MF=E
```

The execute form obtains additional information from the DECB to carry out the READ macro correctly.

WAITF or WAIT

The WAITF macro in DOS must follow each READ or WRITE when records are retrieved or updated directly to allow time for the search and transfer of records to be completed. The WAITF macro may be given a name. The only operand is the file name.

The WAIT macro in OS has the same purpose. Its form is

```
WAIT  ECB=ISAMDECB
```

where ISAMDECB is the name of the DECB identified in a list form READ macro.

WRITE

After a record obtained with a READ macro under DOS has been updated, it is written back to the disk with the WRITE macro in this form:

```
WRITE filename,KEY
```

This causes the record to be written back to the record corresponding to the search argument field named in the KEYARG operand. We should be certain that the contents of the KEYARG field have not been changed between the READ and the WRITE to be sure that the correct record is updated.

The size of the record cannot be changed during an update operation, nor should the record key ever be changed.

Under OS, the WRITE macro follows a READ with the KU type to rewrite the updated record back to its original location. It has this form:

```
WRITE  ISAMDECB,K,MF=E
```

where ISAMDECB is the name of the DECB, K indicates reference is to be made to the key area specified in that block, and MF=E indicates execute form.

PROGRAM 16C: INVENTORY MASTER DIRECT RETRIEVAL AND UPDATE

Our third program reads inventory transactions, retrieves the corresponding records from the master file, and updates the records. The transaction records are in the same format as those from which the file was created in Program 16A. An inventory update report is printed as the transactions are processed.

A transaction code (column 44) of S (Sale) indicates that the quantity on hand is to be reduced by the quantity of the transaction. A code of P (Purchase) means to add the quantity to the quantity on hand. A code of C (Change) means to change the value in the master record if the unit price, reorder point, or reorder quantity is not blank in the transaction record.

Any transaction with a key not matching a key in the master file will be listed as having an invalid key. Any other disk read or write error causes an abnormal termination.

Figure 16–9 shows the assembler listing, and Figure 16–10 shows the program output.

```
  LOC  OBJECT CODE    ADDR1 ADDR2  STMT   SOURCE STATEMENT                                     DOS/VSE ASSEMBLER 21.52 86-04-15

                                      1 ***********************************************************************
                                      2 *                   ALTON R. KINDRED, PROGRAM 16C
                                      3 * THIS PROGRAM UPDATES THE INDEXED SEQUENTIAL INVENTORY MASTER FILE.
                                      4 * THE TRANSACTION CODE IN THE INPUT RECORD DETERMINES THE TYPE OF
                                      5 * UPDATE:        P = PURCHASE, ADD QUANTITY TO QUANTITY ON HAND
                                      6 *                S = SALE, SUBTRACT QUANTITY FROM QUANTITY ON HAND
                                      7 *                C = CHANGE, CHANGE PRICE, REORDER POINT, OR REORDER
                                      8 *                    QUANTITY IF FIELD IS NOT BLANK
                                      9 *                    ANY OTHER TRANSACTION CODE IS INVALID.
                                     10 * AN INVENTORY UPDATE REPORT IS PRINTED TO SHOW THE MASTER RECORD
                                     11 * BEFORE THE UDPATE, THE UPDATE TRANSACTION RECORD, AND THE MASTER
                                     12 * RECORD AFTER THE UPDATE.  UNMATCHED TRANSACTION RECORDS ARE FLAGGED
                                     13 * IN THE UPDATE REPORT.
                                     14 *        REGISTERS USED:
                                     15 *               R09-11:  LINK REGISTERS
                                     16 *               R12:     BASE REGISTER
                                     17 ***********************************************************************
                                     18          PRINT NOGEN
000000                               19 MAINLINE START 0                          SET LOCATION COUNTER
                                     20 *        STM   14,12,12(13)               SAVE REGISTERS FOR OS          OS
000000 05C0                          21          BALR  12,0                       LOAD BASE REGISTER
                             00002   22          USING *,12                       DESIGNATE BASE REGISTER
                                     23 *        ST    13,SAVE+4                  STORE REGISTER 3               OS
                                     24 *        LA    13,SAVE                    LOAD SAVE AREA ADDRESS         OS
                                     25 *        OPEN  (INFILE,(INPUT),ISFILE,(OUTPUT),PRINTER,(OUTPUT))         OS
                                     26          OPEN  INFILE,ISFILE,PRINTER      OPEN FILES                     DOS
00001A 4590 C03E             00040   36          BAL   9,INITIAL                  DO INITIAL PROCESSING
00001E 4590 C056             00058   37          BAL   9,MAINLOOP                 DO MAIN PROCESSING LOOP
000022 4590 C0CC             000CE   38          BAL   9,FINAL                    DO FINAL PROCESSING
                                     39          CLOSE INFILE,ISFILE,PRINTER      CLOSE FILES                    DOS
                                     49          EOJ                              END PROGRAM                    DOS
                                     52 *        CLOSE (INFILE)                   CLOSE FILES                    OS
                                     53 *        CLOSE (ISFILE,,PRINTER)          *                              OS
                                     54 *        L     13,SAVE+4                  LOAD SAVE AREA ADDRESS         OS
                                     55 *        LM    14,12,12(13)               RESTORE REGISTERS              OS
                                     56 *        BR    14                         RETURN TO OS                   OS
                                     57 ***********************************************************************
                                     58 *                  FIRST LEVEL MODULES
                                     59 ***********************************************************************
                                     60 *
                                     61 *                  SET INITIAL VALUES MODULE
                                     62 *
000040 F811 C9E4 CA5E 009E6 00A60    63 INITIAL  ZAP   LINECNT,=P'51'             SET LINE COUNT => 50
000046 92D5 CA18      00A1A          64          MVI   EOFFLAG,C'N'               SET END OF FILE FLAG OFF
00004A 92D5 CA19      00A1B          65          MVI   ERRFLAG,C'N'               SET ERROR FLAG OFF
00004E 45A0 C162             00164   66          BAL   10,CLEAR                   CLEAR PRINT LINE
000052 45A0 C0E0             000E2   67          BAL   10,READRECD                READ TRANSACTION RECORD
000056 07F9                          68          BR    9                          RETURN
                                     69 *
                                     70 *                  MAIN PROCESSING LOOP
                                     71 *
                             00058   72 MAINLOOP EQU   *
000058 95E8 CA18      00A1A          73 DOWHILE  CLI   EOFFLAG,C'Y'               DOWHILE NOT END OF FILE
00005C 4780 C0CA      000CC          74          BE    ENDDO                        *
000060 95E8 CA19      00A1B          75 AND      CLI   ERRFLAG,C'Y'               AND NO ERRORS
000064 4780 C0CA      000CC          76          BE    ENDDO                        *
000068 D204 C850 C708 00852 0070A    77          MVC   KEYFIND,INITEM               MOVE KEY TO KEY ARGUMENT
00006E 45A0 C0FE             00100   78          BAL   10,RDDISK                    READ MASTER FILE
000072 95E8 CA19      00A1B          79 IF       CLI   ERRFLAG,C'Y'                 IF NO ERRORS
000076 4780 C0C2      000C4          80          BE    ENDIF                          *
                             0007A   81 THEN     EQU   *                              THEN
00007A 9110 C2DC      002DE          82 IF1      TM    ISFILEC,B'00010000'            IF RECORD FOUND        DOS
                                     83 *        TM    ISDECB+24,B'10000000'          *                      OS
00007E 4710 C0B0      000B2          84          BO    ELSE1                          *
000082 45A0 C124             00126   85 THEN1    BAL   10,SETMAST                       THEN PRINT MASTER DATA
000086 45A0 C13E             00140   86          BAL   10,PRDETAIL                        *
00008A 45A0 C16E             00170   87          BAL   10,UPDATE                        UPDATE THE RECORD
00008E 45A0 C204             00206   88          BAL   10,WRDISK                        REWRITE THE RECORD
000092 95E8 CA19      00A1B          89 IF2      CLI   ERRFLAG,C'Y'                     IF NO ERRORS
000096 4780 C0AC      000AE          90          BE    ENDIF2                             *
00009A 45A0 C22A             0022C   91 THEN2    BAL   10,SETTRAN                         PRINT TRANS. RECORD
00009E 45A0 C13E             00140   92          BAL   10,PRDETAIL                        *
0000A2 45A0 C124             00126   93          BAL   10,SETMAST                         PRINT UPDATED MASTER
0000A6 45A0 C13F             00140   94          BAL   10,PRDETAIL                        *
0000AA 92F0 C789      0078B          95          MVI   PRLINE,C'0'                        SET FOR DOUBLE SPACE
                             000AE   96 ENDIF2   EQU   *                                ENDIF
0000AE 47F0 C0C2      000C4          97          B     ENDIF1                           *
                             000B2   98 ELSE1    EQU   *                              ELSE
0000B2 D209 C7D1 CA60 007D3 00A62    99          MVC   PRMESG,=CL10'NOT FOUND'          SET UP NOT FOUND MESSAGE
0000B8 45A0 C22A             0022C  100          BAL   10,SETTRAN                       PRINT THE TRANS. RECORD
0000BC 45A0 C13E             00140  101          BAL   10,PRDETAIL                      *
0000C0 92F0 C789      0078B         102          MVI   PRLINE,C'0'                      SET FOR DOUBLE SPACE
                             000C4  103 ENDIF1   EQU   *                              ENDIF
                             000C4  104 ENDIF    EQU   *                            ENDIF
0000C4 45A0 C0E0             000E2  105          BAL   10,READRECD                  READ NEXT RECORD
0000C8 47F0 C056      00058         106          B     DOWHILE                      *
                             000CC  107 ENDDO    EQU   *                          ENDDO
0000CC 07F9                         108          BR    9                          RETURN
                                    109 *
                                    110 *                  FINAL PROCESSING MODULE
                                    111 *
                             000CE  112 FINAL    EQU   *
0000CE 95E8 CA19      00A1B         113 IFERR2   CLI   ERRFLAG,C'Y'               IF FATAL ERROR
0000D2 4770 C0DE      000E0         114          BNE   ENDERR2                      *
                                    115 THENERR2 PDUMP MAINLINE,ENDLITRL            THEN DUMP STORAGE            DOS
                                    121 *        OPEN  (SNAPDCB,(OUTPUT))           *                            OS
                                    122 *        SNAP  DCB=SNAPDCB,ID=1,PDATA=(PSW,REGS),                        OSX
                                    123 *              STORAGE=(MAINLINE,ENDLITRL)                               OS
                                    124 *        CLOSE (SNAPDCB)                    *                            OS
                             000E0  125 ENDERR2  EQU   *                          ENDIF
```

Figure 16–9 Assembler listing of Program 16C

```
  LOC  OBJECT CODE    ADDR1 ADDR2  STMT   SOURCE STATEMENT                                     DOS/VSE ASSEMBLER 21.52 86-04-15

0000E0 07F9                         126          BR    9                          RETURN
                                    127 ************************************************************************
                                    128 *                  SECOND LEVEL MODULES
                                    129 ************************************************************************
                                    130 *
                                    131 *                  READ TRANSACTION MODULE
                                    132 *
0000E2 92D5 CA18       00A1A        133 READRECD MVI   EOFFLAG,C'N'               SET END OF FILE FLAG OFF
                                    134          GET   INFILE,INRECD              READ RECORD
0000F6 47F0 C0FC       000FE        140 IFEOF    B     ENDIFEOF                   IF END OF FILE
0000FA 92E8 CA18       00A1A        141 THENEOF  MVI   EOFFLAG,C'Y'                 THEN SET EOFFLAG ON
                             000FE  142 ENDIFEOF EQU   *                          ENDIF
0000FE 07FA                         143          BR    10                         RETURN
                                    144 *
                                    145 *                  READ MASTER DISK MODULE
                                    146 *
                                    147 RDDISK   READ  ISFILE,KEY                 READ MASTER FILE                DOS
                                    152          WAITF ISFILE                       *                             DOS
                                    157 *        READ  ISDECB,KU,MF=E               *                             OS
                                    158 *        WAIT  ECB=ISDECB                   *                             OS
000118 91EE C2DC       002DE        159 IFERR    TM    ISFILEC,B'11101110'        IF ANY ERRORS                   DOS
                                    160 *        TM    ISDECB+24,B'01111101'        *                             OS
00011C 4780 C122       00124        161          BZ    ENDIFERR                     *
000120 92E8 CA19       00A1B        162 THENERR  MVI   ERRFLAG,C'Y'                 THEN SET ERROR FLAG ON
                             00124  163 ENDIFERR EQU   *                          ENDIF
000124 07FA                         164          BR    10                         RETURN
                                    165 *
                                    166 *                  SET UP MASTER DATA MODULE
                                    167 *
000126 D204 C78A C758 0078C 0075A   168 SETMAST  MVC   PRITEM,INVITEM             SET UP ITEM NUMBER AND DESCR.
00012C D213 C791 C75D 00793 0075F   169          MVC   PRDESCR,INVDESCR           *
000132 D224 C7A7 C9F3 007A9 009F5   170          MVC   PRPRICE,PATRN              EDIT 4 AMOUNTS WITH 1 PATTERN
000138 DE24 C7A7 C771 007A9 00773   171          ED    PRPRICE,INVPRICE           *
00013E 07FA                         172          BR    10                         RETURN
                                    173 *
                                    174 *                  PRINT DETAIL LINE MODULE
                                    175 *
                             00140  176 PRDETAIL EQU   *
000140 F911 C9E4 CA6A 009E6 00A6C   177 IFEOP    CP    LINECNT,=P'50'             IF LINE COUNT => 50
000146 4740 C14C       0014E        178          BL    ENDIFEOP                     *
00014A 45B0 C24A             0024C  179 THENEOP  BAL   11,HEADING                   THEN PRINT HEADING
                             0014E  180 ENDIFEOP EQU   *                          ENDIF
                                    181          PUT   PRINTER,PRLINE             PRINT LINE
00015E FA10 C9E4 CA80 009E6 00A82   187          AP    LINECNT,=P'1'              ADD 1 TO LINE COUNT
000164 9240 C789       0078B        188 CLEAR    MVI   PRLINE,C' '                CLEAR PRINT LINE
000168 D283 C78A C789 0078C 0078B   189          MVC   PRLINE+1(132),PRLINE       *
00016E 07FA                         190          BR    10                         RETURN
                                    191 *
                                    192 *                  UPDATE MODULE
                                    193 *
000170 F236 C9E6 C721 009E8 00723   194 UPDATE   PACK  PKPRICE,INPRICE            PACK AMOUNT FIELDS
000176 F224 C9EA C728 009EC 0072A   195          PACK  PKQOH,INQOH                *
00017C F224 C9ED C72D 009EF 0072F   196          PACK  PKREOP,INREOP              *
000182 F224 C9F0 C732 009F2 00734   197          PACK  PKREOQ,INREOQ              *
000188 960C C9E9       009EB        198          OI    PKPRICE+3,X'0C'            GUARANTEE SIGN
00018C 960C C9EC       009EE        199          OI    PKQOH+2,X'0C'              *
000190 960C C9EF       009F1        200          OI    PKREOP+2,X'0C'             *
000194 960C C9F2       009F4        201          OI    PKREOQ+2,X'0C'             *
000198 D209 C7D1 CA6C 007D3 00A6E   202          MVC   PRMESG,=CL10'UPDATED'      FLAG AS UPDATED
00019E 95D7 C737       00739        203 IF3      CLI   INCODE,C'P'                IF PURCHASE
0001A2 4770 C1AE       001B0        204          BNE   ELSE3                        *
0001A6 FA22 C775 C9EA 00777 009EC   205 THEN3    AP    INVQOH,PKQOH                 THEN ADD QUANT. TO QOH
0001AC 47F0 C202       00204        206          B     ENDIF3                       *
                             001B0  208 ELSE3    EQU   *                          ELSE
0001B0 95E2 C737       00739        209 IF4      CLI   INCODE,C'S'                  IF SALE
0001B4 4770 C1C0       001C2        210          BNE   ELSE4                          *
0001B8 FB22 C775 C9EA 00777 009EC   211 THEN4    SP    INVQOH,PKQOH                   THEN SUBT. QUANT. FROM QOH
0001BE 47F0 C202       00204        212          B     ENDIF4                         *
                             001C2  213 ELSE4    EQU   *                            ELSE
0001C2 95C3 C737       00739        214 IF5      CLI   INCODE,C'C'                    IF CHANGE
0001C6 4770 C1FC       001FE        215          BNE   ELSE5                            *
                             001CA  216 THEN5    EQU   *                                THEN
0001CA D506 C721 CA81 00723 00A83   217 IF6      CLC   INPRICE,=CL7' '                  IF PRICE NOT BLANK
0001D0 4780 C1D8       001DA        218          BE    ENDIF6                             *
0001D4 F236 C771 C721 00773 00723   219 THEN6    PACK  INVPRICE,INPRICE                   THEN CHANGE PRICE
                             001DA  220 ENDIF6   EQU   *                                ENDIF
0001DA D504 C72D CA88 0072F 00A8A   221 IF7      CLC   INREOP,=CL5' '                   IF REORD.PT. NOT BLANK
0001E0 4780 C1E8       001EA        222          BE    ENDIF7                             *
0001E4 F224 C778 C72D 0077A 0072F   223 THEN7    PACK  INVREOP,INREOP                     THEN CHANGE REORD. PT.
                             001EA  224 ENDIF7   EQU   *                                ENDIF
0001EA D504 C732 CA88 00734 00A8A   225 IF8      CLC   INREOQ,=CL5' '                   IF REORD. QTY. NOT BLANK
0001F0 4780 C1F8       001FA        226          BE    ENDIF8                             *
0001F4 F224 C77B C732 0077D 00734   227 THEN8    PACK  INVREOQ,INREOQ                     THEN CHANGE REORD. QTY.
                             001FA  228 ENDIF8   EQU   *                                ENDIF
0001FA 47F0 C202       00204        229          B     ENDIF5                           *
                             001FE  230 ELSE5    EQU   *                              ELSE
0001FE D209 C7D1 CA76 007D3 00A78   231          MVC   PRMESG,=CL10'INVAL.CODE'         FLAG INVALID CODE
                             00204  232 ENDIF5   EQU   *                              ENDIF
                             00204  233 ENDIF4   EQU   *                            ENDIF
                             00204  234 ENDIF3   EQU   *                          ENDIF
000204 07FA                         235          BR    10                         RETURN
                                    236 *
                                    237 *                  WRITE DISK MODULE
                                    238 *
                                    239 WRDISK   WRITE ISFILE,KEY                 REWRITE THE RECORD              DOS
                                    244          WAITF ISFILE                       *                             DOS
                                    249 *        WRITE ISDECB,K,MF=E                *                             OS
                                    250 *        WAIT  ECB=ISDECB                   *                             OS
00021E 91FE C2DC       002DE        251 IFERR3   TM    ISFILEC,B'11111110'        IF ANY ERRORS                   DOS
                                    252 *        TM    ISDECB+24,B'11111101'        *                             OS
000222 4780 C228       0022A        253          BZ    ENDFERR3                     *
000226 92E8 CA19       00A1B        254 THENERR3 MVI   ERRFLAG,C'Y'                 THEN SET ERROR SWITCH ON
                             0022A  255 ENDFERR3 EQU   *                            *
```

Figure 16–9 *(Continued)*

```
  LOC  OBJECT CODE     ADDR1 ADDR2  STMT   SOURCE STATEMENT                                      DOS/VSE ASSEMBLER 21.52 86-04-15

00022A 07FA                          256          BR    10                        RETURN
                                     257 *
                                     258 *                SET UP TRANSACTION RECORD
                                     259 *
00022C D204 C78A C708 0078C 0070A    260 SETTRAN  MVC   PRITEM,INITEM             SET UP ITEM NUMBER AND DESCR.
000232 D213 C791 C70D 00793 0070F    261          MVC   PRDESCR,INDESCR           *
000238 D224 C7A7 C9F3 007A9 009F5    262          MVC   PRPRICF,PATRN             EDIT 4 AMOUNTS WITH 1 PATTERN
00023E DE24 C7A7 C9E6 007A9 009E8    263          ED    PRPRICE,PKPRICE           *
000244 D200 C7CE C737 007D0 00739    264          MVC   PRCODE,INCODE             SET UP CODE
00024A 07FA                          265          BR    10                        RETURN
                                     267 *******************************************************************
                                     268 *                THIRD LEVEL HEADING MODULE
                                     269 *******************************************************************
                                     270 HEADING  PUT   PRINTER,HEAD1             PRINT FIRST HEADING LINE
                                     276          PUT   PRINTER,HEAD2             PRINT SECOND HEADING LINE
                                     282          PUT   PRINTFR,HEAD3             PRINT THIRD HEADING LINE
00027C 92F0 C789       0078B         288          MVI   PRLINE,C'0'               SET FOR DOUBLE SPACE
000280 F810 C9E4 CA8D 009E6 00A8F    289          ZAP   LINECNT,=P'0'             SET LINE COUNT TO ZERO
000286 07FB                          290          BR    11                        RETURN
                                     291 *****************************************************************DOS
                                     292 *                FILE DEFINITIONS AND I/O AREAS                   DOS
                                     293 *****************************************************************DOS
                                     294 INFILE   DTFCD BLKSIZE=80,IOAREA1=INAREA,DEVICE=2540,            DOSX
                                                        DEVADDR=SYS006,EOFADDR=THENEOF,WORKA=YES           DOS
                                     315 *                                                                 DOS
                                     316 ISFILE   DTFIS DSKXTNT=2,IOROUT=RETRVE,KEYLEN=5,NRECDS=10,       DOSX
                                                        RECFORM=FIXBLK,RECSIZE=50,CYLOFL=2,DEVICE=3340,    DOSX
                                                        HINDEX=3340,INDAREA=CORINDEX,INDSIZE=66,           DOSX
                                                        IOAREAR=INVAREA,KEYARG=KEYFIND,KEYLOC=2,           DOSX
                                                        TYPEFLE=RANDOM,VERIFY=YES,WORKR=INVRECD            DOS
                                     407 *                                                                 DOS
                                     408 PRINTER  DTFPR BLKSIZE=133,IOAREA1=PRTAREA,DEVICE=1403,          DOSX
                                                        CTLCHR=ASA,DEVADDR=SYS009,WORKA=YES                DOS
                                     429 *                                                                 DOS
000440                               430 INAREA   DS    CL80                                               DOS
000490                               431 INVAREA  DS    CL500                                              DOS
000684                               432 PRTAREA  DS    CL133                                              DOS
                                     433 *****************************************************************OS
                                     434 *                DEVICE CONTROL BLOCKS AND SAVE AREA              OS
                                     435 *****************************************************************OS
                                     436 *INFILE  DCB   DDNAME=INFILE,BLKSIZE=80,LRECL=80,                OSX
                                     437 *              MACRF=GM,DSORG=PS,EODAD=THENEOF                    OS
                                     438 *                                                                 OS
                                     439 *PRINTER DCB   DDNAME=PRINTER,BLKSIZE=133,LRECL=133,             OSX
                                     440 *              MACRF=PMA,DSORG=PS                                 OS
                                     441 *                                                                 OS
                                     442 *ISFILE  DCB   DDNAME=ISFILE,MACRF=(RU,WU),DSORG=IS,BUFNO=1       OS
                                     443 *                                                                 OS
                                     444 *        READ  ISDECB,KU,ISFILE,'S','S',KEYFIND,MF=L             OS
                                     445 *                                                                 OS
                                     446 *SNAPDCB DCB   DSORG=PS,RECFM=VBA,MACRF=(W),BLKSIZE=1320,        OSX
                                     447 *              LRECL=132,DDNAME=SNAPDD                            OS
                                     448 *                                                                 OS
                                     449 *SAVE    DS    18F                                                OS
                                     451 *******************************************************************
                                     452 *                DATA DEFINITIONS
                                     453 *******************************************************************
000709                               454 INRECD   DS    0CL80
000709                               455          DS    CL1
00070A                               456 INITEM   DS    CL5
00070F                               457 INDESCR  DS    CL20
000723                               458 INPRICE  DS    CL7
00072A                               459 INQOH    DS    CL5
00072F                               460 INREOP   DS    CL5
000734                               461 INREOQ   DS    CL5
000739                               462 INCODE   DS    CL1
00073A                               463          DS    CL31
                                     464 *
000759                               465 INVRECD  DS    0CL50
000759                               466          DS    CL1
00075A                               467 INVITEM  DS    CL5
00075F                               468 INVDESCR DS    CL20
000773                               469 INVPRICE DS    PL4
000777                               470 INVQOH   DS    PL3
00077A                               471 INVREOP  DS    PL3
00077D                               472 INVREOQ  DS    PL3
000780                               473          DS    CL11
                                     474 *
00078B                               475 PRLINE   DS    0CL133
00078B                               476          DS    CL1
00078C                               477 PRITEM   DS    CL5
000791                               478          DS    CL2
000793                               479 PRDESCR  DS    CL20
0007A7                               480          DS    CL2
0007A9                               481 PRPRICE  DS    CL37
0007CE                               482          DS    CL2
0007D0                               483 PRCODE   DS    CL1
0007D1                               484          DS    CL2
0007D3                               485 PRMESG   DS    CL10
0007DD                               486          DS    CL51
                                     487 *
000810                               488 CORINDEX DS    CL66
000852                               489 KEYFIND  DS    CL5
                                     490 *
000857                               491 HEAD1    DS    0CL133
000857 F140404040404040              492          DC    CL29'1'
000874 C9D5E5C5D5E3D6D9              493          DC    CL104'INVENTORY UPDATE REPORT'
                                     494 *
0008DC                               495 HEAD2    DS    0CL133
0008DC F040C9E3C5D44040              496          DC    CL36'0 ITEM'
000900 E4D5C9E34040D8E4              497          DC    CL16'UNIT  QUANTITY'
000910 D9C5D6D9C4C5D940              498          DC    CL81'REORDER  REORDER'
                                     499 *
```

Figure 16–9 *(Continued)*

```
  LOC  OBJECT CODE    ADDR1 ADDR2  STMT   SOURCE STATEMENT                              DOS/VSE ASSEMBLER 21.52 86-04-15

000961                               500 HEAD3    DS    OCL133
000961 40D5E4D4C2C5D940              501          DC    CL12' NUMBER'
00096D C4C5E2C3D9C9D7E3              502          DC    CL24'DESCRIPTION'
000985 D7D9C9C3C54040D6              503          DC    CL17'PRICE  ON HAND'
000996 D7D6C9D5E34040D8              504          DC    CL80'POINT  QUANTITY CODE'
                                     506 *
0009E6                               507 LINECNT  DS    PL2
0009E8                               508 PKPRICE  DS    PL4
0009EC                               509 PKQOH    DS    PL3
0009EF                               510 PKREOP   DS    PL3
0009F2                               511 PKREOQ   DS    PL3
0009F5                               512 PATRN    DS    0CL37
0009F5 4020206B2020214B              513          DC    XL10'4020206B2020214B2020'
0009FF 222222202 06B2021             514          DC    3XL9'2222222020 6B202120'
000A1A                               515 EOFFLAG  DS    CL1
000A1B                               516 ERRFLAG  DS    CL1
000A20                               517          LTORG
000A20 5B5BC2D6D7C5D540              518                =C'$$BOPEN '
000A28 5B5BC2C3D3D6E2C5              519                =C'$$BCLOSE'
000A30 5B5BC2D7C4E4D4D7              520                =CL8'$$BPDUMP'
000A38 0000000000000A90              521                =A(MAINLINE,ENDLITRL)
000A40 00000288                      522                =A(INFILE)
000A44 00000709                      523                =A(INRECD)
000A48 000002C0                      524                =A(ISFILE)
000A4C 00000410                      525                =A(PRINTER)
000A50 0000078B                      526                =A(PRLINE)
000A54 00000857                      527                =A(HEAD1)
000A58 000008DC                      528                =A(HEAD2)
000A5C 00000961                      529                =A(HEAD3)
000A60 051C                          530                =P'51'
000A62 D5D6E340C6D6E4D5              531                =CL10'NOT FOUND'
000A6C 050C                          532                =P'50'
000A6E E4D7C4C1E3C5C440              533                =CL10'UPDATED'
000A78 C9D5E5C1D34BC3D6              534                =CL10'INVAL.CODE'
000A82 1C                            535                =P'1'
000A83 40404040404040                536                =CL7' '
000A8A 4040404040                    537                =CL5' '
000A8F 0C                            538                =P'0'
                        00A90        539 ENDLITRL EQU   *
                        00000        540          END   MAINLINE
```

Figure 16–9 *(Concluded)*

INVENTORY UPDATE REPORT

ITEM NUMBER	DESCRIPTION	UNIT PRICE	QUANTITY ON HAND	REORDER POINT	REORDER QUANTITY	CODE	
17890	QUICK-DOS	219.75	13	15	10		
17890	QUICK-DOS	.00	10	0	0	P	UPDATED
17890	QUICK-DOS	219.75	23	15	10		
32209	PERSONAL FILER	118.95	11	12	12		
32209	PERSONAL FILER	.00	12	0	0	P	UPDATED
32209	PERSONAL FILER	118.95	23	12	12		
49681	QUICK FINGERS WP	348.95	19	15	12		
49681	QUICK FINGERS WP	329.50	0	12	10	C	UPDATED
49681	QUICK FINGERS WP	329.50	19	12	10		
51234	SPACE EXPLORER	59.75	87	100	50		
51234	SPACE EXPLORER	49.95	0	0	0	C	UPDATED
51234	SPACE EXPLORER	49.95	87	100	50		
71225	ZZ ASSEMBLER	79.50	30	25	25		
71225	ZZ ASSEMBLER	.00	2	0	0	S	UPDATED
71225	ZZ ASSEMBLER	79.50	28	25	25		
80317	MAGIC SPREADSHEET	.00	2	0	0	S	NOT FOUND
94631	KIDDIES MATH	29.95	3	5	5		
94631	KIDDIES MATH	.00	1	0	0	X	INVAL.CODE
94631	KIDDIES MATH	29.95	3	5	5		

Figure 16–10 Output from Program 16C

MACROS FOR ADDING AND DELETING RECORDS

Records to be added to an indexed sequential file must have their keys in the same record location as the keys on records already in the file. Adding records is the most time-consuming operation done on indexed sequential files. The key for the record to be added must first be compared with the indexes to determine the track on which the record belongs. If there is already a record there with the same key, the duplicate key error is indicated in bit 5 of filenameC. If there is no duplicate key, the record may be added in any of three places:

1. On the prime track, if the record key is lower than the last key currently on that track. To make room, the last record currently on the track must be moved to the next available location in the overflow area and other records shifted one place on the prime track. The track index entries are then adjusted.
2. In the next available location in the overflow area, if the record key is higher than the last key currently on the prime track, but lower than the highest key in the overflow entry of the track index. In this instance, no records are shifted, but pointers in the track index and on the sequence link field in the overflow records must be adjusted.
3. After the last record previously in the file, if the record key is higher than the key of that record.

Records not deleted by physically removing them from the file. Instead, they are flagged by a special delete code (usually X'FF') in some predetermined byte in the record. To be consistent with OS, DOS users often use the first byte of the record for the delete code. For this reason, the record key should not begin in the first byte of the record.

DTFIS

Records may be added or deleted during either direct or sequential processing. Under DOS, several combinations of DTFIS entries may appear, depending upon our choice of processing methods. Here are some of the more common DTFIS entries:

IOROUT=ADD or ADDRTR

KEYARG=search-argument-field

IOAREAL=I/O-area-name for records to be added

WORKL=work-area-name for records to be added

TYPEFLE=RANDOM, SEQNTL, or RANSEQ

The field named in IOAREAL must contain space for the count area, the key, and a block of data. The work area named in WORKL must hold the key and one logical record.

DCB

Under OS, DCB entries to add or delete records include:

DSORG=IS

MACRF=(RUS,WUA). RUS specifies the READ macro for updating from same buffer. WUA specifies the WRITE macro for updating or for adding new records.

BUFNO=1

DDNAME=DDISFL

READ or GET

It is not necessary to read records from an IS file in order to add new records. However, the add function may be combined with either sequential or direct retrieval for other processing. Records must be read in order to be deleted, since the record must be rewritten with a delete code inserted.

Whenever a record is to be added during sequential retrieval, the ESETL macro must be issued before the record is added.

WRITE or PUT

To add records, the WRITE macro under DOS is used in the form:

```
WRITE filename,NEWKEY
WAITF filename
```

The key to the record to be added and the data for the logical record must first have been placed in the field named in the WORKL operand. If the key to be added duplicates a key in the file, bit 5 of filenameC is set to 1. If no duplication is found, the record is added and the track indexes and sequence link fields are adjusted accordingly.

To delete a record during sequential retrieval, after GET finds the desired record, PUT rewrites it with the delete code. To delete during direct retrieval, after READ filename,KEY finds the record, it is rewritten with the delete code by WRITE filename,KEY.

Under OS, to add a new record to an IS data set, the WRITE macro is written in form

```
WRITE  ISAMDECB,KN,BUFFER,MF=E
WAIT   ECB=ISAMDECB
```

The KN operand indicates a new key is being written. BUFFER is the name of the area containing the new record, including count, key, and data space. MF=E designates the execute form of the WRITE macro. The WAIT macro allows time for the record to be added.

PROGRAM 16D: ADDING AND DELETING INVENTORY RECORDS

Program 16D provides for adding and deleting records in the inventory master file. A transaction code of 'A' specifies addition and 'D' specifies deletion. Any other code is invalid. A log is printed showing each transaction and the action taken.

If a record to be added is a duplicate of one already in the file, or if a record to be deleted cannot be found, an error message is printed. Any other disk errors terminate the program.

The DTFIS requires entries for both IOAREAR and IOAREAL and for WORKR and WORKL. The same work area of 50 bytes can be used for both retrieval and adding records. The I/O area specified in IOAREAL requires 513 bytes to accommodate the count, the key, and the 500-byte data block. IOAREAR requires only 500 bytes for retrieval. The two areas share 500 common bytes.

Figure 16–11 shows the assembler listing, and Figure 16–12 shows the program output.

Programming Tips

- The READ and WRITE macros are used in both DOS and OS for updating, adding, and deleting records directly in IS files. The WAITF macro in DOS or the WAIT macro in OS must follow READ or WRITE to allow the operation to be completed.
- The WRITE macro with NEWKEY in DOS or KN in OS is used to add records to an IS file. WRITE with KEY in DOS or K in OS is used to rewrite a record that has been updated.

PROGRAM 16E: REORGANIZING THE INVENTORY FILE

Whenever an indexed sequential file has an excessive number of records in the overflow area, or whenever additional space is needed, the file is reorganized. This involves reading in the old file sequentially and loading a new one. Any records that were in the overflow area are placed in the prime data area of the new file.

Program 16E reorganizes the inventory master file. The old and new files can share common work areas and overflow areas. Each file needs a 50-byte work area. The I/O area for the new file (NEWMAREA) must contain 513

```
LOC    OBJECT CODE      ADDR1 ADDR2 STMT   SOURCE STATEMENT                                   DOS/VSE ASSEMBLER 13.10 86-04-22

                                       1 ************************************************************************
                                       2 *                  ALTON R. KINDRED, PROGRAM 16D
                                       3 * THIS PROGRAM ADDS AND DELETES RECORDS IN THE INDEXED SEQUENTIAL
                                       4 * INVENTORY MASTER FILE.  TRANSACTION CODES INDICATE THE OPERATION:
                                       5 *          A:  ADD
                                       6 *          D:  DELETE
                                       7 * A LOG IS PRINTED FOR EACH TRANSACTION.  IF THE RECORD TO BE ADDED IS
                                       8 * ALREADY PRESENT, THE RECORD TO BE DELETED IS NOT FOUND, OR THE TRANS-
                                       9 * ACTION CODE IS INVALID, AN ERROR MESSAGE IS PRINTED.
                                      10 *          REGISTERS USED:
                                      11 *                  R09-R11:  LINK REGISTERS
                                      12 *                  R12:      BASE REGISTER
                                      13 ************************************************************************
                                      14          PRINT NOGEN
000000                                15 MAINLINE START 0                           SET LOCATION COUNTER
                                      16 *        STM   14,12,12(13)                 SAVE REGISTERS FOR OS          OS
000000 05C0                           17          BALR  12,0                         LOAD BASE REGISTER
                              00002   18          USING *,12                         DESIGNATE BASE REGISTER
                                      19 *        ST    13,SAVE+4                    STORE REGISTER 3               OS
                                      20 *        LA    13,SAVE                      LOAD SAVE AREA ADDRESS         OS
                                      21 *        OPEN  (INFILE,(INPUT),ISFILE,(OUTPUT),PRINTER,(OUTPUT))         OS
                                      22          OPEN  INFILE,ISFILE,PRINTER        OPEN FILES                     DOS
00001A 4590 C03E              00040   32          BAL   9,INITIAL                    DO INITIAL PROCESSING
00001E 4590 C056              00058   33          BAL   9,MAINLOOP                   DO MAIN PROCESSING LOOP
000022 4590 C0A8              000AA   34          BAL   9,FINAL                      DO FINAL PROCESSING
                                      35          CLOSE INFILE,ISFILE,PRINTER        CLOSE FILES                    DOS
                                      45          EOJ                                END PROGRAM                    DOS
                                      48 *        CLOSE (INFILE)                     CLOSE FILES                    OS
                                      49 *        CLOSE (ISFILE,,PRINTER)            *                              OS
                                      50 *        L     13,SAVE+4                    LOAD SAVE AREA ADDRESS         OS
                                      51 *        LM    14,12,12(13)                 RESTORE REGISTERS              OS
                                      52 *        BR    14                           RETURN TO OS                   OS
                                      53 ************************************************************************
                                      54 *                  FIRST LEVEL MODULES
                                      55 ************************************************************************
                                      56 *
                                      57 *                  INITIAL PROCESSING MODULE
                                      58 *
000040 F811 CA9A CB7E 00A9C 00B80     59 INITIAL  ZAP   LINECNT,=P'51'               SET LINE COUNT => 50
000046 92D5 CAD3      00AD5           60          MVI   EOFFLAG,C'N'                 SET EOF FLAG OFF
00004A 92D5 CAD4      00AD6           61          MVI   ERRFLAG,C'N'                 SET ERROR FLAG OFF
00004E 45A0 C216            00218     62          BAL   10,CLEAR                     CLEAR PRINT LINE
000052 45A0 C0BC            000BE     63          BAL   10,READRECD                  READ FIRST TRANSACTION
000056 07F9                           64          BR    9                            RETURN
                                      65 *
                                      66 *                  MAIN PROCESSING LOOP
                                      67 *
                            00058     68 MAINLOOP EQU   *
000058 95E8 CAD3      00AD5           69 DOWHILE  CLI   EOFFLAG,C'Y'                 DOWHILE NOT END OF FILE
00005C 4780 C0A6      000A8           70          BE    ENDDO                          *
000060 95E8 CAD4      00AD6           71 AND      CLI   ERRFLAG,C'Y'                 AND NO ERRORS
000064 4780 C0A6      000A8           72          BE    ENDDO                          *
000068 45A0 C0DA            000DC     73          BAL   10,SETUP                     SET UP TRANSACTION
00006C D204 CA9C C7F5 00A9E 007F7     74          MVC   KEYFIND,INITEM               SET UP SEARCH ARGUMENT
000072 95C1 C824      00826           75 IF       CLI   INCODE,C'A'                    IF TRAN. CODE = A
000076 4770 C084      00086           76          BNE   ELSE                             *
00007A 45A0 C112            00114     77 THEN     BAL   10,SETREC                        THEN SET UP DISK RECORD
00007E 45A0 C142            00144     78          BAL   10,ADDREC                        ADD RECORD
000082 47F0 C09A      0009C           79          B     ENDIF                            *
                            00086     80 ELSE     EQU   *                              ELSE
000086 95C4 C824      00826           81 IF2      CLI   INCODE,C'D'                      IF TRAN. CODE = D
00008A 4770 C094      00096           82          BNE   ELSE2                              *
00008E 45A0 C184            00186     83 THEN2    BAL   10,DELETREC                        THEN DELETE RECORD
000092 47F0 C09A      0009C           84          B     ENDIF2                             *
                            00096     85 ELSE2    EQU   *                                ELSE
000096 D209 C8CE C880 008D0 00B82     86          MVC   PRMESG,=C'INVAL.CODE'              SET UP ERROR MESSAGE
                            0009C     87 ENDIF2   EQU   *                                ENDIF
                            0009C     88 ENDIF    EQU   *                              ENDIF
00009C 45A0 C1F2            001F4     89          BAL   10,PRDETAIL                    PRINT LINE
0000A0 45A0 C0BC            000BE     90          BAL   10,READRECD                    READ NEXT RECORD
0000A4 47F0 C056      00058           91          B     DOWHILE                        *
                            000A8     92 ENDDO    EQU   *                            ENDDO
0000A8 07F9                           93          BR    9                            RETURN
                                      94 *
                                      95 *                  FINAL PROCESSING MODULE
                                      96 *
                            000AA     97 FINAL    EQU   *
0000AA 95E8 CAD4      00AD6           98 IFERR2   CLI   ERRFLAG,C'Y'                 IF FATAL ERROR
0000AE 4770 C0BA      000BC           99          BNE   ENDERR2                        *
                                     100 THENERR2 PDUMP MAINLINE,ENDLITRL              THEN DUMP STORAGE              DOS
                                     106 *        OPEN  (SNAPDCB,(OUTPUT))               *                              OS
                                     107 *        SNAP  DCB=SNAPDCB,ID=1,PDATA=(PSW,REGS),                             OSX
                                     108 *              STORAGE=(MAINLINE,ENDLITRL)                                    OS
                                     109 *        CLOSE (SNAPDCB)                        *                              OS
                            000BC    110 ENDERR2  EQU   *                            ENDIF
0000BC 07F9                          111          BR    9                            RETURN
                                     112 ************************************************************************
                                     113 *                  SECOND LEVEL MODULES
                                     114 ************************************************************************
                                     115 *
                                     116 *                  READ RECORD MODULE
                                     117 *
0000BE 92D5 CAD3      00AD5          118 READRECD MVI   EOFFLAG,C'N'                 SET END OF FILE FLAG OFF
                                     119          GET   INFILE,INRECD                READ RECORD
0000D2 47F0 C0D8      000DA          125 IFEOF    B     ENDIFEOF                     IF END OF FILE
0000D6 92E8 CAD3      00AD5          126 THENEOF  MVI   EOFFLAG,C'Y'                   SET END OF FILE FLAG ON
                            000DA    127 ENDIFEOF EQU   *                            ENDIF
0000DA 07FA                          128          BR    10                           RETURN
                                     129 *
                                     130 *                  SET UP TRANSACTION MODULE
                                     131 *
0000DC D204 C887 C7F5 00889 007F7    132 SETUP    MVC   PRITEM,INITEM                SET UP ITEM NUMBER AND DESCR.
0000E2 D213 C88E C7FA 00890 007FC    133          MVC   PRDESCR,INDESCR              *
```

Figure 16–11 Assembler listing of Program 16D

```
  LOC  OBJECT CODE      ADDR1 ADDR2  STMT   SOURCE STATEMENT                                           DOS/VSE ASSEMBLER 13.10 86-04-22

0000E8 F236 CAA1 C80E 00AA3 00810    134              PACK   PKPRICE,INPRICE          PACK AMOUNTS
0000EE F224 CAA5 C815 00AA7 00817    135              PACK   PKQOH,INQOH              *
0000F4 F224 CAA8 C81A 00AAA 0081C    136              PACK   PKREOP,INREOP            *
0000FA F224 CAAB C81F 00AAD 00821    137              PACK   PKREOQ,INREOQ            *
000100 D224 C8A4 CAAE 008A6 00AB0    138              MVC    PRPRICE,PATRN            EDIT 4 FIELDS WITH 1 PATTERN
000106 DE24 C8A4 CAA1 008A6 00AA3    139              ED     PRPRICE,PKPRICE          *
00010C D200 C8CB C824 008CD 00826    140              MVC    PRCODE,INCODE            SET UP TRANS. CODE
000112 07FA                          141              BR     10                       RETURN
                                     142 *
                                     143 *                   SET UP RECORD MODULE
                                     144 *
000114 9240 C854       00856         145 SETREC       MVI    INVDELET,C' '            SET UP DISK RECORD
000118 D204 C855 C7F5 00857 007F7    146              MVC    INVITEM,INITEM           *
00011E D213 C85A C7FA 0085C 007FC    147              MVC    INVDESCR,INDESCR         *
000124 F833 C86E CAA1 00870 00AA3    148              ZAP    INVPRICE,PKPRICE         *
00012A F822 C872 CAA5 00874 00AA7    149              ZAP    INVQOH,PKQOH             *
000130 F822 C875 CAA8 00877 00AAA    150              ZAP    INVREOP,PKREOP           *
000136 F822 C878 CAAB 0087A 00AAD    151              ZAP    INVREOQ,PKREOQ           *
00013C D20A C87B CBB4 0087D 00BB6    152              MVC    INVEXPAN,=11C' '         *
000142 07FA                          153              BR     10                       RETURN
                                     154 *
                                     155 *                   ADD RECORD MODULE
                                     156 *
                             00144   157 ADDREC       EQU    *
                                     158              WRITE  ISFILE,NEWKEY            WRITE RECORD TO BE ADDED     DOS
                                     163              WAITF  ISFILE                       *                        DOS
                                     168 *            WRITE  ISDECB,KN,NEWBUF,MF=E        *                        OS
                                     169 *            WAIT   ECB=ISDECB                   *                        OS
00015C 91FE C2B4       002B6         170 IF3          TM     ISFILEC,B'11111110'      IF NO ERRORS                 DOS
                                     171 *            TM     ISDECB+24,B'11111101'      *                          OS
000160 4770 C16C       0016E         172              BNZ    ELSE3                      *
000164 D209 C8CE CB8A 008D0 00B8C    173 THEN3        MVC    PRMESG,=CL10'ADDED'        THEN SO INDICATE
00016A 47F0 C182       00184         174              B      ENDIF3                     *
                             0016E   175 ELSE3        EQU    *                        ELSE
00016E 9104 C2B4       002B6         176 IF4          TM     ISFILEC,B'00000100'        IF DUPLICATE RECORD        DOS
                                     177 *            TM     ISDECB+24,B'00000001'        *                        OS
000172 47E0 C17E       00180         178              BNO    ELSE4                        *
000176 D209 C8CE CB94 008D0 00B96    179 THEN4        MVC    PRMESG,=CL10'DUPL.RECD.'     THEN SO INDICATE
00017C 47F0 C182       00184         180              B      ENDIF4                       *
                             00180   181 ELSE4        EQU    *                          ELSE
000180 92E8 CAD4       00AD6         182              MVI    ERRFLAG,C'Y'                 SET ERROR FLAG ON
                             00184   183 ENDIF4       EQU    *                          ENDIF
                             00184   184 ENDIF3       EQU    *                        ENDIF
000184 07FA                          185              BR     10                       RETURN
                                     186 *
                                     187 *                   DELETE RECORD MODULE
                                     188 *
                             00186   189 DELETREC     EQU    *
                                     190              READ   ISFILE,KEY               READ DISK RECORD             DOS
                                     195              WAITF  ISFILE                     *                          DOS
                                     200 *            READ   ISDECB,KU,,'S',MF=E        *                          OS
                                     201 *            WAIT   ECB=ISDECB                 *                          OS
00019E 91FE C2B4       002B6         202 IF5          TM     ISFILEC,B'11111110'      IF RECORD FOUND              DOS
                                     203 *            TM     ISDECB+24,B'11111101'      *                          OS
0001A2 4770 C1DA       001DC         204              BNZ    ELSE5                      *
0001A6 92FF C854       00856         205 THEN5        MVI    INVDELET,X'FF'             THEN MOVE DELETE CODE
                                     206              WRITE  ISFILE,KEY                 REWRITE RECORD             DOS
                                     211              WAITF  ISFILE                     *                          DOS
                                     216 *            WRITE  ISDECB,K,,'S',MF=E         *                          OS
                                     217 *            WAIT   ECB=ISDECB                 *                          OS
0001C2 91FE C2B4       002B6         218 IF6          TM     ISFILEC,B'11111110'        IF REWRITTEN OK            DOS
                                     219 *            TM     ISDECB+24,B11111101'         *                        OS
0001C6 4770 C1D2       001D4         220              BNZ    ELSE6                        *
0001CA D209 C8CE CB9E 008D0 00BA0    221 THEN6        MVC    PRMESG,=CL10'DELETED'        THEN SHOW AS DELETED
0001D0 47F0 C1D6       001D8         222              B      ENDIF6                       *
                             001D4   223 ELSE6        EQU    *                          ELSE
0001D4 92E8 CAD4       00AD6         224              MVI    ERRFLAG,C'Y'                 SET ERROR SWITCH ON
                             001D8   225 ENDIF6       EQU    *                          ENDIF
0001D8 47F0 C1F0       001F2         226              B      ENDIF5                     *
                             001DC   227 ELSE5        EQU    *                        ELSE
0001DC 9110 C2B4       002B6         228 IF7          TM     ISFILEC,B'00010000'        IF RECORD NOT FOUND        DOS
                                     229 *            TM     ISDECB+24,B'10000000'        *                        OS
0001E0 4780 C1EC       001EE         230              BZ     ELSE7                        *
0001E4 D209 C8CE CBA8 008D0 00BAA    231 THEN7        MVC    PRMESG,=CL10'NOT FOUND'      THEN SO INDICATE
0001EA 47F0 C1F0       001F2         232              B      ENDIF7                       *
                             001EE   233 ELSE7        EQU    *                          ELSE
0001EE 92E8 CAD4       00AD6         234              MVI    ERRFLAG,C'Y'                 SET ERROR SWITCH ON
                             001F2   235 ENDIF7       EQU    *                          ENDIF
                             001F2   236 ENDIF5       EQU    *                        ENDIF
0001F2 07FA                          237              BR     10                       RETURN
                                     238 *
                                     239 *                   PRINT DETAIL LINE MODULE
                                     240 *
                             001F4   241 PRDETAIL     EQU    *
0001F4 F911 CA9A CBB2 00A9C 00BB4    242 IFEOP        CP     LINECNT,=P'50'           IF LINE COUNT => 50
0001FA 4740 C200       00202         243              BL     ENDIFEOP                   *
0001FE 45B0 C222             00224   244 THENEOP      BAL    11,HEADING                 THEN PRINT HEADING
                             00202   245 ENDIFEOP     EQU    *                        ENDIF
                                     246              PUT    PRINTER,PRLINE           PRINT LINE
000212 FA10 CA9A CBBF 00A9C 00BC1    252              AP     LINECNT,=P'1'            ADD 1 TO LINE COUNT
000218 9240 C886       00888         253 CLEAR        MVI    PRLINE,C' '              CLEAR PRINT LINE
00021C D283 C887 C886 00889 00888    254              MVC    PRLINE+1(132),PRLINE     *
000222 07FA                          255              BR     10                       RETURN
                                     256 ***********************************************************************
                                     257 *                   THIRD LEVEL MODULES
                                     258 ***********************************************************************
                                     259 *
                                     260 *                   PRINT HEADING MODULE
                                     261 *
                                     262 HEADING      PUT    PRINTER,HEAD1            PRINT FIRST HEADING LINE
                                     268              PUT    PRINTER,HEAD2            PRINT SECOND HEADING LINE
                                     274              PUT    PRINTER,HEAD3            PRINT THIRD HEADING LINE
```

Figure 16–11 *(Continued)*

```
  LOC  OBJECT CODE    ADDR1 ADDR2  STMT   SOURCE STATEMENT                                   DOS/VSE ASSEMBLER 13.10 86-04-22

000254 92F0 C886        00888       280          MVI   PRLINE,C'0'               SET FOR DOUBLE SPACE
000258 F810 CA9A CBC0 00A9C 008C2   281          ZAP   LINECNT,=P'0'             SET LINE COUNT TO ZERO
00025E 07FB                         282          BR    11                        RETURN
                                    284 *********************************************************************DOS
                                    285 *                  FILE DEFINITIONS AND I/O AREAS                    DOS
                                    286 *********************************************************************DOS
                                    287 INFILE   DTFCD BLKSIZE=80,IOAREA1=INAREA,DEVICE=2540,                DOSX
                                                       DEVADDR=SYS006,EOFADDR=THENEOF,WORKA=YES              DOS
                                    308 *                                                                    DOS
                                    309 ISFILE   DTFIS DSKXTNT=2,IOROUT=ADDRTR,KEYLEN=5,NRECDS=10,           DOSX
                                                       RECFORM=FIXBLK,RECSIZE=50,CYLOFL=2,DEVICE=3340,       DOSX
                                                       HINDEX=3340,INDAREA=CORINDEX,INDSIZE=100,             DOSX
                                                       IOAREAR=INVAREA,KEYARG=KEYFIND,KEYLOC=2,              DOSX
                                                       TYPEFLE=RANDOM,VERIFY=YES,WORKR=INVRECD,              DOSX
                                                       IOAREAL=ADDAREA,WORKL=INVRECD                         DOS
                                    443 *                                                                    DOS
                                    444 PRINTER  DTFPR BLKSIZE=133,IOAREA1=PRTAREA,DEVICE=1403,              DOSX
                                                       CTLCHR=ASA,DEVADDR=SYS009,WORKA=YES                   DOS
                                    465 *                                                                    DOS
000520                              466 INAREA   DS    CL80                                                  DOS
000570                              467 ADDAREA  DS    OCL513                                                DOS
000570                              468          DS    CL8                                                   DOS
000578                              469          DS    CL5                                                   DOS
00057D                              470 INVAREA  DS    CL500                                                 DOS
000771                              471 PRTAREA  DS    CL133                                                 DOS
                                    472 *********************************************************************OS
                                    473 *                  DEVICE CONTROL BLOCKS AND SAVE AREA               OS
                                    474 *********************************************************************OS
                                    475 *INFILE  DCB       DDNAME=INFILE,BLKSIZE=80,LRECL=80,                OSX
                                    476 *                  MACRF=GM,DSORG=PS,EODAD=THENEOF                   OS
                                    477 *                                                                    OS
                                    478 *PRINTER DCB       DDNAME=PRINTER,BLKSIZE=133,LRECL=133,             OSX
                                    479 *                  MACRF=PMA,DSORG=PS                                OS
                                    480 *                                                                    OS
                                    481 *ISFILE  DCB       DDNAME=ISFILE,MACRF=(RUS,WUA),DSORG=IS,BUFNO=1    OS
                                    482 *                                                                    OS
                                    483 *        READ      ISDECB,KU,ISFILE,'S','S',KEYAREA,MF=L             OS
                                    484 *                                                                    OS
                                    485 *SNAPDCB DCB       DSORG=PS,RECFM=VBA,MACRF=(W),BLKSIZE=1320,        OSX
                                    486 *                  LRECL=132,DDNAME=SNAPDD                           OS
                                    487 *                                                                    OS
                                    488 *SAVE    DS        18F                                               OS
                                    490 ***********************************************************************
                                    491 *                  DATA DEFINITIONS
                                    492 ***********************************************************************
0007F6                              493 INRECD   DS    OCL80
0007F6                              494          DS    CL1
0007F7                              495 INITEM   DS    CL5
0007FC                              496 INDESCR  DS    CL20
000810                              497 INPRICE  DS    CL7
000817                              498 INQOH    DS    CL5
00081C                              499 INREOP   DS    CL5
000821                              500 INREOQ   DS    CL5
000826                              501 INCODE   DS    CL1
000827                              502          DS    CL31
                                    503 *
000846                              504 NEWBUF   DS    OCL66
000846                              505          DS    CL16
000856                              506 INVRECD  DS    OCL50
000856                              507 INVDELET DS    CL1
000857                              508 INVITEM  DS    CL5
00085C                              509 INVDESCR DS    CL20
000870                              510 INVPRICE DS    PL4
000874                              511 INVQOH   DS    PL3
000877                              512 INVREOP  DS    PL3
00087A                              513 INVREOQ  DS    PL3
00087D                              514 INVEXPAN DS    CL11
                                    515 *
000888                              516 PRLINE   DS    OCL133
000888                              517          DS    CL1
000889                              518 PRITEM   DS    CL5
00088E                              519          DS    CL2
000890                              520 PRDESCR  DS    CL20
0008A4                              521          DS    CL2
0008A6                              522 PRPRICE  DS    CL37
0008CB                              523          DS    CL2
0008CD                              524 PRCODE   DS    CL1
0008CE                              525          DS    CL2
0008D0                              526 PRMESG   DS    CL10
0008DA                              527          DS    CL51
                                    528 *
00090D                              529 HEAD1    DS    OCL133
00090D F140404040404040             530          DC    CL21'1'
000922 C9D5E5C5D5E3D6D9             531          DC    CL112'INVENTORY ADDITIONS AND DELETIONS REPORT'
                                    532 *
000992                              533 HEAD2    DS    OCL133
000992 F040C9E3C5D44040             534          DC    CL36'0 ITEM'
0009B6 E4D5C9E34040D8E4             535          DC    CL16'UNIT  QUANTITY'
0009C6 D9C5D6D9C4C5D940             536          DC    CL81'REORDER  REORDER'
                                    537 *
000A17                              538 HEAD3    DS    OCL133
000A17 40D5E4D4C2C5D940             539          DC    CL12' NUMBER'
000A23 C4C5E2C3D9C9D7E3             540          DC    CL24'DESCRIPTION'
000A3B D7D9C9C3C5404006             541          DC    CL17'PRICE  ON HAND'
000A4C D7D6C9D5E34040D8             542          DC    CL80'POINT  QUANTITY CODE'
                                    543 *
000A9C                              544 LINECNT  DS    PL2
000A9E                              545 KEYFIND  DS    CL5
000AA3                              546 PKPRICE  DS    PL4
000AA7                              547 PKQOH    DS    PL3
000AAA                              548 PKREOP   DS    PL3
000AAD                              549 PKREOQ   DS    PL3
000AB0                              550 PATRN    DS    OCL37
```

Figure 16–11 *(Continued)*

```
  LOC  OBJECT CODE     ADDR1 ADDR2  STMT   SOURCE STATEMENT                                     DOS/VSE ASSEMBLER 13.10 86-04-22

000AB0 4020206B2020214B              551            DC    XL10'4020206B202021482020'
000ABA 222222202 06B2021             552            DC    3XL9'222222206B202120'
000AD5                               553 EOFFLAG    DS    CL1
000AD6                               554 ERRFLAG    DS    CL1
000AD7                               555 CORINDEX   DS    CL100
000B40                               556            LTORG
000B40 5B5BC2D6D7C5D540              557                  =C'$$BOPEN '
000B48 5B5BC2C3D3D6E2C5              558                  =C'$$BCLOSE'
000B50 5B5BC2D7C4E4D4D7              559                  =CL8'$$BPDUMP'
000B58 00000000000000BC3             560                  =A(MAINLINE,ENDLITRL)
000B60 00000260                      561                  =A(INFILE)
000B64 000007F6                      562                  =A(INRECD)
000B68 00000298                      563                  =A(ISFILE)
000B6C 000004F0                      564                  =A(PRINTER)
000B70 00000888                      565                  =A(PRLINE)
000B74 0000090D                      566                  =A(HEAD1)
000B78 00000992                      567                  =A(HEAD2)
000B7C 00000A17                      568                  =A(HEAD3)
000B80 051C                          569                  =P'51'
000B82 C9D5E5C1D34BC3D6              570                  =C'INVAL.CODE'
000B8C C1C4C4C5C4404040              571                  =CL10'ADDED'
000B96 C4E4D7D34BD9C5C3              572                  =CL10'DUPL.RECD.'
000BA0 C4C5D3C5E3C5C440              573                  =CL10'DELETED'
000BAA D5D6E340C6D6E4D5              574                  =CL10'NOT FOUND'
000BB4 050C                          575                  =P'50'
000BB6 4040404040404040              576                  =11C' '
000BC1 1C                            577                  =P'1'
000BC2 0C                            578                  =P'0'
                      00BC3          579 ENDLITRL   EQU   *
                      00000          580            END   MAINLINE
```

Figure 16–11 *(Concluded)*

INVENTORY ADDITIONS AND DELETIONS REPORT

ITEM NUMBER	DESCRIPTION	UNIT PRICE	QUANTITY ON HAND	REORDER POINT	REORDER QUANTITY	CODE	
28424	SUPER FILER	250.00	20	10	10	A	ADDED
48105	FLEXI-UTILITY	179.95	35	20	20	A	DUPL.RECD.
55003	MATH DRILL	38.20	6	6	6	D	NOT FOUND
73225	TOP DOG INTEG PKG	1,234.50	4	5	5	A	ADDED
74746	INDEX BUILDER	458.25	15	10	10	A	ADDED
94631	KIDDIES MATH	19.95	3	5	5	D	DELETED
95333	BLAZING SORT	15.00	4	3	3	X	INVAL.CODE

Figure 16–12 Output from Program 16D

bytes to hold the count and key fields as well as the 500-byte block. Five hundred of these bytes are the I/O area for the old file (OLDMAREA).

Bit 2 of filenameC of the old file is tested for end of file. Any other bit (except bit 7 for overflow record) causes the program to cancel. Any I/O error on loading the new file causes a cancel.

Figure 16–13 shows the assembler listing.

SUMMARY OF PROCESSING MACROS, I/O AREAS, AND WORK AREAS

A large number of processing macros are used with indexed sequential files. For convenient reference, we show in Figure 16–14 a summary of the macros for each different type of processing.

```
LOC    OBJECT CODE    ADDR1 ADDR2  STMT   SOURCE STATEMENT                                    DOS/VSE ASSEMBLER 13.09 86-04-22

                                      1 *********************************************************************
                                      2 *                  ALTON R. KINDRED, PROGRAM 16E
                                      3 * THIS PROGRAM REORGANIZES THE INVENTORY MASTER INDEXED SEQUENTIAL
                                      4 * FILE.  BOTH THE OLD MASTER AND THE NEW MASTER SHARE THE SAME DATA
                                      5 * PORTION OF THE I/O AREA.  IF ANY ERROR OCCURS DURING EITHER THE
                                      6 * READ OR WRITE OPERATION, THE PROGRAM IS CANCELED.  NO LOG IS
                                      7 * PRINTED FOR THIS OPERATION.
                                      8 *          REGISTERS USED:
                                      9 *                  R10:  LINK REGISTER
                                     10 *                  R12:  BASE REGISTER
                                     11 *********************************************************************
                                     12          PRINT NOGEN
000000                               13 MAINLINE START 0                           SET LOCATION COUNTER
                                     14 *        STM   14,12,12(13)                SAVE REGISTERS FOR OS          OS
000000 05C0                          15          BALR  12,0                        LOAD BASE REGISTER
                          00002      16          USING *,12                        DESIGNATE BASE REGISTER
                                     17 *        ST    13,SAVE+4                   STORE REGISTER 3               OS
                                     18 *        LA    13,SAVE                     LOAD SAVE AREA ADDRESS         OS
                                     19 *        OPEN  (OLDMAST,(INPUT),NEWMAST,(OUTPUT)                          OS
                                     20          OPEN  OLDMAST,NEWMAST             OPEN FILES                     DOS
000016 4590 C036          00038      29          BAL   9,INITIAL                   DO INITIAL PROCESSING
00001A 4590 C066          00068      30          BAL   9,MAINLOOP                  DO MAIN PROCESSING LOOP
00001E 4590 C08C          0008E      31          BAL   9,FINAL                     DO FINAL PROCESSING
                                     32          CLOSE OLDMAST,NEWMAST             CLOSE FILES                    DOS
                                     41          EOJ                               END PROGRAM                    DOS
                                     44 *        CLOSE (OLDMAST,,NEWMAST)          CLOSE FILES                    OS
                                     45 *        L     13,SAVE+4                   LOAD SAVE AREA ADDRESS         OS
                                     46 *        LM    14,12,12(13)                RESTORE REGISTERS              OS
                                     47 *        BR    14                          RETURN TO OS                   OS
                                     48 *********************************************************************
                                     49 *                  FIRST LEVEL MODULES
                                     50 *********************************************************************
                                     51 *
                                     52 *                  INITIAL PROCESSING
                                     53 *
000038 92D5 C575    00577            54 INITIAL  MVI   EOFFLAG,C'N'                SET EDF FLAG OFF
00003C 92D5 C576    00578            55          MVI   ERRFLAG,C'N'                SET ERROR FLAG OFF
                                     56          SETFL NEWMAST                     SET FILE LOAD MODE             DOS
                                     62          SETL  OLDMAST,BOF                 SET SEQ. RETRIEVAL MODE        DOS
                                     71 *        SETL  OLDMAST,B                     *                            OS
000062 45A0 COCC          000CE      72          BAL   10,RDMAST                   READ FIRST REÇORD
000066 07F9                          73          BR    9                           RETURN
                                     74 *
                                     75 *                  MAIN PROCESSING LOOP
                                     76 *
                          00068      77 MAINLOOP EQU   *
000068 95E8 C575    00577            78 DOWHILE  CLI   EOFFLAG,C'Y'                DOWHILE NOT END OF FILE
00006C 4780 C08A    0008C            79          BE    ENDDO                         *
000070 95E8 C576    00578            80 AND      CLI   ERRFLAG,C'Y'                AND NO ERRORS
000074 4780 C08A    0008C            81          BE    ENDDO                           *
000078 45A0 COFA          000FC      82          BAL   10,WRDISK                     WRITE DISK RECORD
00007C 9500 C576    00578            83 IF3      CLI   ERRFLAG,B'00000000'           IF NO ERRORS
000080 4770 C086    00088            84          BNE   ENDIF3                          *
000084 45A0 COCC          000CE      85 THEN3    BAL   10,RDMAST                       THEN READ NEXT RECORD
                          00088      86 ENDIF3   EQU   *                             ENDIF
000088 47F0 C066    00068            87          B     DOWHILE                         *
                          0008C      88 ENDDO    EQU   *                           ENDDO
00008C 07F9                          89          BR    9                           RETURN
                                     90 *
                                     91 *                  FINAL PROCESSING MODULE
                                     92 *
                          0008E      93 FINAL    EQU   *
00008E 95E8 C576    00578            94 IFERR3   CLI   ERRFLAG,C'Y'                IF FATAL ERROR
000092 4770 C09E    000A0            95          BNE   ENDFERR3                      *
                                     96 THENERR3 PDUMP MAINLINE,ENDLITRL             THEN DUMP STORAGE            DOS
                                    102 *        OPEN  (SNAPDCB,(OUTPUT))            *                            OS
                                    103 *        SNAP  DCB=SNAPDCB,ID=1,PDATA=(PSW,REGS),                         OSX
                                    104 *              STORAGE=(MAINLINE,ENDLITRL)                                OS
                                    105 *        CLOSE (SNAPDCB)                     *                            OS
                          000A0     106 ENDFERR3 EQU   *                           ENDIF
                                    107          ESETL OLDMAST                     END SEQ. RETRIEVAL
                                    112          ENDFL NEWMAST                     END FILE LOAD MODE             DOS
0000CC 07F9                         124          BR    9                           RETURN
                                    125 *********************************************************************
                                    126 *                  SECOND LEVEL MODULES
                                    127 *********************************************************************
                                    128 *
                                    129 *                  READ INVENTORY MASTER MODULE
                                    130 *
                                    131 RDMAST   GET   OLDMAST,INVRECD             READ MASTER RECORD
                                    137 *IFEOF   B     ENDIFEOF                    *                              OS
0000DE 9120 C134    00136           138 IFEOF    TM    OLDMASTC,B'00100000'        IF END OF FILE                 DOS
0000E2 4780 COEC    000EE           139          BZ    ELSEEOF                       *                            DOS
0000E6 92E8 C575    00577           140 THENEOF  MVI   EOFFLAG,C'Y'                  THEN SET EOF FLAG ON
0000EA 47F0 COF8    000FA           141          B     ENDIFEOF                      *
                          000EE     142 ELSEEOF  EQU   *                           ELSE
0000EE 91DE C134    00136           143 IFERR    TM    OLDMASTC,B'11011110'          IF OTHER ERRORS              DOS
0000F2 4780 COF8    000FA           144          BZ    ENDIFERR                        *                          DOS
0000F6 92E8 C576    00578           145 THENERR  MVI   ERRFLAG,C'Y'                    THEN SET ERROR FLAG ON
                          000FA     146 ENDIFERR EQU   *                             ENDIF
                          000FA     147 ENDIFEOF EQU   *                           ENDIF
0000FA 07FA                         148          BR    10                          RETURN
                                    149 *
                                    150 *                  WRITE DISK MODULE
                                    151 *
                                    152 WRDISK   WRITE NEWMAST,NEWKEY              WRITE TO NEW FILE              DOS
                                    157 *        PUT   NEWMAST,INVRECD             *                              OS
                                    158 *IFERR2  B     ENDFERR2                    *                              OS
000108 9500 C25C    0025E           159 IFERR2   CLI   NEWMASTC,B'00000000'        IF ANY ERRORS                  DOS
00010C 4780 C112    00114           160          BE    ENDFERR2                      *                            DOS
000110 92E8 C576    00578           161 THENERR2 MVI   ERRFLAG,C'Y'                  THEN SET ERROF FLAG
                          00114     162 ENDFERR2 EQU   *                           ENDIF
000114 07FA                         163          BR    10                          RETURN
```

Figure 16–13 Assembler listing of Program 16E

```
LOC    OBJECT CODE     ADDR1 ADDR2  STMT   SOURCE STATEMENT                                                   DOS/VSE ASSEMBLER 13.09 86-04-22

                                    165 **********************************************************************DOS
                                    166 *                    FILE DEFINITIONS AND I/O AREAS                   DOS
                                    167 **********************************************************************DOS
                                    168 OLDMAST  DTFIS DSKXTNT=2,IOROUT=RETRVE,KEYLEN=5,NRECDS=10,CYLOFL=2,  DOSX
                                                       RECFORM=FIXBLK,RECSIZE=50,DEVICE=3340,HINDEX=3340,     DOSX
                                                       IOAREAS=OLDMAREA,KEYLOC=2,TYPEFLE=SEQNTL,WORKS=YES     DOS
                                    246 *                                                                     DOS
                                    247 NEWMAST  DTFIS DSKXTNT=2,IOROUT=LOAD,KEYLEN=5,NRECDS=10,RECSIZE=50,   DOSX
                                                       RECFORM=FIXBLK,CYLOFL=2,DEVICE=3340,HINDEX=3340,       DOSX
                                                       IOAREAL=NEWMAREA,KEYLOC=2,WORKL=INVRECD,VERIFY=YES     DOS
                                    296 *                                                                     DOS
000344                              297 NEWMAREA DS    0CL513                                                 DOS
000344                              298          DS    CL13                                                   DOS
000351                              299 OLDMAREA DS    CL500                                                  DOS
                                    300 **********************************************************************OS
                                    301 *                    DEVICE CONTROL BLOCKS AND SAVE AREA              OS
                                    302 **********************************************************************OS
                                    303 *OLDMAST DCB   DDNAME=OLDMAST,DSORG=IS,MACRF=GM,EODAD=THENEOF,        OSX
                                    304 *              SYNAD=THENERR                                          OS
                                    305 *                                                                     OS
                                    306 *NEWMAST DCB   DDNAME=NEWMAST,BLKSIZE=500,LRECL=50,CYLOFL=2,          OSX
                                    307 *              MACRF=PM,DSORG=IS,RECFM=FB,KEYLEN=5,OPTCD=YW,RKP=2,    OSX
                                    308 *              SYNAD=THENERR2                                         OS
                                    309 *                                                                     OS
                                    310 *SNAPDCB DCB   DSORG=PS,RECFM=VBA,MACRF=(W),BLKSIZE=1320,             OSX
                                    311 *              LRECL=132,DDNAME=SNAPDD                                OS
                                    312 *                                                                     OS
                                    313 *SAVE    DS    18F                                                    OS
                                    314 **********************************************************************
                                    315 *                    DATA DEFINITIONS
                                    316 **********************************************************************
000545                              317 INVRECD  DS    CL50
000577                              318 EOFFLAG  DS    CL1
000578                              319 ERRFLAG  DS    CL1
000580                              320          LTORG
000580 5B5BC2D6D7C5D540             321                =C'$$BOPEN '
000588 5B5BC2C3D3D6E2C5             322                =C'$$BCLOSE'
000590 5B5BC2E2C5E3C6D3             323                =C'$$BSETFL'
000598 5B5BC2E2C5E3D340             324                =C'$$BSETL '
0005A0 5B5BC2D7C4E4D4D7             325                =CL8'$$BPDUMP'
0005A8 00000000000005C4             326                =A(MAINLINE,ENDLITRL)
0005B0 5B5BC2C5D5C4C6D3             327                =C'$$BENDFL'
0005B8 00000240                     328                =A(NEWMAST)
0005BC 00000118                     329                =A(OLDMAST)
0005C0 00000545                     330                =A(INVRECD)
                       005C4        331 ENDLITRL EQU   *
                       00000        332          END   MAINLINE
```

Figure 16–13 *(Concluded)*

FILE CREATION	SEQUENTIAL RETRIEVAL	DIRECT RETRIEVAL	FILE ADDITION
DOS Macros:			
OPEN	OPEN	OPEN	OPEN
SETFL	SETL	READ,KEY	WRITE,KEY
WRITE,NEWKEY	GET	WAITF	WAITF
ENDFL	PUT	WRITE,KEY	CLOSE
CLOSE	ESETL	WAITF	
	CLOSE	CLOSE	
OS Macros:			
OPEN	OPEN	OPEN	OPEN
PUT	SETL	READ,K or KU	WRITE,KN
CLOSE	GET	WAIT	CLOSE
	PUTX	WRITE,K	
	ESETL	WAIT	
	CLOSE	CLOSE	

Figure 16–14 Summary of processing macros for IS files

FUNCTION	SIZE OF I/O AREA	SIZE OF WORK AREA
Load:		
Unblocked records	C + KL + RL	KL + RL or 10*
Blocked records	C + KL + BL	RL or 10*
Add:		
Unblocked records	C + KL + RL + 10	KL + RL or 10*
Blocked records	C + KL + RL + 10 or C + K + BL*	RL or KL + 10*
Sequential retrieval:		
Unblocked records	KL + RL + 10	KL + RL
Blocked records	BL or RL + 10*	RL
Direct retrieval:		
Unblocked records	RL + 10	RL
Blocked records	BL or RL + 10*	RL

Legend: C = count area, 8 bytes
KL = key length
RL = logical record length
BL = block length (logical record times blocking factor)
* (whichever is longer)

Figure 16–15 Summary of work area and I/O area sizes for IS files

Figure 16–15 shows the sizes of the work areas and I/O areas for file creation, sequential retrieval, direct retrieval, and adding records.

SUMMARY

Indexed sequential files can be processed sequentially or directly. They are probably the most commonly used type of files. They contain indexes, a prime data area, and optional overflow areas. They use count-key-data organization.

The cylinder index is required and gives the highest key on each cylinder. The track index appears on the first track of each cylinder and gives the highest key on each track in that cylinder. The track index has normal and overflow entries. The master index is optional and shows the highest key on each track in the cylinder index.

The prime data area contains the records in sequential order by key. Records may be blocked or unblocked. In DOS records must be fixed in length, but in OS they may be variable.

The cylinder overflow area, which is optional, occupies a specified number of the last tracks on each cylinder. It contains records that overflow from any tracks within the cylinder. The independent overflow area, also optional, is in a separate extent. It receives overflow records from any tracks within the file. Overflow records are never blocked, but have a 10-byte sequence link field pointing to the next record in sequence.

FilenameC is the error and status byte under DOS. This byte, displaced 30 bytes from the start of the DTFIS table, is posted to indicate the result of each disk read or write operation. The programmer must test this byte to determine whether the operation was successful. Under OS, the status byte is displaced 24 bytes from the start of the data event control block (DECB). Its meanings are somewhat different from those of filenameC.

To create the file, all records must be in sequence and there must be no duplicate keys. The I/O area must hold count, key, and block of data. A separate work area is required. Under DOS, special macros SETFL and ENDFL set and end the file load mode. The WRITE macro with the NEWKEY operand writes the new records to the file. Under OS, the PUT macro loads the records into the data set.

GET and PUT macros perform sequential retrieval. The SETL macro indicates whether retrieval will begin at the start of the file, at a specified record, or with the first record of a group. The ESETL macro terminates retrieval.

Under DOS, the READ macro with the KEY operand performs direct retrieval. The key to be located must first be placed in the field named KEYARG. Under OS, the READ macro must appear among the procedural statements in execute form with an operand MF=E, and among the data definitions in list form with an operand MF=L. The list form creates the data event control block.

Records may be updated with either sequential or direct retrieval. PUT in DOS and PUTX in OS indicates that the record obtained with the previous GET is to be rewritten. The WRITE macro with the KEY operand follows READ,KEY to rewrite the updated record in DOS. In OS, a WRITE macro with a K operand rewrites the record previously read with a READ macro with a KU operand.

Records to be added to the file are written in DOS with a WRITE macro with NEWKEY operand. The key to the added record must not duplicate one already in the file. Under OS, records are added with a WRITE macro with a KN operand. Records are deleted by placing a special code, usually X'FF', in one byte of the record on disk.

When the overflow area becomes filled, the file may be reorganized. This involves reading the old file and creating a new one.

TERMS FOR REVIEW

Cylinder index
Cylinder overflow area
Cylinder overflow control record
Data event control block
Direct retrieval
DTFIS
Dummy entry
ENDFL
Error and status byte
ESETL
Execute form
File extension
File loading
File reorganization
FilenameC
Generic key
Independent overflow area
Indexed sequential file
ISAM
KEYARG
List form

Master index	Prime data area	SETFL
Normal entry	Sequence link field	SETL
Overflow entry	Sequential retrieval	Track index

REVIEW QUESTIONS

1. Name and describe the most common operations on indexed sequential files.
2. Name and give the purpose of each of the components of an indexed sequential file.
3. Where is the track index located? What two types of entry does it contain?
4. Where is the cylinder index located with respect to the rest of the file? Where is it often placed during direct retrieval?
5. Describe the structure of records within the overflow area. What is the purpose of the sequence link field?
6. What is the relationship between the cylinder overflow area and the independent overflow area? What determines when each one receives records?
7. If records are unblocked, what is the minimum size of the I/O area when adding records? when retrieving records directly?
8. What is the purpose of the KEYARG operand? What types of processing require it to be used?
9. What is the difference between a WRITE macro followed with the NEWKEY operand and WRITE followed by KEY?
10. What does the WAITF macro do and when is it used?
11. Explain how records are deleted from ISAM files.
12. Explain how records are added to ISAM files.

EXERCISES

1. Write DTFIS entries for a file named INDFILE to be created with records 120 bytes long, blocked 8. The key occupies positions 11 to 16 of the record.
2. Write DTFIS entries for INDFILE (created in Exercise 1) to be retrieved sequentially. Write the necessary processing macros.
3. Write instructions to test filenameC and branch as stated under each of the following conditions:
   a. Branch to ENDIF if no bits set.
   b. Branch to ENDDO if end of file.
   c. Branch to ELSE if any bit other than end of file or if overflow is set.
   d. Branch to ELSE if no record found.
   e. Branch to THEN if duplicate record and to ELSE if out of sequence.

4. Write processing instructions and macros to start sequential retrieval with the first key higher than 15000.
5. Write DTFIS entries to permit records to be added to and deleted from INDFILE as described in Exercise 1 above.

PROGRAMMING PROBLEMS

1. Rewrite Program 14A to read Data Set 3 in Appendix D and create a Salesperson Master Indexed Sequential File. The key to each record is region code and salesperson number, bytes 01 to 07. Year-to-date sales and year-to-date returns should be packed decimal data in the IS file. Records are 36 bytes, with 20 records per block. The format is as follows:

   01–02 Region code
   03–07 Salesperson number
   08–27 Salesperson name
   27–32 Year-to-date sales, packed
   33–36 Year-to-date returns, packed

   List all input records, with an error message for any that are out of sequence or have duplicate keys. Test for disk errors after each WRITE and dump storage if any errors other than out of sequence or duplicate keys occur.
2. Write a program to read the Salesperson Master IS File created in Problem 1, starting with Region 02. Use sequential retrieval with a generic key of 0200000. Produce a Sales Report in the same format as shown in Figure 14–10, except that Region 01 will not be included.
3. Read Data Set 3A in Appendix D and update the Salesperson Master IS File using direct retrieval. To update the master file, add the current month sales from the transaction record to the YTD sales in the master record and the current month returns to the YTD returns. Print a Sales Update Report similar to Figure 14–12. Dump storage if any disk errors occur other than no record found.

17
Vsam Files

OBJECTIVES

After studying this chapter, you should be able to:

- Describe the organization of the control interval and control area of VSAM files
- Describe the logical organization of the three types of VSAM files
- Show the relationship between job control statements, Access Method Services, control block macros, and request macros
- Differentiate between keyed and addressed access of VSAM records
- Differentiate between sequential, direct, and skip sequential processing
- Utilize Access Method Services to define VSAM files
- Use the ACB, RPL, and EXLST control block macros and describe their relationship
- Use the principal request macros to process VSAM files of different types
- Explain how records are added to and deleted from key sequenced data sets
- Explain how error information is made available to the user by VSAM

The Virtual Storage Access Method (VSAM) has been developed for use with DOS/VS or OS/VS and their variations and extensions. The term *virtual storage* refers to the execution of programs by loading them into disk storage rather than main storage. Blocks of the program, called *pages* (usually 4096 bytes each), are brought into main storage as needed until the entire program has been executed. The term *access method* refers to procedures for creating files and retrieving, updating, adding, and deleting records in them.

VSAM virtually eliminates the differences that have existed among the various access methods between DOS and OS for sequential, indexed sequential, and direct files. Like OS, VSAM generally uses the term *data set* to refer to collections of records. In this chapter, we shall tend to use the terms data set and file rather interchangeably.

PHYSICAL ORGANIZATION

The disk space for VSAM data sets is divided into *control intervals*. The size of the control interval varies according to the disk device. VSAM groups control intervals into regions called *control areas*.

Control Intervals

A control interval always contains a whole number of physical blocks. The physical block size, selected by VSAM, is always 512, 1024, 2048, or 4096 bytes. The size of a control interval is not limited to the track capacity or the size of the logical or physical record. Data records may extend across (or *span*) control interval boundaries.

Each physical record in the control interval may contain logical records and unused space. At the end of the last physical block in each control interval is the four-byte control interval definition field (CIDF). The first two bytes of the CIDF give the total length of the physical records, and the last two give the length of the unused space in the control interval.

Preceding the CIDF are the record definition fields (RDF). Each is three bytes long, and they appear in reverse order of the records to which they refer. If no two consecutive records have the same length, there is one RDF for each physical record. If the order of physical records is

REC1, REC2, REC3,.....REC*n*

then the order of the RDFs is

RDF*n*.....RDF3, RDF2, RDF1, CIDF

Where consecutive physical records have different lengths, the format of the RDF is

BYTE	CONTENT
0	X'00'
1–2	Length of physical record to which RDF refers

If two or more consecutive physical records have the same length, only two RDFs are needed for the group of records. The six bytes for the two RDFs have this format:

BYTE	CONTENT
0	X'08'
1–2	Number of consecutive records
3	X'40'
4–5	Length of *each* record

The unused space in the control interval permits records to be inserted at the correct logical position.

Control Areas

VSAM groups control intervals into contiguous space called *control areas*. The size of a control area can range from a minimum of one track to a maximum of one cylinder. Every VSAM data set consists of one or more control areas.

LOGICAL ORGANIZATION

VSAM supports three types of data sets:

1. entry-sequenced data sets (ESDS)
2. key-sequenced data sets (KSDS)
3. relative record data sets (RRDS). All must be placed on direct-access storage devices.

ESDS is similar in concept to sequential organization, KSDS to indexed sequential, and RRDS to direct organization (not covered in this text).

ESDS

Entry-sequenced data set records are stored in the sequence they are initially presented to VSAM. They are normally in ascending sequence, but need not be. A typical ESDS might appear as:

001 002 005 007 011 etc.

ESDS records are processed sequentially by their displacement from the start of the data set, known as the *relative byte address* (RBA). The RBA is in the form of a fullword binary integer. The RBA of the first record is zero. The RBA of the Nth record is equal to the total number of bytes contained in the preceding $N-1$ records. If each logical record is 80 bytes long, then the RBA of the third record is 160. ESDS records may contain duplicate keys, since they are not processed by key.

We may begin sequential retrieval with some record other than the first one in the file by specifying the RBA at which retrieval is to begin. ESDS is useful for records that are to be loaded into tables, for small files kept in sequence, or for extracting records to be sorted.

KSDS

Key-sequenced data set records must be in sequence without duplicates in ascending order when the KSDS is created. Records may be accessed by key or sequentially. You may direct VSAM to leave free space for later insertion of new records in two different ways: (1) leave space at the end of each control interval, or (2) leave some control intervals completely vacant.

On the first track of each control area, a *sequence set* has entries giving the key to the last record on each control interval, together with a pointer to the first record in the control interval. The sequence set is similar to the track index of an indexed sequential file.

As the size of the data set increases, VSAM creates additional *index sets* so that the highest level index will always fit on a single track. The index sets serve a similar purpose to the cylinder and master indexes on indexed sequential files. Figure 17–1 shows a sample of two higher-level indexes, a sequence set, and data records in control intervals.

RRDS

Relative record data set records are arranged in direct relationship to their keys. The record with key 1 is the first record in the data set, and the one with key 50 is the 50th record. Therefore, each key must be unique.

If there is no key for a record location, that location is left empty for possible later insertion of the record. The RRDS might appear as:

001 002 ... 004 ... ... 007 etc.

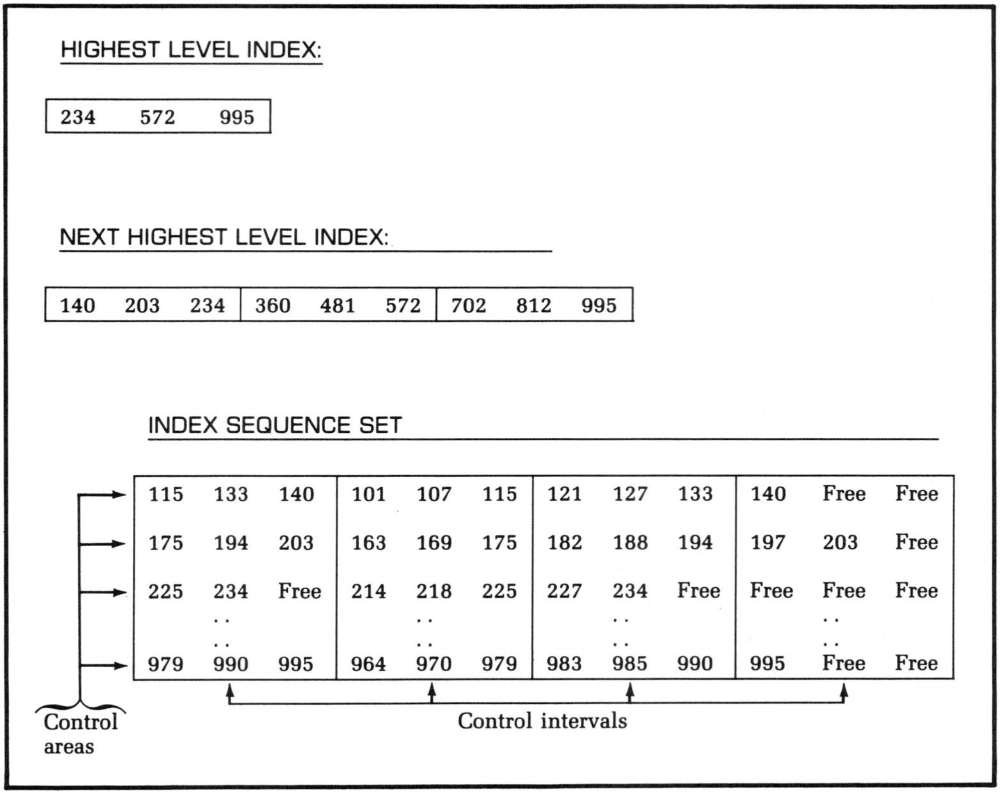

Figure 17–1 KSDS index and data organization

Keys may be transformed by performing some calculation on them. For example, a series of keys of 10, 20, 30, 40,...500 might be converted to relative record numbers 1, 2, 3, 4,...50 by dividing by 10. So long as there are no duplicate keys, any calculation may be used for the transformation.

Comparison of the Three Types

ESDS, KSDS, and RRDS differ from one another in a number of respects. Figure 17–2 shows a comparison of the three types of VSAM organization.

COMPONENTS OF VSAM DATA SETS

VSAM maintains a catalog of information about data sets in three separate components: (1) the *base cluster*, or *cluster;* (2) the *data* component; and (3) the *index* component.

Cluster

The cluster describes the total basic information about a data set required by the VSAM catalog. It includes one or both of the other components. The cluster contains information such as the name of the data set, its organization, number of cylinders or tracks, number of blocks, key length and location, and other pertinent facts.

Data

The data component consists of the set of all control areas that contain control intervals in which data records are stored. All types of organization have the data component.

Index

The index component applies only to KSDS. The index component permits VSAM to translate the primary key of a KSDS record into the RBA of the record. By furnishing the primary key of the desired record in our program, we are able to obtain the desired record without having to read all the preceding records. The index component is organized as a tree structure. The lowest level nodes are the sequence set residing on the first track of each control area. The higher levels include additional indexes created by VSAM for larger data sets.

The entries in any index are in fixed-length blocks called *index control intervals*. The index control interval is always 512, 1024, 2048, or 4096 bytes in length.

CHARACTERISTIC	ESDS	KSDS	RRDS
Sequence of records	In order of creation	By key	By relative record number
Record length	Fixed or variable	Fixed or variable	Fixed only
Access method	By RBA	By key through index or RBA	By relative record number
Change of position	Cannot change RBA	Can change RBA	Cannot change relative record number
Free space	At end of data	Distributed throughout control intervals	Empty record numbers
Reusable space	Cannot delete but can overwrite old record	Space may be reclaimed if record is deleted	Can reuse space of deleted record number

Figure 17–2 Comparison of three types of VSAM organization

Alternate Indexes

The index component of KSDS refers to a *primary* (or *prime*) *key*, which must always be unique. Some other field in a KSDS or ESDS record may be designated as an *alternate key*. The value of an alternate key need not be unique. For ESDS or KSDS we may request an *alternate index* to be constructed. This alternate index is actually a KSDS whose prime keys are the alternate key values from the data records in the base cluster.

For example, a KSDS may have student number as prime key. One field in the record might be major field of study. The alternate index would have the code for each major field of study as a prime key, with pointers to all of the student numbers corresponding to that major.

ACCESSING AND PROCESSING VSAM RECORDS

VSAM provides two methods of accessing records and three ways of processing them. Records may be accessed by address or by key. They may be processed by the sequential, direct, or skip sequential methods.

The types of access and processing that may be performed by each type of organization are shown in Figure 17–3.

Accessing Records

Access by *address* refers to the relative byte address (RBA). Both ESDS and KSDS records may be retrieved by the RBA. RRDS records may not be accessed by this method.

Access by *key* requires use of the record key for KSDS or relative record number for RRDS files. ESDS records may not be accessed by key.

TYPE	KEY	ADDRESS
ESDS		Sequential Direct
KSDS	Sequential Direct Skip sequential	Sequential Direct
RRDS	Sequential Direct Skip sequential	

Figure 17–3 Types of access and processing

Processing Records

The three processing methods are (1) sequential; (2) direct; and (3) skip sequential.

Sequential Processing *Addressed sequential* processing is used to create an ESDS and to add new records at the end of the data set. It is also used to retrieve, update, and flag ESDS records for deletion. VSAM determines the RBA of the record to be created or accessed by maintaining the current RBA and the length of the current record.

Keyed sequential processing is used to create a new KSDS and to sequentially retrieve, update, delete, and add new records. KSDS records can be retrieved sequentially in order by key, even though the records may not be stored physically in that sequence.

Either ESDS or KSDS records may be processed to begin sequential retrieval with a specified record. For ESDS, the RBA of the desired record is given as the search argument for a POINT macro. For KSDS, the key to the desired record is the search argument for POINT. POINT will be discussed in a later section.

Direct Processing ESDS records may be retrieved by *addressed direct* access if the RBA for each desired record is presented to VSAM. Such records may then be updated (without changing length) or flagged for deletion. New records may not be added in this fashion.

KSDS records may be processed through *keyed direct* access. The primary key to the record must be presented. Present records may be retrieved, updated, or deleted. New records may be inserted or added. Records can be processed in any sequence with keyed direct access.

Skip Sequential Processing KSDS records may be processed through *keyed skip sequential* processing. For such processing, the primary key of the desired record must be presented, and records must be processed in *ascending key sequence*. Keyed skip sequential processing may be faster than direct processing if relatively few records are to be processed and the keys of those records are closely grouped.

ACCESS METHOD SERVICES (AMS)

AMS is a VSAM utility program that may be executed under both DOS and OS under the name IDCAMS. It *must* be used to define VSAM catalogs and data sets and to allocate space for them. It *may* be used for other functions such as loading VSAM data sets, printing the contents of VSAM catalogs and data sets, and sorting VSAM data sets.

We will attempt to provide a brief description of only the more common AMS commands. The DOS or OS AMS Manual will provide complete information.

The term *object* in VSAM refers to any of the following seven items that are created or processed through AMS:

1. One and only one master catalog.
2. One or more user catalogs.
3. Data space.
4. The cluster (VSAM data set).
5. Non-VSAM data set.
6. Alternate index.
7. A path connecting an alternate index to a VSAM data set.

The DEFINE command must be used to create a catalog and to create an entry in any existing catalog for any of these VSAM objects.

The DEFINE Command

The DEFINE command has seven variations to define the seven VSAM objects:

FULL COMMAND	ABBREVIATION
DEFINE MASTERCATALOG	DEF MCAT
DEFINE USERCATALOG	DEF UCAT
DEFINE SPACE	DEF SPC
DEFINE CLUSTER	DEF CL
DEFINE NONVSAM	DEF NVSAM
DEFINE ALTERNATEINDEX	DEF AIX
DEFINE PATH	DEF PATH

Through the DEFINE command, space is allocated for objects. Each command is followed by parameters that define the number of bytes per data control interval, number of data control intervals per track, number of tracks per cylinder, number of control areas per cylinder, and other specifications.

CLUSTER The DEFINE CLUSTER command has a number of cluster options. It is followed by the DATA and INDEX parameters, each with a list of options. The general format is:

```
DEFINE  CLUSTER (cluster options)
        DATA (data options)
        INDEX (index options for KSDS only)
        CATALOG (catalog options)
```

Cluster options are enclosed in parentheses following the word CLUSTER. The entries after each of the following keywords are also enclosed in parentheses. They are usually written with one option per line and a continuation character in column 72.

NAME Give the name of the cluster. The name may be up to 44 characters, of which the first must be alphabetic, with a period after each eight or fewer characters, as in VSAM.STUDENT.CLUSTER. There may not be two consecutive periods, nor may the last character be a period.

VOLUME Give the identification of the volume that will contain the cluster.

CYL (p s) or *TRK (p s)* or *REC (p s)* Enter the number of cylinders, tracks, or records to be allocated, where p is the primary allocation and s is the secondary.

FILE Enter the name used in the DOS DLBL statement or the OS DD statement to identify the cluster.

NONINDEXED or *INDEXED* or *NUMBERED* Use NONINDEXED for ESDS, INDEXED for KSDS, or NUMBERED for RRDS.

NOIMBED or *IMBED* For KSDS only, specify whether or not to imbed the index sequence set.

DATA Following the cluster options, the keyword DATA appears. It is followed by the data options enclosed in parentheses. Entries following each of the keywords are also enclosed in parentheses. The data options are:

NAME Specify the name of the data component. It follows the same rules as the name of the cluster. An example of a data component name is VSAM.STUDENT.DATASET.

RECSZ (avg max) Give the average and maximum length of data records. For fixed-length records and RRDS the lengths are the same.

CISZ Give the control interval size. It should be a multiple of 512 between 512 and 8192, or 8192 plus a multiple of 2048 between 10240 and 32768.

KEYS (length offset) For KSDS only, give the length of the primary key and its displacement from the beginning of the record.

FSPC (ci ca) For KSDS only, specify the percent of control interval (ci) space and the percent of control area (ca) space to be left free when the cluster is loaded.

INDEX The index options apply only to KSDS clusters. They follow the keyword INDEX, which follows the DATA options.

NAME Give the name of the index component. An example is VSAM.STUDENT.INDEX.

CISZ Give the size of the control interval for the index component.

Figure 17–4 shows typical job control statements for DOS and OS to run IDCAMS, and Figure 17–5 shows DEFINE CLUSTER statements for processing the VSAM.STUDENT.CLUSTER key-sequenced data set.

```
DOS JOB CONTROL

// DLBL    STUMAST,'VSAM.STUDENT.CLUSTER',,VSAM
// EXTENT  SYS018,VOL1
// ASSGN   SYS018,DISK,VOL=VOL1,SHR
// EXEC    IDCAMS,SIZE=AUTO


OS JOB CONTROL

//STEP001   EXEC   PGM=IDCAMS
//STUMAST   DD     VOL=SER=VOL1,UNIT=3340.
```

Figure 17–4 Job control statements to run IDCAMS for DOS and OS

```
DEFINE CLUSTER   (                                 -
                 NAME (VSAM.STUDENT.CLUSTER)       -
                 FILE (STUMAST)                    -
                 VOL (VOL1)                        -
                 CYL (5 2)                         -
                 INDEXED IMBED                     -
                 )                                 -
DATA             (                                 -
                 NAME (VSAM.STUDENT.DATASET)       -
                 RECORDSIZE (50 50)                -
                 KEYS (9 1)                        -
                 CISZ (8192)                       -
                 )                                 -
INDEX            (                                 -
                 NAME (VSAM.STUDENT.INDEX)         -
                 CISZ (512)                        -
                 )                                 -
```

Figure 17–5 DEFINE CLUSTER statements for key-sequenced data set

CONTROL BLOCK MACROS

All of the preceding definitions and commands appear as job control statements or as parameters to the IDCAMS utility program. Now we shall examine macros that appear within our VSAM program.

Three VSAM macros relate a program to the data or define requests for accessing the data. They are ACB (Access Method Control Block), RPL (Request Parameter List), and EXLST (Exit List). The three together generally supply parameters and specifications similar to those provided by the DTF macro in DOS or the DCB macro in OS.

ACB

The ACB (Access Method Control Block) macro identifies a data set that is to be processed. Much of the information about the cluster has already been provided in the DEFINE CLUSTER command. The ACB indicates the type of access (addressed or keyed) and the type of processing (sequential, direct, or skip sequential).

To use the ACB macro, place ACB in the op code field. The name field is referred to in OPEN, CLOSE, and RPL macros in processing the data set. Each of the operands in the ACB is a keyword followed by an equal sign and an entry. Each operand but the last is followed by a comma. One or more operands may appear on the same line, and a continuation character must be placed in column 72 on each line but the last.

ACB operands are optional and may appear in any sequence. The following operands are typical:

AM=VSAM Use this parameter if VTAM is also used by the system. If omitted, VSAM is assumed.

DDNAME Give the name used as the filename in the DLBL or DD job control statement.

EXLST Give the name of the EXLST macro. This macro provides a list of addresses of routines that handle exits. The address of the end-of-file routine for sequential processing is typical.

MACRF Specify ADR for addressed access or KEY for keyed access. ADR applies to ESDS or KSDS, and KEY to KSDS or RRDS. Specify DIR or SEQ or SKP to indicate whether processing is direct, sequential, or skip sequential. Code IN for input only and OUT to permit retrieval, insertion, update, or addition of records to end of file. Specify NRM or AIX to indicate whether processing is normal or by alternate index.

STRNO Enter total number of RPLs to be used at the same time by the program. The default is 1.

Refer to Program 17 for examples of the ACB macro with KSDS input and output files.

RPL

The RPL (Request Parameter List) macro provides a reference point for GET, PUT, ERASE, and POINT request macros. Rather than refer to the name of the ACB control block, these VSAM macros are in the form

```
GET RPL=RPLname
```

RPLname in this example is the name of an RPL macro that supplies additional information needed to access the record. If a data set is to be accessed in different ways, a separate RPL macro may be coded for each type of access. Some of the typical operands for the RPL macro are:

AM=VSAM Code if this is a VSAM control block rather than VTAM.

ACB Give the name of ACB macro.

AREA Give the name of a work area in which an input record is to be processed or an output record is to be built.

AREALEN Give the length of a logical record in bytes.

ARG Give the name of a field to contain the search argument. This may be a key, a relative record number, or a relative byte address.

KEYLEN Give the length of the key for processing by generic key. The normal key length has been specified in the DEFINE CLUSTER statement.

OPTCD Specify SEQ, DIR, or SKP for processing options. Specify MVE if records are to be moved to or from a work area, or LOC if Locate Mode (records processed in I/O area) is to be used. Specify UPD if record is to be updated or NUP if it is not. Specify (GEN,KEQ) if a record key is to be exactly equal to a generic key or (GEN,KGE) if it should be greater than or equal to the generic key.

RECLEN Specify length of record to be added or inserted.

Program 17 has examples of RPL macros for GET and PUT operations.

EXLST

The EXLST (Exit List) macro provides an optional list of addresses for any exit routines you may specify. Typical operands are:

AM=VSAM Code to indicate a VSAM rather than a VTAM control block.

EODAD Give the name of your end-of-file routine. This routine is entered whenever R15 contains a request return code of X'04'. The request return code is discussed under the section on Request Macros.

LERAD Give the name of the routine to analyze logical errors that occurred during GET, PUT, POINT, or ERASE. This routine is entered if the request return code is X'08'.

SYNAD Give the name of the routine to analyze any physical I/O errors that occur during GET, PUT, POINT, ERASE, or CLOSE. This routine is entered if the request return code is X‘0C’.

REQUEST MACROS

Request macros are designed to be executed at run time. The most common request macros are OPEN, CLOSE, GET, PUT, POINT, and ERASE. OPEN and CLOSE refer to the name of the ACB macro. All others give the RPLname.

Each processing macro sets a request return code in R15. A code of X‘00’ indicates that the operation was performed successfully. Other error codes will be identified under the specific macros.

OPEN

The OPEN macro connects a program to a data set. It may be written in either of these forms:

```
name OPEN ACBname   or          LA    reg,ACBname
                           name OPEN  (reg)
```

Any general register 2 to 12 may be used in the second form. Up to 16 files may be opened with a single OPEN. Although both VSAM and non-VSAM files may be opened in the same OPEN, it is recommended that they not be mixed for debugging.

Return codes following OPEN are placed in R15. They are:

X‘00’ All ACBs were opened successfully.

X‘04’ All ACBS were opened successfully, but a warning message was issued for one or more.

X‘08’ One or more ACBs failed to open.

CLOSE

The CLOSE macro completes all outstanding I/O operations, writes any remaining output buffers, updates catalog entries for the data set, and disconnects the program from the data set. It has either form:

```
name CLOSE ACBname  or          LA     reg,ACBname
                           name CLOSE  (reg)
```

Any general register 2 to 12 may contain the ACBname in the second form. Up to 16 files may be closed with a single CLOSE. Return codes placed in R15 following CLOSE are:

X'00' All ACBs were closed successfully.
X'04' One or more ACBs failed to close.
X'08' Insufficient virtual storage space to close, or close modules could not be located.

GET

The GET, PUT, POINT, and ERASE macros all refer to the RPLname. All place one of the following return codes in R15 following the operation:

X'00' Operation was completed successfully.
X'04' Request not accepted because of an active request from another task for the same RPL. Also set for end of file.
X'08' A logical error occurred.
X'0C' An uncorrectable physical I/O error occurred.

The GET macro retrieves a record from the data set. It may be written in either form:

```
name GET RPL=RPLname or name GET RPL=(reg)
```

where the second form may refer to any general register 2 to 12 containing the address of RPLname. The RPL macro defines the name of a work area to which GET may transfer the accessed record. The OPTCD entry in the RPL macro specifies the access method (ADR or KEY) and the processing method (SEQ, DIR, or SKP).

PUT

The PUT macro writes or rewrites a record in a data set. It may be written in either form:

```
name PUT RPL=RPLname or name PUT RPL=(reg)
```

where the second form may refer to any general register 2 to 12 that contains the address of RPLname. If the OPTCD entry in the RPL macro contained a NUP (no update) operand, PUT stores a new record in the data set. If the operand is UPD, PUT will rewrite an updated record that has been obtained with a GET macro referring to an UPD operand in an OPTCD entry. It is important not to change the key between the GET and PUT if a record is updated.

The PUT macro stores a return code in R15 as mentioned under GET in the preceding section.

POINT

The POINT macro positions VSAM at a specific record in a data set for subsequent sequential processing. It may be written in either form:

```
name POINT RPL=RPLname or name POINT RPL=(reg)
```

where the second form may refer to any general register 2 to 12 containing the address of RPLname.

An RBA, a prime key, or a *generic key* may be used for positioning. A generic key is the high-order portion of a prime key (4000 for keys higher than or equal to 4000). The RBA or key must be moved to the field designated by the ARG parameter in the RPL macro before POINT can be executed. If a generic key is used, the OPTCD parameter in the RPL must specify whether the record key is to be exactly equal to the generic key (GEN,KEQ) or whether the record key should be equal to or greater than the generic key (GEN,KGE).

ERASE

The ERASE macro is used to delete a record from a KSDS or RRDS. The record to be deleted must first be obtained with a GET with an RPL that specifies OPTCD=(UPD, . . .). The record is then deleted by issuing

```
name ERASE RPL=RPLname or RPL=(reg)
```

For ESDS, a record is usually marked for deletion by placing a special code such as X'FF' in a special byte in the record. The program must then bypass a record so indicated. When the entire data set is recopied, deleted records should be omitted.

Figure 17–6 shows the relationship between job control and VSAM macros.

EXECUTABLE CONTROL BLOCK MACROS

There are four macros that generate control blocks at execution time. They are GENCB (generate control block), MODCB (modify control block), TESTCB (test control block), and SHOWCB (show control block).

GENCB

This is an executable macro that creates an ACB, RPL, or EXLST macro at run time rather than assembly time. This feature may eliminate the need to reassemble programs if the format of these macros is modified by later versions of VSAM.

MODCB

This macro permits an ACB, RPL, or EXLST macro to be modified at execution time. For example, an RPL operand might be changed from OPTCD=UPD to OPTCD=NUP at execution time to permit a record to be added instead of updated.

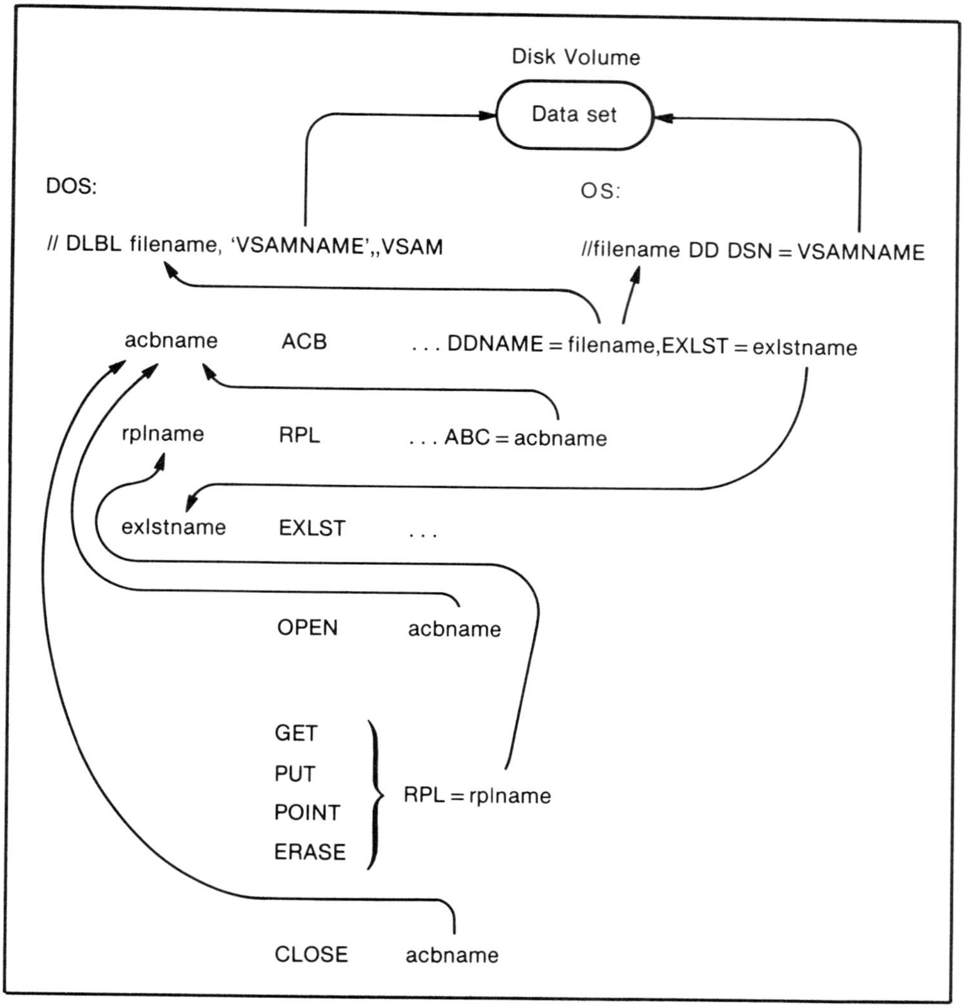

Figure 17–6 Relationship between job control and VSAM macros

TESTCB

This macro is similar to the SHOWCB macro (described more fully below), with one major exception. SHOWCB puts control block information into a user work area for diagnosis. TESTCB compares the value of a control block field with a value that is supplied by the programmer and sets the condition code to show the comparison.

SHOWCB

This is probably the most useful of the executable control block macros. It puts control block information into a user work area following an error on one of the request macros. SHOWCB is written in one of three formats:

```
showname SHOWCB ACB=ACBname or RPL=RPLname or
                EXLST=EXLSTname
```

Each format is followed by keyword parameters specifying the control block information to be made available. SHOWCB is normally used to display error codes resulting from one of the request macros. Some of the SHOWCB keywords are:

AREA Specify address of the area that will receive values specified in the FIELDS keyword.

LENGTH Give length of the AREA field.

OBJECT Specify DATA if fields shown are for the data component or INDEX if they are for the index component of the cluster.

FIELDS Specify one or more mnemonic code words that identify control block fields to be placed in AREA.

For SHOWCB ACB, FIELDS = ERROR provides the error code after execution of an OPEN or CLOSE macro.

For SHOWCB = RPL, three different FIELDS operands are often useful. If FIELDS = FDBK, then AREA refers to a fullword where VSAM will place detailed error codes following execution of a GET, PUT, POINT, or ERASE request macro. The rightmost byte of this fullword will contain the error code, such as:

`X'08'` Record to be stored had duplicate key.

`X'0C'` Record out of sequence or duplicate key for KSDS or RRDS.

`X'10'` No record found.

`X'1C'` No room available to store a record.

The fullword can be tested to determine the specific error and the program can either continue processing or cancel.

If FIELDS = RBA, the relative byte address of the most recently processed logical record is placed in the field named in AREA.

If FIELDS = RECLEN, the length of the field most recently processed is placed in the field named in AREA.

PROGRAM 17: REORGANIZE VSAM FILE

Program 17 is a modification of Program 16E to describe recopying a VSAM file. OLDMAST is the original file, and NEWMAST is the rewritten file. After each request macro, R15 is tested for any error. If any error is indicated, other than end of file, a PDUMP is taken and the program is cancelled. The end-of-file address is obtained through the EXLST macro rather than through testing R15. The GET macro is placed in a separate module that sets EOFFLAG to 'Y' at end of file to control the main processing loop, just as we have done in processing input records throughout the book.

The program itself puts a one-byte code into ERRCODE to show the request macro that was being processed when an error occurred:

CODE	REQUEST MACRO
O	OPEN
G	GET
P	PUT
C	CLOSE

The SHOWCB macro is used to put the specific error code into the fullword FDBKOWD if an error is detected when processing RPLOMAST or into FDBKNWD if the error refers to RPLNMAST.

Figure 17–7 shows the assembler listing.

```
  LOC  OBJECT CODE    ADDR1 ADDR2  STMT   SOURCE STATEMENT                                        DOS/VSE ASSEMBLER 14.38 86-04-14

                                      1 ***********************************************************************
                                      2 *                   ALTON R. KINDRED, PROGRAM 17
                                      3 * THIS PROGRAM REORGANIZES THE INVENTORY MASTER VSAM KSDS FILE.  BOTH
                                      4 * THE OLD MASTER AND THE NEW MASTER SHARE THE SAME DATA WORK AREA.
                                      5 * IF ANY ERROR OCCURS DURING AN OPEN, CLOSE, READ, OR WRITE OPERATION,
                                      6 * THE PROGRAM IS CANCELED.  NO LOG IS PRITED FOR THIS OPERATION.
                                      7 *        REGISTERS USED:
                                      8 *                   R09-R10:  LINK REGISTERS
                                      9 *                   R12:      BASE REGISTER
                                     10 *                   R15:      ERROR CODE FOR VSAM OPERATIONS
                                     11 ***********************************************************************
                                     12          PRINT NOGEN
000000                               13 MAINLINE START 0                         SET LOCATION COUNTER
000000 05C0                          14          BALR  12,0                      LOAD BASE REGISTER
                             00002   15          USING *,12                      DESIGNATE BASE REGISTER
000002 4590 C00E             00010   16          BAL   9,INITIAL                 DO INITIAL PROCESSING
000006 4590 C038             0003A   17          BAL   9,MAINLOOP                DO MAIN PROCESSING LOOP
00000A 4590 C04E             00050   18          BAL   9,FINAL                   DO FINAL PROCESSING
                                     19          EOJ                             END PROGRAM
                                     22 ***********************************************************************
                                     23 *                   FIRST LEVEL MODJLES
                                     24 ***********************************************************************
                                     25 *
                                     26 *                   INITIAL PROCESSING
                                     27 *
000010 41D0 C31A             0031C   28 INITIAL  LA    13,VSAMSAVE               LOAD A(VSAMSAVE AREA) INTO R13
                                     29          OPEN  OLDMAST,NEWMAST           OPEN FILES
000026 12FF                          38 IF       LTR   15,15                     IF OPEN NOT OK
000028 4780 C032       00034         39          BZ    ENDIF                       *
00002C 9206 C319       0031B         40 THEN     MVI   ERRCODE,C'O'                THEN SET ERROR CODE TO 'O'
000030 47F0 C0C0       000C2         41          B     ABEND                       CANCEL
                             00034   42 ENDIF    EQU   *                         ENDIF
000034 45A0 C070             00072   43          BAL   10,READOMST               READ FIRST RECORD
000038 07F9                          44          BR    9                         RETURN
                                     45 *
                                     46 *                   MAIN PROCESSING LOOP
                                     47 *
                             0003A   48 MAINLOOP EQU   *
00003A 95E8 C318       0031A         49 DOWHILE  CLI   EOFFLAG,C'Y'              DOWHILE NOT END OF FILE
00003E 4770 C04C       0004E         50          BNZ   ENDDO                       *
000042 45A0 C09E             000A0   51          BAL   10,WRITNMST                 WRITE NEW RECORD
000046 45A0 C070             00072   52          BAL   10,READOMST                 READ NEXT RECORD
00004A 47F0 C038       0003A         53          B     DOWHILE                     *
                             0004E   54 ENDDO    EQU   *                         ENDDO
00004E 07F9                          55          BR    9                         RETURN
                                     56 *                   FINAL PROCESSING LOOP
                                     57 *
                                     58 FINAL    CLOSE OLDMAST,NEWMAST           CLOSE FILES
000062 12FF                          67 IF3      LTR   15,15                     IF ANY ERRORS
000064 4780 C06E       00070         68          BZ    ENDIF3                      *
000068 92C3 C319       0031B         69 THEN3    MVI   ERRCODE,C'C'                THEN SET ERROR CODE TO 'C'
00006C 47F0 C0C0       000C2         70          B     ABEND                       CANCEL
                             00070   71 ENDIF3   EQU   *                         ENDIF
000070 07F9                          72          BR    9                         RETURN
                                     74 ***********************************************************************
                                     75 *                   SECOND LEVEL MODULES
                                     76 ***********************************************************************
                                     77 *
                                     78 *                   READ OLD MASTER RECORD MODULE
                                     79 *
                                     80 READOMST GET   RPL=RPLOMST               READ VSAM RECORD
000084 47F0 C08E       00090         87 IFEOF    B     ELSEEOF                   IF END OF FILE
000088 92E8 C318       0031A         88 THENEOF  MVI   EOFFLAG,C'Y'                THEN SET EOFFLAG ON
00008C 47F0 C09C       0009E         89          B     ENDIFEOF                    *
                             00090   90 ELSEEOF  EQU   *                         ELSE
00009C 12FF                          91 IF4      LTR   15,15                       IF READ DISK ERROR
000092 4770 C09C       0009E         92          BNZ   ENDIF4                        *
000096 92C7 C319       0031B         93 THEN4    MVI   ERRCODE,C'G'                  THEN SET ERROR CODE TO 'G'
```

Figure 17–7 Listing of Program 17

```
  LOC  OBJECT CODE    ADDR1 ADDR2  STMT   SOURCE STATEMENT                             DOS/VSE ASSEMBLER 14.38 86-04-14

00009A 47F0 C0C0      000C2          94            B      ABEND                          CANCEL
                            0009E    95 ENDIF4    EQU    *                             ENDIF
                            0009E    96 ENDIFEOF  EQU    *                            ENDIF
00009E 07FA                          97            BR     10                          RETURN
                                     98 *
                                     99 *                 WRITE NEW MASTER RECORD MODULE
                                    100 *
                                    101 WRITNMST  PUT    RPL=RPLNMST                 WRITE TO NEW FILE
0000B2 12FF                         108 IF2       LTR    15,15                       IF ANY ERRORS
0000B4 4780 C0BE      000C0         109            BZ     ENDIF2                         *
0000B8 92D7 C319      0031B         110 THEN2     MVI    ERRCODE,C'P'                   THEN SET ERROR CODE TO 'P'
0000BC 47F0 C0C0      000C2         111            B      ABEND                          CANCEL
                            000C0   112 ENDIF2    EQU    *                           ENDIF
0000C0 07FA                         113            BR     10                          RETURN
                                    114 *****************************************************************
                                    115 *                 ABNORMAL END MODULE
                                    116 *****************************************************************
0000C2 50F0 C362            00364   117 ABEND     ST     15,SAVE15                   SAVE TERMINATION CODE
                                    118            SHOWCB RPL=RPLNMST,AREA=FDBKOWD,FIELDS=FDBK,LENGTH=4
                                    170            SHOWCB RPL=RPLOMST,AREA=FDBKNWD,FIELDS=FDBK,LENGTH=4
                                    222            PDUMP MAINLINE,ENDLITRL          DUMP PROGRAM
                                    228            CLOSE OLDMAST,NEWMAST            CLOSE FILES
                                    237            CANCEL ,                         C
                                    241 *****************************************************************
                                    242 *                 FILE DEFINITIONS
                                    243 *****************************************************************
                                    244 OLDMAST   ACB    DDNAME=VSAMFL,MACRF=(KEY,SEQ,IN),EXLST=EOFOMST
                                    276 *
                                    277 RPLOMST   RPL    ACB=OLDMAST,AREA=INVRECD,AREALEN=50,                 X
                                                         OPTCD=(KEY,SEQ,NUP,MVE)
                                    306 *
                                    307 EOFOMST   EXLST  EODAD=THENEOF
                                    318 *
                                    319 NEWMAST   ACB    DDNAME=VSAMFL,MACRF=(KEY,SEQ,OUT)
                                    351 *
                                    352 RPLNMST   RPL    ACB=NEWMAST,AREA=INVRECD,AREALEN=50,RECLEN=80,       X
                                                         OPTCD=(KEY,SEQ,NUP,MVE)
                                    381 *
                                    383 *****************************************************************
                                    384 *                 DATA DEFINITIONS
                                    385 *****************************************************************
0002E8                              386 INVRECD   DS     CL50
00031A                              387 EOFFLAG   DS     CL1
00031B                              388 ERRCODE   DS     CL1
00031C                              389 VSAMSAVE  DS     18F
000364                              390 SAVE15    DS     F
000368                              391 FDBKOWD   DS     F
00036C                              392 FDBKNWD   DS     F
                                    393 *
000370                              394           LTORG
000370 5B5BC2D6D7C5D540             395                  =C'$$BOPEN '
000378 5B5BC2C3D3D6E2C5             396                  =C'$$BCLOSE'
000380 C9D2D8E5E3D4F240             397                  =CL8'IKQVTMS'
000388 5B5BC2D7C4E4D4D7             398                  =CL8'$$BPDUMP'
000390 00000000000003A0             399                  =A(MAINLINE,ENDLITRL)
000398 00000230                     400                  =A(RPLOMST)
00039C 000002B4                     401                  =A(RPLNMST)
                            003A0   402 ENDLITRL  EQU    *
                            00000   403           END    MAINLINE
```

Figure 17–7 *(Concluded)*

SUMMARY

VSAM is a file organization method for DOS and OS systems that have virtual storage. VSAM supports three types of data sets: (1) entry-sequenced data sets (ESDS); (2) key-sequenced data sets (KSDS); and (3) relative-record data sets (RRDS).

ESDS has records in the order of original entry. KSDS records are in sequence according to a key. RRDS records are in order of record number.

All three types of data sets are organized into control intervals (CI), which may have free space left in or at the end of the CI for records to be added. The last physical block in each control interval contains the control interval definition field (CIDF) and a record definition field (RDF) for each record of different length in the CI.

Control intervals are grouped into control areas. Control areas may range in size from a track to a cylinder.

Each data set has a cluster component, a data component, and for KSDS an index component. The index component consists of a sequence set on the first track of each control interval and additional higher level indexes as needed for the size of the data set. The index refers to the prime key of each record. There may be one or more alternate indexes set up for a data set to refer to fields other than the prime key in each record.

VSAM records may be accessed by address or by key. The address is the relative byte address (RBA) giving the displacement from the start of the data set. The key is a unique record identifier for KSDS or a relative record number for RRDS.

VSAM records have three processing methods: (1) sequential, (2) direct, or (3) skip sequential.

Access Method Services (ASM) is a VSAM utility that is required to create a data set and may be used for other optional functions. The DEFINE command supplies parameters that direct ASM to create the cluster, data, and index components by supplying information as to the number of cylinders, tracks, or records; length and position of keys; record size; and type of organization.

Control block macros appear in a VSAM program. The ACB macro indicates the access method and form of processing. The RPL macro specifies the name of the work area and search argument field and various processing options. The EXLST macro gives the name of the end-of-file routine and other possible user exit routines.

Request macros include OPEN, CLOSE, GET, PUT, POINT, and ERASE. They handle reading and writing or rewriting of the records in the data set. The POINT macro positions VSAM at a specified record by address or key. The ERASE macro can delete records from the data set. Each request macro places a request return code in R15 that can be analyzed to determine the reason for unsuccessful I/O operations.

Executable control block macros include GENCB, MODCB, TESTCB, and SHOWCB. The SHOWCB is especially useful in diagnosing errors. It specifies a user area in which VSAM will return detailed error codes.

TERMS FOR REVIEW

Access method control block
Access Method Services
Addressed access
Alternate index
Cluster
Control area
Control interval
Control interval definition field
Data component
Direct processing
Entry-sequenced data set
Executable control block macro
Exit list
Index component
Key-sequenced data set
Keyed access
Object
POINT
Primary key
Record definition field

Relative byte address
Relative record data set
Request macro
Request parameter list
Request return code
Sequence set
Sequential processing
Skip sequential processing
Span

REVIEW QUESTIONS

1. Describe the physical arrangement of a control interval with one physical block per CI, and with more than one physical block.
2. Explain the format and purpose of the control interval definition field (CIDF) and the record definition field (RDF). How does the RDF differ if all records have variable length or if two or more consecutive records have the same length?
3. What happens when records are added to a control interval? Where may they be inserted or added?
4. Distinguish between ESDS, RRDS, and KSDS as to methods of access and processing.
5. What is Access Method Services (AMS), and what is its more important function?
6. What type of information appears in the DEFINE statement for ESDS? What additional information must be supplied for KSDS?
7. What operands appear in an ACB macro? In what part of the program is ACB placed?
8. What is the purpose of the RPL macro? Where in the program does it appear? Can more than one RPL be used with a single data set?
9. What is the purpose of the EXLST macro? What is its more common use?
10. What forms may be used with the OPEN and CLOSE macros? What operands do they have, and what is the maximum number of data sets that can be opened or closed with a single statement?
11. What operands are used with the GET, PUT, POINT, and ERASE macros? What alternative forms may they have?
12. What action must be taken before the GET macro can be used in direct retrieval?
13. How does deletion of a record from an ESDS differ from deletion of a record from a KSDS or RRDS?
14. What is the purpose of the POINT macro, and what must be done before it can be used?
15. How is the request return code made available to the program after each request macro? What is the return code for end of file?
16. How is more detailed information made available to the program about the cause of an I/O error? What executable control block macro is coded for this purpose?

EXERCISES

1. Write a DEFINE statement for a KSDS to occupy three cylinders with 100-byte records. The key is in positions 9 to 16. The data set name is INVMAST, and all components are on volume VOL8.
2. Write a module to read a record from a VSAM ESDS and set a flag if end of file is encountered.

PROGRAMMING PROBLEMS

1. Write a program to read Data Set 2 in Appendix D and create a VSAM key-sequenced data set (KSDS). Create an Inventory Listing similar to Figure 16–6, indicating any records that are out of sequence or have duplicate keys.
2. Write a program to read Data Set 2A in Appendix D and update the VSAM KSDS created in Problem 1. Print an Inventory Update Report similar to Figure 16–10 showing the master record before the update, the transaction data, and the master record after the update. Print a message if the key to the transaction record is not found or if the transaction code is not 'C', 'P', or 'S'.
3. Write a program to read the item number and quantity sold from Data Set 2C in Appendix D. Retrieve the record with the corresponding item number from the VSAM KSDS Inventory Master File that was updated in Problem 2. If the quantity sold is less than the quantity on hand, print a Sales Report showing the item number, description, quantity sold, unit price, and amount of sale. Subtract the quantity sold from the quantity on hand, and rewrite the new quantity back with the updated record to the VSAM file.

   If the quantity sold is not less than the quantity on hand, print the item number, description, quantity on hand, quantity sold (requested), and the message 'INSUFFICIENT STOCK'.

   If the item number from the transaction is not found in the VSAM file, print the item number with the message 'NOT IN FILE'.

18 Floating-Point Operations

OBJECTIVES

After studying this chapter, you should be able to:

- Define floating-point numbers
- Give reasons for using floating-point numbers
- Give examples of floating-point numbers in decimal and hexadecimal form
- Define and give examples of normalization of floating-point numbers
- Explain the effect on precision of numbers of different lengths
- Distinguish between short, long, and extended floating-point numbers
- Define constants in each of the three different forms
- Explain and use floating-point arithmetic instructions
- Convert fixed-point numbers to floating-point form and floating-point numbers to fixed-point form

All numbers used thus far in the text have been *fixed-point numbers*, regarded as integers and processed accordingly. The position of the decimal point is the responsibility of the programmer, who must keep track of where it belongs during arithmetic operations and insert it in the proper position when editing the final results.

With fixed-point numbers one digit position must be reserved in storage for each digit in the number. This means that hexadecimal numbers are limited to about 16 digits, and packed decimal numbers to 31 digits.

FORMAT OF FLOATING-POINT NUMBERS

In scientific work, we often must work with very large or very small numbers. *Floating-point* numbers are convenient for this purpose. They have two main components:

1. A *fraction*, or *mantissa*, representing the value of the entire number (or its most significant digits).
2. An *exponent*, or *characteristic*, representing the number of places the decimal place must be shifted left or right to represent the true value of the number.

High-level scientific programming languages make use of floating-point numbers. They are often said to be in *exponential* form. The exponent is usually indicated with the letter E followed by the exponent, which may be positive or negative. A positive exponent means to shift the decimal point right the number of places indicated, while a negative exponent specifies a left shift.

Most high-level languages accept exponential data for input, with the decimal place shown explicitly or implicitly. The exponent specifies the shift of the decimal point from its explicit or implicit location. Figure 18–1 shows a few examples of decimal numbers, with their equivalent values in floating-point form. In each case, the fraction is limited to eight digits.

The sign of the *number* indicates whether it is positive or negative. The sign of the *exponent* indicates whether the shift of decimal is to the left or right. Zero has a plus sign and both exponent and fraction of zero.

Floating-point numbers can also be expressed in hexadecimal form. The use of the signs, exponent, and fraction is as shown for decimal numbers. Figure 18–2 shows some examples, using X as the exponent to avoid confusion with the hex digit E.

Floating-point numbers are actually stored as 32, 64, or 128 bit binary numbers. For each size, the leftmost bit is the *sign of the fraction*. The next

INPUT FORM	ASSUMED VALUE	STORE AS EXP. FRACTION
12345E+4	123450000	+09 +.12345000
.12345E+4	1234.5	+04 +.12345000
2.5E+4	25000	+05 +.25000000
1234567895E+0	1234567895	+10 +.12345678
1234567895E−5	12345.67895	+05 +.12345678
−75E−6	−.000075	−04 −.75000000
0	0	+00 +.00000000

Figure 18–1 Decimal numbers in exponential form

INPUT FORM	ASSUMED VALUE	STORE AS EXP. FRACTION
40X+2	40.	+02 +.40000000
2A7.83X+2	2A783	+05 +.2A783000
−.F2E3D4C5B6X+3	−F2E.3D4C5B6	+03 −.F2E3D4C5
.8C4X−7	.00000008C4	−07 +.8C400000
−2F7X−8	−.000002F7	−05 −.2F700000
0	0	+00 +.00000000

Figure 18–2 Hexadecimal numbers in exponential form

seven bits represent the exponent in *excess 64 notation*. This means that 64 (X'40') is added to the exponent. The remaining bits represent the fraction. The fraction remains in its true form (not complemented) if negative. Only the sign bit differentiates a positive number from a negative one. Zero has a zero exponent, a zero fraction, and a plus sign.

The hexadecimal numbers in Figure 18–2 are shown in Figure 18–3 in 32-bit form for study. The fraction is limited to 24 bits, or six hex digits, in this form.

The leftmost hex digit represents both the sign of the number and the leftmost three bits of the exponent. Whenever the sign of the fraction is 0 for positive, the value of the leftmost digit can range from X'0' through X'7'. If the sign is 1 for negative, the leftmost digit will be X'8' through X'F'.

PRECISION

The term "precision" refers to the number of nonzero digits that express the value of a number. The fraction .33333333 is more precise than .33, and 92487546 is more precise than 92000000.

Floating-point numbers may be defined, stored, and processed in the following forms:

Short	32 bits	24 bits for fraction
Long	64 bits	56 bits for fraction
Extended	128 bits	112 bits for fraction

In each form, the leftmost bit is the sign of the fraction, and the next seven bits represent the exponent in excess-64 notation. The exponent can therefore range from −64 through +63 (0 through 127, or X'00' through X'7F'). The precision of the fraction in short form is six hex digits, in long form it is 16 hex digits, and in extended form it is 28 hex digits. We will discuss extended form fully in a later section.

EXP. FRACTION	FORM STORED	REMARKS
+02 +.40000000	42400000	X'40' + X'02' = X'42' exponent
+05 +.2A783000	452A7830	
+03 −.F2E3D4C5	C3F2E3D4	Leftmost 1 bit indicates sign
−07 +.8C400000	398C4000	X'40' − X'07' = X'39' exponent
−05 −.2F700000	BB257000	X'C0' − X'05' = X'BB' exponent and sign
+00 +.00000000	00000000	

Figure 18–3 Short floating-point numbers with exponent in excess-64 notation

NORMALIZATION

A floating-point number is said to be *normalized* if it has no leading zeros in the fraction. This refers to leading *hex* zeros, not binary zeros. For example, the hex digit 4 has one leading 0 bit, but would be considered normalized. Consider these examples:

UNNORMALIZED	NORMALIZED	VALUE
45000250	42250000	25.0000
3E000250	3B250000	.0000025

There are instructions that process both normalized and unnormalized data. Most instructions produce a normalized result.

DEFINING FLOATING-POINT CONSTANTS

We may define floating-point constants by specifying one of three types:

E single-precision, short floating-point, 32-bits

D double-precision, long floating-point, 64 bits

L extended precision, extended floating-point, 128 bits

Type E data is aligned on a fullword boundary. Type D or L data is aligned on a doubleword boundary. All types are padded to the *right* with zeros if the value of the data is shorter than the number of bits indicated. Figure 18–4 shows some examples of the three types of numbers. Note that we may use the letter E to represent the exponent in the value of the constant.

FLOATING-POINT INSTRUCTIONS

A large set of instructions is provided for processing floating-point data. As we see in Figure 18–5, most of these are available as both type RR and type RX instructions and for long and short form.

There are four floating-point (FP) registers, numbered 0, 2, 4, and 6. Each is a 64-bit register. The registers process both short and long data. For type RR instructions, both operands must be in the FP registers. For type RX, the first operand is in a FP register, and the second is in main storage. In all other respects, their operation is identical.

The op code for each instruction gives the operation in the first one or two letters. The next letter is either E, D, or X indicating short, long, or extended form. The last letter of the op code is R for type RR instructions.

```
                        ************************************************************************
                        *                 ALTON R. KINDRED, FLOATING-POINT CONSTANTS
                        ************************************************************************
                        *
                        *                 SHORT FORM CONSTANTS
                        *
                                   PRINT DATA
000000                             START 0
000000 42640000                    DC    E'100'
000004 C3100000                    DC    E'-256'
000008 46F808EF                    DC    E'16255215'
00000C 451E23A0                    DC    E'123.45E3'
000010 C2100000                    DC    E'-16'
                        *                 LONG FORM CONSTANTS
000014 00000000
000018 487FFFFFFF000000            DC    D'2147483647'
000020 C11553F7CED91687            DC    D'-1.333'
000028 4410008000000000            DC    D'40965E-1'
000030 483ADE68B1000000            DC    D'987654321'
000038 42199CCCCCCCCCCD            DC    D'.256125E2'
                        *                 EXTENDED FORM CONSTANTS
000040 C11553F7CED91687            DC    L'-1.333'
000048 B32B020C49BA5E35
000050 3011B578C96DB19A            DC    L'.375E-20'
000058 2285FCD6F18AAFA2
000060 512086AC35105260            DC    L'.375E20'
000068 4300000000000000
000070 4880000000000000            DC    L'2147483648'
000078 3A00000000000000
000080 C3FFF3CE075F6FD2            DC    L'-40952378E-4'
000088 B51FF2E48E8A71DE
                                   END
```

Figure 18–4 Long, short, and extended floating-point constants

Load and Store Instructions

The Load instructions (LER, LE, LDR, LD) place the second operand unchanged in the operand-1 FP register. LER and LE do not affect the rightmost 32 bits of the register. The condition code is unaffected.

The Store instructions (STE and STD) place the contents of the operand-1 FP register unchanged into the second operand location in main storage. STE stores only the leftmost 32 bits of the FP register. STD stores all 64 bits. The condition code is unchanged.

Other Load Instructions

Four special type RR Load instructions have functions similar to those of the fixed-point instructions. Both operands must refer to FP register 0, 2, 4, or 6. Load and Test (LTER and LTDR) place the contents of the operand-2 FP register unchanged into the operand-1 FP register. The condition code is set to 0, 1, or 2 to indicate result of zero, negative, or positive. Operand 1 and operand 2 may refer to the same register.

Load Complement (LCER and LCDR) place the second operand into the operand-1 register with the sign bit inverted. The exponent and fraction are not changed. The sign bit is inverted even if the result is zero. The condition code is set to 0, 1, or 2 as in Load and Test.

Load Negative (LNER and LNDR) place the second operand in the operand-1 location with a minus sign. The exponent and fraction are unchanged. The condition code is 0 if the result is zero, and 1 if it is negative.

Load Positive (LPER and LPDR) place the second operand in the operand-1 register with a plus sign. The condition code is set to 0 if the result is zero,

INSTRUCTION	SHORT FORM RR	SHORT FORM RX	LONG FORM RR	LONG FORM RX	EXTENDED FORM RR	EXTENDED FORM RX
Add Normalized	AER	AE	ADR	AD	AXR	
Add Unnormalized	AUR	AU	AWR	AW		
Compare	CER	CE	CDR	CD		
Divide	DER	DE	DDR	DD		
Halve	HER		HDR			
Load	LER	LE	LDR	LD		
Load and Test	LTER		LTDR			
Load Complement	LCER		LCDR			
Load Negative	LNER		LNDR			
Load Positive	LPER		LPDR			
Load Rounded	LRER(1)		LRDR(2)			
Multiply	MER(3)	ME(3)	MDR	MD	MXR	
Multiply Long to Extended					MXDR(4)	MXD(4)
Store		STE		STD		
Subtract Normalized	SER	SE	SDR	SD	SXR	
Subtract Unnormalized	SUR	SU	SWR	SW		

Notes: (1) Load rounded long to short.
(2) Load rounded extended to long.
(3) Multiply short operands, long product.
(4) Multiply long operands, extended product.

Figure 18–5 Floating-point instruction summary

and 2 if it is positive.

Load Rounded (LRER and LRDR) does not have a counterpart fixed-point instruction. The second operand is rounded to the next shorter format, and the result is placed in the operand-1 location. LRER rounds long format to short. LRDR rounds extended format to long. Rounding consists of adding a 1 to bit position 32 of the long format or bit position 72 of the extended second operand, and propagating any carry to the left. The carry may cause the fraction to be shifted one digit to the right and the exponent to be increased by one. The condition code is unchanged.

Addition and Subtraction

The Add Normalized instructions (AER, AE, ADR, and AD) all add the second operand to the first and place the normalized sum in the operand-1 FP register. In performing addition, the smaller exponent must be made equal to the larger before addition can take place. To do this, each time the smaller exponent is increased by one, its fraction is shifted one digit position to the right. This is repeated until the exponents are equal.

Internal circuitry of the machine provides one extra digit called a *guard digit*. The leftmost digit shifted out of a register becomes the guard digit. Where data is not shifted, the guard digit is zero. The guard digit participates in the arithmetic operations. Thus the fraction of the sum of short addition is seven digits, and for long, 15 digits. The extra guard digit provides increased precision when normalization is done.

An exponent overflow interrupt occurs if the exponent exceeds 127. An exponent underflow interrupt occurs if the exponent becomes less than zero.

The condition code for addition may be 0, 1, or 2, for zero, negative, or positive.

Add Unnormalized instructions (AUR, AU, AWR, and AW) add the two operands, and the unnormalized sum is placed in the operand-1 FP register. AUR and AU are short format instructions, and AWR and AW are long format. The operations are like Add Normalized except that the result is not shifted left for normalization and exponent underflow cannot occur.

Subtract Normalized instructions (SER, SE, SDR, SD) subtract the second operand from the first and place the result normalized in the operand-1 register. Execution of Subtract Normalized is identical to Add Normalized except that the sign of the second operand is inverted before the operation takes place.

Subtract Unnormalized instructions (SUR, SU, SWR, SW) subtract the second operand from the first and place the unnormalized difference in the operand-1 register. These instructions are like Add Unnormalized except that the sign bit of the second operand is inverted. The condition codes for both types of subtraction are 0, 1, 2, for results of zero, negative, or positive, respectively.

Compare Instructions

Compare instructions (CER, CE, CDR, CD) compare the first operand with the second and set the condition code accordingly. The comparison is algebraic and similar to the procedure for normalized floating-point subtraction, except that no difference is retained and both operands are unchanged. The condition code is set for 0 if operands are equal, 1 if the first operand is low, and 2 if the first operand is high.

Halve Instructions

Halve instructions (HER and HDR) cause the second operand to be divided by two and the normalized quotient to be placed in the operand-1 FP register. Halving is done by shifting the fraction of the second operand right one bit position. The leftmost bit of the fraction becomes 0 and the rightmost bit becomes the leftmost bit of the guard right. Then the result is normalized and truncated to its proper length. The condition code remains unchanged.

Multiply Instructions

The Multiply instructions are MER, ME, MDR, and MD. In each instance the normalized product of the second operand (multiplier) and first operand (multiplicand) is placed in the operand-1 FP register. MER and ME both multiply short numbers, each with a six-digit fraction, and create a long product of 14 digits, of which the rightmost two digits will always be zeros. MDR and MD multiply two 14-digit long numbers and create a long product that will be truncated to 14 digits.

In floating-point multiplication, both numbers are first normalized. Then the fractions are multiplied and the exponents are added. The sum of the exponents (less 64) is the exponent of the product.

The sign of the product follows the rules of algebra, except that a zero product always has a zero sign. The condition code is unchanged.

Divide Instructions

The Divide instructions are DER, DE, DDR, and DD. The first operand (dividend) is divided by the second operand (divisor) and the normalized quotient is placed in the operand-1 FP register. No remainder is kept.

Floating-point division consists of first normalizing both operands, dividing the fractions, and subtracting the exponents. The difference between the exponents, plus 64, becomes the exponent of the quotient. The condition code remains unchanged.

Extended Format Instructions

Extended format floating-point data contains 128 bits, and all operations require a pair of floating-point registers. The registers can be addressed only as 0 or 4. Each extended format number contains a high-order part of 64 bits and a low-order part of 64 bits. Each part has a sign bit in the leftmost position, an exponent in the next seven bits, and a 56-bit (14 hex digit) fraction. In most instances the sign and exponent of the low-order part are ignored. The 28-digit fraction in the complete number gives the greatest precision available.

The high-order part of the number may be any long floating-point number. It has the sign and exponent for the entire number, and its fraction contains the leftmost 14 digits of the 28-digit fraction of the number. The low-order fraction contains the rightmost 14 digits of the 28-digit fraction.

When the result in extended format is placed in a register pair, the signs of both parts are made the same and, unless the result is true zero, the exponent of the low-order part is made 14 less than that of the high-order part. If the low-order exponent would be less than zero, 128 is added to it.

Five instructions are available to process extended format numbers. Add Normalized (AXR) is a type RR instruction that adds together the contents of FP register pairs 0 and 2 (addressed as 0) and register pairs 4 and 6 (addressed as 4). The two operands are added under the same rules as those for short and long format. The result is normalized in the operand-1 FP register pair. The condition code is set to 0 for zero sum, 1 for negative, and 2 for positive.

Subtract Normalized (SXR) works just like AXR except that the sign of operand 2 is reversed before the operation takes place. The condition code is set to 0, 1, or 2 depending upon the difference.

Multiply (MXR) multiplies two extended format numbers in register pairs 0 and 4 and places the extended product in the operand-1 register pair. MXDR multiplies two long format (14 digit) numbers and places the 28-digit result in the operand-1 register pair. MXD is a type RX instruction in which the second operand is in a doubleword in main storage. None of the multiply instructions set the condition code.

FLOATING-POINT CONVERSION

Unfortunately, there is no machine instruction to convert data from fixed-point to floating-point form. The process is complex and difficult to generalize. We may convert integers of up to nine decimal digits to floating-point by following these steps. We limit the length to nine digits because not all 10-digit numbers can be converted to binary in one general register.

1. Pack the integer into a doubleword.
2. Convert to binary and store in an odd-numbered general register.
3. Make the binary number positive with a LPR instruction.
4. Load the constant X'4E000000' into the next lower even-numbered register. The X'4E' is the exponent for a 14-digit unnormalized integer.
5. Store the general register pair into a doubleword in main storage.
6. Isolate the sign bit of the binary number with an AND instruction.
7. OR the sign bit into the leftmost bit of the doubleword.
8. Load the doubleword into an FP register.
9. Add zero to the FP register to normalize the number.

Zoned Decimal to Floating Integer Conversion

We demonstrate a subprogram to convert a 9-digit zoned decimal number to long floating-point form. The calling program issues these two statements:

```
LA      13,SAVEAREA
CALL    CVFLI,(ZONENBR,FPINT)
```

ZONENBR must be a 9-byte zoned decimal (or character) field with the unpacked number. FPINT is a doubleword to hold the converted long floating-point integer.

Figure 18–6 shows the CVFLI (Convert to Floating-Point Integer) subprogram that makes the conversion and returns the correct value to FPINT in the calling program. The LM instruction places the address of ZONENBR in R2 and that of FPINT in R3. We use the SAV13 and RET13 macros developed in Chapter 12 to keep track of the addresses of the respective save areas. The comments show the results at each step if the value to be converted is 4095.

If the original integer in R8 in Figure 18–6 had been negative, the sign bit of R8 would remain a 1 when ANDed with SGNMSK, and the OR instruction would have set the sign bit to 1. The final result would be

C3FFF000 00000000

Zoned Decimal to Floating Fraction Conversion

We can call the CVFLI subprogram from another subprogram to convert the fractional part of a zoned decimal number to long floating-point form. Again, we limit the fraction to nine decimal digits, since not all 10-digit numbers can be converted to binary.

The approach is to convert the fraction to an integer and then divide the result by D'1000000000', or D'1.0E9'. If the original fraction were 4095, the floating-point value should be equivalent to 000004095/1000000000. If the original fraction were 409500000, the floating-point fraction would be equivalent to 409500000/1000000000.

Our new subprogram is called CVFLF (Convert to Floating-Point Fraction). The calling sequence in the main program is

```
LA      13,SAVEAREA
CALL    CVFLF,(ZONEFRAC,FPFRAC)
```

```
CVFLI     CSECT
          SAVE   (14,12)
          BALR   12,0
          USING  *,12
          SAV13  SAVESUB                RESULT              LOCATED AT
          LM     2,3,0(1)
          PACK   DOUBLE,0(9,2)          000000000004095C    DOUBLE
          CVB    8,DOUBLE               00000FFF            R08
          LPR    7,8                    00000FFF            R07
          L      6,EXPONENT             4E000000 00000FFF   R06-07
          N      8,SGNMSK               00000000            R08
          OR     6,8                    4E000000 00000FFF   R06-07
          STM    6,7,DOUBLE             4E000000 00000FFF   DOUBLE
          LD     0,DOUBLE               4E000000 00000FFF   FP0
          AD     0,=D'0'                43FFF000 00000000   FP0
          STD    0,0(3)                 43FFF000 00000000   FPINT
          RET13  SAVESUB
          RETURN (14,12)
DOUBLE    DS     D
EXPONENT  DC     X'4E000000'
SGNMSK    DC     X'80000000'
SAVESUB   DS     18F
          END
```

Figure 18–6 CVFLI subprogram to convert 9-digit integer to floating-point

ZONEFRAC must be a 9-byte zoned decimal or character field. FPFRAC must be a doubleword to hold the fractional value. The subprogram is shown in Figure 18–7.

The mainline calling program could combine the integer and fraction portions of a number by calling first CVFLI and then CVFLF and adding FPINT and FPFRAC. If the integer were actually nine decimal digits long, the floating-point fraction might be truncated when the two numbers were combined. In long form, there are only 14 hex digits of precision.

Floating to Fixed Integer Conversion

We might use another subprogram to convert a long floating-point integer to fixed-point binary. The range of the integer must be 2,147,483,647 through −2,147,483,648 (X'7FFFFFFF' through X'80000000'), the largest fixed-point values that can fit into a general register. The floating-point number is first *unnormalized* to get all significant digits into the rightmost eight hex digits. We then add the unnormalized value X'4E00000100000000'. This has the effect of complementing the rightmost 32 bits if the number is negative and leaving them unchanged if it is positive. We can demonstrate by using the floating-point values of 4095 and −4095.

Original value:	4095	−4095
FP long form:	4E000000 00000FFF	CE000000 00000FFF
Add adjustment:	4E000001 00000000	4E000001 00000000
Sum:	4E000001 00000FFF	4E000000 FFFFF001

Where the sign of the integer (FPINT) is different from that of the adjustment factor, the subtraction complements the rightmost 32 bits of the number. We can then move the rightmost 32 bits to the desired binary fullword location. Figure 18–8 shows the CVFXI (Convert Floating to Fixed Integer) subprogram.

Programming Tips

- The op code of each floating-point instruction indicates whether its type is RR or RX, as well as the type of data it operates on. E refers to short normalized data, U to short unnormalized, D to long normalized, W to long unnormalized, and X to extended format. All op codes for type RR instructions end with R.
- You can convert a positive binary fullword with value up to 2,147,483,647 to long floating-point form (unnormalized) by placing it in an odd-numbered register and loading the constant X'4E000000' into the next lower even-numbered register. Then store the register pair into a doubleword in storage.

```
CVFLF   CSECT
        SAVE   (14,12)
        BALR   12,0
        USING  *,12
        SAV13  SAVESUB
                                              R2 = A(ZONEFRAC);
        LM     2,3,0(1)                       R3 = A(FPFRAC)
        MVC    CHRFRAC,0(2)                   Move ZONEFRAC to subprogram
        CALL   CVFLI,(CHRFRAC,FPINT)          Convert ZONEFRAC to FP integer
        LD     0,FPINT                        Divide FP integer by 1000000000
        DD     0,=D'1.0E9'                    *
        STD    0,0(3)                         Store at FRFRAC in calling program
        RET13  SAVESUB
        RETURN (14,12)
FPINT   DS     D
SAVESUB DS     18F
CHRFRAC DS     CL9
        END
```

Figure 18–7 CVFLF subprogram to convert 9-digit fraction to floating-point

```
CVFXI   CSECT
        SAVE   (14,12)
        BALR   12,0
        USING  *,12
        SAV13  SAVESUB
        LM     2,3,0(1)                  R2 = A(FPINT); R3 = A(FULLWORD)
        LD     0,0(2)                    Load FPINT into FPR 0
        AW     0,ADJUST                  Add adjustment unnormalized
        STD    0,DOUBLE                  Store result
        MVC    0(4,3),DOUBLE+4           Move rightmost 32 bits to FULLWORD
        RET13  SAVESUB
        RETURN (14,12)
DOUBLE  DS     D
ADJUST  DC     X'4E00000100000000'
SAVESUB DS     18F
        END
```

Figure 18–8 CVFXI subprogram to convert floating integer to fixed-point

```
LE   2,=E'23.75'     Load diameter
HER  0,2             Radius = diameter / 2
LER  4,0             Put radius in FP4
MER  0,4             Square radius
ME   0,=E'3.1416'    Multiply by pi
STD  0,DBL           Store doubleword result
```

Figure 18–9 Calculation of area of a circle

FLOATING-POINT PROCESSING EXAMPLES

Recall that in Chapter 11 we demonstrated a subroutine to calculate the area of a circle. This operation was awkward because of the long decimal numbers resulting from several multiplications. The operation is very simple with short floating-point numbers because the exponent is automatically adjusted for each operation. The result is in long format. Figure 18–9 shows an example.

Long format numbers could be used in all operations in Figure 18–9 by changing literal types and op code letters from E to D. The result would still be in long format.

Another example in Figure 18–10 shows compounding interest daily on a stated principal amount at a given annual rate for a certain number of days. All values except number of days are given in long floating-point form and no rounding is done. The final results will therefore differ somewhat from the same problem done in packed decimal, where each day's interest was rounded to the nearest cent. However, we are freed from concern about placement of the decimal point.

By making the multiplier one plus the daily interest rate, we avoid the necessity of adding the interest to the accumulation each time we multiply. For the data given, the annual interest rate of 0.0975 divided by 365 gives a daily interest rate of 0.0002671. The multiplier is therefore 1.0002671. Each multiplication increases the accumulation by 0.0002671 of its previous value (0.02671 percent).

PROGRAM 18: FORTRAN CALLING PROGRAM AND ASSEMBLER SUBPROGRAM

As we have seen, conversion of data to and from floating-point form is both complex and tedious. The FORTRAN language has a series of subroutines to make these conversions readily available. There is no need for us to attempt to rewrite the FORTRAN compiler. However, it is desirable to gain some understanding about how the conversions are made.

In Chapter 11 we pointed out that subprograms in assembler language could be linked to and called by programs in other languages. Program 18 uses a FORTRAN mainline routine to read in the diameter of a circle with whatever number of decimal places appears in the input record. The FORTRAN program then calls our assembler language subprogram, gives it the address of a short-form floating point number containing the diameter, and provides the address where a long-form floating point area is to be placed. The subprogram does the calculation and returns the results.

```
       LD     0,PRIN           Load principal into FPR0
       LDR    2,0              Set accumulation = principal
       LD     4,RATE           Load annual rate into FPR4
       DD     4,=D'365'        Daily rate = annual rate / 365
       AD     4,=D'1'          Make rate 1 + daily rate
       L      5,DAYS           Set count to number of days
REPEAT EQU    *                REPEAT
       MDR    2,4                Mult. accum by 1 + daily rate
       BCT    5,REPEAT           Subtract 1 from count
UNTIL  EQU    *                UNTIL count = zero
       STD    2,ACCUM          Store accumulation
       .
PRIN   DC     D'23175.87'
RATE   DC     D'.0975'
DAYS   DC     F'725'
ACCUM  DS     D
```

Figure 18–10 Daily compounding of interest for stated number of days

Figure 18–11 shows the FORTRAN mainline program. Figure 18–12 shows the assembler language subprogram, and Figure 18–13 shows the output.

SUMMARY

Floating-point numbers are useful in scientific programming, where very large and very small numbers are often represented. Floating-point numbers contain a signed fraction, or mantissa, and a signed exponent, or characteristic. The fraction represents all or some of the high-order (most significant) digits of the number. The exponent specifies the number of digits the decimal point should be shifted. A positive exponent indicates a right shift, while a negative exponent indicates a left shift.

The precision of the number depends on the number of digits that represent the fraction. The more digits, the higher the precision.

There are three forms of floating-point numbers: (1) short form, or single precision; (2) long form, or double precision; and (3) extended precision. In all forms, the leftmost bit represents the sign of the fraction, 0 for positive and 1 for negative. The next seven bits represent the exponent in excess-64 notation, that is, a value 64 (X'40') higher than the actual exponent. The actual exponents range from −64 through +63, represented as 0 through 127 (X'00' through X'7F').

The remaining bytes of each form of floating-point number represent the fraction. Short form has three bytes (six hex digits) of precision. Long form has seven bytes (14 hex digits), and extended form has 14 bytes (28 hex digits

```
DOS FORTRAN IV 360N-FO-479 3-8          MAINPGM          DATE   04/14/86     TIME    15.18.20        PAGE 0001

               C*************************************************************************
               C                        ALTON R. KINDRED, PROGRAM 18
               C THIS FORTRAN PROGRAM READS IN THE DIAMETER OF A CIRCLE, CALLS AN
               C ASSEMBLER LANGUAGE SUBPROGRAM THAT CALCULATES THE CIRCUMFERENCE
               C AND AREA, AND PRINTS OUT THE RESULTS.
               C*************************************************************************
                     DOUBLE PRECISION AREA
                     WRITE (3,100)
               100   FORMAT (1H1,2X,'DIAMETER',10X,'CIRCUMFERENCE',20X,'AREA'/)
                     READ (1,101, END=999) DIAM
               101   FORMAT (F8.3)
                 2   CALL CIRCLE(DIAM, CIRCUM, AREA)
                     WRITE (3,102) DIAM, CIRCUM, AREA
               102   FORMAT (1H , F10.3, 10X, E14.8, 10X, D22.16)
                     READ (1,101, END=999) DIAM
                     GO TO 2
               999   STOP
                     END
```

Figure 18–11 FORTRAN listing of mainline routine for Program 18

```
  LOC  OBJECT CODE    ADDR1 ADDR2  SOURCE STATEMENT                                            DOS/VSE ASSEMBLER 15.20 86-04-14

                                     ***************************************************************************
                                     *                      ALTON R. KINDRED, SUBPROGRAM TO PROGRAM 18
                                     * THIS SUBPROGRAM IS CALLED BY A FORTRAN PROGRAM THAT SUPPLIES THE
                                     * DIAMETER OF A CIRCLE AS AS A SHORT FORM FLOATING-POINT NUMBER.  THE
                                     * SUBPROGRAM CALCULATES THE CIRCUMFERENCE IN SHORT FORM AND THE AREA
                                     * IN LONG FORM AND RETURNS THESE VALUES TO THE FORTRAN CALLING PROGRAM,
                                     * WHICH PRINTS THEM OUT.
                                     *          REGISTERS USED:
                                     *                   R01:  PARAMETER LIST
                                     *                   R02:  ADDRESS OF DIAMETER
                                     *                   R03:  ADDRESS OF CIRCUMFERENCE
                                     *                   R04:  ADDRESS OF AREA
                                     *                   R12:  BASE REGISTER
                                     *                   R13-15:  STANDARD SUBPROGRAM USAGE
                                     ***************************************************************************
000000                               CIRCLE   CSECT
                                              SAVE   (14,12)                    SAVE REGISTERS
                                    +* SUPERVISOR - SAVE - 5745-SC-SUP - REL. 28.0                        12000028
000000 90EC D00C            0000C   +         STM    14,12,12+4*(14+2-(14+2)/16*16)(13)                  70000025
000004 05C0                                   BALR   12,0                       LOAD BASE REGISTER
                            00006             USING  *,12                       DESIGNATE BASE REGISTER
                                              SAV13  SAVE                       STORE SAVE AREA ADDRESSES
                                    +*THIS MACRO SHOULD ALWAYS FOLLOW SAVE (14,12)
000006 4120 C04A            00050   +         LA     2,SAVE
00000A 5002 0004            00004   +         ST     13,4(2)
00000E 502D 0008            00008   +         ST     2,8(13)
000012 582D 001C            0001C   +         L      2,28(13)
000016 41D0 C04A            00050   +         LA     13,SAVE
00001A 9824 1000            00000             LM     2,4,0(1)                   GET PARAMETER ADDRESSES
00001E 6800 C092            00098             LD     0,=D'0'                    CLEAR FPR0
000022 7802 0000            00000             LE     0,0(2)                     PUT DIAMETER IN FPR0
000026 2420                                   HDR    2,0                        PUT RADIUS IN FPR2
000028 6C00 C042            00048             MD     0,PI                       CIRCUM = RADIUS * PI
00002C 7003 0000            00000             STE    0,0(3)                     STORE CIRCUM IN CALLING PROGRAM
000030 2842                                   LDR    4,2                        STORE RADIUS IN FPR4
000032 2C42                                   MDR    4,2                        SQUARE RADIUS
000034 6C40 C042            00048             MD     4,PI                       A = PI * R * R
000038 6044 0000            00000             STD    4,0(4)                     STORE AREA IN CALLING PROGRAM
                                              RET13  SAVE                       RESTORE SAVE AREA ADDRESS
                                    +*THIS MACRO SHOULD ALWAYS PRECEDE RETURN (14,12)
00003C 58D0 C04E            00054   +         L      13,SAVE+4
                                              RETURN (14,12)                    RETURN TO CALLING PROGRAM
                                    +* SUPERVISOR - RETURN - 5745-SC-SUP - REL. 28.0                      12000028
000040 98EC D00C            0000C   +         LM     14,12,12+4*(14+2-(14+2)/16*16)(13)                  72000025
000044 07FE                         +       BR     14                                                    74000025
                                     *
000046 0000
000048 413243FE5C91D14E              PI       DC     D'3.1416'
000050                               SAVE     DS     18F
                                              END
000098 0000000000000000                              =D'0'
```

Figure 18–12 Assembler listing of subprogram for Program 18

for the fraction). Positive and negative fractions are the same; only the sign bit is different.

Fractions are normalized when the leftmost hex digit is not zero. Where digits are shifted to normalize the fraction, the exponent is decreased by one for each digit position shifted.

Floating-point constants may be defined as type E (short form), type D (long form), or type L (extended form). They are four, eight, or 16 bytes in length, respectively.

All floating-point arithmetic is done in four floating-point registers, numbered 0, 2, 4, and 6. Each register contains 64 bits. Short floating-point operations affect only the leftmost 32 bits of each register. Extended form operations require a pair of FP registers, addressed as 0 or 4.

Most of the floating-point instructions are available in RR or RX types. RR instructions have both operands in FP registers. RX instructions have the first operand in an FP register and the second in main storage. The results are the same regardless of the location of the second operand.

No single machine instruction is available to convert data to or from floating-point form. Separate routines are presented as subprograms to convert zoned decimal integers and fractions to floating-point form. Another subprogram converts floating-point integers to fixed-point integers.

DIAMETER	CIRCUMFERENCE	AREA
25.000	0.78539993E 02	0.4908750000000000D 03
12345.668	0.38785148E 05	0.1197071475188143D 09
5555.555	0.17453328E 05	0.2424073316550985D 08
1.000	0.31415997E 01	0.7854000000000000D 00
73.987	0.23243755E 03	0.4299339366385148D 04
0.125	0.39269996E 00	0.1227187500000000D-01

Figure 18–13 Output from Program 18

TERMS FOR REVIEW

Characteristic	Fraction	Mantissa
Excess-64 notation	Guard digit	Normalization
Exponent	Halve	Precision
Extended form	Long form	Short form
Floating-point number		

REVIEW QUESTIONS

1. In what different formats do floating-point numbers appear? What feature is common among all formats?
2. What is the purpose of the fraction in floating-point numbers? of the exponent?
3. What is the purpose of the sign of the exponent? How is the exponent represented in floating-point constants and results?
4. What is meant by precision? How does precision differ among the different forms of floating-point numbers?
5. What is the purpose of the guard digit?

6. What is the leftmost byte in any FP register that contains a short form unnormalized positive integer? a long form unnormalized positive integer?

EXERCISES

1. Write assembler declaratives to create each of the following values as short, long, and extended form constants:
   a. 100 c. 255 e. 32767 g. 40960
   b. 96.5 d. −512 f. −.0625 h. −100.75E3
2. Show each of the following floating-point numbers in normalized form:
   a. 42010000 c. 4600000A e. 3F000ABC g. 01020000
   b. C4000004 d. C6000965 f. FE000012 h. 3A001234
3. Show each of the following constants as they would appear on the assembler listing:
   a. DC E'768.5' e. DC D'2147483647'
   b. DC E'2500' f. DC D'−217483648'
   c. DC E'65535.25' g. DC D'.8750'
   d. DC E'16777215' h. DC D'−1.1'
4. Assume that FPRO contains 42968000 00000000 and FPR2 contains C3121000 00000000 at the start of each of the following instructions. Show the result of each operation in short or long form, whichever is applicable:
   a. AER 2,0 e. HER 4,2
   b. AUR 2,0 f. MER 0,2
   c. SER 0,2 g. LPER 4,2
   d. LCER 6,0 h. DDR 0,2
5. The factorial of an integer *N* is the product of all integers between 1 and *N*. Write a floating-point routine to produce the factorial of 50.
6. One way to determine the square root of a positive number *X* is to divide it by any number *Y* to obtain a quotient *Z*. If *Y* is not equal to *Z*, compute a new *Y*, which is the average of the old *Y* and *Z*, and divide again. Write floating-point instructions to repeat this procedure until *Y* = *Z* or until the difference between *Y* and *Z* is less than 0.0001. *Y* is then the square root.
7. Write a subprogram that will convert a four-digit fraction from character form to short floating-point form and return it to a specified location in the calling program. Show the calling sequence in the main program.
8. How does adding the value X'4E00000100000000' to an unnormalized long form number complement the rightmost 32 bits of a negative number? Demonstrate by using the values D'200' and D'-200'.

PROGRAMMING PROBLEMS

1. Write a program to do floating-point calculations and present the results through a PDUMP or SNAP. Use the following data definitions to define four sets of data and space for the results of the calculations:

```
         PRINT   DATA
FIRST    DC      D'10,100,255,3.14159'
SECOND   DC      D'64,-25,150,4096'
SUM      DS      4D
DIFFRNCE DS      4D
PRODUCT  DS      4D
QUOTIENT DS      4D
```

   Write a loop to be executed four times. Initialize a separate general register with the address of each of the operands named. Using FIRST and SECOND as operands, perform long-form addition, subtraction, multiplication, and division, storing the results in the corresponding named doublewords (FIRST + SECOND = SUM, FIRST − SECOND = DIFFRNCE, etc.).

   Then add 8 to each address and repeat the operations. After completing the loop four times, issue a PDUMP or SNAP macro. Each pair of operands and the four results should appear in a column in the dump. Compare the floating-point constants and verify the results in the dump.

A
Glossary

Access method control block: A VSAM macro that identifies a data set that is to be processed.

Access Method Services: A utility program that defines VSAM catalogs and data sets, allocates space for them, and, optionally, loads, deletes, and prints the contents of VSAM catalogs and data sets.

Access time: The length of time between the request for a disk record and the time it is available for processing.

ADDR1 and ADDR2: On the assembler source statement listing, columns giving the addresses within the program space of the first and second operands named in the instruction.

Address calculation: A method of locating a record in a positional table by multiplying its relative record location (less one) by the number of bytes in each table entry.

Address constant: A binary constant defined as type A giving the address of an instruction, file, record, or field.

Address modification: A method of altering the effective address of one or more operands between successive iterations of a loop.

Addressed access: In VSAM, retrieval or storage of a data record (1) that is identified by its relative byte address or (2) that sequentially follows the previous record.

Addressability error: A program error caused by (1) failure to establish a base register or (2) referring to an address more than 4095 bytes from the address in a base register.

Alternate index: In VSAM, a key-sequenced data set in which the key refers to some field other than the prime key, and the entries contain pointers to records containing that key value.

Alternate track: A disk track chosen to hold data because the originally selected track was defective.

AND: A logical operation in which a bit is set to 1 only if both corresponding bits in two operands are 1s.

Arithmetic-logic unit (ALU): The part of the central processing unit that carries out arithmetic operations, shifting of data within registers, and logical instructions affecting individual bits.

Array: A series of data elements of the same type and number of bytes.

ASA control character: A code placed in the first byte of a printed record that controls spacing and skipping of the paper.

Assembler: A computer program that translates statements written in assembler language into the machine language of a specific computer.

Assembler declarative: An instruction to the assembler defining a constant to be placed in the object program or an amount of space to be reserved for a record or field.

Assembler directive: An instruction to the assembler specifying some option to be exercised at assembly time but having no effect on the object program.

Assembly time: The period of time during which the assembler is translating the source statements into the machine language object code.

Attributes: Data maintained by the assembler about each name used in a program, such as length, location, type, length of name, and number of digits in a number.

Base address: A location within a program from which the displacement, or distance, to other locations may be calculated.

Base register: One of the 16 general registers that holds a base address for the entire program or for specific instructions.

Base-displacement addressing: A method of determining the effective address by adding together the contents of a base register, the displacement stated in the instruction, and (optionally) an index register.

Binary constant: A value defined as type B using only the digits 0 and 1.

Binary numbers: A number system based on the digits 0 and 1 only.

Bit: A shortened form of binary digit, which can be only 0 or 1.

Block: An arrangement of more than one logical record grouped into a single unit for transfer to or from magnetic disk or tape.

Block length field: The first four bytes of a block of variable-length records that contain a binary value indicating the number of bytes contained in the block.

Block-multiplexor: A channel capable of moving many bytes of data between main storage and high-speed devices such as tape or disk in a continuous stream or burst. See Selector channel.

Body: In macro definitions, the conditional assembly statements, data definitions, and machine instructions that determine the source statements to be generated when the macro is invoked.

Boolean logic: A system of symbolic logic based on the digits 0 and 1.

Burst mode: A method of transmitting data along a channel in a continuous high-speed stream.

Byte: One storage location capable of holding eight data bits.

Byte-multiplexor: A channel that intersperses one or more bytes of data from several low-speed devices as they move between main storage and the devices.

CALL: A macro commonly used to pass parameters and transfer control to a subprogram.

Called module: A subprogram, designed to do a specific task, that receives parameters from a calling module.

Calling module: A program or module that issues a CALL macro to pass parameters and transfer control to another module.

Calling sequence: A list of addresses of data, or the data itself, that is passed from a main module or program to a subroutine or subprogram.

Carriage control tape: A paper tape punched with holes in certain channels to control spacing and skipping on printed forms.

Central processing unit (CPU): The heart of a computer system, containing the control unit and the arithmetic-logic unit, that directs the execution of instructions.

Channel: (1) A special-purpose computer that carries out input and output operations between the central processing unit and external devices; (2) one row on a magnetic tape; (3) one row on a carriage control tape.

Channel command word: A direction to a channel giving the operation to be carried out, the storage location of the data, and the number of bytes to be moved.

Characteristic: See Exponent.

Check protection symbol: A special symbol, usually an asterisk or dollar sign, placed in front of the first significant digit on a check or other document to prevent altering the amount.

Cluster: The totality of basic information that VSAM maintains about a data set, including a data component and an index component.

CNOP (Conditional No-Op): An assembler instruction that can produce from zero to three halfword instructions depending upon the current setting of the location counter.

Coding: Writing source program statements in a specific computer language to reflect the design and logic of the program.

Collating sequence: The order in which data will be placed when compared or sorted based upon the code used to represent letters, digits, or special characters.

Communication region: An area in the supervisor giving the current date and information about the job currently being executed.

Compare arithmetic: A class of machine instructions that consider the signs of the numbers being compared to determine their relative values. Contrast with Compare logical.

Compare logical: A class of machine instructions that compare data based solely on the value of the bits from left to right. Contrast with Compare arithmetic.

Compound condition: A decision based on more than one comparison or set of relationships.

Concatenation: The joining together of two or more words or characters.

Condition code: Two bits in the arithmetic-logic unit that reflect the results of comparisons or certain arithmetic or logical operations.

Conditional assembly: Statements within macro definitions that cause certain source statements to be generated or not depending upon conditions encountered at assembly time.

Conditional branch: A machine instruction that causes control to be transferred to some other instruction based upon the setting of the condition code.

Control area: A contiguous space, ranging from one track to one cylinder, on a VSAM data set that holds a grouping of control intervals.

Control break: A change between the content of some field within one record and the content of the corresponding field in the preceding record.

Control interval: The unit of information that is read from or written to a VSAM storage device by the operating system.

Control interval definition field (CIDF): The last record in a VSAM control interval giving the total length of data records and the length of unused space within the control interval.

Control module: A module whose main purpose is to cause other modules (subroutines or subprograms) to be executed.

Control unit: That portion of the central processing unit that decodes and executes machine instructions and directs the channel to carry out input/output instructions.

Core dump: A display or printout of main storage and the content of certain registers and indicators in the computer.

Count-key-data organization: An arrangement of records on magnetic disk files.

Cross-Reference Listing: An optional output of the assembler showing each name used in the program, together with its length, location, statement in which defined, and statements that refer to it.

Cyclic check bytes: A two-byte field at the end of each disk record that contains a code verifying the parity of the data in the record.

Cylinder: The series of disk tracks located directly above one another that can be read or written without moving the read-write assembly.

Cylinder index: On an indexed sequential file, a listing of the highest key on each cylinder, together with a pointer to the appropriate cylinder.

Cylinder overflow area: On an indexed sequential file, one or more of the highest-numbered tracks on a cylinder that receive records as additions are made to that cylinder.

Cylinder overflow control record (COCR): On an indexed sequential, a pointer to the next available location in the overflow area.

Data component: In VSAM, the set of all control areas that contain control intervals in which data records are stored.

Data definition: An assembler declarative that gives the type, length, and value of constants or the length of storage areas required within a program.

Data event control block (DECB): An area generated within the expansion of a READ or WRITE macro in which OS passes information about I/O operations.

Data set: In OS, a collection of records. See File.

Data transfer rate: A measure of the number of bits or bytes that may be sent in a given interval of time from one location or device to another.

Decimal digit: One of the numerals 0 through 9.

Desk checking: A method of visually and mentally reviewing a computer program for correctness before submitting it to the assembler.

Destination field: A data element that receives data moved or modified from some other location.

Detail line: A line printed as a result of processing a single record.

Detail-printed report: A report printing information about each record processed.

Device: A piece of equipment or hardware that is part of a computer system.

Diagnostics: Messages printed by the assembler indicating errors in source programs and their possible causes.

Digit selector: A special code in an edit pattern that causes a packed decimal digit to be formatted for printing.

Direct-access storage device (DASD): A type of equipment that permits data to be stored in or retrieved from any location as readily as any other.

Direct retrieval: The ability to go directly to a record in a file without having to search each preceding record.

Direct processing: Storing and retrieving records without having to start at the beginning of a file. Contrast with Sequential processing.

Disk label: A magnetic record giving the location and characteristics of a file on magnetic disk.

Displacement: A distance, expressed in bytes, from a base address.

DLBL (Disk label): A job control statement in which data is supplied for creating or processing a disk label.

Documentation: Supporting papers that provide specifications and characteristics about systems and programs.

Double-register shift: The ability to move the bits within an even-odd pair of registers to the right or left.

Doubleword: An eight-bit binary floating-point number, normally starting on an address evenly divisible by eight.

DSECT: An assembler declarative instruction designating the start of a dummy section.

DTFIS: A macro in which are supplied the name and characteristics of an indexed sequential file.

DTFMT: A macro in which are supplied the name and characteristics of a magnetic tape file.

DTFSD: A macro in which are supplied the name and characteristics of a sequential file on magnetic disk.

Dummy entry: A record placed in an index, table, or file to hold space that will later be filled or to indicate the end of data.

Dummy section: The description of the appearance of data that occurs more than once within a program, without actually reserving space for the data.

Duplication factor: In a data definition, a number indicating how many times the data described occurs.

EBCDIC: Extended Binary Coded Decimal Interchange Code. A method of representing digits, letters, or special characters with an arrangement of eight bits.

Edit: To arrange numeric data for printing by suppressing leading zeros and inserting decimal points, commas, signs, and dollar signs.

Edit pattern: A collection of codes specifying the format in which numeric data is to be printed.

Effective address: The sum of the value in a base register, an index register if used, and a displacement in a machine instruction; the actual location of an operand.

End-of-tape marker: A special reflective strip placed near the end of a reel of magnetic tape to indicate that no more data should be written beyond that point.

ENDFL: A macro used to terminate loading of an indexed sequential file and to cause the indexes to be updated and completed.

ENTRY: An assembler declarative instruction that identifies a name defined in one program or subprogram that will be referred to in another program or subprogram.

Entry-sequenced data set (ESDS): In VSAM, a logical method of storing records in a data set in the sequence in which they are presented to the operating system.

Error and status byte: In an indexed sequential file, a one-byte field in which bits are set to reflect conditions encountered as the file is processed.

ESETL: A macro used to terminate sequential processing of an indexed sequential file.

Even-odd register pair: Two general registers in which the even-numbered register is assumed to be on the left and the odd-numbered register on the right; used in binary multiplication and division, and double-register shift operations.

Excess-64 notation: A method of representing the exponent of a floating-point number as a binary value 64 higher than the actual exponent.

EXCLUSIVE OR: A logical operation in which a result bit is set to 1 only if the corresponding bits of the two operands are different, that is, one bit is a 0 and the other a 1.

Execute form: With indexed sequential data sets under OS, a form of the READ macro appearing among procedural statements that refers to a data event control block for additional information.

Execute instruction (EX): A machine instruction that performs a single instruction out of the normal sequence and returns immediately to the following instruction in sequence. It ORs the contents of the register specified as the first operand with the second byte of the instruction that is executed.

Execution cycle: That interval during which the control unit causes a machine instruction to be carried out.

Execution time: That period of time during which a computer program is run, or executed. Contrast with Assembly time.

Exit list: A VSAM macro that provides an optional list of addresses for user exit routines such as end-of-file processing or analyzing errors.

Explicit length: A number that indicates how many bytes are to be processed in any operand in a machine instruction. Contrast with Implicit length.

Explicit register addressing: A reference in a machine instruction to the actual base or index register and displacement to be used as an operand.

Exponent: That part of a floating-point number that specifies how many places the decimal point is to be moved to the left or right. Also called Characteristic.

Extended form: A floating-point number consisting of 128 bits, or two doublewords.

Extended mnemonics: A group of conditional branch instructions in which the op code generates both the machine instruction op code and the mask that tests the condition code.

EXTENT: A job control statement that supplies data about the location of a disk file.

Exterior label: A gummed label or tag placed on a reel of tape or disk pack to identify the volume visually.

External address: An address needed by a program of some area or instruction that is not defined within the program.

External Symbol Dictionary (ESD): A list of external addresses created by the assembler for use by the linkage editor.

EXTRN: An assembler declarative statement identifying a name referenced in one program but defined in another. See External address.

Factor matching: A method of searching a table by comparing the key of each table entry with a key argument supplied within the program.

Field separator: A special code in an edit pattern that permits more than one numeric field to be edited with a single pattern.

File: A collection of records organized for a particular purpose.

File definition: A group of operands that give the name and characteristics of an input or output file to be used in a program.

File extension: In an indexed sequential file, adding records to an existing file, all of which have keys higher than the last key previously in the file.

File label: A magnetic record identifying a tape or disk file.

File loading: Creating a new file on magnetic tape or disk; most commonly refers to an indexed sequential file.

File reorganization: Copying an existing file on magnetic disk and creating a new file to rearrange records previously in an overflow area.

FilenameC: The name applied to the error and status byte of an indexed sequential file.

Fill character: The first byte in an edit pattern. It replaces leading zeros as numeric data is edited.

Fixed-point number: A binary number considered to be always an integer. Contrast with Floating-point number.

Floating-point number: A binary number consisting of a fraction that represents the digits contained in the number, and an exponent that indicates the position of the decimal point to represent the true value of the number. Contrast with Fixed-point number.

Fraction: The bits of a floating-point number that represent the digits it contains. Also called Mantissa.

Fullword: A 32-bit signed binary number. When located in main storage, normally it must begin at an address evenly divisible by 4.

General register: A component in the arithmetic-logic unit that holds a 32-bit binary value for arithmetic operations or addressing.

Generic key: On an indexed sequential file, a key argument containing one or more high-order letters or digits of the starting key to be found for sequential retrieval.

Global: In a macro definition, a SET symbol that is defined to be recognized in other definitions or in open code. Contrast with Local.

Group-printed report: A report containing one line summarizing totals for more than one record of the same class or group. Contrast with Detail-printed report.

Guard digit: In floating-point arithmetic, an additional digit provided to preserve precision during computation.

Halfword: A 16-binary number, normally placed in main storage to begin at an even-numbered address.

Halve: A floating-point operation that divides a number by two.

Hardware: A general name for the equipment and devices of a computer system.

Head selection: An electronic switch that determines which track within a cylinder on disk will be processed by the read-write assembly.

Header label: A magnetic tape file label that precedes the first data record in the file.

Header statement: The first statement in a macro definition, containing only the op code MACRO.

Hexadecimal numbers: A set of 16 digits, represented as 0 to 9 and A to F, widely used to represent combinations of four bits.

Home address field: A record identifying the cylinder and head number of a specific disk track.

Immediate instruction: A machine instruction having as its second operand a single byte of data appearing in the second byte of the instruction itself.

Implicit length: The length given when a record or field is defined and thereafter assumed whenever its name is used as an operand. Contrast with Explicit length.

Independent overflow area: On an indexed sequential file, a separate extent that may receive overflow records from any cylinder.

Index component: A tree structure that may contain one or more levels pointing to the prime or alternate keys in a VSAM data set.

Index point: On a disk track, a designation of the physical beginning of the track.

Index register: In a type RX machine instruction, a general register that may contain a value to be added to the base register and displacement to form the effective address.

Indexed sequential file: A type of file organization that contains two or more levels of indexes, a prime data area, and optional overflow areas.

Initial program load (IPL): The act of loading the supervisor into main storage to begin normal operations at the start of day or after a power interruption.

Initialization: Operations necessary to begin operations or to prepare for repetitive functions, such as clearing totals and setting initial values.

Input/output channel: Special purpose hardware that moves data between the central processing unit and external devices.

Insert Character (IC): A machine operation that places a single byte of data into the rightmost eight bits of a general register without disturbing the other 24 bits.

Instruction cycle: That interval of time during which the control unit fetches an instruction from main storage, decodes it, and prepares to execute it.

Interior label: A magnetic record that identifies a tape or disk file. Contrast with Exterior label.

Intermediate total: A total consisting of one or more lower-level totals and which itself becomes a part of a higher-level total. Contrast with Minor and Major totals.

Interrecord gap: A space between records recorded magnetically on tape or disk.

Invoke: To use, or call, a macro, subroutine, or subprogram.

IOREG: An operand in the definition of a disk or tape containing blocked records. It specifies a register that will contain a pointer to the current record to be processed in the I/O area.

ISAM: An abbreviation for Indexed Sequential Access Method, the instructions that process indexed sequential files.

Job control language (JCL): The statements or instructions used to communicate with the operating system.

Job stream: A series of job control statements and input to programs that permit jobs to be executed one after another without intervention of a human operator.

Key: A data element that uniquely identifies a record within a file.

Key-sequenced data set (KSDS): A VSAM data set having one or more index components to permit access sequentially or by key.

KEYARG: An operand in a disk file definition that specifies the name of a field that will contain the key of a record to be located within the file.

Keyed access: A method of retrieving records from VSAM key-sequenced or relative record data sets by referring to an identifier, or key, field in the record.

Keyword parameter: An operand for a macro that is identified by a word followed by an equal sign and the value for the operand. Contrast with Positional parameter.

LBLTYP (Label type): A job control statement requesting that the linkage editor allow space for checking labels when loading tape or disk files.

Length code: An operand in the second byte of type SS instructions that specifies the length of one or both operands in main storage.

Linkage: A connection between two modules so that either can refer to data or instructions in the other.

Linkage editor: A program in the operating system that can join two or more modules together and relocate addresses as necessary to permit communication among modules.

Linkage editor map: A record produced by the linkage editor showing the names of modules linked together, along with their addresses at execution time.

Link register: A general register in which is placed the return address before branching to a subroutine or subprogram.

List form: With indexed sequential data sets under OS, a form of the READ macro that appears among data definitions with information to carry out the input operation.

Literal: A constant defined in a machine instruction in assembler language.

Literal pool: An area, normally at the end of a program, containing the literals defined in a program.

Load module: The output of the linkage editor, consisting of one or more object modules with all addresses relocated and ready for execution.

Load point marker: A reflective strip near the start of a reel of magnetic tape designating the point at which data may be recorded. Contrast with End-of-reel marker.

Local: In a macro definition, a SET symbol defined to be recognized only within that one macro. Contrast with Global.

Location counter: An accumulator used by the assembler to keep track of the address of each machine instruction, file definition, and data definition in a program.

Logical instructions: A set of machine instructions capable of modifying the content of individual bits within operands.

Logical record: A grouping of data elements relating to a single person, object, or item. Contrast with Physical record.

Long form: A 64-bit floating point number.

Longitudinal check byte: A byte at the end of each physical record or magnetic tape that verifies the parity of each channel on the tape.

Loop: Another name for repetition structure or iteration structure. A series of instructions executed repeatedly until some condition causes termination.

Machine instruction: A statement in assembler language that is translated directly into machine language.

Macro definition: A formal statement of instructions to be generated whenever a macro is used, or invoked.

Macro instruction: A statement in assembler language that causes one or more other statements to be generated.

Main storage: An area of numbered locations into which all data or instructions must be placed for processing by a computer.

Mainline loop: That portion of a computer program that is repeated to process each record in turn until no data remains.

Major total: The most inclusive total created by multiple-level control break processing.

Mantissa: The fraction of a floating-point number. Also called Fraction.

Mask: A code for processing data in which a 1 indicates the position of a bit or byte to be processed and a 0 indicates the position to be ignored.

Master index: In an indexed sequential file, a list pointing to the last key on each track of the cylinder index.

Medium: A type of material on which data is recorded, such as paper, magnetic tape or disk, or visual display screen. Contrast with Device.

Message character: A code in an edit pattern representing a decimal point, comma, sign, or other character to be inserted into a number to be printed.

Minor total: The lowest level at which totals are taken during control break processing.

Model statement: In a macro definition, a statement that either (1) generates a source statement at assembly time or (2) states conditions under which source statements will be generated.

Module: A group of instructions to perform some specific task. Often used interchangeably with Subroutine or Subprogram.

Move Inverse (MVCIN): A machine instruction that causes the relative position of bytes within a field to be reversed as they are moved.

Move numeric (MVN): A machine instruction that moves only the rightmost, or numeric, bits of each byte from one field to another.

Move with offset (MVO): A machine instruction that causes each byte in a field to be offset four bits to the left as the bytes are moved from right to left from one field to another.

Move zones (MVZ): A machine instruction that moves only the leftmost, or zone, bits of each byte from one field to another.

Multifile volume: A disk pack or reel of magnetic tape that contains more than one file.

Multiple base registers: More than one general register designated to contain an address from which displacements to various locations with a program are calculated. Usually necessary on programs containing more than 4096 bytes.

Multiple field editing: The ability to perform an edit operation on more than one packed decimal field with a single edit pattern.

Multiple-level table: An arrangement of data in which each entry in a table contains one or more other tables.

Multiple-level totals: A series of progressive totals in which each higher level total contains the sum of other lower totals, as in city, county, and state totals for population.

Multiple record format: The description of records where more than one type of record may appear in a single file.

Multiplexor channel: A special purpose computer capable of interleaving data from more than one low-speed input/output device along the same path. Contrast with Selector channel.

Multiprogramming: The capability of having more than one computer program in main storage at the same time and executing them concurrently.

Multivolume file: A file requiring more than one disk pack or reel of magnetic tape.

Nested IF statements: A program logical structure in which either or both of the

THEN or ELSE options in an IF structure contains one or more additional IF structures to determine what actions are to be taken.

Nonsequential disk file: A file organized to permit direct retrieval of a specific record, such as indexed sequential, direct organization, or relative record file.

NOP (No-op): A machine instruction that does nothing but proceed to the next instruction in sequence.

Normal entry: On an indexed sequential file, that portion of the track index that points to the highest key on each track in the prime data area. Contrast with Overflow entry.

Normalization: An arrangement of floating-point numbers such that the first hexadecimal digit in the fraction is not zero.

Numeric bits: The four rightmost bits of a byte. Contrast with Zone bits.

Object: In VSAM, a term applied to a catalog, data set, index, or non-VSAM data set.

Object code: Machine language instructions and data constants created by a language translator such as an assembler or compiler.

Object module: The machine language output of a complete program or control section from an assembler or compiler.

One-way selection: A type of conditional statement that causes one or more instructions to be executed if a condition is true but merely bypassed if the condition is false.

One-way test: See One-way selection.

Ones complement: A binary number derived by changing all the zeros in an original number to ones and all the ones to zeros.

Op code: That portion of a machine instruction that states what operation is to be performed on the operands described in the instruction.

Operand: The addresses of data, or the actual data, on which operations are to be performed as specified by the op code of a machine instruction.

Operating system: A collection of programs providing operations common to most applications, such as loading programs, performing input/output operations, maintaining libraries, and sorting records.

OR: A logical machine instruction in which each bit within a byte or field is set to 1 if either of the corresponding bits in the two operands is a 1.

ORG: An assembler directive that permits the location counter to be reset to some specified value.

Overflow entry: On an indexed sequential file, that part of the track index that refers to the last record from a given track that is in the overflow area, together with a pointer to the record with the lowest key in the overflow area that came from that track. Contrast with Normal entry.

Overlapping fields: Two fields of data containing one or more bytes in common.

Pack: A machine instruction that changes zoned decimal or character data into packed decimal form.

Packed decimal: An arrangement of data in which each decimal digit is represented in a four-bit code, with the last four bits of the field representing the sign of the number.

Pad character: A code representing the value to be placed in each byte if the receiving field is longer than the sending field in data movement.

Padding: The act of supplying additional characters, usually zeros or blanks, to fill out a field longer than the data defined to fill it.

Parameter: An address or data element supplied to a macro, subroutine, or subprogram that is to process that data.

Parameter list: A sequence of parameters, usually in the form of consecutive addresses.

Parity bit: An extra bit provided with a byte of data to validate accuracy of hardware operations, usually by providing that the total number of bits set to 1 will always be odd.

PDUMP (Partial dump): A macro that causes certain registers, indicators, and a portion of main storage to be printed out or displayed in hexadecimal form for analysis or debugging.

Physical record: The actual data transferred to or from a magnetic disk or tape file during a single input/output operation. See Block. Contrast with Logical record.

Place value: The magnitude associated with a digit depending upon its position within a number.

POINT: A VSAM macro that sets a pointer at a specific record in a data set for subsequent sequential processing.

Positional parameter: An address of data or the actual data whose meaning is determined by its position within a list of operands supplied to a macro, subroutine, or subprogram.

Positional table: An organization of data in which the key to a table entry is directly related to its location or position within the table.

Posttest loop: A program logical structure in which certain statements are performed at least once before a condition is tested to see if they should be repeated. Contrast with Pretest loop.

Pretest loop: A program logical structure in which a test is made prior to performing the statements in a loop to see if they should be continued or terminated. Contrast with Posttest loop.

Precision: A measure of the number of digits used to represent the value of a number.

Primary (or prime) key: In VSAM, a unique identifier for each record in a key-sequenced data set.

Prime data area: In an indexed sequential file, that portion of each cylinder where data records are placed as the file is created before any records are sent to the overflow area.

Priming read: The reading of the first input record during the initialization phase of program logic.

PRINT GEN: An assembler directive instruction that causes statements generated by a macro to be printed on the assembler source statement listing.

Processing module: A portion of a program that does some specific task without calling or invoking another module. Contrast with Control module.

Program flowchart: A graphic representation of program logic using a limited set of symbols and connecting lines.

Program relocation: The ability to adjust addresses in an object module so that it can be executed from different locations within main storage.

Program Status Word (PSW): A 64-bit binary record in which the control unit records such information as the length of the current instruction, the condition code, address of the next instruction, and cause of interrupt, if any.

Prototype statement: In a macro definition, a statement showing the name of the macro and the format of the operands to be used when the macro is invoked.

Pseudocode: The use of ordinary English words, along with a few key words and indentation, to represent program logic.

Read-write assembly: On magnetic tape or disk drives, the hardware mechanism that records or senses bits representing the data in each record. Also called Read-write head.

Read-write head: See Read-write assembly.

Record definition field: A three-byte control information field giving the length of each record in a VSAM data set.

Record length field: The first four bytes of each variable-length record, containing a binary number indicating the length of the record in bytes.

Record Zero: The first record on a disk track, used by the operating system to maintain statistics about the track.

Register conventions: The standard way in which general registers are to be used when linking to subroutines or subprograms, to permit their use by different programming languages.

Relative address: The location of some byte or field in relation to some other location that is named, usually expressed as plus or minus a certain number of bytes.

Relative byte address (RBA): A fullword binary integer specifying the position of a record relative to the beginning of a VSAM data set.

Relative record data set (RRDS): A VSAM organization in which the key to each record indicates its position within the data set.

Relative track: The number of a disk track with regard to its position (1) on a disk pack or (2) within a file extent.

Relocation Dictionary (RLD): An optional listing by the assembler giving the location and type of address constants that must have their values changed by the linkage editor.

Relocation factor: The amount added to address constants by the linkage editor.

Repetition structure: A program logical structure in which one or more instructions are repeated until some condition occurs to cause termination. Also called Iteration structure or Loop.

Request macro: In VSAM, a macro designed to be executed at run time to initiate an action such as opening or closing a data set or retrieving or updating records.

Request parameter list (RPL): A VSAM macro supplying information needed about a data set for the execution of request macros.

Request return code: An error or status code returned in general register 15 by one of the VSAM request macros.

RETURN: A macro used at the end of a subprogram to cause an orderly return to the calling program.

Rolling totals: The act of adding totals from a lower level to the next higher level in multiple-level control break processing.

Root: The fixed-length portion of a variable-length record.

Rotational delay: The time spent waiting for a disk to rotate until the desired record is under the read-write assembly.

Rounding: The act of adding a specified amount, usually 5, to the leftmost digit to be dropped to cause the last retained digit to be closer to the actual value of the number.

RR (Register to register) instruction: A type of machine instruction in which both operands refer to general registers.

RS (Register to storage) instruction: A type of machine instruction in which the first and third operands refer to general registers and the second operand to a location in main storage.

Run time: That period of time during which a program is being executed. Also called Execution time. Contrast with Assembly time.

RX (Register to indexed storage) instruction: A type of machine instruction in which the first operand refers to a general register and the second to a location in main storage. An index register may contain a value to specify a part of the main storage address.

S (Storage and implied operand) instruction: A type of machine instruction four bytes in length, having a two-byte op code and a single operand in base-displacement form.

SAVE: A macro normally used at the beginning of a subprogram to store designated general registers in an area defined in the calling program.

Save area: An area, normally containing 18 fullwords, where the contents of general registers are stored so that the registers may be reused by a subprogram.

Scaling: Determining the number of digits to left and right of a decimal point that numbers will have as a result of various arithmetic operations.

Scan: To search for a specific value; normally to search a variable-length record for a specific code that separates, or delimits, the fields within the record.

Search argument: A value for which a matching key is to be found in a file or table.

Seek time: The period of time required for the read-write assembly on a disk drive to reach the desired cylinder.

Selection structure: A program logical structure in which one series of instructions will be executed if a condition is true and another series if the condition is false.

Selector channel: A special purpose computer for the transfer of data between main storage and high-speed devices such as magnetic tape or disk. Contrast with Multiplexor channel.

Sentinel: A special code or record that designates the end of a file or table.

Sequence check: A method of verifying that the records in a file or table are in the desired order.

Sequence link field: In an indexed sequential file, a 10-byte pointer attached to each record in the overflow area that designates the address of the next record, if any, belonging to a specific track.

Sequence set: In VSAM, an index on the first track of each control area giving the key to the last record on each control interval, together with a pointer to the first record in the control interval. Similar to the Track index in ISAM.

Sequence structure: A program logical structure in which instructions are executed one after another with no deviation.

Sequence symbol: In conditional assembly statements, the name given to a statement to be referred to in branching.

Sequential processing: A method of handling the records in a file in the order in which they appear in the file.

Sequential retrieval: Reading records from a file or table (1) in order of their physical appearance or (2) with indexed sequential files, in ascending order of their keys.

SET symbol: In macro definitions, a type of parameter to which a value can be assigned.

SETFL: A macro that initializes indexes in preparation for creating, or loading, an indexed sequential file.

SETL: A macro that specifies how the records of an indexed sequential file are to be retrieved sequentially.

Short form: A 32-bit floating-point binary number.

SI (Storage immediate) instruction: A type of machine instruction in which the first operand is a location in main storage and the second operand is contained in the second byte of the instruction itself.

Sign: A code indicating whether a number is positive or negative.

Significance indicator: In an edit instruction, a flag or signal that indicates whether a nonzero digit has been selected for editing.

Significance starter: In an edit instruction, a special code that causes the significance indicator to be set ON even if no nonzero digit has been selected.

Single-level table: A type of data organization in which each table entry contains no data elements that occur more than once. Contrast with Multiple-level table.

Single-level totals: A type of control break processing in which only one key is compared between successive records and a total taken when the key changes. Contrast with Multiple-level totals.

Single-register shift: A machine instruction that can move the individual bits within a general register to the right or left.

Skip sequential processing: A method of retrieving records from VSAM key-sequenced data sets where the primary key is presented and records must be processed in ascending key sequence.

Software: A general name for computer programs and supporting documentation.

Source field: A data element that is to be moved to another location or to perform some operation on another data element. Contrast with Destination field.

Source statements: Statements written by the programmer in some language that are to be translated into machine language.

Span: In VSAM data sets, a condition where one record extends across control interval boundaries.

SS (Storage to storage) instruction: A type of machine instruction in which both operands are located in main storage. The instruction must give the length of one or both operands.

Store character (STC): A machine instruction that moves the rightmost byte of a general register to a single byte location in main storage.

Structured programming: An organized method of developing and writing computer programs by constructing a hierarchy of modules, each of which controls other modules or performs a specific task.

Sublist: In macro definitions, a series of items separated by commas and enclosed within parentheses.

Subprogram: A module assembled separately and later linked to a calling module.

Subroutine: A module to perform some specific task, assembled with a main program or control section.

Substring: A sequence of characters that are part of a longer sequence, such as a word.

Supervisor: The main control of an operating system. It controls the loading of programs, execution of all input/output operations, and the service of interrupts.

Symbol: The name assigned to a file, record, data element, or instruction.

Symbolic parameter: A variable symbol used to supply information to a macro definition to determine what source statements are to be generated.

Table: An orderly arrangement of data consisting of a key, or identifier, for each entry, together with data elements giving attributes or characteristics of that entry.

Table argument: The key, identifier, or value that identifies a table entry.

Table entry: One discrete element of a table, logically equivalent to one row of data that may contain more than one column.

Table function: A field that gives a characteristic of a table entry.

Table key: See Table argument.

Tape density: A measure of the number of bits per inch recorded on each channel of magnetic tape.

Tape transfer rate: The speed at which data is read from or written to magnetic tape. It is a function of tape speed and recording density.

Test under Mask (TM): A machine instruction that determines which individual bits within a byte are set to 0 and which to 1.

Text insertion: In macro definitions, the ability to cause data or instructions to be placed as written into a source program.

Text manipulation: In macro definitions, the ability to create new words and operands in generated source statements to meet conditions encountered at assembly time.

Text modification: In macro definitions, the ability to specify different names or operands to appear in generated source statements when macros are used.

TLBL (Tape label): A job control statement with operands that describe the data to be used in magnetic tape labels.

Total line: A line on a report that shows one or more accumulated amounts from processing detail records.

Track capacity table: A reference giving the number of records of different sizes that can be placed on each track of certain types of disk units.

Track index: On indexed sequential files, an index giving the highest key on each track of a cylinder with a pointer to the first record on the corresponding track.

Trailer label: A magnetic record placed at the end of a disk file or volume that identifies the file and gives a count of the number of physical records recorded in that part of the file. Contrast with Header label.

Trailer statement: The op code MEND that identifies the end of a macro definition.

Translate instruction (TR): A machine instruction that uses a 256-byte table to cause any eight-bit code in a byte within an operand to be replaced by any other desired eight-bit code.

Translate and Test (TRT): A machine instruction that uses a 256-byte table to scan a record for certain characters that separate variable-length fields or serve some other useful purpose.

Truth tables: An organization of alternate conditions, usually TRUE and FALSE or 0 and 1, to indicate the result of various compound conditions.

Two-way selection: A logical program structure in which one set of actions is taken if a condition is true and an alternative set if false.

Two-way test: See Two-way selection.

Twos complement: A binary number formed by changing all zeros in the original number to ones and all ones to zeros, and then adding one to the result. It is used to represent the negative of the original number.

Unconditional branch: A transfer of control to some instruction other than the next one in sequence, without considering whether any condition is true or false.

Unpack: A machine instruction that converts data from packed decimal to zoned decimal format.

V-type constant: An address constant naming a field not defined within the program where the constant appears. It is assembled as all zeros, and replaced by the linkage editor.

Variable-length record: A form of record not always having the same number of bytes. The first four bytes of the record contain a binary number giving the length of the record.

Variable symbol: In a macro definition, a name beginning with an ampersand (&) that is replaced wherever it appears with a name supplied by the programmer.

Volume: A disk pack or reel of magnetic tape.

Volume label: A magnetic record that identifies a disk pack or reel of magnetic tape.

Volume Table of Contents (VTOC): A disk directory containing the labels of all files on a disk pack.

Wrap-around: A term applied to an arrangement where logically (1) general register 15 is followed by general register 0 or (2) bits shifted out of one end of a general register are shifted into the other end.

ZAP (Zero and add packed): A machine instruction that moves a packed decimal number from one field to another, truncating bytes if the destination field is shorter than the source and padding with zeros if the destination field is longer.

Zero suppression: In editing, changing leading zeros to blanks before the number is printed.

Zone bits: The leftmost four bits of a byte. Contrast with Numeric bits.

Zoned decimal: A number in which each decimal digit occupies a full byte, with the sign represented in the zone bits of the rightmost byte of the field.

B Machine Instruction Summary

ADD: AR (RR) or A (RX) The second operand in the form of a 32-bit signed binary fullword is added to the first operand in a general register. The sum replaces the first operand. CC: Yes.

ADD DECIMAL: AP (SS) The second operand is added to the first, and the sum replaces the first operand. Both operands must be valid packed decimal numbers. The maximum length of each operand is 16 bytes. CC: Yes.

ADD HALFWORD: AH (RX) The second operand, a 16-bit signed binary halfword in main storage, is added to the first operand in a general register. CC: Yes.

ADD LOGICAL: ALR (RR) or AL (RX) The second operand is added to the first, and the sum replaces the first operand in a general register. Both operands are 32-bit unsigned binary integers. CC: Yes.

ADD NORMALIZED, extended: AXR (RR) The second operand is added to the first and the sum replaces the first operand. Both operands are 128-bit signed floating-point numbers and must refer to floating-point registers 0 or 4. The sum is shifted so that the leftmost hex digit of the fraction is not zero. CC: Yes.

ADD NORMALIZED, long: ADR (RR) or AD (RX) The second operand is added to the first, and the normalized sum replaces the first operand in a floating-point register. Both operands are 64-bit signed floating-point numbers. The first operand (and with ADR the second operand) must refer to FP register 0, 2, 4, or 6. CC: Yes.

ADD NORMALIZED, short: AER (RR) or AE (RX) The second operand is added to the first, and the normalized sum replaces the first operand in a floating-point register. Both operands and the sum are 32-bit signed floating-point numbers. CC: Yes.

ADD UNNORMALIZED, long: AWR (RR) or AW (RX) The second operand is added to the first, and the unnormalized sum replaces the first operand in a floating-point register. Both operands and the sum are 64-bit signed floating-point numbers. CC: Yes.

ADD UNNORMALIZED, short: AUR (RR) or AU (RX) The second operand is added to the first, and the unnormalized sum replaces the first operand in a floating-point register. Both operands and the sum are 32-bit signed floating-point numbers. CC: Yes.

AND: NR (RR), N (RX), NI (SI), or NC (SS) The AND of the first and second operands is placed in the first operand location. The AND is applied left to right to each pair of bits. If both corresponding bits are ones, the resulting bit is one; otherwise, the result is zero. NC can operate on a maximum of 256 bytes. CC: 0 if result is all zeros; 1 if not zeros.

BRANCH AND LINK: BALR (RR) or BAL (RX) Bits 32-63 of the Program Status Word are placed in the first operand general register, and a branch is made to the address specified in the second operand. The effect is to place the address of the following instruction into the first operand register. If the second operand of a BALR instruction is zero, no branch is made. CC: Unchanged.

BRANCH ON CONDITION: BCR (RR) or BC (RX) The first operand is a four-bit mask to test the condition code. The four condition codes (0, 1, 2, and 3) correspond, left to right, with mask bit values of 8, 4, 2, 1. If the condition code setting agrees with any of the mask bits, a branch is made to the address specified in the second operand. CC: Unchanged.

BRANCH ON COUNT: BCTR (RR) or BCT (RX) The first operand general register is decremented by one. If the result is not zero, a branch is made to the address specified in the second operand. However, if the second operand of BCTR is zero, no branch is made. CC: Unchanged.

BRANCH ON INDEX HIGH: BXH (RS) The first operand general register is incremented and compared with a value. If the sum is higher than the compare value, a branch is made to the second operand address. If the third operand is an even-numbered general register, that register contains the increment and the next-higher odd-numbered register contains the compare value. If the third operand is an odd-numbered general register, it contains both the increment and the compare value. CC: Unchanged.

BRANCH ON INDEX LOW OR EQUAL: BXLE (RS) Operates like BXH, except that the branch is made if the sum in the first operand is less than or equal to the compare value. CC: Unchanged.

COMPARE: CR (RR) or C (RX) The first operand is compared with the second, and the condition code is set accordingly. Both operands are 32-bit signed binary integers. CC: Yes.

COMPARE, long: CDR (RR) or CD (RX) The first operand is compared with the second, and the condition code is set accordingly. Both operands are 64-bit floating-point numbers. The first operand (and with CDR the second operand) must refer to FP registers 0, 2, 4, or 6. CC: Yes.

COMPARE, short: CER (RR) or CE (RX) The first operand is compared with the second, and the condition code is set accordingly. Both operands are 32-bit floating-point numbers. CC: Yes.

COMPARE AND SWAP: CS (RS) or CDS (RS) The first and second operands are compared. If they are equal, the third operand is stored at the second-operand location. If they are unequal, the second operand is loaded into the first-operand location. For CS, the first and third operands are 32-bit numbers occupying general registers. The second operand is a fullword in main storage. For CDS, the first and third operands are 64-bit binary numbers, each occupying an even-odd pair of general registers. The second operand is a doubleword in main storage. CC: Yes.

COMPARE DECIMAL: CP (SS) The first operand is compared with the second, and the condition code is set accordingly. Both operands are packed decimal numbers in main storage, with a maximum length of 16 bytes. CC: Yes.

COMPARE HALFWORD: CH (RX) The first operand is compared with the second, and the condition code is set accordingly. The first operand is a fullword in a general register. The second operand is a 16-bit signed binary number in main storage. CC: Yes.

COMPARE LOGICAL: CLR (RR), CL (RX) , CLI (SI), or CLC (SS) The first operand is compared with the second, and the condition code is set accordingly. Comparison is left to right, byte by byte, and ends upon finding an inequality or the end of the field. For CLC, a maximum of 256 bytes may be compared. CC: Yes.

COMPARE LOGICAL CHARACTERS UNDER MASK: CLM (RS) The first operand is compared with the second operand under control of a mask, and the condition code is set accordingly. The four bits of the third operand form a mask to correspond, left to right, with the four bytes in the general register specified as the first operand. The byte positions corresponding to ones in the mask are considered as a contiguous field to be compared with the second operand. CC: Yes.

COMPARE LOGICAL LONG: CLCL (RR) The first operand is compared with the second operand, and the condition code is set accordingly. Both operands refer to the even-numbered register of an even-odd pair. The even-numbered register of the first operand contains the address of the first field, and the odd-numbered register its length. The even-numbered register of the second operand contains the address of the second field, and the odd-numbered register its length in the rightmost three bytes. The leftmost eight bits of the odd-numbered register contain a pad byte to be used to extend the shorter field as comparison is made. CC: Yes.

CONVERT TO BINARY: CVB (RX) The second operand, a packed decimal number in a doubleword in main storage, is converted to 32-bit signed binary form and placed in the general register specified as the first operand. Invalid data in the second operand causes a data exception. An attempt to convert a value outside the range of 2,147,483,647 through -2,147,483,648 causes a fixed-point-divide exception. CC: Unchanged.

CONVERT TO DECIMAL: CVD (RX) The 32-bit signed binary number in the first operand general register is converted to packed decimal form and placed in a doubleword in main storage. CC: Unchanged.

DIVIDE: DR (RR) or D (RX) The first operand is divided by the second and is replaced by the quotient and the remainder. The first operand must designate the even-numbered register of an even-odd pair. The dividend is a 64-bit signed binary integer. The divisor, quotient, and remainder are all 32-bit signed binary integers. The remainder is placed in the even-numbered register and the quotient in the odd-numbered register, replacing the dividend. If the size of the dividend and divisor would create a quotient too large to be expressed as a 32-bit signed integer, a fixed-point divide exception occurs, and the operation is suppressed. CC: Unchanged.

DIVIDE, long: DDR (RR) or DD (RX) The first operand is divided by the second operand, and the normalized quotient replaces the first operand. No remainder is preserved. The first operand must designate one of the floating-point registers 0, 2, 4, or 6. The second operand is in another FP register (DDR) or in a doubleword in storage (DD). Both operands and the quotient are 64-bit floating-point numbers. When the divisor fraction is zero, a floating-point divide interruption occurs. An exponent-overflow exception occurs when the characteristic of the quotient would exceed 127 and the fraction is not zero. An exponent-underflow exception occurs when the characteristic of the quotient would be less than zero and the fraction is not zero. CC: Unchanged.

DIVIDE, short: DER (RR) or DD (RX) Same as DIVIDE, long, except that both operands and the quotient are 32-bit floating-point numbers. CC: Unchanged.

DIVIDE DECIMAL: DP (SS) The first operand is divided by the second operand and is replaced by the quotient and remainder. Both operands and the results are packed decimal integers. The remainder occupies the rightmost bytes of the first operand (dividend) field and is the length of the divisor. The remaining leftmost bytes of the dividend field contain the quotient. The divisor length cannot exceed 15 digits and sign and must be less than the dividend length; otherwise, a specification exception occurs. If the divisor is zero or the quotient is too large to be represented in the bytes allowed for it, a decimal-divide exception occurs. CC: Unchanged.

EDIT: ED (SS) The first operand is an edit pattern whose length may be as large as 256 bytes. The second operand (source) is one or more packed decimal numbers. The second operand is changed to zoned format and modified as specified by the edit pattern. The edited result replaces the first operand. The edit pattern consists of a fill character, digit selectors, significance starter, and message characters. The fill character, usually a blank, replaces leading zeros. Digit selectors cause one decimal digit to be placed in zoned format in the edit pattern. Message characters provide commas, decimal points, signs, or other characters. The significance starter acts like a digit selector but also turns the significance indicator ON, effective with the following byte. If the leftmost four bits of a byte in the source field do not contain a decimal digit code (X'0' through X'9'), a data exception occurs. CC: Yes.

EDIT AND MARK: EDMK (SS) Same as EDIT except that the address of the byte in the edit pattern where the first non-zero digit appears is placed in general register 1 if the significance indicator was OFF at the time of selection. CC: Yes.

EXCLUSIVE OR: XR (RR), X (RX), XI (SI), or XC (SS) The EXCLUSIVE OR of the first and second operands is placed in the first operation location. The EXCLUSIVE OR works on corresponding bits, left to right. If the bits are different, the resulting bit is 1; if they are alike, the result is 0. XC requires one length code, which can be as long as 256 bytes. CC: 0 if all resulting bits are zero; 1 if not.

EXECUTE: EX (RX) The second operand must refer to a single instruction outside the main path of the program. The rightmost byte of the general register specified as the first operand is ORed with the second byte of the instruction specified by the second operand; then the second operand instruction is executed and control returns to the instruction following EX. The ORing does not change either the contents of the first operand register or the second operand instruction, but only the effect of the instruction to be executed. If the first operand specifies R0, no ORing takes place. CC: Unchanged by EX, but may be changed by the target instruction.

HALVE: HER (RR) or HDR (RR) The second operand is divided by 2, and the normalized quotient is placed in the first operand location. Both operands must designate floating-point registers 0, 2, 4, or 6. HER refers to a 32-bit floating-point number, and HDR to a 64-bit FP number. CC: Unchanged.

INSERT CHARACTER: IC (RX) The single byte at the second-operand location is inserted into the rightmost byte of the general register specified by the first operand. The leftmost 24 bits of the register remain unchanged. CC: Unchanged.

INSERT CHARACTERS UNDER MASK: ICM (RS) Bytes from contiguous locations beginning at the second-operand location are inserted into the first-operand register under control of a mask. The four bits of the third operand, left to right, make a mask corresponding to the four bytes of the general register specified as the first operand. The byte positions corresponding to ones in the mask are filled, left to right, with bytes from successive storage locations beginning at the second-operand address. Bytes in the register corresponding to zeros in the mask are unchanged. CC: Yes.

LOAD: LR (RR) or L (RX) The 32-bit binary integer at the second operand location is placed unchanged in the general register specified as the first operand. CC: Unchanged.

LOAD, long: LDR (RR) or LD (RX) The 64-bit floating-point number in the second operand location is placed unchanged in the first operand location. The first operand (and second operand for LDR) must designate FP register 0, 2, 4, or 6. CC: Unchanged.

LOAD, short: LER (RR) or LE (RX) Same as LOAD, long, except that the operands are 32-bit floating-point numbers. CC: Unchanged.

LOAD ADDRESS: LA (RX) The address of the second operand is placed in the general register specified as the first operand. The same register may be specified as R1, X2, and B2. The contents of general register 0 are ignored if it is specified as X2 or B2. CC: Unchanged.

LOAD AND TEST: LTR (RR), LTDR (RR), or LTER (RR) The second operand is placed unchanged in the first-operand location, and the condition code is set as determined by its sign and magnitude. LTR refers to two general registers. For LTDR and LTER, both operands must refer to floating-point register 0, 2, 4, or 6. LTDR refers to a 64-bit FP number, while LTER refers to a 32-bit number. CC: Yes.

LOAD COMPLEMENT: LCR (RR), LCDR (RR), or LCER (RR) For LCR, the twos complement of a 32-bit binary number in the second-operand general register is placed into the first operand register. LCDR and LCER place the contents of the second operand floating-point register into the first operand FP register with the sign bit reversed. Both operands must refer to FP registers 0, 2, 4, or 6. LCDR refers to a 64-bit FP number, while LCER refers to a 32-bit number. CC: Yes.

LOAD HALFWORD: LH (RX) The 16-bit binary halfword in main storage specified by the second operand is loaded into the first-operand general register. The sign bit of the halfword is propagated throughout the leftmost 16 bits of the register. CC: Unchanged.

LOAD MULTIPLE: LM (RS) The set of general registers starting with the one specified by the first operand and continuing through that specified as the third operand is loaded from storage beginning at the second-operand address and continuing consecutively as many locations as needed. General register 0 is assumed to follow R15 for this operation. CC: Unchanged.

LOAD NEGATIVE: LNR (RR), LNDR (RR), or LNER (RR) The contents of the second operand is made negative and placed in the first-operand register. LNR operates on 32-bit signed binary integers. LNDR and LNER must refer to floating-point registers 0, 2, 4, or 6. LNDR refers to 64-bit FP numbers, and LNER refers to 32-bit numbers. Zero values are unchanged. CC: 0 if result is zero; 1 if less than zero.

LOAD POSITIVE: LPR (RR), LPDR (RR), or LPER (RR) The absolute value of the second operand is placed in the first operand register. LPR works on 32-bit signed binary integers. LPDR refers to 64-bit floating point numbers, and LPER to 32-bit FP numbers. CC: Yes.

LOAD ROUNDED: LRDR (RR) or LRER (RR) The second operand is rounded to the next shorter floating-point form, and the result is placed in the first-operand location. LRDR rounds an extended FP number in FP register pair 0 or 4 to long form. LRER rounds a long FP number in FP register 0, 2, 4, or 6 to short form. CC: Unchanged.

MOVE: MVC (SS) The second operand is placed in the first-operand location. Each operand is processed left to right, with each byte being stored before the next byte in the source field is fetched. Fields may overlap. The length of the first operand determines the number of bytes to be moved. The first operand may indicate a maximum length of 256. CC: Unchanged.

MOVE IMMEDIATE: MVI (SI) The second operand specifies a single character in the second byte of the instruction. This byte is moved to the first-operand location. CC: Unchanged.

MOVE INVERSE: MVCIN (SS) The second operand is placed in the first-operand location with the left-to-right sequence of the bytes inverted. The first-operand address designates the leftmost byte of the first operand. The second-operand address designates the rightmost byte of the second operand. The first operand may specify a maximum length of 256. CC: Unchanged.

MOVE LONG: MVCL (RR) The second operand is placed in the first-operand location, provided overlapping of operand locations does not affect the final contents of the first-operand location. If the first operand is longer than the second, the remaining rightmost bytes are filled with padding bytes. Both operands must specify the even-numbered register of an even-odd pair. The first-operand even register contains the address of the first operand, and the odd register its length. The second-operand even register contains the address of the second operand, and the odd register its length. The first byte of the second-operand odd register contains the padding byte. CC: Yes.

MOVE NUMERICS: MVN (SS) The rightmost four bits of each byte in the second operand replace the corresponding bits in each byte of the first operand. The leftmost four bits of each byte in the first operand remain unchanged. Each operand is processed left to right. The length of the first operand determines the number of bytes to be moved, to a maximum of 256. CC: Unchanged.

MOVE WITH OFFSET: MVO (SS) The second operand is placed in the first operand location, but shifted four bits to the left. Movement is right to left, and excess positions in the first operand are padded with binary zeros. The rightmost four bits of the last byte of the first operand are unchanged. A maximum length of 16 can be specified for each operand. CC: Unchanged.

MOVE ZONES: MVZ (SS) The leftmost four bits of each byte in the second operand replace the corresponding bits in each byte of the first operand. The rightmost four bits of each byte in the first operand remain unchanged. The length of the first operand determines the number of bytes to be moved, to a maximum of 256. CC: Unchanged.

MULTIPLY: MR (RR) or M (RX) The second word of the first operand is multiplied by the second operand, and the doubleword product is placed at the first-operand location. The first operand specifies the even register of an even-odd pair. Both the multiplicand and multiplier are 32-bit signed binary integers. The product is a 64-bit signed binary integer. CC: Unchanged.

MULTIPLY, extended: MXR (RR) The normalized product of the first and second operand is placed in the first-operand location. All numbers are extended (128-bit) floating-point numbers. Both operands must specify FP register 0 or 4. CC: Unchanged.

MULTIPLY, long: MDR (RR), MD (RX), MXDR (RR), or MXD (RX) The normalized product of the first and second operand is placed in the first-operand location. For all instructions, both operands are long (64-bit) floating point numbers. MDR and MD produce an eight-byte product; MXDR and MXD produce an extended (128-bit) product. R1 of MDR and MD and R2 of MD and MXD must specify FP register 0, 2, 4, or 6. R1 of MXDR or MXD must designate FP register 0 or 4. CC: Unchanged.

MULTIPLY, short: MER (RR) or ME (RX) The normalized product of the first and second operand is placed in the first-operand location. The operands are both short (32-bit) floating-point numbers, and the product is a long (64-bit) FP number. R1 for both instructions, and R2 for MER, must specify FP registers 0, 2, 4, or 6. CC: Unchanged.

MULTIPLY DECIMAL: MP (SS) The product of the first and second operands is placed in the first-operand location. Both operands and the product are packed decimal numbers. The multiplicand cannot exceed 16 bytes. The multiplier cannot exceed eight bytes and must be shorter than the multiplicand. The multiplicand must have at least as many bytes of high-order zeros as the number of bytes in the multiplier; otherwise, a data exception occurs. CC: Unchanged.

MULTIPLY HALFWORD: MH (RX) The first operand is multiplied by the second operand, and the product is placed at the first-operand location. The second operand is a 16-bit signed binary integer in main storage. The first operand and the product are 32-bit signed binary integers. Any general register may be specified for the first operand. Only the rightmost 32 bits of the product are retained. CC: Unchanged.

OR: OR (RR), O (RX), OI (SI), or OC (SS) The OR of the first and second operands is placed in the first-operand location. The OR operation is applied bit by bit, left to right. If both of the corresponding bits are zeros, the result is 0; if either or both of the corresponding bits is 1, the result is 1. For OC, the length of the first operand controls the number of bytes processed, and may be as long as 256 bytes. CC: 0 if all result bits are zero; otherwise, 1.

PACK: PACK (SS) The second operand is changed from zoned to packed format and the result is placed in the first-operand location. The operation proceeds from right to left. The zone and numeric bits of the rightmost byte of the second operand are exchanged. In all other bytes of the second operand, only the four numeric bits are selected and placed, two sets per byte, in the first operand location. If the first operand is longer than needed to hold the zone bits of the second operand, it is padded to the left with binary zeros. CC: Unchanged.

SHIFT AND ROUND DECIMAL: SRP (SS) Format: D1(L1,B),D2(B2),I3 The first operand is shifted in the direction and for the number of decimal-digit positions specified by the second operand. For a right shift, rounding is done by using the I3 operand. The first operand is a packed-decimal number. Only the digits are shifted; the sign does not move. Zeros are supplied for the vacated digit positions. The result replaces the first operand. Only bits 26–31 of the second operand specify the shift value. Values of 0–31 specify left shifts of 0–31 digits. Negative values specify right shifts. Negative values are represented by subtracting from 64 (for instance, 63, shift 1 digit; 62, shift 2 digits). For a right shift, the I3 field, bits 12–15 of the instruction, are used as a decimal rounding digit. CC: Yes.

SHIFT LEFT DOUBLE: SLDA (RS) The rightmost 63 bits of an even-odd pair of registers designated by the first operand are shifted left the number of bit positions specified by the second operand. The leftmost sign bit does not shift. The first operand must indicate the even-numbered register. Bit positions 12–15 of the instruction are ignored. If one or more bits unlike the sign is shifted out of bit position 1 of the even register, an overflow occurs. Vacated positions to the right of the odd-numbered register are filled with binary zeros. The effect of a shift of one bit position is to double the value of the signed binary integer. CC: Yes.

SHIFT LEFT DOUBLE LOGICAL: SLDL (RS) All bits of the first operand are shifted left the number of bits specified by the second-operand address. The first operand must specify the even-numbered register of an even-odd pair. Bits positions 12–15 of the instruction are ignored. Bits shifted out of the register are lost. Vacated positions to the right of the register are filled with zeros. CC: Unchanged.

SHIFT LEFT SINGLE: SLA (RS) The rightmost 31 bits of the 32-bit signed binary integer in the general register specified as the first operand are shifted left the number of bits specified in the second operand. The sign bit does not shift. This instruction is similar to SLDA except that only 31 data bits in a single register are shifted. CC: Yes.

SHIFT LEFT SINGLE LOGICAL: SLL (RS) All 32 bits in the general register specified as the first operand are shifted left the number of bits specified in the second operand. This instruction is similar to SLDL except that the contents of only one register are affected. CC: Unchanged.

SHIFT RIGHT DOUBLE: SRDA (RS) Similar to SLDA except that the 63 data bits in the even-odd register pair shift to the right. The sign bit fills in bit positions vacated on the left of the number. CC: Yes.

SHIFT RIGHT DOUBLE LOGICAL: SRDL (RS) Similar to SRDA except that all 64 bits in the even-odd register pair shift to the right. The vacated bit positions at the left are filled with binary zeros. CC: Unchanged.

SHIFT RIGHT SINGLE: SRA (RS) The 31 data bits in the general register specified as the first operand are shifted right the number of bit positions specified in the second operand. The sign bit is not shifted. The sign bit fills vacated positions to the left of the number. A right shift of one bit position is equivalent to division by 2 with rounding downward. CC: Yes.

SHIFT RIGHT SINGLE LOGICAL: SRL (RS) All 32 bits in the general register specified as the first operand are shifted right the number of bit positions specified in the second operand. Bits 12–15 of the instruction are ignored. Vacated positions at the left of the register are filled with binary zeros. CC: Unchanged.

STORE: ST (RX), STD (RX), STE (RX) The first operand is stored at the second-operand location. For ST, 32 bits representing a signed binary integer are stored. ST refers to a general register, and STD and STE must refer to floating-point registers 0, 2, 4, or 6. STD stores a long (64-bit) FP number, and STD a short (32-bit) FP number. CC: Unchanged.

STORE CHARACTER: STC (RX) The rightmost byte of the general register specified as the first operand are placed unchanged in a single byte at the second-operand location. CC: Unchanged.

STORE CHARACTERS UNDER MASK: STCM (RS) Bytes selected from the general register specified as the first operand are stored in contiguous bytes at the second-operand location under control of a mask. The third operand is the four-bit mask which corresponds, left to right, with the four bytes of the general register designated as the first operand. The bytes corresponding to 1 bits in the mask are placed in the same order in successive and contiguous storage locations beginning at the second-operand address. The first operand field is unchanged. CC: Unchanged.

STORE HALFWORD: STH (RX) The rightmost 16 bits of the general register designated as the first operand are stored in two bytes at the second-operand location. CC: Unchanged.

STORE MULTIPLE: STM (RS) The contents of the set of general registers starting with the one specified as the first operand and ending with the register designated as the third operand are stored in successive locations starting at the second-operand address. Registers are stored in ascending order of register numbers, with register 0 following register 15. CC: Unchanged.

SUBTRACT: SR (RR) or S (RX) The second operand is subtracted from the first operand, and the difference is placed in the first-operand location. Both operands and the result are 32-bit signed binary integers. CC: Yes.

SUBTRACT DECIMAL: SP (SS) The second operand is subtracted from the first operand, and the difference is placed in the first-operand location. Both operands and the result are packed decimal numbers. Either operand may be up to 16 bytes in length. CC: Yes.

SUBTRACT HALFWORD: SH (RX) The second operand is subtracted from the first operand, and the difference is placed in the first-operand location. The second operand is a 16-bit signed binary integer. The first operand and the difference are 32-bit signed binary integers. CC: Yes.

SUBTRACT LOGICAL: SLR (RR) or SL (RX) The second operand is subtracted from the first operand, and the difference is placed in the first-operand location. Both operands and the difference are treated as 32-bit unsigned binary integers. Logical subtraction is done by adding the ones complement of the second operand and a low-order one to the first operand. CC: Yes.

SUBTRACT NORMALIZED: SER (RR), SE (RX), SDR (RR), SD (RX), or SXR (RR) The second operand is subtracted from the first operand, and the normalized difference is placed in the first-operand location. SER and SE refer to short (32-bit) floating-point numbers. SDR and SD refer to long (64-bit) FP numbers. SXR refers to extended (128-bit) FP numbers. The R1 field of SER, SE, SDR, and SD, and the R2 field of SER and SDR must designate FP register 0, 2, 4, or 6. The R1 and R2 fields of SXR must designate FP register 0 or 4. CC: Yes.

SUBTRACT UNNORMALIZED: SUR (RR), SU (RX), SWR (RR), or SW (RX) The second operand is subtracted from the first operand, and the unnormalized difference is placed in the first-operand location. SUR and SU refer to short (32-bit) floating-point numbers, and SWR and SW refer to long (64-bit) FP numbers. The R1 and R2 fields must designate FP register 0, 2, 4, or 6. CC: Yes.

SUPERVISOR CALL: SVC (RR) This instruction causes a supervisor-call interruption, with the second byte of the instruction providing the interruption code. Bits 8–15 of the instruction, with eight high-order zeros supplied, are placed in the supervisor-call interruption code that is stored in the course of the interruption. CC: Unchanged and saved as part of the old Program Status Word; replaced by a new CC as part of the SVC interruption.

TEST UNDER MASK: TM (SI) The second operand is an eight-bit mask used to select bits of the first operand, and the result is indicated in the condition code. The bits of the mask correspond one for one with the bits of the byte in storage to be tested. A mask bit of 1 indicates that the storage bit is to be tested; a mask bit of zero causes the storage bit to be ignored. CC: 0 if all tested bits are zero; 1 if tested bits are mixed zeros and ones; 3 if tested bits are all ones.

TRANSLATE: TR (SS) Each byte in the first operand forms an index to be added to the second operand location. The byte in the indexed location replaces the first operand byte. The length of the first operand may be up to 256 bytes. The second operand is a 256-byte table containing the values to replace the original bytes. The operation proceeds left to right until the first-operand field is exhausted. CC: Unchanged.

TRANSLATE AND TEST: TRT (SS) Each byte in the first operand forms an index to be added to the second operand location. The second operand refers to a 256-byte table. The operation proceeds left to right until the first operand field is exhausted. The first operand field, which may be as long as 256 bytes, remains unchanged. If the indexed location contains binary zeros, the operation proceeds to the next byte of the first operand. If the indexed location is nonzero, the nonzero byte from the table is inserted into the rightmost byte of general register 2, the address of the first-operand byte is placed in general register 1, and the condition code is set. CC: 0 if all indexed bytes were zero; 1 if a nonzero function byte was found before the last byte of the first operand; 2 if a nonzero function byte was found at the last byte of the first operand.

UNPACK: UNPK (SS) The second operand in packed decimal format is changed to zoned decimal and placed in the first-operand location. Both operands require length codes with a maximum of 16 bytes. The operation proceeds for right to left. The zone and numeric bits in the rightmost byte of the packed field are exchanged and placed in the rightmost byte of the first operand. Each remaining decimal digit is selected and placed in the numeric bit positions of the first-operand byte. Zone bits of 1111 are supplied in all first-operand bytes but the rightmost one. Leading zero numeric bits and 1111 zone bits are supplied if the first operand is longer than necessary to hold the packed decimal number. CC: Unchanged.

ZERO AND ADD: ZAP (SS) The second operand is placed in the first-operand location. The second operand and result are packed decimal numbers. This is equivalent to an addition to zero. Only the second operand is checked for valid sign and digit codes. Extra high-order zeros are supplied for the shorter operand if needed. If the first operand is too short to contain all significant digits of the second operand, decimal overflow occurs, the operation is completed, and condition code 3 is set. CC: Yes.

C
IBM System/370 Reference Summary*

PREFACE

This publication is intended primarily for use by S/370 assembler language application programmers. It contains basic machine information summarized from the *System/370 Principles of Operation* (GA22-7000) about System/370 Models 115 through 195; the 3031, 3032, 3033, 3081, 3083, and 3084 Processor Complexes; and the 4321, 4331, 4341, 4361, and 4381 Processors. It also contains frequently used information from the OS/VS, DOS/VSE, and VM/370 assembler language manual (GC33-4010), command codes for various I/O devices, and a multi-code translation table. This publication will be updated from time to time. However, the above manuals and others cited in this booklet are the authoritative reference sources and will be first to reflect changes.

The floating-point and extended-precision floating-point instructions, as well as the instructions listed below, are not provided on every model. For instructions that are provided on a particular model, either as standard or op-

Sixth Edition (July 1984)

This edition is a major revision and makes obsolete the previous edition, GX20-1850-4. Additions include new printer, tape, and DASD command codes. Minor technical and editorial revisions have been made throughout.

References in this publication to IBM products, programs, or services do not imply that IBM intends to make these available in all countries in which IBM operates.

Requests for copies of this and other IBM publications should be made to your IBM representative or to the IBM branch office serving your locality.

Please direct any comments on the contents of this publication to the address on the front cover. IBM may use or distribute whatever information you supply in any way it believes appropriate without incurring any obligation to you.

tional features on that model, the user should refer to the appropriate System Library manual.

Facility	**Instructions**
Branch and save	BAS, BASR
Channel-set switching	CONCS, DISCS
Conditional swapping	CS, CDS
CPU timer and clock comparator	SCKC, SPT, STCKC, STPT
Direct control	RDD,WRD
Dual address space	EPAR, ESAR, IAC, IVSK, LASP, MVCP, MVCS, MVCK, PC, PT, SAC, SSAR
Extended facility	IPTE, TPROT
Move inverse	MVCIN
Multiprocessing	SPX, SIGP, STAP, STPX
PSW-key handling	IPK, SPKA
Storage-key-instruction extensions	ISKE, RRBE, SSKE
Suspend and resume	RIO
Test block	TB
Translation	LRA, PTLB, RRB, STNSM, STOSM

The operation of the following I/O instructions may differ depending on the model, the designated channel, and the installed facilities: CLRCH, CLRIO, HDV, and SIOF. To determine the operation, the user should refer to the appropriate System Library manual.

MACHINE INSTRUCTION FORMATS

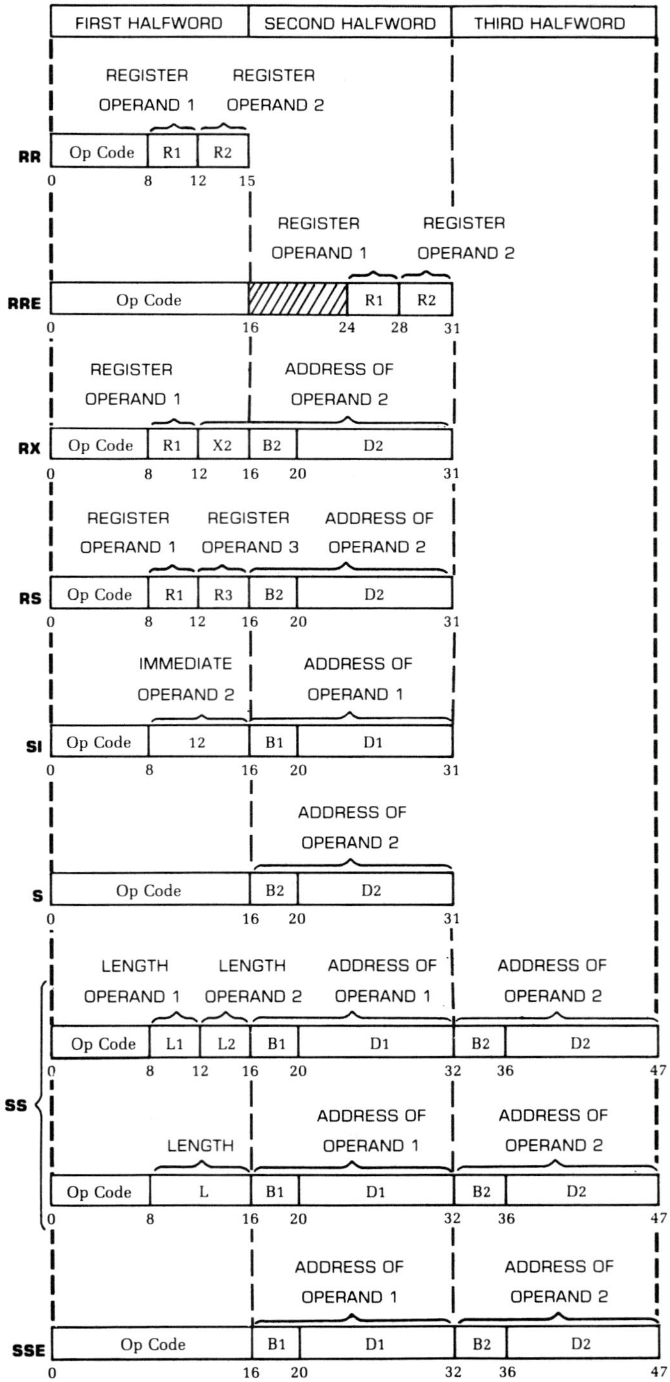

MACHINE INSTRUCTIONS

NAME	MNEMONIC	OP CODE	FORMAT	OPERANDS
Add (c)	AR	1A	RR	R1,R2
Add (c)	A	5A	RX	R1,D2(X2,B2)
Add Decimal (c)	AP	FA	SS	D1(L1,B1),D2(L2,B2)
Add Halfword (c)	AH	4A	RX	R1,D2(X2,B2)
Add Logical (c)	ALR	1E	RR	R1,R2
Add Logical (c)	AL	5E	RX	R1,D2(X2,B2)
AND (c)	NR	14	RR	R1,R2
AND (c)	N	54	RX	R1,D2(X2,B2)
AND (c)	NI	94	SI	D1(B1),I2
AND (c)	NC	D4	SS	D1(L,B1),D2(B2)
Branch and Link	BALR	05	RR	R1,R2
Branch and Link	BAL	45	RX	R1,D2(X2,B2)
Branch and Save	BASR	0D	RR	R1,R2
Branch and Save	BAS	4D	RX	R1,D2(X2,B2)
Branch on Condition	BCR	07	RR	M1,R2
Branch on Condition	BC	47	RX	M1,D2(X2,B2)
Branch on Count	BCTR	06	RR	R1,R2
Branch on Count	BCT	46	RX	R1,D2(X2,B2)
Branch on Index High	BXH	86	RS	R1,R3,D2(B2)
Branch on Index Low or Equal	BXLE	87	RS	R1,R3,D2(B2)
Clear Channel (c,p)	CLRCH	9F01	S	D2(B2)
Clear I/O (c,p)	CLRIO	9D01	S	D2(B2)
Compare (c)	CR	19	RR	R1,R2
Compare (c)	C	59	RX	R1,D2(X2,B2)
Compare and Swap (c)	CS	BA	RS	R1,R3,D2(B2)
Compare Decimal (c)	CP	F9	SS	D1(L1,B1),D2(L2,B2)
Compare Double and Swap (c)	CDS	BB	RS	R1,R3,D2(B2)
Compare Halfword (c)	CH	49	RX	R1,D2(X2,B2)
Compare Logical (c)	CLR	15	RR	R1,R2
Compare Logical (c)	CL	55	RX	R1,D2(X2,B2)
Compare Logical (c)	CLI	95	SI	D1(B1),I2
Compare Logical (c)	CLC	D5	SS	D1(L,B1),D2(B2)
Compare Logical Characters under Mask (c)	CLM	BD	RS	R1,M3,D2(B2)
Compare Logical Long (c)	CLCL	0F	RR	R1,R2
Connect Channel Set (c,p)	CONCS	B200	S	D2(B2)
Convert to Binary	CVB	4F	RX	R1,D2(X2,B2)
Convert to Decimal	CVD	4E	RX	R1,D2(X2,B2)
Diagnose (p)		83		Model-dependent
Disconnect Channel Set (c,p)	DISCS	B201	S	D2(B2)
Divide	DR	1D	RR	R1,R2
Divide	D	5D	RX	R1,D2(X2,B2)
Divide Decimal	DP	FD	SS	D1(L1,B1),D2(L2,B2)
Edit (c)	ED	DE	SS	D1(L,B1)D2(B2)
Edit and Mark (c)	EDMK	DF	SS	D1(L,B1),D2(B2)
Exclusive OR (c)	XR	17	RR	R1,R2
Exclusive OR (c)	X	57	RX	R1,D2(X2,B2)
Exclusive OR (c)	XI	97	SI	D1(B1),I2
Exclusive OR (c)	XC	D7	SS	D1(L,B1),D2(B2)
Execute	EX	44	RX	R1,D2(X2,B2)
Extract Primary ASN (s)	EPAR	B226	RRE	R1
Extract Secondary ASN (s)	ESAR	B227	RRE	R1

c. Condition code is set
n. New condition code is loaded
p. Privileged instruction
s. Semiprivileged instruction
x. Extended-precision floating-point

MACHINE INSTRUCTIONS (Cont'd)

NAME	MNEMONIC	OP CODE	FORMAT	OPERANDS
Halt Device (c,p)	HDV	9E01	S	D2(B2)
Halt I/O (c,p)	HIO	9E00	S	D2(B2)
Insert Address Space Control (c,s)	IAC	B224	RRE	R1
Insert Character	IC	43	RX	R1,D2(X2,B2)
Insert Characters under Mask (c)	ICM	BF	RS	R1,M3,D2(B2)
Insert PSW Key (s)	IPK	B20B	S	
Insert Storage Key (p)	ISK	09	RR	R1,R2
Insert Storage Key Extended (p)	ISKE	B229	RRE	R1,R2
Insert Virtual Storage Key (s)	IVSK	B223	RRE	R1,R2
Invalidate Page Table Entry (p)	IPTE	B221	RRE	R1,R2
Load	LR	18	RR	R1,R2
Load	L	58	RX	R1,D2(X2,B2)
Load Address	LA	41	RX	R1,D2(X2,B2)
Load Address Space Parameters (c,p)	LASP	E500	SSE	D1(B1),D2(B2)
Load and Test (c)	LTR	12	RR	R1,R2
Load Complement (c)	LCR	13	RR	R1,R2
Load Control (p)	LCTL	B7	RS	R1,R3,D2(B2)
Load Halfword	LH	48	RX	R1,D2(X2,B2)
Load Multiple	LM	98	RS	R1,R3,D2(B2)
Load Negative (c)	LNR	11	RR	R1,R2
Load Positive (c)	LPR	10	RR	R1,R2
Load PSW (n,p)	LPSW	82	S	D2(B2)
Load Real Address (c,p)	LRA	B1	RX	R1,D2(X2,B2)
Monitor Call	MC	AF	SI	D1(B1),I2
Move	MVI	92	SI	D1(B1),I2
Move	MVC	D2	SS	D1(L,B1),D2(B2)
Move Inverse	MVCIN	E8	SS	D1(L,B1),D2(B2)
Move Long (c)	MVCL	0E	RR	R1,R2
Move Numerics	MVN	D1	SS	D1(L,B1),D2(B2)
Move to Primary (c,s)	MVCP	DA	SS	D1(R1,B1),D2(B2),R3
Move to Secondary (c,s)	MVCS	DB	SS	D1(R1,B1),D2(B2),R3
Move with Key (c,s)	MVCK	D9	SS	D1(R1,B1),D2(B2),R3
Move with Offset	MVO	F1	SS	D1(L1,B1),D2(L2,B2)
Move Zones	MVZ	D3	SS	D1(L,B1),D2(B2)
Multiply	MR	1C	RR	R1,R2
Multiply	M	5C	RX	R1,D2(X2,B2)
Multiply Decimal	MP	FC	SS	D1(L1,B1),D2(L2,B2)
Multiply Halfword	MH	4C	RX	R1,D2(X2,B2)
OR (c)	OR	16	RR	R1,R2
OR (c)	O	56	RX	R1,D2(X2,B2)
OR (c)	OI	96	SI	D1(B1),I2
OR (c)	OC	D6	SS	D1(L,B1)D2(B2)
Pack	PACK	F2	SS	D1(L1,B1),D2(L2,B2)
Program Call (s)	PC	B218	S	D2(B2)
Program Transfer (s)	PT	B228	RRE	R1,R2
Purge TLB (p)	PTLB	B20D	S	
Read Direct (p)	RDD	85	SI	D1(B1),I2
Reset Reference Bit (c,p)	RRB	B213	S	D2(B2)

c. Condition code is set
n. New condition code is loaded
p. Privileged instruction
s. Semiprivileged instruction
x. Extended-precision floating-point

MACHINE INSTRUCTIONS (Cont'd)

NAME	MNEMONIC	OP CODE	FORMAT	OPERANDS
Rest Reference Bit Extended (c,p)	RRBE	B22A	RRE	R1,R2
Resume I/O (c,p)	RIO	9C02	S	D2(B2)
Set Address Space Control (s)	SAC	B219	S	D2(B2)
Set Clock (c,p)	SCK	B204	S	D2(B2)
Set Clock Comparator (p)	SCKC	B206	S	D2(B2)
Set CPU Timer (p)	SPT	B208	S	D2(B2)
Set Prefix (p)	SPX	B210	S	D2(B2)
Set Program Mask (n)	SPM	04	RR	R1
Set PSW Key from Address (s)	SPKA	B20A	S	D2(B2)
Set Secondary ASN (s)	SSAR	B225	RRE	R1
Set Storage Key (p)	SSK	08	RR	R1,R2
Set Storage Key Extended (p)	SSKE	B22B	RRE	R1,R2
Set System Mask (p)	SSM	80	S	D2(B2)
Shift and Round Decimal (c)	SRP	FO	SS	D1(L1,B1),D2(B2),I3
Shift Left Double (c)	SLDA	8F	RS	R1,D2(B2)
Shift Left Double Logical	SLDL	8D	RS	R1,D2(B2)
Shift Left Single (c)	SLA	8B	RS	R1,D2(B2)
Shift Left Single Logical	SLL	89	RS	R1,D2(B2)
Shift Right Double (c)	SRDA	8E	RS	R1,D2(B2)
Shift Right Double Logical	SRDL	8C	RS	R1,D2(B2)
Shift Right Single (c)	SRA	8A	RS	R1,D2(B2)
Shift Right Single Logical	SRL	88	RS	R1,D2(B2)
Signal Processor (c,p)	SIGP	AE	RS	R1,R3,D2(B2)
Start I/O (c,p)	SIO	9C00	S	D2(B2)
Start I/O Fast Release (c,p)	SIOF	9C01	S	D2(B2)
Store	ST	50	RX	R1,D2(X2,B2)
Store Channel ID (c,p)	STIDC	B203	S	D2(B2)
Store Character	STC	42	RX	R1,D2(X2,B2)
Store Characters under Mask	STCM	BE	RS	R1,M3,D2(B2)
Store Clock (c)	STCK	B205	S	D2(B2)
Store Clock Comparator (p)	STCKC	B207	S	D2(B2)
Store Control (p)	STCTL	B6	RS	R1,R3,D2(B2)
Store CPU Address (p)	STAP	B212	S	D2(B2)
Store CPU ID (p)	STIDP	B202	S	D2(B2)
Store CPU Timer (p)	STPT	B209	S	D2(B2)
Store Halfword	STH	40	RX	R1,D2(X2,B2)
Store Multiple	STM	90	RS	R1,R3,D2(B2)
Store Prefix (p)	STPX	B211	S	D2(B2)
Store Then AND System Mask (p)	STNSM	AC	SI	D1(B1),I2
Store Then OR System Mask (p)	STOSM	AD	SI	D1(B1),I2
Subtract (c)	SR	1B	RR	R1,R2
Subtract (c)	S	5B	RX	R1,D2(X2,B2)
Subtract Decimal (c)	SP	FB	SS	D1(L1,B1),D2(L2,B2)
Subtract Halfword (c)	SH	4B	RX	R1,D2(X2,B2)
Subtract Logical (c)	SLR	1F	RR	R1,R2
Subtract Logical (c)	SL	5F	RX	R1,D2(X2,B2)
Supervisor Call	SVC	0A	RR	I
Test and Set (c)	TS	93	S	D2(B2)
Test Block (c,p)	TB	B22C	RRE	R1,R2

c. Condition code is set
n. New condition code is loaded
p. Privileged instruction
s. Semiprivileged instruction
x. Extended-precision floating-point

MACHINE INSTRUCTIONS (Cont'd)

NAME	MNEMONIC	OP CODE	FORMAT	OPERANDS
Test Channel (c,p)	TCH	9F00	S	D2(B2)
Test I/O (c,p)	TIO	9D00	S	D2(B2)
Test Protection (c,p)	TPROT	E501	SSE	D1(B1),D2(B2)
Test under Mask (c)	TM	91	SI	D1(B1),I2
Translate	TR	DC	SS	D1(L,B1),D2(B2)
Translate and Test (c)	TRT	DD	SS	D1(L,B1),D2(B2)
Unpack	UNPK	F3	SS	D1(L1,B1),D2(L2,B2)
Write Direct (p)	WRD	84	SI	D1(B1),I2
Zero and Add (c)	ZAP	F8	SS	D1(L1,B1),D2(L2,B2)

c. Condition code is set
n. New condition code is loaded
p. Privileged instruction
s. Semiprivileged instruction
x. Extended-precision floating-point

FLOATING-POINT INSTRUCTIONS

NAME	MNEMONIC	OP CODE	FORMAT	OPERANDS
Add Normalized, Extended (c,x)	AXR	36	RR	R1,R2
Add Normalized, Long (c)	ADR	2A	RR	R1,R2
Add Normalized, Long (c)	AD	6A	RX	R1,D2(X2,B2)
Add Normalized, Short (c)	AER	3A	RR	R1,R2
Add Normalized, Short (c)	AE	7A	RX	R1,D2(X2,B2)
Add Unnormalized, Long (c)	AWR	2E	RR	R1,R2
Add Unnormalized, Long (c)	AW	6E	RX	R1,D2(X2,B2)
Add Unnormalized, Short (c)	AUR	3E	RR	R1,R2
Add Unnormalized, Short (c)	AU	7E	RX	R1,D2(X2,B2)
Compare, Long (c)	CDR	29	RR	R1,R2
Compare, Long (c)	CD	69	RX	R1,D2(X2,B2)
Compare, Short (c)	CER	39	RR	R1,R2
Compare, Short (c)	CE	79	RX	R1,D2(X2,B2)
Divide, Long	DDR	2D	RR	R1,R2
Divide, Long	DD	6D	RX	R1,D2(X2,B2)
Divide, Short	DER	3D	RR	R1,R2
Divide, Short	DE	7D	RX	R1,D2(X2,B2)
Halve, Long	HDR	24	RR	R1,R2
Halve, Short	HER	34	RR	R1,R2
Load, Long	LDR	28	RR	R1,R2
Load, Long	LD	68	RX	R1,D2(X2,B2)
Load, Short	LER	38	RR	R1,R2
Load, Short	LE	78	RX	R1,D2(X2,B2)
Load and Test, Long (c)	LTDR	22	RR	R1,R2
Load and Test, Short (c)	LTER	32	RR	R1,R2
Load Complement, Long (c)	LCDR	23	RR	R1,R2
Load Complement, Short (c)	LCER	33	RR	R1,R2
Load Negative, Long (c)	LNDR	21	RR	R1,R2
Load Negative, Short (c)	LNER	31	RR	R1,R2
Load Positive, Long (c)	LPDR	20	RR	R1,R2
Load Positive, Short (c)	LPER	30	RR	R1,R2
Load Rounded, Extended to Long (x)	LRDR	25	RR	R1,R2
Load Rounded, Long to Short (x)	LRER	35	RR	R1,R2
Multiply, Extended (x)	MXR	26	RR	R1,R2
Multiply, Long	MDR	2C	RR	R1,R2
Multiply, Long	MD	6C	RX	R1,D2(X2,B2)
Multiply, Long to Extended (x)	MXDR	27	RR	R1,R2
Multiply, Long to Extended (x)	MXD	67	RX	R1,D2(X2,B2)
Multiply, Short to Long	MER	3C	RR	R1,R2
Multiply, Short to Long	ME	7C	RX	R1,D2(X2,B2)
Store, Long	STD	60	RX	R1,D2(X2,B2)
Store, Short	STE	70	RX	R1,D2(X2,B2)
Subtract Normalized, Extended (c,x)	SXR	37	RR	R1,R2
Subtract Normalized, Long (c)	SDR	2B	RR	R1,R2
Subtract Normalized, Long (c)	SD	6B	RX	R1,D2(X2,B2)
Subtract Normalized, Short (c)	SER	3B	RR	R1,R2
Subtract Normalized, Short (c)	SE	7B	RX	R1,D2(X2,B2)
Subtract Unnormalized, Long (c)	SWR	2F	RR	R1,R2
Subtract Unnormalized, Long (c)	SW	6F	RX	R1,D2(X2,B2)
Subtract Unnormalized, Short (c)	SUR	3F	RR	R1,R2
Subtract Unnormalized, Short (c)	SU	7F	RX	R1,D2(X2,B2)

c. Condition code is set
n. New condition code is loaded
p. Privileged instruction
s. Semiprivileged instruction
x. Extended-precision floating-point

CONDITION CODES

Condition Code Setting	0	1	2	3
Mask Bit Value	8	4	2	1
General Instructions				
Add, Add Halfword	zero	<zero	>zero	overflow
Add Logical	zero, no carry	not zero, no carry	zero, carry	not zero, carry
AND	zero	not zero	—	—
Compare, Compare Halfword	equal	1st op low	1st op high	—
Compare and Swap/Double	equal	not equal	—	—
Compare Logical	equal	1st op low	1st op high	—
Exclusive OR	zero	not zero	—	—
Insert Characters under Mask	all zeros	1st bit one	1st bit zero	—
Load and Test	zero	<zero	>zero	—
Load Complement	zero	<zero	>zero	overflow
Load Negative	zero	<zero	—	—
Load Positive	zero	—	>zero	overflow
Move Long	length equal	length low	length high	overlap
OR	zero	not zero	—	—
Shift Left Double/Single	zero	<zero	>zero	overflow
Shift Right Double/Single	zero	<zero	>zero	—
Store Clock	set	not set	error	not oper
Subtract, Subtract Halfword	zero	<zero	>zero	overflow
Subtract Logical	—	not zero, no carry	zero, carry	not zero, carry
Test and Set	1st bit zero	1st bit one	—	—
Test under Mask	all zeros	mixed	—	all ones
Translate and Test	all zeros	incomplete	complete	—
Decimal Instructions				
Add Decimal	zero	<zero	>zero	overflow
Compare Decimal	equal	1st op low	1st op high	—
Edit, Edit and Mark	zero	<zero	>zero	—
Shift and Round Decimal	zero	<zero	>zero	overflow
Subtract Decimal	zero	<zero	>zero	overflow
Zero and Add	zero	<zero	>zero	overflow
Floating-Point Instructions				
Add Normalized	zero	<zero	>zero	—
Add Unnormalized	zero	<zero	>zero	—
Compare	equal	1st op low	1st op high	—
Load and Test	zero	<zero	>zero	—
Load Complement	zero	<zero	>zero	—
Load Negative	zero	<zero	—	—
Load Positive	zero	—	>zero	—
Subtract Normalized	zero	<zero	>zero	—
Subtract Unnormalized	zero	<zero	>zero	—
I/O Instructions				
Clear Channel	reset signaled	—	chan busy	not oper
Clear I/O	no operation in progress	CSW stored	chan busy	not oper
Halt Device	interruption pending/busy	CSW stored	channel working	not oper

CONDITION CODES (Cont'd)

Condition Code Setting	0	1	2	3
Mask Bit Value	8	4	2	1
Halt I/O	interruption pending	CSW stored	burst op stopped	not oper
Resume I/O	successful	—	—	not oper
Start I/O, SIOF	successful	CSW stored	busy	not oper
Store Channel ID	ID stored	CSW stored	busy	not oper
Test Channel	available	interruption pending	burst mode	not oper
Test I/O	available	CSW stored	busy	not oper
Control Instructions				
Connect/Disconnect Channel Set	successful	connected to another CPU	—	not oper
Insert Address Space Control	zero	one	—	—
Load Address Space Parameters	parameters loaded	pri not available	sec not avail or not auth	space-sw event
Load Real Address	translation available	ST entry invalid	PT entry invalid	length violation
Move to Primary/ Secondary	len $\leq$ 256	—	—	len > 256
Move with Key	len $\leq$ 256	—	—	len > 256
Reset Reference Bit/ Extended	R=0, C=0	R=0, C=1	R=1, C=0	R=1, C=1
Set Clock	set	secure	—	not oper
Signal Processor	accepted	stat stored	busy	not oper
Test Block	usable	not usable	—	—
Test Protection	can fetch, can store	can fetch, can't store	can't fetch, can't store	translation not avail

SOME EDIT AND EDMK PATTERN CHARACTERS (hex)

20—digit selector
21—start of significance
22—field separator

40—blank
4B—period
5B—dollar sign

5C—asterisk
6B—comma
C3D9—CR

ASSEMBLER INSTRUCTIONS†

FUNCTION	MNEMONIC	MEANING
Data definition	DC	Define constant
	DS	Define storage
	CCW	Define channel command word
Program sectioning and linking	START	Start assembly
	CSECT	Identify control section
	DSECT	Identify dummy section
	DXD*	Define external dummy section
	CXD*	Cumulative length of external dummy section
	COM	Identify blank common control section
	ENTRY	Identify entry-point symbol
	EXTRN	Indentify external symbol
	WXTRN	Identify weak external symbol
Base register assignment	USING	Use base address register
	DROP	Drop base address register
Control of listings	TITLE	Identify assembly output
	EJECT	Start new page
	SPACE	Space listing
	PRINT	Print optional data
Program Control	ICTL	Input format control
	ISEQ	Input sequence checking
	PUNCH	Punch a card
	REPRO	Reproduce following card
	ORG	Set location counter
	EQU	Equate symbol
	OPSYN*	Equate operation code
	PUSH*	Save current PRINT or USING status
	POP*	Restore PRINT or USING status
	LTORG	Begin literal pool
	CNOP	Conditional no operation
	COPY	Copy predefined source coding
	END	End assembly
Macro definition	MACRO	Macro definition header
	MNOTE	Request for error message
	MEXIT	Macro definition exit
	MEND	Macro definition trailer
Conditional assembly	ACTR	Conditional assembly loop counter
	AGO	Unconditional branch
	AIF	Conditional branch
	ANOP	Assembly no operation
	GBLA	Define global SETA symbol
	GBLB	Define global SETB symbol
	GBLC	Define global SETC symbol
	LCLA	Define local SETA symbol
	LCLB	Define local SETB symbol
	LCLC	Define local SETC symbol
	SETA	Set arithmetic variable symbol
	SETB	Set binary variable symbol
	SETC	Set character variable symbol

†Source: GC33-4010 for OS/VS, VM/370, and DOS/VSE.
*OS/VS and VM/370 only.

EXTENDED MNEMONIC INSTRUCTIONS†

USE	EXTENDED CODE* (RX OR RR)	MEANING	MACHINE INSTR.* (RX OR RR)
General	B or BR	Unconditional Branch	BC or BCR 15,
	NOP or NOPR	No Operation	BC or BCR 0,
After Compare Instructions (A:B)	BH or BHR	Branch on A High	BC or BCR 2,
	BL or BLR	Branch on A Low	BC or BCR 4,
	BE or BER	Branch on A Equal B	BC or BCR 8,
	BNH or BNHR	Branch on A Not High	BC or BCR 13,
	BNL or BNLR	Branch on A Not Low	BC or BCR 11,
	BNE or BNER	Branch on A Not Equal B	BC or BCR 7,
After Arithmetic Instructions	BO or BOR	Branch on Overflow	BC or BCR 1,
	BNO or BNOR	Branch on No Overflow	BC or BCR 14,
	BP or BPR	Branch on Plus	BC or BCR 2,
	BM or BMR	Branch on Minus	BC or BCR 4,
	BNP or BNPR	Branch on Not Plus	BC or BCR 13,
	BNM or BNMR	Branch on Not Minus	BC or BCR 11,
	BNZ or BNZR	Branch on Not Zero	BC or BCR 7,
	BZ or BZR	Branch on Zero	BC or BCR 8,
After Test under Mask Instruction	BO or BOR	Branch if Ones	BC or BCR 1,
	BM or BMR	Branch if Mixed	BC or BCR 4,
	BZ or BZR	Branch if Zeros	BC or BCR 8,
	BNO or BNOR	Branch if Not Ones	BC or BCR 14,
	BNM or BNMR	Branch if Not Mixed	BC or BCR 11,
	BNZ or BNZR	Branch if Not Zeros	BC or BCR 7,

†Source: GC33-4010 for OS/VS, VM/370 and DOS/VSE.
*Second operand, not shown is D2(X2,B2) for RX format and R2 for RR format.

CNOP ALIGNMENT

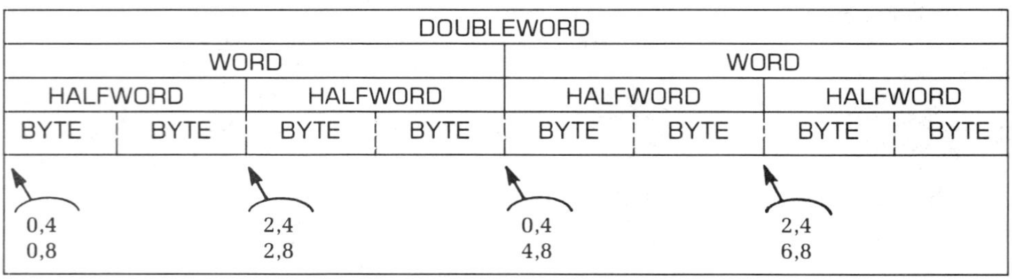

SUMMARY OF CONSTANTS†

TYPE	IMPLIED LENGTH, BYTES	ALIGNMENT	FORMAT	TRUNCATION/ PADDING
C	—	Byte	Characters	right
X	—	Byte	Hexadecimal digits	left
B	—	Byte	Binary digits	left
F	4	Word	Fixed-point binary	left
H	2	Halfword	Fixed-point binary	left
E	4	Word	Short floating-point	right
D	8	Doubleword	Long floating-point	right
L	16	Doubleword	Extended floating-point	right
P	—	Byte	Packed decimal	left
Z	—	Byte	Zoned decimal	left
A	4	Word	Value of address	left
Y	2	Halfword	Value of address	left
S	2	Halfword	Address in base-displacement form	—
V	4	Word	Externally defined address value	left
Q*	4	Word	Symbol naming a DXD or DSECT	left

†Source: GC33-4010 for OS/VS, VM/370, and DOS/VSE.
*OS/VS and VM/370 only.

I/O COMMAND CODES

Standard Command-Code Assignments (CCW bits 0-7)

x x x x	0 0 00	Invalid Command	mmmm	0100	Sense
mmmm	mm01	Write	0 0 0 0	0100	—Basic Sense
mmmm	mm10	Read	1 1 1 0	0100	—Sense ID
0 0 0 0	0 0 10	—Read IPL	x x x x	1000	Transfer in Channel
mmmm	mm11	Control	mmmm	1100	Read Backward
0 0 0 0	0 0 11	—Control No Operation			

x—Bit ignored   m—Modifier bit for specific type of I/O device

Standard Meanings of Bits of First Sense Byte

BIT	DESIGNATION	BIT	DESIGNATION
0	Command reject	4	Data check
1	Intervention required	5	Overrun
2	Bus-out check	6	(Device—dependent)
3	Equipment check	7	(Device—dependent)

Console Printer Channel Commands

Write, No Carrier Return	01	Sense	04
Write, Auto Carrier Return	09	Audible Alarm	0B
Read Inquiry	0A	No Operation	03

Direct Access Storage Devices

Use this chart to find the proper column in the DASD Channel Commands table (Page) and to find order numbers for DASD reference manuals. See DASD manuals for restrictions.

CONTROLLER	CKD DEVICES 2305	3330 3333	3340 3344	3350	3375	3380	FBA DEVICES 3310	3370	CONTROLLER MANUAL
DASD-A1							col6		GA26-1660
DASD-A4			col2						GA33-1526
DASD-A6			col2						GA33-1566
DASD-A7								col6	GA33-1539
DDA-30		col2							GA33-1510
DDA-40			col2						GA33-1506
IFA		col2	col2						GA24-3632
ISC		col2	col2	col2					GA26-1620
ISC-SA		col2		col2					GA32-0036
2835	col1								GA26-1589
3830-1		col2*							GA26-1592
3830-2		col2	col2	col2					GA26-1617
3830-3		col2		col2					GA32-0036
3880-1		col2	col2	col2	col4			col6	GA26-1661
3880-2		col2	col2	col2	col4	col4		col6	GA26-1661
3880-3						col4			GA26-1661
3880-4					col4			col6	GA26-1661
3880-11 (ND)		col2		col2					GA32-0061
3880-11 (PD)				col2					GA32-0061
3880-11 (PP)				col3					GA32-0061
3880-11						col5			GA32-0067
Device Manual	GA26 1589	GA26 1615	GA26 1619	GA26 1638	GA26 1666	GA26 1664	GA26 1660	GA26 1657	

DASD-A1 = 4321/4331/4361 DASD Adapter for 3310
DASD-A4 = 4321/4331 DASD Adapter for 3340/3344
DASD-A6 = 4361 DASD Adapter for 3340/3344
DASD-A7 = 4321/4331/4361 DASD Adapter for 3370
DDA-30 = S/370 125-0, -2 Direct Disk Attachment for 3330/3333
DDA-40 = S/370 115-0, -2, 125-0, -2 Direct Disk Attachment for 3340/3344
IFA = S/370 135, 135-3, 138 Integrated File Adapter
ISC = Integrated storage controller
ISC-SA = Integrated storage controller with staging adapter
ND = Nonpaging director
PD = Paging director, direct mode
PP = Paging director, paging mode
* = 3333 does not attach to 3830-1

I/O COMMAND CODES (Cont'd)

DASD Channel Commands

CHANNEL COMMAND	HEX CODE	2305	3330 3340 3350	PAGE SWAP 3350	3375 3380	DATA CACHE 3380	FBA 3310 3370	TYPICAL TRANSFER COUNT
		1	2	3	4	5	6	
Control								
No Operation	03	X	X	X	X	X	X	None
Seek	07	X	X	X	X	X		6
Seek Cylinder	0B	X	X	X	X	X		6
Space Count	0F	X	X		X	X		3
Recalibrate (No-Op on 2305-1, -2)	13	X	X		X	X		None
Restore (executed as No-Op)	17	X	X		X	X		None
Seek Head	1B	X	X	X	X	X		6
Set File Mask	1F	X	X		X	X		1
Set Sector (3340 RPS is optional)	23	X	X	X	X	X		1
Vary Sensing	27	X						1
Orient (No-Op on 2305-2)	2B	X						None
Set High Performance Storage Limits	3B					X		10
Locate	43						X	8
Locate Record	47				(a)			16
Suspend Multipath Reconnection	5B				(b)	X		None
Define Extent	63				(a)	X	X	16
Set Subsystem Mode	87					X		2
Set Paging Parameters	8B			X				10
Discard Block	8F			X				2 + (5 × n)
Set Path Group ID	AF				(b)	X		12
Search								
Search Key Equal (*A9)	29	X	X		X	X		KL
Search ID Equal (*B1)	31	X	X	X	X	X		5
Search Home Address Equal (*B9)	39	X	X		X	X		4
Search Key High (*C9)	49	X	X		X	X		KL
Search ID High (*D1)	51	X	X		X	X		5
Search Key Equal or High (*E9)	69	X	X		X	X		KL
Search ID Equal or High (*F1)	71	X	X		X	X		5
Read								
Read Initial Program Load	02	X	X		X	X	X	DL or 512
Read Data (*86)	06	X	X	X	X	X		DL
Read Key & Data (*8E)	0E	X	X		X	X		KL + DL
Read Count (*92)	12	X	X		X	X		8
Read Record Zero (*96)	16	X	X		X	X		8 + KL + DL
Read Home Address (*9A)	1A	X	X		X	X		5
Read Count Key & Data (*9E)	1E	X	X		X	X		8 + KL + DL
Read Sector (3340 RPS is optional)	22	X	X		X	X		1
Read	42						X	512 × n
Read Multiple Count Key & Data	5E		(c,d)		X	X		n × (8 + KL + DL)
		1	2	3	4	5	6	

a Speed-matching-buffer feature
b Dynamic path switching (3380-AA4 only)
c Not valid for 3330 or 3333 on ISC-SA or 3830-1; DDA-40, IFA, ISC and 3830-2, -3 require 3344/3350 microcode
d Not valid on DDA-30
e Not valid on IFA, ISC-SA or 3330-1; not valid on 3330, 3333, 3340, or 3344 devices
f Without string-switch, executed as Basic Sense on DASD-A1, -A4, -A6, -A7 (for Unconditional Reserve, see note g)
g Not valid on DDA-30, DDA-40, DASD-A4, -A6
h String-switching feature
j Channel-switching feature
k Valid only for 3880-11 paging director
m Valid only for 3880-1, -2, -11
* Multi-track command codes (standard)
\# Also called "Read Diagnostic Status 1"

I/O COMMAND CODES (Cont'd)

DASD Channel Commands

CHANNEL COMMAND	HEX CODE	2305	3330 3340 3350	PAGE SWAP 3350	3375 3380	DATA CACHE 3380	FBA 3310 3370	TYPICAL TRANSFER COUNT
		1	2	3	4	5	6	
Write								
Write Special Count Key & Data	01	X	X					8+KL+DL
Write Data	05	X	X	X	X	X		DL
Write Key & Data	0D	X	X		X	X		KL+DL
Erase	11	X	X		X	X		8+KL+DL
Write Record Zero	15	X	X		X	X		8+KL+DL
Write Home Address	19	X	X		X	X		5, 7, or 11
Write Count Key & Data	1D	X	X		X	X		8+KL+DL
Write	41						X	512 × n
Write Update Data	85				(a)			DL
Write Update Key & Data	8D				(a)			KL+DL
Write Count Key & Data Next Track	9D				(a)			8+KL+DL
Sense								
Basic Sense	04	X	X	X	X	X	X	24
Unconditional Reserve (e,f,g)	14		(h,j)		(b,h,j)	X	(h,j)	24
Read Buffered Log	24	X						128
Sense Path Group ID	34				(b)	X		12
Sense Subsystem Status	54		(k)			X		40
Read Device Characteristics	64						X	32
Sense Subsystem Counts	74		(k)			X		80
Device Release (d,f)	94	(j)	(h,j)		(b,h,j)	X	(h,j)	24
Read and Reset Buffered Log (d)	A4		X		X	X	X	24 or 32
Device Reserve (d,f)	B4	(j)	(h,j)		(b,h,j)	X	(h,j)	24
Sense ID (c,d)	E4		X	X	X	X	X	7
Diagnostic								
Diagnostic Write Home Address	09				X	X		27 or 28
Diagnostic Read Home Address	0A				X	X		27 or 28
Diagnostic Sense # (g)	44	X	X					16 or 512
Diagnostic Load (g)	53	X	X					1
Diagnostic Write (g)	73	X	X					8 or 512
Diagnostic Sense/Read	C4		(m)		X	X	X	variable
Diagnostic Control	F3						X	4+n
		1	2	3	4	5	6	

a Speed-matching-buffer feature
b Dynamic path switching (3380-AA4 only)
c Not valid for 3330 or 3333 on ISC-SA or 3830-1; DDA-40, IFA, ISC and 3830-2, -3 require 3344/3350 microcode
d Not valid on DDA-30
e Not valid on IFA, ISC-SA or 3330-1; not valid on 3330, 3333, 3340, or 3344 devices
f Without string-switch, executed as Basic Sense on DASD-A1, -A4, -A6, -A7 (for Unconditional Reserve, see note g)
g Not valid on DDA-30, DDA-40, DASD-A4, -A6
h String-switching feature
j Channel-switching feature
k Valid only for 3880-11 paging director
m Valid only for 3880-1, -2, -11
* Multi-track command codes (standard)
# Also called "Read Diagnostic Status 1"

I/O COMMAND CODES (Cont'd)

Card Reader and Card Punch Channel Commands

3504, 3505 Card Readers/3525 Card Punch (GA21-9124)

COMMAND	BINARY		HEX	BIT MEANINGS	
Sense	0000	0100	04	SS	Stacker
Feed, Select Stacker	SS10	F011		00	1
Read Only*	11D0	F010		01/10	2
Diagnostic Read (invalid for 3504)	1101	0010	D2	F	Format Mode
Read, Feed, Select Stacker*	SSD0	F010		0	Unformatted
Write RCE Format*	0001	0001	11	1	Formatted
3504, 3505 only				D	Data Mode
Write OMR Format†	0011	0001	31	0	1—EBCDIC
				1	2—Card image
3525 only					
Write, Feed, Select Stacker	SSD0	0001		L	Line Position
Print Line*	LLLL	L101		(5-bit binary value)	

*Special Feature on 3525. †Special feature.

Magnetic-Tape Channel Commands (Cont'd)

Use column A, B, C, D, or E.

A = 3410/3411 (GA32-0022)
B = 3420-3, -5, -7 (GA32-0020)
C = 3420-4, -6, -8 (GA32-0021)
D = 3430 (GA32-0076)
E = 8809 (GA26-1659)

		A B C D E			A B C D E
No Operation	03	X X X X X	Modeset-1 800/Odd/Y/N	93	1 1 3 .
Rewind	07	X X X X X	Set High Spd/Long Gap	93	. X
Rewind Unload	0F	X X X X X	Data Security Erase	97	X X X X X
Modeset-1 200/Odd/Y/N	13	1 2 3 .	Modeset-1 800 Evn/N/N	A3	1 1 3 . .
Set Long Gap	13	. X	Modeset-1 800/Evn/N/Y	AB	1 1 3 . .
Erase Gap	17	X X X X X	Modeset-1 800/Odd/N/N	B3	1 1 3 . .
Request Track-In-Error	1B	X X X X .	Modeset-1 800/Odd/N/Y	BB	1 1 3 . .

X = Valid command
. = Invalid command
Blank = N/A
1 = No action occurs unless the 7-track feature is installed.
2 = No action occurs unless the 7-track feature is installed; if installed, density is set to 200 BPI by 3803-2 Tape Control, 556 BPI by 3803-1.
3 = Valid command, but no action occurs.
4 = No action occurs unless the 800 BPI density feature is installed.
5 = No action occurs unless the 1600 BPI density feature is installed.
6 = Requires two-channel switch feature.

Modeset-1 sets: density (200/556/800 BPI)/parity (even/odd)/data converter (Y = on/N = off)/translator (Y = on/N = off) for 7-track drives.
Modeset-2 sets: density (800/1600/6250 BPI) for 9-track drives.

Magnetic-Tape Channel Commands

Use column A, B, C, D, or E.

A = 3410/3411 (GA32-0022)
B = 3420-3, -5, -7 (GA32-0020)
C = 3420-4, -6, -8 (GA32-0021)
D = 3430 (GA32-0076)
E = 8809 (GA26-1659)

Command	Code	A	B	C	D	E
Write Tape Mark	1F	X	X	X	X	X
Modeset-1 200/Evn/N/N	23	1	2	3	.	
Set Normal Gap	23				.	X
Backspace Block	27	X	X	X	X	X
Modeset-1 200/Evn/N/Y	2B	1	2	3	.	.
Backspace File	2F	X	X	X	X	X
Modeset-1 200/Odd/N/N	33	1	2	3	.	
Set High Spd/Norm Gap	33				.	X
Forward Space Block	37	X	X	X	X	X
Modeset-1 200/Odd/N/Y	3B	1	2	3	.	.
Forward Space File	3F	X	X	X	X	X
Modeset-1 556/Odd/Y/N	53	1	1	3	.	
Set Low Spd/Long Gap	53				.	X
Modeset-1 556/Evn/N/N	63	1	1	3	.	
Set Low Spd/Norm Gap	63				.	X
Modeset-1 556/Evn/N/Y	6B	1	1	3	.	.
Modeset-1 556/Odd/N/N	73	1	1	3	.	.
Modeset-1 556/Odd/N/Y	7B	1	1	3	.	.
Set Low Speed	83	.	.	.	.	X
Modeset-2 1600 BPI PE	C3	4	4	5	X	3
Modeset-2 800 BPI NRZI	CB	4	4	3	.	.
Modeset-2 6250 BPI GCR	D3	.	.	5	X	.
Set High Speed	E3	.	.	.	.	X
Write	01	X	X	X	X	X
Read	02	X	X	X	X	X
Read Backward	0C	X	X	X	X	.
Basic Sense	04	X	X	X	X	X
Read/Reset Buffered Log	A4	.	.	.	.	X
Release	D4	.	6	6	.	.
Sense ID	E4	.	.	.	X	X
Reserve	F4	.	6	6	.	.
Diagnostic Mode Set	0B	.	X	X	.	.
Set Diagnose	4B	.	X	X	X	.
Loop Write-To-Read	8B	.	X	X	X	X

X = Valid command
. = Invalid command
Blank = N/A
1 = No action occurs unless the 7-track feature is installed.
2 = No action occurs unless the 7-track feature is installed; if installed, density is set to 200 BPI by 3803-2 Tape Control, 556 BPI by 3803-1.
3 = Valid command, but no action occurs.
4 = No action occurs unless the 800 BPI density feature is installed.
5 = No action occurs unless the 1600 BPI density feature is installed.
6 = Requires two-channel switch feature.

Modeset-1 sets: density (200/556/800 BPI)/parity (even/odd)/data converter (Y = on/N = off)/translator (Y = on/N = off) for 7-track drives.
Modeset-2 sets: density (800/1600/6250 BPI) for 9-track drives.

I/O COMMAND CODES (Cont'd)

Printer Channel Commands

COMMANDS VALID FOR ALL PRINTERS
(Except 3800-3 when in Page Mode)

Command	Code
No Operation	03
Space 1 Line Immediate	0B
Space 2 Lines Immediate	13
Space 3 Lines Immediate	1B
Block Data Check	73
Allow Data Check	7B
Skip to Channel 1 Immediate	8B
Skip to Channel 2 Immediate	93
Skip to Channel 3 Immediate	9B
Skip to Channel 4 Immediate	A3
Skip to Channel 5 Immediate	AB
Skip to Channel 6 Immediate	B3
Skip to Channel 7 Immediate	BB
Skip to Channel 8 Immediate	C3
Skip to Channel 9 Immediate	CB
Skip to Channel 10 Immediate	D3
Skip to Channel 11 Immediate	DB
Skip to Channel 12 Immediate	E3
Write Without Spacing	01
Write and Space 1 Line	09
Write and Space 2 Lines	11
Write and Space 3 Lines	19
Write and Skip to Channel 1	89
Write and Skip to Channel 2	91
Write and Skip to Channel 3	99
Write and Skip to Channel 4	A1
Write and Skip to Channel 5	A9
Write and Skip to Channel 6	B1
Write and Skip to Channel 7	B9
Write and Skip to Channel 8	C1
Write and Skip to Channel 9	C9
Write and Skip to Channel 10	D1
Write and Skip to Channel 11	D9
Write and Skip to Channel 12	E1
Basic Sense	04

3800-3 PAGE MODE COMMANDS
(See Note X)

Command	Code
No Operation	03
Load Font Index	0F
Load Font Control	1F
Load Font	2F
Execute Order Any State	33
Load Font Equivalence	3F
Delete Font	4F
Begin Page Segment	5F
Delete Page Segment	6F
Include Page Segment	7F
Execute Order Home State	8F
Load Copy Control	9F
Begin Page	AF
End Page	BF
Load Page Description	CF
Begin Overlay	DF
Delete Overlay	EF
Write Factored Text Control	0D
Write Text	2D
Write Image Control	3D
Write Image	4D
End	5D
Load Page Position	6D
Basic Sense	04
Sense Intermediate Buffer	14
Sense Error Log	24
Sense ID	E4

3800-1 Reference: GA26-1635
3800-3 Reference: GA32-0050

Note X: Other 3800-3 commands are rejected with command retry; the retry will succeed because Page Mode will have been reset.

Note Y: For 3800-3 only, the Set Home State (97) command will be rejected with command retry; the retry will succeed because Page Mode will have been set.

I/O COMMAND CODES (Cont'd)

Printer Channel Commands (Cont'd)

IMPACT PRINTERS—ADDITIONAL COMMANDS

Printer	Column	Reference
1403-N1	A	GA24-3312
3203-1, -2	B	GA33-1515
3203-4	C	GA33,1515
3203-5	C	GA33-1529
3211	C	GA24-3543
4248 ‹3211 mode›	C	GA24 3927
3262-1, -11	D	GA24 3733
3262-5 ‹3262-1 mode›	D	GA24 3036
4245	D	GA33 1541
3262-5 ‹4248 mode›	E	GA24 3936
4248 ‹native mode›	E	GA24 3927

Use column A, B, C, D, or E		A	B	C	D	E
Unfold	23	.		X	X	X
Execute Order	33	.		.	.	X
Fold	43	.	.	X	X	X
Advance to End of Sheet	5B	.	X	.	.	.
Load Forms Control Buffer	63	.	X	X	X	X
Raise Cover	6B	.		1	2	
Signal Attention	6B	.	.			3
Skip to Channel 0 Immediate	83	.	.	4	.	2
Clear Printer	87	.	.	.	X	X
UCS Gate Load	EB	X	2	.	.	.
Load UCS Buffer and Fold	F3	X	X	.	.	
Verify Band ID	F3			.	.	X
Load UCS Buffer (No Fold)	FB	X	X	X	X	
Verify Band ID	FB					X
Release CU and Device	14	5	.	.	.	
Sense Intermediate Buffer	14		.	.	.	X
Release CU, Reserve Device	34	5	.	.	.	.
Reserve CU, Release Device	54	5	.	.	.	.
Reserve CU and Device	74	5	.	.	.	.
Release Device	94	5	.	.	.	.
Reserve Device	B4	5	.	.	.	.
Release CU	D4	5	.	.	.	.
Sense ID	E4		X	.	X	X
Reserve CU	F4	5		.	.	.
Read Band ID	0A	.	.			X
Diagnostic Read PLB	02	X		X	6	2
Diagnostic Write	05	7	.	8	6	2
Diagnostic Check Read	06	X	.	X	X	2
Diagnostic Gate	07	.	.	X	X	2
Diagnostic Read UCS Buffer	0A	.	.	X	X	
Diagnostic Read FCB	12	.	.	X	X	X

X = Valid; = Invalid; Blank = N/A
1 = No action occurs (except 3211)
2 = No action occurs.
3 = No action occurs (except 4248).
4 = 3211 only (no action occurs on 4248 ‹3211 mode› and 3203-4).
5 = Two-channel switch feature only.
6 = No action occurs (except 4245).
7 = 1403-N1 also uses command codes 0D, 15, 1D, 8D, 95, 9D, A5, AD, B5, BD, C5, CD, D5, DD, and E5.
8 = 3211 and 4248 ‹3211 mode› only.

I/O COMMAND CODES (Cont'd)

3800-1, 3—ADDITIONAL COMMANDS
(Except 3800-3 when in Page Mode; see Note Y)

End of Transmission	07
Mark Form	17
Load Copy Number	23
Execute Order Any State	33
Initialize Printer	37
Load Forms Overlay Seq Control	43
Select Translate Table 0	47
Load Writable Char Gen Module	53
Select Translate Table 1	57
Load Forms Control Buffer	63
Select Translate Table 2	67
Select Translate Table 3	77
Load Translate Table	83
Clear Printer	87
Load Graphic Char Modification	25
Load Copy Modification	35
Sense Intermediate Buffer	14
Sense Error Log	24
Sense ID	E4

CODE TABLES

DEC.	HEX	INST. (RR)	GRAPHICS AND CONTROLS BCDIC	EBCDIC(1)	ASCII	7-TRACK TAPE BCDIC(2)	CARD CODE EBCDIC	BINARY
0	00			NUL	NUL		12-0-1-8-9	0000 0000
1	01			SOH	SOH		12-1-9	0000 0001
2	02			STX	STX		12-2-9	0000 0010
3	03			ETX	ETX		12-3-9	0000 0011
4	04	SPM		SEL	EOT		12-4-9	0000 0100
5	05	BALR		HT	ENQ		12-5-9	0000 0101
6	06	BCTR		RNL	ACK		12-6-9	0000 0110
7	07	BCR		DEL	BEL		12-7-9	0000 0111
8	08	SSK		GE	BS		12-8-9	0000 1000
9	09	ISK		SPS	HT		12-1-8-9	0000 1001
10	0A	SVC		RPT	LF		12-2-8-9	0000 1010
11	0B			VT	VT		12-3-8-9	0000 1011
12	0C			FF	FF		12-4-8-9	0000 1100
13	0D	BASR		CR	CR		12-5-8-9	0000 1101
14	0E	MVCL		SO	SO		12-6-8-9	0000 1110
15	0F	CLCL		SI	SI		12-7-8-9	0000 1111
16	10	LPR		DLE	DLE		12-11-1-8-9	0001 0000
17	11	LNR		DC1	DC1		11-1-9	0001 0001
18	12	LTR		DC2	DC2		11-2-9	0001 0010
19	13	LCR		DC3	DC3		11-3-9	0001 0011
20	14	NR		RES/ENP	DC4		11-4-9	0001 0100
21	15	CLR		NL	NAK		11-5-9	0001 0101
22	16	OR		BS	SYN		11-6-9	0001 0110
23	17	XR		POC	ETB		11-7-9	0001 0111
24	18	LR		CAN	CAN		11-8-9	0001 1000
25	19	CR		EM	EM		11-1-8-9	0001 1001
26	1A	AR		UBS	SUB		11-2-8-9	0001 1010
27	1B	SR		CU1	ESC		11-3-8-9	0001 1011
28	1C	MR		IFS	FS		11-4-8-9	0001 1100
29	1D	DR		IGS	GS		11-5-8-9	0001 1101
30	1E	ALR		IRS	RS		11-6-8-9	0001 1110
31	1F	SLR		ITB/IUS	US		11-7-8-9	0001 1111
32	20	LPDR		DS	SP		11-0-1-8-9	0010 0000
33	21	LNDR		SOS	!		0-1-9	0010 0001
34	22	LTDR		FS	"		0-2-9	0010 0010
35	23	LCDR		WUS	#		0-3-9	0010 0011
36	24	HDR		BYP/INP	$		0-4-9	0010 0100
37	25	LRDR		LF	%		0-5-9	0010 0101
38	26	MXR		ETB	&		0-6-9	0010 0110
39	27	MXDR		ESC	'		0-7-9	0010 0111
40	28	LDR		SA	(		0-8-9	0010 1000
41	29	CDR		SFE	)		0-1-8-9	0010 1001
42	2A	ADR		SM/SW	*		0-2-8-9	0010 1010
43	2B	SDR		CSP	+		0-3-8-9	0010 1011

1. Two columns of EBCDIC graphics are shown. The first gives IBM standard U.S. bit pattern assignments. The second shows the T-11 and TN text printing chains (120 graphics.)
2. Add C (check bit) for odd or even parity as needed, except as noted.
3. For even parity use CA.
Note: This character is an EBCDIC superscript character.

CODE TABLES (Cont'd)

DEC.	HEX	INST. (RR)	GRAPHICS AND CONTROLS BCDIC	EBCDIC(1)	ASCII	7-TRACK TAPE BCDIC(2)	CARD CODE EBCDIC	BINARY
44	2C	MDR		MFA	,		0-4-8-9	0010 1100
45	2D	DDR		ENQ	-		0-5-8-9	0010 1101
46	2E	AWR		ACK	.		0-6-8-9	0010 1110
47	2F	SWR		BEL	/		0-7-8-9	0010 1111
48	30	LPER			0		12-11-0-1-8-9	0011 0000
49	31	LNER			1		1-9	0011 0001
50	32	LTER		SYN	2		2-9	0011 0010
51	33	LCER		IR	3		3-9	0011 0011
52	34	HER		PP	4		4-9	0011 0100
53	35	LRER		TRN	5		5-9	0011 0101
54	36	AXR		NBS	6		6-9	0011 0110
55	37	SXR		EOT	7		7-9	0011 0111
56	38	LER		SBS	8		8-9	0011 1000
57	39	CER		IT	9		1-8-9	0011 1001
58	3A	AER		RFF	:		2-8-9	0011 1010
59	3B	SER		CU3	;		3-8-9	0011 1011
60	3C	MER		DC4	<		4-8-9	0011 1100
61	3D	DER		NAK	=		5-8-9	0011 1101
62	3E	AUR			>		6-8-9	0011 1110
63	3F	SUR		SUB	?		7-8-9	0011 1111

1. Two columns of EBCDIC graphics are shown. The first gives IBM standard U.S. bit pattern assignments. The second shows the T-11 and TN text printing chains (120 graphics.)
2. Add C (check bit) for odd or even parity as needed, except as noted.
3. For even parity use CA.
Note: This character is an EBCDIC superscript character.

TWO-CHARACTER BSC DATA LINK CONTROLS

Function	EBCDIC	ASCII
ACK-0	DLE,X'70'	DLE,0
ACK-1	DLE,X'61'	DLE,1
WACK	DLE,X'6B'	DLE,;
RVI	DLE,X'7C'	DLE,<

CODE TABLES (Cont'd)

DEC.	HEX	INST. (RX)	GRAPHICS AND CONTROLS BCDIC	EBCDIC(1)		ASCII	7-TRACK TAPE BCDIC(2)	CARD CODE EBCDIC	BINARY
64	40	STH	SP	SP	SP	@	(3)	no punches	0100 0000
65	41	LA		RSP		A		12-0-1-9	0100 0001
66	42	STC				B		12-0-2-9	0100 0010
67	43	IC				C		12-0-3-9	0100 0011
68	44	EX				D		12-0-4-9	0100 0100
69	45	BAL				E		12-0-5-9	0100 0101
70	46	BCT				F		12-0-6-9	0100 0110
71	47	BC				G		12-0-7-9	0100 0111
72	48	LH				H		12-0-8-9	0100 1000
73	49	CH				I		12-1-8	0100 1001
74	4A	AH		¢	¢	J		12-2-8	0100 1010
75	4B	SH	.	.	.	K	B A 8 2 1	12-3-8	0100 1011
76	4C	MH	¤)	<	<	L	B A 8 4	12-4-8	0100 1100
77	4D	BAS	[	(	(	M	B A 8 4 1	12-5-8	0100 1101
78	4E	CVD	<	+	+	N	B A 8 4 2	12-6-8	0100 1110
79	4F	CVB	‡	|	|	O	B A 8 4 2 1	12-7-8	0100 1111
80	50	ST	&+	&	&	P	B A	12	0101 0000
81	51					Q		12-11-1-9	0101 0001
82	52					R		12-11-2-9	0101 0010
83	53					S		12-11-3-9	0101 0011
84	54	N				T		12-11-4-9	0101 0100
85	55	CL				U		12-11-5-9	0101 0101
86	56	O				V		12-11-6-9	0101 0110
87	57	X				W		12-11-7-9	0101 0111
88	58	L				X		12-11-8-9	0101 1000
89	59	C				Y		11-1-8	0101 1001
90	5A	A		!	!	Z		11-2-8	0101 1010
91	5B	S	$	$	$	[	B 8 2 1	11-3-8	0101 1011
92	5C	M	*	*	*		B 8 4	11-4-8	0101 1100
93	5D	D	]	)	)	[illegible]	B 8 4 1	11-5-8	0101 1101
94	5E	AL	;	;	;	^	B 8 4 2	11-6-8	0101 1110
95	5F	SL	Δ	¬	¬	_	B 8 4 2 1	11-7-8	0101 1111
96	60	STD	-	-	-	`	B	11	0100 0000
97	61		/	/	/	a	A 1	0-1	0110 0001
98	62					b		11-0-2-9	0110 0010
99	63					c		11-0-3-9	0110 0011

CODE TABLES (Cont'd)

DEC.	HEX	INST. (RX)	GRAPHICS AND CONTROLS BCDIC	EBCDIC(1)	ASCII	7-TRACK TAPE BCDIC(2)	CARD CODE EBCDIC	BINARY
100	64				d		11-0-4-9	0110 0100
101	65				e		11-0-5-9	0110 0101
102	66				f		11-0-6-9	0110 0110
103	67	MXD			g		11-0-7-9	0110 0111
104	68	LD			h		11-0-8-9	0110 1000
105	69	CD			i		0-1-8	0110 1001
106	6A	AD		¦	j		12-11	0110 1010
107	6B	SD	,	,	k	A 8 2 1	0-3-8	0110 1011
108	6C	MD	%(	%	l	A 8 4	0-4-8	0110 1100
109	6D	DD	γ	—	m	A 8 4 1	0-5-8	0110 1101
110	6E	AW	\	›	n	A 8 4 2	0-6-8	0110 1110
111	6F	SW	◆	?	o	A 8 4 2 1	0-7-8	0110 1111
112	70	STE			p		12-11-0	0111 0000
113	71				q		12-11-0-1-9	0111 0001
114	72				r		12-11-0-2-9	0111 0010
115	73				s		12-11-0-3-9	0111 0011
116	74				t		12-11-0-4-9	0111 0100
117	75				u		12-11-0-5-9	0111 0101
118	76				v		12-11-0-6-9	0111 0110
119	77				w		12-11-0-7-9	0111 0111
120	78	LE			x		12-11-0-8-9	0111 1000
121	79	CE		'	y		1-8	0111 1001
122	7A	AE	ƀ	:	z	A 2	2-8	0111 1010
123	7B	SE	#=	#	{	8 2 1	3-8	0111 1011
124	7C	ME	@'	@	¦	8 4	4-8	0111 1100
125	7D	DE	:	'	}	8 4 1	5-8	0111 1101
126	7E	AU	>	=	~	8 4 2	6-8	0111 1110
127	7F	SU	✓	"	DEL	8 4 2 1	7-8	0111 1111

CODE TABLES (Cont'd)

DEC.	HEX	INST AND FORMAT	GRAPHICS AND CONTROLS BCDIC	EBCDIC(1)		ASCII	7-TRACK TAPE BCDIC(2)	CARD CODE EBCDIC	BINARY
128	80	SSM S						12-0-1-8	1000 0000
129	81			a	a			12-0-1	1000 0001
130	82	LPSW S		b	b			12-0-2	1000 0010
131	83	Diagnose		c	c			12-0-3	1000 0011
132	84	WRD SI		d	d			12-0-4	1000 0100
133	85	RDD SI		e	e			12-0-5	1000 0101
134	86	BXH RS		f	f			12-0-6	1000 0110
135	87	BXLE RS		g	g			12-0-7	1000 0111
136	88	SRL RS		h	h			12-0-8	1000 1000
137	89	SLL RS		i	i			12-0-9	1000 1001
138	8A	SRA RS						12-0-2-8	1000 1010
139	8B	SLA RS			{			12-0-3-8	1000 1011
140	8C	SRDL RS			≤			12-0-4-8	1000 1100
141	8D	SLDL RS			(See Note			12-0-5-8	1000 1101
142	8E	SRDA RS			+ See Note			12-0-6-8	1000 1110
143	8F	SLDA RS			+			12-0-7-8	1000 1111
144	90	STM RS						12-11-1-8	1001 0000
145	91	TM SI		j	j			12-11-1	1001 0001
146	92	MVI SI		k	k			12-11-2	1001 0010
147	93	TS S		l	l			12-11-3	1001 0011
148	94	NI SI		m	m			12-11-4	1001 0100
149	95	CLI SI		n	n			12-11-5	1001 0101
150	96	OI SI		o	o			12-11-6	1001 0110
151	97	XI SI		p	p			12-11-7	1001 0111
152	98	LM RS		q	q			12-11-8	1001 1000
153	99			r	r			12-11-9	1001 1001
154	9A							12-11-2-8	1001 1010
155	9B				}			12-11-3-8	1001 1011
156	9C	See below			⌑			12-11-4-8	1001 1100
157	9D	See below			) See Note			12-11-5-8	1001 1101
158	9E	See below			±			12-11-6-8	1001 1110
159	9F	See below			■			12-11-7-8	1001 1111
160	A0				° See Note			11-0-1-8	1010 0000
161	A1			~				11-0-1	1010 0001
162	A2			s	s			11-0-2	1010 0010
163	A3			t	t			11-0-3	1010 0011

S Format

9C00 — SIO
9C01 — SIOF
9C02 — RIO
9D00 — TIO
9D01 — CLRIO
9E00 — HIO
9E01 — HDV
9F00 — TCH
9F01 — CLRCH
B200 — CONCS
B201 — DISCS
B202 — STIDP
B203 — STIDC
B204 — SCK
B205 — STCK
B206 — SCKC
B207 — STCKC
B208 — SPT
B209 — STPT
B20A — SPKA
B20B — IPK
B20D — PTLB
B210 — SPX
B211 — STPX
B212 — STAP
B213 — RRB
B218 — PC
B219 — SAC

RRE Format

B221 — IPTE
B223 — IVSK
B224 — IAC
B225 — SSAR
B226 — EPAR
B227 — ESAR
B228 — PT
B229 — ISKE
B22A — RRBE
B22B — SSKE
B22C — TB

SSE Format

E500 — LASP
E501 — TPROT

Note: This character is an EBCDIC superscript character.

CODE TABLES (Cont'd)

DEC.	HEX	INST. AND FORMAT	GRAPHICS AND CONTROLS BCDIC	EBCDIC(1)	ASCII	7-TRACK TAPE BCDIC(2)	CARD CODE EBCDIC	BINARY
164	A4			u u			11-0-4	1010 0100
165	A5			v v			11-0-5	1010 0101
166	A6			w w			11-0-6	1010 0110
167	A7			x x			11-0-7	1010 0111
168	A8			y y			11-0-8	1010 1000
169	A9			z z			11-0-9	1010 1001
170	AA						11-0-2-8	1010 1010
171	AB			└			11-0-3-8	1010 1011
172	AC	STNSM SI		┌			11-0-4-8	1010 1100
173	AD	STOSM SI		[			11-0-5-8	1010 1101
174	AE	SIGP RS		≥			11-0-6-8	1010 1110
175	AF	MC SI		•			11-0-7-8	1010 1111
176	B0			^{0} See Note			12-11-0-1-8	1011 0000
177	B1	LRA RX		^{1} See Note			12-11-0-1	1011 0001
178	B2	See below		^{2} See Note			12-11-0-2	1011 0010
179	B3			^{3} See Note			12-11-0-3	1011 0011
180	B4			^{4} See Note			12-11-0-4	1011 0100
181	B5			^{5} See Note			12-11-0-5	1011 0101
182	B6	STCTL RS		^{6} See Note			12-11-0-6	1011 0110
183	B7	LCTL RS		^{7} See Note			12-11-0-7	1011 0111
184	B8			^{8} See Note			12-11-0-8	1011 1000
185	B9			^{9} See Note			12-11-0-9	1011 1001
186	BA	CS RS					12-11-0-2-8	1011 1010
187	BB	CDS RS		┘			12-11-0-3-8	1011 1011
188	BC			┐			12-11-0-4-8	1011 1100
189	BD	CLM RS		]			12-11-0-5-8	1011 1101
190	BE	STCM RS		≠			12-11-0-6-8	1011 1110
191	BF	ICM RS		—			12-11-0-7-8	1011 1111

S Format

9C00 — SIO
9C01 — SIOF
9C02 — RIO
9D00 — TIO
9D01 — CLRIO
9E00 — HIO
9E01 — HDV
9F00 — TCH
9F01 — CLRCH
B200 — CONCS
B201 — DISCS
B202 — STIDP
B203 — STIDC
B204 — SCK
B205 — STCK
B206 — SCKC
B207 — STCKC
B208 — SPT
B209 — STPT
B20A — SPKA
B20B — IPK
B20D — PTLB
B210 — SPX
B211 — STPX
B212 — STAP
B213 — RRB
B218 — PC
B219 — SAC

RRE Format

B221 — IPTE
B223 — IVSK
B224 — IAC
B225 — SSAR
B226 — EPAR
B227 — ESAR
B228 — PT
B229 — ISKE
B22A — RRBE
B22B — SSKE
B22C — TB

SSE Format

E500 — LASP
E501 — TPROT

Note: This character is an EBCDIC superscript character.

CODE TABLES (Cont'd)

DEC.	HEX	INST. (SS)	GRAPHICS AND CONTROLS BCDIC	EBCDIC(1)	ASCII	7-TRACK TAPE BCDIC(2)	CARD CODE EBCDIC	BINARY
192	C0		?	/		B A 8 2	12-0	1100 0000
193	C1		A	A	A	B A 1	12-1	1100 0001
194	C2		B	B	B	B A 2	12-2	1100 0010
195	C3		C	C	C	B A 2 1	12-3	1100 0011
196	C4		D	D	D	B A 4	12-4	1100 0100
197	C5		E	E	E	B A 4 1	12-5	1100 0101
198	C6		F	F	F	B A 4 2	12-6	1100 0110
199	C7		G	G	G	B A 4 2 1	12-7	1100 0111
200	C8		H	H	H	B A 8	12-8	1100 1000
201	C9		I	I	I	B A 8 1	12-9	1100 1001
202	CA			SHY			12-0-2-8-9	1100 1010
203	CB						12-0-3-8-9	1100 1011
204	CC			⑀			12-0-4-8-9	1100 1100
205	CD						12-0-5-8-9	1100 1101
206	CE			⑂			12-0-6-8-9	1100 1110
207	CF						12-0-7-8-9	1100 1111
208	D0		!	}		B 8 2	11-0	1101 0000
209	D1	MVN	J	J	J	B 1	11-1	1101 0001
210	D2	MVC	K	K	K	B 2	11-2	1101 0010
211	D3	MVZ	L	L	L	B 2 1	11-3	1101 0011
212	D4	NC	M	M	M	B 4	11-4	1101 0100
213	D5	CLC	N	N	N	B 4 1	11-5	1101 0101
214	D6	OC	O	O	O	B 4 2	11-6	1101 0110
215	D7	XC	P	P	P	B 4 2 1	11-7	1101 0111
216	D8		Q	Q	Q	B 8	11-8	1101 1000
217	D9	MVCK	R	R	R	B 8 1	11-9	1101 1001
218	DA	MVCP					12-11-2-8-9	1101 1010
219	DB	MVCS					12-11-3-8-9	1101 1011
220	DC	TR					12-11-4-8-9	1101 1100
221	DD	TRT					12-11-5-8-9	1101 1101
222	DE	ED					12-11-6-8-9	1101 1110
223	DF	EDMK					12-11-7-8-9	1101 1111
224	E0		‡	\		A 8 2	0-2-8	1110 0000
225	E1			NSP			11-0-1-9	1110 0001
226	E2		S	S	S	A 2	0-2	1110 0010
227	E3		T	T	T	A 2 1	0-3	1110 0011

S Format

9C00 — SIO
9C01 — SIOF
9C02 — RIO
9D00 — TIO
9D01 — CLRIO
9E00 — HIO
9E01 — HDV
9F00 — TCH
9F01 — CLRCH
B200 — CONCS
B201 — DISCS
B202 — STIDP
B203 — STIDC
B204 — SCK
B205 — STCK
B206 — SCKC
B207 — STCKC
B208 — SPT
B209 — STPT
B20A — SPKA
B20B — IPK
B20D — PTLB
B210 — SPX
B211 — STPX
B212 — STAP
B213 — RRB
B218 — PC
B219 — SAC

RRE Format

B221 — IPTE
B223 — IVSK
B224 — IAC
B225 — SSAR
B226 — EPAR
B227 — ESAR
B228 — PT
B229 — ISKE
B22A — RRBE
B22B — SSKE
B22C — TB

SSE Format

E500 — LASP
E501 — TPROT

Note: This character is an EBCDIC superscript character.

CODE TABLES (Cont'd)

DEC.	HEX	INST. (SS)	GRAPHICS AND CONTROLS BCDIC	EBCDIC(1)	ASCII	7-TRACK TAPE BCDIC(2)	CARD CODE EBCDIC	BINARY
228	E4		U	U	U	A 4	0-4	1110 0100
229	E5	See below	V	V	V	A 4 1	0-5	1110 0101
230	E6		W	W	W	A 4 2	0-6	1110 0110
231	E7		X	X	X	A 4 2 1	0-7	1110 0111
232	E8	MVCIN	Y	Y	Y	A 8	0-8	1110 1000
233	E9		Z	Z	Z	A 8 1	0-9	1110 1001
234	EA						11-0-2-8-9	1110 1010
235	EB						11-0-3-8-9	1110 1011
236	EC			⑁			11-0-4-8-9	1110 1100
237	ED						11-0-5-8-9	1110 1101
238	EE						11-0-6-8-9	1110 1110
239	EF						11-0-7-8-9	1110 1111
240	F0	SRP	0	0	0	8 2	0	1111 0000
241	F1	MVO	1	1	1	1	1	1111 0001
242	F2	PACK	2	2	2	2	2	1111 0010
243	F3	UNPK	3	3	3	2 1	3	1111 0011
244	F4		4	4	4	4	4	1111 0100
245	F5		5	5	5	4 1	5	1111 0101
246	F6		6	6	6	4 2	6	1111 0110
247	F7		7	7	7	4 2 1	7	1111 0111
248	F8	ZAP	8	8	8	8	8	1111 1000
249	F9	CP	9	9	9	8 1	9	1111 1001
250	FA	AP		|			12-11-0-2-8-9	1111 1010
251	FB	SP					12-11-0-3-8-9	1111 1011
252	FC	MP					12-11-0-4-8-9	1111 1100
253	FD	DP					12-11-0-5-8-9	1111 1101
254	FE						12-11-0-6-8-9	1111 1110
255	FF			EO			12-11-0-7-8-9	1111 1111

S Format

9C00 — SIO
9C01 — SIOF
9C02 — RIO
9D00 — TIO
9D01 — CLRIO
9E00 — HIO
9E01 — HDV
9F00 — TCH
9F01 — CLRCH
B200 — CONCS
B201 — DISCS
B202 — STIDP
B203 — STIDC
B204 — SCK
B205 — STCK
B206 — SCKC
B207 — STCKC
B208 — SPT
B209 — STPT
B20A — SPKA
B20B — IPK
B20D — PTLB
B210 — SPX
B211 — STPX
B212 — STAP
B213 — RRB
B218 — PC
B219 — SAC

RRE Format

B221 — IPTE
B223 — IVSK
B224 — IAC
B225 — SSAR
B226 — EPAR
B227 — ESAR
B228 — PT
B229 — ISKE
B22A — RRBE
B22B — SSKE
B22C — TB

ANSI-DEFINED PRINTER CONTROL CHARACTERS
(A in RECFM field of DCB)

Code	Action before printing record
blank	Space 1 line
0	Space 2 lines
—	Space 3 lines
+	Suppress space
1	Skip to line 1 on new page

CONTROL REGISTERS

CR	BITS	NAME OF FIELD	ASSOCIATED WITH	INIT.*
0	0	Block-multiplexing control	Block-multiplexing	0
	1	SSM-suppression control	SSM instruction	0
	2	TOD-clock-sync control	Multiprocessing	0
	3	Low-addr-protection control	Low-address protection	0
	4	Extraction-authority control	Dual address space	0
	5	Secondary-space control	Dual address space	0
	7	Storage-key exception control	Storage-key 4K-byte block	0
	8-12	Translation format	Dynamic address trans	0
	13	Page-fault-assist control	MVS assists	0
	16	Malfunc-alert subclass mask	Multiprocessing	0
	17	Emergency-signal subcl mask	Multiprocessing	0
	18	External-call subclass mask	Multiprocessing	0
	19	TOD-clk sync-chk subcl mask	Multiprocessing	0
	20	Clk-comparator subclass mask	Clock comparator	0
	21	CPU-timer subclass mask	CPU timer	0
	22	Service-signal subclass mask	Service signal	0
	24	Interval-timer subclass mask	Interval timer	1
	25	Interrupt-key subclass mask	Interrupt key	1
	26	External-signal subcl mask	External signal	1
1	0-7	Primary segment-table length	Dynamic address trans	0
	8-25	Primary segment-table origin	Dynamic address trans	0
	31	Space-switch-even control	Dual address space	0
2	0-31	Channel masks	Channels	1
3	0-15	PSW-key mask	Dual address space	0
	16-31	Secondary ASN	Dual address space	0
4	0-15	Authorization index	Dual address space	0
	16-31	Primary ASN	Dual address space	0
5	0	Subsystem-linkage control	Dual address space	0
	8-24	Linkage-table origin	Dual address space	0
	25-31	Linkage-table length	Dual address space	0
6	0	VM assists	VM assists	0
	1	Virtual problem state	Extended facility	0
	2	ISK-SSK inhibit	VM assists	0
	3	S/360 operations only	VM assists	0
	4	SVC inhibit	VM assists	0
	5	Shadow-tbl-valid'n inhibit	VM assists	0
	6	Expanded VM and CP	VM assists	0
	7	Virtual interval timer	VM assists	0
	8-28	Virtual-machine param list		0
	29	VM assists for MVS	Extended facility	0
7	0-7	Secondary segment-tbl length	Dual address space	0
	8-25	Secondary segment-tbl origin	Dual address space	0
8	16-31	Monitor masks	MC instruction	0
9	0	Successful-branching-event mask	Program-event recording	0
	1	Instruction-fetching-event mask	Program-event recording	0
	2	Storage-alteration-event mask	Program-event recording	0
	3	GR-alteration-event mask	Program-event recording	0
	16-31	PER general-register masks	Program-event recording	0
10	8-31	PER starting address	Program-event recording	0
11	8-31	PER ending address	Program-event recording	0

*Value after initial CPU reset.

CONTROL REGISTERS

CR	BITS	NAME OF FIELD	ASSOCIATED WITH	INIT.*
14	0	Check-stop control	Machine-check handling	1
	1	Synch-MCEL control		1
	2	I/O-extended-logout control	I/O extended logout	0
	4	Recovery-report subclass mask	Machine-check handling	0
	5	Degradation-report subclass mask		0
	6	Ext.-damage report subclass mask		1
	7	Warning subclass mask		0
	8	Asynch.-MCEL control		0
	9	Asynch.-fixed-log control		0
	12	ASN-translation control	Dual address space	0
	20-31	ASN-first-table origin		0
15	8-28	MCEL address	Machine-check handling	512

*Value after initial CPU reset.

PROGRAM-STATUS WORD (EC Mode)

0R00 0TIE	PSW key	CMWPS	0	CC	Program mask	0000 0000
0	8	12	17	18	20	24 — 31

0000 0000	Instruction address
32	40 — 63

1 (R) Program-event-recording mask
2 (T = 1) DAT mode
6 (I) Input/output mask
7 (E) External mask
12 (C = 1) Extended-control mode
13 (M) Machine-check mask
14 (W = 1) Wait state
15 (P = 1) Problem state
16 (S = 1) Address-space control
18-19 (CC) Condition code
20 Fixed-point-overflow mask
21 Decimal-overflow mask
22 Exponent-underflow mask
23 Significance mask

PROGRAM-STATUS WORD (BC Mode)

Channel Masks	E	PSW key	CMWP	Interruption code
0	7	8	12	16 — 31

ILC	CC	Program mask	Instruction address
32	34	36	40 — 63

0–5 Channel 0 to 5 masks
6 Mask for channel 6 and up
7 (E) External mask
12 (C = 0) Basic-control mode
13 (M) Machine-check mask
14 (W = 1) Wait state
15 (P = 1) Problem state
32–33 (ILC) Instruction-length code
34–35 (CC) Condition code
36 Fixed-point-overflow mask
37 Decimal-overflow mask
38 Exponent-underflow mask
39 Significance mask

PROGRAM INTERRUPTION CODES

0001	Operation exception	0010	Segment translation excp
0002	Privileged operation excp	0011	Page translation exception
0003	Execute exception	0012	Translation specification excp
0004	Protection exception	0013	Special operation exception
0005	Addressing exception	0017	ASN-translation spec excp
0006	Specification exception	001C	Space-switch event
0007	Data exception	001F	PC-translation spec excp
0008	Fixed-point overflow excp	0020	AFX translation excp
0009	Fixed-point divide excp	0021	ASX translation excp
000A	Decimal overflow exception	0022	LX translation excp
000B	Decimal divide exception	0023	EX translation excp
000C	Exponent overflow excp	0024	Primary authority excp
000D	Exponent underflow excp	0025	Secondary authority excp
000E	Significance exception	0040	Monitor event
000F	Floating-point divide excp	0080	PER event (code may be combined with another code)

EXTERNAL INTERRUPTION CODES

Code (binary)		Condition	Code (binary)	Condition
00000000	1eeeeeee	Interval timer	00010010 00000000	Malfunction alert
00000000	e1eeeeee	Interrupt key	00010010 00000001	Emergency signal
00000000	ee1eeeee	External sig 2	00010010 00000010	External call
00000000	eee1eeee	External sig 3	00010000 00000011	TOD-clock-sync check
00000000	eeee1eee	External sig 4	00010000 00000100	Clock comparator
00000000	eeeee1ee	External sig 5	00010000 00000101	CPU timer
00000000	eeeeee1e	External sig 6	00100100 00000001	Service signal
00000000	eeeeeee1	External sig 7		

e- if 1, the bit indicates a concurrent external interruption condition.

FIXED STORAGE LOCATIONS

AREA, DEC.	ADDR TYPE	HEX ADDR	EC ONLY	FUNCTION
0–7	A	0		Initial-program-loading PSW
0–7	R	0		Restart new PSW
8–15	A	8		Initial-program-loading CCW1
8–15	R	8		Restart old PSW
16–23	A	10		Initial-program-loading CCW2
24–31	R	18		External old PSW
32–39	R	20		Supervisor-call old PSW
40–47	R	28		Program old PSW
48–55	R	30		Machine-check old PSW
56–63	R	38		Input/output old PSW
64–71	R	40		Channel-status word (see diagram)
72–75	R	48		Channel-address word (see diagram)
80–83	R	50		Interval timer

*May vary among models; see System Library manuals for specific model.
A = Absolute address
L = Logical address
R = Real address

FIXED STORAGE LOCATIONS (Cont'd)

AREA, DEC.	ADDR TYPE	HEX ADDR	EC ONLY	FUNCTION
84–87	L	54		Trace-table designation (0 control, 8-31 address)
88–95	R	58		External new PSW
96–103	R	60		Supervisor-call new PSW
104–111	R	68		Program new PSW
112–119	R	70		Machine-check new PSW
120–127	R	78		Input/Output new PSW
128–131	R	80		External-interruption parameter for service signal
132–133	R	84		CPU address associated with external interruption, or unchanged
132–133	R	84	X	CPU address associated with external interruption, or zeros
134–135	R	86	X	External-interruption code (see table)
136–139	R	88	X	SVC interruption (0-12 zeros, 13-14 ILC, 15:0, 16-31 code)
140–143	R	8C	X	Program interrupt (0-12 zeros, 13-14 ILC, 15:0, 16-31 code)
144–147	R	90	X	Translation-exception ID (see table)
148–149	R	94		Monitor class (0-7 zeros, 8-15 class number)
150–151	R	96	X	PER code (0-3 code, 4-15 zeros)
152–155	R	98	X	PER address (0-7 zeros, 8-31 address)
156–159	R	9C		Monitor code (0-7 zeros, 8-31 code)
164–167	L	A4		MVS-assist parameter list (MAPL) address
168–171	R	A8		Channel ID (0-3 type, 4-15 model, 16-31 max, IOEL length)
172–175	R	AC		I/O-extended-logout address (0-7 unused, 8-31 address)
176–179	R	B0		Limited channel logout (see diagram)
185	R	B9	X	Measurement byte (0-1 delay, 2-4 count, 5-7 zeros)
186–187	R	BA	X	I/O address
216–223	A	D8		Store-status CPU-timer save area
216–223	R	D8		Machine-check CPU-timer save area
224–231	A	E0		Store-status clock-comparator save area
224–231	R	E0		Machine-check clock-comparator save area
232–239	R	E8		Machine-check-interruption code (see diagram)
244–247	R	F4		External-damage code (see table)
248–251	R	F8		Failing-storage address (0-5 zeros, 6-31 address)
252–255	R	FC		Region code*
256–263	A	100		Store-status PSW save area
256–351	R	100		Fixed-logout area*
264–267	A	108		Store-status prefix save area
268–271	A	10C		Store-status model-dependent save area*
352–383	A	160		Store-status floating-point-register save area
352–383	R	160		Machine-check floating-point-register save area
384–447	A	180		Store-status general-register save area
384–447	R	180		Machine-check general-register save area
448–511	A	1C0		Store-status control-register save area
448–511	R	1C0		Machine-check control-register save area
795	L	31B		CPU identity for DAS tracing

*May vary among models; see System Library manuals for specific model.
A = Absolute address
L = Logical address
R = Real address

CHANNEL-ADDRESS WORD (hex 48)

Key	S	000	Channel-Program Address
0	4		8 31

4(S) Suspend-control bit

CHANNEL-COMMAND WORD

Command code	Data address
0	8 31

Flags	0	//////	Byte count
32	39	40	48 63

CD – bit 32 (80) causes use of data-address portion of next CCW.
CC – bit 33 (40) causes use of command code and data address of next CCW.
SLI – bit 34 (20) causes suppression of possible incorrect-length indication.
Skip – bit 35 (10) suppresses transfer of information to main storage.
PCI – bit 36 (08) causes a channel-program-controlled interruption.
IDA – bit 37 (04) causes bits 8-31 of CCW to specify location of first IDAW.
Suspend – bit 38 (02) causes suspension before execution of this CCW.

CHANNEL-STATUS WORD (hex 40)

Key	S	L	CC	CCW address
0	4	5	6	8 31

Unit status	Channel status	Byte count
32	40	48 63

4 Suspended (only in CCW stored by PCI)
5 Logout pending
6-7 Deferred condition code
32 (80) Attention
33 (40) Status modifier
34 (20) Control-unit end
35 (10) Busy
36 (08) Channel end
37 (04) Device end
38 (02) Unit check
39 (01) Unit exception
40 (80) Program-controlled interruption
41 (40) Incorrect length
42 (20) Program check
43 (10) Protection check
44 (08) Channel-data check
45 (04) Channel-control check
46 (02) Interface-control check
47 (01) Chaining check
48-63 Residual byte count for the last CCW used

LIMITED CHANNEL LOGOUT (hex B0)

0	SCU id	Detect	Source	00	Field validity flags	TT	0	IA	Seq.
0	1	4	8	13	15	24	26	27	29 31

4 CPU
5 Channel
6 Main-storage control
7 Main storage
8 CPU
9 Channel
10 Main-storage control
11 Main storage
12 Control unit
15 Full chan logout
16–18 Reserved (000)
19 Sequence code
20 Unit status
21 CCW addr. and key
22 Channel address
23 Device address
24–25 Type of termination
 00 Interface disconnect
 01 Stop, stack or normal
 10 Selective reset
 11 System reset
27 (I) Interface inoperative
28 (A) I/O-error alert
29-31 Sequence code

EXTERNAL DAMAGE CODE (hex F4)

BITS	MEANING
0–1	Reserved (zeros)
2	External secondary report
3	Channel not operational
4	Channel-control failure
5	I/O-instruction timeout
6	I/O-interruption timeout
7–31	Reserved (zeros)

MACHINE-CHECK INTERRUPTION CODE (hex E8)

MC conditions	000 00	Time	Stg. error	0	Validity Indicators
0	9	14	16	19	20 … 31

0000 0000 0000 00	Val.	MCEL length
32	46	48 … 63

0 System damage
1 Inst.-proc'g damage
2 System recovery
3 Intvl-timer damage
4 Timing-facil. damage
5 External damage
6 Not assigned (0)
7 Degradation
8 Warning

14 Backed up
15 Delayed
16 Uncorrected
17 Corrected
18 Key uncorrected
20 PSW bits 12-15
21 PSW mask and key
22 Prog. mask and CC
23 Instruction address

24 Failing-stg. address
25 Region code
26 External-damage code
27 Floating-pt registers
28 General registers
29 Control registers
30 Logout
31 Storage logical
46 CPU timer
47 Clock comparator

DYNAMIC ADDRESS TRANSLATION

Dynamic Address Translation Format

CNTL REG 0 BITS 8–12	SEGMENT SIZE	PAGE SIZE	VIRTUAL-ADDRESS FIELDS	SEGMENT INDEX	PAGE INDEX	BYTE INDEX
0 1 0 0 0	64K	2K	Bits 0–7 are ignored	8–15	16–20	21–31
0 1 0 1 0	1M	2K		8–11	12–20	21–31
1 0 0 0 0	64K	4K		8–15	16–19	20–31
1 0 0 1 0	1M	4K		8–11	12–19	20–31

Any other combination of bits 8–12 of control register 0 is invalid for translation. 1M-byte segments are not provided on some models; 2K-byte pages are not provided on some models.

Segment-Table Entry

PT length	0000*	Page-table origin	P	C	I
0	4	8	29	30	31

*Normally zeros; ignored on some models.
29 (P) Segment protection
30 (C) Common segment
31 (I) Segment-invalid bit

Page-Table Entry (4K)

Page-frame real address	I	EA	//////
0	12	13	15

12 (I) Page-invalid bit
13-14 (EA) Extended-address bits

Page-Table Entry (2K)

Page-frame real address	I	O	
0	13	14	15

13 (I) Page-invalid bit

TRANSLATION-EXCEPTION ID (hex 90)

INTERRUPTION CODE	ID
0010,0011	0 secondary address 1–7 zeros, 8–31 address
001C	0 old space-sw-event ctl bit, 1–15 zeros, 16–31 old PASN
0020,0021,0024,0025	0–15 zeros, 16–31 ASN
0022,0023	0–11 zeros, 12–31 PC number

DUAL-ADDRESS-SPACE CONTROL

Program-Call Number

//////////	Linkage index	Entry index	
0	12	24	31

Linkage-Table Entry

I	000 0000	Entry-table origin	ETL	
0	1	8	26	31

0 (I) LX-invalid bit

26–31 (ETL) Entry-table length

Entry-Table Entry

Authorization key mask	ASN	0000 0000	Entry instruction address	P
0	16	32	40	63

Entry parameter	Entry key mask	//////////	
64	96	112	127

63(P) Entry problem state

ASN-First-Table Entry

I	000 0000	ASN-second-table origin	0000	
0	1	8	28	31

0 (I) AFX-invalid bit

ASN-Second-Table Entry

I	000 0000	Authority-table origin	00	Authorization index	Authority-table length	0000	
0	1	8	30	32	48	60	63

STL	Segment-table origin	//////	X	V	000 0000	Linkage-table origin	LTL	
64	72	90	95	96	97	104	121	127

0 (I) ASX-invalid bit

64–71(STL) Segment-table length

95 (X) Space-switch-event bit

96 (V) Subsystem-linkage control

121–127 (LTL) Linkage-table length

Trace-Table-Entry Header

Current-entry control	First-entry control	Last-entry control	
0	32	64	95

HEXADECIMAL AND DECIMAL CONVERSION

From hex: locate each hex digit in its corresponding column position and note the decimal equivalents. Add these to obtain the decimal value.

From decimal: (1) locate the largest decimal value in the table that will fit into the decimal number to be converted, and (2) note its hex equivalent and hex column position. (3) Find the decimal remainder. Repeat the process on this and subsequent remainders.

Note: Decimal, hexadecimal, and binary equivalents of all numbers from 0 to 255 are listed in the code tables.

HEXADECIMAL COLUMNS											
6		5		4		3		2		1	
HEX	DEC	HEX	DEC	HEX	DEC	HEX	DEC	HEX	DEC	HEX	DEC
0	0	0	0	0	0	0	0	0	0	0	0
1	1,048,576	1	65,536	1	4,069	1	256	1	16	1	1
2	2,097,152	2	131.072	2	8,192	2	512	2	32	2	2
3	3,145,728	3	196,608	3	12,288	3	768	3	48	3	3
4	4,194,304	4	262,144	4	16,384	4	1,024	4	64	4	4
5	5,242,880	5	327,680	5	20,480	5	1,280	5	80	5	5
6	6,291,456	6	393,216	6	24,576	6	1,536	6	96	6	6
7	7,340,032	7	458,752	7	28,672	7	1,792	7	112	7	7
8	8,388,608	8	524,288	8	32,768	8	2,048	8	128	8	8
9	9,437,184	9	589,824	9	36,864	9	2,304	9	144	9	9
A	10,485,760	A	655,360	A	40,960	A	2,560	A	160	A	10
B	11,543,336	B	720,896	B	45,056	B	2,816	B	176	B	11
C	12,582,912	C	786,432	C	49,152	C	3,072	C	192	C	12
D	13,631,488	D	851,968	D	53,248	D	3,328	D	208	D	13
E	14,680,064	E	917,504	E	57,344	E	3,584	E	224	E	14
F	15,728,640	F	983,040	F	61,440	F	3,840	F	240	F	15
0 1 2 3		4 5 6 7		0 1 2 3		4 5 6 7		0 1 2 3		4 5 6 7	
BYTE				BYTE				BYTE			

POWERS OF 2

2^n	n
256	8
512	9
1 024	10
2 048	11
4 096	12
8 192	13
16 384	14
32 768	15
65 536	16
131 072	17
262 144	18
524 288	19
1 048 576	20
2 097 152	21
4 194 304	22
8 388 608	23
16 777 216	24
33 554 432	25
67 108 864	26

2^{0}	$= 16^{0}$
2^{4}	$= 16^{1}$
2^{8}	$= 16^{2}$
2^{12}	$= 16^{3}$
2^{16}	$= 16^{4}$
2^{20}	$= 16^{5}$
2^{24}	$= 16^{6}$
2^{28}	$= 16^{7}$
2^{32}	$= 16^{8}$
2^{36}	$= 16^{9}$
2^{40}	$= 16^{10}$
2^{44}	$= 16^{11}$
2^{48}	$= 16^{12}$
2^{52}	$= 16^{13}$
2^{56}	$= 16^{14}$
2^{60}	$= 16^{15}$

POWERS OF 16

16^n	n
1	0
16	1
256	2
4 096	3
65 536	4
1 048 576	5
16 777 216	6
268 435 456	7
4 294 967 296	8
68 719 476 736	9
1 099 511 627 776	10
17 592 186 044 416	11
281 474 976 710 656	12
4 503 599 627 370 496	13
72 057 594 037 927 936	14
1 152 921 504 606 846 976	15

D Data for Programming Problems

DATA SET 1, PERSONNEL RECORD

```
01-09 Social security number              54-57 Job code
10-29 Name                                58    Pay type (A=annual; W=weekly;
30    Sex (M or F)                                          H=hourly)
31-36 Date of birth (MMDDYY)              59-66 Pay rate (999999V99)
37-42 Date employed (MMDDYY)              67-72 Unused
43-46 Department                          73-78 Date terminated (MMDDYY)
47-50 Office                              79-80 Termination code
51-53 Phone
```

```
0         1         2         3         4         5         6         7         8
12345678901234567890123456789012345678901234567890123456789012345678901234567890

435465879NINA CLOCK           F010562043084123401034779982H00000745
882099317BESS FRIEND          F051731122859123401044802339A04527500
086429731HORACE KOLLAR        M072443092454123401054823228A04850000
001237864COLE SLAW            M100858061885407211372289007H00000698
267378498IDA NOE              F122539011960203811823467034W00031525
819203746FREDA FELONS         F083146032582457734914079734H00000850
807968572ISADOR SHUTT         M113026050849203811833471075A06570000
773984752ARNO MOORE           M060950041476457734914084321W00045285
456389015LON MOORE            M031449082373407211372283924W00048075
983758280JIMMY DELOCK         M042653022978705360226118842H00000998
135782468BELLA DABOLL         F060660103083705360236129074H00000732
259837185MARY MAKER           F012831107549461903784720 84A03745950
500499388OTTO KLAVE           M010822012646946190388481077A07012500
908978675ERNA LIVEN           F091929062750680365436413052W00036375
807968574FLO FAST             F083055020377680365446428077H00000895
432554387RHONDA BOUT          F072660042183500751945979072H00000625
335744790SAL MONELLA          M042153082778500751955988742H00000910
441193847LUKE EMIA            M022956030881247924592179265H00000895
532058379DELAND O'COTTON      M121247090668203811843481397A05430000
102938475GALE WORNING         F053143120765407211274382850W00052000
491025837FREDA O'PREST        F082342012963247924602181488A04381000
880077223BRUCE ELLIS          M033128082549500751965991001A06550000
079682340ALDA WAY             F071558050380680365456439072H00000955
089786235DEWEY FLOWERS        M020360033084247924602189442H00000710
125689074JUNIOR MEMBER        M042964052485500751976009966H00000760
300698273MACK ORONI           M011124072449986596439651753A05932800
8079263840 LEO MARJARIN       M031743091368986596549662438W00056050
```

```
294837205ORSON WAGON         M06265212097824792461219680 2H00000935
738059280LEIGH Z KIDD        M09035911188251135643582968 0H00000842
007798345MARIAN HASTE        F12086208168351135644583990 4H00000815
937495222PHIL ERRUP          M11093706046024792462220453 0W00050650
349285703FRANK LEE MYDEER    M10302904025498659655967196 6A04456800
970873923BURR ITZKOLD        M07043802216151135645584207 5W00052300
789043221SIM ULATION         M07274701196968036546644326 8W00048300
588293852MINNIE MUM          F08223607285924792463221423 8W00054950
352073842MAXIE MUM           M05094009276350075198601446 7W00051000
```

DATA SET 2, INVENTORY RECORD

```
01    Delete code                    34-38 Quantity on hand
02-06 Item number                    39-43 Reorder point
07-26 Item description               44-48 Reorder quantity
27-33 Unit price                     49    Transaction code (A=add; D=delete;
                                              C=change; P=purchase; S=sale)
```

```
0         1         2         3         4         5         6         7         8
12345678901234567890123456789012345678901234567890123456789012345678901234567890

 11105DOBBERTS            0003728002380020000100
 11378PALPITRANTS         0005507004460045000120
 12480ZEBETHONS           0015050000830007500024
 14709FAIRLEQUINTS        0256000000040000500002
 18237GABBERWONKS         0000379015500100001000
 20573MONOMAXILLATORS     0008729006280055000200
 26987ABNEWICKIES         0052595000470005000010
 28075TRELLICASTERS       0004975001380012000048
 39071FORBICULES          0003335000890007500050
 40793PRESBYLOCKS         0022750000510005000050
 50378DILLAPATCHES        0000049045980500005000
 64906HOBBACLAIMERS       0004873000560005000060
 74299RIPLEYZIPS          0009595001020010000060
 73962LEMMOLUGENS         0000948005570060000300
 84492PABLITORROS         0004507002410020000100
 84492BUFFERPINS          0000989003350035000120
 95802QUAXITONIC          0008433000980008000036
 96086RAMOROMS            0000427006500070000100
```

DATA SET 2A, INVENTORY UPDATE

```
01    Delete code                    34-38 Quantity on hand
02-06 Item number                    39-43 Reorder point
07-26 Item description               44-48 Reorder quantity
27-33 Unit price                     49    Transaction code (A=add; D=delete;
                                              C=change; P=purchase; S=sale)
```

```
0         1         2         3         4         5         6         7         8
12345678901234567890123456789012345678901234567890123456789012345678901234567890

 10300                           00050          P
 12480                           00024          P
 26987                           00003          S
 40739                           0007900065     C
 45237                           00015          S
 50378                    0000037          03000C
 74299RIPPLEZIPS          0008940               C
 84492                           00025          S
 90927                           00010          X
```

DATA SET 2B, ITEMS ADDED OR DELETED

```
01    Delete code                    34-38 Quantity on hand
02-06 Item number                    39-43 Reorder point
07-26 Item description               44-48 Reorder quantity
27-33 Unit price                     49    Transaction code (A=add; D=delete;
                                             C=change; P=purchase; S=sale)
```

```
0        1         2         3         4         5         6         7         8
12345678901234567890123456789012345678901234567890123456789012345678901234567890

 11105                                          D
 11307                                          D
 12105DOBBERTS            0003450002380020000100A
 26987ABNEWICKIES         0052595000470005000010A
 40000                                          X
 52476CERTIFLAPS          0001575001000005000200A
```

DATA SET 2C, INVENTORY ITEMS SOLD

```
01    Unused                         34-38 Quantity sold
02-06 Item number                    39-80 Unused
07-33 Unused
```

```
0        1         2         3         4         5         6         7         8
12345678901234567890123456789012345678901234567890123456789012345678901234567890

 18237                           00005
 95802                           00015
 20573                           00050
 52800                           00036
 96086                           00025
 50378                           01200
 74299                           00012
 14709                           00006
 10543                           00008
 28075                           00015
```

DATA SET 3, SALESPERSON RECORD

```
01-02 Region                         28-36 Year-to-date sales (9999999V99)
03-07 Salesperson number             37-43 Year-to-date returns (99999V99)
08-27 Salesperson name               44-80 Unused
```

```
0        1         2         3         4         5         6         7         8
12345678901234567890123456789012345678901234567890123456789012345678901234567890

0113579BILLY RUBIN         0078294370692381
0124897CASSIE BLANCA       0145000200395932
0149862MAE B KNOTT         0023794950504916
0239075JERRY TALL          0094527830374289
0253069FLOYD OY            0042893851159739
0619836OTTO KNOWBETTER     0021987650739240
0640729RHODES COLLAR       0059837420839572
0680721CLARA FYE           0097538230975117
0944492EUBIE HAYVE         0084253950473926
0952628D LIONEL ROHR       0147058260527693
1120598AMOS KEETO          0077483960655432
```

```
1130293LIBBIE RAITED       0044882290739285
1158270MAUDE LIN           0149283751047926
1560827BELLE CANTO         0072819361483925
1830622CHRIS MASEEVE       0089756340982753
1880628PHYLLIS KUPP        0015500420895730
2142908VYONNE TUNNOE       0198756360452739
2189703LYMAN LEMON         0085938470698325
2547829TOM FULERY          0077264370425391
2579881HUGH STONE          0056394821092857
```

DATA SET 3A, SALESPERSON RECORD UPDATE

```
01-02 Region                          28-36 Current month sales
03-07 Salesperson number              37-43 Current month returns
08-27 Unused
```

```
0        1         2         3         4         5         6         7         8
12345678901234567890123456789012345678901234567890123456789012345678901234567890
```

```
1158270                    0015807270052797
0944492                    0007987230079208
1130293                    0018078240708226
0952628                    0032879551259833
2579881                    0008073290079901
5002341                    0000050250004597
1880628                    0009728530069802
0860721                    0009728530002857
```

DATA SET 4, STUDENT COURSE RECORD

```
01-09 Student number                  36-41 Course number and section (999V99)
10-29 Student name                    42-43 Credit hours (9V9)
30-32 Year and term (99V9)            44    Grade
33-35 Course abbreviation             45-80 Unused
```

```
0        1         2         3         4         5         6         7         8
12345678901234567890123456789012345678901234567890123456789012345678901234567890
```

```
287953640JACQUES E STRAPP    872ACC21010230B
287953640JACQUES E STRAPP    872BIO10010640B
287953640JACQUES E STRAPP    872COC13000330A
287953640JACQUES E STRAPP    872ENC10010730A
428973017BURROUGHS DEEPER    872CIS23210130B
428973017BURROUGHS DEEPER    872GER20010230C
428973017BURROUGHS DEEPER    872LIT20240130B
697582903JUDY IZZOM          872COP24010340B
697582903JUDY IZZOM          872REL20000530A
870963512BRUNO BEER          872COC10010730D
870963512BRUNO BEER          872HPE15030420B
870963512BRUNO BEER          872SPC16000430W
908978632AILEEN WINDWARD     872BUS15010220B
908978632AILEEN WINDWARD     872COP15100330C
908978632AILEEN WINDWARD     872HIS13010430B
908978632AILEEN WINDWARD     872Z0022000240D
```

DATA SET 5, STUDENT TEST SCORES

```
01-09 Student number                   39-41 Test 4 score
10-29 Student name                     42-44 Test 5 score
30-32 Test 1 score                     45-47 Final exam score
33-35 Test 2 score                     48-80 Unused
36-38 Test 3 score
```

```
0        1         2         3         4         5         6         7         8
12345678901234567890123456789012345678901234567890123456789012345678901234567890

245367489DOT EDLIN           086079075088072081
408927831RON DELAY           075078082081074077
809728349MARGIE NALL         059063066061062066
410857293IONA PORSCHE        092071053086072083
502938471CHERRY BAUM         094098088093097096
019275832MARION LAITE        072077084076081078
920583728RAFER DETEEM        065073081069072079
250639481KEN TUCKIE          074085090078082086
072958387TURNER ROUND        072074084087092095
056195837PERCY VEER          098092094095100099
844592280DAN DELYON          055061037048054052
309298473REGGIE STIR         073079074072084077
409582739KELLY GREEN         089091084080092087
304928572EPPIE GRAHAM        075079082088084085
209384668JAY WALKER          082081080079068077
440722593SUNNY DAY           072045063075064064
166598732FERLIN FLAGS        100095093100092095
```

DATA SET 6, BANK CUSTOMER RECORD

```
01-09 Customer number                  64-65 State
10-29 Customer name                    66-70 Zip
30-49 Street address                   71-80 Unused
50-63 City
```

```
0        1         2         3         4         5         6         7         8
12345678901234567890123456789012345678901234567890123456789012345678901234567890

132453658DIANA RISE          8 SEMI CIRCLE       FOREST LAWN   CA91406
148793057DUSTIN DE·CORNER    351 LASSITUDE WAY   WINDY RIDGE   NM80782
158302753JENNIFER GOTT       3426 MEMORY GAP     LONESOME      UT70822
189705327PETE ZARREA         798 PEPPERONI ROAD  CHIQUITA      TX50782
204837175HOMER UNN           493 HICKORY OAK     LOUISVILLE    KY49872
253820567PHIL A MIGNON       34 CUTLER BEND      OMAHA         NE50287
298740295FULLER BOLOGNIE     9738 WINDY SIDE     CHICAGO       IL50928
349287500JOANNA FRIEND       3797 MEADOWBROOK    PALM CITY     AR70982
349287500LESTER MOYLE        45 PEACEFUL DRIVE   SILENT        SD57829
379087423CASSIE BLANCA       872 BOGART AVE      CASBAH GLEN   LA40782
402895308MILLIE GRAHAM       96 METRIC BLVD      SILICON CITY  CA95072
459928307CHRIS P KRAKERCZ    1047 BAKER ST       COOK CITY     IL52682
498707258CARRIE MEBACK       799 DOMINION WAY    RICHMOND      VA27500
559978236UPSON DOWNS         588 ROLLER COAST    FAR ROCKAWAY  NY04372
540987283RAZ METAZZ          802 JAZZ HAVEN      NEW ORLEANS   LA41793
597028735HENRIETTA LOTT      104 CALORIE HAVEN   PLENTIFUL     TX58273
614879203ROSETTA LITTLE      4 DIET ST           LEAN          VA10728
689702841ROB U BLIND         595 CROOKED WAY     HOLDUP        OK60872
798725283BILL E KLUBB        22 SCOTLAND YARD    COPP CITY     TN42703
```

DATA SET 6A, BANK CUSTOMER TRANSACTIONS

```
01-09 Customer number                      11-19 Transaction amount (9999999V99)
10    Transaction code (C=check,
        D=deposit,S=service charge,
        I=interest)

0         1         2         3         4         5         6         7         8
12345678901234567890123456789012345678901234567890123456789012345678901234567890

189705327D000500000
189705327C000013528
189705327C000035589
349287500D000075000
349287500C000006450
402895308D000287329
402895308C000001875
498707258I000021857
507283729D000050000
540987283D001200000
540987283C000980027
624879203D000050033
624879203C000004822
624879203C000002187
624879203S000000450
802319702D000002500
```

DATA SET 7, VARIABLE LENGTH RECORDS

```
Name, maximum 20 bytes
Account number, maximum 6 bytes
Balance, maximum 7 bytes

0         1         2         3         4         5         6         7         8
12345678901234567890123456789012345678901234567890123456789012345678901234567890

BELLE E AKERS,324872,15750
ALEXANDER BROTHERS,298703,4079382
JERRY TALL,407285,452986
JUSTIN CASE,987280,9987251
LETTA SPRAY,684920,75283
JEANIE ALOGY,97387022,70293
BEN EVALENT,762352,970163627
PHYLLIS TEEN,902874,549
```

E

Answers to Exercises

CHAPTER 1

1. PRETEST LOOP

```
Initialize
DOWHILE NOT end condition:
  Process data
  Output information
  Get more data
ENDO
```

POSTTEST LOOP

```
Initialize
REPEAT:
  Process data
  Output information
  Get more data
UNTIL end condition
```

2. ONE-WAY TEST

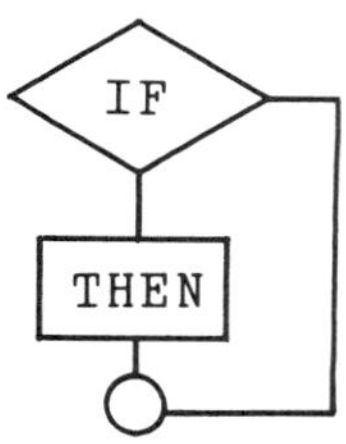

TWO-WAY TEST

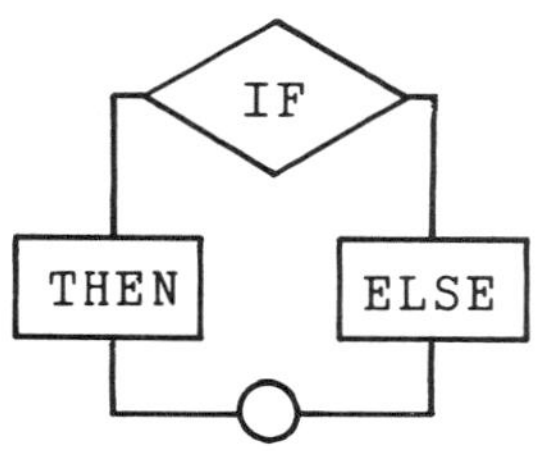

3. a. X'C3D7E4'
   b. X'5BF3F74BF4F8'
   c. X'616140D1D6C240E3C5E2E3'
   d. X'C1D3E3D6D5'
4. a. 17269
   b. 11643
   c. 48813
   d. 64206
5. a. X'10F5'
   b. X'D431'
   c. X'14A0'
   d. X'3039'
6. a. X'BFDC'
   b. X'1473A'
   c. X'6C34'
   d. X'3BDF'
7. a. X'5E' b. X'F2' c. X'97' d. X'13'
8. a. B'00110111' b. B'01011001' c. B'11101011' d. B'00011111'

CHAPTER 2

1. X'E7E8E9' X'F3F4F7' X'C9C2D44040' X'5C5C5C5C5C'

2.
```
INRECD   DS  0CL80
INACCT   DS  CL5
         DS  CL5
INDESCR  DS  CL15
         DS  CL20
INQUANT  DS  CL5
         DS  CL30
```

3.
```
HEAD1  DS  0CL132
       DC  CL27' '
       DC  CL105'CHECK REGISTER'
HEAD2  DS  0CL132
       DC  CL25' '
       DC  CL11'CHECK'
       DC  CL28'INVOICE'
       DC  CL68'NET'
HEAD3  DS  0CL132
       DC  CL7' '
       DC  CL17'PAYEE'
       DC  CL13'NUMBER'
       DC  CL11'AMOUNT'
       DC  CL14'DISCOUNT'
       DC  CL70'AMOUNT'
```

4.
```
HEADING  CNTRL  PRINTER,SK,1
         PUT    PRINTER,HEAD1
         CNTRL  PRINTER,SP,1
         PUT    PRINTER,HEAD2
         CNTRL  PRINTER,SP,1
         LA     5,40
         BR     9
```

5.
```
         GET    INTRANS,INWORK
```

6.
```
         BALR   8,0
         USING  *,8
```

CHAPTER 3

1.
```
MVI  PRLINE,C' '
MVC  PRLINE+1(131),PRLINE
```

2. a.
```
MVI  PRNAME,C'*'
MVC  PRNAME+1(19),PRNAME
```
b.
```
MVC  PRNAME,=20C'*'
```

3. a. `MVC  PRLINE+30(8),INAMOUNT`
b. `MVC  PRZIP(5),INRECD+69`
c. `MVC  PRCODE(1),INRECD+29`
d. `MVC  PRLINE+58(3),INRECD`

4. a. X'F9F8F7'
b. X'404040'
c. X'C1C2C3C1C2C3'
d. X'5BF9F84BF7F5'

5. a. X'C1C2C4' X'0ABD' b. X'F1F2F34040'
X'0000000123'

```
6. IF       CLI  A,C'5'
            BNH  ELSE
   AND      CLI  B,C'3'
            BNL  ELSE
   THEN     .
            B    ENDIF
   ELSE     .
   ENDIF    EQU  *
```

```
7. IF       CLI  A,C'5'
            BH   THEN
   OR       CLI  B,C'3'
            BNL  ELSE
   THEN     .
            B    ENDIF
   ELSE     .
   ENDIF    EQU  *
```

```
8. IF       CLC  INRECD+20(5),=C'12345'
            BE   ELSE
   THEN     .
            B    ENDIF
   ELSE     .
   ENDIF    EQU  *
```

CHAPTER 4

1. a. X'F2F3C7'
   b. X'F0F0F2F3C7'
   c. X'F0F0F2F3D7'
   d. X'F3C7'
   e. X'F2F3F7'
   f. X'F2F3F74040'
   g. X'000000237D'
   h. X'237C'

2. 45F 450

3. 000004 Interrupt for data exception; invalid sign.

4. a. X'0C'
   b. X'00000C'
   c. X'38875D'
   d. X'0C0C'
   e. X'125C'
   f. X'5C'
   g. X'38875D'
   h. X'125C125C'

```
5.          ZAP  COUNT,=P'0'
   DOWHILE  CP   COUNT,=P'50'
            BNL  ENDDO
            (BODY OF LOOP)
            AP   COUNT,=P'1'
            B    DOWHILE
   ENDDO    EQU  *
```

```
6. IF       CLI  INRECD+79,C'1'
            BL   ENDIF
   AND      CLI  INRECD+79,C'3'
            BH   ENDIF
   THEN     AP   COUNT,=P'1'
   ENDIF    EQU  *
```

7.
```
         MVC   PRTOTAL,PATRN
         ED    PRTOTAL,PKTOTAL
         .
         .
PKTOTAL  DS    PL5
PATRN    DC    XL13'40206B2020206B2020214B2020'
PRTOTAL  DS    CL13
```

8. X'000012345F'

X'FFFFFFF4F5'

CHAPTER 5

1.
```
ZAP   DOUBLE,B              or    ZAP   DOUBLE,B
MP    DOUBLE,=P'100'              SRP   DOUBLE,2,0
AP    DOUBLE,A                    AP    DOUBLE,A
```
The sum will have two decimal places.

2. 9999.9   999.999   99999.99999

3.
```
ZAP   DOUBLE,HOURS              or    ZAP   DOUBLE,HOURS
MP    DOUBLE,RATE                     MP    DOUBLE,RATE
AP    DOUBLE,=P'50'                   SRP   DOUBLE,62,5
MVN   DOUBLE+6(1),DOUBLE+7            ZAP   WAGES, DOUBLE
ZAP   WAGES,DOUBLE(7)
```

4.
```
ZAP   DOUBLE,TOTSCORE         9999
MP    DOUBLE,=P'100'          9999V00
DP    DOUBLE,STUCOUNT         9999V99
AP    DOUBLE(6),=P'5'
MVO   DOUBLE(6),DOUBLE(5)     9999V9
ZAP   TESTAVG,DOUBLE(6)
```

5.
```
ZAP   DOUBLE,PRIN             9999V99
MP    DOUBLE,RATE             9999V999999
MP    DOUBLE,=P'30'           999999V999999
DP    DOUBLE,=P'365'          999999V999999
SRP   DOUBLE(6),60,5          999999V99
ZAP   MONTHINT,DOUBLE(6)
```

6.
a.
```
AP    DOUBLE,=P'5000'
MVN   DOUBLE+5(1),DOUBLE+7
ZAP   ANSWER,DOUBLE(6)
```
b.
```
AP    DOUBLE,=P'500'
MVO   DOUBLE,DOUBLE(6)
ZAP   ANSWER,DOUBLE
```
c.
```
AP    DOUBLE,=P'50'
MVN   DOUBLE+6(1),DOUBLE+7
ZAP   ANSWER,DOUBLE(7)
```
d.
```
AP    DOUBLE,=P'5'
MVO   DOUBLE,DOUBLE(7)
ZAP   ANSWER,DOUBLE
```

7.
```
ZAP   DOUBLE,=P'43287'
SRP   DOUBLE,5,0
DP    DOUBLE,=P'124.5'
SRP   DOUBLE(5),62,5
ZAP   RESULT,DOUBLE(5)
```

8.
```
HEAD1  DS   0CL133
       DC   CL1'1
       DC   CL30' '
       DC   CL102'REPORT TITLE'
HEAD2  DS   0CL133
       DC   CL1'0'
       DC   CL10' '
       DC   3CL20'COLUMN'
       DC   CL62' '
HEAD3  DS   0CL133
       DC   CL1' '
       DC   CL10' '
       DC   CL20'HEAD 1'
       DC   CL20'HEAD 2'
       DC   CL82'HEAD 3'
```

CHAPTER 6

1. a. X'8416' b. X'8C64' c. X'85' d. X'8C40'

2.

BYTE	1	2	3	4	5	6
RR:	OP	R1 R2				
RX:	OP	R2 X2	B2 D2	D2 D2		
RS:	OP	R1 R3	B2 D2	D2 D2		
SI:	OP	I2	B1 D1	D1 D1		
SS:	OP	L1 L2	B1 D1	D1 D1	B2 D2	D2 D2
SS:	OP	L2	B1 D1	D1 D1	B2 D2	D2 D2

3.

	IMPLICIT		EXPLICIT	
RR:	AR	4,8	AR	4,8
RX:	L	4,FULL(7)	L	4,28(7,12)
RS:	STM	4,6,FULL	STM	4,6,28(12)
SI:	MVI	PRLINE,C' '	MVI	232(12),C' '
SS:	MVC	PRNAME,INNAME	MVC	240(20,12),168(12)
SS:	AP	PKTOT,PKAMT	AP	362(5,12),345(4,12)

4.
a. BC 8,ELSE — BZ ELSE
b. BC 1,ENDIF — BO ENDIF
c. BC 13,ENDDO — BNH ENDDO
d. BC 15,DOWHILE — B DOWHILE

5.
a. MVI 30(8,4),0(3)
b. CLC 77(3,3),45(4)
c. PACK 37(5,3),37(5,3)

CHAPTER 7

1. a. X'2330B0' c. X'233184'
   b. X'23347A' d. X'233584'
2. a. X'F3F7F5F6' c. X'00051C'
   b. X'D5' d. X'00000000'
3. X'2336F8' The name IJDFAZZW appears at X'233708'.

4. X‘2734CF’ and X‘2734D0’
5. X‘23242E’
6. X‘403630’

CHAPTER 8

1.
```
            GET   INFILE,INRECD
            MVC   SAVEKEY,INKEY
DOWHILE     CLI   EOFFLAG,C'Y'
            BE    ENDDO
IF          CLC   INKEY,SAVEKEY
            BH    ENDIF
THEN        MVC   PRERRMSG,=CL28'OUT OF SEQUENCE OR    X
                  DUPLICATE'
ENDIF       PUT   PRINTER,PRLINE
            MVC   SAVEKEY,INKEY
            GET   INFILE,INRECD
            B     DOWHILE
ENDDO       EQU   *
```

2. Change three statements as follows:
```
IF          CLC   INKEY,SAVEKEY
            BNL   ENDIF
THEN        MVC   PRERRMSG,=CL28'OUT OF SEQUENCE'
```

3.
```
MAINLOOP    EQU   *
DOWHILE     CLI   EOFFLAG,C'Y'
            BE    ENDDO
IF          CLC   INMAJKEY,SVMAJKEY
            BE    ELSE
THEN        BAL   10,MINTOTAL
            BAL   10,INTTOTAL
            BAL   10,MAJTOTAL
            MVI   PRCNTRL,C'0'
            AP    LINECNT,=P'4'
            B     ENDIF
ELSE        EQU   *
IF2         CLC   ININTKEY,SVINTKEY
            BE    ELSE2
THEN2       BAL   10,MINTOTAL
            BAL   10,INTTOTAL
            MVI   PRCNTRL,C'0'
            AP    LINECNT,=P'3'
            B     ENDIF2
ELSE2       EQU   *
IF3         CLC   INMINKEY,SVMINKEY
            BE    ENDIF3
THEN3       BAL   10,MINTOTAL
            MVI   PRCNTRL,C'0'
            AP    LINECNT,=P'2'
ENDIF3      EQU   *
ENDIF2      EQU   *
```

```
ENDIF      EQU  *
           BAL  10,SETUP
           BAL  10,PRDETAIL
           BAL  10,ADD
           BAL  10,READRECD
           B    DOWHILE
ENDDO      EQU  *
           BR   9
```

4.
```
AP  PKMINTOT,PKAMOUNT   at detail time
AP  PKINTTOT,PKAMOUNT
AP  PKMAJTOT,PKAMOUNT
AP  PKFINTOT,PKAMOUNT
```

5.
```
AP  PKMINTOT,PKAMOUNT   at detail time
AP  PKINTTOT,PKMINTOT   at minor total time
AP  PKMAJTOT,PKINTTOT   at intermediate total time
AP  PKFINTOT,PKMAJTOT   at major total time
```

CHAPTER 9

1.

128	64	32	16	8	4	2	1		
0	0	0	1	0	0	0	1	=	17
0	0	0	1	1	1	0	1	=	29
0	0	1	1	0	0	0	0	=	48
0	0	1	1	1	1	1	1	=	63
0	1	1	0	0	0	1	1	=	99
1	0	0	0	0	0	0	0	=	128
1	1	1	1	1	1	1	0	=	254

2. 15 62 85 133 146

3.

S	64	32	16	8	4	2	1		
0	0	0	0	0	1	1	1	=	7
0	0	1	0	0	0	0	0	=	32
0	1	0	0	1	1	1	1	=	79
0	1	1	1	1	1	1	1	=	127
1	1	1	1	1	1	1	1	=	−1
1	1	1	0	0	0	0	0	=	−32
1	0	0	1	1	1	0	0	=	−100

4. 21 120 −128 −123 −5

5. 0010 0011 0111 1111 11001100 (overflow) 0011 1101 (overflow) 1110 0000

6. X'05' X'F0' X'00FF' X'03E8'
X'FFFFFFF9' X'0000007F' X'0000FFFF' X'FFFFF000'

7. X'0000001AC' X'00000428'

8. 32767 = X'7FFF' −32768 = X'8000'

9. 2147483647 = X'7FFFFFFF' −2147483648 = X'80000000'

10. a.
```
         AH   7,=H'5'
```
b.
```
         A    7,CONS
         .
CONS     DC   F'5'
```
c.
```
         L    8,=F'5'
         AR   7,8
```
d.
```
         LA   7,5(7)
```

11.
```
L     7,=F'12345678'
M     6,=F'4739'
A     7,=F'5000'
D     6,=F'10000'
CVD   6,DOUBLE
MVC   PRANSWER,PATRN
ED    PRANSWER,DOUBLE+3
```

12.
```
L     7,=F'4238729'
M     6,=F'1175'
D     6,=F'365'
A     7,=F'5000'
SR    6,6
D     6,=F'10000'
ST    7,DAYINT
```

CHAPTER 10

1.
```
            USING CRSDUMMY,7
            .
CRSDUMMY    DSECT
CRSNBR      DS     CL7
CRSDESCR    DS     CL20
CRSSEMHR    DS     PL2'99.9'
```

2.
```
TABLE       DS     0CL90
            DC     CL4'1234'
            DC     CL2'05'
            DC     CL6'123456'
            DC     CL6'001234'
            DC     CL4'2345'
            DC     CL2'10'
            DC     CL6'234567'
            DC     CL6'002345'
            DC     CL4'3456'
            DC     CL2'15'
            DC     CL6'345678'
            DC     CL6'003456'
            DC     CL4'4567'
            DC     CL2'20'
            DC     CL6'456789'
            DC     CL6'004567'
            DC     CL4'5678'
            DC     CL2'25'
            DC     CL6'567890'
            DC     CL6'005678'
```

To hold equivalent data in decimal or binary form, lengths would be:

PACKED DECIMAL			BINARY	
SPCODE	DS	PL3	DS	H
BRCHNBR	DS	PL1	DS	H
SALES	DS	PL4	DS	F
RETURNS	DS	PL4	DS	F
Total lengths		12		12

3.
```
         LA     5,10
         LA     6,TABLE
REPEAT   GET    INFILE,INRECD
         MVC    0(22,6),INRECD
         LA     6,22(6)
         BCT    5,REPEAT
UNTIL    EQU    *
```

4.
```
         LA     6,TABLE
         ZAP    COUNT,=P'0'
         GET    INFILE,INRECD
DOWHILE  CLC    INKEY,=C'99999'
         BE     ENDDO
         MVC    0(5,6),INKEY
         LA     7,INSCORE
         LA     6,5(6)
         LA     5,6
REPEAT   PACK   0(2,6),0(3,7)
         LA     7,3(7)
         LA     6,2(6)
         BCT    5,REPEAT
UNTIL    EQU    *
         AP     COUNT,=P'1'
         GET    INFILE,INRECD
         B      DOWHILE
ENDDO    EQU    *
```

5.
```
         GET    INFILE,INRECD
IF       CLC    INAGE,=C'18'
         BL     ELSE
AND      CLC    INAGE,=C'60'
         BH     ELSE
THEN     PACK   DOUBLE,INAGE
         CVB    7,DOUBLE
         SH     7,=H'18'
         MH     7,=H'15'
         LA     8,TABLE
         AR     7,8
         MVC    TABWORK,0(7)
         B      ENDIF
ELSE     MVC    ERRMSG,=C'INVALID AGE'
ENDIF    EQU    *
```

CHAPTER 11

```
1.              COMRG
                MVC       PRDATE,0(1)
                GETIME     STANDARD
                ST        1,PKTIME
                MVC       PRTIME,PATRN
                ED        PRTIME,PKTIME

2.  GETLARGE    EQU       *                     SUBROUTINE
    IF          CR        2,3
                BL        ELSE
    THEN        LR        4,2
                B         ENDIF
    ELSE        LR        4,3
    ENDIF       EQU       *
                BR        10
                .
                LA        2,375                 MAINLINE CALLING
    *                                           SEQUENCE
                LA        3,248
                BAL       10,GETLARGE
                ST        4,LARGE

3.  GETLARGE    EQU       *                     SUBROUTINE
    IF          CP        0(3,2),0(3,3)
                BL        ELSE
    THEN        ZAP       0(3,4),0(3,2)
                B         ENDIF
    ELSE        ZAP       0(3,4),0(3,3)
    ENDIF       EQU       *
                BR        10
                .
                LA        2,PKFIRST             MAINLINE CALLING
    *                                           SEQUENCE
                LA        3,PKSECOND
                LA        4,PKLARGE
                BAL       10,GETLARGE

4.  MAINLINE    START     0                     ENTRY
                ENTRY     TABLE                 ENTRY
    TABLE       DS        CL240
                LA        15,=V(SUBR)           EXTRN
                EXTRN     ADCON                 EXTRN
    ADCON       DC        A(SUBR2)

5.  SUBR        CSECT     0                     SUBROUTINE
    *                                           (PARTIAL)
                SAVE      (14,12)
                BALR      12,0
                USING     *,12
                L         2,0(1)
                PUT       (2),PRRECD
                .
                OPEN      PRINTER               MAINLINE CALLING
    *                                           SEQUENCE
                LA        13,SAVE
                CALL      SUBR,(PRINTER)
```

6.
```
SUBR      CSECT  0                      SUBROUTINE
*                                       (PARTIAL)
          SAVE   (14,12)
          BALR   12,0
          USING  *,12
IF        CLI    OPENFLAG,C'Y'
          BE     ENDIF
THEN      OPEN   PRINTER
          MVI    OPENFLAG,C'Y'
ENDIF     EQU    *
          .
PRINTER   DTFPR  DEVADDR=SYS009, etc.
OPENFLAG  DC     CL1'N'
```

CHAPTER 12

1.
```
          MACRO
          HEADING
HEAD1     DS     0CL133
          DC     CL55'1'
          DC     CL70'SOFTWARE ENTERPRISES, INC'
PRPAGE    DS     CL4
          DC     CL4' '
          MEND
```

2.
```
          MACRO
&NAME     ADD4   &R1,&FULL
          LCLA   &RFIRST,&NUMBER
&RFIRST   SETA   &R1
&NAME     EQU    *
.REPEAT   A      &RFIRST,&FULL
&RFIRST   SETA   &RFIRST+1
.IF       AIF    (&RFIRST LE 15).ENDIF
.THEN     ANOP
&RFIRST   SETA   &RFIRST-16
.ENDIF    ANOP
&NUMBER   SETA   &NUMBER+1
          AIF    (&NUMBER LE 4).REPEAT
          MEND
```

3.
```
          MACRO
&NAME     ADDB    &R,&WORD1,&WORD2,&WORD3
          LCLC    &H1,&H2,&H3
.IF       AIF     (T'&WORD1 NE 'H').ENDIF
.THEN     ANOP
&H1       SETC    'H'
.ENDIF    ANOP
.IF2      AIF      (T'&WORD2 NE 'H').ENDIF2
.THEN     ANOP
&H2       SETC     'H'
.ENDIF2   ANOP
.IF3      AIF      (T'&WORD3 NE 'H').ENDIF3
.THEN3    ANOP
&H3       SETC     'H'
.ENDIF3   ANOP
```

```
&NAME      L&H1      &R,&WORD1
           A&H2      &R,&WORD2
           ST&H3     &R,&WORD3
           MEND
```

4.
```
           MACRO
&NAME      ADD5      &P1,&SUM
           LCLA      &DISP
&NAME      ZAP       &SUM,=P'0'
.REPEAT    AP        &SUM,&P1+&DISP(3)
&DISP      SETA      &DISP+3
           AIF       (&DISP LE 12).REPEAT
           MEND
```

5.
```
           LCLC      &STR
&STR       SETC      '&P1(1,3)'.'&P2(5,3)'
```

6.
```
           MACRO
&NAME      EXCH      &R1,&R2
.IF        AIF       (&R1 LE 15 AND &R2 LE 15).ELSE
.THEN      MNOTE     64,'REGISTERS NOT BETWEEN 0 AND 15'
           MEXIT
.ELSE      ANOP
&NAME      CNOP      0,4
           ST        &R1,SAVE&SYSNDX
           LR        &R1,&R2
           L         &R2,SAVE&SYSNDX
           B         *+8
SAVE&SYSNDX       DS   F
           MEND
```

CHAPTER 13

1.
```
IF         TM     STATUS,B'00110000'
           BNZ    ENDIF
AND        TM     STATUS,B'00000010'
           BNO    ENDIF
THEN       EQU    *
```

2.
```
           MVC    PRSCORES(31),PATRN
           ED     PRSCORES(31),SCORES
ENDIF      EQU    *
           .
SCORES     DS     5PL2
PRSCORES   DS     CL31
PATRN      DS     0CL31
           DC     XL1'40'
           DC     5XL6'202120222222'
```

3.
```
           LA     7,TABLE
           LA     5,10
           LA     6,PRTEMP
REPEAT     MVC    0(4,6),PATRN
           LA     1,3(6)
           EDMK   0(4,6),0(7)
           BCTR   1,0
```

```
IF          CP      0(2,7),=P'0'
            BNL     ENDIF
THEN        MVI     0(1),C'-'
ENDIF       EQU     *
            LA      7,2(7)
            LA      6,4(6)
            BCT     5,REPEAT
UNTIL       EQU     *
            .
TABLE       DS      10PL2
PRTEMP      DS      10CL4
PATRN       DC      XL4'40202120'
```

4. a. `SRL    7,28`
   b. `SLDL   6,32`
   c. `SLDL   7,24`
      `SRDL   6,48`

5.
```
LA     6,DEST
LA     7,1000
LA     8,SOURCE
LA     9,800
O      9,X'F0000000'
MVCL   6,8
```

6.
```
IC     4,BYTE1
STC    4,BYTE2
```

7. `ICM    7,B'1001',INRECD`

8. `CLM    7,B'1011',CHECK`

9.
```
            LA      3,255
REPEAT      STC     3,TABLE(3)
            BCT     3,REPEAT
UNTIL       EQU     *
            STC     3,TABLE
            MVC     TABLE+240(10),=
                    XL10'00010203040506070809'
```

10.
```
            MVI     TABLE+107,X'01'
            LA      5,INDATA
            TRT     0(80,5),TABLE
IF          BZ      ELSE
THEN        SR      1,5
            BCTR    1,0
            EX      1,PACKINST
            LA      5,2(1,5)
            B       ENDIF
ELSE        MVC     ERRMSG,=C'NO COMMA FOUND'
ENDIF       EQU     *
            .
TABLE       DC      256X'00'
PACKINST    PACK    DOUBLE,0(0,5)
```

CHAPTER 14

1. CALCULATIONS REQUIRED

Number of blocks (NB) = Number of records (NR) / Blocking factor (BF)
Block length (BL) = Record length (RL) * Blocking factor (BF)
Inches = (NB * BL / Density) + 0.6 * NB

a. NB = 10000 / 1 = 10000 BL = 100 * 1 = 100
   Inches = (10000 * 100 / 800) + 0.6 * 10000
   = 1250 + 6000 = 7250

b. NB = 10000 / 100 = 100 BL = 100 * 100 = 10000
   Inches = (100 * 10000 / 800) + 0.6 * 100
   = 1250 + 60 = 1310

c. NB = 5000 / 10 = 500 BL = 250 * 10 = 2500
   Inches = (500 * 2500 / 1600) + 0.6 * 500
   = 781.25 + 300 = 1081.25

d. NB = 5000 / 40 = 125 BL = 125 * 40 = 5000
   Inches = (125 * 5000 / 1600) + 0.6 * 125
   = 390.625 + 75 = 465.625

2. Minimum = 4 + 120 + 18 = 142
   Maximum = 4 + 120 + (15 * 18) = 394

3.
```
LA     4,TAPE1
LA     5,TAPE2
LA     6,PRINTER
OPEN   (4),(5),(6)
```

4.
```
TAPEIN  DTFMT  BLKSIZE=960,RECSIZE=120,                X
               IOAREA=TAPEAREA,                        X
               RECFORM=FIXBLK,DEVADDR=SYS011,          X
               TYPEFLE=INPUT,                          X
               IOREG=(5),EOFADDR=THENEOT,              X
               FILABL=STD
TAPEIN  DCB    DDNAME=TAPEIN,BLKSIZE=960,              X
               RECSIZE=120,                            X
               MACRF=GL,DSORG=PS,RECFM=FB
```

5.
```
         OPEN  OLDMAST,TRANFLE,NEWMAST,ERRFLE
         BAL   10,READTRAN
         BAL   10,READMAST
DOWHILE  CLC   MASTKEY,=C'99999'
         BNE   DO
AND      CLC   TRANKEY,=C'99999'
         BE    ENDDO
DO       EQU   *
IF       CLC   MASTKEY,TRANKEY
         BNE   ELSE
THEN     BAL   10,UPDATE
         BAL   10,READTRAN
         B     ENDIF
ELSE     EQU   *
IF2      BNL   ELSE2
THEN2    BAL   10,WRITMAST
         BAL   10,READMAST
         B     ENDIF2
```

```
ELSE2    BAL    10,WRITERR
         BAL    10,READTRAN
ENDIF2   EQU    *
ENDIF    EQU    *
         B      DOWHILE
ENDDO    CLOSE  NEWMAST,TRANFLE,OLDMAST,ERRFLE
         EOJ
```

CHAPTER 15

1.

	LRL	LR/B	BL	KEY	B/T	LR/T
a.	120	10	1200	No	6	60
b.	120	10	1200	Yes	5	50
c.	500	3	1500	No	5	15
d.	500	6	3000	No	2	12
e.	94	20	1880	Yes	4	80

2.
```
// DLBL STUCRSE,'STUDENT COURSE FILE',99/365,SD
// EXTENT SYS018,VOL50,1,1,50,20
```

3.
```
OUTDISK DTFSD BLKSIZE=808,RECSIZE=160,                X
              IOAREA1=DKAREA,                         X
              DEVADDR=SYS011,DEVICE=3340,             X
              RECFORM=FIXBLK,                         X
              TYPEFLE=OUTPUT,IOREG=(5),VERIFY=YES
```

4.
```
INDISK  DTFSD BLKSIZE=800,RECSIZE=160,                X
              IOAREA1=DKAREA,                         X
              DEVADDR=SYS011,DEVICE=3340,             X
              RECFORM=FIXBLK,                         X
              TYPEFLE=INPUT,WORKA=YES
```

5.
```
        OPEN  INTRANS,DKFILE,ERRFLE
        BAL   10,READTRAN
        BAL   10,READDISK
        MVI   UPDTSW,C'N'
DOWHILE CLC   TRANKEY,=C'99999'
        BNE   DO
AND     CLC   DISKKEY,=C'99999'
        BE    ENDDO
DO      EQU   *
IF      CLC   DISKKEY,TRANKEY
        BNL   ELSE
THEN    EQU   *
IF2     CLI   UPDTSW,C'Y'
        BNE   ENDIF2
THEN2   BAL   10,WRDISK
        MVI   UPDTSW,C'N'
ENDIF2  EQU   *
        BAL   10,READDISK
        B     ENDIF
ELSE    EQU   *
IF3     BNE   ELSE3
```

```
THEN3    BAL    10,UPDATE
         MVI    UPDTSW,C'Y'
         B      ENDIF3
ELSE3    EQU    *
         BAL    10,WRERROR
ENDIF3   EQU    *
         BAL    10,READTRAN
ENDIF    EQU    *
         B      DOWHILE
ENDDO    CLOSE  INTRANS,DKFILE,ERRFLE
         EOJ
```

CHAPTER 16

1.
```
INDFILE  DTFIS   DSKXTNT=2,IOROUT=LOAD,                   X
                 KEYLEN=6,NRECDS=8,                       X
                 RECFORM=FIXBLK,RECSIZE=120,              X
                 CYLOFL=2,                                X
                 DEVICE=3340,HINDEX=3340,                 X
                 IOAREAL=INDAREA,                         X
                 KEYLOC=11,VERIFY=YES,WORKL=INDRECD
```

2.
```
INDFILE  DTFIS   DSKXTNT=2,IOROUT=RETRVE,                 X
                 KEYLEN=6,                                X
                 NRECDS=8,RECFORM=FIXBLK,                 X
                 RECSIZE=120,                             X
                 CYLOFL=2,DEVICE=3340,                    X
                 HINDEX=3340,                             X
                 IOAREAS=INVAREA,WORKS=YES,               X
                 KEYLOC=11,                               X
                 TYPEFLE=SEQNTL
         OPEN    INDFILE
         SETL    INDFILE,BOF
         GET     INDFILE,INDRECD
         ESETL   INDFILE
         CLOSE   INDFILE
```

3. a.
```
TM   INDFILEC,B'11111111'
BZ   ENDIF
```
b.
```
TM   INDFILEC,B'00100000'
BO   ENDDO
```
c.
```
TM   INDFILEC,B'11011110'
BNZ  ELSE
```
d.
```
TM   INDFILEC,B'00010000'
BO   ELSE
```
e.
```
TM   INDFILEC,B'00000100'
BO   THEN
TM   INDFILEC,B'00000010'
BO   ELSE
B    ENDIF
```

4.
```
            OPEN    INDFILE
            MVC     ISKEY,=C'15000'
            SETL    INDFILE,GKEY
            GET     INDFILE,INDRECD
            ESETL   INDFILE
            CLOSE   INDFILE
```

5.
```
INDFILE     DTFIS   DSKXTNT=2,IOROUT=ADDRTR,                X
                    KEYLEN=6,NRECDS=20,                     X
                    RECFORM=FIXBLK,RECSIZE=120,             X
                    CYLOFL=2,DEVICE=3340,                   X
                    HINDEX=3340,INDAREA=CORINDEX,           X
                    INDSIZE=100,                            X
                    IOAREAR=INVAREA,KEYARG=KEYFIND,         X
                    KEYLOC=2,                               X
                    TYPEFLE=RANDOM,VERIFY=YES,              X
                    WORKR=INDRECD,                          X
                    IOAREAL=ADDAREA,WORKL=INDRECD
```

CHAPTER 17

1.
```
DEFINE CLUSTER     (                                        X
                    NAME (VSAM.INVMAST.CLUSTER)             X
                    VOLUME (VOL8)                           X
                    CYL (3 1)                               X
                    FILE (INVMAST)                          X
                    INDEXED IMBED                           X
                   )                                        X
       DATA        (                                        X
                    NAME (VSAM.INVMAST.DATASET)             X
                    RECSZ (100 100)                         X
                    CISZ (4096)                             X
                    KEYS (8 9)                              X
                    FSPC (10 10)                            X
                   )                                        X
       INDEX       (                                        X
                    NAME (VSAM.INVMAST.INDEX)               X
                    CISZ (512)                              X
                   )
```

2.
```
READRECD   GET   RPL=VSAMIN
IFEOF      B     ELSEEOF
THENEOF    MVI   EOFFLAG,C'Y'
           B     ENDIFEOF
ELSEEOF    EQU   *
IFERR      LTR   15,15
           BZ    ENDIFERR
THENERR    MVI   ERRFLAG,C'Y'
ENDIFERR   EQU   *
ENDIFEOF   EQU   *
           BR    10
```

CHAPTER 18

1.

	VALUE	SHORT FORM	LONG FORM	EXTENDED FORM
a.	100	42640000	4264000000000000	42640000000000003400000000000000
b.	96.5	41608000	4160800000000000	41608000000000003400000000000000
c.	255	42FF0000	42FF000000000000	42FF0000000000003400000000000000
d.	−512	C3200000	C320000000000000	C3200000000000000B50000000000000
e.	32767	447FFF00	447FFF0000000000	447FFF00000000003600000000000000
f.	−0.0625	C0100000	C010000000000000	C0100000000000000B20000000000000
g.	40960	44A00000	44A0000000000000	44A00000000000003600000000000000
h.	−100.75E3	C51898E0	C51898E000000000	C51898E000000000B700000000000000

2. a. 41100000 c. 41A00000 e. 3CABC000 g. 00200000
   b. BF400000 d. C3965000 f. FA120000 h. 38123400

3. a. 43300800 b. 439C4000 c. 44FFFF40 d. 46FFFFFF
   e. 487FFFFFF000000 f. C880000000000000 g. 40E0000000000000 h. C11199999999999A

4. a. C28A8000 b. C50008A8 c. 431B7800 d. C2968000
   e. C2908000 f. C4A9E680 g. 43121000 h. C085509B37327DC9

5.

```
         LD    0,ONE
         LD    2,ONE
REPEAT   MDR   0,2
         AD    2,ONE
         CD    2,FIFTY
         BNH   REPEAT
UNTIL    EQU   *
         STD   0,FACT50
         .
ONE      DC    D'1'
FIFTY    DC    D'50'
FACT50   DS    D  (Value is 7649EEBC961ED268)
```

6.

```
         LD     4,X              LOAD NUMBER X
         SDR    0,0              Z = 0
         LD     2,Y              Y = TRIAL SQUARE ROOT
REPEAT   EQU    *                REPEAT
         ADR    2,0                Y = (Y + Z) / 2
         HDR    2,2                *
         LDR    0,4                Z = X / Y
         DDR    0,2                *
         LDR    6,0                DIFF = Z - Y
         SDR    6,2                *
         LPDR   6,6                DIFF = ABS(DIFF)
         CDR    0,2                Z = Y?
         BE     UNTIL              YES, Y = ROOT
         CD     6,=D'.0001'        (DIFF < .0001) ?
         BNL    REPEAT             YES, Y = ROOT
UNTIL    EQU    *                UNTIL Y = Z OR (Y - Z)
*                                < .0001
         STD    2,ROOT           STORE ROOT
```

```
         .
X        DC     D'54321.278'
Y        DC     D'5555'
ROOT     DS     D (Value is 42E911BA0C3071A48)
```

7. CALLING PROGRAM

```
             LA     13,SAVE
             CALL   CVFLF4,(ZONEFRAC,FPFRAC)
             .
ZONEFRAC     DC     Z'9843'
FPFRAC       DS     E
SAVE         DS     18F
```

SUBPROGRAM TO CONVERT FOUR-DIGIT NUMBER TO FLOATING-POINT FRACTION

```
CVFLF4       CSECT
             SAVE     (14,12)
             BALR     12,0
             USING    *,12
             SAV13    SAVESUB
             LM       2,3,0(1)          R2=A(ZONEFRAC);
*                                       R3=A(FPFRAC)
             PACK     DOUBLE,0(4,2)     PACK ZONEFRAC
             CVB      8,DOUBLE          CONVERT TO BINARY
             LPR      7,8               MAKE IT POSITIVE
             L        6,EXPONENT        GIVE R6 THE
*                                       EXPONENT
             N        8,SGNMSK          PRESERVE SIGN ONLY
*                                       IN R8
             OR       6,8               GIVE R6 THE SIGN
             STM      6,7,DOUBLE        TRANSFER R6-R7 TO
*                                       FP REG.
             LD       0,DOUBLE          *
             AD       0,=D'0'           NORMALIZE
             DD       0,=D'10000'       CONVERT TO 4-DIGIT
*                                       FRACTION
             STE      0,0(3)            STORE FRACTION IN
*                                       CALLING PROGRAM
             RET13    SAVESUB
             RETURN   (14,12)
DOUBLE       DS       D
EXPONENT     DC       X'4E000000'
SGNMSK       DC       X'80000000'
SAVESUB      DS       18F
             END
```

8.

Original Value =>	+200	−200
FP long form =>	4E000000 000000C8	CE000000 000000C8
Add adjustment =>	4E000001 00000000	4E000001 00000000
Sum =>	4E000001 000000C8	4E000000 FFFFFF38

Index

A 6
B 7
C 8
D 9
E 0
F 1
G 2
H 3
I 4
J 5